Reproducible Leader's Guide

# How To Make Clean Copies From This Book

## *You may make copies of portions of this book with a clean conscience if*

- you (or someone in your organization) are the original purchaser;
- you are using the copies you make for a noncommercial purpose (such as teaching or promoting your ministry) within your church or organization;
- you follow the instructions provided in this book.

## *However, it is ILLEGAL for you to make copies if*

- you are using the material to promote, advertise or sell a product or service other than for ministry fund-raising;
- you are using the material in or on a product for sale; or
- you or your organization are not the original purchaser of this book.

By following these guidelines you help us keep our products affordable.

Thank you,
Gospel Light



**Gospel Light *LittleKidsTime™* Curriculum**

**Publisher,** William T. Greig
**Senior Consulting Publisher,** Dr. Elmer L. Towns
**Publisher, Research, Planning and Development,** Billie Baptiste
**Managing Editor,** Lynnette Pennings, M.A.
**Senior Consulting Editor,** Wesley Haystead, M.S.Ed.
**Senior Editor, Biblical and Theological Issues,** Bayard Taylor, M.Div.
**Senior Advisor, Biblical and Theological Issues,** Dr. Gary S. Greig
**Senior Editor,** Sheryl Haystead
**Editor,** Karen McGraw
**Editorial Team,** Amanda Abbas, Mary Gross, Julie Smith
**Contributing Editors,** Alan Davenport, Sheri Hammons, Melanie Harvey, Fran Kashchy, Carol Niblett, Cindi Schneider, Margaret Self
**Designer,** Zelle Olson

# How to Use *LittleKidsTime*

## *A few children, one leader*

**If you teach alone, follow these simple steps:**

1. Read "*My Great Big God* Overview" on page 6 to get a clear view of what this course is about.

2. Look at "Advice & Answers for Schedule Planning" on pages 7-9. Choose the schedule that best fits your situation and decide which centers you will include.

3. Read the tip articles (pp. 11-20) for each center you will lead, taking note of the ways you can make each center an effective learning experience for the children in your class.

## *Several children, more than one teacher*

**If you teach with one or more other teachers, follow the above three steps and add one more!**

4. Decide if each teacher will lead his or her class in all of the activities or if each teacher will lead only one activity for children as they move between the centers.

## *Lots of children, several teachers, a director or coordinator*

**If you are the children's director or coordinator of *LittleKidsTime*, follow the above steps and add two more!**

5. Pay special attention to "Getting & Keeping the Very Best Staff" on pages 21-22. Remember to start recruiting early—several months before *LittleKidsTime* begins.

6. Read "Questions & Answers for a Terrific Program" on page 23 for tips on how to distribute and store curriculum, special ways to involve parents and more!

# Contents

**How to Use *LittleKidsTime***

A step-by-step *LittleKidsTime* introduction for teachers or leaders—get a head start on a year's worth of sharing God's love with little ones.

***My Great Big God* Overview • 6**

**Advice & Answers for Schedule Planning • 7**

**Basic Materials • 10**

**Active Game Center Tips • 11**

**Art Center Tips • 12**

**Block Center Tips • 13**

**Science Center Tips • 14**

**Bible Story Center Tips • 15**

**Worship Center Tips • 16**

**Read-Aloud Story and Activity Center Tips • 18**

**Kindergarten Puzzle Center Tips • 19**

**Instant Activities Tips • 20**

**Getting & Keeping the Very Best Staff • 21**

**Questions & Answers for a Terrific Program • 23**

**Snacks • 24**

**Play-Dough Recipes • 27**

**Leading the Young Child Toward Jesus • 28**

**Lesson 1** Baby in a Basket • Exodus 2:1-10 • **29**

**Lesson 2** Escape from Egypt • Exodus 12:31-38; 13:20-22 • **37**

**Lesson 3** A Path Through the Sea • Exodus 14—15:20 • **45**

**Lesson 4** A Desert Surprise • Exodus 15:22-25; 16 • **53**

**Lesson 5** Hannah's Prayer • 1 Samuel 1; 2:18,19 • **61**

**Lesson 6** Helping at the Tabernacle • 1 Samuel 1:28; 2:11,18-21,26 • **69**

**Lesson 7** Samuel Listens and Obeys • 1 Samuel 3 • **77**

**Lesson 8** Samuel Obeys God • 1 Samuel 16:1-13 • **85**

**Lesson 9** David Helps His Family • 1 Samuel 16:11,12,18; 17:34,35 • **93**

**Lesson 10** David Visits His Brothers • 1 Samuel 17:12-20 • **101**

**Lesson 11** David and Jonathan Are Kind • 1 Samuel 16:15-23; 18:1-4; 19:1-7 • **109**

**Lesson 12** David and Saul • 1 Samuel 26 • **117**

**Lesson 13** David and Mephibosheth • 1 Samuel 20:14-17,42; 2 Samuel 9 • **125**

**Lesson 14** Mary Hears Good News • Matthew 1:18-25; Luke 1:26-56 • **133**

**Lesson 15** Jesus Is Born • Luke 2:1-7 • **141**

**Lesson 16** Angels Tell the News • Luke 2:8-20 • **149**

**Lesson 17** Wise Men Give Gifts • Matthew 2:1-12 • **157**

**Lesson 18** Jesus Tells of God's Love • Matthew 6:25-34; Luke 12:22-31 • **165**

**Lesson 19** Jesus Stops the Storm • Matthew 8:23-27; Mark 4:1,35-41 • **173**

**Lesson 20** Jesus Heals a Blind Man • John 9:1-11,35-38 • **181**

**Lesson 21** Jesus Feeds 5,000 • Mark 6:30-44; John 6:1-14 • **189**

**Lesson 22** The Forgiving King • Matthew 18:21-35 • **197**

**Lesson 23** The Good Samaritan • Luke 10:25-37 • **205**

**Lesson 24** The Good Shepherd • Luke 15:3-7 • **213**

**Lesson 25** The Loving Father • Luke 15:11-24 • **221**

**Lesson 26** The Greatest of All • Mark 9:33-37; Luke 9:46-48 • **229**

**Lesson 27** People Praise Jesus • Matthew 21:1-11,15,16; Luke 19:28-38 • **237**

**Lesson 28** Jesus Dies and Lives Again • Matthew 26:1-4,47-50; 27:11-66; John 18—20:20 • **245**

**Lesson 29** Thomas Sees Jesus • John 20:19-31 • **253**

**Lesson 30** Jesus Lives Today • Matthew 28:16-20; John 21:1-14; Acts 1:3-11 • **261**

**Lesson 31** The Lame Man Walks • Acts 3:1-16 • **269**

**Lesson 32** Barnabas Shares • Acts 4:32-37 • **277**

**Lesson 33** Food for Widows • Acts 6:1-7 • **285**

**Lesson 34** Philip and the Ethiopian • Acts 8:26-40 • **293**

**Lesson 35** Paul Meets Jesus • Acts 9:1-20 • **301**

**Lesson 36** Paul Escapes in a Basket • Acts 9:20-28 • **309**

**Lesson 37** Peter Helps Dorcas • Acts 9:32-43 • **317**

**Lesson 38** Peter Escapes from Prison • Acts 12:1-18 • **325**

**Lesson 39** Paul Helps a Lame Man • Acts 14:8-20 • **333**

**Lesson 40** Jacob and Esau • Genesis 25:19-28 • **341**

**Lesson 41** An Unfair Trade • Genesis 25:27-34 • **349**

**Lesson 42** Jacob's Tricks • Genesis 27:1-45 • **357**

**Lesson 43** Esau Forgives Jacob • Genesis 32:3-21; 33:1-11 • **365**

**Lesson 44** Daniel Obeys God • Daniel 1 • **373**

**Lesson 45** The Fiery Furnace • Daniel 3 • **381**

**Lesson 46** The Writing on the Wall • Daniel 5 • **389**

**Lesson 47** The Lions' Den • Daniel 6 • **397**

**Lesson 48** Ruth Loves Naomi • Ruth 1—2:23 • **405**

**Lesson 49** Jonah and the Big Fish • Jonah • **413**

**Lesson 50** Josiah Reads God's Words • 2 Chronicles 34—35:19 • **421**

**Lesson 51** Jeremiah Obeys • Jeremiah 36 • **429**

**Lesson 52** Nehemiah Helps Build Walls • Nehemiah 1—2; 4:1-6; 6:15,16; 12:27,43 • **437**

# My Great Big God overview

Welcome to a year's worth of great learning!

*My Great Big God* will help the young children you teach grow more aware of God's love, care and help in their everyday lives. Young children have unique needs. Their understanding of the world is limited. And their most effective method of learning is through play! *My Great Big God* will give each one a chance to actively explore Bible truths in ways that involve the whole child. They will discover ways to do what they have learned in class, so Bible truths are applied in ways that have real meaning for their lives.

## Special Features

• Every lesson includes a colorful Bible Story poster as part of the Bible story presentation. The back of each poster contains that lesson's Bible story in a slightly longer version for older children. These beautiful pictures help you keep children focused on the story!

• During each class session, children may participate in several different active learning experiences that will help focus children's minds as you relate the day's lesson to their lives. Each activity is related to the session's lesson focus, God's Word & Me, and many are related to the Bible Story as well. Noncompetitive, active games provide a change of pace and a chance to move large muscles. Art projects give children an opportunity to creatively manipulate a variety of art materials. Building, lifting and carrying blocks give children opportunities to develop motor skills. Science activities help them explore God's world and the wonderful things He has created. The Bible story helps children connect Bible truths to their own world. And the Worship Center helps you lead children in singing, praying and speaking God's Word.

• Each activity is designed to meet the needs and abilities of the majority of preschool children. However, the developmental differences that exist between younger and older preschoolers are also addressed. At the bottom of each activity center are two suggested options. For Younger Children provides simplification or alternate ideas for the younger children in your group. For Older Children provides challenges and enrichment ideas for kindergartners and other older children.

• The activities suggested on the final page of each lesson provide another chance to customize each session for your unique group of children and the unique needs of your program. For both younger and older children, the Read-Aloud Story and Activity Center features a contemporary story and activity page related to that session's lesson focus. Kindergartners will enjoy the challenge of puzzles provided in the Kindergarten Puzzle Center. The Instant Activities can be used at any time in the session to provide a change of pace, to extend the session or to allow for transitions at the beginning or end of the session.

• Because teachers are the heart of any teaching time, *My Great Big God* is especially easy for teachers to use. Every lesson opens with a Teacher's Devotional to give teachers insight and background in understanding how the lesson's focus applies to their own lives. The Leader's Guide is reproducible, so the members of the teaching team can be given copies to use as part of their preparation for teaching.

Additionally, each member of the teaching team can be given a copy of the page for the center to which he or she has been assigned. Each center's page includes the Bible verse (God's Word) and the lesson focus (God's Word & Me). As a result, the team members understand the goal of the lesson and how their centers tie into achieving that goal.

## Prayerful Preparation

When you and your team members are full of eagerness and understanding of the lesson at hand, your children will be eager to learn, too! As you pray and organize this course to meet the needs of your group, ask God what He wants to do during this time. Invite Him to make you sensitive to ways you can be part of what He wants to accomplish. Although these children are young, the foundations for understanding that you lay will make an eternal difference as they grow to understand our great big God!

# Advice & Answers for Schedule Planning

## *How much time is needed for each session?*

The answer to this question is another question: How much time do you need each session to take? This course is designed to meet the needs of multiple time frames and a wide variety of needs. Selecting from the variety of activities provided in each session will allow you to make the session last for however long you will be meeting with your children. See the scheduling options below for suggestions that will meet the needs of a majority of programs.

## *What are the special needs of young children?*

As you develop your schedule, consider a few of the special needs of the children you serve:

• The children in your care will not be able to sit still for long periods of time. Some will not be able to sit still for any period of time! Be sure to alternate seated activities with activities that allow children to exercise their large muscles (active games, blocks, playground play, etc.). If children attend a portion of the adult worship service before the *LittleKidsTime* session begins, provide a large-motor activity at the beginning of the session.

• Schedules and timetables have no meaning to the preschool child. Instead of having a predetermined length of time for each center, it is best if young children move freely between the centers as their interests direct them. The activity centers are designed to be open-ended, with no set beginning or end. Provide as many centers as you have teachers or helpers, with each teacher or helper taking responsibility for one center. A child may play the game for a few minutes and then move to the Block Center to build for a while before returning to play the game some more. This kind of flexibility allows children to experience as many or as few of the centers as they want!

• Because the Bible Story Center and the Worship Center do have a specific beginning and end, we recommend that you group all the children together for these centers. You may choose to have the Worship Center immediately after the Bible Story Center, instead of trying to get children all together and seated quietly at two different times in the session.

• For children to be able to move freely between the centers, all of the *LittleKidsTime* activity centers should take place in the same room. You may wish to create a large sign with a drawing or a magazine picture on it to identify each center: for instance, a crayon for the Art Center, jumping children for the Active Game Center, blocks for the Block Center, a magnifying glass for the Science Center, etc. This makes it easy for children to identify the different centers.

## *What activity centers are provided in the Leader's Guide?*

• The Active Game Center provides a change of pace and a chance for young bodies to move. All the games for young children should be noncompetitive.

• The Art Center activities provide enjoyable and meaningful art experiences for children.

• The Block Center encourages children to lift, carry and build with blocks, giving them opportunities to develop motor skills, use their imaginations, care for materials and make decisions.

• The Science Center provides the kind of firsthand experiences that are essential for young children to learn. Exploring God's creation helps a child begin to sense the extent of God's love, His care and His wisdom.

• The Bible Story Center allows Bible truths to impact the mind, feelings and behavior of a young child, by relating those truths to the child's world of family, home and friends.

• The Worship Center actively involves young children in the basic elements of worship: music, God's Word and prayer.

• In the Read-Aloud Story and Activity Center, a contemporary story picture from *Read-Aloud Story and Activity Book* helps each child understand and apply the session's Bible truth to his or her own life.

• The Kindergarten Puzzle Center provides puzzles to engage your kindergartners and provide a springboard for Bible learning.

• Instant Activities are not a separate center but are simple, quick activities that you can use at any time during your session. There are two suggested ideas for each session.

## How do we plan each session?

Each teacher takes responsibility for one or more activities, interacting with each child as he or she visits the activity center. Helpers and teachers not actively leading an activity move freely with children and/or assist other teachers as needed.

Once you have chosen the activities for each session, plan who will lead and who will help with each center. Make a copy of each of the chosen activities for the teacher or teachers who will lead the activities. Give the copies to teachers in plenty of time for them to do their necessary preparation. Also give each teacher and helper a copy of each session's devotional. The devotional will help them prepare their hearts and minds in the week before each session.

Doing this preparation early will go a long way to help you avoid last-minute panic! Planning a month or more in advance will ensure that your teachers are well prepared to serve the children in their care.

For help in staffing and recruiting, make a planning page to be completed on a weekly or monthly basis (see samples).

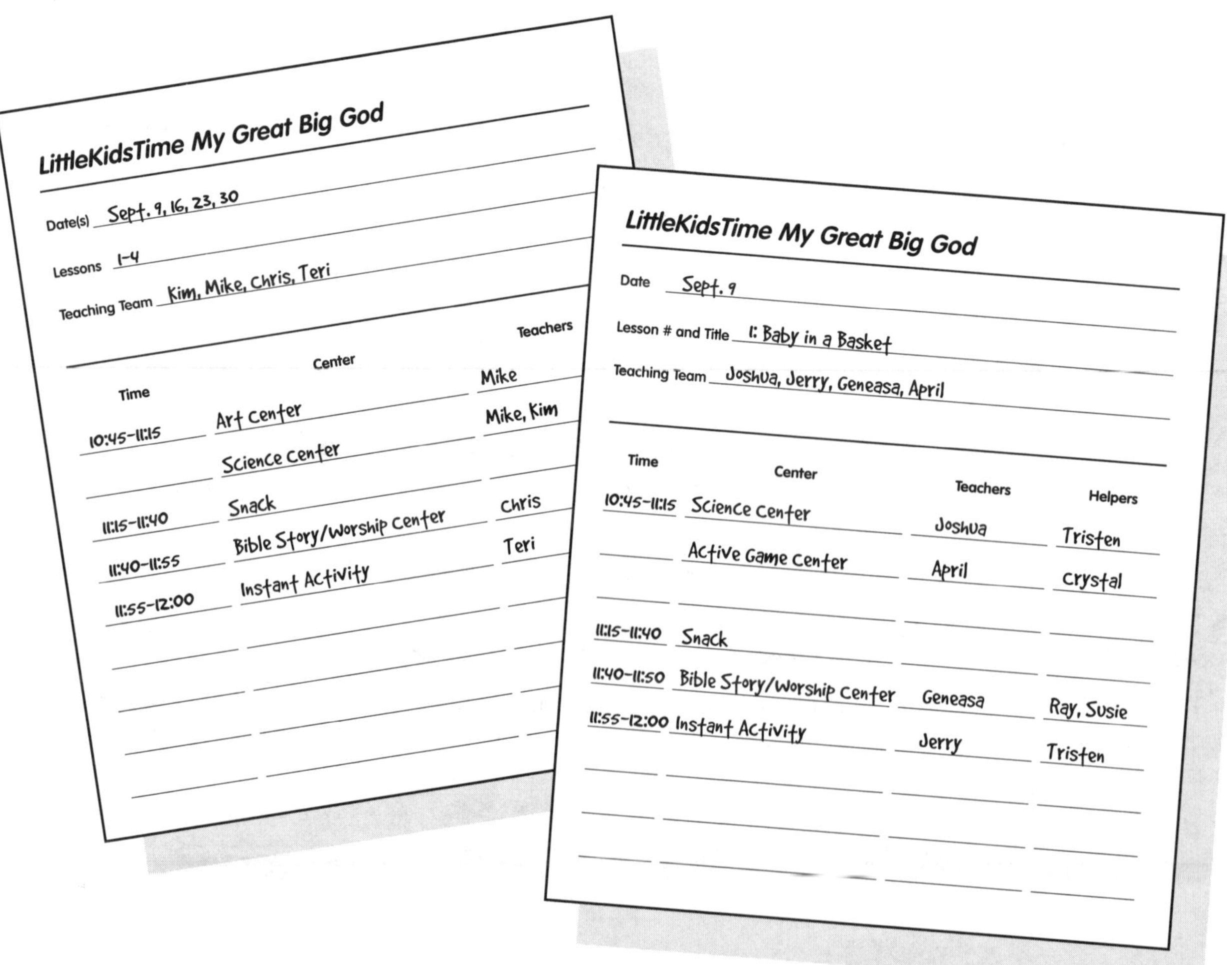

**LittleKidsTime My Great Big God**

Date(s) Sept. 9, 16, 23, 30

Lessons 1-4

Teaching Team Kim, Mike, Chris, Teri

| Time | Center | Teachers |
|---|---|---|
| 10:45-11:15 | Art Center | Mike |
| | Science Center | Mike, Kim |
| 11:15-11:40 | Snack | |
| 11:40-11:55 | Bible Story/Worship Center | Chris |
| 11:55-12:00 | Instant Activity | Teri |

**LittleKidsTime My Great Big God**

Date Sept. 9

Lesson # and Title 1: Baby in a Basket

Teaching Team Joshua, Jerry, Geneasa, April

| Time | Center | Teachers | Helpers |
|---|---|---|---|
| 10:45-11:15 | Science Center | Joshua | Tristen |
| | Active Game Center | April | Crystal |
| 11:15-11:40 | Snack | | |
| 11:40-11:50 | Bible Story/Worship Center | Geneasa | Ray, Susie |
| 11:55-12:00 | Instant Activity | Jerry | Tristen |

### What are some schedule options?

Below are some sample schedule options. Adapt these sample schedules to the needs and interests of your church. Other centers can be added or substituted in order to meet the needs of younger or older children. In addition to the centers suggested in this curriculum, you may wish to include snacks (see recipes on p. 24) and/or supervised playtime outdoors.

**Option 1**
**(60-75 minutes)**

**Activity Centers***
20-30 minutes

Active Game
Art
Blocks

**Snack and/or supervised outdoor play**
25 minutes

**Bible Story Center and Worship Center**
10-15 minutes

**Instant Activities**
5 minutes

* Select from the Active Game Center, Art Center, Block Center, Science Center, Read-Aloud Story and Activity Center and Kindergarten Puzzle Center.

**Option 2**
**(60-90 minutes)**

**Adult Worship**
15-20 minutes

**Activity Centers***
20-30 minutes

Active Game
Art
Blocks

**Snack and/or supervised outdoor play**
15-25 minutes

**Bible Story Center and Worship Center**
10-15 minutes

* Select from the Active Game Center, Art Center, Block Center, Science Center, Read-Aloud Story and Activity Center and Kindergarten Puzzle Center.

**Option 3**
**(75-90 minutes)**

**Activity Centers***
20-30 minutes

Active Game
Art
Science

**Snack and/or supervised outdoor play**
25 minutes

**Bible Story Center and Worship Center**
10-15 minutes

**Activity Centers***
20 minutes

Blocks
Kindergarten Puzzles
Read-Aloud Story and Activity

* Select from the Active Game Center, Art Center, Block Center, Science Center, Read-Aloud Story and Activity Center and Kindergarten Puzzle Center.

# Basic Materials

### *Active Game Center*

- Beanbags
- Several soft balls in various sizes
- Masking tape and/or yarn
- Colored construction paper
- Functional scissors

### *Art Center*

- Newspaper (to protect surfaces)
- Functional scissors
- Usable glue bottles and sticks
- Working markers
- Usable crayons and chalk
- An adequate supply of tape
- Colored construction paper
- Stapler
- Paint smocks (or old shirts)
- Butcher paper or newsprint end rolls (ask at your local newspaper office)

### *Block Center*

- Wooden or cardboard blocks in different sizes, shapes and colors
- Toy cars and trucks
- Toy people
- Toy animals
- Toy trees
- Signs (traffic signs, building signs, etc.)
- Recyclable materials (cardboard sheets, boxes and tubes, film canisters, wooden spools, etc.)

### *Science Center*

- Several magnifying glasses
- A variety of nature items (rocks, shells, living plants, sticks, etc.)
- Large tubs for water or sand play
- Fabrics in a variety of textures
- Newspaper (to protect surfaces)
- Measuring cups
- Bowls in a variety of sizes
- Several spoons and ladles
- Plastic or paper dinnerware (plates, bowls, cups, napkins, etc.)

### *Worship Center*

- A variety of rhythm instruments

# Active Game Center Tips

The Active Game Center can be the perfect place for children to let off steam, work out the wiggles and be open to conversation that relates the focus of the day's lesson to children's lives.

## *Creating a Playing Area*

Set up a game area. You may have little space in your classroom for a game area, so consider alternatives: outdoor areas, a gymnasium or a vacant area of the church from which sound will not carry and disturb others.

Once you have chosen the area, plan what you will need:

• Will you need to move furniture?

• Will you need to mark boundaries? Use chalk or rope outdoors; yarn or masking tape works indoors. (Remove masking tape from carpets after each session.)

• How much space will you need? Review the game procedures to plan what amount and shape of space will be needed.

From time to time, take stock of your classroom area. Is it time to remove that large table or unused bookshelf? Should the chairs be rearranged or the rug put in a different place? Small changes in arrangement can result in more usable space!

## *Basic Materials*

Some of the games require no materials at all. Other games require items that can be found in most classrooms or homes. The following supplies are used in many of the games: beanbags, several soft balls in various sizes, masking tape and/or yarn, colored construction paper and functional scissors. Having these basic game materials on hand will greatly simplify teacher preparation.

## *Leading the Game*

Games for young children are really not games in the strictest sense of the word. They do not involve a long list of rules and restrictions. Rather, games with young children are easygoing and noncompetitive. There are no winners or losers! A child may follow the rules for a while, but as excitement builds the rules will simply slip away as children begin to enjoy themselves. The fun is in the doing, not in the end result of winning or losing.

Explain the game clearly in a step-by-step fashion. Demonstrate the actions, if needed. Then get the children involved! Children will learn the game best by actually playing it.

## *Guiding Conversation*

Using guided conversation turns a game activity into discovery learning! Make use of the Talk About conversation suggestions provided in the curriculum. These conversation starters will help you relate the child's activity to the lesson focus. Keep in mind the lesson focus and Bible verse for each lesson. Then your natural conversation can tie children's activities to the lesson's Bible truths. Briefly telling parts of the Bible story can also help make the connection.

# Art Center Tips

The Art Center is a place where young children can become absorbed in a creative activity that helps focus their minds as you relate the day's lesson to their lives. Each art activity is related to the session's lesson focus, God's Word & Me, and many are related to the Bible story as well.

## Basic Materials

No one enjoys a long wait for the right crayon, so make sure you have plenty of the following supplies on hand: newspaper (to protect surfaces), functional scissors, usable glue bottles and sticks, working markers, usable crayons and chalk, an adequate supply of tape, colored construction paper, stapler, paint smocks (or old shirts) and butcher paper or newsprint end rolls (ask at your local newspaper office).

## Before Every Activity

Preparation is the key to making an art experience a joyful, creative one. Before children arrive at your center, cover the work tables with newspaper, securing it with masking tape, if needed. Set out materials in an orderly fashion, making sure you have enough materials for the number of children who will visit the Art Center.

If table space is limited, set out materials on a nearby shelf or supply table. Allow children to get and return materials to the appropriate places.

Ask older children to help younger ones with tasks such as stapling, cutting, etc. during the Art Center time.

## Guiding Conversation

Use the conversation suggestions in the Talk About section to help children relate the art activity to the lesson, and the lesson focus to their daily lives. As children create, they are relaxed and eager to talk. Guided conversation will take the activity beyond art to discovery of Bible truth.

Especially for young children, the goal of an art activity is not a product that looks pretty. The value lies in the process the child goes through as his or her attention is focused. Take advantage of those moments when a child says "Look at my picture!" Instead of responding with "That's nice," focus on the child. Relate the child's work and interest to the lesson focus. Use "I see . . ." statements to affirm the value of the child's work while helping him or her see how his or her work relates to the lesson focus (God's Word & Me). **Jacob, I see you drew a lot of stars on your paper. I'm glad that God made the stars. We can thank God for all the great things He has made!**

Avoid making value judgments ("That's nice" or "How pretty!"). First, any child who then does not hear such a positive judgment will feel inadequate. Second and more important, focusing on the visual appeal of the artwork will not help the child better understand the lesson. How a child's work looks is far less important than the child's process of creating that work. Comment on colors, lines, materials and techniques the child used. **Kathy, I see you glued yarn on your paper. Tell me about your work.** As you invite children to tell you about their work, many opportunities will arise for you to use the conversation suggestions in the Talk About section of the lesson or to make comments that will help children understand the lesson focus. **Thank you for telling me about your project, Kathy. I saw that you handed the glue to April. Thank you, Kathy, for being kind. We show God's love by being kind to others.**

# Block Center Tips

Blocks are important learning tools for all young children. Block building provides firsthand experiences in practicing biblical concepts such as sharing, helping, taking turns and exercising self-control. Many activities are Bible story related and all connect to the lesson focus, God's Word & Me.

## *Basic Materials*

Blocks, blocks and more blocks! Provide many different sizes, shapes and colors of wooden and cardboard blocks. Blocks for children under three years of age should be lightweight and easy to manipulate. Provide enough blocks so that several children can build at the same time. Four- and five-year-olds need a larger number and variety of blocks. A set of wooden unit blocks is a versatile learning tool that stimulates creative building for this age.

## *Accessory Toys*

The value of block building is enhanced for all children by a variety of accessory toys that encourage dramatic play. Sturdy toy cars and trucks should be a part of every block area. Other accessory toys include toy people, toy animals and toy trees. Four- and five-year-olds enjoy using signs (traffic signs, building signs, etc.) in dramatic play.

A variety of cardboard sheets, boxes and tubes can stimulate young imaginations as they build with blocks. Also consider carpet squares, fabric pieces, wallpaper and other home remodeling materials, sheets or blankets, film canisters and wooden spools.

## *Building Guidelines*

Block building helps a child develop physically, mentally, socially and spiritually. When it comes to playing with blocks, the fewer rules there are, the more meaningful block play will be. However, a few guidelines are necessary for safety and efficient use of the blocks.

• Guide children to build several feet away from the block shelves, so children may get to the blocks without knocking down someone else's construction. A strip of masking tape or a chalk line on the floor about two feet from the shelves serves as a silent reminder.

• The floor of the block area should be carpeted with a smooth rug to provide a warm, level surface for building, while at the same time reducing noise.

• Block constructions should rise no higher than the child's chin.

• Knocking down a block tower is a lot of fun, but children can only knock down their own building; they must ask permission before knocking down someone else's construction.

## *Guiding Conversation*

A teacher's conversation with young builders offers many opportunities to help children know and do what God's Word says. Specific ideas for guiding children in block building are given in the Talk About section of each Block Center. The conversation suggestions are planned to relate the lesson focus and Bible verse to the child's block-building activities.

Occasionally, a block building project will be suggested to help children become familiar with Bible-times life (building a sheepfold or flat-roofed house) or something in the Bible story. This block-building activity will enable them to listen with increased understanding to the Bible story.

Building with blocks is a favorite activity for young children. It stimulates young imaginations. As a result, a child will sometimes decide to build structures of his or her own choosing instead of completing the activity suggested in the Leader's Guide. However a child decides to work, either singly or with others, completing the suggested activity or building structures of their own design, building with blocks is a valuable activity. Be sure to look for ways to tie their activities to the lesson focus, God's Word & Me.

# Science Center Tips

The wonder and excitement of a hands-on examination of God's world presents teachers with a variety of opportunities to help young children learn about God and themselves. Each Science Center involves children in an activity directly related to the lesson focus and the Bible verse and/or story.

## *Basic Materials*

Though each science activity provides a unique experience for children, there are certain materials to keep on hand. Having these things on hand will enhance the experiences of the children and/or ease teacher preparation: several magnifying glasses, a variety of nature items (rocks, shells, living plants, sticks, etc.), large tubs for water or sand play, fabrics in a variety of textures, newspaper (to protect surfaces), measuring cups, bowls in a variety of sizes, several spoons and ladles, plastic or paper dinnerware (plates, bowls, cups, napkins, etc.).

## *Science and the Young Child*

For young children, science is all about experiencing the physical world and recognizing the science in the things they do every day: mixing, digging, pouring, inventing, improvising, taking apart and moving. Through repetition and exploration of the world in ways that are meaningful to them, children explore basic science concepts and begin to understand how the world works, how to measure it, how to make sense of it and how to connect it to their own world.

Learning begins as a sensory experience. Science activities enhance a child's development of his or her five senses: touching, tasting, smelling, hearing and seeing. Using their senses to explore God's world helps children begin to sense the extent of God's love, His care and His wisdom.

## *Guiding Conversation*

An essential part of the teacher's role is to provide words for a child, helping him or her identify the experience and relate God to the event. Once this relationship is made, the child is able to think about God (Jesus, the Bible story, the Bible verse or lesson focus) in terms of a firsthand experience. Without such guidance, science activities become just so many interesting experiences. Use the conversation suggestions in the Talk About section of each Science Center.

# Bible Story Center Tips

The Bible stories and Bible verses in this course correlate with Gospel Light's *Movers and Shakers* Sunday School curriculum. By focusing on one Bible story and verse at a time, children are provided with the repetition so necessary for early childhood learners. Also, older children who have already heard the Bible story in Sunday School can help you tell the story.

## *Storytelling Tips*

Most of us can still remember a childhood story told by a good storyteller. What makes a good storyteller so memorable? A good storyteller draws listeners into the story, helping them imagine the story themselves and thus making it their own. You may not feel like one of the world's great storytellers, but young children are a forgiving and easily fascinated audience when any adult makes the effort to draw them into a story. Here are some ideas and tips to help you become more confident, communicative and memorable!

• Each story has several suggested motions (found in the Leader's Guide) to increase the involvement of the children as they listen to the story. Repeat the suggested motions at appropriate moments in the story and even add your own! Adapt the motions for your particular needs. For instance, many of the suggested motions are full-body movements, such as walking in place. If you have a large group, you may want to change this motion to walking your fingers instead.

• Consider having a partner for storytelling. One person can tell the story as the other leads children in the suggested motions.

• While the Bible story is being told, other teachers and helpers sit separately among the children. Encourage them to fully participate with children, doing the motions, reacting appropriately and having fun! Their listening presence will encourage children to listen attentively as well, and they can help redirect the attention of children back to the storyteller if needed.

• For variety, dress in a Bible-times costume and tell the story in the first person ("I," "we"). Practice telling the story, imagining how the people in the story felt and what they saw. Describe these ideas to the children for particularly effective storytelling.

• Use dramatic facial expressions and vary your tone of voice according to the story action.

• Occasionally, use a puppet to introduce or tell the story. If you enjoy using puppets, consider using the puppet often. You might ask the puppet the introductory question at the beginning of the story before asking children the question.

• If children heard the Bible story in Sunday School before coming to *LittleKidsTime* or indicate a familiarity with the story, ask volunteers to tell some of the story action. Be sure to clarify and supplement information as needed.

## *Bible Story Picture Tips*

Make good use of the posters available in the *LittleKidsTime Bible Story Pictures.* This pack of large, colorful posters is designed to make you a star storyteller! Use these posters as the focal point of your story time. Showing visuals of Bible story people and places enhances and clarifies children's understanding. Pictures also help children perceive the story as having really happened.

• If your class is made up mainly of older preschoolers, read the story as it is printed on the back of the poster. If your class is mainly two- and three-year-olds, display the poster as you tell the story printed in the Leader's Guide.

• Use these pictures to help recapture wandering attentions. Ask simple questions or give simple directions anytime children need to refocus on the Bible story. **Blake, point to someone in the picture who looks happy. The man is happy because God helped him!**

• To extend the time in the Bible Story Center or as a quick review, ask simple questions about the poster. **This is a picture of people from today's Bible story. Dani, how do you think the people feel? Rob, what do you think is happening? What is going to happen next?**

# Worship Center Tips

The goal of the Worship Center is to help children participate in meaningful worship at their level of experience. It can be a fine small-group time or an excellent large-group time. Activities involving prayer, God's Word and lesson-related songs, as well as a variety of options you can use to enrich or extend the children's worship experience, are provided in the Worship Center.

## A Time of Worship

Adults sometimes see children's worship time as an easy way to occupy kids with singing or a way to teach children to worship in the same way adults do. But children need informal worship opportunities at their own level of understanding. Worship experiences designed to meet children's needs help them respond in love and praise to their heavenly Father.

Worship is indeed a time to show reverence and respect for God, but it doesn't mean always sitting still and being quiet. The activities offered in the Worship Center involve young children in a variety of ways to help them interact with each other and with teachers in praising God and hearing His Word.

## A Place of Worship

Worship is also enhanced by setting apart a place especially for praising God. To create a space in your classroom for the Worship Center, prayerfully consider the ages and abilities of the children in your group, the kind of worship experience appropriate for them and the time and space available.

Consider ideas such as displaying a picture of Jesus, spreading a rug on the floor upon which children sit, and playing a song related to that week's lesson at the beginning of each Worship Center time. This creates an invitation to worship. Using the same opening song each time can be used as a signal to begin worship.

If taking an offering, singing a particular response or placing candles on an altarpiece are part of your church's adult worship, occasionally add those elements to the Worship Center as well. Give a simple explanation to help children understand why each of these acts is part of worship.

Keep in mind that the Worship Center is not a place for entertainment or observation; your goal is to see every child participate in a positive way that is in keeping with his or her development.

## Sing to God

Every lesson features a song related to the lesson focus and a Scripture song to help children remember the related Bible verse. A wide variety of musical styles is represented, making it easy for you to customize your worship time to include your children's favorites. Consider making audiocassette copies of the reproducible *Shake It Up!* songs to help children become familiar with the songs used during this course.

### Leading songs

Children may participate by singing, clapping their hands or playing rhythm instruments. Help children understand that all these activities have one goal: to honor and praise God. Your enthusiastic participation sets the tone—it is the strongest teaching about worship that the children will receive.

Learning new songs can be difficult for some teachers. Listen to each session's songs on the *Shake It Up!* cassette/CD. Play the songs again and sing along several times (listen to the audiocassette or CD as you drive in your car, while you cook, etc.). Depending on the ages and abilities of your children, you may want to choose three or four favorite songs from the *Shake It Up!* cassette/CD and repeat them often rather than teaching two new songs every four to five sessions.

As you play a song, sing along with the song, inviting children to join in with you. If you can, occasionally use live musicians or play an instrument yourself instead of using the audiocassette or CD to keep children's interest high. Even if at first children only watch you and do not sing along, they are still participating at their level. Children may sing at a later time as you continue to incorporate music into the sessions.

### Choosing additional songs

If your church chooses to lead children in additional worship songs, select songs with the same prayer and sensitivity with which you'd plan adult worship. Utilizing simple worship choruses and hymns from among your own church's favorites will prepare children for the transition to adult-level worship in a gradual, age-appropriate manner. In this way, children will become familiar with a body of songs used in adult worship.

Whatever songs you use, be sure to explain any words or concepts that are unfamiliar to children. Use a children's Bible dictionary if needed. For example, **The word "Lord" is another name for God. When we sing about the Lord, we are singing about God!** If you cannot put the words or concepts of any song into terms a young child can truly understand, recognize that the song is probably appropriate only for adult worship.

## Hear and Say God's Word

The simple verse activity provided encourages children to hear and/or say the Scripture with understanding in a creative way. As children repeat the activity, they learn the verse naturally and easily.

## Pray to God

Prayer is an integral part of worship. Don't deny children this privilege because they seem too young to hold still with folded hands and bowed heads for long periods of time. Instead, involve children in prayer in ways that will help them understand that prayer is something they can do. Keep prayer times short and use the activities suggested to make them times of high involvement. Remember that your prayers give children a model for prayer that they will follow. Keep your prayers brief. Use simple words. Long sentences and long prayers make prayer seem boring and not something a child would want to do.

# Read-Aloud Story and Activity Center Tips

The *Read-Aloud Story and Activity Book* provides ideal activities for all children in the program, from the youngest ones in *LittleKidsTime* to older kindergartners. Each child will participate at his or her level of development and will enjoy it if you read the story aloud while they color and complete the activity page.

The pages may be used at a variety of times—as a separate activity center, for early arrivals, for children who finish other activities ahead of time or for children who need a quiet change of pace. You may also occasionally substitute the sheets for another activity suggested in your curriculum or offer them in addition to the suggested activities.

## Preparation

• Prepare pages by making a double-sided photocopy for each child in your class. It's easiest to copy at one time all the pages needed for four or five lessons rather than photocopying on a weekly basis. Store the pages in marked folders for easy use. Have extra photocopies on hand, especially during holiday times, so there are enough for visitors.

• Provide crayons or markers for children to use in coloring the pages.

• Plan ahead for those pages that require extra materials (tape, construction paper, etc.).

## Guiding Conversation

While children are coloring, read the story aloud. Use the Let's Talk About the Story ideas to encourage conversation with the children. If you are unable to read the story aloud and ask the questions, label each page with the child's name to send home. Encourage parents to read and discuss the story at home.

"I will praise you, O Lord." 2 Samuel 22:50
Connect the dots. Color the picture.

# Kindergarten Puzzle Center Tips

Puzzles from *The Big Book of Kindergarten Puzzles* provide a variety of puzzles and activities to challenge kindergartners as they practice the same skills they are learning in kindergarten. These mazes, picture puzzles, matching and counting activities all reflect different levels of difficulty. Complete instructions, conversation ideas and Bonus Ideas make it easy for you to use in every session as a regular center or as an occasional change of pace.

There are two puzzles for each of the lessons in *My Great Big God.* The puzzles highlight the 52 Bible verses in the curriculum, with two puzzles focusing on each verse. One puzzle reinforces the verse through the lesson's Bible story. The second puzzle presents a modern life application of the verse. Both types of puzzles will engage your kindergartner and provide a springboard for Bible learning. Complete instructions for use are included in the front of the book.

## Preparation

• Photocopy the puzzle(s) you have selected for use. Make one copy of the selected puzzle(s) for each child, plus a few extras for visitors or for children who want to start over. Leave the back of each paper blank for children to use for each puzzle's Bonus Idea.

• Check the puzzle's directions and Bonus Idea for any extra materials you will need. In addition to pencils, some puzzles may require crayons, colored pencils, scissors or glue sticks.

## Guiding Conversation

Talk with children during and after their puzzle work. Your conversation can tie the children's work to the session's Bible story and verse. The printed copy on each puzzle will help you communicate the important link between the Bible story and verse and the everyday lives of your children. Soon you'll find that asking the right questions and effectively guiding conversation become second nature!

# Instant Activities Tips

*The Big Book of Instant Activities* provides simple, quick activities that you can use at any time during your session. There are two suggested ideas for each session.

These activities can provide a needed change of pace, extend the session's time schedule or provide transitions at the beginning or end of the session. Geared to interest both the youngest and the oldest preschooler, these activities will engage every child in your class!

## *Preparation*

Most of the Instant Activities require NO preparation. Some require a bit, using materials you have at hand, such as paper and markers. Read the brief, easy-to-follow instructions, and you and your children are ready for fun.

## *Why use Instant Activities?*

From a child's viewpoint, the best part about Instant Activities is that the activities are fun! Enjoy these activities with the children you guide. Add a smile to your words. If you're happy and enthusiastic, the children will reflect your joy.

From a teacher's viewpoint, you will appreciate the valuable learning experiences incorporated into each Instant Activity. A variety of types of activities provide for a variety of learning experiences for your children.

- Circle Time Activities address the needs of young children's brief attention spans. These activities can recapture wandering attention and allow wiggly bodies to move in appropriate ways.
- Finger Play Activities appeal to a child's imagination and sense of rhythm. Repeat finger plays often, so children become familiar with them.
- Get-Acquainted Activities provide opportunities for children to respond to their names and to learn the names of others in the group. These experiences help each child to feel that he or she belongs—that your classroom is a place where he or she is loved, valued and accepted.
- Movement Activities meet the need of young children for plenty of opportunities to move their whole bodies. The activities require open space, indoors or outdoors, as children enjoy expending their energy at the same time they develop large-motor skills.
- Music Activities help regain a child's wandering attention faster than almost anything else! Young children are attracted to music and movement, even if they don't always sing along.
- Quiet Activities provide children with a welcome break from active involvement. Children will enjoy quiet activities individually or in small groups.

Circle Time Activities 15

All Eyes on Me!

**Procedure:** Children sit in a circle. Say, **One, two, three; All eyes on me!**

Children look at you carefully. **Now close your eyes.** Turn around and change one item of your appearance (remove a watch, put on glasses, add a sweater or scarf, etc.). At your signal, children open their eyes and try to guess what has changed. Repeat game, changing a different item of your appearance for each round.

Amazing Animal List

**Materials:** Large sheet of paper, marker.

**Procedure:** Show children the paper. **Let's think of the names of enough animals to fill this whole paper!** Children take turns naming animals. On sheet of paper, print name of each animal. Give hints if children have difficulty thinking of animals that have not already been named. **I'm thinking of an animal with a very long trunk.** Or make the sound of that animal.

Continue activity until paper is full. Then lead children in counting all the animal names on the paper.

**Variation:** Challenge children to fill up additional papers with other lists: names of people to show love to, favorite foods, names of colors, etc.

# Getting & Keeping the Very Best Staff

One of the most important elements in staffing a successful *LittleKidsTime* program is planning how you will recruit and organize your staff. However you do it, keep in mind that the best learning and the most fun take place when there is a teacher or helper for every four to six children.

The optimum plan for staffing is to have the same teachers in place for six months to one year. Both teachers and children benefit from regular interaction. Having long-term teachers creates a wonderful opportunity for spiritual growth in children as they build relationships with adults who are faithful in demonstrating God's love.

While it may be easier to recruit teachers to teach one session at a time, such short-term staffing creates other problems. Many churches have found that rotating teachers frequently not only makes learning and growth difficult for children but also creates a heavy workload in administration (distributing curriculum, orienting a constant stream of new teachers, etc.).

Here are some options if long-term commitment is difficult in your situation.

• Ask teachers to teach for a shorter time period—three or four months at a time instead of a year.

• Find two teams of teachers and helpers who will each teach for a month. Then plan to rotate the two teams so that they alternate monthly. Over the course of a year, teachers and children become familiar with each other and can benefit from regular interaction.

• If you must rotate teachers more frequently (weekly or biweekly), have regular greeters or leaders who are present every week.

## Recruiting Tips

Recruiting teachers and helpers is one of the key tasks to making *LittleKidsTime* an effective and fun learning experience for the children of your church and community. Keep the following tips in mind as you seek the volunteers and then match their talents to the tasks to be done:

• Pray for guidance in finding the people God wants to serve in this ministry.

• Start early!

• Keep all the leaders of your Sunday School and other children's ministries aware of and praying about staffing needs.

• Write a job description for each *LittleKidsTime* staff position.

• Make a list of potential teachers and helpers. Consider a wide variety of sources for volunteers: church membership list, new members' classes, suggestions from adult teachers or leaders, lists of previous and current teachers and survey forms. Get recommendations from present teachers. Don't overlook singles, senior citizens, youth and collegians. Be sure to follow your church's established procedures for screening volunteers.

• Look for team members with interests and abilities in specific areas. For example, the teaching team for 24 children might consist of four to six adults: one who prepares and leads the Bible Story Center, one who prepares and leads the Worship Center and four more who each lead a different activity center. When not actively involved with leading a center, team members act as helpers. You may wish to have the leaders of the Bible Story Center and the Worship Center each lead an activity center, or one person might lead both the Bible Story and Worship Centers.

• Recruit a separate team of teachers and leaders for each center. Each team might consist of two or more adults who enjoy teaching together; or consider asking a family with teenagers to work together to form a teaching team.

• Prayerfully prioritize your prospect list. Determine which job description best fits each person's strengths and gifts.

• Personally contact the prospects. Sending a personal letter or a flyer to each prospect is a good first step. Follow up with a phone call to answer any questions or to see if the prospect has made a decision.

• Provide new volunteers with all the needed materials, forms, helpful hints and training that will help them to succeed. For all teachers and helpers, you may want to schedule one or more training meetings at which you distribute curriculum, review schedules and procedures, learn the songs together, etc.

• During the volunteer's time of service, make sure the volunteer knows who will be available to answer questions or lend a helping hand. Look for specific actions and services contributed by the volunteer and offer your thanks.

• Plan a thank-you brunch or pizza dinner or lunch for teachers and their families. Even the ones who don't attend will be grateful for your appreciation!

### *Recruiting Announcements*

The teachers and helpers who will be your *LittleKidsTime* teachers and helpers will appreciate clear, concise information about the program—and a little added inspiration couldn't hurt! Here are some attention-grabbing recruiting announcements.

## WE WANT YOU!

Yes, YOU can fascinate, teach and amaze! Help us as we teach an exciting new course to our preschoolers. Our new *LittleKidsTime* program, *My Great Big God*, is filled with age-appropriate ways to teach young children about God! Active game and block activities, enjoyable songs and worship activities, science discoveries and a variety of other centers will make teaching God's Word easy and delightful!

If you'd like to see great things every single Sunday, we're now taking applications for teachers who can show God's love to young children, use their imaginations and have fun learning more about God's Word!

*My Great Big God* will start on ________ (date)

and continue through________ (date) at ________ (times).

Explore God's Word for a little kid's world!

## WANT TO LEARN MORE ABOUT GOD?

You can! Let our new *LittleKidsTime* program, *My Great Big God*, help you learn as you teach our little kids all about God! You'll find there is no better way to learn more about God and His Word than to teach young children in this kid-friendly program.

*My Great Big God* has exciting songs, Bible stories and worship activities. But that's not all! You'll be able to expand little kids' minds with awesome art projects, amazing science experiences, adaptable games and active block building. All it needs to be the best is YOU! Act now to ensure your spot as a teacher or helper who helps children explore God's Word for a little kid's world!

# Questions & Answers for a Terrific Program

## *What's the best way to distribute and store LittleKidsTime curriculum?*

When you first receive your curriculum, pull out the perforated pages and place them in a binder. Use dividers to separate the main sections of the book: planning pages, lesson pages, etc.

At the beginning of the program, photocopy all the lesson pages, making multiple copies of the first page of each lesson (one for each teacher or helper). Also make multiple copies of the tips page for each activity center (one of the appropriate center for each teacher or helper).

Distribute the appropriate pages to teachers and helpers at a *LittleKidsTime* orientation meeting, or mail them to teachers a week or so before their teaching assignments begin. (If pages will be distributed periodically throughout the year, store the photocopied pages in a separate notebook.)

## *How can we build enthusiasm for LittleKidsTime?*

Children of all ages will respond positively to your efforts to create interest in *LittleKidsTime.*

• Plan theme days such as Fruit Day (everyone is served a specific fruit for a snack), Crazy Hat Day (everyone wears a funny- or silly-looking hat), Color Day (everyone wears clothes of a certain color) or, for Sunday evening or weekday programs, Parent Day (parents and/or grandparents attend *LittleKidsTime* with their children or grandchildren).

• Design a name tag just for the children who attend *LittleKidsTime.*

• Make or decorate T-shirts for *LittleKidsTime* participants to wear.

• Create a special name or logo for your *LittleKidsTime* program and use it on all publicity, recruiting letters, T-shirts, name tags and classroom signs.

These special attention-getting ideas can be used all year long to kick off the beginning of *LittleKidsTime,* as a way to reach out to the community or as "shot-in-the-arm" ideas at any time during the year when you feel enthusiasm and attendance are lagging.

## *How can we make LittleKidsTime challenging enough for kindergartners?*

Throughout *LittleKidsTime,* options are suggested in each center for ways to increase the challenge in that activity for older children. *The Big Book of Kindergarten Puzzles* can provide a challenge to kindergartners. If your group is large enough to divide into classes, group older children in a separate class.

• As you tell the story in the Bible Story Center, one or more of the older children can demonstrate the motions for younger children to copy.

• At the Active Game Center, older children can help to demonstrate games.

• At the Art Center, older children can help younger ones with gluing, cutting, etc.

• In the Worship Center, older children may enjoy helping to lead songs or making up motions to do as they sing.

# Snacks

Be sure to advise parents whenever food is used during a session. Post a note to alert parents so that they will be able to tell you of any food allergies the children may have. Also, registration forms often ask parents to list food allergies. Check these forms first before selecting snacks.

### Neat Treat

1 6-ounce package dried fruit

1 cup nuts

1 cup sunflower seeds

½ cup raisins

Mix together and serve in small paper cups.

### Banana Pudding

Make instant banana pudding. Add sliced bananas and serve in small paper cups with plastic spoons.

### Vegetable Slices

Prepare fresh vegetable slices. Use carrots, celery, etc. You may wish to provide yogurt, ranch dressing or cottage cheese for a dip.

### **Peanut Butter Balls** (serves 16)

1 cup powdered sugar

1 cup powdered milk

2 cups peanut butter

2 cups graham cracker crumbs or wheat germ

Mix sugar, milk and peanut butter. Form into balls. Roll the balls in crumbs or wheat germ.

### **No-Bake Cookies** (serves 16)

1 cup raisins

1 cup finely chopped dates

½ cup honey

½ cup graham cracker crumbs

Mix raisins, dates and honey. Form balls. Roll in graham cracker crumbs.

### **Moon Balls** (serves 16)

2 cups nonfat dry milk

1 cup honey

1 cup peanut butter

1 cup granola or crushed-flake cereal

Mix milk, honey and peanut butter. Chill for an hour or more. Shape into balls and roll in cereal.

### Quesadillas

Cut flour tortillas in half. Cover with cheese spread, fold and serve sandwich style. (These are good served warm, too!)

### **Celery and Pineapple Sticks** (serves 12)

6 stalks celery

1 8-ounce package cream cheese

1 small can crushed pineapple

Cut celery stalks in half. Mash cream cheese. Drain pineapple. Mix pineapple and cream cheese. Spread on celery.

**One-Cup Salad** (serves 8-10)

1 cup diced bananas

1 cup fruit cocktail

1 cup tiny marshmallows

1 cup crushed pineapple

1 cup sour cream or plain yogurt

Mix and chill and serve in small paper cups.

**Oatmeal Bars**

2 cups oatmeal (uncooked)

¾ cup brown sugar

½ cup or 1 stick butter or margarine

dash of baking soda

Boil sugar, butter or margarine and soda. Add oatmeal and blend. Spread mixture in a well-greased 8-inch square pan (or equivalent) and bake at 350° for 10 minutes. Cut into bars while warm. Serve when cool.

**Fresh Fruit Mix**

Combine equal parts of fresh sliced peaches and blueberries or blackberries. Serve in small paper cups.

**Open-Face Sandwiches**

Mix peanut butter and drained crushed pineapple. Spread on whole wheat bread. Cut in fourths.

**Cereal Snack**

Pour dry cereal into a bowl. Children take a handful and put on napkin or in a cup and eat.

**Applesauce**

Serve prepared applesauce in small paper cups. Provide one quart for 15 children.

**Carrot Sticks**

Wash carrots. Leave skin on. Cut into small bite-size pieces.

**Muffins**

Prepare bran, blueberry or cranberry muffins. Use a small-cup muffin tin if available.

**Fruit Cubes and Dip**

1 cup plain yogurt

4 tablespoons orange or apple juice concentrate

Fresh and/or dried fruit

Combine yogurt and juice concentrate in a bowl. Cut fruit into bite-size pieces. Dip fruit in yogurt mixture and eat.

**Orange Pops**

Pour orange juice (or another juice) into small paper cups. Put a plastic spoon in each cup. Freeze until solid. Children hold frozen-juice pops by the spoon handles, tear off cups and lick!

## Yogurt

Serve frozen or chilled yogurt in small paper cups with plastic spoons. Provide one quart yogurt for every
15 children.

## Cereal Cookies (serves 16)

1 cup corn syrup

1 cup peanut butter

8 cups puffed rice cereal

Mix syrup and peanut butter together. Add cereal and mix until coated. Spoon onto waxed paper. Let set before serving.

## Finger Jello

Dissolve four envelopes unflavored gelatin in one cup cold water. Dissolve one 6-ounce box of any flavor gelatin in four cups boiling water. Then mix the two gelatins together and pour into a 9x13-inch (23x33-cm) pan. Refrigerate until firm. Cut in squares and serve.

## Rolled Bananas

½ banana for each child

1 tablespoon lemon juice (for each ½ banana)

2 tablespoons coconut or wheat germ (for each ½ banana)

Cut banana into 3 or 4 slices, dip in lemon juice, roll in coconut or wheat germ.

## Fruit

Prepare (or children prepare) any type of fresh fruit that is in season.

## Ants on a Log

Spread peanut butter on celery sticks. Place raisins on top of peanut butter.

## Cheese and Crackers

Serve sliced cheese and crackers. Or children use a cheese spread to decorate their own crackers.

## Fruit Leather

Purchase rolls of fruit leather from your local grocery store. One roll should serve two children.

## No-Bake Cookies (serves 16)

1 ¾ cups finely crushed vanilla wafers

1 cup powdered sugar

¼ cup melted butter or margarine

¼ cup undiluted orange juice

Mix ingredients together. Roll into balls. Roll balls in some powdered sugar. Refrigerate and serve.

## Cereal Scramble

1 cup each of three different kinds of unsweetened cereal

½ cup pretzels

½ stick melted butter or margarine

Mix all ingredients gently. Spread on baking sheet. Bake at 300° for 30 minutes. Stir occasionally. Store in a tightly covered container.

# Play-Dough Recipes

Children enjoy the unending variety of shapes that results from molding, squeezing, rolling and pounding dough. This activity becomes even more fun when the children mix the dough themselves. Here are some recipes for different textures. Three of the recipes require no baking and could be made by the children during the class session.

**Recipe One**

2 parts flour

1 part salt

1 tablespoon alum

Add water and dry tempera to achieve desired consistency and color.

**Recipe Two**

4 cups flour

2 cups salt

food coloring

¼ cup salad oil

⅛ cup soap flakes

2 cups water

⅛ cup alum

Mix ingredients well.

**Recipe Three**

1 ½ cups flour

1 cup cornstarch

1 cup salt

1 cup warm water

Mix ingredients well.

**Recipe Four**

1 cup flour

1 cup water and food coloring

½ cup salt

1 tablespoon cooking oil

2 teaspoons cream of tartar

Cook over medium heat until consistency of mashed potatoes. Do not boil. Knead until cool.

With all recipes, if dough is sticky, dust with flour. If dough is stiff, add water. All recipes need to be stored in airtight containers. Recipe Three hardens nicely and can be painted if sculptures are to be preserved.

# Leading the Young Child Toward Jesus

When we have presented Jesus by both our actions and our words, a foundation is laid for a child to receive Christ as Savior. Every lesson may create an opportunity to talk with a young child who wants to know more about Jesus.

•The young child is easily attracted to Jesus. Jesus is a warm, sympathetic person who obviously likes children, and children readily like Him. These early perceptions prepare the foundation for the child to receive Christ as Savior and to desire to follow His example in godly living. While some children at this age level (especially from Christian homes) may indeed pray to become a member of God's family, accepting Jesus as their Savior, expect wide variation in children's readiness for this important step. Allow the Holy Spirit room to work within His own timetable.

• Talk individually with children. Something as important as a child's personal relationship with Jesus Christ can be handled more effectively alone than in a group. Ask questions that will help you determine what the child understands. Open-ended what-do-you-think questions give you a chance to hear what's really going on in the child's mind and heart. "What do you like best about Jesus?" will help a child give words to his or her thoughts and feelings about Him.

• Talk simply. Phrases such as "born again" or "Jesus in my heart" are symbolic and far beyond a young child's understanding. Focus on how God makes people a part of His family:

- **God loves us, but we have done wrong things (sinned).**
- **God says sin must be punished.**
- **God sent Jesus to take the punishment for the wrong things we have done.**
- **We can tell God that we have done wrong and tell Him we are sorry for our sin.**
- **We can ask Jesus to be our Savior.**
- **Then we become a part of God's family.**

Share this information whenever a child seems interested but only for as long as the interest lasts. Lay a good foundation for a lifetime of solid spiritual growth!

Lesson 1

# Baby in a Basket

## Bible Story

Exodus 2:1-10

God's Word
"God cares about you." (See 1 Peter 5:7.)
God's Word & Me
God shows His care for me by giving me people who love me.

## Teacher's Devotional

Every parent knows how stressful it can be to adjust to a new baby, but the experience of Moses' family far exceeds anything most of us will ever know. Imagine trying to quiet a crying baby so that soldiers won't come to kill him! Pharaoh had ordered all Hebrew baby boys to be thrown into the Nile River. Moses' parents had either to risk losing their baby or to see him die. So they did put him in the Nile—but in a waterproof basket, trusting God to do something miraculous. And God honored their faith!

Of course, we know the rest of the story: God protected Moses and used him mightily. Now think about your own life. You've seen God protect you, probably many times. Pause to consider what His plans may be for you! Those plans may not look big to you. They may even be hidden from your sight right now. But rest assured, they are of eternal importance!

There are no little plans in God's eyes. What you are doing at this moment is part of the amazing tapestry He is weaving for you—and through you—for you will touch many others. He has led you and protected you just as He protected Moses. Take joy in watching His plans unfold!

## Teacher's Planning

1. Choose which centers you will provide and the order in which children will participate in them. For tips on schedule planning, see page 7.
2. Plan who will lead each center. For staffing tips and ideas, see page 21.

Lesson 1

# Active Game Center: Hidden Basket

## Collect

Bible, basket.

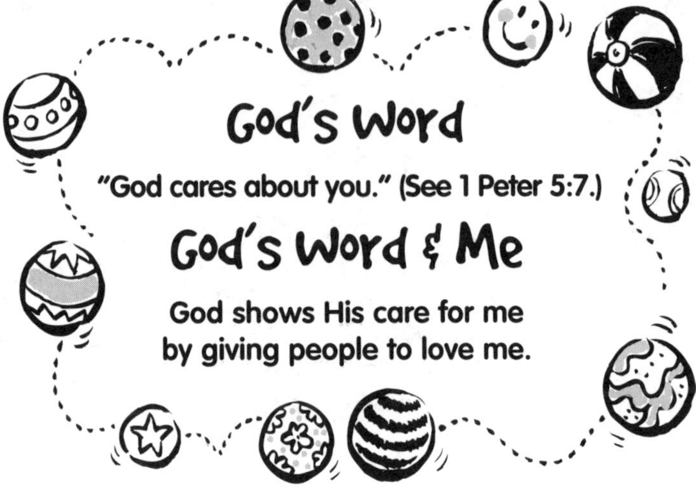
God's Word
"God cares about you." (See 1 Peter 5:7.)
God's Word & Me
God shows His care for me by giving people to love me.

## Do

1. Select two volunteers to close their eyes as you hide the basket in the classroom. Be sure basket can be seen but is not in too obvious a place. **Let's help Shawna and Noel find the basket. Don't make any noise when they are far from the basket. Start clapping when they move close to the basket.**
2. Volunteers begin to move around classroom. Lead children in clapping faster and louder as the volunteers move closer and closer to the basket. Repeat as time allows.

## Talk About

Story Book
A
B
C
D

- **Baby Moses' mother cared for him by making a special basket. Let's play a game to find a hidden basket.**
- **What are some ways your mother cares for you?**
- **God cared for baby Moses by giving him people to love him. Our Bible says, "God cares about you." God shows His care by giving us people who love us!**
- **What are some ways babies are cared for by the people who love them?**
- **Who has God given to care for you? What are ways your babysitter cares for you?**
- Pray briefly, **Thank You, God, for caring for us.**

### For Younger Children

Give verbal hints to help children find the basket: **The basket is near a door.**

### For Older Children

After finding basket, children select new volunteers and also hide the basket for the next round of play.

# Art Center: Paper-Plate Puppet People

## Collect

Bible, two paper plates for each child, markers, stapler.

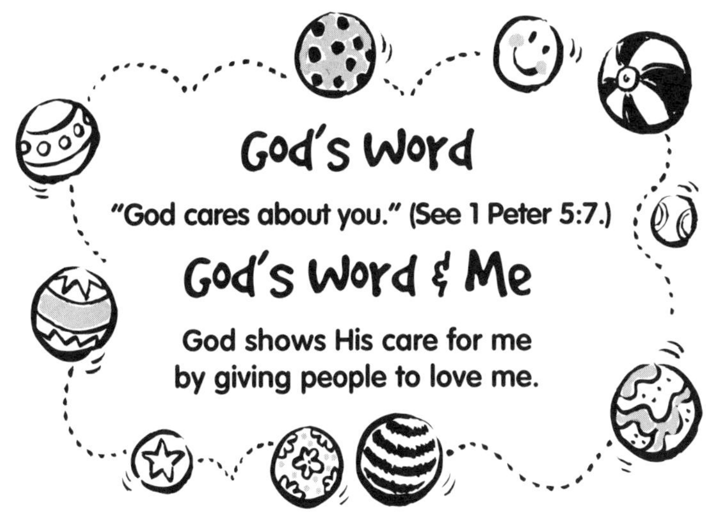
God's Word
"God cares about you." (See 1 Peter 5:7.)
God's Word & Me
God shows His care for me by giving people to love me.

## Do

1. On the back of the plates, children draw faces of two people who care for them, one face on each plate.
2. Children place paper plates together with faces on the outside. Staple at the top and sides, leaving bottom unstapled so that children can insert their hands. Children use puppets to act out ways people in their families care for each other.

## Talk About

- **Our Bible says, "God cares about you." God cares about each one of us! God gives us people who love us. Let's make puppets that show people who love us.**
- **Who cooks dinner for you? Who helps you take a bath? Get ready for bed? Get dressed? These are ways people care for you!**
- **What other things does your dad do to show his love for you? Our Bible says, "God cares about you," Richie. God planned for people to take care of you.**
- **Who are some other people who love you?** Pray briefly, **Dear God, thank You for giving me people to care for me.**

## For Younger Children

Instead of using two paper plates and stapling them together, children draw one face on a paper plate and hold up paper-plate puppet.

## For Older Children

Provide lengths of yarn. Children glue yarn to top edges of plates to form hair.

# Block Center: Road Blocks

## Collect

Bible, construction paper in a variety of colors, markers, scissors, blocks.

## Prepare

Make several street signs (Stop, Yield, etc.) from construction paper and markers.

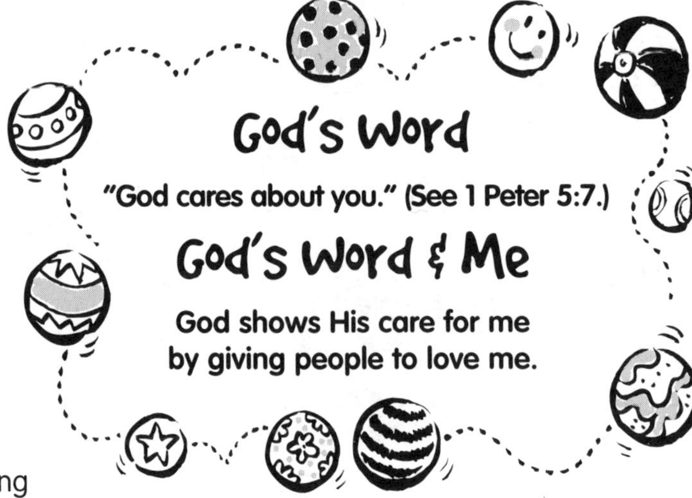
God's Word
"God cares about you." (See 1 Peter 5:7.)
God's Word & Me
God shows His care for me by giving people to love me.

## Do

1. Children use blocks to outline a road wide enough to walk down. Then along the road, children build buildings and place signs you prepared.
2. Suggest family roles to interested children. Walk down the road with pretend family as you ask the questions below.

## Talk About

- **Let's pretend we're a family and go for a walk on a road! Where do you want to go?**
- **God planned for families to have fun together. That's one way to show love for each other. What are some of the fun things you do with the people who love you?**
- **The Bible says, "God cares about you." God gives people to keep you safe. What is a way people help each other when they walk down the street? When they ride in a car?** (Hold hands as they walk. Look both ways before crossing the street. Wear seat belts.)

## For Younger Children

Children make a road without signs or buildings. If a child hesitates to walk down the road, offer to walk along with the child. Your companionship will encourage participation.

## For Older Children

Children make one or more intersections in their road. Assign a volunteer to an intersection. Volunteer acts like a stoplight, holding up a red sheet of paper to cue children to stop walking, and holding up a green sheet of paper to cue children to start walking.

# Science Center: Sink or Float?

## Collect

Bible; toy and household objects that float or sink (plastic toy, penny, pebble, pencil, spoon, etc.), at least one item for each child; dishpan with water; several towels.

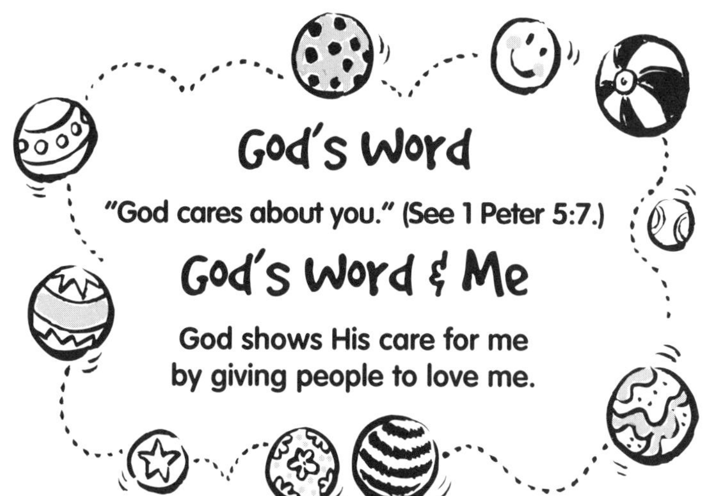

### God's Word

**"God cares about you." (See 1 Peter 5:7.)**

### God's Word & Me

**God shows His care for me by giving people to love me.**

## Do

1. Show children the toys and objects you brought. Children take turns placing items in water. As each item is placed into water, ask, **Do you think this pencil will float or sink?**
2. Children remove items from water, placing items that float in one pile and items that sink in another pile. Children dry hands with towels.

## Talk About

- **In our Bible story, a mother made a basket so that her baby could float safely on a river. Let's find some things that float.**
- **Moses' mother took care of her baby. What are some ways babies are cared for? Who feeds a baby? Gives a baby a bath?**
- **Our Bible says, "God cares about you." God gave you your family to love you and help you.** Pray briefly, **Thank You, God, for caring for us.**
- **God cares for us and gives us people to keep us safe. Who are some people who love you? What is something they do to take care of you?**

## For Younger Children

Provide more than one dishpan so that younger children have several opportunities to experiment with items. If you use more than two dishpans, be sure to have additional helpers.

## For Older Children

Provide several empty plastic water or soda bottles. Completely fill some of the plastic bottles with water, fill some partially and leave some unfilled. Place lids on bottles. Allow children time to experiment with the different bottles to determine why some of the bottles sink, why some float and why some only partially float.

Lesson 1 • Exodus 2:1-10

# Bible Story Center

## Collect

Bible, Picture 5 from *Bible Story Pictures.*

### God's Word

**"God cares about you." (See 1 Peter 5:7.)**

## Tell the Story

### God's Word & Me

**God shows His care for me by giving people to love me.**

Use the pictured motions (keywords in bold) or show Picture 5. For older children, tell the version of the story on the back of Picture 5.

**What is something people do to care for a baby? Listen to hear who God planned to take care of baby Moses.**

Our Bible tells us about a special family. This family had a dad, a mom, a big sister, a big brother and a **baby** brother. The baby's name was Moses.

Moses' family loved him very much. Moses' family took good care of him. Every day they fed baby Moses. They wrapped baby Moses in soft blankets. Every day they played with baby Moses. God planned for Moses to have a family to care for him.

But there was a mean king who wanted to hurt Moses. Moses' family must have been scared! God helped Moses' mom plan a way to keep her baby safe.

Moses' mom made a special basket. She put soft blankets in the basket. Then she carefully laid Moses in the basket. Moses' mom carried the basket with Moses to the river. She placed the basket on top of the water. Moses' big sister stayed with the basket and **watched** over Moses.

The king's daughter came to the river. The king's daughter wasn't mean. She was kind. She saw the basket. When she opened it, she found Moses crying. "This poor baby," she said. The king's daughter felt sorry for Moses. "This baby needs someone to care for him." Moses' big sister heard this. She went to the king's daughter.

"I will go get someone to care for the baby," Moses' big sister said. Then she **ran** to get Moses' mom.

Moses' mom took good care of him. The king's daughter made sure the mean king did not hurt the **baby**. Moses' family was glad God helped them keep Moses safe.

## God's Word & Me

**Who took care of baby Moses?** (Mother, sister, family, princess.) **God showed His care for baby Moses by giving people to love him! God gives people to care for us, too. Who are some of the people God gives to love you? What are some of the things they do to take care of you?** (Cook food to eat. Give clothes to wear. Help when sick.)

# Worship Center

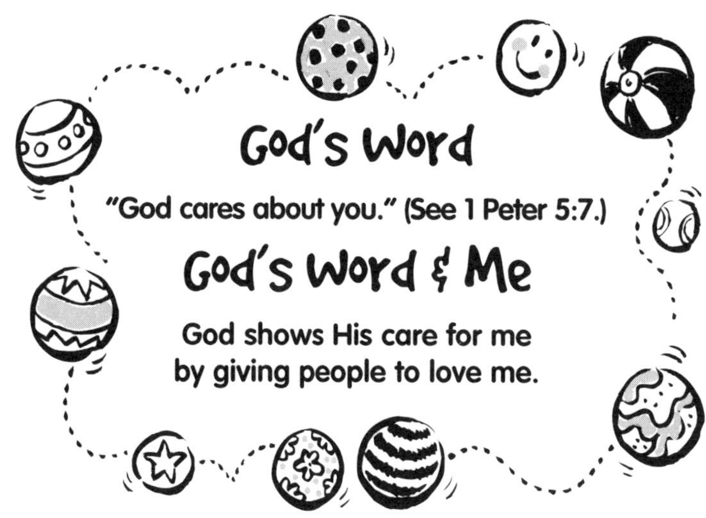

## God's Word

**"God cares about you." (See 1 Peter 5:7.)**

## God's Word & Me

**God shows His care for me by giving people to love me.**

### Collect

Bible, *Shake It Up!* songbook and cassette/CD and player, "God Cares About You" and "All I Need" word charts (pp. 9 and 6 in songbook).

## Sing to God

Play "God Cares About You." Invite children to sing along with you. **Let's sing a song about God's love.** Lead children in singing song and doing suggested motions. **Who are some people God cares about?**

## Hear and Say God's Word

Holding your Bible open to 1 Peter 5:7, say verse aloud. **Our Bible says, "God cares about you." God gives people to love and care for us.** Lead children in saying the verse. First the boys say "God cares" and then the girls say "About you." Have children repeat the verse in this manner several times, alternating which group says the phrases.

## Pray to God

**Let's thank God that He cares for us.** To complete the following prayer, volunteers take turns naming people who care for them: **Thank You, God, for the people who love and care for us. Thank You for . . .**

## Sing to God

In closing the worship time, play "All I Need." Invite children to sing along with you and do suggested motions. **What are some of the good things God gives us?** (Food, water, houses, pets, friends, teachers, etc.)

### Options

1. To make the Bible verse activity more of a challenge for older children, ask them to repeat verse and replace the word "you" with another child's name. The named child then repeats verse, using a different child's name. Continue until each child has a turn.
2. Ask children to tell ways people care for them. Print children's responses on large sheet of paper. Display paper so that it is visible to parents when children are dismissed.

Lesson 1

# Read-Aloud Story and Activity Center

## Collect

A copy of Story Picture 1 (pp. 7-8 from *Read-Aloud Story and Activity Book*) for each child and yourself, crayons or markers.

## Prepare

Color your copy of Story Picture 1.

## Do

**Listen to find out what this family is doing.** Read story and show completed Story Picture 1. Distribute pictures. Use conversation suggestions in Let's Talk About the Story as children complete their pages.

# Kindergarten Puzzle Center

## Collect

Copies of Puzzles 1 and 2 (p. 9 and p. 11 from *The Big Book of Kindergarten Puzzles)* for each child, pencils, crayons or markers.

## Do

Children complete the puzzles and color pages.

# Instant Activities

These activities can be used at any time during this session: when children need a change of pace, to extend the session, or during transition time at the beginning or end of the session.

## Collect

*The Big Book of Instant Activities.*

## Do

Guide children to complete "We'll Clap for You!" and/or "Match Me" (p. 73 and/or p. 114 from *The Big Book of Instant Activities).*

Lesson 2

# Escape from Egypt

## Bible Story

Exodus 12:31-38; 13:20-22

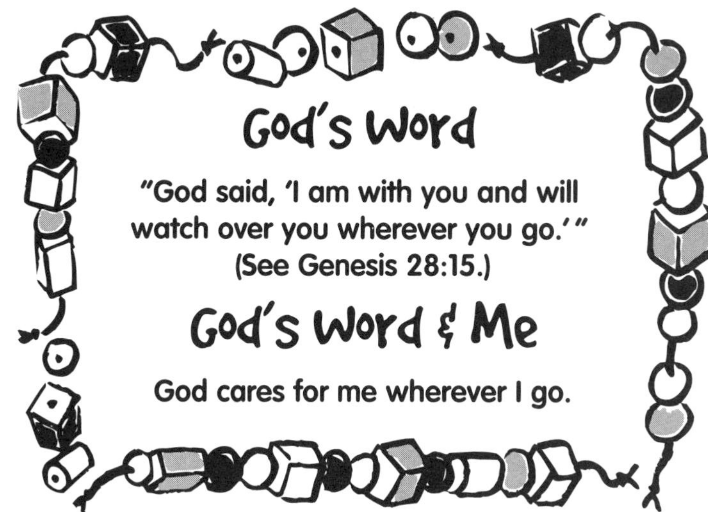

God's Word
"God said, 'I am with you and will watch over you wherever you go.'" (See Genesis 28:15.)
God's Word & Me
God cares for me wherever I go.

## Teacher's Devotional

Where is the loneliest place you have ever been? In a foreign country? Along a stretch of deserted highway? Such places bring the word "god-forsaken" to mind. The desert through which God's people traveled to get to the Promised Land was also a place many would describe as godforsaken. The Sinai Desert is desolate! But was it indeed godforsaken?

Think of what happened in that lonely place—some of history's most astounding miracles, short of Jesus' resurrection. God guided His people by cloud and fire, parted the Red Sea and destroyed the Pharaoh's army. He kept His people safe through tremendous dangers—in this place that looked godforsaken to many of His own people!

Sometimes we come to places in our lives where we think, *This is it. There's no solution. This place in which I am is absolutely godforsaken. It's hopeless.* It's easy to forget God's presence—the Israelites proved that. But a place where He is not? It doesn't exist! No matter how the place looks to you, He's there, waiting to hear you and meet you where you are.

## Teacher's Planning

1. Choose which centers you will provide and the order in which children will participate in them. For tips on schedule planning, see page 7.
2. Plan who will lead each center. For staffing tips and ideas, see page 21.

Lesson 2

# Active Game Center: Stop and Go

## Collect

Bible, yarn, one sheet each of red and green construction paper.

## Prepare

Place a yarn line at each end of the playing area.

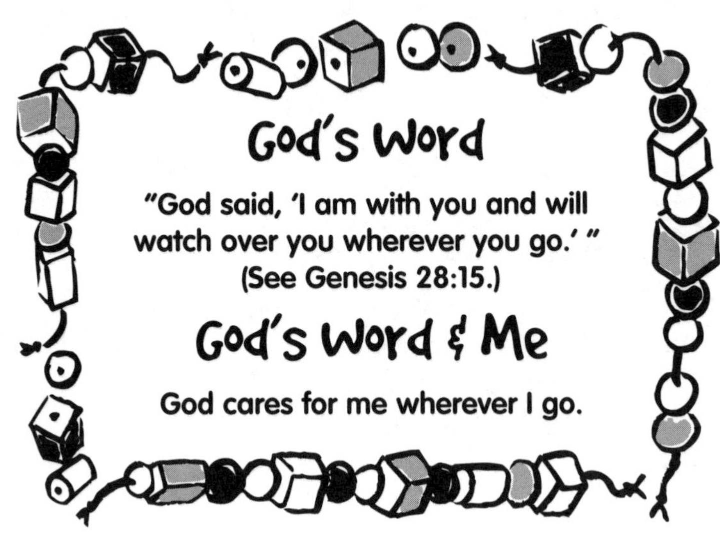

God's Word
"God said, 'I am with you and will watch over you wherever you go.'"
(See Genesis 28:15.)
God's Word & Me
God cares for me wherever I go.

## Do

1. Play a game like Red Light, Green Light. All children stand behind one of the yarn lines. Stand behind other yarn line to lead the first round of the game.
2. Hold up the sheets of construction paper, one at a time. Instruct children to walk toward you when you hold up the green sheet and to freeze when you hold up the red sheet. After all the children reach you, a volunteer becomes the leader and another round is played. Repeat as time allows.

## Talk About

- **Our Bible tells us, "God said, 'I am with you and will watch over you wherever you go.'" God is with us wherever we go. He takes care of us. Let's play a game to remind us of God's promise.**
- **Where do you like to go with your family?**
- **What are some of the things you see when you travel in your car? When you go for a walk?**
- Pray briefly, **Dear God, thank You for always watching over us.**

## For Younger Children

Lead each round of play. Younger children playing the game may need verbal clues such as "Walk" and "Freeze" to reinforce the color clues.

## For Older Children

Add a yellow paper for older children. When yellow paper is shown, children move in slow motion.

Lesson 2

# Art Center: Pack It Up

## Collect

Bible, catalog pictures of items to pack in a suitcase, scissors, yarn, ruler, construction paper in a variety of colors, transparent tape, hole punch.

## Prepare

Cut out catalog pictures, preparing enough pictures so that each child will have several to choose from. Cut two 8-inch (20.5-cm) yarn lengths for each child.

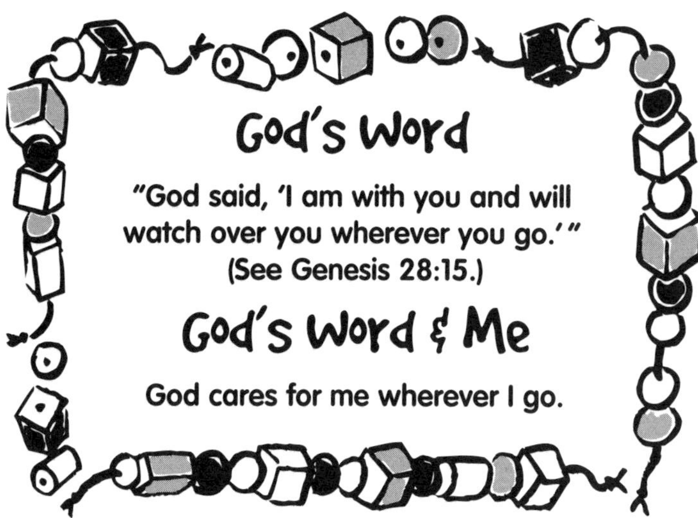

God's Word
**"God said, 'I am with you and will watch over you wherever you go.'" (See Genesis 28:15.)**
God's Word & Me
**God cares for me wherever I go.**

## Do

1. Each child tapes together two sheets of construction paper as shown in sketch. In the outside edges of the papers, help children punch two holes. Help children thread a yarn length through each set of holes and tie ends together to form handles.
2. Children select catalog pictures and tape them to the inside of their paper suitcases.

# Talk About

- **In our Bible story today, God's people went on a long trip. Let's pretend we're going on a trip, too. We'll make suitcases to take on our pretend trip.**
- **Have you ever gone on a trip? Where did you go?**
- **What did you do to get ready for your trip?**
- **In our Bible we read, "God said, 'I am with you and will watch over you wherever you go.'"** Pray briefly, **Thank You, God, for being with us wherever we go.**

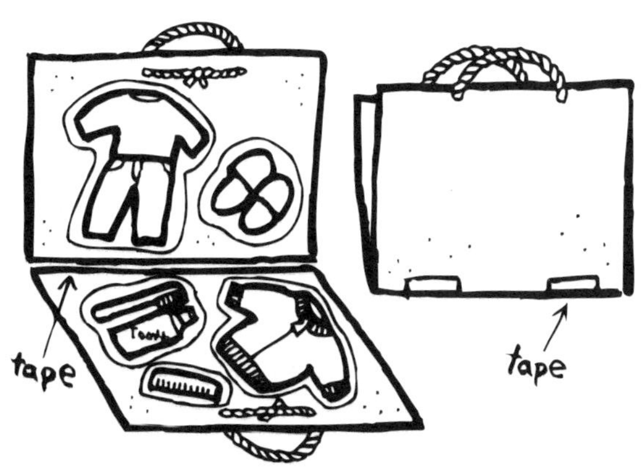

tape
tape

## For Younger Children

Instead of making suitcases, children make a collage by taping onto a large sheet of butcher paper, pictures of things to take on a trip.

## For Older Children

Children decorate the outside of their suitcases with words and pictures cut from a travel brochure, or color it with markers.

 

# Block Center: Camp Out

## Collect

Bible, white paper, scissors, glue, cotton balls, blocks, construction paper, toy animals, toy people.

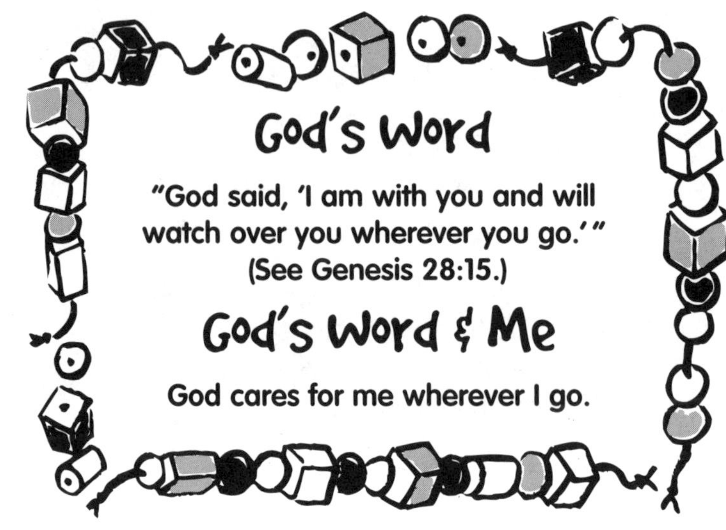
God's Word
"God said, 'I am with you and will watch over you wherever you go.'"
(See Genesis 28:15.)
God's Word & Me
God cares for me wherever I go.

## Prepare

Cut a cloud shape from white paper. Glue cotton balls on cloud shape.

## Do

1. Children outline a campground with blocks and make tents from sheets of construction paper. Children set up toy animals and toy people.
2. Use cloud shape you prepared to signal children it is time to move to a new campground. Children gather up tents, toy animals and toy people and follow you as you lead them to a new area of the room. Children outline a new campground and set up tents, toy animals and toy people.

## Talk About

- **Moses and God's people followed a cloud by day. At night, God put a large fire in the sky. Whenever God's people moved, they had to make a new campground. Let's build a place to camp!**
- **Have you ever had to move to a new house? What did you do to get ready to move?**
- **What do you think God's people took on their trip?** (Clothes, food, water, etc.)
- **Our Bible tells us that God said, "I am with you and will watch over you wherever you go." How can we show that we are glad God watches over us?** (Sing songs of praise to God. Pray to God to tell Him thanks.)

## For Younger Children

Children build one campground and don't move to another area.

## For Older Children

Children fold index cards in half to make stand-up cards. Then children draw animal and people pictures on cards to make moveable figures.

# Science Center: Texture Walk

## Collect

Bible, a variety of materials with different textures (cardboard, towels, bubble wrap, newspaper, sandpaper, etc.).

## Prepare

Arrange the different materials to create a path through the room.

### God's Word

**"God said, 'I am with you and will watch over you wherever you go.'" (See Genesis 28:15.)**

### God's Word & Me

**God cares for me wherever I go.**

## Do

1. Children remove their shoes. Then children form a line and follow you as you lead them along the path you created. **Let's pretend we're walking to a park.** Ask questions to guide children in describing the different textures.
2. Select a volunteer. Volunteer chooses a destination for the walk (store, grandmother's house, church, etc.) and leads the other children along the path in a manner of his or her choice: crawling, hopping on one foot, walking backward, etc.

## Talk About

- **Wherever we go, God cares for us! Let's go on a pretend walk and talk about some of the ways God cares for us.**
- **What does it feel like to walk on cardboard? What sound does walking on cardboard make?** Repeat for each texture.
- **In our Bible we read, "God said, 'I am with you and will watch over you wherever you go.'" That means God is with us when we go to the park. Where are some other places you go? God is with you whenever you go there.**

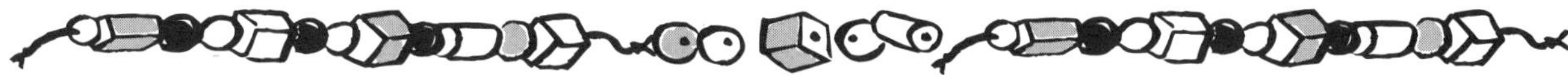

## For Younger Children

Young children may need your help to verbalize answers. **Shanda, the cardboard feels smooth, doesn't it? The towel feels soft and cuddly. What else is soft and cuddly?**

## For Older Children

Ask a volunteer to remove his or her shoes and close his or her eyes. Lead volunteer in walking across one of the textures to identify it. Repeat with several volunteers.

# Bible Story Center

## Collect

Bible, Picture 6 from *Bible Story Pictures.*

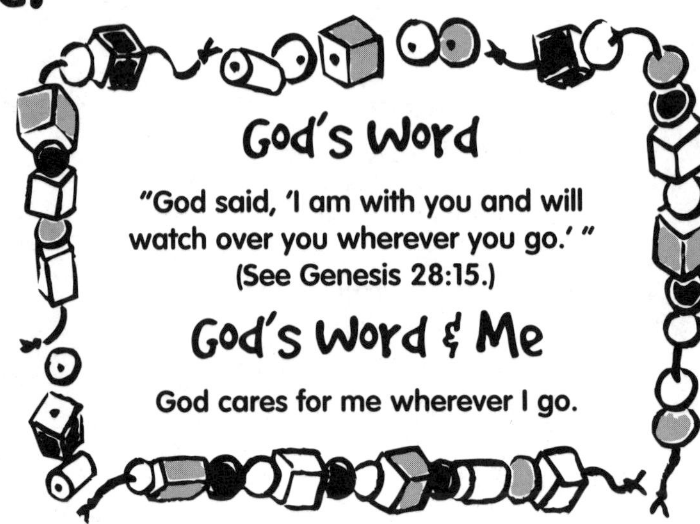

### God's Word

**"God said, 'I am with you and will watch over you wherever you go.' " (See Genesis 28:15.)**

### God's Word & Me

**God cares for me wherever I go.**

## Tell the Story

Use the pictured motions (keywords in bold) or show Picture 6. For older children, tell the version of the story on the back of Picture 6.

**Have you ever been on a long trip? What did you do to get ready? Today we're going to hear about a long trip God's people took a long time ago.**

Our Bible tells about when God wanted His people to go to a new home far away. God told Moses to be the leader. God said, "I will be with you."

How **excited** the people were! "We will need food to eat," they said. So moms cooked special food to take on the trip. "And we will need water to drink," they said. So boys and girls filled water bags. "What will we wear and where will we sleep?" they asked. So grandmas **tied** clothes and blankets into big bundles. "And what about all our animals?" they asked. So dads got the sheep, goats, cows and donkeys ready to go.

Soon it was time to start on the long, long trip. Moses told the people, "**God** will take care of us. God will lead us and show us the way." And God did that in a very special way. During the day, God put a big white cloud in the sky. The people followed the cloud. During the night, God put fire in the sky. The fire showed the people God was with them.

**Step**, step, step—moms and dads, aunts and uncles, grandmas and grandpas walked down the road. Steppety-step, steppety-step—boys and girls walked down the road. Clippety-clop, clippety-clop—sheep, goats, cows and donkeys walked down the road. All of the people and animals walked behind God's cloud.

The people were glad they were going to a new home. They were glad God showed them He was with them. The people knew God was taking care of them on their long, long trip.

## God's Word & Me

**How did Moses and God's people find their way as they traveled?** (God showed them.) **God was with His people as they traveled to a new land. God is with us everywhere we go, too! Where are some of the places you go?** (Park, friend's house, church, store, etc.) **What is a way God cares for you when you go to the park?**

# Worship Center

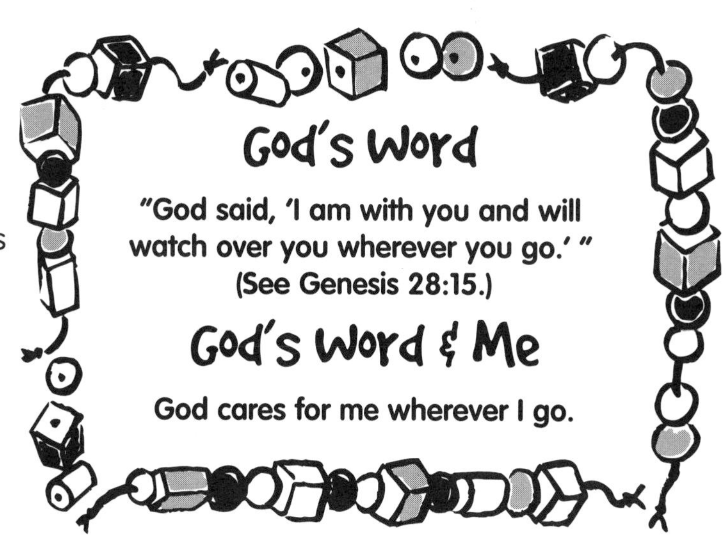
God's Word
"God said, 'I am with you and will watch over you wherever you go.' "
(See Genesis 28:15.)
God's Word & Me
God cares for me wherever I go.

## Collect

Bible, *Shake It Up!* songbook and cassette/CD and player, "God Cares About You" and "All I Need" word charts (pp. 9 and 6 in songbook).

## Sing to God

Play "God Cares About You." Invite children to sing along with you. **Let's sing a song about God's love.** Lead children in singing song and doing suggested motions. **Where are some of the places you go?** Volunteers respond. **Remember whenever you are at the library that God cares for you!**

## Hear and Say God's Word

Holding your Bible open to Genesis 28:15, say verse aloud. **What does God promise us in today's Bible verse?** (He will always be with us. He will always watch over us.) Then lead children in repeating the verse. Children clap their hands on each word of the verse except the word "you." Whenever children say the word "you," they point to a different child in the class. Repeat several times.

## Pray to God

As you say the following prayer, point to a child and pause for the child to say his or her name, thereby completing the phrase. **Dear God, thank You for caring for ___________.** Repeat once for each child in your class. If you have a large class, point to more than one child each time you repeat the phrase.

## Sing to God

In closing the worship time, play "All I Need." Invite children to sing along with you and do suggested motions. **Who loves you? God cares for us by giving us people who love us!**

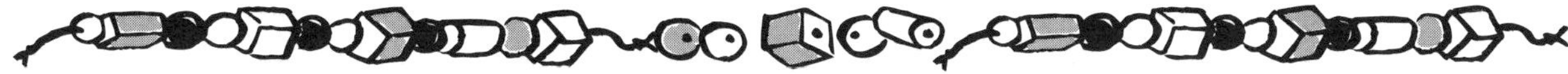

## Options

1. On a large sheet of paper, print the words "God cares for me at." During the first song activity ask children to name some of the places where they go. Print children's responses on paper; then place paper where parents can read responses when they pick up their children.
2. Older children lead other children in doing the motions suggested for "God Cares About You" and/or "All I Need."

Lesson 2

# Read-Aloud Story and Activity Center

## Collect

A copy of Story Picture 2 (pp. 9-10 from *Read-Aloud Story and Activity Book*) for each child and yourself, crayons or markers.

"God said, 'I am with you and will watch over you wherever you go.'"
Story Picture 2

## Prepare

Color your copy of Story Picture 2.

## Do

**Listen for ways Casey's family helped him.** Read story and show completed Story Picture 2. Distribute pictures. Use conversation suggestions in Let's Talk About the Story as children complete their pages.

# Kindergarten Puzzle Center

## Collect

Copies of Puzzles 3 and 4 (p. 13 and p. 15 from *The Big Book of Kindergarten Puzzles*) for each child, pencils, crayons or markers.

## Do

Children complete the puzzles and color pages.

# Instant Activities

These activities can be used at any time during this session: when children need a change of pace, to extend the session, or during transition time at the beginning or end of the session.

## Collect

*The Big Book of Instant Activities.*

## Do

Guide children to complete "Animal Moves" and/or "All Eyes on Me!" (p. 17 and/or p. 16 from *The Big Book of Instant Activities).*

Lesson 3

# A Path Through the Sea

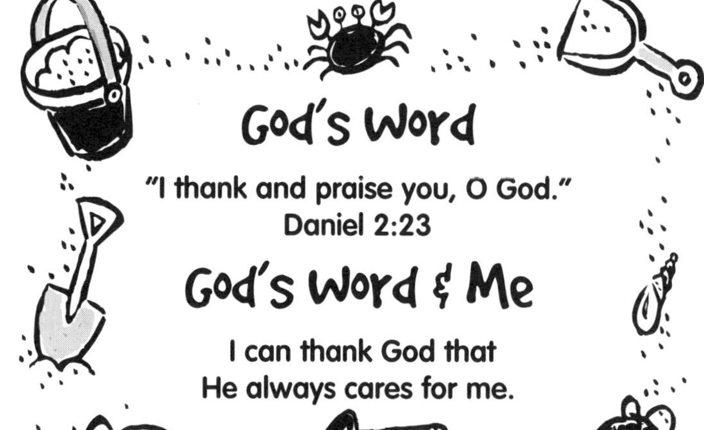

### God's Word

**"I thank and praise you, O God."**
**Daniel 2:23**

### God's Word & Me

**I can thank God that He always cares for me.**

## Bible Story

Exodus 14—15:20

## Teacher's Devotional

Safety is one of the basic needs of every human being. Unless a person feels safe, it is very difficult to fulfill any other life need.

Today's lesson focuses on how God kept His people safe. God's safety program was unique. It was unlike anything from a personnel office—no safety guidelines or accident reports were necessary. It was very simple: God told the people what to do, they obeyed Him, and He protected them! When God sent the wind that held back the water, they could have said, "Now this is ridiculous. There's no way those walls of water won't fall on us. We'll drown—and be the laughingstock of the world, to boot!" But the Israelites took the risk of obeying God, even as they heard the armies of Pharaoh coming.

Safety is a relative term! Our lives may look as impossibly unsafe as that path through the sea. But in the care of God, in the arms of Jesus Christ, we can take that first step. Believe the unbelievable. Risk obeying the Lord, no matter how the circumstances look. You'll be loved and led. And you'll have your own stories to tell of what God has done in your life!

## Teacher's Planning

1. Choose which centers you will provide and the order in which children will participate in them. For tips on schedule planning, see page 7.
2. Plan who will lead each center. For staffing tips and ideas, see page 21.

# Active Game Center: Household Help

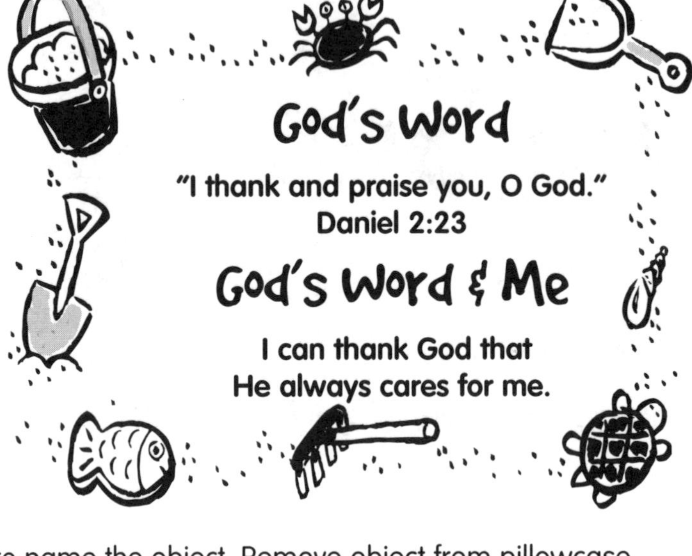
God's Word
"I thank and praise you, O God."
Daniel 2:23
God's Word & Me
I can thank God that
He always cares for me.

## Collect

Bible, a variety of household items (toy, spoon, napkin, child's sweater, soap, book, etc.), large paper grocery bag, pillowcase.

## Prepare

Place household items in bag.

## Do

1. Take an item from bag and secretly place in pillowcase. Children take turns feeling object through pillowcase. After everyone has had a turn, call on a volunteer to name the object. Remove object from pillowcase.

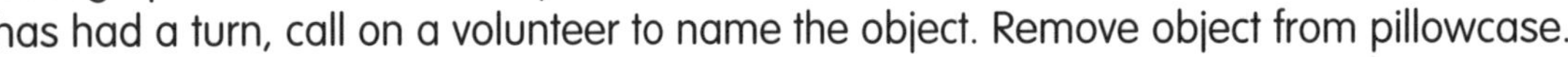

2. Talk about ways the object can be used to help people in families. Repeat with other items.

## Talk About

- **One way God cares for us is by giving us people who live with us and care for us. Let's play a game and talk about some of the ways family members take care of each other.**
- **Who are the people in your family? What are some of the ways your father helps take care of the people in your family?** Repeat using other family members.
- **Our Bible says, "I thank and praise you, O God." We can thank and praise God because He always cares for us.**
- **Who helps you take a bath? Cooks dinner? Reads you stories? Helps you get dressed?**
- **How does it make you feel to know God gave you all these people to take care of you? We can thank God that He always cares for us.**

## For Younger Children

Children take turns pulling objects out of large paper bag. If children have difficulty identifying object, tell what the object is and how it can be used to help others.

## For Older Children

Children act out ways the object can be used to help people in their families.

Lesson 3

# Art Center: Shoe-Print Path

## Collect

Bible; construction paper; crayons; scissors; two large sheets of blue paper, pieces of blue fabric or blue towels.

### God's Word

**"I thank and praise you, O God."**
**Daniel 2:23**

### God's Word & Me

**I can thank God that He always cares for me.**

## Do

1. Children form pairs and take turns standing on a sheet of construction paper as their partners outline their shoes. Children decorate and cut out their paper shoes.
2. Help children make a path by laying their paper shoes in a line. At the end of the path, place the two large sheets of blue paper, pieces of blue fabric or blue towels to create a pretend sea.
3. Lead children on a pretend trip by walking along the path. When you reach the pretend sea, stop walking. Separate papers, fabric pieces or towels to open up a path for children to cross.

## Talk About

- **In today's Bible story, God kept His people safe on a very long trip. He helped them cross a big sea. Let's make shoe prints and pretend we're going on a long trip and crossing a sea.**
- **Our Bible says, "I thank and praise you, O God." We can thank God for caring for us. Lorrie, what do you want to thank God for? That's right! God gives us feet.**
- **What can your feet do?** Encourage children to demonstrate walking, jumping, skipping, etc. **What can other parts of your body do?** (Hands clap, arms hug, eyes see, knees bend, etc.)

## For Younger Children

Outline children's feet for them. Children don't cut out paper shoes but place the whole paper on the floor to create the path.

## For Older Children

After crossing the pretend sea, children celebrate and thank God for His help by clapping their hands, jumping up and down and/or playing rhythm instruments (tambourines, maracas, etc.).

# Block Center: Care Centers

## Collect

Bible, *Shake It Up!* cassette/CD and player, blocks, toys (toy animals, toy people, toy cars, toy airplanes, etc.).

### God's Word

**"I thank and praise you, O God."**
**Daniel 2:23**

### God's Word & Me

**I can thank God that He always cares for me.**

## Do

Children play with blocks, building familiar places they go (store, church, park, etc.).

## Talk About

- **Our Bible story today tells about boys and girls and mothers and fathers who walked a long, long way to a new home. And God cared for them everywhere they went. God cares for us wherever we go, too! Let's use our blocks to build some of the places where we go.**
- **Our Bible says, "I thank and praise you, O God." We can thank God that He always cares for us. Joy, what place are you building? God cares for you at the store.**

- **We can show our thanks to God for caring for us. One way to show our thanks to God is by praying.** Pray briefly, **Dear God, thank You for caring for us. We love You.**
- **We can sing songs about God. Singing is one way to thank and praise God.** As children work, play "God Cares About You." Invite children to sing the song with you.

## For Younger Children

Children will also want to build structures of their own choosing. Talk about God's care at the places children build.

## For Older Children

Children play a stacking game. Each child takes a turn naming something for which he or she wishes to thank God. As the item is named, child places a block on top of another, forming a tower.

Lesson 3

# Science Center: Air on Water

## Collect

Bible, towels, shallow baking dish of water, Styrofoam peanuts; optional—other small items that float (leaves, tiny paper cups, etc.).

## Prepare

Cover working area with towels. Place baking dish in the center of the towels.

God's Word
"I thank and praise you, O God."
Daniel 2:23
God's Word & Me
I can thank God that
He always cares for me.

## Do

1. Children make ripples on the surface of the water in the baking dish by gently blowing. Have children experiment with the effect of blowing hard compared to blowing gently.
2. Place Styrofoam peanuts on the water. Children blow Styrofoam peanuts across water. (Optional: Children experiment with other small items that float.)

## Talk About

- **In our Bible story, God's people thanked Him for sending a big wind. The wind made a dry path through a big sea. Let's make a small wind to blow on the water.**
- **God sent the wind to help His people. What are some of the ways God helps you?** (Gives people to love us. Listens to our prayers.)
- **I'm glad God always cares for us and helps us. We can thank Him for His care. Our Bible says, "I thank and praise you, O God." Lily, what do you want to thank God for?**

## For Younger Children

Provide a baking dish for every two to three children so that each child will have time to experiment.

## For Older Children

Children experiment with color by adding drops of food coloring to water and blowing on water to mix colors.

# Bible Story Center

## Collect

Bible, Picture 7 from *Bible Story Pictures.*

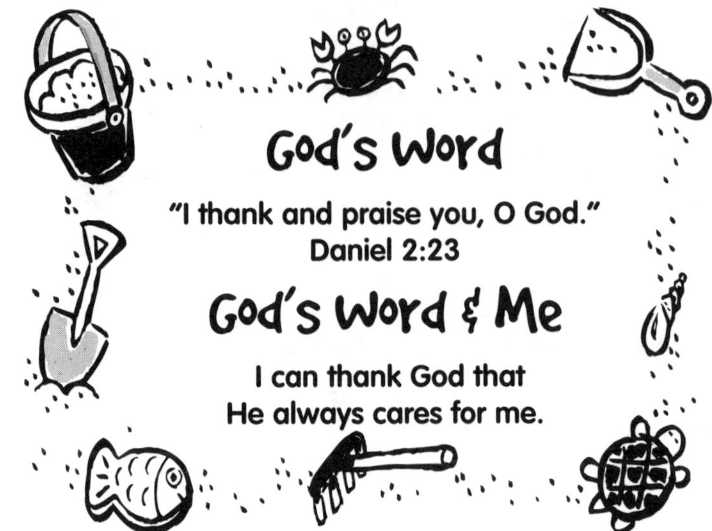
God's Word
"I thank and praise you, O God."
Daniel 2:23
God's Word & Me
I can thank God that
He always cares for me.

## Tell the Story

Use the pictured motions (keywords in bold) or show Picture 7. For older children, tell the version of the story on the back of Picture 7.

**Have you ever seen a really big windstorm? What happened? Today we're going to hear what happened when God caused a very big wind to blow.**

God's people were on a long trip. God told Moses where to go and where to stop. Steppety-step, steppety-step—the people walked and **walked** and walked. Clippety-clop, clippety-clop—the animals also walked and walked and walked. God's people were going to a new home far away.

One day God's people stopped in front of a big sea. They **looked** around. All they could see was lots and lots of water in front of them. The people felt afraid. They didn't know how to get across the water. There were no boats to ride in. There was no bridge to walk across.

Moses knew the people felt afraid. Moses said, "Don't be afraid. God will help us." Moses held his hand up over the water, just as God told him to do. Then God sent a great big wind to **blow** the water out of the way. O-o-o! How the wind blew! O-o-o! The wind blew some of the water to one side. O-o-o! The wind blew some of the water to the other side. Right in the middle of the water was a dry path for the people and animals to walk on. They walked all the way to the other side without even getting their feet wet!

Then God told Moses to hold his hand over the water again. The wind stopped. All the water splashed together again and covered up the dry path. The people were very happy that God had helped them. They sang songs to God. Some women played **tambourines**. They wanted to show their thanks to God for His care and help.

## God's Word & Me

**How did God's people thank God for His help?** (They sang songs and played tambourines.) **God's people sang songs to show their thanks to God. We can show thanks to God for His care, too!**

# Worship Center

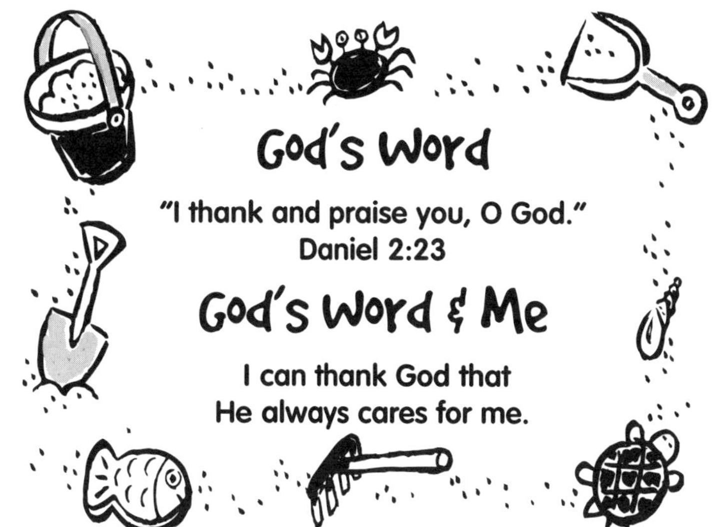
God's Word
"I thank and praise you, O God."
Daniel 2:23
God's Word & Me
I can thank God that
He always cares for me.

## Collect

Bible, *Shake It Up!* songbook and cassette/CD and player, "All I Need" and "God Cares About You" word charts (pp. 6 and 9 in songbook), large sheet of paper, marker.

## Prepare

On paper, print the words "We thank You, God, for _________."

## Sing to God

Play "All I Need." Invite children to sing along with you. **Let's sing about how God cares for us.** Lead children in singing song and doing suggested motions. **We sang about many different things God gives us. Which do you want to thank God for today?** On paper, print children's responses. Place paper where parents can read it when they pick up their children.

## Hear and Say God's Word

Holding your Bible open to Daniel 2:23, say verse aloud. **What two things does this verse tell us we can do?** (Thank and praise God.) Then lead children in repeating the verse by clapping their hands on each word. Repeat with other motions: stomping feet, clapping hands over heads, slapping knees, etc.

## Pray to God

Lead children in prayer, thanking God that He always cares for us. Include in your prayer the items mentioned by children during song activity.

## Sing to God

In closing the worship time, play "God Cares About You." Invite children to sing along with you. Lead children in singing song and doing suggested motions. **God always cares for us. We can thank Him every day!**

## Options

1. With parents' permission, videotape children as they sing songs and do the motions. Show videotape at the end of the session as parents come to pick up their children.
2. If you take a weekly offering during this worship time, explain to children that the money is used to help people learn about God. **Giving money is one way to thank God for caring for us.**

# Read-Aloud Story and Activity Center

## Collect

A copy of Story Picture 3 (pp. 11-12 from *Read-Aloud Story and Activity Book*) for each child and yourself, crayons or markers.

## Prepare

Color your copy of Story Picture 3.

## Do

**Listen to find out what this girl is looking for.** Read story and show completed Story Picture 3. Distribute pictures. Use conversation suggestions in Let's Talk About the Story as children complete their pages.

# Kindergarten Puzzle Center

## Collect

Copies of Puzzles 5 and 6 (p. 17 and p. 19 from *The Big Book of Kindergarten Puzzles)* for each child, pencils, crayons or markers.

## Do

Children complete the puzzles and color pages.

# Instant Activities

These activities can be used at any time during this session: when children need a change of pace, to extend the session, or during transition-time at the beginning or end of the session.

## Collect

*The Big Book of Instant Activities.*

## Do

Guide children to complete "God Gave Me Feet" and/or "Say Your Name" (p. 49 and/or p. 71 from *The Big Book of Instant Activities).*

# A Desert Surprise

## Bible Story

Exodus 15:22-25; 16

God's Word
"Lord, you are good to us."
(See Psalm 86:5.)
God's Word & Me
God shows love to me by giving me food and water.

## Teacher's Devotional

God's people were following the cloud and the fire through the desert on their long journey to the land promised by God. But then a crisis developed. They hadn't found a source of water for three days. Once again, the situation didn't look hopeful. Unless they found water soon, they'd die—all of them. At last they did find water, but it was not fit to drink. It was tainted and bitter. The people complained angrily to Moses.

We don't know why the water was not fit to drink, but we know that God (as always) could turn a problem into an opportunity. This dilemma created a classic example of a teachable moment! These people were very aware of their need for water. Every eye was on Moses. It makes no apparent sense, but God pointed out a tree or large log and told Moses to throw it into the water. And while all those parched people looked intently on, Moses listened, obeyed—and Israel learned.

God always has something new for us to learn. And He certainly creates teachable moments in our lives! When we feel our need most keenly, He teaches us most effectively. Be teachable. Learn God's lessons, even in the hardest situation. And be ready to live out what you learn before your little ones as you trust, obey and rejoice.

## Teacher's Planning

1. Choose which centers you will provide and the order in which children will participate in them. For tips on schedule planning, see page 7.
2. Plan who will lead each center. For staffing tips and ideas, see page 21.

# Active Game Center: Food Fun

## Collect

Bible, yarn, toy foods or magazine pictures of food.

## Prepare

Place a yarn line at each end of the play area. Place toy foods or magazine pictures of food in a pile behind one yarn line.

### God's Word

**"Lord, you are good to us." (See Psalm 86:5.)**

### God's Word & Me

**God shows love to me by giving me food and water.**

## Do

1. Children line up behind line opposite the pile of toy foods or pictures of food.
2. At your signal, the first child in each line walks quickly to the pile of toy foods or food pictures and selects one to bring back to the starting line. The next child repeats action. Continue until each child has a turn. Invite volunteers to tell the foods they collected. Repeat game as time permits.

## Talk About

- **In today's Bible story, God's people picked their food up from the ground each morning. Let's play a game by picking up pretend food!**
- **Haley, what food did you take? Is it a food you like? What are some of your favorite foods?**
- **Our Bible says, "Lord, you are good to us." God is good to us and gives us food and water.**
- **What are some other good things God gives you?** (Friends, families, pets, etc.)

## For Younger Children

Instead of making lines with yarn, make three circles in different areas of the room. Place some of the toy foods or pictures in each circle. Children pretend to travel from one place to another, carrying toy foods or pictures.

## For Older Children

After collecting foods, children group them into breakfast, lunch and dinner items.

# Art Center: Pizza Party!

## Collect

Bible, white paper or poster board, markers (several red and yellow, plus other colors), scissors; optional—yellow and/or white yarn, ruler, glue.

## Prepare

Draw a large circle on white paper or poster board and cut out—one for each child. (Optional: Cut yellow and/or white yarn into 2- to 3-inch [5- to 7.5-cm] lengths.)

### God's Word

**"Lord, you are good to us."**
**(See Psalm 86:5.)**

### God's Word & Me

**God shows love to me by giving me food and water.**

## Do

Distribute circles to children. Using markers, children color sauce on their pizza and color the crust. (Optional: Children glue on pieces of yarn for cheese.)

## Talk About

- **In our Bible story, God gave His people good water and manna. God gives us food and water to show His love for us. Let's make a pretend pizza.**
- **Pizza is one of my favorite foods. God made tomatoes to grow so that we can have tomato sauce. God makes wheat for flour. Where does cheese come from? I'm glad God made cows and other animals and plants so that we can have good food to eat. What is your favorite food?**
- **The Bible says, "Lord, you are good to us." God gives us good food for lunch. What do you like to eat for lunch?** Pray briefly, thanking God for the foods children mention.

## For Younger Children

Before class, cut out construction-paper pizza toppings (see below). Children glue toppings to pizzas.

## For Older Children

Children cut construction paper into shapes to represent different pizza toppings to be glued on pizzas: black circles for olives, red circles for pepperoni, green strips for peppers, white semicircles for mushrooms, etc.

Lesson 4

# Block Center: Farm Food

## Collect

Bible, construction paper in a variety of colors, scissors, blocks; optional—grocery-store advertisements.

## Prepare

Cut construction paper into shapes to represent different foods grown on a farm: yellow strips for corn, orange circles for pumpkins, green oblongs for watermelons, etc. (Optional: Cut food pictures from grocery-store advertisements.)

### God's Word

**"Lord, you are good to us."**
**(See Psalm 86:5.)**

### God's Word & Me

**God shows love to me by giving me food and water.**

## Do

Children use blocks to outline fields and lay construction-paper shapes in rows as if planting rows of crops. (Optional: Use food pictures from grocery-store advertisements instead of paper shapes.)

## Talk About

- **Our Bible story tells about the special way God gave food and water to His people. Let's pretend we're farmers who are growing food!**
- **What kinds of food grow on farms?** Show construction paper shapes and name foods.
- **The Bible says, "Lord, you are good to us." God has planned a way for us to have food. God made the plants that grow food so that we would have good things to eat.**
- Pray briefly, **Dear God, thank You for all the good food You give us. We love You.**

## For Younger Children

Outline a field with masking tape. Children place blocks on masking-tape line. (Note: Remove tape immediately after activity.)

## For Older Children

Children outline a pond near their fields. **God gives us water to drink. What kinds of food can you find in water?** Children draw and cut out construction-paper fish to put in the pond.

# Science Center: Seed Matchup

## Collect

Bible, fruits and vegetables with seeds (apple, watermelon, squash, peach, corn, tomato, cucumber, etc.), knife, glue, index cards, resealable plastic bags, marker.

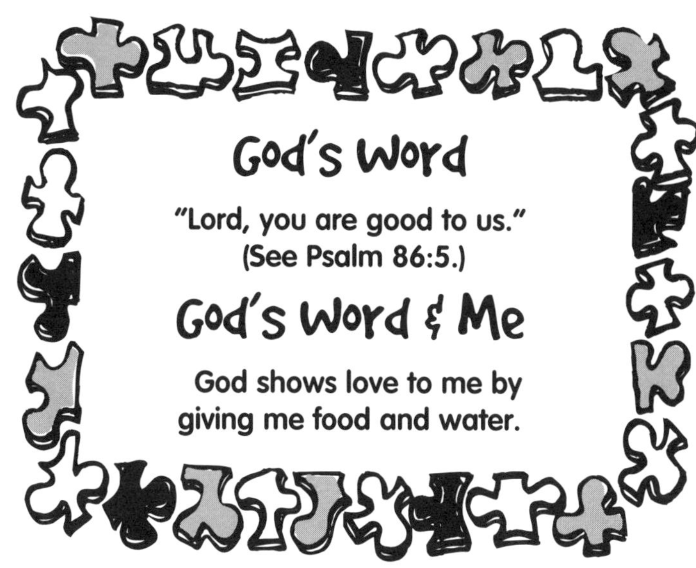
God's Word
"Lord, you are good to us."
(See Psalm 86:5.)
God's Word & Me
God shows love to me by giving me food and water.

## Prepare

Cut food items in half. From one half of each item, extract seeds and glue to an index card. Place half of item with seeds in a resealable plastic bag.

Post a note alerting parents to the use of food in this activity. Also check registration forms for possible food allergies.

## Do

1. Show children the fruit and vegetable halves in the plastic bags. Ask children to name each one.
2. Hand the seed cards to several children and ask them to match the seeds to the fruit or vegetable the seeds came from.

## Talk About

- **Our Bible says, "Lord, you are good to us." God is good by giving us all kinds of foods to eat. Let's look inside some fruits and vegetables.**
- **Sue, what is your favorite kind of fruit? Paul, what is your favorite vegetable?**
- **What other kinds of food do you like to eat? What do you like to drink?**

## For Younger Children

Instead of matching fruits and vegetables to their seeds, children smell and taste pieces of the foods.

## For Older Children

Bring additional pieces of fruit or vegetables some children may not be familiar with, such as star fruit, mango, kiwi and avocado. Volunteers take turns smelling and tasting them.

# Bible Story Center

## Collect

Bible, Picture 8 from *Bible Story Pictures.*

## God's Word

**"Lord, you are good to us." (See Psalm 86:5.)**

## God's Word & Me

**God shows love to me by giving me food and water.**

## Tell the Story

Use the pictured motions (keywords in bold) or show Picture 8. For older children, tell the version of the story on the back of Picture 8.

**What did you have for breakfast today? Where did you get the food you ate? Today we're going to hear about one way God gave food to His people.**

God's people were on a long trip. They **walked** through the desert. The desert is a hot place. There are not many trees for shade. There is not much water to drink, but there is a lot of hot sand. God's people walked across the hot, hot sand. Step, step, step.

For three days, God's people had no water. "We are thirsty!" they all said. Then someone shouted, "Water!" They saw beautiful cool water. The people ran to the water. They took big **drinks**. Yuk! The water tasted bad! "We can't drink this water," the people said. "Where will we get good water?" they asked Moses.

Moses asked God what to do. God told Moses to throw a special piece of wood into the water. The special piece of wood made the water taste good. Everyone drank the good-tasting water.

God's people had brought food with them from their old home. That food was almost gone. There were no stores to buy more food. "We're hungry," the people said. "What shall we eat?" the people asked Moses. Again Moses talked to God. That night God sent many birds to the people's camp. Now the people had plenty of meat to eat. They were **happy**.

But God gave them even more. The next morning the ground was covered with little white flakes. "What is it?" the people asked.

"This is the bread God sent," Moses said. The people **picked up** the bread and tasted it. It was good! The bread was called manna.

God cared for His people. The people thanked God for His gifts of food and water.

## God's Word & Me

**What kind of food did God give to His people?** (Birds. Manna.) **God showed His love for His people in the desert by giving them food to eat and water to drink. What did you have for breakfast?** Volunteers respond. **God shows His love for us by giving us good food and water, too!**

# Worship Center

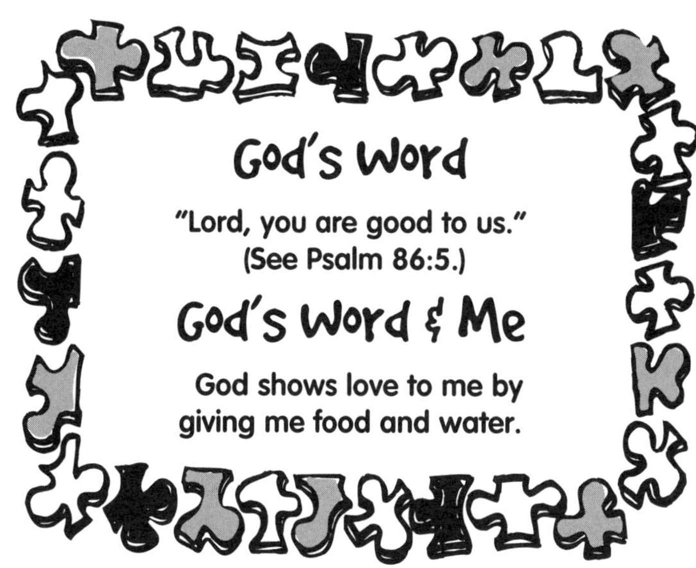
God's Word
"Lord, you are good to us."
(See Psalm 86:5.)
God's Word & Me
God shows love to me by
giving me food and water.

## Collect

Bible, *Shake It Up!* songbook and cassette/CD and player, "All I Need" and "God Cares About You" word charts (pp. 6 and 9 in songbook).

## Sing to God

Play "All I Need." Invite children to sing along with you. **Let's sing together about some of the good things God gives us!** Lead children in singing song and doing suggested motions. **Besides food and water, what are some of the other things this song tells us God gives us to show His love?** (A house to live in. People who love us.)

## Hear and Say God's Word

Holding your Bible open to Psalm 86:5, say verse aloud. **What does this verse tell us about God?** (He is good to us.) Then lead children in repeating the Bible verse several times. As the children are repeating the verse with you, point to one or more children. You and the children say the name of every child pointed at instead of the word "us." Repeat until every child has had his or her name said.

## Pray to God

Children repeat the following prayer after you, one phrase at a time: **Dear God, . . . thank You for being so good to us. . . . We give You thanks. . . . In Jesus' name, amen.**

## Sing to God

In closing the worship time, play "God Cares About You." Invite children to sing along with you and do suggested motions. **God shows He cares about you by giving you food and water. What are some other ways God shows His love? What other things has God given you?** Volunteers respond.

## Option

At the top of a large sheet of paper, print "God gives me . . ." During "God Cares About You" song activity, print children's responses on large sheet of paper. Tape to wall where parents will be able to see it when they pick up their children.

# Read-Aloud Story and Activity Center

## Collect

A copy of Story Picture 4 (pp. 13-14 from *Read-Aloud Story and Activity Book*) for each child and yourself, crayons or markers.

## Prepare

Color your copy of Story Picture 4.

## Do

**Listen to find out what animals this boy met.** Read story and show completed Story Picture 4. Distribute pictures. Use conversation suggestions in Let's Talk About the Story as children complete their pages.

# Kindergarten Puzzle Center

## Collect

Copies of Puzzles 7 and 8 (p. 21 and p. 23 from *The Big Book of Kindergarten Puzzles)* for each child, pencils, crayons or markers.

## Do

Children complete the puzzles and color pages.

# Instant Activities

These activities can be used at any time during this session: when children need a change of pace, to extend the session, or during transition time at the beginning or end of the session.

## Collect

*The Big Book of Instant Activities.*

## Do

Guide children to complete "Eat It or Not" and/or "God's Garden" (p. 111 and/or p. 22 from *The Big Book of Instant Activities).*

Lesson 5

# Hannah's Prayer

## Bible Story

1 Samuel 1; 2:18,19

God's Word
"I love the Lord." Psalm 116:1
God's Word & Me
I talk to God to show my love for Him and to ask for His help.

## Teacher's Devotional

Imagine the intensity with which Hannah must have loved Samuel! He was the child for whom she'd poured out her heart to God, even promising to return him to the Lord. Samuel was Hannah's living proof that God hears! Proof of Hannah's love for God was seen in her gift of Samuel to do godly work at the Tabernacle.

She must also have loved Samuel with a passion simply because he wasn't hers to keep. She must have spent every possible moment with him, listening closely to him, teaching him everything she thought he could understand, delighting in him. It had to be difficult to leave her child with Eli at the Tabernacle, but she had prepared Samuel for this day. She knew she had done all she could and that God would take care of him.

These little ones we teach are a gift from God, too—every one of them! And their time with us is certainly short. Very soon they'll be grown enough to leave us. We must love them and teach them now with the passion and intensity that Hannah had. God will hear us as He did Hannah and give us an intense love for each of them—if we ask Him. The truths we teach them through our lives and our love will lay a foundation for a strong faith in the God who hears.

## Teacher's Planning

1. Choose which centers you will provide and the order in which children will participate in them. For tips on schedule planning, see page 7.
2. Plan who will lead each center. For staffing tips and ideas, see page 21.

Lesson 5

# Active Game Center: Dress Up!

## Collect

Bible, yarn, Bible-times costume; optional—3-foot (.9-m) fabric length, scissors, man's tie.

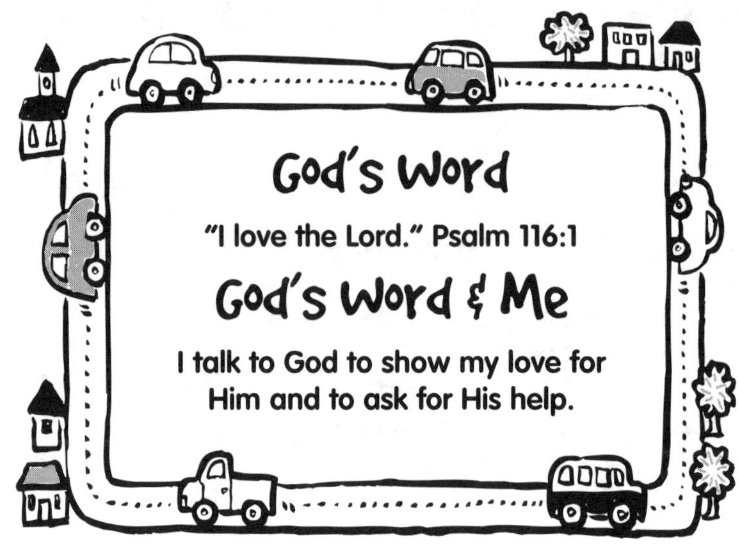
God's Word
"I love the Lord." Psalm 116:1
God's Word & Me
I talk to God to show my love for Him and to ask for His help.

## Prepare

Place a yarn line at one end of the playing area. Place Bible-times costume at the other end. (Optional: To make costume: Fold length of fabric in half and cut a slit along the center of the fold to make a neck opening. Man's tie serves as belt.) (Note: If you have a large class, provide one costume for each group of five to six children.)

## Do

Children line up behind the costume. The first child puts on the costume, walks quickly to the yarn line on the opposite side of the playing area and then returns to starting point. After first child takes off the costume, the second child puts on the costume and repeats actions. Continue until every child has a turn.

## Talk About

- **Our Bible story today is about a woman named Hannah. Hannah loved God. Hannah asked God for a baby. God answered her prayer. Hannah had a baby boy named Samuel. Hannah made Samuel a coat every year.**
- **Let's pretend we're Samuel and we're putting on our new coat.**
- Show open Bible. **The Bible says, "I love the Lord." When we talk to God, we can tell Him we love Him.** Briefly pray with children, expressing love to God.

## For Younger Children

Help children put the costume on and off. Don't use the man's tie as a belt.

## For Older Children

As each child reaches yarn line, he or she says the words of the Bible verse, "I love the Lord."

# Art Center: Paper People

## Collect

Bible, length of butcher paper, markers, white paper, scissors, tape.

## Prepare

On the butcher paper, draw a simple outline of a church (see sketch a). Include a feature that will identify your church (steeple, logo, etc.). Fold white paper and cut out paper dolls (see sketch b), preparing approximately four dolls for each child.

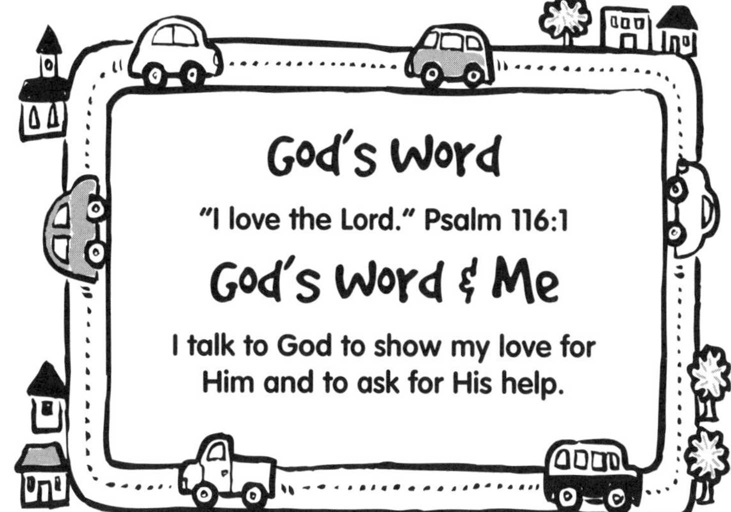
God's Word
"I love the Lord." Psalm 116:1
God's Word & Me
I talk to God to show my love for Him and to ask for His help.

## Do

Ask each child to tell you who came to church with him or her today. Give child the appropriate number of paper dolls, cutting additional paper dolls if needed. Children color dolls to represent the people with whom they came to church. Tape dolls to butcher paper.

## Talk About

- **In our Bible story today, Hannah and Elkanah went to talk to God at a special place called the Tabernacle. Hannah asked God for a baby. Where are some places you talk to God?**
- **When we come to our church, we can talk to God and ask for His help, too. Let's make a big picture of people coming to church.**
- **Who are the people who came to church with you today? Our Bible says, "I love the Lord." We come to church to show our love for God.**

## For Younger Children

Instead of coloring paper dolls, children draw on the church outline the people who came to church with them.

## For Older Children

Children draw and cut out clothing from colored paper or fabric scraps and glue clothing to their paper dolls.

Lesson 5

# Block Center: Favorite Places

## Collect

Bible, *Shake It Up!* cassette/CD and player, yarn, scissors, blocks.

## Prepare

Cut yarn into various lengths from approximately 8 inches (20.5 cm) to 2 feet (61 cm) long.

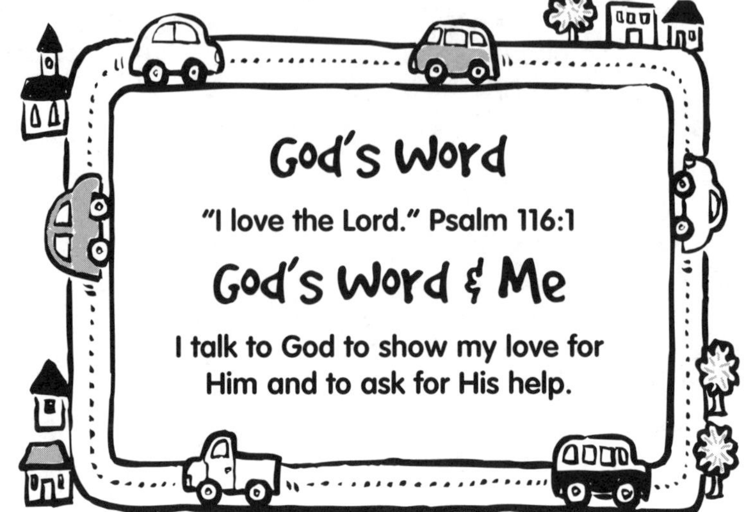
God's Word
"I love the Lord." Psalm 116:1
God's Word & Me
I talk to God to show my love for Him and to ask for His help.

## Do

Children use blocks and lengths of yarn to build familiar places (park, home, church, school, etc.). Children may use yarn to tie blocks together, to make lines between blocks or to create different shaped areas.

## Talk About

- **Our Bible says, "I love the Lord." We show love for God by talking to Him and asking Him for help. We can talk to God anywhere we go! Let's build some of our favorite places.**
- **Where is one of your favorite places to go? Why do you like to go there? What are some of the things you do when you go there?**
- **What are some things you can thank God for when you are at the park?** (Trees. Friends. Flowers.)
- **One way to show our love for God is to sing songs about Him.** As they build with blocks, sing with children "I Love the Lord" from *Shake It Up!*

## For Younger Children

Instead of building representational places, children will enjoy building structures of their own design, such as towers. Here's a good safety rule: A child's tower can be no higher than his or her chin. Be consistent in enforcing this rule. Soon children will remember it as they build.

## For Older Children

Provide recyclable materials (paper plates, cups, straws, small boxes, etc.) for children to use.

# Science Center: Feel and Match

## Collect

Bible, several pairs of items with a variety of textures (rubber balls, felt squares, sandpaper pieces, coins, fake-fur swatches, socks, hand towels, etc.), three paper grocery bags.

## Prepare

Place one set of items in each of two of the paper grocery bags.

### God's Word

**"I love the Lord." Psalm 116:1**

### God's Word & Me

**I talk to God to show my love for Him and to ask for His help.**

## Do

1. Children take turns selecting an item from one bag and feeling the item to become familiar with it.
2. For each child, select the item from the second bag that matches the one the child has examined. Place item in third paper bag. Place another item in the third bag. Child reaches but doesn't look into third bag, feeling both items until he or she finds the matching item. Repeat for each child.

## Talk About

- **In our Bible story today, a woman named Hannah asked God to send her a baby boy. God did! Hannah named the baby Samuel. As Samuel grew up, Hannah made a new coat for him to wear every year. Samuel's coat probably felt soft and warm. Today we're going to feel lots of different things.**
- **Our Bible says, "I love the Lord." The word "Lord" is another name for God. I love God because of the way He made my hands so that I can touch and feel things. What are some other things you can do with your hands? Let's thank God for our hands and tell God how much we love Him.** Briefly pray with children.

## For Younger Children

Use only a few objects with very different textures (rubber balls, felt squares, sandpaper pieces, etc.).

## For Older Children

Use different pieces of clothing: leather gloves, wool socks, cotton handkerchiefs or bandannas, velvet ribbons, T-shirts, silk scarves, etc.

# Bible Story Center

## Collect

Bible, Picture 10 from *Bible Story Pictures.*

God's Word
"I love the Lord." Psalm 116:1
God's Word & Me
I talk to God to show my love for Him and to ask for His help.

## Tell the Story

Use the pictured motions (keywords in bold) or show Picture 10. For older children, tell the version of the story on the back of Picture 10.

**Where is a special place you like to go? What do you do there? In today's story, we'll find out about a special place where Bible-times people went to show their love for God.**

Hannah and her husband, Elkanah (ehl-KAY-nuh), loved each other and God very much. But Hannah and Elkanah had **no children**. Hannah felt very sad.

Hannah and Elkanah went to a special place to worship God. The special place was called the Tabernacle. Hannah **prayed** to God. "Dear God, please give me a baby boy. When he is old enough, I will bring him to the Tabernacle to be Your helper."

Eli lived at the Tabernacle. He prayed to God and taught others about God. "I pray God gives you what you ask," Eli told Hannah. Hannah and Elkanah went home.

After many, many days, a **baby** boy was born to Hannah. Hannah named the baby Samuel. Every day Samuel grew taller and stronger. Hannah took good care of little Samuel. She cooked good food for him to eat. She made clothes for him to wear. And best of all, Hannah taught little Samuel about God.

Finally, the day came when Samuel was big enough to go to the Tabernacle. Hannah, Elkanah and Samuel went to the Tabernacle. Samuel stayed there with Eli to learn to be God's helper, just as his mother Hannah had promised.

Every year Samuel's mother made a special new coat for him. And every year she had to make a bigger and bigger coat! Do you know why? Because Samuel **GREW**, just like you do. And as he grew a little taller and a little stronger, Samuel also grew to love God!

## God's Word & Me

**What did Hannah ask God at the Tabernacle?** (To give her a baby boy.) **Hannah showed her love for God by praying to Him. She asked God for help when she wanted a baby. We can talk to God, too. We can show our love for God and ask for His help. What are some of the places where you talk to God?**

# Worship Center

## Collect

Bible, *Shake It Up!* songbook and cassette/CD and player, "I Love the Lord" and "A Little Bit More" word charts (pp. 15 and 12 in songbook).

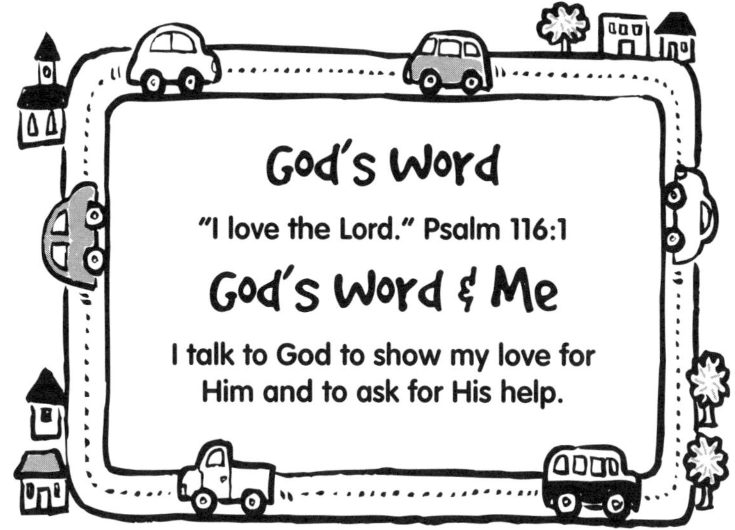
God's Word
"I love the Lord." Psalm 116:1
God's Word & Me
I talk to God to show my love for Him and to ask for His help.

## Sing to God

Play "I Love the Lord." Invite children to sing along with you. **Let's sing about our love for God!** Lead children in singing song and doing suggested motions. **Every day we can talk to God and tell Him how much we love Him.**

## Hear and Say God's Word

Holding your Bible open to Psalm 116:1, say verse aloud. **When we come to church, we can tell God how much we love Him.** Volunteers respond. Lead children in repeating the verse two or three times. Then add the word "at" and a time of day ("I love the Lord at bedtime."). Children echo the phrase after you. Repeat several times, using different times of the day, week or seasons of the year.

## Pray to God

Lead children in prayer. **Dear God, we love You. Thank You for helping us when we ask. In Jesus' name, amen.**

## Sing to God

In closing the worship time, play "A Little Bit More." Invite children to sing along with you and do suggested motions. **What does this song say our hands can do?** (Help others.) **When we talk to God, we can ask for His help to help others! God will always hear us when we talk to Him.**

## Options

1. Provide one or two rhythm instruments for children to use while singing "I Love the Lord" and "A Little Bit More." Children hand the instruments to other children before each song is sung and before each repetition of the songs.
2. Older children lead the rest of the group in doing the motions for "I Love the Lord" and/or "A Little Bit More."

# Read-Aloud Story and Activity Center

## Collect

A copy of Story Picture 5 (pp. 15-16 from *Read-Aloud Story and Activity Book*) for each child and yourself, crayons or markers.

## Prepare

Color your copy of Story Picture 5.

## Do

**Listen to find out what this girl prayed.** Read story and show completed Story Picture 5. Distribute pictures. Use conversation suggestions in Let's Talk About the Story as children complete their pages.

# Kindergarten Puzzle Center

## Collect

Copies of Puzzles 9 and 10 (p. 25 and p. 27 from *The Big Book of Kindergarten Puzzles*) for each child, pencils, crayons or markers.

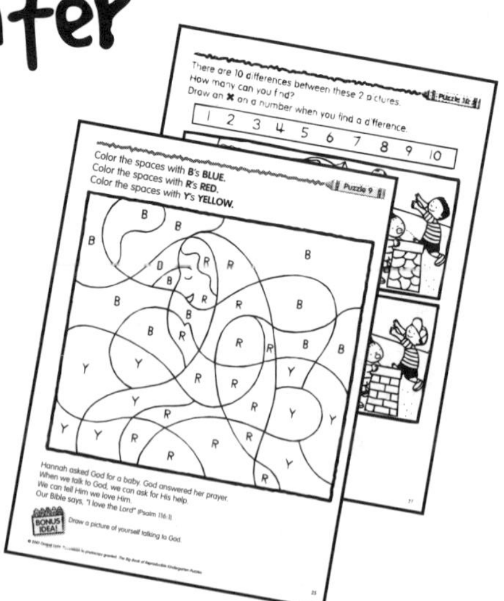

## Do

Children complete the puzzles and color pages.

# Instant Activities

These activities can be used at any time during this session: when children need a change of pace, to extend the session, or during transition time at the beginning or end of the session.

## Collect *The Big Book of Instant Activities.*

## Do

Guide children to complete "Roll, Roll, Roll Your Hands" and/or "Hot Potato" (p. 101 and/or p. 67 from *The Big Book of Instant Activities).*

Lesson 6

# Helping at the Tabernacle

## Bible Story

1 Samuel 1:28; 2:11,18-21,26

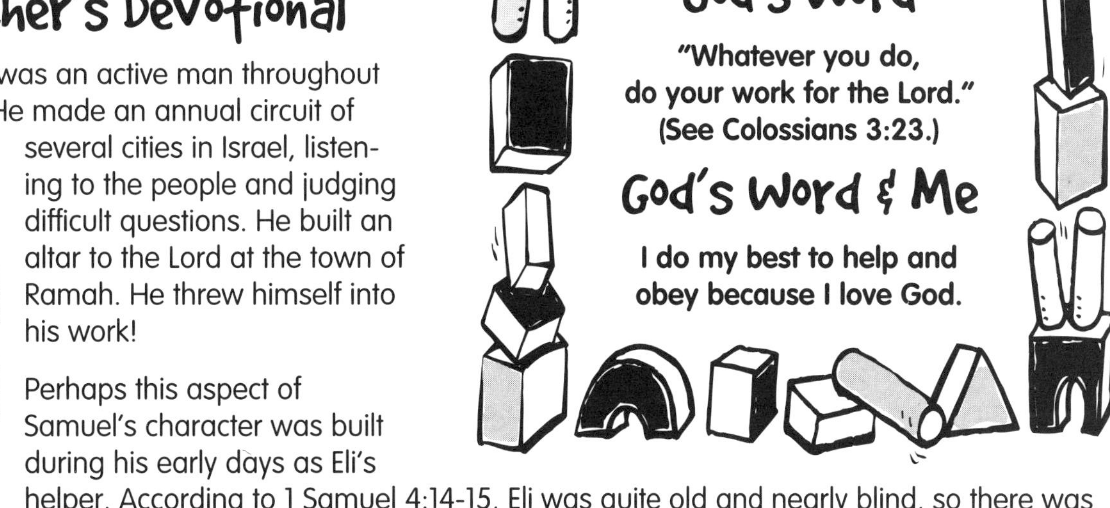
God's Word
"Whatever you do,
do your work for the Lord."
(See Colossians 3:23.)
God's Word & Me
I do my best to help and
obey because I love God.

## Teacher's Devotional

Samuel was an active man throughout his life. He made an annual circuit of several cities in Israel, listening to the people and judging difficult questions. He built an altar to the Lord at the town of Ramah. He threw himself into his work!

Perhaps this aspect of Samuel's character was built during his early days as Eli's helper. According to 1 Samuel 4:14-15, Eli was quite old and nearly blind, so there was a great deal that young Samuel was able to do to help. And he must have loved doing it, for children love to feel that what they do is important.

Children know that grown-up work is important. They so want their work to be important, too! A child who doesn't want to help may have been discouraged from helping at home or told that his or her work isn't good or valuable.

Since work is what each of us do all of our lives, do your best work today! Work to affirm every child's efforts. Each child's satisfaction in doing good work is worth extra effort from you! Let the children in your class know that you—and God—value their work.

## Teacher's Planning

1. Choose which centers you will provide and the order in which children will participate in them. For tips on schedule planning, see page 7.
2. Plan who will lead each center. For staffing tips and ideas, see page 21.

Lesson 6

# Active Game Center: Target Sweep

## Collect

Bible, masking tape, paper, basket or box, one broom (whisk, child-sized or regular) for every four to five children.

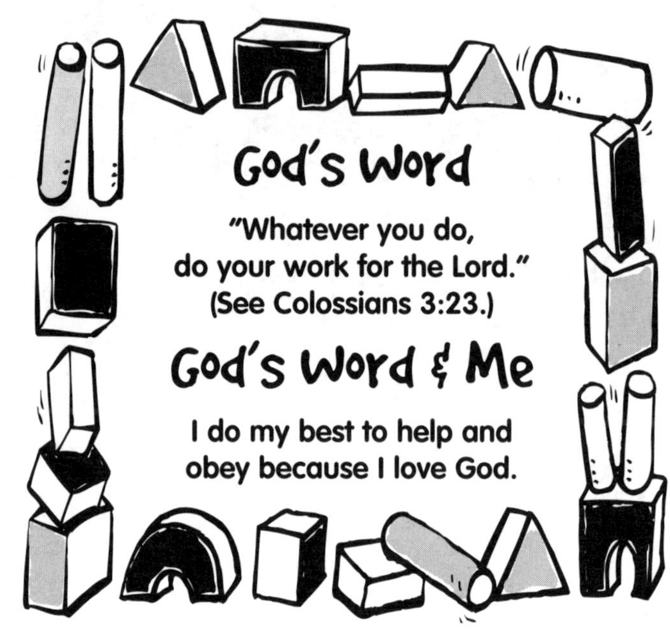

God's Word
"Whatever you do, do your work for the Lord." (See Colossians 3:23.)
God's Word & Me
I do my best to help and obey because I love God.

## Prepare

On floor, make a large masking-tape square. Make a masking-tape line on the opposite side of the playing area. (Note: Remove tape immediately after use.)

## Do

1. Children crumple paper into balls and place in basket or box. Children line up behind masking-tape line. Hand a broom to the first child in the line and place basket or box next to him or her.
2. At your signal, the first child selects a paper ball and drops it onto the floor. He or she uses broom to sweep ball onto masking-tape square. Child returns to line and hands broom to the next child who repeats action. Continue until each child has a turn. Next, children sweep balls from masking-tape square back to starting line, placing paper ball back in basket or box. Repeat as time and interest allow.

## Talk About

- **In our Bible story, Samuel helped at the Tabernacle. One way he may have helped was by sweeping the floor. Let's play a sweeping game!**
- **The Bible says, "Whatever you do, do your work for the Lord." "Lord" is another name for God. How can you help a brother or sister? How can you help a grandparent?**

## For Younger Children

Children do not use paper balls but simply make sweeping motions with the broom as they move across the playing area.

## For Older Children

Each child writes the first letter of his or her name on paper before crumpling it into a ball. After each round of play, pick a paper ball, open it and tell the letter. Children whose names begin with that letter tell ways to help.

# Art Center: Table Tabernacle

## Collect

Bible, butcher paper, tape, markers.

## Prepare

Tape butcher paper to a table. Draw an outline of the Tabernacle. Include a road leading up to the Tabernacle.

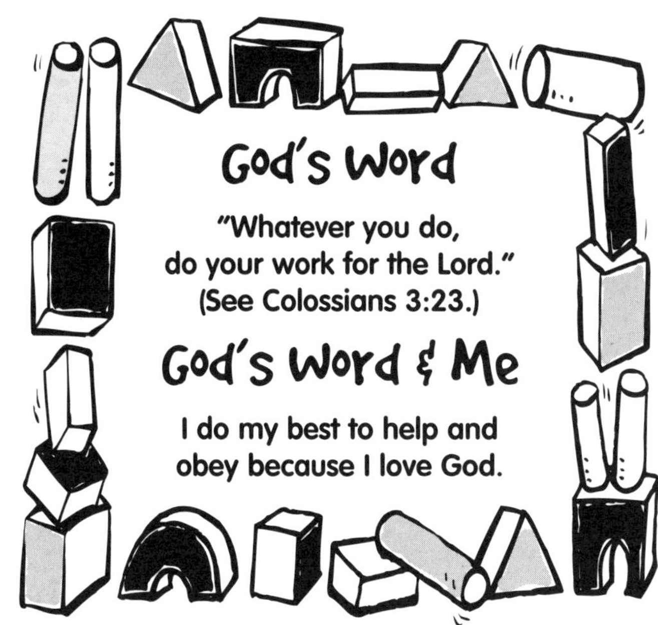
God's Word
"Whatever you do,
do your work for the Lord."
(See Colossians 3:23.)
God's Word & Me
I do my best to help and
obey because I love God.

## Do

Children use markers to decorate the Tabernacle and draw people traveling on the road to the Tabernacle.

## Talk About

- **In our Bible story today, a boy named Samuel helped at the Tabernacle. Let's decorate a Tabernacle drawing and draw some people on their way to the Tabernacle.**
- **The Bible says, "Whatever you do, do your work for the Lord." "Lord" is another name for God. This verse reminds us to do our best work. When Samuel helped at the Tabernacle, he did his best work. We can do our best work when we help others, too.**
- **What is one way you help someone in your family? What is one way you help a friend?**

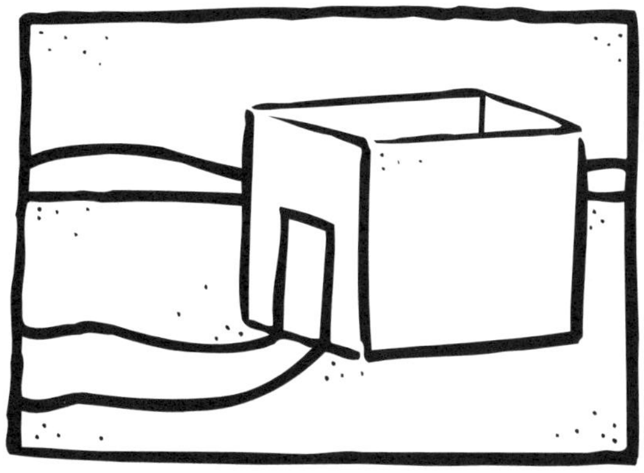

## For Younger Children

Simplify activity by drawing only the Tabernacle for children to color.

## For Older Children

Provide fabric swatches, scissors and glue. Children cut fabric swatches and glue fabric to drawing to decorate Tabernacle, to create clothing for people or to make trees and flowers for the path.

# Block Center: Where We Work

## Collect

Bible, blocks, toy people, toy vehicles.

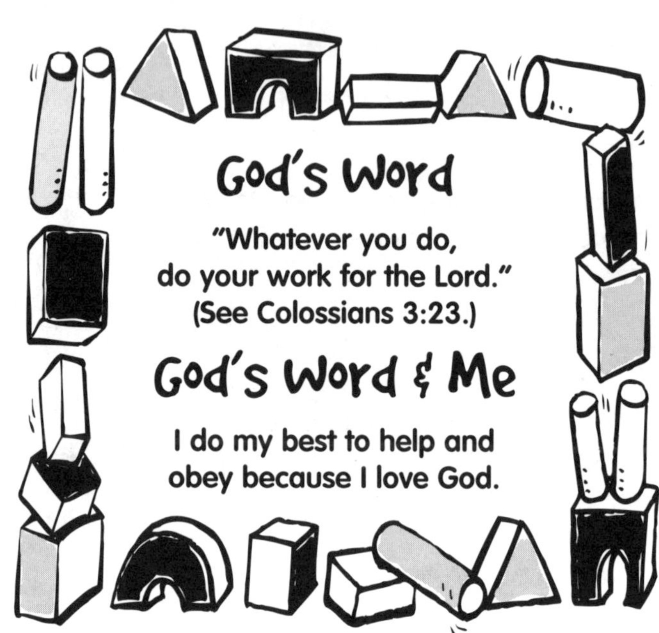
God's Word
"Whatever you do,
do your work for the Lord."
(See Colossians 3:23.)
God's Word & Me
I do my best to help and
obey because I love God.

## Do

1. Children use blocks to build different places where people work.
2. Children use toys to act out different ways people work in these places. For example, a child might make an airport and pretend to fly toy airplanes, or a child may make a restaurant and use a toy figure to serve food.

## Talk About

- **The Bible says, "Whatever you do, do your work for the Lord." This verse tells us that we should always do our best work. Let's build some places where people work and help others.**
- **What kind of work do people do at an airport?** (Carry suitcases. Fly airplanes.) **What kind of work do people do at a grocery store?** (Put food on shelves. Put groceries in bags.)
- **What kind of work do people do at your home?** (Cook food. Wash car. Stack papers.) **What kind of work can you do at your home?**

## For Younger Children

Do not expect children's block work to actually look like the places they say they are building. Avoid the tendency to correct a child's work. Simply allow children the freedom to build in a way that is meaningful to them.

## For Older Children

Children use construction paper and markers to make signs for the places they build. On another sheet of paper, print words they ask for so that children can copy them on their signs.

Lesson 6

# Science Center: Cleaning Coins

## Collect
Bible, newspaper, several dirty coins, water, three bowls, paper towels, liquid soap, measuring cup, vinegar, tablespoon, salt.

## Prepare
Spread newspaper over the activity area.

### God's Word
**"Whatever you do, do your work for the Lord." (See Colossians 3:23.)**

### God's Word & Me
**I do my best to help and obey because I love God.**

## Do

1. Show children the coins you brought. **What do you think might be a good way to clean these coins?** Allow several children to respond. **Let's see if water helps clean the coins.** Pour some water into one of the bowls. Drop a few coins in the water. Allow several volunteers to try rubbing coins with paper towels. Add liquid soap to water and invite several different volunteers to wash coins again.
2. After several minutes, pour ½ cup vinegar in third bowl. Add one tablespoon salt and stir. Drop coins in mixture and lead children in counting to 25 as they watch the mixture clean the coins. Remove coins and rinse in water. Children dry coins with paper towels.

## Talk About

- **In our Bible story today, a boy named Samuel did his best work to help others. One way he may have helped was by keeping a big candlestick clean and shiny. Let's see if we can clean some coins so that they are shiny.**
- **The Bible says, "Whatever you do, do your work for the Lord." This verse tells us that we should always do our best work. We can do our best when we help others.**
- **Who is someone you can help at your house? Who can you help in our classroom?**

## For Younger Children
Children use water to wash and dry classroom objects.

## For Older Children
Children mix vinegar and salt and then take turns dropping coins into mixture to be cleaned. Be sure to provide at least one coin for each child to clean.

# Bible Story Center

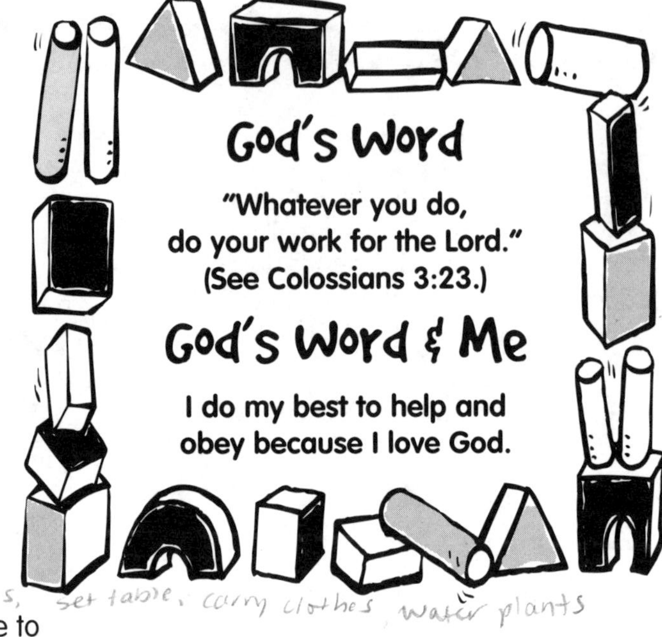
God's Word
"Whatever you do,
do your work for the Lord."
(See Colossians 3:23.)
God's Word & Me
I do my best to help and
obey because I love God.

## Collect

Bible, Picture 11 from *Bible Story Pictures.*

## Tell the Story

Use the pictured motions (keywords in bold) or show Picture 11. For older children, tell the version of the story on the back of Picture 11.

**What is the first thing you do when you wake up in the morning? Today we're going to learn what Samuel did every day when he woke up in the Tabernacle.**

"Samuel, Samuel," Eli called. "Samuel, it's time to **wake up** and start a new day at God's Tabernacle," he said.

Eli had a special job at the Tabernacle. He prayed to God for others. And Eli taught people about God. Samuel helped Eli and took care of the Tabernacle.

Sometimes Eli would say, "Today you may polish the candlesticks." Samuel obeyed. He rubbed and **rubbed** the candlesticks. Samuel rubbed them until they were shiny and bright.

"We will need some firewood from the woodpile," Eli told Samuel. "Please get some more wood." Samuel obeyed Eli. He carried firewood from the woodpile to the Tabernacle for Eli.

Eli told Samuel other jobs to do. And Samuel obeyed all Eli said. When all the work was finished, Eli said, "**Open** the doors to the Tabernacle. Let the people come inside."

Many people came inside to thank God and to sing glad songs to Him. When all the people went home, Eli would **call** Samuel to close the doors.

Every day Samuel grew taller and stronger. And every day Samuel learned more and more about God. Samuel did a good job of helping Eli at the Tabernacle. Samuel obeyed God by doing his best.

## God's Word & Me

**What are some of the chores Samuel probably did at the Tabernacle?** (Polished candlesticks. Carried firewood. Swept floor. Opened and closed the doors.) **Samuel did his best to help and obey Eli. Samuel loved God. We can show we love God by doing our best to help and obey, too! Who is someone you can help at home?** (Mom, Dad, grandparent, baby-sitter, etc.) **What is something you can do to help your mother?**

# Worship Center

## Collect

Bible, *Shake It Up!* songbook and cassette/CD and player, "A Little Bit More" and "I Love the Lord" word charts (pp. 12 and 15 in songbook).

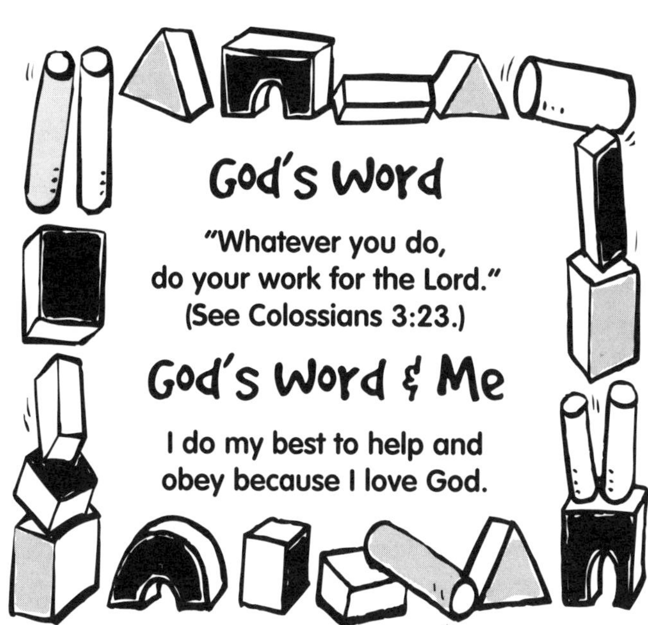
God's Word
"Whatever you do,
do your work for the Lord."
(See Colossians 3:23.)
God's Word & Me
I do my best to help and
obey because I love God.

## Sing to God

Play "A Little Bit More." Invite children to sing along with you. **Let's sing a song about obeying!** Lead children in singing song and doing suggested motions. **According to the song, what do our hands do?** (Help others.) **Doing our best to help others is one way to show that we love God!**

## Hear and Say God's Word

Holding your Bible open to Colossians 3:23, say verse aloud. **"Lord" is another name for God. We can do our best to help and obey because we love God.** Lead children in repeating the verse a few times in this manner: Say the verse very quietly the first time and then a bit louder each time you repeat the verse, until you are speaking in a normal speaking voice. Continue repeating verse, getting softer on each repetition, until speaking very quietly again.

## Pray to God

**We can ask God to help us do our best to help and obey.** Children repeat prayer, phrase by phrase after you. **Dear God, . . . help us to always . . . do our best . . . to help and obey. . . . We want to do our best . . . because we love You. . . . In Jesus' name, amen.**

## Sing to God

In closing the worship time, play "I Love the Lord." Invite children to sing along with you and do suggested motions. **We can show our love for God by helping and obeying. Who can you help today?**

## Options

1. If you take a weekly offering during this worship time, explain to children that the money is used to help people learn about God. Giving money is one way to show our love for God.
2. Children think of things they can do this week to help the people in their families. Record children's responses on a large sheet of paper. Display paper where parents will see it when they pick up their children.

# Read-Aloud Story and Activity Center

## Collect

A copy of Story Picture 6 (pp. 17-18 from *Read-Aloud Story and Activity Book*) for each child and yourself, crayons or markers.

## Prepare

Color your copy of Story Picture 6.

## Do

**Listen for ways this family helped at church.** Read story and show completed Story Picture 6. Distribute pictures. Use conversation suggestions in Let's Talk About the Story as children complete their pages.

# Kindergarten Puzzle Center

## Collect

Copies of Puzzles 11 and 12 (p. 29 and p. 31 from *The Big Book of Kindergarten Puzzles)* for each child, pencils, crayons or markers.

## Do

Children complete the puzzles and color pages.

# Instant Activities

These activities can be used at any time during this session: when children need a change of pace, to extend the session, or during transition time at the beginning or end of the session.

## Collect

*The Big Book of Instant Activities.*

## Do

Guide children to complete "Measuring Song" and/or "Stringing Things" (p. 98 and/or p. 122 from *The Big Book of Instant Activities).*

Lesson 7

# Samuel Listens and obeys

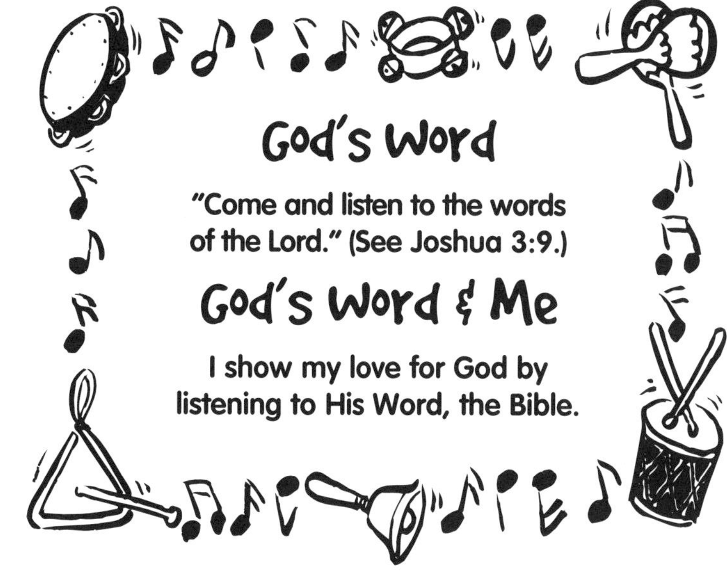
God's Word
"Come and listen to the words of the Lord." (See Joshua 3:9.)
God's Word & Me
I show my love for God by listening to His Word, the Bible.

## Bible Story

1 Samuel 3

## Teacher's Devotional

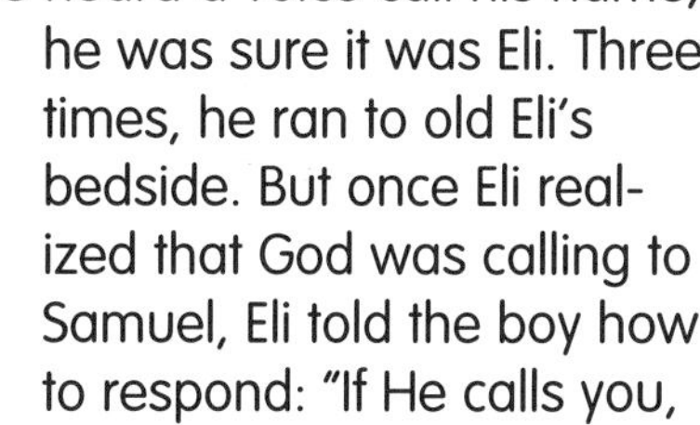

Samuel lay quietly, almost asleep. When he heard a voice call his name, he was sure it was Eli. Three times, he ran to old Eli's bedside. But once Eli realized that God was calling to Samuel, Eli told the boy how to respond: "If He calls you, say, 'Speak, Lord, for your servant is listening.' " Can you imagine how excited Samuel was? He must have lain down, full of anticipation. And "the Lord came and stood there" (1 Samuel 3:10). He talked with Samuel, preparing him for the work he was to do.

In our noisy world, it's difficult sometimes even to find a quiet place to rest—let alone prepare for God to speak to us! Listening is hard work! But as we quiet our souls, tune out the world, search God's Word and pray, we can anticipate—as Samuel did—that His Word will tell us what we need to know.

Listen, too, for God's voice in the needs of the children you teach. Ask the Lord, "What do I need to understand about this child? How can I communicate Your love to this one?" James assures us that if we ask for wisdom, in faith, God will answer (see James 1:5,6). Keep your ears—and your heart—open.

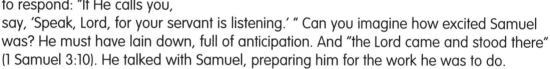

## Teacher's Planning

1. Choose which centers you will provide and the order in which children will participate in them. For tips on schedule planning, see page 7.
2. Plan who will lead each center. For staffing tips and ideas, see page 21.

# Active Game Center: Seat Swap

## Collect

Bible, *Shake It Up!* cassette/CD and player, two beanbags or other small objects.

### God's Word

**"Come and listen to the words of the Lord." (See Joshua 3:9.)**

### God's Word & Me

**I show my love for God by listening to His Word, the Bible.**

## Do

1. Children sit in a circle. (Note: If you have more than eight or ten children, you may wish to form additional circles.) Hand beanbags or other objects to children on opposite sides of the circle.
2. Play "I Love the Lord" from cassette/CD. Children pass beanbags or other objects as music plays. When music is stopped, the two children holding the beanbags or other objects stand, run around the outside of the circle and switch places. Repeat game as time allows.

## Talk About

- **Our Bible tells us, "Come and listen to the words of the Lord." Let's play a game where we have to listen carefully.**
- **When someone tells us a Bible story, we are listening to God's Word. When are times people tell Bible stories to you?**
- **One thing God's Word tells us to do is to be kind to others. What can you do to be kind while playing this game?** (Pass the beanbag or object instead of throwing it.)
- **Nathan and Chandler, you are listening to the music. You can listen to God's Word, too!**

## For Younger Children

Children form a circle. As music plays, children follow each other, walking around the circle. When music stops, children sit down. Repeat as time allows.

## For Older Children

After children switch places, they say the words of the Bible verse together.

# Art Center: Puppet Talk

## Collect

Bible, two small paper bags for each child, markers; optional—yarn, scissors, glue.

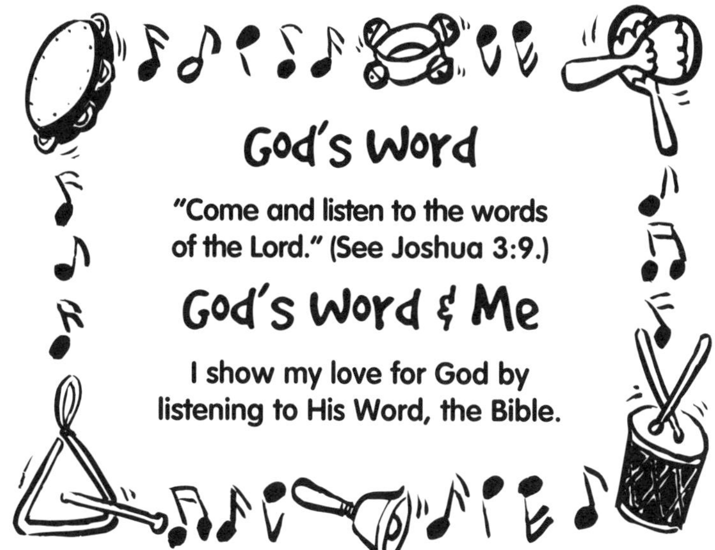
God's Word
"Come and listen to the words of the Lord." (See Joshua 3:9.)
God's Word & Me
I show my love for God by listening to His Word, the Bible.

## Do

1. Children draw Samuel's face on the bottom of one paper bag and draw Eli's face on the bottom of the other paper bag. (Optional: Children cut short lengths of yarn and glue onto puppets for hair. Children glue yarn for a beard for Eli.) Children draw arms and clothes on the paper bags.
2. Children put their hands inside the bags and act out story by moving flaps up and down to show Samuel and Eli talking (see sketch a).

## Talk About

- **Today's Bible story is about a boy named Samuel. One night while Samuel was sleeping, he heard someone call his name three times. Eli told Samuel that it was the Lord talking to Samuel. Eli told Samuel to say "Speak to me, Lord. I'm listening." Let's make puppets and act out what happened in our Bible story.**
- **The Bible says, "Come and listen to the words of the Lord." "Lord" is another name for God. Samuel listened to God's words. When are some times you can listen to God's words in the Bible?** (When I hear a Bible story.)

## For Younger Children

Photocopy a simple drawing of a face (see sketch b). Cut out two faces for each child to color and then glue to his or her paper bags.

## For Older Children

Provide construction paper. Children draw and cut out clothing for their puppets. Children glue clothing to puppets.

 

Lesson 7

# Block Center: Beds of Blocks

## Collect

Bible, blocks; optional—fabric pieces or blankets.

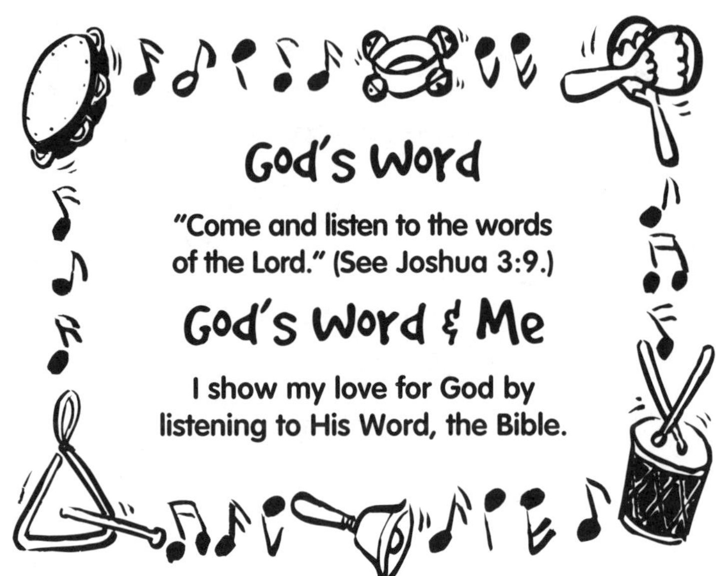
God's Word
"Come and listen to the words of the Lord." (See Joshua 3:9.)
God's Word & Me
I show my love for God by listening to His Word, the Bible.

## Do

1. Children arrange blocks to outline a bed. (Optional: Children use fabric pieces or blankets to finish making their beds.)
2. Children lie down in their block beds and pretend to sleep. Call each child by name. Named child responds by sitting up and saying "I am listening" and then joins teacher. Repeat activity by calling other children by name.

## Talk About

I am listening

- **In our Bible story today, Samuel woke up several times when he heard someone calling his name. Let's pretend we're Samuel and get up when our names are called.**
- **When Samuel heard his name called, he thought Eli was calling him. But Eli told him it was the Lord. Samuel listened to the Lord.**
- **Our Bible says, "Come and listen to the words of the Lord." We can listen to God's Word, the Bible. Who reads Bible stories to you? Who tells you Bible verses?**
- **Let's find out if Naomi knows how to listen. Naomi, bring me a long block. Good for you! You know how to listen and obey!**

## For Younger Children

Use masking tape to outline a large bed on floor. Children place blocks on outline and use as one big bed. When called by name, children simply get up and join you. (Note: Remove tape after use.)

## For Older Children

Children take turns acting out the roles of Samuel and Eli as you retell story events. Be prepared to repeat story several times during the Block Center.

Lesson 7

# Science Center: Listen to the Sounds

## Collect

Bible; two each of a variety of small items (gravel, marbles, rice, cotton balls, pasta, paper clips, buttons, jingle bells, coins, etc.); several clean, small dairy-product containers and lids; masking tape.

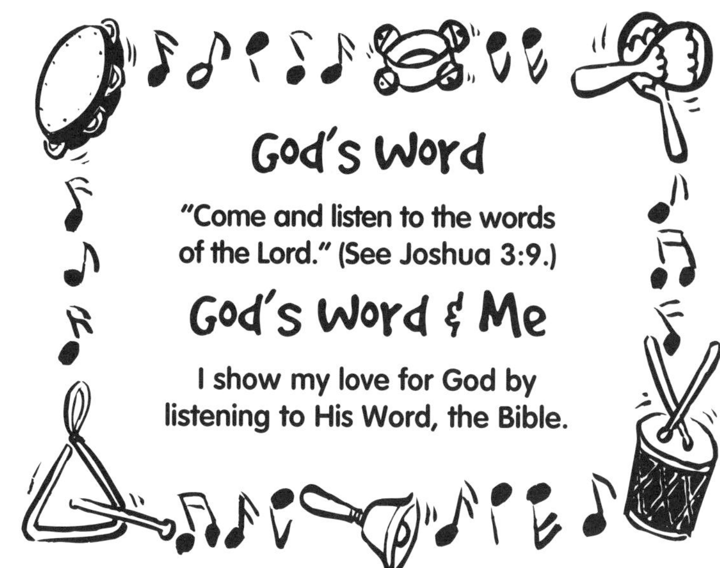
God's Word
"Come and listen to the words of the Lord." (See Joshua 3:9.)
God's Word & Me
I show my love for God by listening to His Word, the Bible.

## Prepare

Place one kind of item in each container, reserving one of each kind of item. Place lids on containers and tape securely.

## Do

Children take turns shaking containers one at a time and guessing what item might be in each container. Show items you reserved. Children shake containers again, trying to identify which container holds each item shown. After children have guessed the contents of each container, open container and reveal item. Replace lid and secure tape on each container before repeating activity.

## Talk About

- **The Bible says, "Come and listen to the words of the Lord." We can listen to the words of the Lord when we hear stories and verses from the Bible, God's Word. "Lord" is another name for God. Let's practice listening to some different kinds of sounds.**
- **I love the sound of rain on the roof. What are some of your favorite sounds? God made our ears. We can show our love for Him by listening to His Word, the Bible.**
- **I can make sounds with my hands by clapping them. What are some sounds you can make with your hands? With your feet? With your mouth?**

## For Younger Children

Children shake containers freely instead of waiting for turns. After several minutes, lead children in guessing what might be in each container.

## For Older Children

Lead children in comparing the different sounds and classifying them: loudest, softest, most pleasant, least pleasant, etc.

Lesson 7 • 1 Samuel 3

# Bible Story Center

## Collect

Bible, Picture 12 from *Bible Story Pictures.*

God's Word
"Come and listen to the words of the Lord." (See Joshua 3:9.)
God's Word & Me
I show my love for God by listening to His Word, the Bible.

## Tell the Story

Use the pictured motions (keywords in bold) or show Picture 12. For older children, tell the version of the story on the back of Picture 12.

**What sounds do you hear at night when you are in your bed? Today we're going to hear about a boy who heard something very unusual when he was in his bed.**

Samuel **yawned** a big yawn and stretched his arms. It was bedtime and Samuel felt very sleepy. After he got himself ready for bed, he lay down and closed his eyes. Then something strange happened! Just as Samuel was going to sleep, he heard someone call, "Samuel! Samuel!" Samuel sat straight up in his bed! "Eli must be calling me," he said. Samuel jumped out of his bed. He **ran** to where Eli slept. "Here I am. You called me?" Samuel asked.

Eli looked surprised. "I did not call you," Eli said. "Go back to bed, Samuel." Samuel went to his bed and lay down.

Everything was quiet again. "Samuel! Samuel!" Samuel heard the voice again. Samuel ran to Eli. "Here I am. You called me?" Samuel asked. "**No**," Eli said. "I did not call you. Now go back to bed." So Samuel went back to his bed and lay down.

A third time Samuel heard the voice. "Samuel! Samuel!" And once again he ran to Eli. "Here I am. You called me?" Samuel asked. Then Eli knew God was calling Samuel.

"When you hear the voice again," Eli told Samuel, "say 'Speak to me, God. I am listening.' " Samuel went back to his bed and lay down.

Soon Samuel **heard** the voice again, "Samuel! Samuel!" Samuel said, "Speak to me, God. I am listening." Then something wonderful happened. God spoke to Samuel. God told Samuel how to obey Him. And Samuel listened carefully to all God told him. Samuel was glad he obeyed Eli.

## God's Word & Me

**What woke Samuel up in the middle of the night?** (Someone was calling his name.) **Samuel showed his love for God by listening to Him. We can show our love for God by listening to His Word, the Bible. When do you hear stories from God's Word?**

# Worship Center

## Collect

Bible, *Shake It Up!* songbook and cassette/CD and player,"A Little Bit More" and "I Love the Lord" word charts (pp. 12 and 15 in songbook).

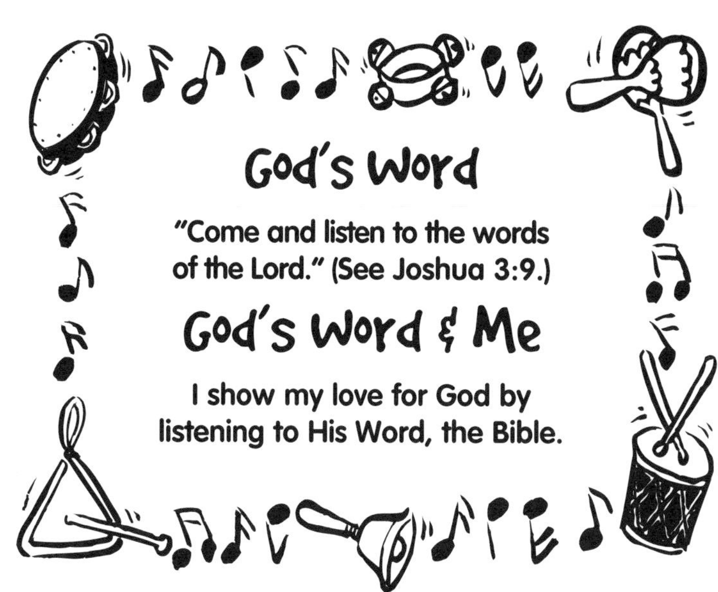
God's Word
"Come and listen to the words of the Lord." (See Joshua 3:9.)
God's Word & Me
I show my love for God by listening to His Word, the Bible.

## Sing to God

Play "A Little Bit More." Invite children to sing along with you. **Let's sing a song about growing up.** Lead children in singing song and doing suggested motions. **What does the song tell us we hear?** (God's Word.)

## Hear and Say God's Word

Holding your Bible open to Joshua 3:9, say verse aloud. **What does the Bible tell us to listen to?** (The words of the Lord.) **"Lord" is another name for God.** Show children the following motions to use when saying the verse: use hand to beckon when you say the word "come," cup your hand to your ear when you say the word "listen," point up when you say the phrase "the Lord." Lead children in saying the verse and doing the motions several times.

## Pray to God

**We can thank God for His Word, the Bible.** Invite volunteers to each say this brief thank-you prayer: **Thank You, God, for the Bible.**

## Sing to God

In closing the worship time, play "I Love the Lord." Invite children to sing along with you and do suggested motions. **This song tells us we can show love for the Lord every day.**

## Options

1. Provide one or two rhythm instruments for children to use while singing "A Little Bit More" and "I Love the Lord." Children exchange instruments each time the songs are sung.
2. During the verse activity, invite individuals or pairs to do the motions while you and other children say the verse.

 

# Read-Aloud Story and Activity Center

## Collect

A copy of Story Picture 7 (pp. 19-20 from *Read-Aloud Story and Activity Book*) for each child and yourself, crayons or markers.

## Prepare

Color your copy of Story Picture 7.

## Do

**Listen to find out what the boy was missing.** Read story and show completed Story Picture 7. Distribute pictures. Use conversation suggestions in Let's Talk About the Story as children complete their pages.

## Collect

Copies of Puzzles 13 and 14 (p. 33 and p. 35 from *The Big Book of Kindergarten Puzzles)* for each child, pencils, crayons or markers.

## Do

Children complete the puzzles and color pages.

# Instant Activities

These activities can be used at any time during this session: when children need a change of pace, to extend the session, or during transition time at the beginning or end of the session.

## Collect

*The Big Book of Instant Activities.*

## Do

Guide children to complete "Who's Talking?" and/or "Reach High" (p. 126 and/or p. 84 from *The Big Book of Instant Activities).*

Lesson 8

# Samuel obeys God

## Bible Story

1 Samuel 16:1-13

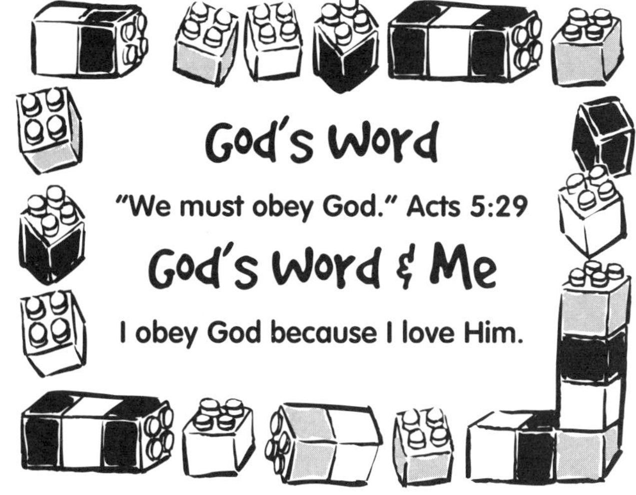

God's Word
"We must obey God." Acts 5:29
God's Word & Me
I obey God because I love Him.

## Teacher's Devotional

We hear a great deal today about self-esteem—or the lack of it. How is it that

our society produces an abundance of human beings who don't feel that they are worth anything?

Perhaps it's because we're taught all the wrong ways to measure our value. Society values a pretty or handsome exterior, wealth, fame and superior performance. Such values aren't new. They're simply the same superficial appearances that have always been around.

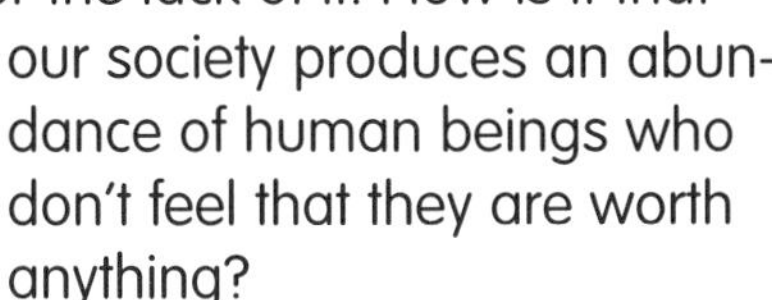

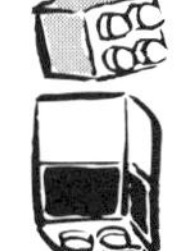

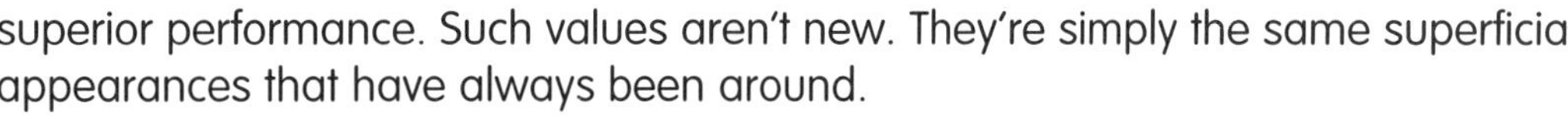

When Samuel went to anoint God's choice for a new king, he thought Eliab was the man. Eliab was tall and probably handsome. But the Lord said, "Do not consider his appearance or his height, for . . . the Lord does not look at the things man looks at. Man looks at the outward appearance, but the Lord looks at the heart" (1 Samuel 16:7).

The children in your class will be attacked all their lives by the world's shallow measures of self-worth. A deeply effective way to combat this is to treat each child as if he or she is of infinite value, because each one is! By your words and actions, help your children grasp the truth that what God sees in their hearts is what is important. His love for them—and you!—doesn't depend on exteriors or performance.

## Teacher's Planning

1. Choose which centers you will provide and the order in which children will participate in them. For tips on schedule planning, see page 7.
2. Plan who will lead each center. For staffing tips and ideas, see page 21.

# Active Game Center: Shape Shuffle

## Collect

Bible, masking tape, scissors, four colors of construction paper, masking tape.

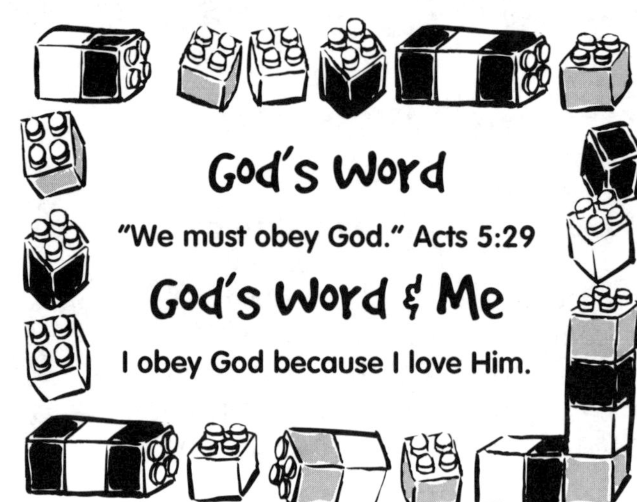
God's Word
"We must obey God." Acts 5:29
God's Word & Me
I obey God because I love Him.

## Prepare

On the floor, make a large X with two masking-tape lines. Cut each color of construction paper into a different shape (for example, red circle, blue triangle, green star and yellow square). Tape one shape in each of the areas created by the X. (If you have a large group, prepare more than one X and additional shapes.) (Note: Remove tape immediately after use.)

## Do

1. Help children identify the colors and shapes in each section of the X. Then direct children to different areas. **Stand in the section with the green shape.** Continue, using all colors and shapes.
2. Make the directions progressively more difficult to encourage children to use their imaginations. **Stand in the section with a shape like a piece of pizza.** Also include some directions that may have children move to more than one section. **Stand in a section with a color in a stoplight.**

## Talk About

- **Our Bible tells us, "We must obey God." We obey God because we love Him. Let's play a game by obeying some directions.**
- **Alonzo, you did a good job following directions. When you follow directions, you are obeying!**
- **What are some ways you obey your parents? Your teachers? Your baby-sitters? When is it hard to obey?**

## For Younger Children

Make a duplicate of each shape. Hold that shape up as you give directions.

## For Older Children

With each direction, include a motion for children to perform. **Stand on one foot in the section with a red circle.** Vary the motion with each direction.

# Art Center: Helping Hands Mural

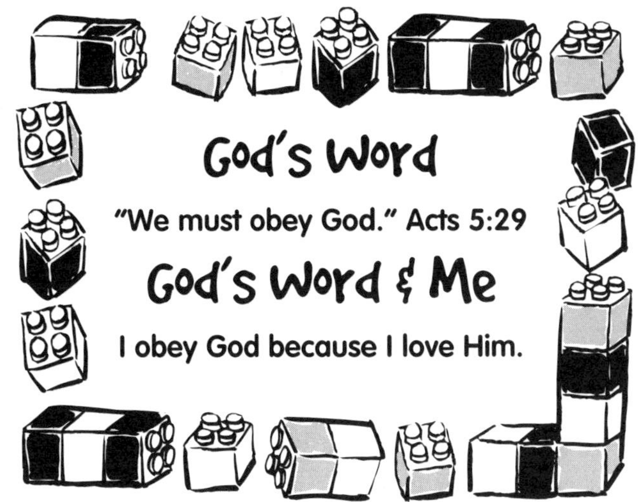
God's Word
"We must obey God." Acts 5:29
God's Word & Me
I obey God because I love Him.

## Collect

Bible, large sheet of butcher paper, markers, pencils, tape.

## Prepare

Along the top of the paper print in large letters "We obey God and do what's right!"

## Do

Children use pencils to trace their hands on paper. Then children trace over and decorate the hand outlines with markers. Children make as many hands as time allows. (Note: If you have a large class, prepare a paper for every group of four to six children.) Tape mural to wall.

## Talk About

We obey God and

- **Our Bible says, "We must obey God." We can use our hands when we obey. Let's make pictures of our hands.**
- **How do you use your hands to obey and do what's right at home? At church? At the park?**
- **When your mother drops something, what do you do? Helping is a way to obey God.**
- **Travis, you are doing a good job of following my directions. You know how to obey!**
- **What is one way we can obey God and do what's right by using our hands?** (Help someone stand up who has fallen down. Make the bed when Mom says to. Put away toys. Open the door for someone.)

## For Younger Children

Teacher or older children trace younger children's hands.

## For Older Children

Use tempera paint to make handprints. Fold several paper towels to make a paint pad. Place in shallow pan and pour paint on pad to saturate it. Repeat for as many colors as desired. Cover table with newspaper. Children place hand on paint pad and then on paper, cleaning hands before switching colors.

# Block Center: Keep the Sheep

## Collect

Bible, blocks; optional—cotton balls.

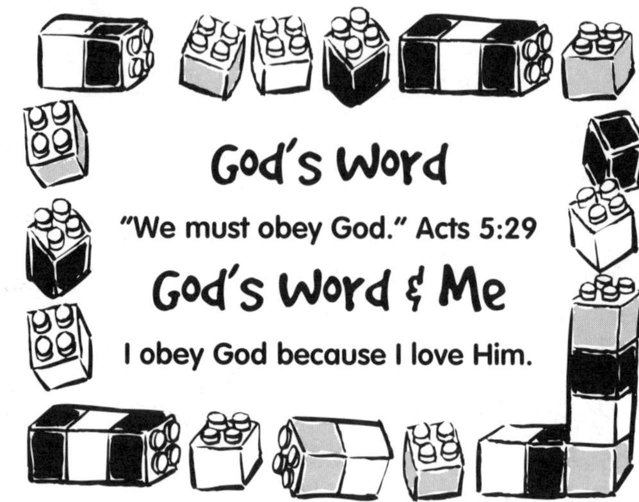
God's Word
"We must obey God." Acts 5:29
God's Word & Me
I obey God because I love Him.

## Do

1. Children make sheepfolds by using blocks to outline squares.
2. Children use additional blocks as if they were sheep. (Optional: Children use cotton balls for sheep.) Announce, **It's nighttime! It's time for the sheep to go into their sheepfolds.** Children move sheep into sheepfolds. Then say, **It's morning time! Time to take the sheep out to eat grass and drink water.** Repeat several times as children come and go from the Block Center.

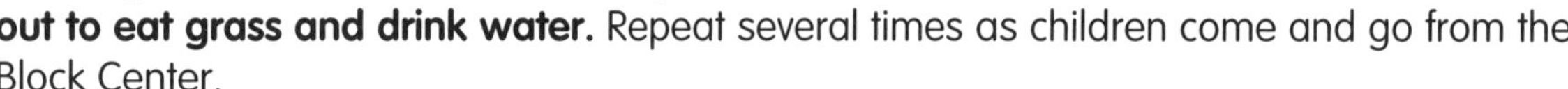

## Talk About

- **In our Bible story, David obeyed his father by caring for his family's sheep. Let's make pens for sheep, called sheepfolds.**
- **David took good care of his family's sheep. David loved God and wanted to do what was right. What are some of the things David did to care for his family's sheep?** (Found grass for the sheep to eat. Gave them water to drink.)
- **Our Bible says, "We must obey God." What jobs do you do at your house? When you obey, you are showing your love for God!**
- **Natalie, you put your sheep into the sheepfold like a good shepherd! You know how to obey.**

## For Younger Children

Make masking-tape squares on floor to represent sheepfolds. Children place blocks on masking-tape lines. If your floor is carpeted, remove masking tape immediately after use.

## For Older Children

Each child counts the sheep as they are put in the sheepfold. Each time you announce nighttime, designate a different number (one, two, three or four) of sheep to be led into each sheepfold.

Lesson 8

# Science Center: Bottled Fun

## Collect

Bible, empty plastic water or soda bottle with lid, water, food coloring, vegetable oil, duct tape; optional—plastic or metallic confetti.

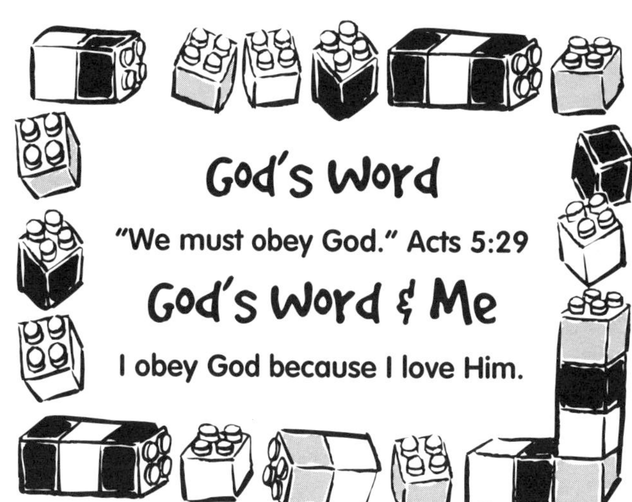
God's Word
"We must obey God." Acts 5:29
God's Word & Me
I obey God because I love Him.

## Do

1. Invite children to help you with the following tasks: Fill ⅔ of the bottle with water. Add a few drops of food coloring and fill remainder with vegetable oil. (Optional: Add plastic or metallic confetti.) Attach lid, securing with tape.
2. Children play with bottle, watching oil and water separate, shaking bottle fast and slow, swirling it, turning it upside down, etc. (Note: If you have more than six children, make additional bottles.)

## Talk About

- **In our Bible story, Samuel obeyed God. He poured oil on David's head to show that God had chosen David to be the next king. We're going to experiment with oil today.**
- As children follow your directions to make bottle, comment on the ways they obey. **Megan, thank you for putting the food coloring in the bottle. You obeyed.**
- **Our Bible says, "We must obey God."** Pray briefly, **Dear God, we love You. Help us obey You.**

## For Younger Children

Instead of making a bottle in class, before class, prepare several of the following bags, at least one for every pair of children: Partially fill a small, resealable plastic bag with oil, water, corn syrup or other liquid. Add food coloring and additional objects (plastic or metallic confetti; or a few buttons, beads or shells). Seal the bag. Place inside a second bag and seal. Secure closure with duct tape.

## For Older Children

Children make their own water and oil bottles. In addition to plastic or metallic confetti, you may wish to provide buttons, beads, shells, sand or other objects for children to use. Provide funnels to make pouring liquids easier for children.

# Bible Story Center

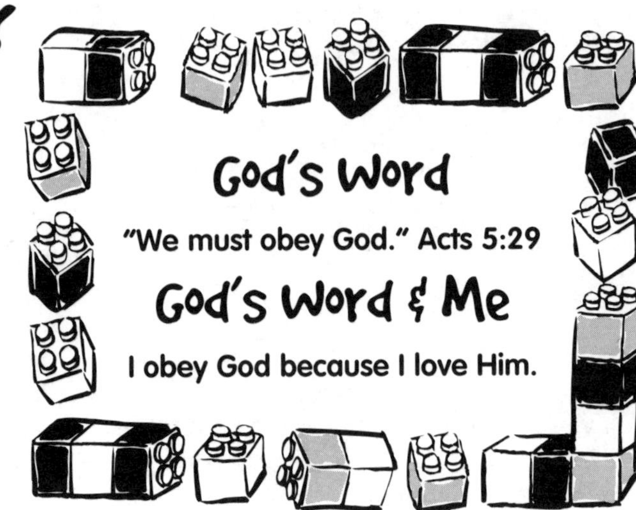
God's Word
"We must obey God." Acts 5:29
God's Word & Me
I obey God because I love Him.

## Collect

Bible, Picture 13 from *Bible Story Pictures.*

## Tell the Story

Use the pictured motions (keywords in bold) or show Picture 13. For older children, tell the version of the story on the back of Picture 13.

**Do you have brothers or sisters? What are their names? Today we're going to hear about a boy who had seven older brothers!**

Our Bible tells about a boy named Samuel who grew up to be a leader of God's people. Samuel loved and obeyed God. Samuel did what was **right** and good.

One day God said to Samuel, "I have chosen a new leader, a king, for My people. I want you to show the people their new king. Find a man named Jesse," God said. "I have chosen one of Jesse's sons to be the new king. When you get to Bethlehem, I will show you which son I have chosen."

So Samuel obeyed God. Step, step, step. Samuel went to Bethlehem. Then he talked to Jesse. Samuel looked at Jesse's sons. The oldest one was tall and **strong**. *Surely this is the one God wants to be king,* Samuel thought. But God said, "No, he is not the one. The one I have chosen loves Me very much." **One, two**, three, four, five, six, seven sons walked by Samuel. Each time God said "No, I have not chosen this one to be king." *Who could the king be?* wondered Samuel.

Samuel asked Jesse, "Do you have any more sons?"

"I have one more son," Jesse answered. "David is his name. He is out in the hills taking care of our sheep."

"Tell David to come here to me," Samuel said. Soon David **walked** in. David loved God very much. Samuel looked at David. Then God said, "This is the one I have chosen to be the new king." God had chosen David to be king. And Samuel had obeyed God by doing what God had told him to do.

## God's Word & Me

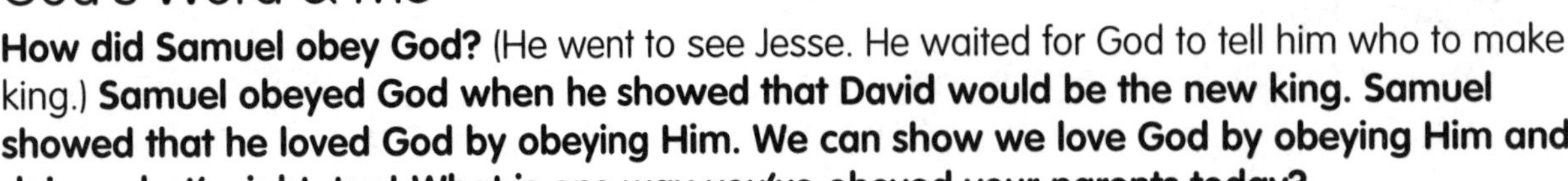

**How did Samuel obey God?** (He went to see Jesse. He waited for God to tell him who to make king.) **Samuel obeyed God when he showed that David would be the new king. Samuel showed that he loved God by obeying Him. We can show we love God by obeying Him and doing what's right, too! What is one way you've obeyed your parents today?**

# Worship Center

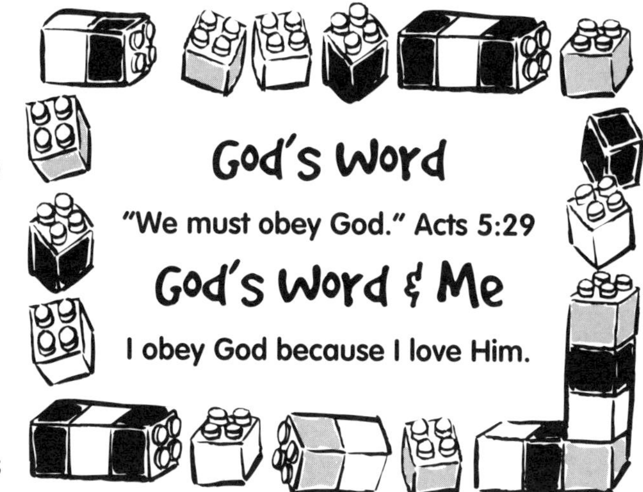
God's Word
"We must obey God." Acts 5:29
God's Word & Me
I obey God because I love Him.

## Collect

Bible, *Shake It Up!* songbook and cassette/CD and player, "I Love the Lord" and "A Little Bit More" word charts (pp. 15 and 12 in songbook).

## Sing to God

Play "I Love the Lord." Invite children to sing along with you. **Let's tell God we love Him as we sing this song.** Lead children in singing song and doing suggested motions. **We obey God because we love Him. In the Bible God tells us to help others. What is one way to obey God by helping others in our class?** (Hand someone a block. Share markers when drawing.)

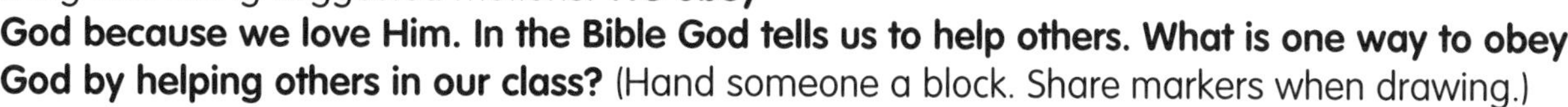

## Hear and Say God's Word

Holding your Bible open to Acts 5:29, say verse aloud. **When we do right, we obey God. What right things can you do when playing with a friend?** (Share. Take turns. Play fairly.) Lead children in repeating verse by echoing phrases after you: "We must/obey God." Point to children when it is their turn to speak. Repeat verse several times in this manner.

## Pray to God

Lead children in a brief prayer. **Dear God, thank You for showing us ways to obey You and do what's right. Help us show our love for You everywhere we go. In Jesus' name, amen.**

## Sing to God

In closing the worship time, play "A Little Bit More." Invite children to sing along with you and do suggested motions. **What does this song say we do every day?** (Grow up. Do what's right.)

## Options

1. In the verse activity, vary the manner in which the first group speaks (singsong, loud, soft, whisper, low, high, etc.). Second group echoes in the same manner of speaking.
2. Older children lead other children in doing the motions suggested for "I Love the Lord" and/or "A Little Bit More."

# Read-Aloud Story and Activity Center

## Collect

A copy of Story Picture 8 (pp. 21-22 from *Read-Aloud Story and Activity Book*) for each child and yourself, crayons or markers.

## Prepare

Color your copy of Story Picture 8.

## Do

**Listen to hear how this boy felt.** Read story and show completed Story Picture 8. Distribute pictures. Use conversation suggestions in Let's Talk About the Story as children complete their pages.

# Kindergarten Puzzle Center

## Collect

Copies of Puzzles 15 and 16 (p. 37 and p. 39 from *The Big Book of Kindergarten Puzzles)* for each child, pencils, crayons or markers.

## Do

Children complete the puzzles and color pages.

# Instant Activities

These activities can be used at any time during this session: when children need a change of pace, to extend the session, or during transition time at the beginning or end of the session.

## Collect

*The Big Book of Instant Activities.*

## Do

Guide children to complete "Friend Find" and/or "What's Your Answer?" (p. 66 and/or p. 87 from *The Big Book of Instant Activities).*

Lesson 9

# David Helps His Family

## Bible Story

1 Samuel 16:11,12,18; 17:34,35

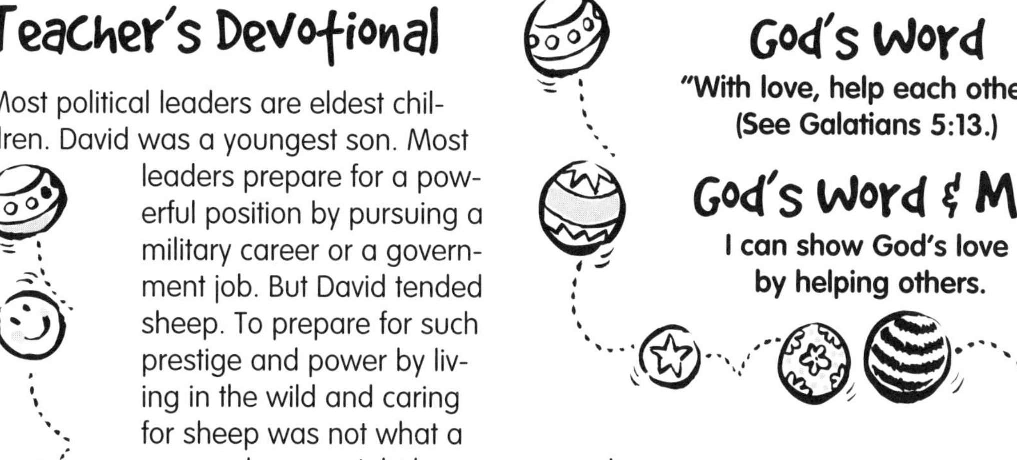

## God's Word

**"With love, help each other." (See Galatians 5:13.)**

## God's Word & Me

**I can show God's love by helping others.**

## Teacher's Devotional

Most political leaders are eldest children. David was a youngest son. Most leaders prepare for a powerful position by pursuing a military career or a government job. But David tended sheep. To prepare for such prestige and power by living in the wild and caring for sheep was not what a career planner might have suggested!

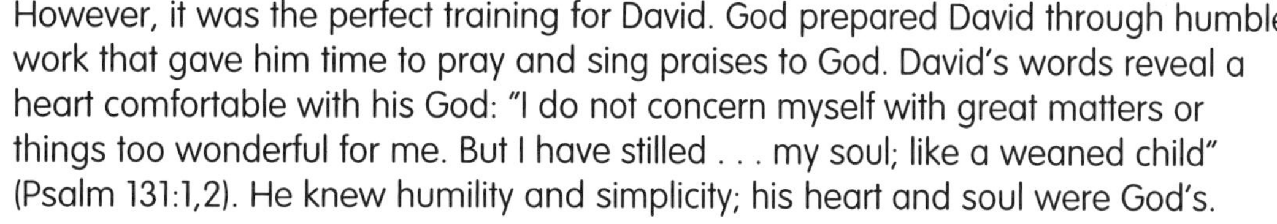

However, it was the perfect training for David. God prepared David through humble work that gave him time to pray and sing praises to God. David's words reveal a heart comfortable with his God: "I do not concern myself with great matters or things too wonderful for me. But I have stilled . . . my soul; like a weaned child" (Psalm 131:1,2). He knew humility and simplicity; his heart and soul were God's.

Your preparation to be a teacher may be as unconventional as David's was for the throne! You may even think you are not prepared at all. But still your soul. Open yourself to God's Spirit and ask Him to change you and draw out those abilities He's put within you. He can help you make creative use of every bit of your class time, for He promises wisdom if you ask confidently (see James 1:5-8). Give God your heart as David did, and He will prepare you as He did David!

## Teacher's Planning

1. Choose which centers you will provide and the order in which children will participate in them. For tips on schedule planning, see page 7.
2. Plan who will lead each center. For staffing tips and ideas, see page 21.

 

# Active Game Center: Help the Sheep

## Collect

Bible, green towel, blue towel, cardboard box, cotton balls, plastic spoons.

God's Word
"With love, help each other."
(See Galatians 5:13.)
God's Word & Me
I can show God's love
by helping others.

## Prepare

Place towels and box in different areas of the classroom. Place cotton balls, two or three for each child, in box.

## Do

Say, **The sheep need to eat.** Each child places a cotton ball on a spoon and carries the ball to the green towel, which represents grass. Continue the activity using the following directions: **The sheep need to drink.** Children carry the cotton balls to the blue towel, which represents water. **The sheep need to sleep.** Children carry the cotton balls to the box, which represents a sheepfold. Repeat directions as time permits.

## Talk About

- **In our Bible story, David helped his family by caring for their sheep. Let's play a game and pretend to care for sheep.**
- **David found green grass and good water for the sheep. When the sheep had eaten all the grass in one place, what do you think David did? When a sheep got lost, what do you think David did?**
- **Our Bible says, "With love, help each other." We show God's love when we help each other. What are some ways you've helped others at your house?**

## For Younger Children

Children carry cotton balls in cups instead of on spoons.

## For Older Children

Before moving the cotton balls from one area to another, children count them. **David probably counted his sheep to make sure none got lost. Let's count our sheep, too!**

# Art Center: Pasture Pictures

## Collect

Bible, butcher paper, marker, construction paper (green, blue, brown and yellow), glue sticks, cotton balls.

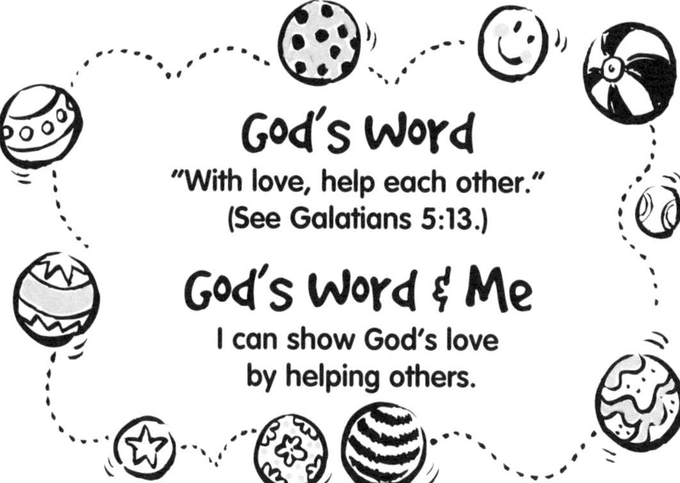
God's Word
"With love, help each other."
(See Galatians 5:13.)
God's Word & Me
I can show God's love
by helping others.

## Prepare

On a sheet of butcher paper, draw a simple outline of a landscape (see sketch). Prepare one sheet for each group of six to eight children.

## Do

Children tear colored construction paper into pieces. Children glue construction-paper pieces onto landscape, filling it in like a mosaic. When the landscape is completed, children glue on cotton balls to represent sheep. Attach completed mural to classroom or hallway walls.

## Talk About

- **David showed God's love by helping to care for his family's sheep. Let's make a picture to show ways David cared for the sheep.**
- **What did David find for the sheep to eat? To drink? Let's make plenty of grass and water in our picture.**
- **What other ways did David help his sheep?** (Kept them safe, etc.)
- **The Bible says, "With love, help each other." David helped his family by caring for the sheep. What are some ways you could help your family today?**
- **Who are some other people you could help? When we help others, we show God's love.**

## For Younger Children

Before class, use paper cutter to cut construction paper into pieces.

## For Older Children

Provide additional colors of paper and a variety of materials (chenille wires, tissue paper, felt squares, etc.) for children to use.

 

Lesson 9

# Block Center: Block Bus

## Collect

Bible, blocks.

## Do

Children lay blocks in the outline of a bus, large enough for the children to sit inside. When pretend bus is finished, children take seats and pretend to ride the bus to church or other familiar places.

### God's Word

**"With love, help each other."**
**(See Galatians 5:13.)**

### God's Word & Me

**I can show God's love by helping others.**

## Talk About

- **Our Bible tells us, "With love, help each other." Let's help each other build a bus with our blocks!**
- **Julia, I see you are carrying long blocks to build the bus. Thank you for helping. You are doing just what our Bible verse says to do.**
- **What are some other ways we help each other in our classroom?**
- Watch for ways to interpret children's interactions in terms of the lesson focus. **Marty, moving over so Cynthia would have more room to build was a loving thing to do. Our Bible says, "With love, help each other." You know about helping!**
- **Who can you help at your home?**

## For Younger Children

Before class, place chairs in two rows that are close together. Place one chair in front for the driver. Children place blocks in a large rectangle around the chairs to form bus.

## For Older Children

Cut the center from a paper plate and hand to child pretending to be the bus driver. Child pretends paper-plate ring is the steering wheel. Cut out four large black circles for tires. Ask children to tape to the sides of the bus.

# Science Center: Music Glasses

## Collect

Bible, at least five or six glasses or jars, water, metal spoons.

## Prepare

Fill glasses or jars with varying amounts of water.

God's Word
"With love, help each other."
(See Galatians 5:13.)
God's Word & Me
I can show God's love
by helping others.

## Do

Children use spoons to tap on glasses or jars and listen to the different sounds produced.

## Talk About

- **In today's Bible story, David helped his family by taking care of his family's sheep. David played his harp and sang songs while caring for the sheep. Let's make our own musical sounds!**
- **What kinds of instruments do you have at home? Who plays those instruments?**
- **What are some of the instruments you hear at church?**
- **Our Bible tells us, "With love, help each other." What are some ways you can help others at home? At church? At the park?**
- Pray briefly, **Dear God, please show us ways to help others.**

## For Younger Children

Be sure to use containers with wide bases: baby food jars, mason jars, glass bowls, etc. This will help ensure containers won't tip over.

## For Older Children

Children line glasses up from lowest to highest tone.

# Bible Story Center

God's Word
"With love, help each other."
(See Galatians 5:13.)
God's Word & Me
I can show God's love
by helping others.

## Collect

Bible, Picture 14 from *Bible Story Pictures.*

## Tell the Story

Use the pictured motions (keywords in bold) or show Picture 14. For older children, tell the version of the story on the back of Picture 14.

**What is something you have to wait your turn for? Listen to find out what David had to wait his turn to do.**

The Bible tells about a boy named David. One day his father said, "David, you are old enough to do an important job. You are old enough to take care of our sheep." David felt **happy**! He was glad to be a helper with the sheep

His father said, "You are old enough to **find** grass for our sheep to eat. You are old enough to find water for them to drink. And you are old enough to bring them safely home at night."

"I will take good care of our sheep," David said. David worked hard taking care of the sheep. He listened carefully to the sheep. "Baa! Baa! Baa!" the sheep said. David knew they were thirsty. Step, step, step—David walked to find cool water for the sheep to drink. "Baa! Baa! Baa!" the sheep said. David knew the sheep were hungry. Step, step, step—David walked to find a place where green grass grew for the sheep to eat.

While the sheep rested, David often **played his harp** and sang happy songs about God. One day David saw a lion creeping toward the sheep. The lion grabbed one of the sheep in its mouth. David jumped up and chased the lion. David caught the lion and pulled the sheep out of its mouth. Gently David **patted** the sheep and took it back to the other sheep.

David loved God. David was glad to be a good helper for his family.

## God's Word & Me

**What did David find for his sheep to eat?** (Green grass.) **For the sheep to drink?** (Water.) **David helped his family by caring for their sheep. David showed God's love by helping others. We can show God's love by helping others, too! What have you done today to help someone?**

# Worship Center

## Collect

Bible, *Shake It Up!* songbook and cassette/CD and player, "With Love" and "What Are You Gonna Do?" word charts (pp. 20 and 18 in songbook).

God's Word
"With love, help each other."
(See Galatians 5:13.)
God's Word & Me
I can show God's love
by helping others.

## Sing to God

Play "With Love." Invite children to sing along with you. **Let's sing a song about helping others.** Lead children in singing song and doing suggested motions. **What does this song tell us God says we should do?** (Help each other.)

## Hear and Say God's Word

Holding your Bible open to Galatians 5:13, say verse aloud. **How are we to help each other?** (With love.) Lead children in saying the Bible verse in the following manner: When children say the words "With love," they clap their hands on each word. When children say the words "Help each other," they slap their knees on each word. Repeat as time allows.

## Pray to God

Invite volunteers to name people they can help. Close in prayer, using the names of the people mentioned by children. **Dear God, we love You. Please show us ways we can help ____________. In Jesus' name, amen.**

## Sing to God

Play "What Are You Gonna Do?" to close the worship time. Invite children to sing along with you and do suggested motions. **What can you do today to show God's love by helping someone?** Volunteers respond.

## Options

1. During prayer activity, briefly tell an age-appropriate example of a time someone helped you.
2. If you take a weekly offering during this worship time, explain to children that the money is used to help people learn about God. **Giving money is one way to show God's love.**

 

# Read-Aloud Story and Activity Center

"With love, help each other."

## Collect

A copy of Story Picture 9 (pp. 23-24 from *Read-Aloud Story and Activity Book*) for each child and yourself, crayons or markers.

## Prepare

Color your copy of Story Picture 9.

## Do

**Listen to find out what these children are doing.** Read story and show completed Story Picture 9. Distribute pictures. Use conversation suggestions in Let's Talk About the Story as children complete their pages.

# Kindergarten Puzzle Center

## Collect

Copies of Puzzles 17 and 18 (p. 41 and p. 43 from *The Big Book of Kindergarten Puzzles)* for each child, pencils, crayons or markers.

## Do

Children complete the puzzles and color pages.

# Instant Activities

These activities can be used at any time during this session: when children need a change of pace, to extend the session, or during transition time at the beginning or end of the session.

## Collect

*The Big Book of Instant Activities.*

## Do

Guide children to complete "David's Sheep" and/or "Feel for It" (p. 79 and/or p. 20 from *The Big Book of Instant Activities).*

Lesson 10

# David Visits His Brothers

## Bible Story

1 Samuel 17:12-20

## Teacher's Devotional

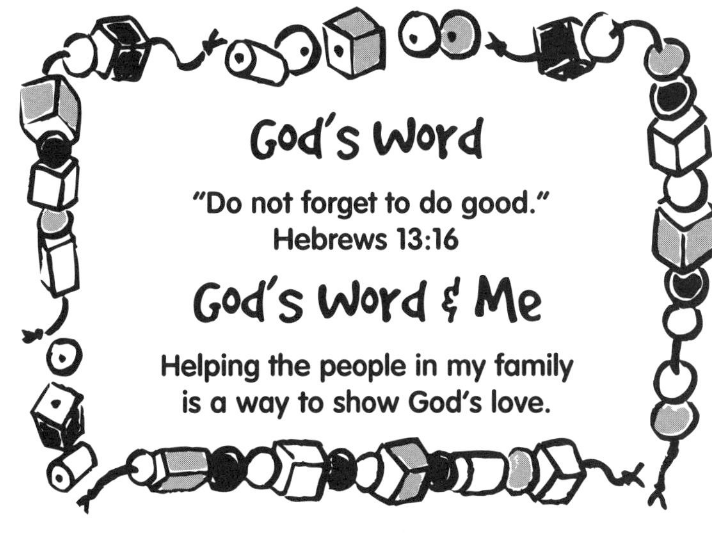
God's Word
"Do not forget to do good."
Hebrews 13:16
God's Word & Me
Helping the people in my family
is a way to show God's love.

Class time just seems to disappear, doesn't it? Children arrive, the activity swirls and the last child goes out the door in a cloud of dust. Your job is finished. But your effect has only begun!

Every child goes away with more than projects and papers. (We all know how often these scatter to the floor of the car!) Every child also takes home an attitude, an understanding, a feeling. Stop to picture each child's face. Imagine what each one took from the last session. Some may have taken home frustration. Some may have taken joy and acceptance. But whatever the child took home, it impacted his or her family. The family may be one you will never see. But if your loving attitude has reached the child, you will be reaching the family, too.

When the activity whirls and the tension builds, pause to remember that acting out God's love and patience will have lasting effects—reaching even people you may never see! As you teach each child about who God is and what He's like, teach with more than words; teach with your life.

## Teacher's Planning

1. Choose which centers you will provide and the order in which children will participate in them. For tips on schedule planning, see page 7.
2. Plan who will lead each center. For staffing tips and ideas, see page 21.

# Active Game Center: Table Tasks

## Collect

Bible; paper or plastic plates, cups and utensils—at least one item for each child; large paper bag; yarn.

## Prepare

Place a table at one end of the playing area. Place plates, cups and utensils in bag. Place bag on floor in front of table. Make a yarn line at other end of the playing area.

God's Word
"Do not forget to do good."
Hebrews 13:16
God's Word & Me
Helping the people in my family
is a way to show God's love.

## Do

1. Children line up behind yarn line. Each child takes a turn to walk to the table, select an item from bag, place item on the table and return to starting point. Continue until each child has a turn.
2. For the second round, children take turns walking to the table, removing items one at a time and placing the items in the bag. Continue setting and clearing the table as time allows.

## Talk About

- **Our Bible tells us, "Do not forget to do good." Helping our families is a way to do something good. We can help our families by setting the table before we eat and clearing the table after we eat. Let's play a game of setting and clearing a table!**
- **What are some good things you can do to help your family at meal times?**
- **What are some of the other jobs people in your family do to help each other?** (Wash clothes. Cook food.)

## For Younger Children

Use only paper or plastic plates and cups and not utensils.

## For Older Children

Tape a magazine picture or simple drawing of a proper place setting on a wall behind the table. Children place items in correct positions.

# Art Center: Paper Picnic

God's Word
"Do not forget to do good."
Hebrews 13:16
God's Word & Me
Helping the people in my family
is a way to show God's love.

## Collect

Bible, markers, paper lunch bags, markers, scissors, ruler, stapler; optional—magazines or grocery-store advertisements.

## Prepare

Draw cut line on paper lunch bags (see sketch a), one bag for each child. (Optional: Cut out pictures of food from magazines or grocery-store advertisements.)

## Do

Children cut bags along cut line. Keeping bags flat, children decorate bag with markers. As children work, cut a strip approximately 1-inch (2.5-cm) wide from the cutoff portions of the bags. When children finish decorating bags, staple strips to bags to form handles for picnic baskets (see sketch b). (Optional: Children choose two or three food pictures to put in their picnic baskets.)

## Talk About

a.
b.
cut
c.

- **In our Bible story, David helped his family by bringing food to his brothers. We can show God's love by helping the people in our families, too.**
- **Let's pretend we're packing food to take with us on a picnic. What are some of your favorite foods? What do you like to eat on a picnic?**
- **At my house, I help my family by mowing the lawn. The Bible says, "Do not forget to do good." What can you do to help your family and do good?**

## For Younger Children

Instead of making a paper picnic basket, children glue food pictures to paper plates (see sketch c). Place plates in a picnic basket. Walk with children to another area of the classroom. Children unpack basket to enjoy a pretend picnic.

## For Older Children

Provide a large sheet of butcher paper. After children complete their paper picnic baskets, they cut fringe along all sides of butcher paper and decorate to create a picnic blanket. Drawing ants and ladybugs on blanket is a fun touch. Children place baskets on blanket for picnic.

# Block Center: "House-Help" Appliances

## Collect

Bible, one or more large cardboard boxes, blocks.

God's Word
"Do not forget to do good."
Hebrews 13:16
God's Word & Me
Helping the people in my family
is a way to show God's love.

## Do

Lead children to choose which household appliance they want the cardboard box(es) to be (refrigerator, stove, washing machine, dryer, dishwasher, vacuum, etc.). Children use blocks and act out ways family members use the appliance to help each other. For instance, children use blocks as food and place in box as if it were a refrigerator.

## Talk About

- **Our Bible tells us, "Do not forget to do good." Helping our families is a way to show God's love. Let's use the boxes and blocks to show ways family members help each other.**
- **What job can a clothes dryer help you do for your family?** Repeat for several appliances.
- **What is one way you did good by helping your family this morning? What did you do with your pajamas?**
- To help children think of helping actions, ask, **Who helps you have clean clothes? What does your grandmother do? How can you help her?**

## For Younger Children

Instead of using boxes, children build block houses and use toy people. As children play with toy people, talk with them about ways to help family members.

## For Older Children

Children draw details (knobs, doors, etc.) on cardboard appliances.

# Science Center: Taste Test

## Collect

Bible, a variety of Bible-times foods (raisins, dates, pita bread, olives, hard cheese, cream cheese, etc.), bowls or other containers, paper, marker, plastic knives and spoons, paper plates, napkins; optional—premoistened towelettes.

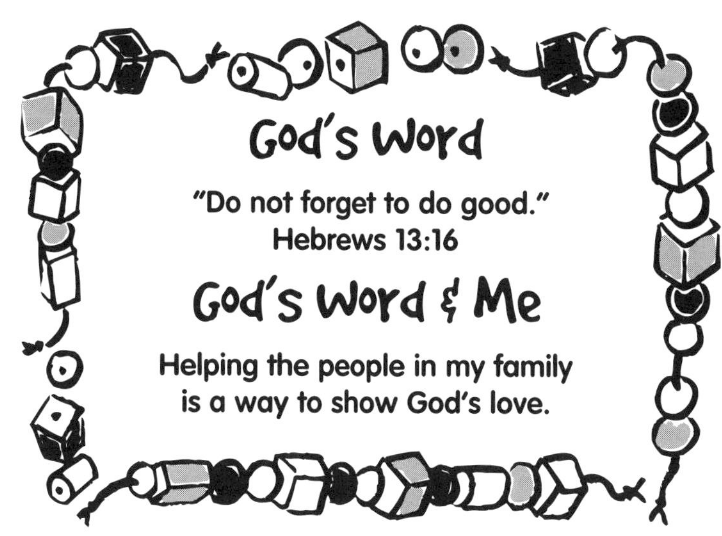
God's Word
"Do not forget to do good."
Hebrews 13:16
God's Word & Me
Helping the people in my family
is a way to show God's love.

## Prepare

Place foods in individual bowls or other containers. Cut larger food into bite-size pieces. Post a note alerting parents to the use of food in this activity. Also check registration forms for possible food allergies.

## Do

1. Children wash hands before beginning activity. (Optional: If you do not have a sink nearby, provide premoistened towelettes with which children can clean their hands.)
2. Children use utensils to select different food items, place them on a plate and enjoy tasting each food.

## Talk About

- **In today's Bible story, David helped his family by bringing food to his brothers. Let's taste some foods that David might have taken to his brothers.**
- **David showed God's love by helping his family. How do you help your family?**
- **Who in your family helps you? How? The Bible says, "Do not forget to do good." Helping the people in our families is a way to do good.**

## For Younger Children

Limit food items to crackers, cheese cubes and raisins.

## For Older Children

Before eating, lead children in sorting foods according to color, size and shape.

Lesson 10 • 1 Samuel 17:12-20

# Bible Story Center

## Collect

Bible, Picture 15 from *Bible Story Pictures.*

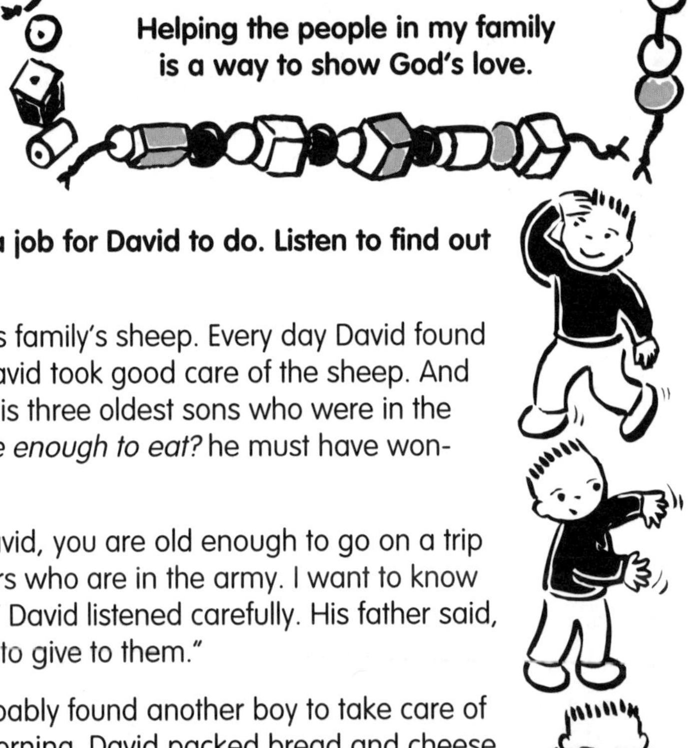

### God's Word

**"Do not forget to do good."**
**Hebrews 13:16**

### God's Word & Me

**Helping the people in my family is a way to show God's love.**

## Tell the Story

Use the pictured motions (keywords in bold) or show Picture 15. For older children, tell the version of the story on the back of Picture 15.

**I have a job at my house. Once a week I wash my car. What is a job you like to do? Today we'll hear about a time when David's father had a job for David to do. Listen to find out what David did to help.**

Every day David **found** green grass for his family's sheep. Every day David found cool water for them to drink. Every day David took good care of the sheep. And every day, David's father thought about his three oldest sons who were in the army. *What are they doing? Do they have enough to eat?* he must have wondered.

One day David's father said to David, "David, you are old enough to go on a trip by yourself. Please go to see your brothers who are in the army. I want to know how they are doing. I can't go see them." David listened carefully. His father said, "**Pack** some bread and cheese and corn to give to them."

David made plans right away. David probably found another boy to take care of his family's sheep. Then early the next morning, David packed bread and cheese and corn in sacks. Very carefully he loaded the sacks on his donkey. "Good-bye, David," his father called as David walked down the road. "Be careful."

"I'll be careful," David said. "Good-bye!" **Clippety-clop**, clippety-clop went the donkey's feet on the rocky road.

After a while David saw the tents of the army camp. Then he saw his brothers. David ran to meet his brothers. "I **brought** you some food from home," David told them. The brothers must have been very glad to get the food. David was glad he could help his father by bringing food to his brothers. David was a good helper. David loved God.

## God's Word & Me

**What was the job David's father, Jesse, asked him to do?** (Take food to his brothers in the army.) **David showed God's love by helping his father and brothers. When we help the people in our families, we show God's love, too! What is something you can do today to help the people in your family?**

# Worship Center

God's Word
"Do not forget to do good."
Hebrews 13:16
God's Word & Me
Helping the people in my family
is a way to show God's love.

## Collect

Bible, *Shake It Up!* songbook and cassette/CD and player, "What Are You Gonna Do?" and "With Love" word charts (pp. 18 and 20 in songbook).

## Sing to God

Play "What Are You Gonna Do?" Invite children to sing along with you. **Let's sing together!** Lead children in singing song and doing suggested motions. **What are some other ways you can show God's love by helping people in your family?** (Help Mom water the plants. Help my sister clear the table. Obey Dad when it's time for bed or a bath.)

## Hear and Say God's Word

Holding your Bible open to Hebrews 13:16, say verse aloud. **What are we not supposed to forget?** (To do good.) Children sit in a large circle. Lead children in repeating the verse several times. When saying the words "Do not forget," children stand. When saying the words "To do good," children sit down.

## Pray to God

**We can thank God for the people in our family. We can ask God to help us do good things for our family.** Volunteers complete the following sentence prayer by adding the name of family members: **Thank You, God, for __________.** Close prayer by asking for God's help to show love to the people in our families.

## Sing to God

In closing the worship time, play "With Love." Invite children to sing along with you and do suggested motions. **Who is someone you've helped today?** Give examples of ways you saw children help in your room this morning. Use children's names. **Katie, you helped Tony today. You handed him the glue in the Art Center today. You showed God's love when you helped!**

## Options

1. With parents' permission, videotape children as they sing songs and do the motions. Show videotape at the end of the session as parents come to pick up their children.
2. Children think of things they can do this week to help the people in their families. Record children's responses on a large sheet of paper. Display paper where parents will see it when they pick up their children.

 

# Read-Aloud Story and Activity Center

"Do not forget to do good."
1
2
3
4
5

## Collect

A copy of Story Picture 10 (pp. 25-26 from *Read-Aloud Story and Activity Book*) for each child and yourself, crayons or markers.

## Prepare

Color your copy of Story Picture 10.

## Do

**Listen for ways this family helped each other.** Read story and show completed Story Picture 10. Distribute pictures. Use conversation suggestions in Let's Talk About the Story as children complete their pages.

# Kindergarten Puzzle Center

## Collect

Copies of Puzzles 19 and 20 (p. 45 and p. 47 from *The Big Book of Kindergarten Puzzles)* for each child, pencils, crayons or markers.

## Do

Children complete the puzzles and color pages.

# Instant Activities

These activities can be used at any time during this session: when children need a change of pace, to extend the session, or during transition time at the beginning or end of the session.

## Collect

*The Big Book of Instant Activities.*

## Do

Guide children to complete "Tape Travel" and/or "Use Your Eyes" (p. 86 and/or p. 48 from *The Big Book of Instant Activities).*

Lesson 11

# David and Jonathan Are Kind

## Bible Story

1 Samuel 16:15-23; 18:1-4; 19:1-7

God's Word
"A friend loves at all times."
Proverbs 17:17
God's Word & Me
Being kind to my friends shows God's love.

## Teacher's Devotional

The relationship between Jonathan and David is the Bible's classic example of friendship. The love may have been equal on both sides of this friendship, but the effects were different for each one. David, it seems, couldn't lose; he had a dear friend in Jonathan. Saul was hunting David down, but Saul's son was an openhearted, genuine ally.

David already knew he would become king, based on God's promise. Jonathan probably knew this, too. For Jonathan, God's promise meant that he would never become king. In one sense, he had nothing to gain from his friendship with David. Every bit of help he gave David took him further from the possibility of ever sitting on the throne himself. But Jonathan's love was pure and free of personal interest, born out of trust in and surrender to God (see 1 Samuel 20:13-15).

Friendship that is free of personal interest is truly rare. But it's the kind we need to teach our little ones—by the example of our lives! Be the kind of friend who gives each child genuine respect. Teach loving friendships by being a true friend to every child.

## Teacher's Planning

1. Choose which centers you will provide and the order in which children will participate in them. For tips on schedule planning, see page 7.
2. Plan who will lead each center. For staffing tips and ideas, see page 21.

# Active Game Center: Gift Pass

## Collect

Bible, *Shake It Up!* cassette/CD and player, box (shoebox or smaller), wrapping paper, scissors, tape, ribbon.

## Prepare

Cut wrapping paper to fit box, and tape to box. Tie ribbon on box.

## God's Word

**"A friend loves at all times."**
**Proverbs 17:17**

## God's Word & Me

**Being kind to my friends shows God's love.**

## Do

Children form a circle, sitting on the floor. As you play "What Are You Gonna Do?" children pass gift box around the circle. After a few moments, stop the music. Child holding the box when the music stops names a friend.

## Talk About

- **Our Bible tells us, "A friend loves at all times." Giving gifts is one way we can show love for our friends. Let's play a game using a gift box.**
- **What gift has someone given you? Today in our Bible story, a man named Jonathan gave gifts to his friend David.**
- **Our Bible tells us, "A friend loves at all times." Who is a friend you can show love to today?**
- **Being kind to our friends is one way to show God's love. What is something kind that someone did for you today?**

## For Younger Children

Younger children may hesitate or feel too shy to name friends if they are holding the box when the music stops. Instead say, **Kevin has the box. Kevin can be kind to his friends.**

## For Older Children

Children pass more than one gift box around the circle. When music stops, each child holding a box acts out a way to be kind to a friend.

Lesson 11

# Art Center: Rock Art

## Collect

Bible; newspaper; smooth, flat rocks; markers; masking tape; optional—wiggle eyes, pieces of yarn, chenille wires, nature objects (sticks, shells, acorns, pinecones, etc.), glue.

## Prepare

Spread newspaper over table.

God's Word
"A friend loves at all times."
Proverbs 17:17
God's Word & Me
Being kind to my friends
shows God's love.

## Do

1. Children use markers to decorate rocks. Suggest children draw faces, animals, flowers or other designs. (Optional: Children glue wiggle eyes, pieces of yarn, chenille wires or nature objects onto rocks.)
2. Place a strip of masking tape on each rock. Child or you writes child's name on strip.

## Talk About

- **In our Bible story today, Jonathan showed kindness by giving gifts to his friend David. We can show God's love by being kind to our friends, too. Let's show kindness as we decorate rocks.**
- **Angelica, I like seeing you show kindness to Brett by sharing the markers with him. Our Bible says, "A friend loves at all times." Being kind is a way to show God's love.**
- **Who can you show kindness to at your house? At the park? At church?**

## For Younger Children

Help children focus on showing kindness. **I see Edgar handing Ashley a marker. Edgar is a kind friend. Seth, thank you for being kind and picking up Sarah's marker from the floor.**

## For Older Children

Each child decorates two rocks, giving second rock to a friend or family member.

Lesson 11

# Block Center: Block House

## Collect

Bible, masking tape, blocks, toy people.

## Prepare

Use masking tape to outline a street with several intersections. (Note: Remove masking tape immediately after activity.)

## Do

Children use blocks to make the homes of their friends along the street outline. Children use toy people to act out visiting the homes.

God's Word
"A friend loves at all times."
Proverbs 17:17
God's Word & Me
Being kind to my friends
shows God's love.

## Talk About

- **Our Bible tells us, "A friend loves at all times." One way we show God's love is by being kind to our friends. Let's build houses for our friends, and then pretend we're going to visit them.**
- **Winnie, whose home are you visiting? When you play with your friend, what do you like to do? How can you be kind when you are playing with dolls?**
- **Who are some of your friends?**
- **What are some other ways to show kindness when you go to a friend's home?** (Say "please" and "thank you." Be careful with his or her toys. Help put away toys before leaving.)

## For Younger Children

Children build structures of their own choosing. As you observe their play, discuss children's kind actions. **Dallas, thank you for handing a block to Judy. That is a kind thing to do. Being kind is a way to show God's love. You're doing what our Bible says to do!**

## For Older Children

On large index cards, children write, or dictate for you to write, names of friends. Place cards by the homes.

# Science Center: Name That Sound

## Collect

Bible, a variety of items with which to make sounds (coins, kitchen timer, bell, guitar, whistle, keys, maracas, Autoharp, blocks, etc.), large paper grocery bag.

## God's Word

**"A friend loves at all times." Proverbs 17:17**

## God's Word & Me

**Being kind to my friends shows God's love.**

## Prepare

Place items in large paper grocery bag.

## Do

1. Ask children to close their eyes. One at a time, use each item in bag to make a sound. As each item is sounded, children try to guess the item.
2. Allow time for children to experiment by using items to make the various sounds.

## Talk About

- **In our Bible story today, David showed God's love by playing music for and being kind to King Saul. King Saul listened to David's music. Let's listen to some different kinds of sounds.**
- **The Bible says, "A friend loves at all times." We can show God's love and be kind to our friends.**
- **Ansley, who are some of your friends? What can you do to be kind to Sara?**
- **I see that Katie is being kind by waiting for a turn to play the maraca. Katie is showing God's love.**

## For Younger Children

Children experiment with making sounds before you place items in the bag.

## For Older Children

In addition to items you collected, children experiment with using a variety of recyclable materials to make sounds (cardboard tubes, paper cups, paper plates, cans, etc.).

# Bible Story Center

## Collect

Bible, Picture 16 from *Bible Story Pictures.*

God's Word
"A friend loves at all times."
Proverbs 17:17
God's Word & Me
Being kind to my friends
shows God's love.

## Tell the Story

Use the pictured motions (keywords in bold) or show Picture 16. For older children, tell the version of the story on the back of Picture 16.

**Who are some of your friends? Today's Bible story is about two friends, David and Jonathan, who showed love and friendship to one another.**

King Saul felt grumpy and sad. King Saul felt so **grumpy** and sad that everyone tried to think of a way to make him feel happy. One of the king's helpers had an idea. "King Saul," the helper said, "if someone could play happy music on the harp, you might feel happy." King Saul thought that was a good idea!

The helper said. "David plays the harp very well. **God** is with him."

A helper went to talk to David's father. Step, step, step. David was taking care of his family's sheep. But his father said he could go help the king.

Soon David came to live in the king's house. David loved God and was glad to help King Saul by **playing** his harp. David's music helped King Saul feel happy again.

David liked living in the king's house. One of the people David liked best in the king's house was King Saul's son. His name was Jonathan. They became best friends. David and Jonathan made a special promise to each other. "We will ALWAYS be good friends!" they said. "We will ALWAYS help each other."

One day Jonathan did something to show how much he liked David. "David, I am **giving** you my coat," Jonathan said. Then Jonathan brought his best bow and arrow to David. "You may have my bow and arrow, too." Jonathan said.

David knew that Jonathan was his good friend. And Jonathan knew David was his good friend.

## God's Word & Me

**How did Jonathan show his love for his friend David?** (Gave him a coat. Gave him a bow and arrow.) **Giving gifts is one way Jonathan showed God's love and kindness to David. We can show God's love and be kind to our friends, too! How can you be kind to your friends at church today?** (Share toys. Give a hug. Say nice words.)

# Worship Center

## Collect

Bible, *Shake It Up!* songbook and cassette/CD and player, "With Love" and "What Are You Gonna Do?" word charts (pp. 20 and 18 in songbook).

God's Word
"A friend loves at all times."
Proverbs 17:17
God's Word & Me
Being kind to my friends
shows God's love.

## Sing to God

Play "With Love." Invite children to sing along with you. **Let's sing a song about showing love!** Lead children in singing song and doing suggested motions. **Helping others is one way to be kind and show God's love! Who is someone you've helped today?**

## Hear and Say God's Word

Holding your Bible open to Proverbs 17:17, say verse aloud. **What does this verse tell us a friend always does?** (Loves.) Lead children in repeating the verse two or three times. Then replace the words "all times" with a time of day (morning, lunchtime, bedtime, etc.). Children echo the phrase after you. Repeat several times, using different times of the day, days of the week or seasons of the year.

## Pray to God

Children repeat the following prayer after you, phrase by phrase: **Dear God, . . . thank You for loving us. . . . Please help us . . . to be kind . . . and show love . . . to our friends. . . . In Jesus' name, amen.**

## Sing to God

In closing the worship time, play "What Are You Gonna Do?" Invite children to sing along with you and do suggested motions. **What are some ways you can show God's love by being kind to your friends today?** (Share toys and snacks. Let a friend take the first turn on the swings. Give a hug. Say kind words.)

## Options

1. Before class, on a large sheet of paper, print the words you will be using as substitutions in the Bible verse. During Hear and Say God's Word, display paper and point to each word as you use it while repeating the Bible verse.
2. Provide rhythm instruments for children to use when singing the songs.

# Read-Aloud Story and Activity Center

## Collect

A copy of Story Picture 11 (pp. 27-28 from *Read-Aloud Story and Activity Book*) for each child and yourself, crayons or markers.

"A friend loves at all times."

## Prepare

Color your copy of Story Picture 11.

## Do

**Listen to find out what a boy did to be kind.** Read story and show completed Story Picture 11. Distribute pictures. Use conversation suggestions in Let's Talk About the Story as children complete their pages.

# Kindergarten Puzzle Center

## Collect

Copies of Puzzles 21 and 22 (p. 49 and p. 51 from *The Big Book of Kindergarten Puzzles)* for each child, pencils, crayons or markers.

## Do

Children complete the puzzles and color pages.

# Instant Activities

These activities can be used at any time during this session: when children need a change of pace, to extend the session, or during transition time at the beginning or end of the session.

## Collect

*The Big Book of Instant Activities.*

## Do

Guide children to complete "The Friend Song" and/or "Where Is It?" (p. 66 and/or p. 88 from *The Big Book of Instant Activities).*

Lesson 12

# David and Saul

## Bible Story

1 Samuel 26

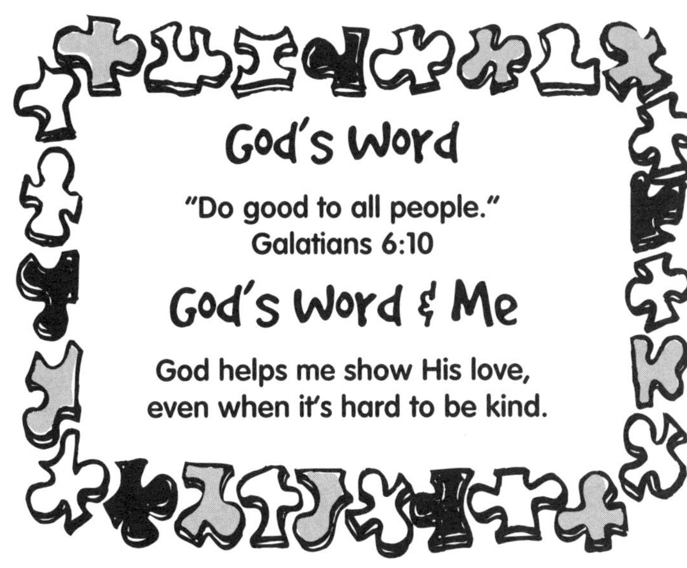
God's Word
"Do good to all people."
Galatians 6:10
God's Word & Me
God helps me show His love, even when it's hard to be kind.

## Teacher's Devotional

Saul was a tormented man—either murderously pursuing David or else apologizing to him in moments of clarity. David was in constant danger. Saul's deadly hatred surely caused stress for David.

Several times, David had the chance to kill Saul. What a golden opportunity! God had already said David would rule. Since Saul was trying to kill him, the Lord's anointed, why not kill Saul in self-defense? It would be looked upon as just—most people see killing in self-defense as both legally and morally justified.

But David's attitude was quite different. He called Saul the Lord's anointed and would not kill him, no matter how he was urged. David was willing to remain in danger to preserve the life of the madman who wanted to kill him! David was willing to wait for God's timing. He was humble, not grasping after power, even power he knew would rightfully be his. Since God had promised, David could wait for His perfect timing.

May we have such humility and graciousness! We too can humbly wait for the Lord. When we talk about those who threaten or disagree with us, we can express gracious understanding. That will greatly impact our children, for it is living out God's kindness.

## Teacher's Planning

1. Choose which centers you will provide and the order in which children will participate in them. For tips on schedule planning, see page 7.
2. Plan who will lead each center. For staffing tips and ideas, see page 21.

# Active Game Center: Beanbag Baskets

## Collect

Bible, several beanbags, wastebasket.

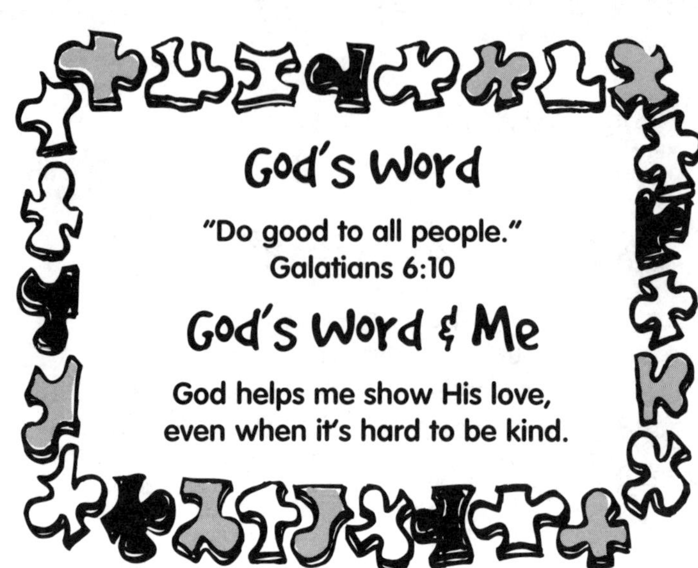
God's Word
"Do good to all people."
Galatians 6:10
God's Word & Me
God helps me show His love,
even when it's hard to be kind.

## Do

Children take turns tossing beanbags into wastebasket. Older children will enjoy the challenge of standing at a designated distance from the basket. Younger children will need to stand close to the basket.

## Talk About

- **Sometimes it's hard to be kind. But God will help us. Our Bible tells us, "Do good to all people." Let's play a game and talk about ways to do good and kind things.**
- **I see Brynne waiting quietly to take her turn. What would happen if people did not wait for a turn playing our game?**
- **When are some other times you need to wait quietly?** (When others are talking. When others are on the swings. When someone else is playing with a toy you want to play with.)
- **Waiting quietly for your turn is a good thing to do. God will help us do good things and be kind, even when it's hard for us.**

## For Younger Children

Instead of tossing beanbags into a wastebasket, children toss beanbags onto a large sheet of paper or a towel that has been spread on the floor.

## For Older Children

Instead of tossing beanbags into a wastebasket, children toss them onto a paper grid. Print numbers or draw geometric shapes on separate sheets of paper. Tape papers to floor in a grid pattern. Children choose a paper as a target before tossing beanbag.

Lesson 12

# Art Center: Body Art

## Collect

Bible, butcher paper, measuring stick, scissors, crayons, markers, rubber bands.

## Prepare

Cut one 3-foot (.9-m) length of butcher paper for each child.

### God's Word

**"Do good to all people."**
**Galatians 6:10**

### God's Word & Me

**God helps me show His love, even when it's hard to be kind.**

## Do

1. One at a time, ask each child to lie on a sheet of butcher paper. Use a crayon to outline his or her body. Print "Tony is big enough to do good things" on the paper (see sketch a).
2. Children use crayons and/or markers to draw and color their facial features, hair and clothing. When children are finished, roll pictures and secure with a rubber band. Print each child's name on the outside of his or her picture.

## Talk About

- **Our Bible tells us, "Do good to all people." As you grow bigger, you can do good things in more and more ways. Let's make a picture of you.**
- **Lindsay, you are helping me by holding very still while I draw around you. Helping others is a way to do something good.**
- **What are some good things you can do at church when you are building with blocks?**
- **What are some ways you can do good at home? What can you do when it's time for your bath? When it's time to go to bed? When your mom says "Time to come with me"?**

## For Younger Children

Instead of coloring body outlines, give each child a copy of a person outline (see sketch b). Children color outline.

## For Older Children

Children cut out body outlines. Tape outlines to walls or hallways outside the classroom.

# Block Center: Cave Dwellings

## Collect

Bible, blocks, toy people.

## Do

Children use blocks to form hills and cave openings and then use toy people to act out King Saul's search for David.

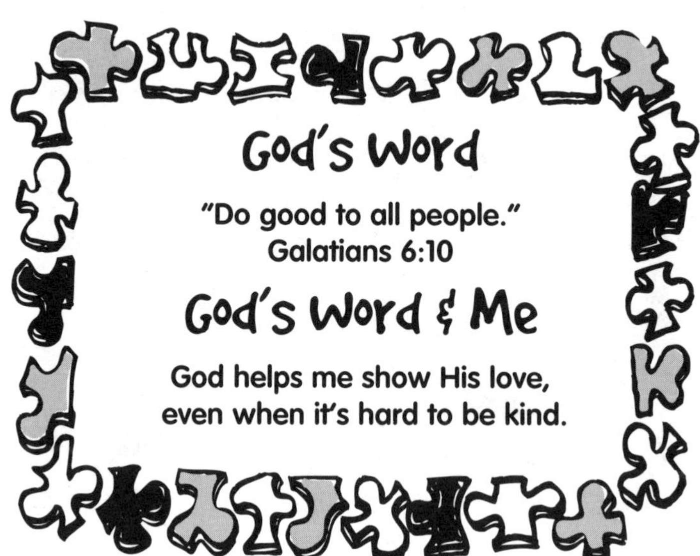
God's Word
"Do good to all people."
Galatians 6:10
God's Word & Me
God helps me show His love,
even when it's hard to be kind.

## Talk About

- **In our Bible story today, King Saul searched for David on hills and in caves. Let's make some hills and caves and act out the Bible story!**
- **King Saul and his soldiers were looking for David because Saul was angry at David. King Saul wanted to hurt David. Even though King Saul wanted to hurt him, David was kind to him. When are some times it might be hard to be kind and do good things?** (When someone laughs at you. When someone won't share with you.)
- **What are some good things you can do for your friends? Your family?**
- **Saying kind words is a good thing to do. When are times it might be hard to say kind words to others?**
- **God wants us to be kind and do good things for others. Our Bible says, "Do good to all people." God will always help us to show His love by being kind and doing good things.**

## For Younger Children

Give guidance by suggestions and questions. **Philip, Heidi needs another long block for her cave. You have lots of long blocks. What can you do to help Heidi? That was a good thing to do!**

## For Older Children

Provide play dough and twigs. Children make trees by standing twigs in small lumps of play dough.

# Science Center: Do-Good Cookies

## Collect

Bible, 1 cup raisins, 1 cup finely chopped dates, ½ cup honey, ½ cup graham cracker crumbs, 2 medium mixing bowls, plastic wrap, paper, marker, tape, large spoon, paper plates, napkins, damp paper towels; optional—premoistened towelettes.

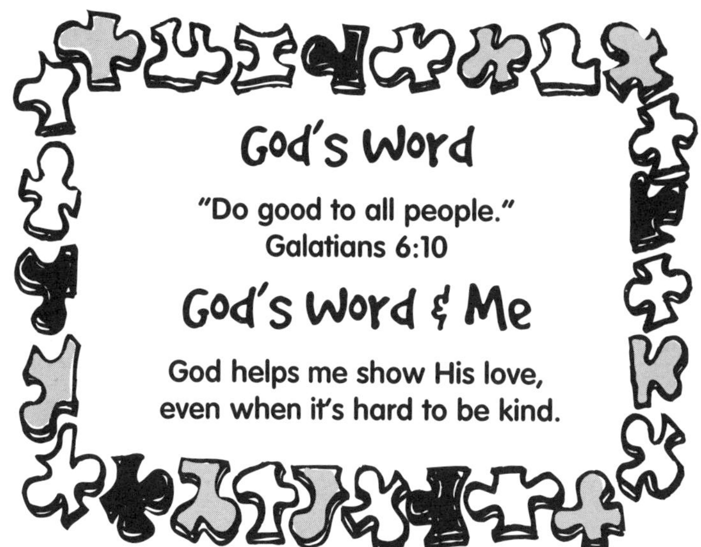
God's Word
"Do good to all people."
Galatians 6:10
God's Word & Me
God helps me show His love, even when it's hard to be kind.

## Prepare

Place raisins, chopped dates and honey in a mixing bowl. Place graham cracker crumbs in second mixing bowl. Cover bowls with plastic wrap. (Note: This recipe makes 16 cookies. Repeat process for more cookies if needed.)

Post a note alerting parents to the use of food in this activity. Also check registration forms for possible food allergies.

## Do

1. Children wash hands. (Optional: Children use premoistened towelettes to clean hands.) Children take turns mixing raisins, dates and honey together using large spoon. After ingredients are thoroughly mixed, children form dough into balls and then roll balls in graham crackers to coat.
2. When ready to eat snack, volunteers place cookies on plates and serve to other children. Other volunteers pass out napkins and use damp paper towels to clean up area.

## Talk About

- **Our Bible tells us, "Do good to all people." Let's do good and make good things to eat!**
- **Kelly, you've had a turn to stir. Now you may choose a friend to have a turn. What is a way you help prepare dinner at home?** (Tear lettuce for a salad. Set the table.)
- **Chelsea, I like the way you gave cookies to others before taking one for yourself. When you let others go first, you are doing a good thing and being kind. And that shows God's love!**

## For Younger and Older Children

Provide enough ingredients to make an extra cookie for each child. Place extra cookie in a resealable plastic bag. Child chooses a family member he or she can be kind to and give the cookie.

 

# Bible Story Center

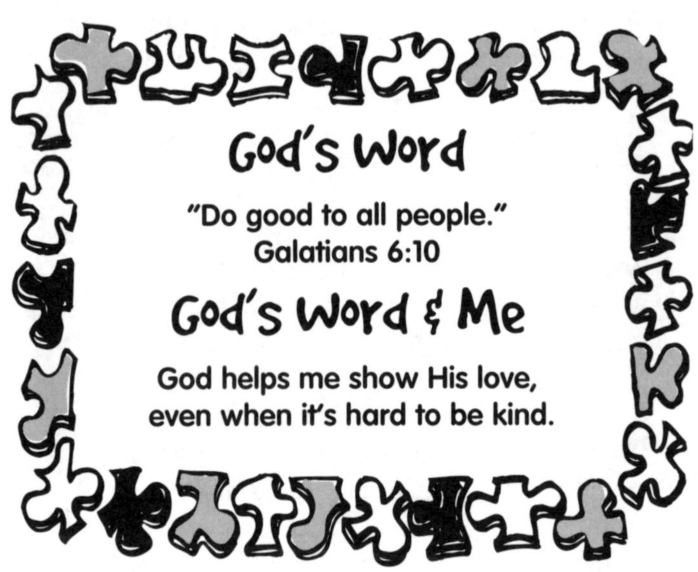
God's Word
"Do good to all people."
Galatians 6:10
God's Word & Me
God helps me show His love,
even when it's hard to be kind.

## Collect

Bible, Picture 17 from *Bible Story Pictures.*

## Tell the Story

Use the pictured motions (keywords in bold) or show Picture 17. For older children, tell the version of the story on the back of Picture 17.

**Have you ever been camping? Where did you sleep? Today we're going to hear about a time David was kind to King Saul when King Saul was sleeping outside on the ground.**

Step, step, step. King Saul and his men looked for David all day. King Saul was **angry** with David. King Saul wanted to find David and hurt him. Finally, King Saul and his men stopped for the night and set up their camp. King Saul slept on the ground. His men slept all around him.

While King Saul and his men were asleep, David and his men found King Saul's camp. Very quietly, David and his friend Abishai (AB-uh-shi) **tiptoed** up to King Saul.

"Here's our chance," whispered Abishai. "King Saul wants to hurt you. Let's hurt him!"

"No!" whispered David. "That would be wrong. Let's just take his spear and water jug." So David and Abishai picked up the king's spear and water jug.

They quietly ran to the top of a high hill. "Wake up!" David **shouted**. David held up King Saul's spear and jug. "See what happened while you slept!" King Saul and his men heard the shouting. They looked around and saw King Saul's spear and jug were gone. "Is that you, David?" King Saul called out.

"Look!" David shouted. "I have your spear. Let one of your men come and get it. I could have hurt you, but I did not."

King Saul was sorry for the way he had treated David. David turned around and walked back to his men. He could have hurt King Saul, but he **didn't**. David showed love for God by being kind to King Saul.

## God's Word & Me

**Where did David and his friends find King Saul and his soldiers?** (Asleep on the ground.) **David was kind to King Saul, even though it must have been very hard. It's not always easy to be kind to others. God will always help us to be kind. When might it be hard to be kind to others?** (When others say mean things. When others do mean things.)

# Worship Center

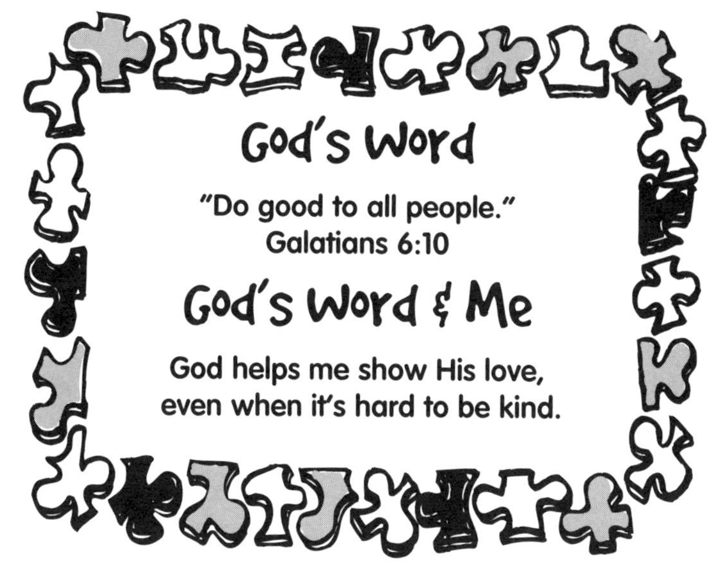
God's Word
"Do good to all people."
Galatians 6:10
God's Word & Me
God helps me show His love,
even when it's hard to be kind.

## Collect

Bible, *Shake It Up!* songbook and cassette/CD and player, "What Are You Gonna Do?" and "With Love" word charts (pp. 18 and 20 in songbook).

## Sing to God

Play "What Are You Gonna Do?" Invite children to sing along with you. **Let's sing a song together!** Lead children in singing song and doing suggested motions. **When are some times it might be hard to show God's love and be kind?** (When someone won't share a toy. When someone says mean words. When you're really tired or unhappy.) **When it's hard to be kind, we can ask God for His help! He will always help us show His love to others.**

## Hear and Say God's Word

Holding your Bible open to Galatians 6:10, say verse aloud. **What are some good things to do?** (Share toys. Help put away blocks.) Then lead children in repeating the verse several times. As the children are repeating the verse with you, point to one child. You and the children say that child's name instead of the words "all people." Repeat until every child has had a turn.

## Pray to God

**We can ask God to help us to be kind.** Invite volunteers to each say this brief thank-you prayer: **Dear God, please help me to be kind.**

## Sing to God

In closing the worship time, play "With Love." Invite children to sing along with you and do suggested motions. **God wants us to be kind and help each other, even when it's hard.**

## Options

1. If you take an offering during this time, explain to children that giving money is one way to do good things for others. Describe one mission project your church uses offering money to support.

2. Add motion to the verse activity. Children line up and follow the first child in the line, walking around the classroom. Say verse aloud, replacing the words "all people" with the name of the first child in the line. After his or her name is said, that child moves to the end of the line and the next child becomes the line leader. Repeat verse until every child has had a chance to be the line leader.

# Read-Aloud Story and Activity Center

## Collect

A copy of Story Picture 12 (pp. 29-30 from *Read-Aloud Story and Activity Book*) for each child and yourself, crayons or markers.

## Prepare

Color your copy of Story Picture 12.

## Do

**Listen for ways this boy was kind to this girl.** Read story and show completed Story Picture 12. Distribute pictures. Use conversation suggestions in Let's Talk About the Story as children complete their pages.

# Kindergarten Puzzle Center

## Collect

Copies of Puzzles 23 and 24 (p. 53 and p. 55 from *The Big Book of Kindergarten Puzzles)* for each child, pencils, crayons or markers.

## Do

Children complete the puzzles and color pages.

# Instant Activities

These activities can be used at any time during this session: when children need a change of pace, to extend the session, or during transition time at the beginning or end of the session.

## Collect

*The Big Book of Instant Activities.*

## Do

Guide children to complete "I'll Touch" and/or "Hula Hoop Pass" (p. 43 and/or p. 82 from *The Big Book of Instant Activities).*

Lesson 13

# David and Mephibosheth

## Bible Story

1 Samuel 20:14-17,42; 2 Samuel 9

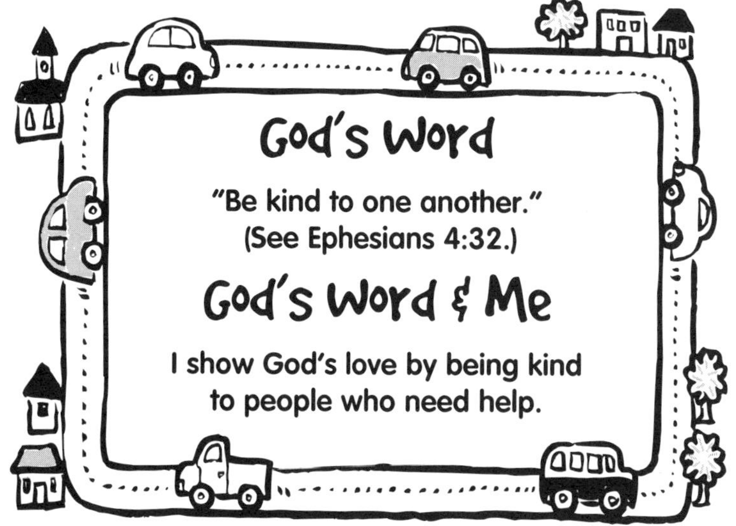
God's Word
"Be kind to one another."
(See Ephesians 4:32.)
God's Word & Me
I show God's love by being kind to people who need help.

## Teacher's Devotional

Mary Poppins, that famous and fictional British nanny, once commented to her charges that some promises are "piecrust promises—easily made, easily broken." How hurtful that kind of promise is to a child! A child must rely absolutely on the adults in charge; there is no other choice. That dependence quickly teaches a child whether or not his or her world is reliable. When an adult fulfills or breaks a promise, it sends a powerful message to a child about who can or can't be counted on.

Thank God that His promises don't change! He never leaves us, and He never breaks His promises. He may do things we don't understand at times, but we can look at His character and His track record, and we can be reassured that He is faithful. In a world where promises are often the "piecrust" kind, where we all have been hurt by unreliable people, God's trustworthiness is a genuine comfort.

Be a promise-keeper as David was. Don't make vague promises you can't keep. Ask the Holy Spirit to bring to your remembrance even the little things you promise. God promises to do this for you, so you can make promise-keeping real to your little ones!

## Teacher's Planning

1. Choose which centers you will provide and the order in which children will participate in them. For tips on schedule planning, see page 7.
2. Plan who will lead each center. For staffing tips and ideas, see page 21.

# Active Game Center: Line Leaders

## Collect

Bible.

## Do

1. Play a game like Follow the Leader. Children form a single-file line. Lead children in walking around the room and acting out some of the motions someone might do to get ready for a visitor (sweep the floor, pick up toys, set the table, etc.).
2. After leading children for a few moments, move aside. The first child in line leads the other children in a motion that you call out. After a few moments, ask that child to move to the end of the line. The next child becomes the leader, and the game continues. If a child does not wish to lead the line, he or she simply moves to the end of the line. Continue until each child has had an opportunity to lead the line.

### God's Word

**"Be kind to one another." (See Ephesians 4:32.)**

### God's Word & Me

**I show God's love by being kind to people who need help.**

## Talk About

- **In our Bible story today, King David was kind and invited Mephibosheth to live with him in the palace. Mephibosheth needed help because he couldn't walk very well. Let's play a game and pretend we're getting ready for visitors to come to our home.**
- **What are some of the things your family does when visitors are coming to your home?**
- **What are some of the things you can do to help your mother or father get ready for visitors?**
- **The Bible says, "Be kind to one another." Being kind to visitors is a way to show God's love. What are some other ways to be kind?**
- **What is a way to be kind to a friend when you're playing together?**

## For Younger Children

Since children this age would have difficulty leading the others, remain the line leader.

## For Older Children

Children think up their own motions as they lead the other children.

# Art Center: Kindness Collage

## Collect

Bible, newspaper, construction paper, a variety of art materials (confetti, stickers, yarn, chenille wires, feathers, etc.), glue.

## Prepare

Cover table with newspaper.

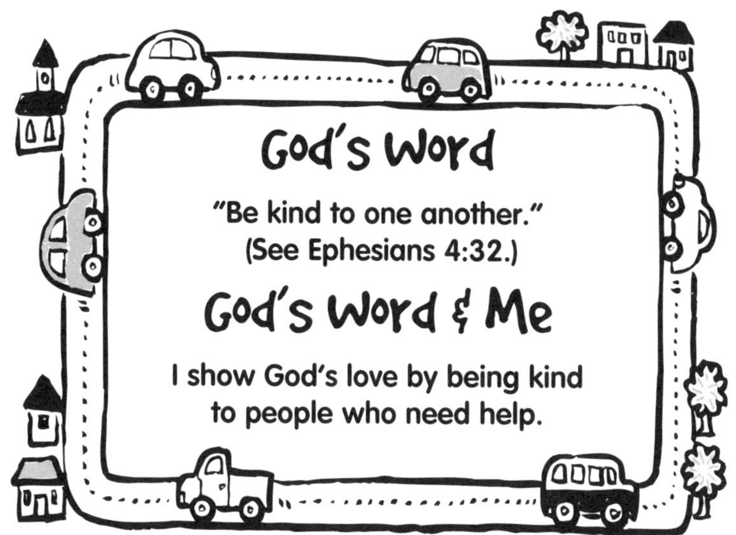
God's Word
"Be kind to one another."
(See Ephesians 4:32.)
God's Word & Me
I show God's love by being kind
to people who need help.

## Do

Give each child a sheet of construction paper. Child glues art materials onto paper to make a collage. Participate in this activity with children, taking advantage of opportunities to talk about ways to be kind.

## Talk About

- **The Bible says, "Be kind to one another." We can show God's love by being kind to people who need help. Today we're going to make collages. As we make our collages, we can be kind to each other.**
- **I see that Nathaniel shared the glue with Matthew. Thank you, Nathaniel, for being kind. You helped Matthew.**
- **Thank you, Serena, for picking up the feather for me. I needed help, and you were kind to me.**
- **We're helping each other and being kind as we make our collages. What are some other ways to be kind to our friends at church? Tung, how can you be kind to a friend who is playing at your house?**

## For Younger Children

Limit the number of art materials you provide so that younger children are not overwhelmed by the number of choices available. Select two or three materials only.

## For Older Children

On each child's sheet of paper print the word "KIND" in large letters. Children glue art materials over the letters.

# Block Center: Helpful Places

## Collect

Bible, blocks, toy people, toy cars.

## Do

1. Children build places where people help others (hospital, restaurant, police station, fire station, school, etc.).
2. Children use toy people and toy cars to act out ways to help others in the places they build.

### God's Word

**"Be kind to one another."**
**(See Ephesians 4:32.)**

### God's Word & Me

**I show God's love by being kind to people who need help.**

## Talk About

- **Our Bible tells us, "Be kind to one another." There are many places in our town where people are kind to others. Let's build some of these places with blocks!**
- **Where are some of the places you can go if you need help? Where would you go if you were hurt? If there was a fire? If you were lost?** (Hospital, fire station, police station, school, church, etc.) **Who are some of the people who help you there?** (Nurses. Doctors. Firefighters. Police officers. Teachers.)
- **Who are some of the people who help others in the place you are building? What are some of the ways they help others?**
- Pray briefly, **Dear God, thank You for loving us. Please show us ways to be kind and help others.**

## For Younger Children

Avoid crowding the block area. Lay a strip of masking tape about three feet (.9 m) from where you store your blocks. Instruct children to always build on the other side of the masking-tape line. Children will then have room to remove and return blocks without knocking down anyone else's work.

## For Older Children

On a large sheet of butcher paper or light-colored fabric, draw several streets and intersections, creating a pretend town. Children build fire stations, libraries, stores, schools, etc. along the streets.

Lesson 13

# Science Center: Walk the Line

## Collect

Bible, yarn; optional—chalk.

## Prepare

Create a straight line using yarn. (Optional: Play game outside and draw a chalk line.) If you have more than six children, make more than one line.

God's Word
"Be kind to one another."
(See Ephesians 4:32.)
God's Word & Me
I show God's love by being kind to people who need help.

## Do

Invite children to take turns walking along the line in a variety of ways: marching, tiptoeing, sliding, one foot in front of the other, heel-to-toe, straddling the line, etc. You may also vary activity by placing yarn in a curve, circle, zigzag or other shape.

Talk About

- **Today in our Bible story, Mephibosheth had trouble walking because his feet had been hurt. When Mephibosheth needed help, King David was kind and helped him. Let's look at some of the things our feet can do!**
- **God made our feet able to do lots of things. What other ways can we move along this line?**
- **Our Bible tells us, "Be kind to one another." We can show God's love by being kind to people who need help. When might your grandma need help? Your little sister?**

## For Younger Children

Steady children who are having difficulty walking in a straight line: hold their hands as they walk.

## For Older Children

Lay a 2x4-inch (5x10-cm) board on the floor. Children use it like a balance beam, walking carefully, one foot in front of the other.

# Bible Story Center

## Collect

Bible, Picture 18 from *Bible Story Pictures.*

God's Word
"Be kind to one another."
(See Ephesians 4:32.)
God's Word & Me
I show God's love by being kind
to people who need help.

## Tell the Story

Use the pictured motions (keywords in bold) or show Picture 18. For older children, tell the version of the story on the back of Picture 18.

**When has your mom or dad promised to take you to a park or to a playground? We're glad when people keep their promises. Listen to find out how David kept a promise he made to his friend Jonathan.**

When David became the king, he tried to do good because he loved God. One day, King David was **sad**. David remembered his good friend Jonathan who was dead. They had promised always to help each other and to help each other's children.

*How can I help Jonathan now?* King David thought. *Maybe there is someone from his family that I could help.*

"Is anyone from Jonathan's family still living?" King David asked his helper.

"There is only one person still alive," the helper said. "He is Jonathan's son, Mephibosheth (mih-FIHB-eh-shehth). His **feet** are hurt, and he cannot walk very well."

"Bring Mephibosheth to see me right away," King David said. Soon the helper brought Mephibosheth. He walked very slowly toward King David. Mephibosheth felt afraid. He **bowed** before King David.

"Oh, Mephibosheth, don't be afraid," King David said. "I promised your father that I would help his children. I want to do as I promised. I want to help you."

Mephibosheth was surprised. "Oh, thank you," Mephibosheth said.

King David said, "I want you and your family to come and live with me. I will give you good food to **eat**. I will give you nice clothes to wear." So Mephibosheth lived with King David. King David was kind and did the good things that he said he would do.

## God's Word & Me

**How did David help Mephibosheth?** (David asked Mephibosheth and his family to come live at the palace.) **David showed God's love by helping Mephibosheth. When we are kind to people who need help, we are showing God's love, too! What can you do today if someone falls down on the playground?** (Get a teacher to help. Help the person stand up again.) **It is good to help others. That's a way to show God's love!**

# Worship Center

## Collect

Bible, *Shake It Up!* songbook and cassette/CD and player, "With Love" and "What Are You Gonna Do?" word charts (pp. 20 and 18 in songbook).

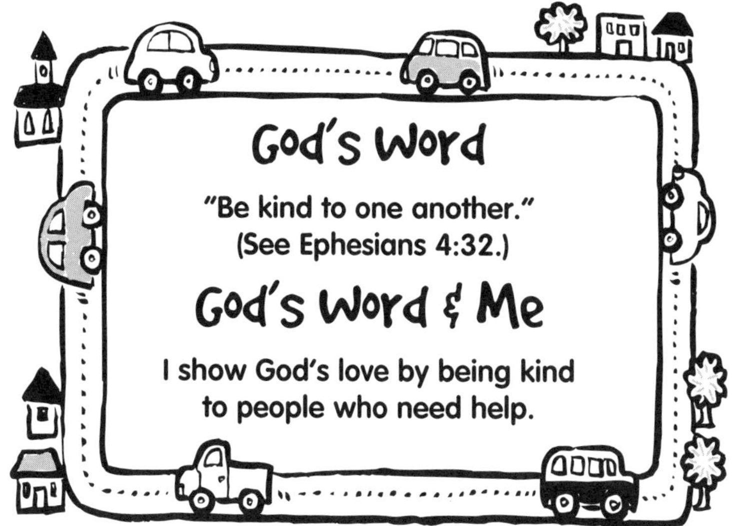
God's Word
"Be kind to one another."
(See Ephesians 4:32.)
God's Word & Me
I show God's love by being kind to people who need help.

## Sing to God

Play "With Love." Invite children to sing along with you. **Let's sing a song together!** Lead children in singing song and doing suggested motions. **This song tells us to help others.**

## Hear and Say God's Word

Holding your Bible open to Ephesians 4:32, say verse aloud. **Who are we supposed to be kind to?** (One another.) **We can show God's love by being kind to others.** Then lead children in repeating the verse several times. As the children are repeating the verse with you, point to a child. You and the children say that child's name instead of the words "one another." Repeat until every child has had his or her name used.

## Pray to God

Lead children in prayer, asking for God's help in being kind to people who need help.

## Sing to God

In closing the worship time, play "What Are You Gonna Do?" Invite children to sing along with you and do suggested motions. **What is something you can do today to help someone?** (Help Mom get supper ready. Help my sister pick up toys.)

## Options

1. During verse activity, children name people they know or categories of people (police officer, teacher, cowboy, etc.) and insert in place of the words "one another."
2. Invite a musician from your church to play one or more of the suggested songs for this lesson on a guitar, flute, trumpet, etc. Explain to children that by coming to play for them, the musician is being kind and showing God's love.

# Read-Aloud Story and Activity Center

## Collect

A copy of Story Picture 13 (pp. 31-32 from *Read-Aloud Story and Activity Book*) for each child and yourself, crayons or markers.

## Prepare

Color your copy of Story Picture 13.

## Do

**Listen to find out what happened to this boy.** Read story and show completed Story Picture 13. Distribute pictures. Use conversation suggestions in Let's Talk About the Story as children complete their pages.

# Kindergarten Puzzle Center

## Collect

Copies of Puzzles 25 and 26 (p. 57 and p. 59 from *The Big Book of Kindergarten Puzzles)* for each child, pencils, crayons or markers.

## Do

Children complete the puzzles and color pages.

# Instant Activities

These activities can be used at any time during this session: when children need a change of pace, to extend the session, or during transition time at the beginning or end of the session.

## Collect

*The Big Book of Instant Activities.*

## Do

Guide children to complete "Partners" and/or "I Have Ten Fingers" (p. 69 and/or p. 40 from *The Big Book of Instant Activities).*

Lesson 14

# Mary Hears Good News

## Bible Story

Matthew 1:18-25; Luke 1:26-56

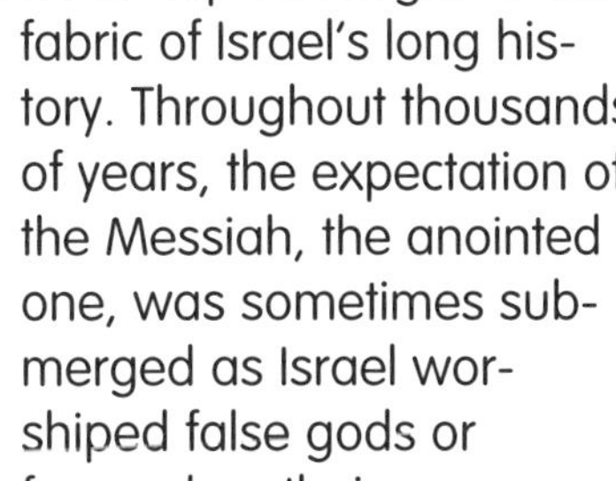

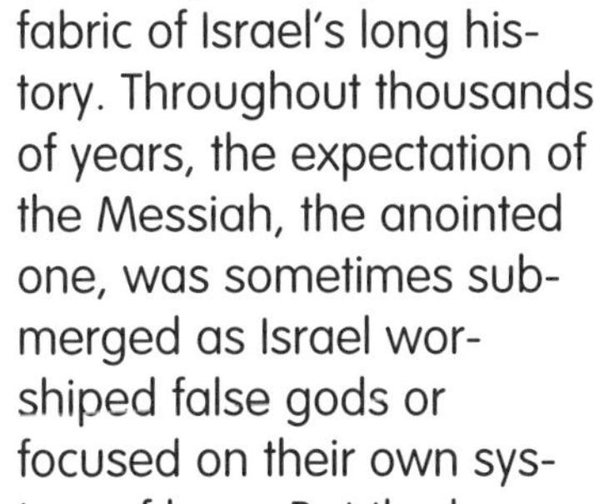

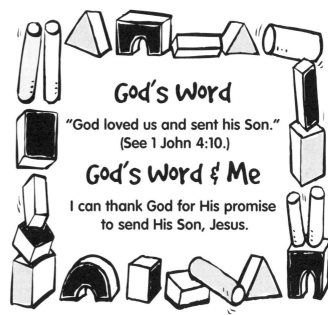

### God's Word

**"God loved us and sent his Son."**
**(See 1 John 4:10.)**

### God's Word & Me

**I can thank God for His promise to send His Son, Jesus.**

## Teacher's Devotional

The promise of a coming Messiah wove a bright thread of hope throughout the fabric of Israel's long history. Throughout thousands of years, the expectation of the Messiah, the anointed one, was sometimes submerged as Israel worshiped false gods or focused on their own system of laws. But the hope was never abandoned, and it shone brightest in times of great difficulty. This hope caused people to do extraordinary things and to joyfully suffer astounding troubles.

Unlike the prophets of old, we are not only privileged to know about the fulfillment of this promise, but we have also experienced Him. We have been sought out in love by the Messiah, in whom dwells all the fullness of God! The deliverer has extended His promise of freedom, originally given to Israel, to each of us. The fulfillment of this promise is so deep, this love is so lavish, that it's beyond us to fully understand. But we can share the joy and excitement of the reality of Jesus with the children in our classes. Read 1 John 4:7-12 and realize once again that Jesus is the fulfillment of God's promise! Lead your children in celebrating and thanking God as the celebration of this season begins.

## Teacher's Planning

1. Choose which centers you will provide and the order in which children will participate in them. For tips on schedule planning, see page 7.
2. Plan who will lead each center. For staffing tips and ideas, see page 21.

# Active Game Center: Trim the Tree

## Collect

Bible, large sheet of butcher paper, green marker, masking tape, scissors, variety of colored construction paper.

## Prepare

On butcher paper, draw a Christmas tree with a star on top. Post paper tree low on wall. Cut out construction-paper circles to make paper ornaments.

### God's Word

**"God loved us and sent his Son." (See 1 John 4:10.)**

### God's Word & Me

**I can thank God for His promise to send His Son, Jesus.**

## Do

1. Children select paper ornaments. Make masking-tape loops for the backs of the ornaments.
2. Each child takes a turn to stand several feet from tree, close his or her eyes and walk toward the tree, trying to place ornament onto tree. If an ornament misses the tree, child simply moves it onto the tree after opening eyes.

## Talk About

- **In our Bible story God's people waited a long time for Jesus to be born. God's people were glad God promised to send His Son, Jesus. We can be glad for God's promise, too.**
- **We celebrate Christmas each year to show our thanks to God for sending His Son, Jesus. One way to get ready for Christmas is to decorate a Christmas tree. What are some things your family does to get ready for Christmas?**
- **Our Bible says, "God loved us and sent his Son." Why did God send His Son?** (He loves us.) **We are glad God sent Jesus.**

## For Younger Children

Print children's names on their ornaments before children place them on the tree.

## For Older Children

Children print their names on ornaments and/or cut out their ornaments. Instead of closing their eyes, older children wear a blindfold.

Lesson 14

# Art Center: Good-News Cards

## Collect

Bible, white paper, photocopier, scissors, 12x16-inch (30.5x40.5-cm) construction paper, glue, a variety of art materials (metallic pens, stickers, wrapping paper pieces, ribbons, etc.).

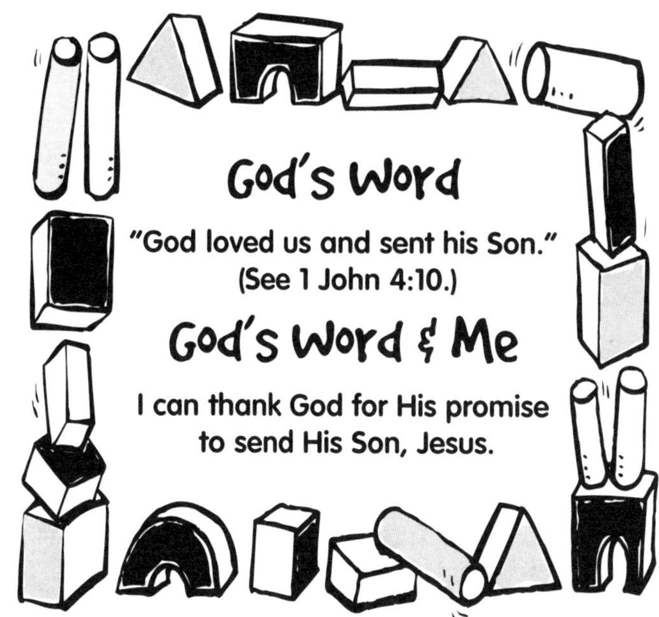
God's Word
"God loved us and sent his Son."
(See 1 John 4:10.)
God's Word & Me
I can thank God for His promise
to send His Son, Jesus.

## Prepare

On white paper, print the following sentences three or four times: "Good news! God loved us and sent His Son, Jesus." Make copies and cut apart so that each child will have a copy. Cut construction paper in half to form one 6x9-inch (15x23-cm) rectangle for each child.

## Do

1. Children fold construction-paper rectangles in half to form cards. Distribute photocopied sentences. Children glue sentences inside their cards and write their names under the sentences (see sketch a). (Note: Print the names of children who are unable to do so themselves.)
2. Children decorate the cards using art materials (see sketch b).

## Talk About

- **In today's Bible story, the angels told the shepherds the good news that Jesus was born. Let's make good-news cards.**
- **At Christmas, we can tell our friends the good news that God sent His Son, Jesus. Nathaniel, who do you want to give your good-news card to?**
- **I'm glad God kept His promise to send His Son, Jesus. That's very good news!** Pray, **Thank You, God, for sending Your Son, Jesus.**

## For Younger Children

Prefold construction-paper rectangles to form cards. Reopen cards. During activity, children fold cards again.

## For Older Children

Children cut and trim wrapping paper and other materials. Provide bell- and star-shaped cookie cutters for children to trace around and cut out shapes.

# Block Center: Baby Blocks

## Collect

Bible, blocks, baby dolls, doll blankets.

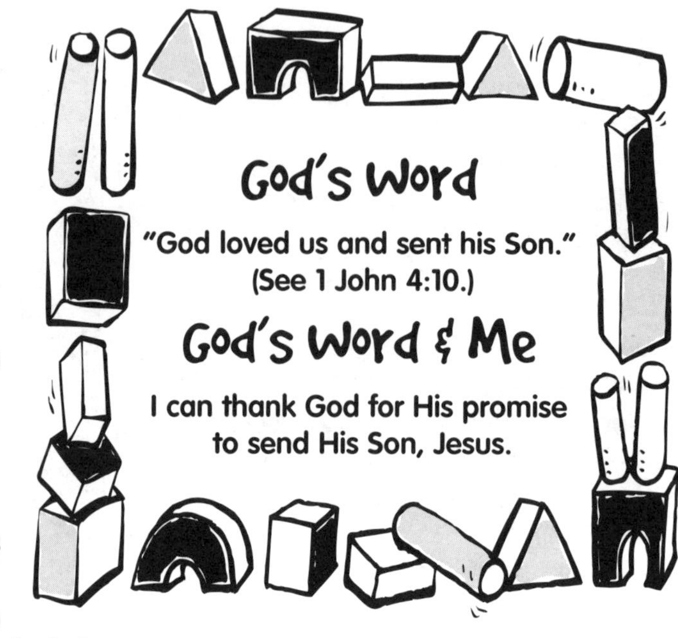
God's Word
"God loved us and sent his Son."
(See 1 John 4:10.)
God's Word & Me
I can thank God for His promise to send His Son, Jesus.

## Do

1. Children use blocks to build beds.
2. Using baby dolls and doll blankets, children act out ways to care for babies (laying baby in bed, wrapping baby in a blanket, feeding baby, etc.).

## Talk About

- **Our Bible story today tells about God's promise to send a special baby to Mary and Joseph. God even told them what to name the baby. What was the baby's name? Let's build beds and show ways people care for babies!**
- Encourage participation by building with the blocks yourself. Then invite a child to help you. **Chloe, I'm building a bed for babies to sleep in. Would you please bring me more blocks?**
- **What do you think your family did to take care of you when you were a baby? What must parents do for babies?**
- **Our Bible tells us, "God loved us and sent his Son." We can thank God for doing what He promised and sending His Son, Jesus.** Pray briefly, **Thank You, God, for sending Jesus.**

## For Younger Children

Demonstrate how to wrap dolls in blankets. **Mothers often wrap their babies like this. The babies stay nice and warm.** Children wrap dolls in blankets.

## For Older Children

Children assign names to dolls. Print names on index cards. Children tape cards to the beds.

# Science Center: Snack Science

## Collect

Bible, paper, marker, package of instant pudding, large bowl, milk, measuring cup, large spoon, plastic cups and spoons, paper towels.

## Prepare

Post a note alerting parents to the use of food in this activity. Also check registration forms for possible food allergies.

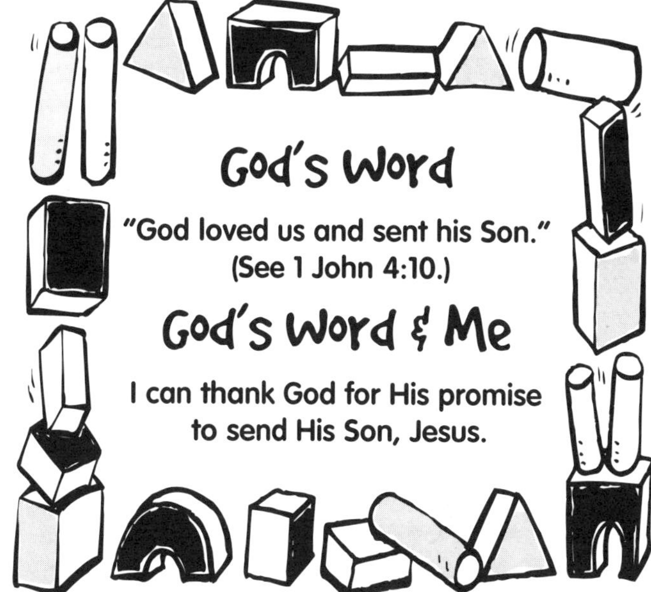
God's Word
"God loved us and sent his Son."
(See 1 John 4:10.)
God's Word & Me
I can thank God for His promise to send His Son, Jesus.

## Do

1. One child empties pudding into the bowl. Another child adds milk according to package directions. The rest take turns stirring the pudding. Lead children in counting to five as each child stirs. (Note: If you have a large group, provide one set of materials for every six to eight children.)
2. Pour pudding into individual cups. Ask the questions below as children wait (no more than five minutes) for pudding to set before eating. Children use paper towels to clean up.

## Talk About

- **Our Bible says, "God loved us and sent his Son." God's people waited a long time for Jesus to be born. But they knew God would do what He promised. Let's work together to make a snack and see what happens when we wait.**
- **When was a time you had to wait for something you wanted? How did you feel when the waiting was over?**
- **Why is it sometimes hard to wait when you're playing with your friends?**
- **God's people waited for Jesus to come. They knew God always does what He promises! We can thank God for doing what He promised. Thank You, God, for sending Jesus to be born.**

## For Younger Children

Put ingredients in bowl for children to stir. Children add animal crackers or sprinkles to their pudding.

## For Older Children

Give each child one-third of a banana and a plastic knife. Children slice bananas and add them to their pudding cups.

# Bible Story Center

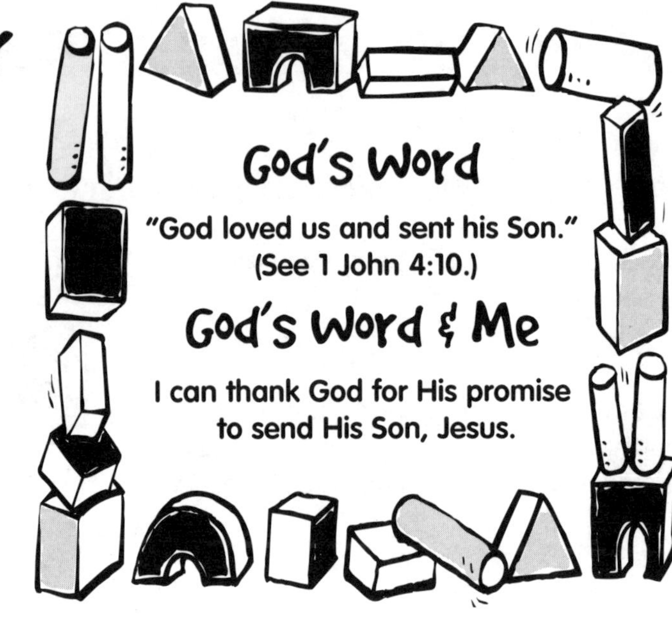
God's Word
"God loved us and sent his Son."
(See 1 John 4:10.)
God's Word & Me
I can thank God for His promise
to send His Son, Jesus.

## Collect

Bible, Picture 27 from *Bible Story Pictures.*

## Tell the Story

Use the pictured motions (keywords in bold) or show Picture 27. For older children, tell the version of the story on the back of Picture 27.

**A promise is something someone tells you he or she will do, and the person does it! Has someone ever made you a promise? Listen to find out what special promise God gave to Mary.**

A long, long time ago, God promised He would send His special Son. God's people waited and waited and waited. They wanted God to send His Son. One person who waited for God's promise was a young woman named Mary.

One day Mary was alone. She **looked up**. Standing right there beside her was an angel! Mary had never seen an angel before!

"Hello, Mary," the angel said. "God is with you." Mary was surprised and afraid. "Don't be afraid, Mary," the angel said. "God loves you. He has chosen you to be the mother of a very special baby. You will name the baby Jesus. He will be very great. This special baby will be God's own Son!" Mary was **glad** to hear this promise!

How exciting! Mary hurried to tell her cousin Elizabeth the wonderful news. Mary **walked** into Elizabeth's house. Just then God let Elizabeth know that Mary was going to be the mother of His Son, Jesus. Elizabeth said, "Mary, you're a special woman and your baby is very special!" Mary was glad. She thanked God. She told God she loved Him.

Very soon a man named Joseph was going to be Mary's husband. One night Joseph was **asleep**. An angel talked to him in a dream. "Mary is going to have a special baby. He is God's Son," the angel said. "You will name Him Jesus." Joseph was glad God was sending His Son, Jesus. Joseph was glad he could help care for this special baby God had promised.

## God's Word & Me

**God's people had to wait a long time for something very special to happen. What did they wait for?** (God to send His Son, Jesus.) **We can thank God for doing what He promised—sending His Son, Jesus! Singing songs to God and praying to Him are two of the ways we can show our thanks for His promise.**

# Worship Center

## Collect

Bible, *Shake It Up!* songbook and cassette/CD and player, "God Loved Us" and "Good News" word charts (pp. 25 and 23 in songbook).

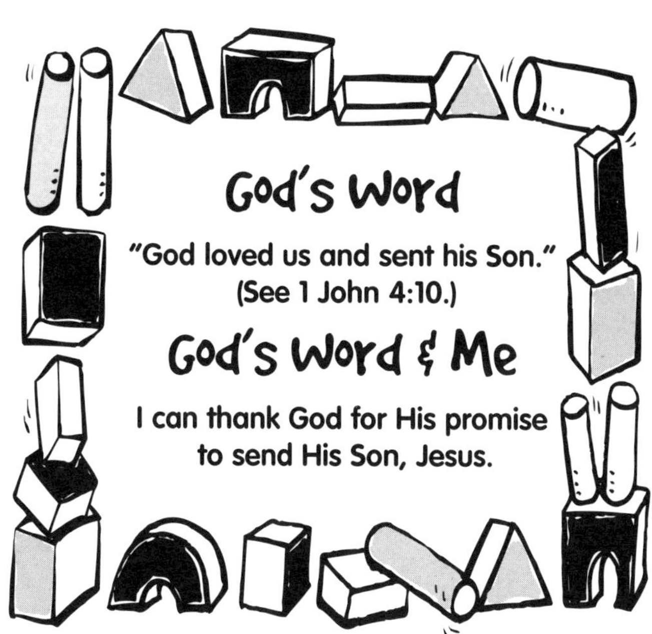
God's Word
"God loved us and sent his Son."
(See 1 John 4:10.)
God's Word & Me
I can thank God for His promise to send His Son, Jesus.

## Sing to God

Play "God Loved Us." Invite children to sing along with you. **Let's sing a song about God's love.** Lead children in singing song and doing suggested motions. **God showed His love by sending Jesus to be born. We sing songs to show we're glad Jesus was born!**

## Hear and Say God's Word

Holding your Bible open to 1 John 4:10, say the verse to the class. **God's Son is Jesus. We can thank God for doing what He promised. God sent Jesus to be born.** Lead children in repeating the verse and clapping their hands on each word. Vary the motion by asking children to stomp their feet, pat their heads, slap their legs, etc.

## Pray to God

Children repeat the following prayer, phrase by phrase: **Dear God, . . . thank You for loving us . . . and sending Your Son, Jesus. . . . We love You. . . . In Jesus' name, amen.**

## Sing to God

In closing the worship time, play "Good News." Invite children to sing along with you and do suggested motions. **What is the good news?** (Baby Jesus was born.)

## Options

1. Older children lead other children in doing the motions suggested for "God Loved Us" and/or "Good News."
2. If you collect a weekly offering, introduce it by saying, **Giving money to our church is one way to thank God for sending His Son, Jesus.** Then briefly describe one or more ways the money is used.

Lesson 14

# Read-Aloud Story and Activity Center

## Collect

A copy of Story Picture 14 (pp. 33-34 from *Read-Aloud Story and Activity Book*) for each child and yourself, crayons or markers.

## Prepare

Color your copy of Story Picture 14.

## Do

**Listen to find out why a family came to see these trees.** Read story and show completed Story Picture 14. Distribute pictures. Use conversation suggestions in Let's Talk About the Story as children complete their pages.

# Kindergarten Puzzle Center

## Collect

Copies of Puzzles 27 and 28 (p. 61 and p. 63 from *The Big Book of Kindergarten Puzzles)* for each child, pencils, crayons or markers.

## Do

Children complete the puzzles and color pages.

# Instant Activities

These activities can be used at any time during this session: when children need a change of pace, to extend the session, or during transition time at the beginning or end of the session.

## Collect

*The Big Book of Instant Activities.*

## Do

Guide children to complete "The Feeling Song" and/or "Shape Sighting" (p. 20 and/or p. 23 from *The Big Book of Instant Activities).*

Lesson 15

# Jesus Is Born

## Bible Story

Luke 2:1-7

## Teacher's Devotional

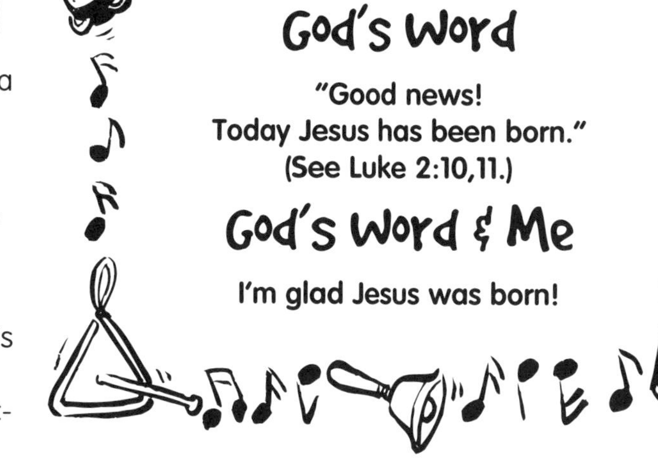
God's Word
"Good news!
Today Jesus has been born."
(See Luke 2:10,11.)
God's Word & Me
I'm glad Jesus was born!

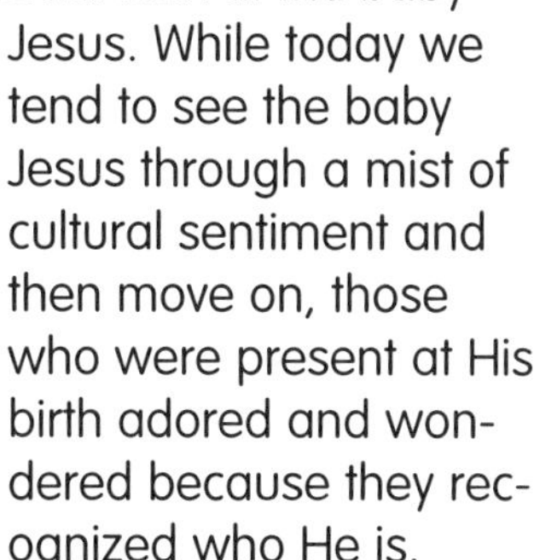

During this season, the world takes a brief, sentimental look at the baby Jesus. While today we tend to see the baby Jesus through a mist of cultural sentiment and then move on, those who were present at His birth adored and wondered because they recognized who He is.

To these people who had waited for the reality of God's promise to appear, awe and praise must have been a natural response. This baby proved their covenant with God was real. God had not forgotten them! Their ancestors had not died in vain! At long last, God had shown Himself in a new and living way to those who had waited to see Him and longed to know Him.

Read the first two chapters of Hebrews. These chapters may seem to be unusual reading for Christmas, but they are a powerful foundation from which to venture beyond the sentimental. Consider who came in the person of the baby. The depth of what was happening that night in Bethlehem is astounding! The fullness of time had come. The words of Zechariah 9:9 were fulfilled: "See, your king comes to you."

## Teacher's Planning

1. Choose which centers you will provide and the order in which children will participate in them. For tips on schedule planning, see page 7.
2. Plan who will lead each center. For staffing tips and ideas, see page 21.

# Active Game Center: Good News Toss

## Collect

Bible, large sheet of butcher paper, marker, beanbag; optional—magazine pictures of Christmas items (angel, Christmas tree, ornament, star, etc.), glue.

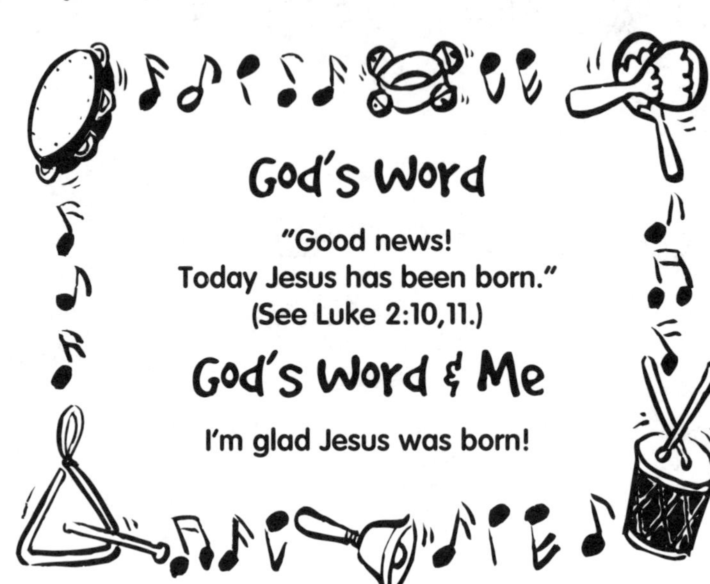
God's Word
"Good news!
Today Jesus has been born."
(See Luke 2:10,11.)
God's Word & Me
I'm glad Jesus was born!

## Prepare

Divide butcher paper into four or more sections. Draw a picture of a Christmas item in each section. (Optional: Glue magazine pictures in sections of butcher paper.)

## Do

Children stand approximately 3 feet (.9 m) from butcher paper. One at a time, children toss beanbag onto the butcher paper.

## Talk About

- **In our Bible story today, angels told shepherds the good news that Jesus was born. We celebrate Christmas to remember Jesus' birth. Let's play a game to remind us of things we see at Christmastime.**
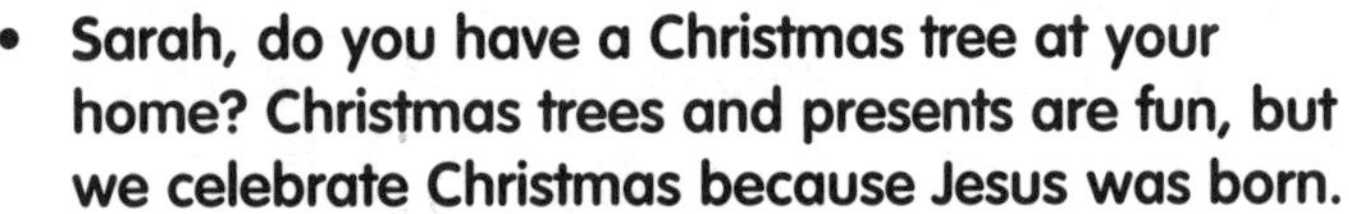
- **Sarah, do you have a Christmas tree at your home? Christmas trees and presents are fun, but we celebrate Christmas because Jesus was born.**

- **Our Bible says, "Good news! Today Jesus has been born." What reminds you of Jesus at Christmastime?**
- **I'm glad Jesus was born!** Pray briefly, **Thank You, God, that Jesus was born.**

## For Younger Children

Younger children stand closer to butcher paper.

## For Older Children

Children select a section of the butcher paper to use as a target. Some children may wish to experiment with tossing the beanbag between their legs or with their eyes closed.

# Art Center: Beaded ornaments

## Collect

Bible, ribbon, scissors, ruler, chenille wires, assorted craft beads (pony beads or larger), fine-tipped pen.

## Prepare

Cut ribbon into 8-inch (20.5-cm) lengths, cutting at least one for each child.

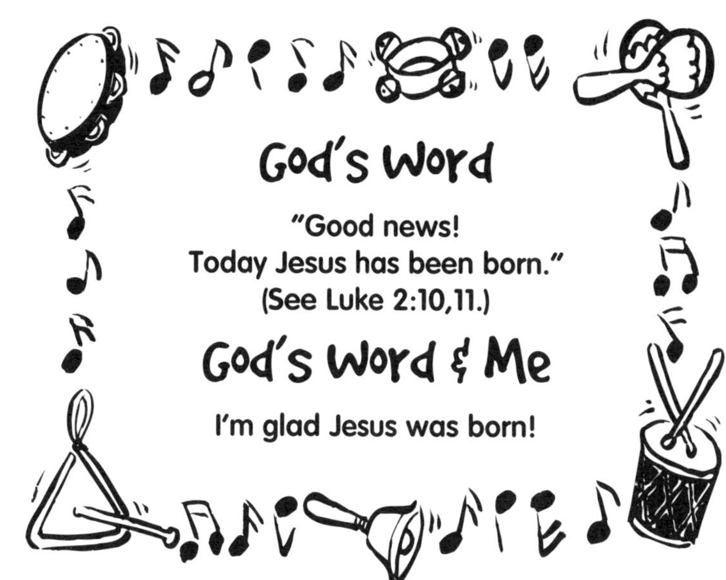
God's Word
"Good news!
Today Jesus has been born."
(See Luke 2:10,11.)
God's Word & Me
I'm glad Jesus was born!

## Do

1. Help each child put a bead on one end of chenille wire. Twist wire so that bead acts as a stopper. Children thread beads onto wire from other end, stopping about ½ inch (1.3 cm) from the end.
2. Help children twist the two ends of the wire together. Children can shape the wire into a wreath, candy cane or other shape.
3. Attach ribbon to ornament and tie into a bow. Use pen to print each child's name on the ribbon.

## Talk About

- **Our Bible says, "Good news! Jesus has been born." We are happy that Jesus was born! Let's make Christmas ornaments.**
- **We make ornaments for our Christmas trees as a way to celebrate Jesus' birthday. What kind of Christmas decorations do you have inside your home? Outside?**
- **Your family will be glad to have your Christmas decoration. We made them because we are glad Jesus was born!** Pray briefly, **Dear God, thank You that Jesus was born.**

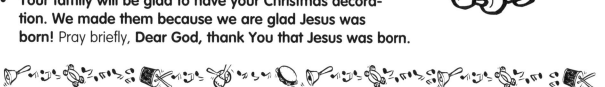

## For Younger Children

Use colorful circle-shaped cereal instead of beads.

## For Older Children

Cut additional, short lengths of chenille wire for children to attach to their ornaments. Children can create a striker for a bell, holly berries for a wreath, etc.

Lesson 15

# Block Center: Stable Blocks

## Collect

Bible; blocks; straw, hay or raffia; toy animals or animals from a nativity set.

## Do

Children use blocks and straw, hay or raffia to build a stable and manger for animals.

### God's Word

**"Good news! Today Jesus has been born." (See Luke 2:10,11.)**

### God's Word & Me

**I'm glad Jesus was born!**

## Talk About

- **Our Bible tells about a time when Mary and Joseph went to Bethlehem. Lots of other people also went to Bethlehem. Mary and Joseph looked and looked to find a place to sleep. Where did they finally stay?** (A stable.) **A stable is a building where animals live. Let's use our blocks to build a stable!**
- **When nighttime comes, where do animals sleep? Many animals sleep in a barn or a stable. Mary and Joseph stayed in a stable with the animals. What kinds of animals sleep in a stable?**
- **Our Bible tells us, "Good news! Today Jesus has been born." Jesus was born while Mary and Joseph were in the stable. Where do babies usually sleep? Where do you think Mary laid baby Jesus down to sleep?** (A manger.) **A manger is a box that animals eat from. Let's put lots of hay in the manger, so it will be nice and soft for baby Jesus.**
- **I'm glad Jesus was born!** Pray briefly, **Thank You, God, for sending Your Son, Jesus.**

## For Younger Children

Make a large masking-tape square on floor for the stable. Children use blocks to outline masking-tape stable and build a manger. Children act out different animals that might live in the stable. (Note: Remove masking tape immediately after activity.)

## For Older Children

Children build a road leading up to the stable and use toy people or nativity figures to act out the Bible story as you briefly tell the story. Expect to repeat the Bible story many times as children come and go from the Block Center.

# Science Center: Texture Touch

## Collect

Bible; straw, hay or raffia; piece of wood; faux or real fur; sheepskin; swatch of soft fabric (flannel, fleece, brushed cotton, etc.).

## Do

Children touch and explore the textures of the various items. Use suggestions below to talk about objects in the stable that had the same texture as each item.

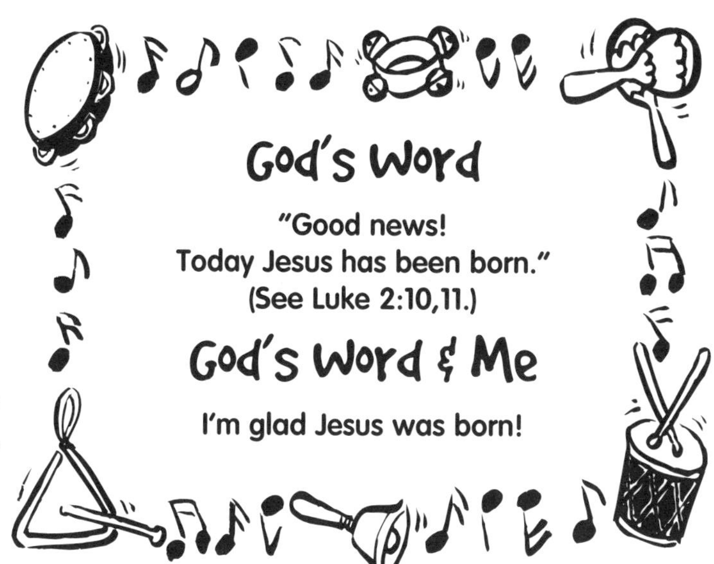

### God's Word

**"Good news! Today Jesus has been born." (See Luke 2:10,11.)**

### God's Word & Me

**I'm glad Jesus was born!**

## Talk About

- **I'm glad baby Jesus was born! In today's Bible story, baby Jesus was born in a stable! A stable is a place where animals sleep. Let's feel some things that may have been in that stable.**
- **Jay Bea, why do you think there was hay in the stable? Mary laid hay in the manger for Jesus to sleep on. The manger is a box animals eat from.**
- **Many buildings are made of wood. Norm, what is something in our room that is made of wood?**
- **What kinds of animals have fur? What animals live in a stable or a barn?**
- **Leah, what do babies wear? Mary probably used soft fabric like this to keep baby Jesus nice and warm.**
- **Our Bible says, "Good news! Today Jesus has been born." I'm glad Jesus was born! Are you glad too?** Pray briefly, **Dear God, we are glad you sent Jesus to be born. We love You.**

## For Younger Children

Bring an unbreakable nativity set. Help children identify nativity objects made of the same materials as those you brought.

## For Older Children

Give each child a small piece of each differently textured item. Children glue items to paper plates.

 

# Bible Story Center

## Collect

Bible, Picture 28 from *Bible Story Pictures.*

God's Word
"Good news!
Today Jesus has been born."
(See Luke 2:10,11.)
God's Word & Me
I'm glad Jesus was born!

## Tell the Story

Use the pictured motions (keywords in bold) or show Picture 28. For older children, tell the version of the story on the back of Picture 28.

**Do you or anyone you know have a baby brother or sister at home? Listen to find out what happened when God sent a very special baby to be born.**

One day Joseph said to Mary, "We must go to Bethlehem. We must write our names in the king's book." So Joseph and Mary began to **pack** for their trip. When all their things were packed, they started to go to Bethlehem.

Mary probably rode on a donkey. **Clippety-clop**, clippety-clop—the donkey's feet went clippety-clop against the rocks on the road. Joseph walked beside her. It was a long, hard, bumpy ride for Mary. It was almost time for Mary to have a baby. Mary and Joseph knew that this baby would be very, very special. This baby would be God's Son, Jesus.

Soon it was almost nighttime. Mary was tired! How much farther would they have to go? Finally they saw the town of Bethlehem ahead.

But when Mary and Joseph got to Bethlehem, the town was FULL of people! There was no place for them to **sleep**. Every room was full. So Mary and Joseph went to a stable where animals were kept. They slept on the hay.

There in the stable, in the quiet nighttime, **baby** Jesus was born. Mary wrapped baby Jesus in warm clothes. Then she laid Him on soft hay in the manger. (The manger is a box animals eat from. It made a comfortable bed for baby Jesus.)

Mary and Joseph took good care of baby Jesus. Jesus is God's special Son!

## God's Word & Me

**Mary and Joseph were so happy baby Jesus was born. I'm glad Jesus, God's Son, was born! Aren't you glad, too? At Christmastime, what are some ways to show we are glad Jesus was born?** (Sing songs about Jesus' birth. Decorate Christmas trees. Give gifts to people.)

# Worship Center

## Collect

Bible, *Shake It Up!* songbook and cassette/CD and player, "Good News" and "God Loved Us" word charts (pp. 23 and 25 in songbook).

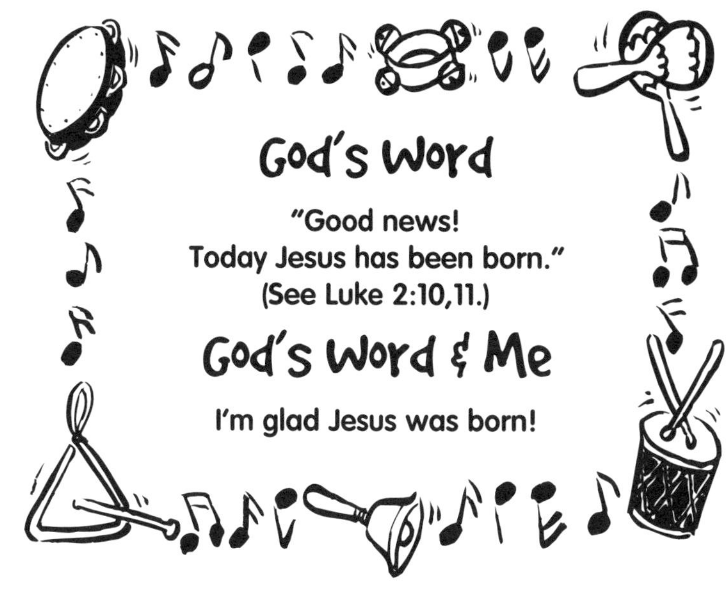
God's Word
"Good news!
Today Jesus has been born."
(See Luke 2:10,11.)
God's Word & Me
I'm glad Jesus was born!

## Sing to God

Play "Good News." Invite children to sing along with you. **Let's sing a song about some very good news!** Lead children in singing song and doing suggested motions. **This song tells us the very best news ever: Jesus was born! I'm glad that Jesus was born. Clap your hands if you're glad Jesus was born!**

## Hear and Say God's Word

Holding your Bible open to Luke 2:10,11, say verse aloud. **What good news does this Bible verse tell us?** (Today Jesus has been born.) Lead children in saying the Bible verse together a few times. Ask all children with a certain characteristic to say the verse together (everyone wearing red, everyone with brown hair, everyone wearing tennis shoes, etc.). Choose several categories and repeat the Bible verse several times.

## Pray to God

Lead children in repeating the following prayer, phrase by phrase: **Dear God, we are glad that You love us. We are glad You sent Your Son, Jesus, to be born. We love You. In Jesus' name, amen.**

## Sing to God

In closing the worship time, play "God Loved Us." Invite children to sing along with you and do suggested motions. **Why did God send His Son, Jesus?** (God loved us.)

## Options

1. Provide rhythm instruments for children to use while singing "Good News" and "God Loved Us."

2. With parents' permission, videotape children as they sing songs and do the motions. Show videotape at the end of the session as parents come to pick up their children.

# Read-Aloud Story and Activity Center

## Collect

A copy of Story Picture 15 (pp. 35-36 from *Read-Aloud Story and Activity Book*) for each child and yourself, crayons or markers.

## Prepare

Color your copy of Story Picture 15.

## Do

**Listen to find out what game these children played.** Read story and show completed Story Picture 15. Distribute pictures. Use conversation suggestions in Let's Talk About the Story as children complete their pages.

# Kindergarten Puzzle Center

## Collect

Copies of Puzzles 29 and 30 (p. 65 and p. 67 from *The Big Book of Kindergarten Puzzles)* for each child, pencils, crayons or markers.

## Do

Children complete the puzzles and color pages.

# Instant Activities

These activities can be used at any time during this session: when children need a change of pace, to extend the session, or during transition time at the beginning or end of the session.

## Collect

*The Big Book of Instant Activities.*

## Do

Guide children to complete "That First Christmas" and/or "Hidden Picture" (p. 60 and/or p. 112 from *The Big Book of Instant Activities).*

Lesson 16

# Angels Tell the News

## Bible Story

Luke 2:8-20

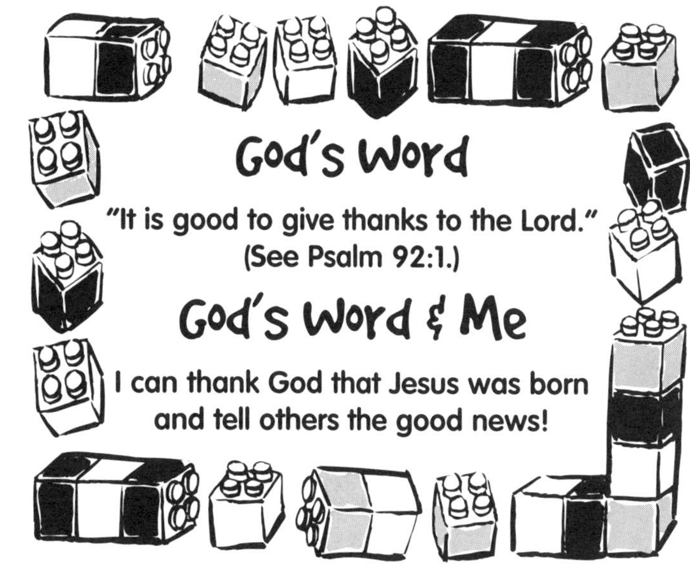
God's Word
"It is good to give thanks to the Lord."
(See Psalm 92:1.)
God's Word & Me
I can thank God that Jesus was born
and tell others the good news!

## Teacher's Devotional

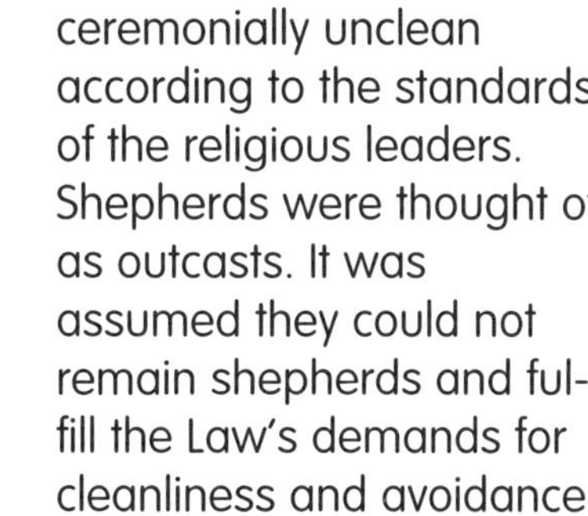

Consider the delightful paradox in today's Bible story: Shepherds were ceremonially unclean according to the standards of the religious leaders. Shepherds were thought of as outcasts. It was assumed they could not remain shepherds and fulfill the Law's demands for cleanliness and avoidance of contact with dead animals. So to whom did God first announce His Son's arrival? To people who felt they could not fulfill the demands of the Law! God proved that His grace and His Messiah were for everyone. Since we're as unable to fulfill the Law as the shepherds were, that's good news!

Ponder this paradox for a moment. God has chosen you to share His good news, just as surely as He chose those shepherds. Share His joy and good news with the little ones you love! Then lead your class to express thanks to God for the gift of His Son. Just as the shepherds left the manger with words of praise on their lips, let your words announce your joy and thankfulness. Echo the words of the apostle Paul: "Thanks be to God for his indescribable gift!" (2 Corinthians 9:15).

## Teacher's Planning

1. Choose which centers you will provide and the order in which children will participate in them. For tips on schedule planning, see page 7.
2. Plan who will lead each center. For staffing tips and ideas, see page 21.

Lesson 16

# Active Game Center: Chain Game

## Collect

Bible, red and green construction paper, scissors, markers, tape.

## Prepare

Cut construction paper into 6x2-inch (15x5-cm) strips. Make sure there are two or three strips for each child. Place paper strips in different places around classroom.

### God's Word

**"It is good to give thanks to the Lord." (See Psalm 92:1.)**

### God's Word & Me

**I can thank God that Jesus was born and tell others the good news!**

## Do

1. Children move around the room, looking for paper strips. When a strip is found, the child uses markers to decorate the strip. Instruct children to take only one strip of paper at a time.
2. As children finish decorating strips, assist them in taping strips to form links, creating a paper chain. Children continue searching for, decorating and forming links with paper strips until all have been found or as time allows. Hang chain from classroom walls or around doorway.

## Talk About

- **Our Bible says, "It is good to give thanks to the Lord." At Christmas we can thank God that Jesus was born and tell others the good news. Let's make a Christmas decoration for our classroom.**
- **What are some of the special things your family does to celebrate Christmas?**
- **Who can you tell about Jesus' birth? What cay you say?**
- **At Christmas we thank God for sending Jesus to be born.** Pray briefly, **Thank You, God, that Jesus was born.**

## For Younger Children

Be alert to younger children who may have difficulty finding strips. Offer verbal clues. **Look under the table. Check higher on the bookshelf.** If needed, take the child by hand and lead him or her directly to a strip.

## For Older Children

Children count the links as they are added to chain. Start counting over when children reach 20 links.

# Art Center: Paper-Plate Angels

## Collect

Bible, two paper plates for each child, scissors, red construction paper, chenille wires, hole punch, stapler, markers, glue; optional—heart-shaped stickers.

## Prepare

For each child, cut one paper plate in half for wings. Cut 1-inch (2.5-cm) hearts from red construction paper. Cut chenille wires into 6-inch (15-cm) lengths. Punch two holes at the top of the paper plate.

God's Word
"It is good to give thanks to the Lord."
(See Psalm 92:1.)
God's Word & Me
I can thank God that Jesus was born and tell others the good news!

## Do

1. Each child arranges the cut halves of a paper plate in back of a whole paper plate to form wings. Help children staple plates together. Children draw eyes and hair. Then children glue construction-paper heart over staple to form the mouth. (Optional: Children stick heart-shaped sticker over staple instead of red construction paper and glue.)
2. Help children thread chenille wires through holes and twist to secure at back to form a halo. Halo may also act as a hanger.

## Talk About

- **In our Bible story the angels told the shepherds the good news that Jesus was born. Let's make angels to remind us of this good news.**
- **The angels we made will remind us of the angels who told the shepherds about Jesus. What other things remind you of Jesus' birthday? Who can tell you about Jesus' birth?**
- **Our Bible says, "It is good to give thanks to the Lord." I am thankful that Jesus was born!** Invite children to join you as you pray briefly, **Dear God, thank You for sending Jesus to be born!**

## For Younger Children

Provide lace for children to glue to wings.

## For Older Children

Children cut paper plate in half to form wings.

Lesson 16

# Block Center: Blocks of Thanks

## Collect

Bible, blocks.

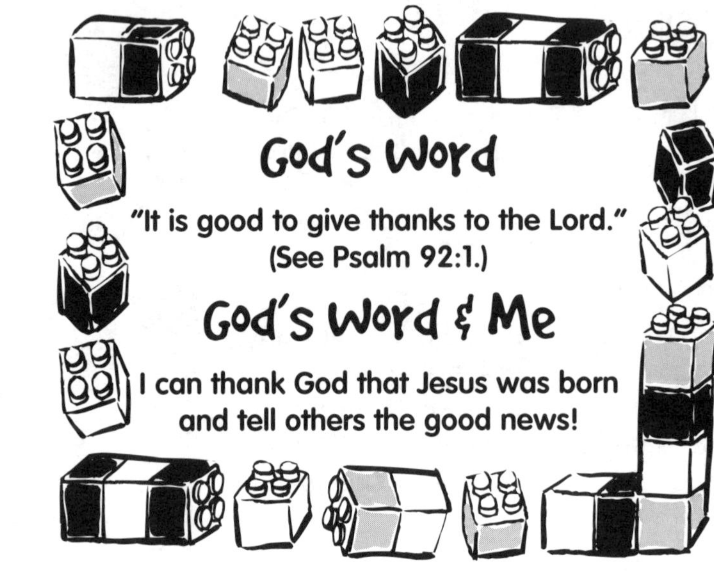
God's Word
"It is good to give thanks to the Lord."
(See Psalm 92:1.)
God's Word & Me
I can thank God that Jesus was born and tell others the good news!

## Do

Children build things for which they want to thank God.

## Talk About

- **Our Bible tells us, "It is good to give thanks to the Lord." "Lord" is another name for God. At Christmas, we celebrate and thank God for Jesus' birth. Let's build some other things to thank God for.**
- **Susie, what is something you are thankful for when you are tired and want to lie down? You can build a bed!**
- **Larry is building his house because he's thankful that God gave him a house to live in. What are some other things at Larry's house that he can thank God for?**
- **I thank God for the good news that Jesus was born! Bret, who is someone you can tell the good news to?**
- **Thank you for handing Beth a block, Joey. That was very kind of you. God gives us things we need. We can thank Him, too!** Pray briefly, **Thank You, God, for sending Jesus to be born.**

## For Younger Children

Do not expect young children to be able to make representational objects. They will simply enjoy stacking blocks and carrying blocks from one place to another.

## For Older Children

Bring in a variety of cardboard tubes (oatmeal boxes, wrapping-paper tubes, toilet-paper and paper-towel cores, etc.) and masking tape. Children incorporate tubes as they build with blocks, taping blocks and tubes together as desired.

# Science Center: Jingle Bells

## Collect

Bible, a variety of bells (jingle, sleigh, hand, bicycle, kitchen timer, etc.).

## Do

Children explore the bells, ringing them and listening to their sounds. Use the conversation suggestions below to lead children in comparing and contrasting the sounds the bells make.

### God's Word

**"It is good to give thanks to the Lord." (See Psalm 92:1.)**

### God's Word & Me

**I can thank God that Jesus was born and tell others the good news!**

## Talk About

- **Our Bible says, "It is good to give thanks to the Lord." We are thankful that Jesus was born! We celebrate Christmas to show our thanks to God. Some people play bells when they sing songs at Christmas. Let's listen to some different kinds of bells.**
- **These bells make different sounds. Debbie, which bells make a high sound? Mandy, which bells make a low sound?**
- **What are some other kinds of bells?** (Doorbells, church bells, school bells, etc.)
- **We sing songs to thank God that Jesus was born. What are some other things we do to show our thanks for Jesus?** (Decorate our houses. Give gifts.) **The most important thing that ever happened was that Jesus was born. And that's good news we can tell everyone we know!**

## For Younger Children

Include a variety of rhythm instruments for children to play.

## For Older Children

After children have had several moments to examine bells, gather bells. Ask children to close their eyes as you ring one of the bells. Children tell which bell was played.

Lesson 16 • Luke 2:8-20

# Bible Story Center

## Collect

Bible, Picture 29 from *Bible Story Pictures.*

God's Word
"It is good to give thanks to the Lord."
(See Psalm 92:1.)
God's Word & Me
I can thank God that Jesus was born and tell others the good news!

## Tell the Story

Use the pictured motions (keywords in bold) or show Picture 29. For older children, tell the version of the story on the back of Picture 29.

**What do you see when you look at the sky at night? Listen to find out what some shepherds saw in the sky on one very special night.**

Some shepherds were in the fields at night. They were watching their sheep. All the sheep were sleeping. Stars **twinkled** high in the nighttime sky. Everything was still and quiet.

Suddenly, the shepherds saw a bright light in the dark sky. *What could this be?* they wondered. Then they saw an angel! The shepherds were very **afraid**.

"Do not be afraid," the angel said. "I have good news to tell you. Today in Bethlehem, a Savior has been born for you. You will find this special baby lying in a manger." Before the shepherds could say a word, the sky was FULL of angels. The angels thanked God that Jesus was born. Then the angels left and went back to heaven. The nighttime sky grew dark and quiet again.

The shepherds said, "Let's go right now and find this special baby." The shepherds **hurried** as fast as they could go. They ran down the hillside. Then they ran along the road to Bethlehem. When they came to the stable, they saw Mary and Joseph. Quietly the shepherds came near to see the baby. And in the manger lay baby Jesus, just as the angel had said.

The shepherds were excited and happy about baby Jesus. "Jesus is born!" they **told** everyone they saw. Then the shepherds went back to their sheep. And all the while they praised and thanked God for sending His Son, Jesus.

## God's Word & Me

**After visiting the baby Jesus, what did the shepherds do?** (Told others that Jesus was born.) **The shepherds were so thankful that Jesus was born, they told everyone they saw! We can tell others about Jesus, too! Who can you tell about Jesus' birth?**

# Worship Center

## Collect

Bible, *Shake It Up!* songbook and cassette/CD and player, "Good News" and "God Loved Us" word charts (pp. 23 and 25 in songbook).

God's Word
"It is good to give thanks to the Lord."
(See Psalm 92:1.)
God's Word & Me
I can thank God that Jesus was born
and tell others the good news!

## Sing to God

Play "Good News." Invite children to sing along with you. **Let's sing a song about some very good news!** Lead children in singing song and doing suggested motions. **Who is someone you would like to tell the good news that Jesus was born?**

## Hear and Say God's Word

Holding your Bible open to Psalm 92:1, say verse aloud. **What is it good to do?** ("Give thanks to the Lord.") Lead children in repeating the verse by echoing phrases after you: "It is good/to give thanks/to the Lord." Point to children when it is their turn to speak. Repeat verse several times in this manner.

## Pray to God

Lead children in prayer, thanking God that Jesus was born and asking for His help to tell others the good news.

## Sing to God

In closing the worship time, play "God Loved Us." Invite children to sing along with you and do suggested motions. **This song tells us the good news that God loves us and sent His Son. I'm so glad that God loves us!**

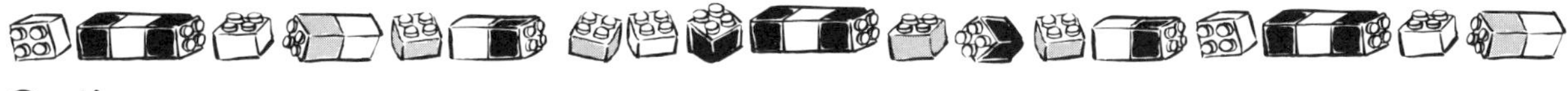

## Options

1. During verse activity, lead children in saying the words in different manners (loudly, softly, in a high voice, in a low voice, whisper, fast, slow, etc.).
2. As part of the prayer activity, ask children to name things for which they want to thank God. Volunteers then choose one of the things mentioned and thank God aloud.

# Read-Aloud Story and Activity Center

## Collect

A copy of Story Picture 16 (pp. 37-38 from *Read-Aloud Story and Activity Book*) for each child and yourself, crayons or markers.

## Prepare

Color your copy of Story Picture 16.

## Do

**Listen to find out what one boy couldn't find.** Read story and show completed Story Picture 16. Distribute pictures. Use conversation suggestions in Let's Talk About the Story as children complete their pages.

# Kindergarten Puzzle Center

## Collect

Copies of Puzzles 31 and 32 (p. 69 and p. 71 from *The Big Book of Kindergarten Puzzles)* for each child, pencils, crayons or markers.

## Do

Children complete the puzzles and color pages.

# Instant Activities

These activities can be used at any time during this session: when children need a change of pace, to extend the session, or during transition time at the beginning or end of the session.

## Collect

*The Big Book of Instant Activities.*

## Do

Guide children to complete "Ring the Bells" and/or "Eyes Open, Eyes Closed" (p. 59 and/or p. 112 from *The Big Book of Instant Activities).*

Lesson 17

# Wise Men Give Gifts

## Bible Story

Matthew 2:1-12

## Teacher's Devotional

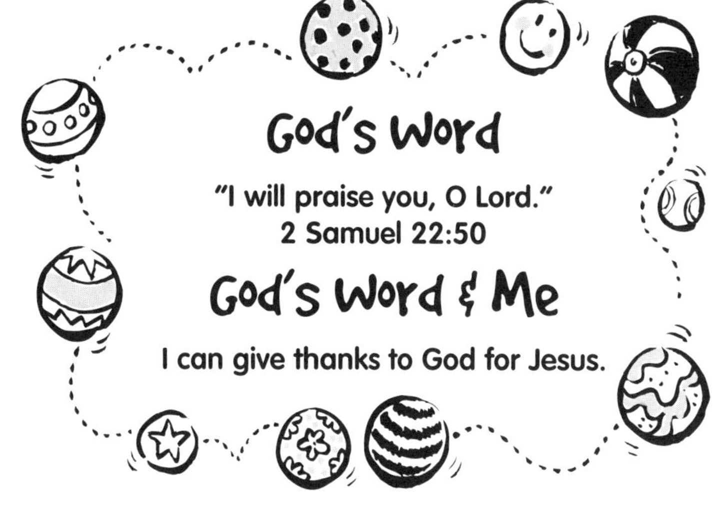
God's Word
"I will praise you, O Lord."
2 Samuel 22:50
God's Word & Me
I can give thanks to God for Jesus.

By the earliest traditions of the Church, there were 12 wise men who followed the star and came to worship Jesus. The later tradition of three wise men, or magi, probably arose from the Scripture record of three kinds of gifts given to the young Messiah. Their gifts for Him were wonderful symbols of who He is!

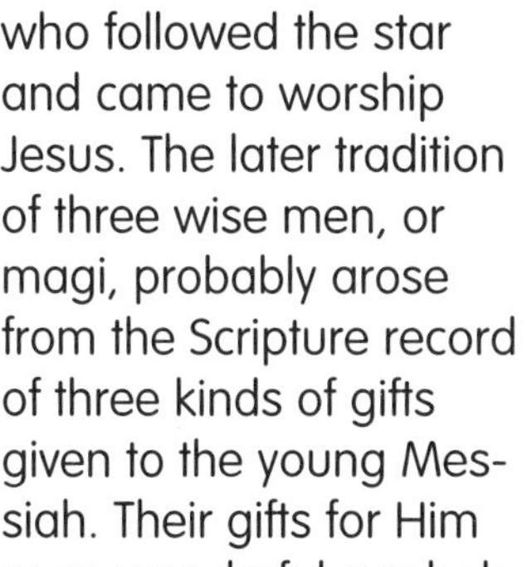

In some ancient kingdoms, no one dared come to the king without a gift. Gold, the king of metals, was the fitting gift for a king. Frankincense is the gift for a priest, for it was used in Temple worship. And myrrh, a gummy resin with antibacterial properties, was used for many kinds of healing and for embalming the dead. Jesus, then a little child in Bethlehem, became our King, our great high priest, our healer and our final sacrifice (see Hebrews 7:26-28). Jesus truly deserved these gifts!

Yet when we come to the King, He asks us to come with empty hands. All He wants for us to bring Him is ourselves. He then pours out His gifts on us as He rules our lives, intercedes for us, heals us and forgives us. These gifts far exceed any riches available in this world. We are blessed to be children of the King!

## Teacher's Planning

1. Choose which centers you will provide and the order in which children will participate in them. For tips on schedule planning, see page 7.
2. Plan who will lead each center. For staffing tips and ideas, see page 21.

# Active Game Center: Star Path

## Collect

Bible, yellow construction paper, marker, masking tape, stones, gold spray paint, incense, bottle of cologne; optional—star stickers.

## Prepare

Draw stars on 20 to 30 sheets of yellow construction paper. Tape papers to floor in an interesting path, ending at a point out of sight from the first star. (Optional: Instead of drawing stars, place star stickers on paper.) Spray stones with gold paint. When dry, place at end of path with incense and bottle of cologne.

### God's Word

**"I will praise you, O Lord."**
**2 Samuel 22:50**

### God's Word & Me

**I can give thanks to God for Jesus.**

## Do

Children follow the path of stars to discover the items at the end of the path. Repeat several times. Each time, ask children to move in a different way (walk, hop, walk backward, etc.).

## Talk About

- **In today's Bible story, the wise men followed a star to find Jesus. They gave Jesus gifts to worship Him. We are thankful for Jesus and worship Him, too. Let's follow some stars and see what we find!**
- If a child mentions the wise men visiting Jesus at the stable, simply tell the story correctly, rather than saying the child is wrong. **The wise men followed God's special star for a long, long time. When they found Jesus at Mary and Joseph's house, Jesus was no longer a baby. He was a little boy!**
- **Our Bible says, "I will praise you, O Lord." "Lord" is another name for God.** Pray briefly, **Thank You, God, for sending Jesus to be born.**

## For Younger Children

Some children will be more likely to walk on the path if you invite them to hold your hand and walk with you.

## For Older Children

Children count the stars as they follow path. Invite children to rearrange path after following it once.

# Art Center: Toothpick Stars

## Collect

Bible, construction paper, colored toothpicks, glue.

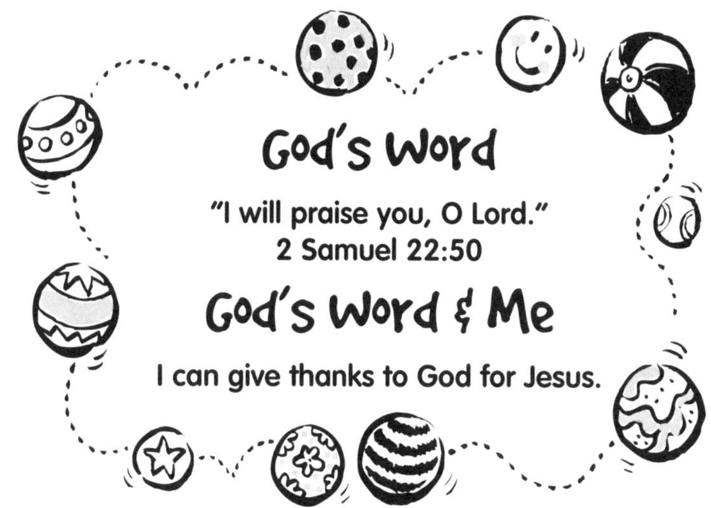
God's Word
"I will praise you, O Lord."
2 Samuel 22:50
God's Word & Me
I can give thanks to God for Jesus.

## Prepare

Following the directions below, make a sample star picture.

## Do

Children make stars on construction paper by placing colored toothpicks in a dot of glue, points together. (Note: Put away sample picture you made, so as children begin activity, they will be prevented from copying your work.)

## Talk About

- **In today's Bible story, wise men followed a star and found Jesus. They gave Jesus gifts and worshiped Him. Let's make star pictures. Our pictures will remind us to thank God for Jesus.**
- **When can you see stars in the sky? How many stars do you think are in the sky? Who made all the stars?**
- **Our Bible says, "I will praise you, O Lord." "Lord" is another name for God. We praise God at Christmas for sending Jesus to be born.**
- **God showed how much He loved us when He sent Jesus to be born. We celebrate Christmas to remember God's love and His special gift to us of His Son, Jesus.** Pray briefly, **Dear God, thank You for sending Your Son, Jesus.**

## For Younger Children

Instead of gluing toothpicks, children place star stickers on a sheet of dark blue, black or dark purple construction paper.

## For Older Children

In addition to or instead of gluing toothpicks, on their papers children trace around star-shaped cookie cutters. Then children color star shapes.

# Block Center: Super Stars

## Collect

Bible, blocks.

## Do

Children use blocks to outline one or more large stars and place blocks in the outlines to fill them in.

### God's Word

**"I will praise you, O Lord."**
**2 Samuel 22:50**

### God's Word & Me

**I can give thanks to God for Jesus.**

## Talk About

- **In our Bible story there is a very bright star. The wise men followed the star to find Jesus! The wise men thanked God for Jesus. Let's make a very big star to remind us that we can be thankful for Jesus.**
- **Where do we see star shapes at Christmastime?** (Tree ornaments. Lights on houses. Cookies.)
- **At Christmas we celebrate Jesus' birthday. Langdon, what are some things your family does to celebrate your birthday? At Christmas, we decorate the house, eat special food and give gifts. We show that we love Jesus and are thankful that He was born.**
- **Our Bible says, "I will praise you, O Lord." "Lord" is another name for God. We can give thanks to God for Jesus.** Pray briefly, **Dear God, thank You for Jesus!**

## For Younger Children

With masking tape, outline a very large star on floor of activity area. Make the star as large as space allows. Children place blocks on masking-tape lines. (Note: Remove masking tape from carpet immediately after activity.)

## For Older Children

Give children other materials with which to outline star shapes (yarn, ribbon, string, etc.).

# Science Center: Paper Matches

## Collect

Bible, a variety of wrapping paper, scissors, transparent tape, index cards, large paper bag.

## Prepare

Cut wrapping paper into various shapes (star, circle, square, heart, etc.). Make one shape for each child, cutting at least two of every shape and every design of paper. Tape shapes to index cards. Place cards in paper bag.

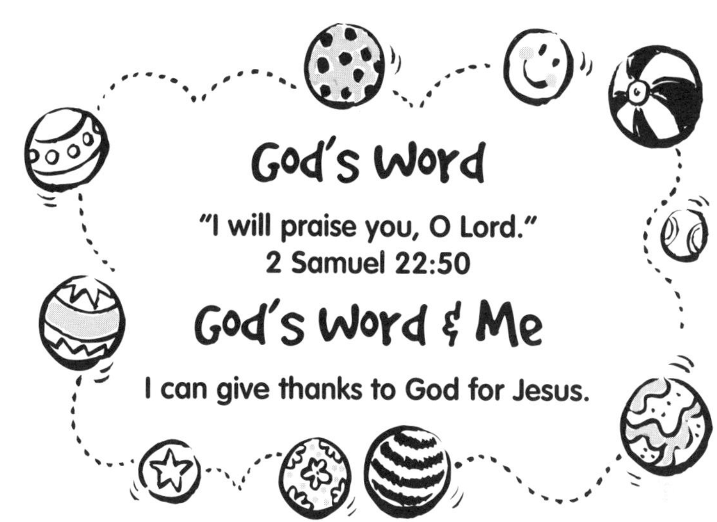
God's Word
"I will praise you, O Lord."
2 Samuel 22:50
God's Word & Me
I can give thanks to God for Jesus.

## Do

1. Children take turns selecting a card from the paper bag. Ask children to match their cards with another child's card according to the shape on the card. Next, ask children to match their cards according to the wrapping-paper design.
2. Gather the cards for the next round of play. For each round, vary the way children select a card (hide cards in classroom for children to find, place upside-down in a grid pattern, etc.).

## Talk About

- **Our Bible says, "I will praise you, O Lord." "Lord" is another name for God. We can thank God that Jesus was born. Let's look at something that we often see at Christmastime.**
- **Whose birthday is Christmas?** (Jesus' birthday.) **We can thank God for Jesus' birth.**
- **This pretty paper can wrap Christmas presents. When you get a gift, what do you say? We can thank God for sending Jesus as a gift to us.** Pray briefly, **Dear God, thank You for Jesus.**

## For Younger Children

Keep the game very simple. Children select cards by reaching into the paper bag. After each round, put cards back in paper bag for children to select again.

## For Older Children

Place cards face-down in a grid pattern. Children play a game of Concentration, matching cards according to either shape or wrapping-paper design.

Lesson 17 • Matthew 2:1-12

# Bible Story Center

## Collect

Bible, Picture 30 from *Bible Story Pictures.*

## God's Word

**"I will praise you, O Lord."**
**2 Samuel 22:50**

## God's Word & Me

**I can give thanks to God for Jesus.**

## Tell the Story

Use the pictured motions (keywords in bold) or show Picture 30. For older children, tell the version of the story on the back of Picture 30.

**Have you ever played Follow the Leader? What are the rules? Listen to find out what some wise men followed to find where little Jesus lived.**

**Clop**, clop, clop went the camels' feet. The camels carried the wise men on their backs. The wise men had seen a very bright star high in the sky. They knew the star meant a special child had been born. The wise men wanted to see this special child.

After many nights, the wise men came to a big city. "Where is the special child God has sent?" the wise men **asked** everyone they met. "We saw His star. We want to see Him."

"The special child is to be born in Bethlehem," a man told the wise men. "Bethlehem is close by," said the wise men. "Let's hurry and find the child." The wise men climbed up on the camels' backs and started toward Bethlehem.

**"Look!"** said one wise men as they came to the town. "There's the star!" As the wise men got closer, the star shone above one house. The wise men got down off the camels' backs. They opened their saddle bags and carefully took out beautiful gifts. The wise men found Mary and Jesus. Jesus was a little boy now. The wise men gave Jesus their gifts. They **gave** Him gold and some sweet-smelling perfumes.

The wise men were glad to see Jesus. They must have been very thankful to God for Jesus.

## God's Word & Me

**What did the wise men see that told them something important had happened?** (A very bright star.) **The wise men followed the star and found Jesus. They gave Him gifts and thanked God for Jesus. We can give thanks to God for Jesus. What are some ways to show our thanks to God?** (Pray to God. Sing songs to Him.)

# Worship Center

## Collect

Bible, *Shake It Up!* songbook and cassette/CD and player, "God Loved Us" and "Good News" word charts (pp. 25 and 23 in songbook), magazine pictures of items for which to thank God (families, food, home, church, school, water, etc.).

God's Word
"I will praise you, O Lord."
2 Samuel 22:50
God's Word & Me
I can give thanks to God for Jesus.

## Sing to God

Play "God Loved Us." Invite children to sing along with you. **Let's sing a song about God's love!** Lead children in singing song and doing suggested motions. **At Christmas, we like to give gifts, but this song tells us about the very best gift ever. The best gift was when God gave us His Son, Jesus!**

## Hear and Say God's Word

Holding your Bible open to 2 Samuel 22:50, say verse aloud. **What does this verse tell us we can do?** (Praise the Lord.) Lead children in saying the verse as a group several times. Then have children form a circle. Each child says one word of the verse in order around the circle. Repeat the verse in this manner several times, making sure each child gets to say a word at least two different times.

## Pray to God

Hold facedown the magazine pictures you prepared. **These are pictures of things for which we can thank God.** Ask a volunteer to select and show a picture. **Angela, what is your picture? Your picture shows a family! God gives us our families.** Repeat for all pictures with different volunteers. Ask volunteers to say a brief prayer, thanking God for the items in their pictures. **Let's thank God for sending His Son, Jesus, to be born.** Close in prayer, thanking God for sending Jesus.

## Sing to God

In closing the worship time, play "Good News." Invite children to sing along with you and do suggested motions. **What good news this is! Jesus was born to show God's love. God loves us, and we love Him, too!**

## Options

1. Older children lead other children in doing the motions suggested for "God Loved Us" and/or "Good News."
2. Ask children to name things for which they are thankful to God. Print children's responses on a large sheet of paper and tape to a wall for parents to read when they pick up their children.

# Read-Aloud Story and Activity Center

## Collect

A copy of Story Picture 17 (pp. 39-40 from *Read-Aloud Story and Activity Book*) for each child and yourself, crayons or markers.

## Prepare

Color your copy of Story Picture 17.

## Do

**Listen to find out what this girl asked about a star.** Read story and show completed Story Picture 17. Distribute pictures. Use conversation suggestions in Let's Talk About the Story as children complete their pages.

# Kindergarten Puzzle Center

## Collect

Copies of Puzzles 33 and 34 (p. 73 and p. 75 from *The Big Book of Kindergarten Puzzles)* for each child, pencils, crayons or markers.

## Do

Children complete the puzzles and color pages.

# Instant Activities

These activities can be used at any time during this session: when children need a change of pace, to extend the session, or during transition time at the beginning or end of the session.

## Collect

*The Big Book of Instant Activities.*

## Do

Guide children to complete "I'm a Camel" and/or "Look at It!" (p. 56 and/or p. 84 from *The Big Book of Instant Activities).*

Lesson 18

# Jesus Tells of God's Love

God's Word
"I will sing of the Lord's great love forever."
Psalm 89:1
God's Word & Me
God cares for me and
all the things He has made.

## Bible Story

Matthew 6:25-34; Luke 12:22-31

## Teacher's Devotional

In one way or another, we are told almost every day that we should worry about our health, our hair, our credit—the list of potential worries goes on and on.

Worry is what we experience when we feel we've got to take care of something ourselves, that responsibility rests entirely on our shoulders. But Jesus said that worry characterized pagans, those who do not know the loving fatherhood of God (see Matthew 6:32). Someone who has no relationship with the heavenly Father should worry: there is no God to whom he or she can go for real help! But for a child of God, nothing could be further from the truth! When we have done what we can, we can trust God to do what we cannot.

We must be responsible for those things over which we truly have responsibility! Often, however, our problem is not irresponsibility but falling prey to the world's definition of responsibility, fretting over what we can't control. God promises to go beyond what we are able to do to take care of our every need—if we will seek Him first! As we stop in our self-imposed struggles and rest in Him, we'll find His love never fails!

## Teacher's Planning

1. Choose which centers you will provide and the order in which children will participate in them. For tips on schedule planning, see page 7.
2. Plan who will lead each center. For staffing tips and ideas, see page 21.

# Active Game Center: Clapping Clues

## Collect

Bible, toy bird or artificial flower.

## God's Word

**"I will sing of the Lord's great love forever." Psalm 89:1**

## God's Word & Me

**God cares for me and all the things He has made.**

## Do

1. Play a game of Hot and Cold. Ask a volunteer to close his or her eyes. Place the toy bird or artificial flower somewhere in the classroom. Make sure the object is in plain sight. (Note: If you have a large class, invite volunteers to play two at a time.)
2. Volunteer begins to look for the hidden object. Lead the rest of the children in clapping to indicate whether or not the volunteer is close to the object. If volunteer is very far from object, clap very lightly or not at all. As the volunteer gets closer to object, clap louder and faster. Continue action until the object is found. Repeat with new volunteers as time allows.

## Talk About

- **Our Bible says, "I will sing of the Lord's great love forever." God loves and cares for everything He has made. Let's play a game to look for something God has made.**
- **Where do birds sleep? Stephen, what do birds use to make a nest? God made birds, so they know how to make nests to sleep in. What do you sleep in?**
- **God gave the flowers beautiful petals to wear. Petra, what is your favorite thing to wear? Who bought it for you? God showed He cares for you when He gave you people to buy you clothes to wear.**

## For Younger Children

Children do not clap to give directions. Instead, give verbal clues as needed: **The bird is near a chair.** If volunteer is hesitant to move around the classroom, invite volunteer to choose a friend to search with, or have an adult helper walk with the child and hold his or her hand.

## For Older Children

Once an older volunteer has found the object, let him or her choose the next volunteer and hide the object for the next search.

# Art Center: Flour-Dough Flowers

## Collect

Bible, mixing bowl, measuring cup, flour, cornstarch, salt, warm water, food coloring, large spoon, paper plates, marker.

God's Word
"I will sing of the Lord's great love forever."
Psalm 89:1
God's Word & Me
God cares for me and
all the things He has made.

## Do

1. Volunteers add dough ingredients one at a time to mixing bowl: 1½ cups flour, 1 cup cornstarch, 1 cup salt, 1 cup warm water, several drops of food coloring. Children take turns stirring dough until well mixed. If dough is sticky, dust with flour. If dough is stiff, add a little water. (Note: Recipe makes about 3 cups of dough, enough for 10 to 12 children.)
2. Children use dough to create flowers or birds (see sketch a). When finished, children place dough creations on paper plates on which their names have been written.

## Talk About

- **Our Bible says, "I will sing of the Lord's great love forever." God cares for everyone and everything He has made! Let's use dough to make birds and flowers.**
- **God cares for the birds. What is one thing God gave the birds to care for them?**
- **Mary, what is your favorite color flower? I like flowers, because they smell so good and look so pretty. Levi, what good things does God give the flowers to help them grow?** (Water and sunlight.)
- **God loves and cares for us even more than the birds and flowers! God gave each one of us the people in our family to care for us. Billie, what is one thing someone in your family did this morning to help care for you?**

## For Younger Children

Instead of leading children to make dough, purchase play dough with which children can work.

## For Older Children

Demonstrate hand-rolling dough into small balls. Attach balls to each other to make bird shapes (see sketch b).

 

Lesson 18

# Block Center: Block Party

## Collect

Bible, blocks.

## Do

Children build with blocks. To stimulate imaginative use of blocks, lay several blocks at right angles. When a child asks what you are making, you might ask, **What do you think it looks like?** Often a child will immediately begin to incorporate the blocks into an idea he or she has for building.

God's Word
"I will sing of the Lord's great love forever."
Psalm 89:1
God's Word & Me
God cares for me and all the things He has made.

## Talk About

- **In our Bible story today, Jesus told people of God's great love. Jesus said that God gave the birds food to eat. Jesus said that God gave the flowers beautiful petals. God cares for everything He created—especially you and me! Let's build with our blocks.**
- **Jessica, you have strong arms to lift that long block! I'm glad God made your arms, so they can lift heavy blocks. God loves and cares about you.**
- **Jacob, did you know God cares about you, even more than He cares about the flowers and the birds? God cares for us. God loves us!**
- **Our Bible says, "I will sing of the Lord's great love forever." Let's thank God that He cares for us and all the things He's made.** Pray briefly, **Thank You, God, for caring for us. Thank You for caring for all the wonderful things You have made.**

## For Younger Children

In addition to building with blocks, place a large box at one end of the activity area. Children carry blocks over to box and place blocks inside box. Young children will also enjoy carrying blocks from box back to their storage area.

## For Older Children

Make sure to instruct children to build no higher than their chins. Also tell children that taking apart or knocking down block structures may only be done with the permission of the builder.

Lesson 18

# Science Center: Bird Talk

## Collect

Bible, one or more objects having to do with birds (live bird in bird cage, feathers, bird's nest, pictures of birds and nests, etc.).

God's Word
"I will sing of the Lord's great love forever."
Psalm 89:1
God's Word & Me
God cares for me and
all the things He has made.

## Do

Guide children in observing the bird-related objects. Ask simple questions to increase children's awareness of bird features and to hear what they already know about birds.

## Talk About

- **In our Bible story, Jesus told others about God's love. Jesus told how God cares for flowers and birds. Let's look at ways God cares for birds!**
- **Birds don't have skin like we have. Lee, what has God made to cover birds? Do we have feathers? Why are feathers just right for a bird? The bird's feathers have oil on them to help keep the bird dry. Feathers also help a bird fly.**
- **Why do you think God made claws on the bird's feet?** (To hold onto a branch.) **God has made the bird just right! God cares for birds.**

- **God cares for the birds He has made. But God cares about you even more than the birds! God loves you. Our Bible says, "I will sing of the Lord's great love forever."**
- **Rachel, who did God make to help care for you? God loves you and me and all the things He has created!**

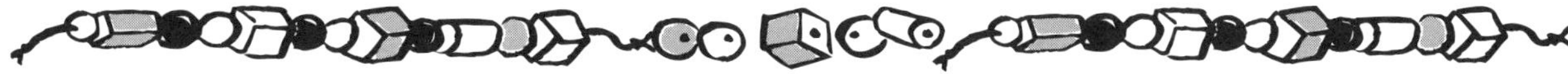

## For Younger Children

To extend the activity, lead children in walking around the room, waving arms like birds and twittering and chirping.

## For Older Children

After looking at objects, teach children several different bird sounds (cawing like a crow, clucking like a chicken, hooting like an owl, crowing like a rooster, cooing like a dove, etc.). Tape-record children making bird sounds. Play back tape so that children can hear themselves.

# Bible Story Center

## Collect

Bible, Picture 31 from *Bible Story Pictures.*

God's Word
"I will sing of the Lord's great love forever."
Psalm 89:1
God's Word & Me
God cares for me and
all the things He has made.

## Tell the Story

Use the pictured motions (keywords in bold) or show Picture 31. For older children, tell the version of the story on the back of Picture 31.

**If you had a pet bird, what would you do to take care of it? If you had a garden, how would you take care of the flowers? Listen to hear what Jesus told us about the ways God cares for birds and flowers—and us!**

One day Jesus was sitting on a hill talking with His friends. "**Look** at those birds up in the sky," Jesus said. "Just think about those birds." Jesus' friends watched as the birds flew high in the air. The birds ate the grain that grew in the fields. At night they had a place to sleep in the trees.

"Those birds don't plant the seeds they eat," Jesus said. "But God, your Father in heaven, feeds each one. He cares about them."

Then Jesus might have bent down and **picked** a beautiful flower. "Think about the way the flowers grow," Jesus said. "Flowers don't sew their leaves onto their stems with a needle and thread. Yet even kings do not wear clothes as beautiful as this flower." Jesus' friends listened.

Then Jesus said, "God makes beautiful flowers. And He cares about them. He sends **rain**. He sends the warm sun to help the flowers grow. If God does that for the flowers, He will surely take care of you! He loves you much more than birds and flowers. Do not worry about what to eat or what to wear. Our Father in heaven knows just what you need. Always try to love and **obey** God. He will take care of you. He loves you."

## God's Word & Me

**What does God give the birds? What does He give the flowers?** (Food to eat. Beautiful colored petals.) **Jesus wanted people to know how much God cares for each of us. God cares for you and me and ALL the things He has made! What has God given to show His care for you?**

# Worship Center

God's Word
"I will sing of the Lord's great love forever."
Psalm 89:1
God's Word & Me
God cares for me and
all the things He has made.

## Collect

Bible, *Shake It Up!* songbook and cassette/CD and player, "I Will Sing" and "Every Day" word charts (pp. 30 and 27 in songbook).

## Sing to God

Play "I Will Sing." Invite children to sing along with you. **Let's sing a song about God's great love!** Lead children in singing song and doing suggested motions. **According to this song, when are some times we can sing?**

## Hear and Say God's Word

Holding your Bible open to Psalm 89:1, say verse aloud. **"Lord" is another name for God. When we talk about singing to the Lord, we mean singing to God. We like to sing to God because He loves us.** Then lead children in singing the words of the verse to the tune of "Mary Had a Little Lamb":

I will sing of the Lord's great love,<br>
The Lord's great love, the Lord's great love.<br>
I will sing of the Lord's great love,<br>
Forever and forever.

## Pray to God

One at a time, call on children to name a person and complete the following prayer: **Dear God, thank You for loving and caring for __________. We love You. In Jesus' name, amen.**

## Sing to God

In closing the worship time, play "Every Day." Invite children to sing along with you and do suggested motions. **Jesus loves us every day. We can sing to Jesus and show Him our love every day, too!**

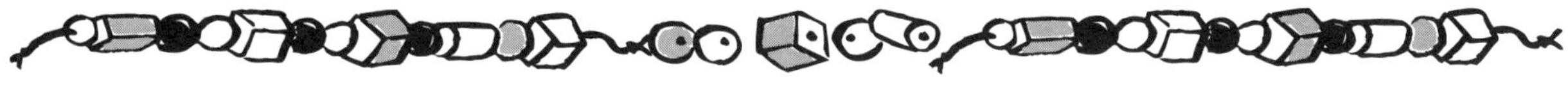

## Options

1. Children experiment with singing the words of the verse to other familiar tunes ("Row, Row, Row Your Boat," "Are You Sleeping?" etc.).
2. If you take an offering during this worship time, explain to children that giving money to God's church is one way to thank God for caring for us.

# Read-Aloud Story and Activity Center

## Collect

A copy of Story Picture 18 (pp. 41-42 from *Read-Aloud Story and Activity Book*) for each child and yourself, crayons or markers.

"I will sing of the Lord's great love forever."

## Prepare

Color your copy of Story Picture 18.

## Do

**Listen to find out what these children are looking for.** Read story and show completed Story Picture 18. Distribute pictures. Use conversation suggestions in Let's Talk About the Story as children complete their pages.

# Kindergarten Puzzle Center

## Collect

Copies of Puzzles 35 and 36 (p. 77 and p. 79 from *The Big Book of Kindergarten Puzzles)* for each child, pencils, crayons or markers.

## Do

Children complete the puzzles and color pages.

# Instant Activities

These activities can be used at any time during this session: when children need a change of pace, to extend the session, or during transition time at the beginning or end of the session.

## Collect

*The Big Book of Instant Activities.*

## Do

Guide children to complete "God's Creation" and/or "Dogs and Cats" (p. 21 and/or p. 79 from *The Big Book of Instant Activities).*

Lesson 19

# Jesus Stops the Storm

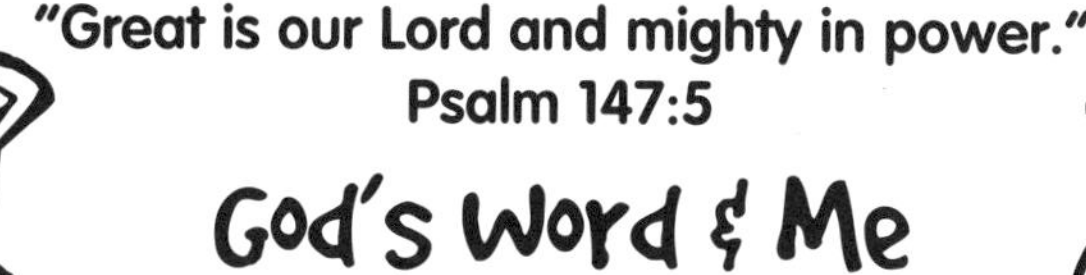

## God's Word

**"Great is our Lord and mighty in power."**
**Psalm 147:5**

## God's Word & Me

**I can ask Jesus for help, because of His great power.**

## Bible Story

Matthew 8:23-27; Mark 4:1,35-41

## Teacher's Devotional

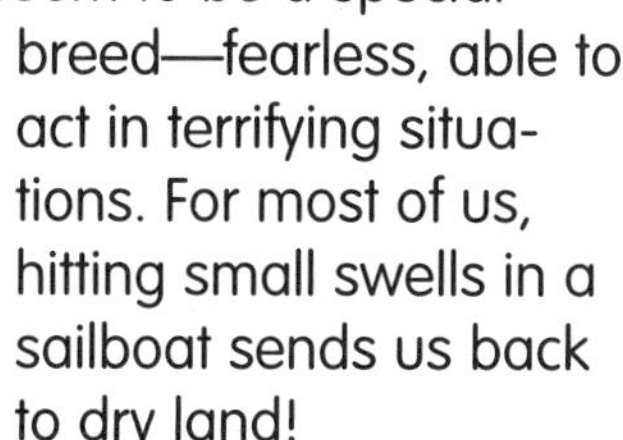

To those who spend their lives on land, sailors seem to be a special breed—fearless, able to act in terrifying situations. For most of us, hitting small swells in a sailboat sends us back to dry land!

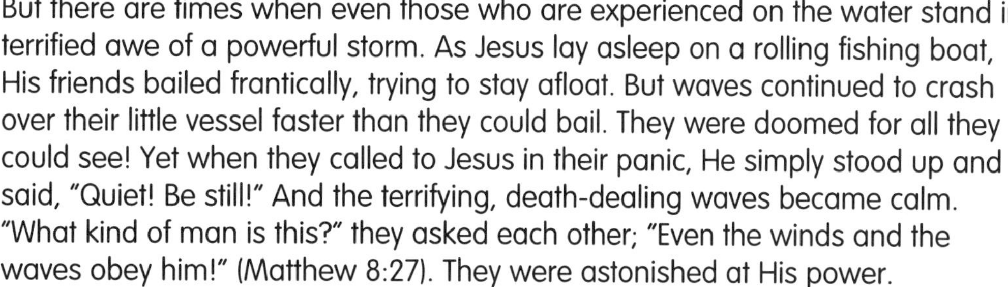

But there are times when even those who are experienced on the water stand in terrified awe of a powerful storm. As Jesus lay asleep on a rolling fishing boat, His friends bailed frantically, trying to stay afloat. But waves continued to crash over their little vessel faster than they could bail. They were doomed for all they could see! Yet when they called to Jesus in their panic, He simply stood up and said, "Quiet! Be still!" And the terrifying, death-dealing waves became calm. "What kind of man is this?" they asked each other; "Even the winds and the waves obey him!" (Matthew 8:27). They were astonished at His power.

We're so like those friends of Jesus! We too often wait until a situation is critical before we call on Him. We're sure we can handle it ourselves—until we begin to sink! Yet Jesus is always there to still the storm, stop the terror. His power has never diminished. He "is the same yesterday and today and forever" (Hebrews 13:8). All we have to do is ask!

## Teacher's Planning

1. Choose which centers you will provide and the order in which children will participate in them. For tips on schedule planning, see page 7.

2. Plan who will lead each center. For staffing tips and ideas, see page 21.

# Active Game Center: Boat Race

## Collect

Bible, *Shake It Up!* cassette/CD and player, masking tape.

## Prepare

Use masking tape to create a square, a circle and a triangle—each large enough that four or five children can stand inside. (Note: Remove masking tape immediately after activity.)

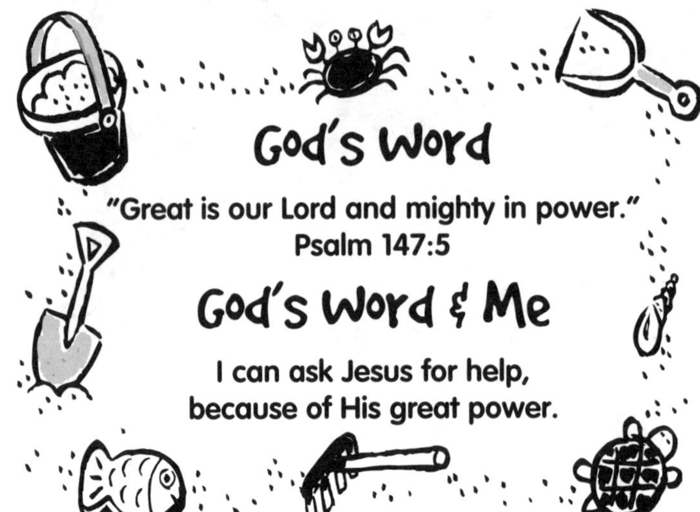
God's Word
"Great is our Lord and mighty in power."
Psalm 147:5
God's Word & Me
I can ask Jesus for help,
because of His great power.

## Do

1. Play "Every Day" as children walk around the room. When music stops, children move to stand in one of the masking-tape shapes.
2. **Let's pretend these shapes are boats.** Give children in each boat a different motion to perform. Refer to masking-tape boats by their shapes. **Everyone in the square boat jump up high! Everyone in the circle boat clap your hands. Everyone in the triangle boat rub your arms.** Repeat activity as time allows.

## Talk About

- **Our Bible story tells about a time Jesus helped His friends on a boat. Let's play a game and pretend to be in a boat!**
- **If you were in a boat, Ray, what are some of the things you would see? How might you feel if there was a big storm? Jesus' friends were glad He helped them in a big storm. We can ask God for help anytime!**
- **Our Bible says, "Great is our Lord and mighty in power." "Lord" is another name for God.** Pray briefly, **Thank You, God, for helping us when we're afraid.**

## For Younger Children

Don't distinguish between boats. Instead of doing different motions, all children do the same motion.

## For Older Children

Instead of giving directions according to the boat shape, ask children to perform motions according to children's initials. **Everyone whose name begins with a *C* or *J* jump up high!**

Lesson 19

# Art Center: Sea Scene

## Collect

Bible, yarn or ribbon, scissors, ruler, paper plates, markers, blue plastic wrap, transparent tape, hole punch.

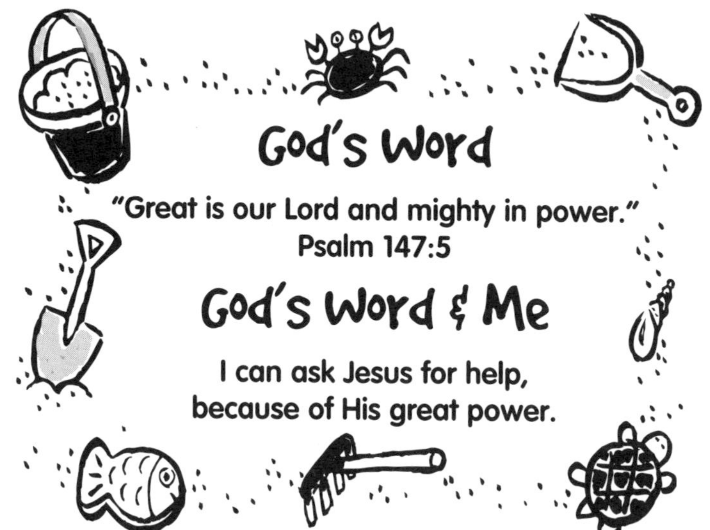
God's Word
"Great is our Lord and mighty in power."
Psalm 147:5
God's Word & Me
I can ask Jesus for help,
because of His great power.

## Prepare

Cut one 6-inch (15-cm) length of yarn or ribbon for each child.

## Do

1. Children use markers to decorate paper plates with underwater scenes, drawing fish, starfish, sea horses, underwater plants, etc.
2. When finished drawing their scenes, assist children in covering paper plate with a sheet of blue plastic wrap. Secure with tape.
3. Punch two holes at the top of the paper-plate scene. Children thread yarn or ribbon through the holes and tie ends together to create a hanger for their pictures.

## Talk About

- **In today's Bible story, Jesus and His friends traveled in a boat. A big storm came and Jesus' friends were afraid. Jesus' friends asked Him for help, and Jesus made the storm stop! Let's make some pictures of a lake or sea.**
- **Our Bible says, "Great is our Lord and mighty in power." "Lord" is another name for God. When we say God is "mighty in power," we mean that God is so powerful, He can do anything! Jesus is so powerful, He can help us every day.**
- Pray briefly, **Dear God, thank You for Jesus' great power and for His help.**

## For Younger Children

On plates, children place stickers or glue purchased precut shapes of fish and underwater objects.

## For Older Children

Children draw scenes using colored chalk. When finished, children may smudge gently with tissues to give an underwater effect.

Lesson 19

# Block Center: Block Boats

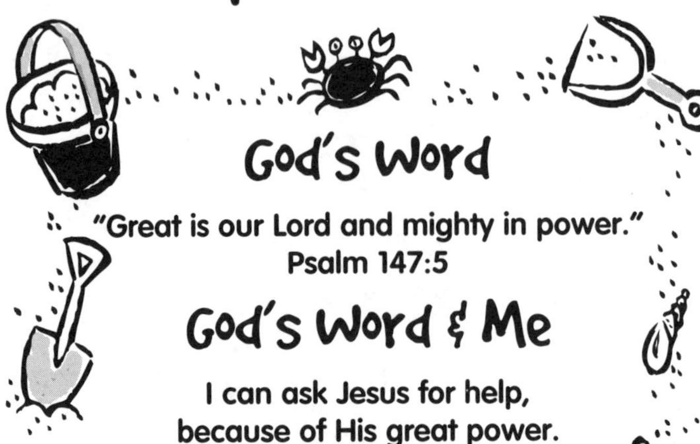
God's Word
"Great is our Lord and mighty in power."
Psalm 147:5
God's Word & Me
I can ask Jesus for help,
because of His great power.

## Collect

Bible, blocks, a blue covering (blue plastic tarp, blue blanket, several large sheets of blue construction paper, blue bedsheet, etc.).

## Do

1. Place blue covering on floor. Children pretend covering is water and use blocks to build boats on it.
2. Begin laying the outline of a boat. As children enter into the activity, move back and become an interested observer, ready to relate children's activity to today's lesson.

## Talk About

- **In today's Bible story, Jesus and His friends were in a boat during a big storm. Jesus' helped them and kept them all safe! Let's use our blocks to build some boats.**
- **One day Jesus and His friends were out in a boat. A strong wind started blowing. The boat rocked back and forth so much that Jesus' friends were afraid.**
- **His friends shouted for Jesus to help them. What did Jesus do?**
- **Jesus said, "Quiet! Be still!" And the storm stopped! Jesus has great power. Our Bible says, "Great is the Lord and mighty in power." "Lord" is another name for God. When we say God is "mighty in power," we mean God is so powerful He can do anything!**
- **Jesus helped His friends when they were afraid. When are you afraid? We can ask Jesus for help, because Jesus helps us when we are afraid.**

### For Younger Children

Instead of building boats with blocks, children pretend blocks are boats and play with them on the pretend water.

### For Older Children

Children use blocks to build a boat large enough for several children to sit inside. Children act out the story as you use the suggestions above to briefly retell it.

# Science Center: Fruit Floats

## Collect

Bible, grapefruit and/or orange, knife, large bowl or dishpan, water, spoons, paper towels.

## Prepare

Cut fruit in half. Scoop out insides. Fill large bowl or dishpan halfway with water. (Note: For a large class, prepare one setup for every six to eight children.)

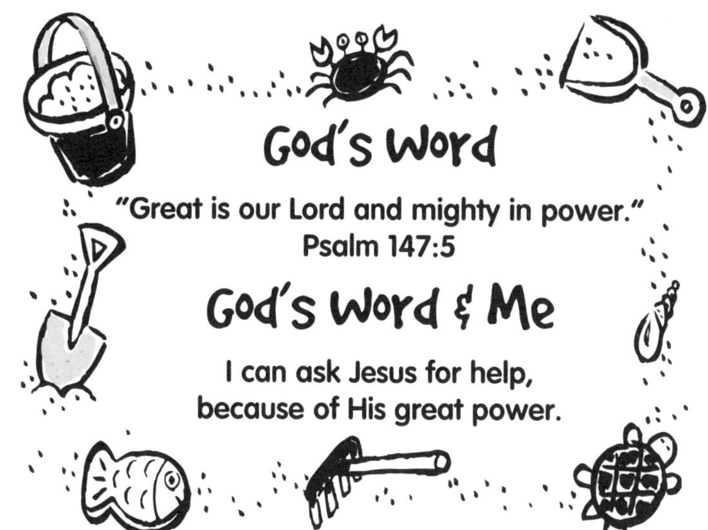
God's Word
"Great is our Lord and mighty in power."
Psalm 147:5
God's Word & Me
I can ask Jesus for help,
because of His great power.

## Do

Float grapefruit and/or orange halves in large bowl or dishpan of water. Children watch what happens as they take turns placing spoonfuls of water in fruit boats. Use paper towels to clean up spills.

## Talk About

- **Our Bible tells of a time Jesus and His friends were in a boat. A strong wind began to blow. The boat rocked so much that water got inside the boat. Let's see what happens when too much water gets in a boat!**
- **Jesus' friends were very afraid when the storm began. But they were glad when Jesus helped them! Wendy, when might you feel afraid? Jesus helps you when you are afraid.**
- **Our Bible says, "Great is our Lord and mighty in power." "Lord" is another name for God. We can ask God for help, because of His great power!**
- Pray briefly, **Thank You, God, for Your great power. Thank You for helping us when we're afraid.**

## For Younger Children

When water spills or splashes on the table, speak matter-of-factly. **Carissa, I see the water spilled on the table. Here is a towel to wipe it up.** Help the child as needed. Then thank the child for his or her help. **Thank you, Carissa. Cleaning up spills is a way to help us all!**

## For Older Children

Children make boat shapes from foil and float them in water.

Lesson 19 • Matthew 8:23-27; Mark 4:1,35-41

# Bible Story Center

## Collect

Bible, Picture 32 from *Bible Story Pictures*.

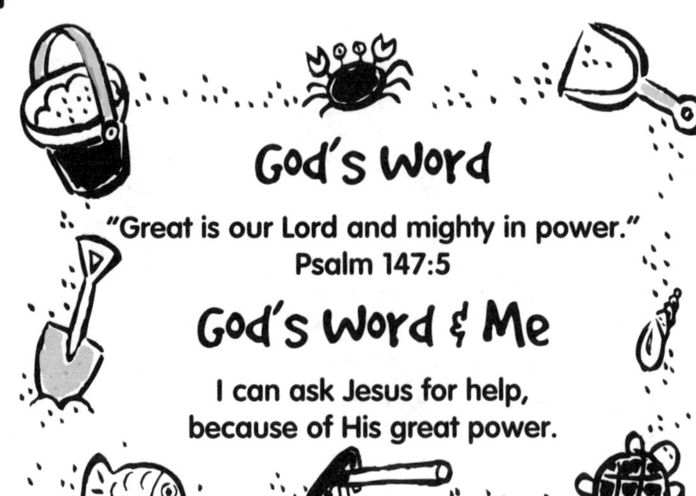
God's Word
"Great is our Lord and mighty in power."
Psalm 147:5
God's Word & Me
I can ask Jesus for help, because of His great power.

## Tell the Story

Use the pictured motions (keywords in bold) or show Picture 32. For older children, tell the version of the story on the back of Picture 32.

**What happens in a very big storm? Listen to find out how Jesus stopped a very big storm.**

One night Jesus and His friends were sailing across the lake in their boat. Jesus was very tired. He lay down in the back of the boat. Soon He was **asleep**.

Suddenly, the wind began to blow. Ooooooo! Ooooooo! The wind **blew** harder and harder. The little waves got bigger and bigger. Splish-splash! Splish-splash! The big waves hit hard against the little boat. Water splashed into the boat. Splash! Splash! Splash! The boat was filling with water.

"I'm afraid," one of Jesus' friends might have shouted.

"Jesus! Help us!" shouted another friend. "Don't You care that our boat is sinking?"

Jesus woke up. He felt the strong winds blowing. He saw the big waves splashing. Jesus stood up and said, "Quiet! Be still!" And **just like that**, the wind stopped blowing. The big waves stopped splashing. Splish. Splish. The little waves rocked the boat gently again.

"Why were you so afraid?" Jesus asked His friends. "Don't you know that I love you?"

Jesus' friends were surprised that the winds and the waves had obeyed Jesus. Jesus' friends were **glad** Jesus helped them when they were afraid.

## God's Word & Me

**What did Jesus do to help His friends?** (Jesus stopped a very big storm.) **Jesus helped His friends when they were afraid. Jesus has great power. We can ask Jesus for help, too! When are some times you are afraid? Whenever you're afraid, you can ask Jesus to help you!**

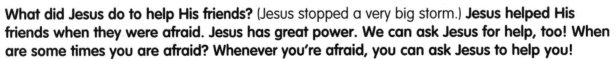

# Worship Center

## Collect

Bible, *Shake It Up!* songbook and cassette/CD and player, "Every Day" and "I Will Sing" word charts (pp. 27 and 30 in songbook).

God's Word
"Great is our Lord and mighty in power."
Psalm 147:5
God's Word & Me
I can ask Jesus for help,
because of His great power.

## Sing to God

Play "Every Day." Invite children to sing along with you. **Let's sing a song about Jesus' help.** Lead children in singing song and doing suggested motions. **I'm glad Jesus uses His great power to help us every day!**

## Hear and Say God's Word

Holding your Bible open to Psalm 147:5, say verse aloud. **When we say God is "mighty in power," we mean that God is so powerful, He can do anything!** Then lead children in repeating the verse after you a few times in this manner: Say the verse very quietly the first time and then a little bit louder each time you repeat the verse until you are speaking in a normal speaking voice. Continue repeating verse, getting softer on each repetition until speaking very quietly again.

## Pray to God

**Dear God, thank You for showing us that You have power to help us when we are afraid. We are glad You love us and care for us. In Jesus' name, amen.**

## Sing to God

In closing the worship time, play "I Will Sing." Invite children to sing along with you and do suggested motions. **When are some times we can sing of God's great love?** Children respond with examples from the song or their own ideas.

## Options

1. Invite a musician from your church to play one or more of the suggested songs for this lesson on a guitar, flute, trumpet, etc.
2. Provide rhythm instruments for children to use while singing "Every Day" and "I Will Sing."

# Read-Aloud Story and Activity Center

## Collect

A copy of Story Picture 19 (pp. 43-44 from *Read-Aloud Story and Activity Book*) for each child and yourself, crayons or markers.

## Prepare

Color your copy of Story Picture 19.

## Do

**Listen to find out where this family is going.** Read story and show completed Story Picture 19. Distribute pictures. Use conversation suggestions in Let's Talk About the Story as children complete their pages.

# Kindergarten Puzzle Center

## Collect

Copies of Puzzles 37 and 38 (p. 81 and p. 83 from *The Big Book of Kindergarten Puzzles)* for each child, pencils, crayons or markers.

## Do

Children complete the puzzles and color pages.

# Instant Activities

These activities can be used at any time during this session: when children need a change of pace, to extend the session, or during transition time at the beginning or end of the session.

## Collect

*The Big Book of Instant Activities.*

## Do

Guide children to complete "Name Cheer" and/or "Sock Game" (p. 68 and/or p. 121 from *The Big Book of Instant Activities).*

Lesson 20

# Jesus Heals a Blind Man

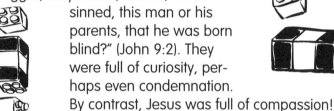

## God's Word

"The Lord is good to all." Psalm 145:9

## God's Word & Me

I can see many ways Jesus shows love to me.

## Bible Story

John 9:1-11,35-38

## Teacher's Devotional

As Jesus' friends passed by a blind beggar, they asked, "Rabbi, who sinned, this man or his parents, that he was born blind?" (John 9:2). They were full of curiosity, perhaps even condemnation. By contrast, Jesus was full of compassion!

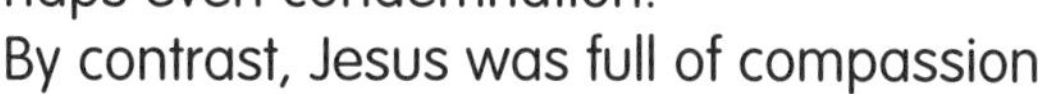

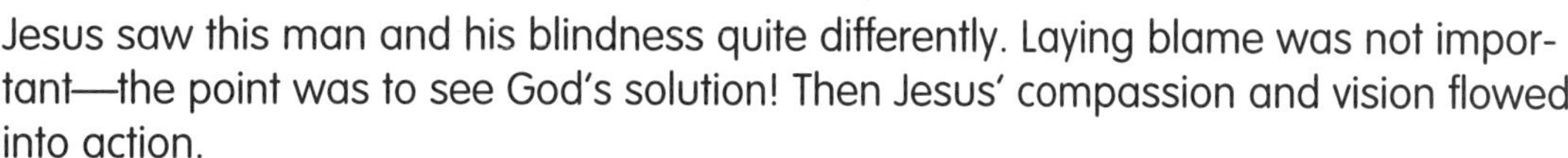

Jesus saw this man and his blindness quite differently. Laying blame was not important—the point was to see God's solution! Then Jesus' compassion and vision flowed into action.

When we see the troubled child, the homeless person, the disabled person, it's natural to wonder, *Why?* But to respond the way Jesus did, we must first see the person as one created in God's image. Beyond asking ourselves, *Why?* we need to ask ourselves, *What am I going to do? How can I help the work of God to be shown in this person's life?* Then we are ready to commit ourselves to helping care for that need.

We can't miraculously solve the problems of all those who are hurting around us. But when we first see such a person as God sees him or her, we are ready to ask God to show the way to share His love with that person.

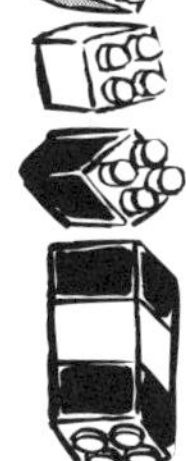

## Teacher's Planning

1. Choose which centers you will provide and the order in which children will participate in them. For tips on schedule planning, see page 7.
2. Plan who will lead each center. For staffing tips and ideas, see page 21.

# Active Game Center: Cups Galore!

## Collect

Bible, disposable cups in a variety of patterns and colors (several of each pattern), yarn.

## Prepare

Place all but one cup of each pattern and color on floor or table. Make a yarn line approximately 5 feet (1.5 m) away. (Note: If you have a large group, prepare more than one setup.)

### God's Word

**"The Lord is good to all." Psalm 145:9**

### God's Word & Me

**I can see many ways Jesus shows love to me.**

## Do

1. Children line up behind the yarn line. Hold up one of the cups. The first child in line walks quickly to the cups and searches for and selects a cup that matches the cup you are holding up. Taking cup, child returns to the back of the line. Repeat until all the matching cups are found. Hold up a cup with a different pattern or color. Repeat for all cups.
2. Children look at and compare their cups to identify colors and patterns, and then sort cups by matching them. Repeat as time allows.

## Talk About

- **In our story today, Jesus showed His love by making a blind man's eyes see. I can see many ways Jesus shows His love to me. Let's use our eyes to play a matching game.**
- **Our Bible tells us, "The Lord is good to all." "Lord" is another name for God. God is good to give us eyes to see. What are some other good things God has done for us?**

## For Younger Children

After all the cups have been selected, children stack cups.

## For Older Children

After children have matched and sorted cups, remove all but one cup of each pattern and color. Ask children to look at the cups closely. Then children close their eyes. Remove one cup and hide from children's view. Children open their eyes and try to identify which cup is missing by describing it. Repeat, replacing hidden cup after each round.

# Art Center: Color Petals

## Collect

Bible, construction paper in a variety of colors, scissors, ruler, paper plates, glue, markers.

## Prepare

Cut construction paper into 1- to 2-inch (2.5- to 5-cm) triangles.

## Do

Children choose triangles and glue them to the edges of a paper plate to form a flower. Children use markers to decorate their flowers.

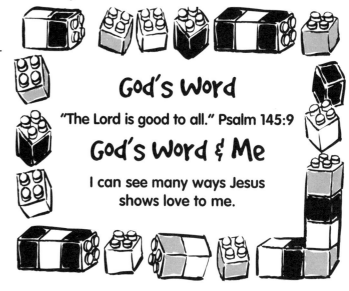

### God's Word

**"The Lord is good to all." Psalm 145:9**

### God's Word & Me

**I can see many ways Jesus shows love to me.**

## Talk About

- **In our Bible story today, Jesus showed His love by making a blind man's eyes see. Let's use our eyes while we make colorful flowers.**
- **Zach, what colors are you using to make your flower? God made our eyes so that we can see colors. What else can you do with your eyes? Can you wink? Can you blink? Show me how.**
- Help children notice similarities and differences in colors, shapes and textures. **How many green crayons do you see on the table, Dana? Are they all the same kind of green? Which ones are the same? Which ones are different? I'm glad God has made our eyes to see!**
- **God is good to give us eyes to see! Our Bible says, "The Lord is good to all." "Lord" is another name for God.** Pray briefly, **Thank You, God for the many ways You show You love us.**
- **What else would you like to thank God for? We can see many ways Jesus shows He loves us.**

## For Younger Children

Children glue cotton balls to the centers of their flowers. Spritz with a bit of perfume or cologne.

## For Older Children

Children cut out triangle petals and green strips for stems.

Lesson 20

# Block Center: Tall Towers

## Collect

Bible, yarn, scissors, measuring stick, blocks.

## Prepare

Cut yarn into varying lengths from 10 inches (25.5 cm) to 3 feet (.9 m).

## Do

Hand each child a length of yarn. Children build towers as tall as their pieces of yarn are long.

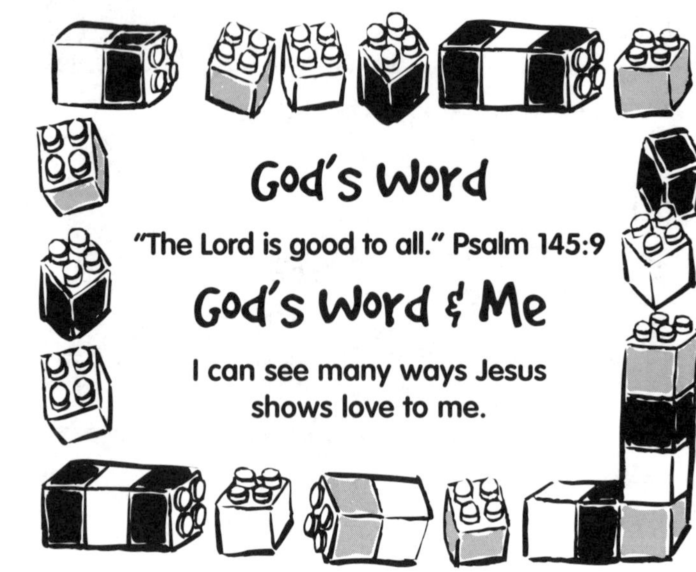
God's Word
"The Lord is good to all." Psalm 145:9
God's Word & Me
I can see many ways Jesus shows love to me.

## Talk About

- **Today in our Bible story, Jesus made a blind man's eyes see! Let's use our eyes to measure and build towers of blocks.**
- **Brittany, how do you know how tall to make your tower? Who made your eyes? God made everything. God shows His love in many ways.**
- **God made us just right! God made** (point to eyes; pause to let volunteers say "eyes")**, so we can** (pause to let children complete the sentence). Repeat with nose, ears, mouth and fingers.
- **The Lord is good to make our eyes just right. Our Bible tells us, "The Lord is good to all." "Lord" is another name for God.** Pray briefly, **Thank You, God, for being good to us and loving us.**

## For Younger Children

Children may not be interested in building towers. Young children will likely not build any objects at all but simply carry blocks from place to place and/or make piles with the blocks. Do not interfere with their free play. Simply tailor your discussion to incorporate their actions with the lesson focus.

## For Older Children

Children use measuring sticks to measure towers. Children may also work in pairs or groups to create a line of blocks on the floor that is as long as their pieces of yarn tied together.

Lesson 20

# Science Center: Cartons of Color

## Collect

Bible; newspaper; red, blue and yellow food coloring; three or four white Styrofoam egg cartons; water; cotton swabs.

## Prepare

Spread newspaper over activity area. Add several drops of red food coloring to one section of each Styrofoam egg carton. Repeat in new sections for each color. Add water to other sections of the egg cartons.

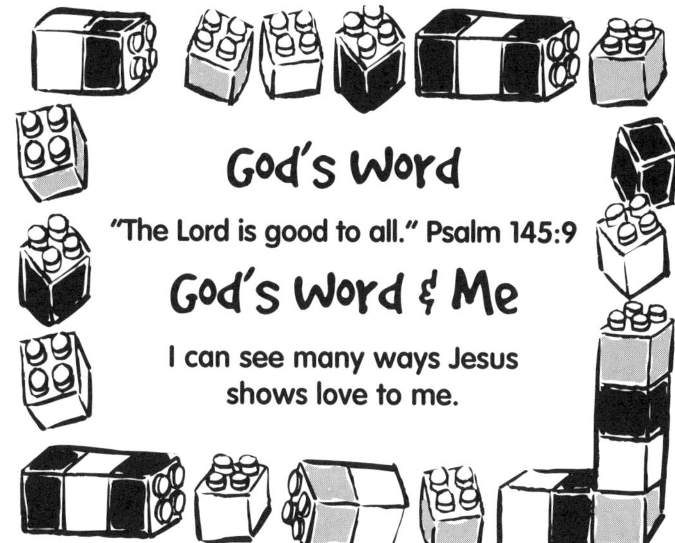

### God's Word

**"The Lord is good to all." Psalm 145:9**

### God's Word & Me

**I can see many ways Jesus shows love to me.**

## Do

Children identify colors. Then children use cotton swabs to stir color into clear water and watch the water change color. Children discover new colors by mixing the colors.

## Talk About

- **In our Bible story, Jesus showed love to a blind man. Jesus made the blind man's eyes see! Let's use our eyes and look at different colors.**
- **Jennifer, I wonder what would happen if you mixed two of our colors. What happened?**
- **What color do blue and red make? Blue and yellow? Yellow and red? What did God make that is yellow? Red?**
- **Our Bible says, "The Lord is good to all." "Lord" is another name for God. God is good for giving us eyes to see.** Pray briefly, **Dear God, thank You for being good to us and loving us.**

## For Younger Children

Tape Styrofoam egg cartons to table. Children take turns experimenting with colors one at a time as you assist.

## For Older Children

Children use cotton swabs to drip colored water onto coffee filters, observing the way the colors blend and run together.

# Lesson 20 • John 9:1-11,35-38

# Bible Story Center

## Collect

Bible, Picture 39 from *Bible Story Pictures.*

## God's Word

**"The Lord is good to all." Psalm 145:9**

## God's Word & Me

**I can see many ways Jesus shows love to me.**

## Tell the Story

Use the pictured motions (keywords in bold) or show Picture 39. For older children, tell the version of the story on the back of Picture 39.

**What can you see if you close your eyes? People who are blind can't see anything. It's like their eyes are always closed! Listen to find out how a blind man felt after Jesus made his eyes see.**

One day a man was sitting beside the road. He could not see the green grass. He could not see the yellow flowers. He could not see the blue sky. He could not see the children playing. He could not see with his eyes. The man was blind. But he could hear. And this is what he heard. **Step**, step, step. Step, step, step. The blind man heard someone walking along the road.

The blind man felt someone **put cool mud** on his eyes. He heard someone say, "Go now and wash in the pool of water." It was Jesus talking to him!

The blind man went right away to the pool and **washed** the mud off his eyes. As he washed, something wonderful happened!

"I can see!" the man probably shouted. "I can see green grass and yellow flowers. I can see the blue sky. I can see children playing."

Soon people came to see what had happened. "Isn't this the man who was blind?" they asked.

The man was so **excited**. He must have shouted, "I AM the man who used to be blind! A man named Jesus put mud on my eyes and told me to wash in the pool. I did what He said and now I can see!" And everywhere the man went, he told that Jesus had made his blind eyes see.

## God's Word & Me

**What happened when the blind man cleaned his eyes like Jesus told him?** (He could see.) **Jesus showed His love by helping the blind man see. How does Jesus show His love to us?** (He is always with us. He listens when we pray. He helps us when we ask.)

# Worship Center

## Collect

Bible, *Shake It Up!* songbook and cassette/CD and player, "Every Day" and "I Will Sing" word charts (pp. 27 and 30 in songbook).

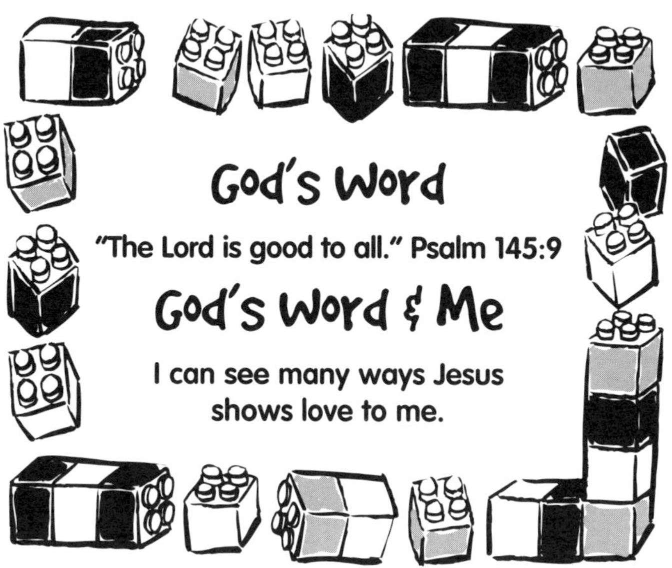

God's Word
"The Lord is good to all." Psalm 145:9
God's Word & Me
I can see many ways Jesus shows love to me.

## Sing to God

Play "Every Day." Invite children to sing along with you. **Let's sing a song together!** Lead children in singing song and doing suggested motions. **Every day, in many ways, we can see ways Jesus shows His love for us.**

## Hear and Say God's Word

Holding your Bible open to Psalm 145:9, say verse aloud. **The verse tells us that God is good to all. That means God is good to everyone! God loves each of us!** Lead children in repeating the Bible verse several times. As the children are repeating the verse with you, point to one or two children. You and the children say those children's names instead of the word "all." Repeat for every child.

## Pray to God

Lead children in repeating the following prayer, phrase by phrase: **Dear God, . . . thank You . . . for making our eyes. . . . You love us so much. . . . We love you. . . . In Jesus' name, amen.**

## Sing to God

In closing the worship time, play "I Will Sing." Invite children to sing along with you and do suggested motions. **What is it we are singing about?** (The Lord's great love.) **God loves us in so many ways!**

## Options

1. During prayer activity, ask children to name things that show ways God loves us. Print children's responses on a large sheet of paper and place where parents can read it when children are dismissed.
2. During verse activity, when a child is pointed to, he or she names a person, another child in the room, a family member, a friend, etc. Repeat verse using the suggested person's name.

 

# Read-Aloud Story and Activity Center

## Collect

A copy of Story Picture 20 (pp. 45-46 from *Read-Aloud Story and Activity Book*) for each child and yourself, crayons or markers.

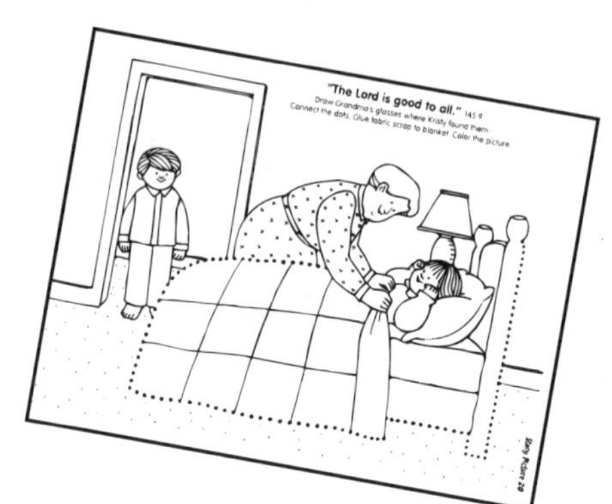


## Prepare

Color your copy of Story Picture 20.

## Do

**Listen to find out what this grandma is looking for.** Read story and show completed Story Picture 20. Distribute pictures. Use conversation suggestions in Let's Talk About the Story as children complete their pages.

# Kindergarten Puzzle Center

## Collect

Copies of Puzzles 39 and 40 (p. 85 and p. 87 from *The Big Book of Kindergarten Puzzles)* for each child, pencils, crayons or markers.

## Do

Children complete the puzzles and color pages.

# Instant Activities

These activities can be used at any time during this session: when children need a change of pace, to extend the session, or during transition time at the beginning or end of the session.

## Collect

*The Big Book of Instant Activities.*

## Do

Guide children to complete "God Made My Ears" and/or "Matchup" (p. 50 and/or p. 115 from *The Big Book of Instant Activities).*

Lesson 21

# Jesus Feeds 5,000

## Bible Story

Mark 6:30-44; John 6:1-14

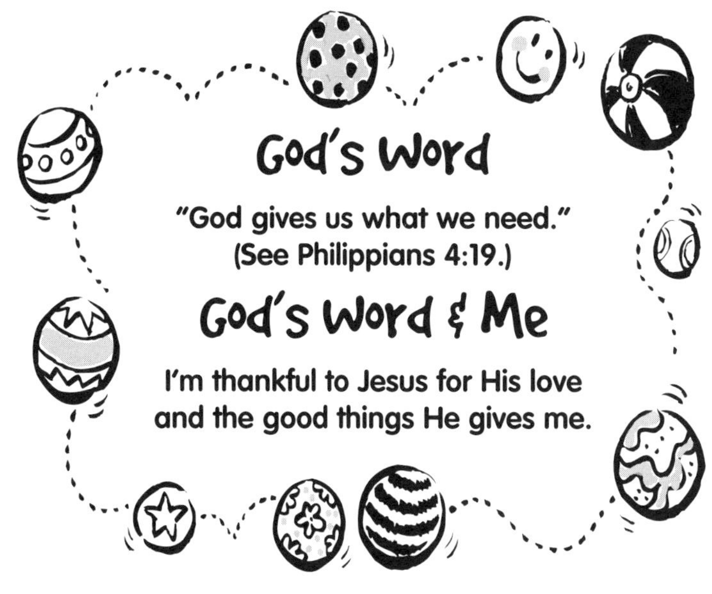
God's Word
"God gives us what we need."
(See Philippians 4:19.)
God's Word & Me
I'm thankful to Jesus for His love and the good things He gives me.

## Teacher's Devotional

We see Jesus' demonstrations of love through His miracles. It's delightful to note Jesus' few words in such situations. Rabbis of the day often talked around every side of a problem, citing this passage or that teacher. By comparison, Jesus was relatively silent. His deeds did much of the talking instead!

When a huge crowd of hungry people faced Jesus and His friends, Jesus asked Philip, "Where shall we buy bread for these people to eat?" Philip had no idea! He began to talk about the problem. There was the philosophical side: Why had these people not brought food? What made Jesus' friends responsible for them? Then there was the practical side: In this remote place, how could they find a source of food? And who was going to pay for it? Jesus must have smiled a bit at His friends' consternation. He knew what to do.

When Andrew brought a small boy with a lunch to Jesus, Jesus said the words that were needed: thanks to the Father who always provides. And quietly, beautifully, every hungry one was fed. Jesus knew the Father is the One to talk to first—and last!

## Teacher's Planning

1. Choose which centers you will provide and the order in which children will participate in them. For tips on schedule planning, see page 7.
2. Plan who will lead each center. For staffing tips and ideas, see page 21.

Lesson 21

# Active Game Center: Fish Walk

## Collect

Bible, *Shake It Up!* cassette/CD and player, construction paper, markers.

## Prepare

Draw a fish on one sheet of construction paper. Place sheets of paper on the floor to create a large circle or square. There should be one sheet for each child.

### God's Word

**"God gives us what we need."**
**(See Philippians 4:19.)**

### God's Word & Me

**I'm thankful to Jesus for His love and the good things He gives me.**

## Do

1. Play "Every Day" as children walk around the outside of the paper circle or square.
2. When you stop the music, children stand on the nearest paper. Child standing on the paper with the fish drawn on it tells something that God has given him or her.

## Talk About

- **In our Bible story, Jesus fed a lot of people with five small loaves of bread and two fish. Let's play a game and talk about the good things Jesus gives us!**
- **Our Bible tells us, "God gives us what we need." One of the things God gives us is good food to eat. Heather, what is your favorite food to eat? What other foods do you like to eat?**
- **I like to pray before I eat. Why do we pray before we eat? Praying is one way to thank Jesus for His love and the good things He gives us.** Pray briefly, **Thank You, God, for giving us what we need.**

## For Younger Children

Young children develop physical skills more quickly than verbal skills. Instead of telling something that God has given him or her, ask child standing on fish paper to point to his or her eyes, clothes, ears, nose, shoes, mouth, etc. **God gave us our eyes to see. God loves us and gives us many good things!**

## For Older Children

Children give examples of things God gives them, beginning with a specified letter of the alphabet. **Lucinda, what is something God gives you that begins with the letter *L*?**

# Art Center: Edible Jewelry

## Collect

Bible, yarn, scissors, measuring stick, circle-shaped dry cereal, transparent tape, paper, marker.

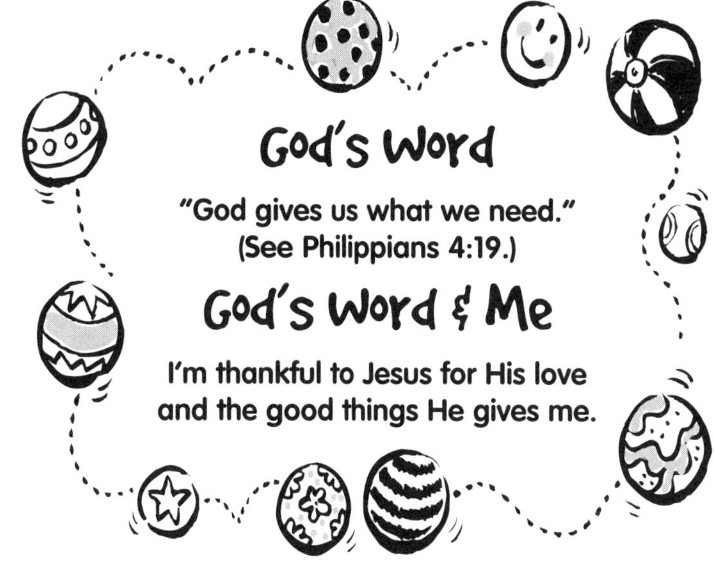
God's Word
"God gives us what we need."
(See Philippians 4:19.)
God's Word & Me
I'm thankful to Jesus for His love
and the good things He gives me.

## Prepare

Cut one 2- to 3-foot (.6- to .9-m) length of yarn for each child. Tie a piece of cereal to one end. Wrap the other end with tape for children to use as a needle.

Post a note alerting parents to the use of food in this activity. Also check registration forms for possible food allergies.

## Do

Children string cereal onto yarn. When each child is finished, tie necklace loosely around child's neck so that necklace can be lifted on and off over the child's head.

## Talk About

- **In today's Bible story, Jesus gave food to a lot of people. Let's make a necklace we can eat!**
- **When do you usually eat cereal? Tim, what are some other foods you eat at breakfast? I'm glad Jesus gives us lots of good things to eat!**
- **Our Bible says, "God gives us what we need." This means God gives us more than good food. He also gives us people to love and care for us. Who are some of the people God has given you? What is something they do to take care of you?**
- Pray briefly, **Thank You, God, for all the good things You give us.**

## For Younger Children

Provide white paper and markers. Instead of making necklaces, younger children draw on paper and snack on cereal.

## For Older Children

In addition to necklaces, older children make armbands. Help children tie armbands around wrists.

# Block Center: Picnic Blocks

## Collect

Bible, blocks, toy food, paper plates.

## Do

Children build a picnic table and then set the table with toy food and paper plates, enjoying a pretend picnic.

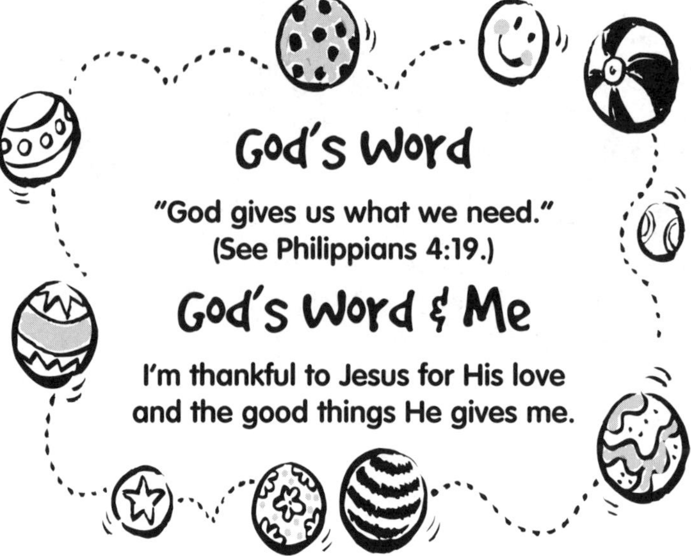
God's Word
"God gives us what we need."
(See Philippians 4:19.)
God's Word & Me
I'm thankful to Jesus for His love and the good things He gives me.

## Talk About

- **Our Bible story today tells about a very special picnic. A boy gave Jesus his lunch. He had two fish and five little loaves of bread. Jesus fed THOUSANDS of people from that little bit of food! Let's build a table and pretend to eat good food at a picnic!**
- **Denissa, do you ever eat a picnic lunch outside? What food do you like to have in your lunch?**
- **Patty, you can carry two blocks at the same time! Who made your strong hands? You are growing stronger and bigger. What good food do you like to eat? Jesus loves you and gives you good things to eat!**
- **Teddy, you have laid the ends of your blocks so that they make a straight side for our table. God gave you eyes to see where to lay the blocks. What are some other good things God has given you?**
- **Our Bible says, "God gives us what we need." God gives us good food and other things we need because He loves us!** Pray briefly, **Dear God, thank You for loving us. Thank You for giving us the good things we need.**

## For Younger Children

Use a large box for the picnic table, or set out a beach towel or blanket. Children use blocks to outline a path to the picnic area.

## For Older Children

In addition to a picnic table, children build other places where they eat. Provide fast-food bags and containers for children to use in pretending to eat lunch or dinner.

# Science Center: Smell Well

## Collect

Bible, a variety of scented food items (lemon, orange, chocolate, tuna, vinegar, spaghetti sauce, bubble gum, banana, spices, etc.), small film or dairy containers with lids, cotton balls.

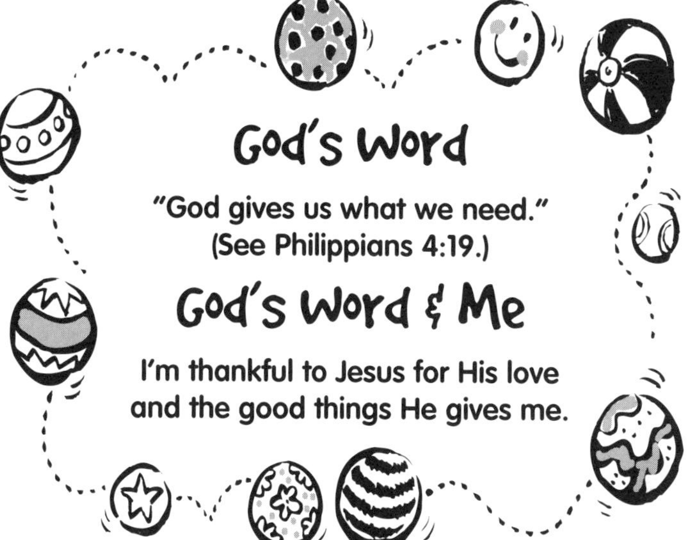
God's Word
"God gives us what we need."
(See Philippians 4:19.)
God's Word & Me
I'm thankful to Jesus for His love and the good things He gives me.

## Prepare

Place pieces of solid food items in containers. For liquids, place on cotton balls in containers and add a bit of liquid. Place lids on containers.

## Do

Children close their eyes. Take the lid off one container and hold for each child to sniff. After each child has had a turn, children guess what the scent is. (Note: With the lids on the containers, the smells can become very concentrated. After you remove the lid, wait a moment before asking children to sniff the contents.)

## Talk About

- **In today's Bible story, Jesus fed THOUSANDS of people with two fish and some bread. Let's smell some different kinds of food.**
- **Our Bible says, "God gives us what we need." We need food to grow strong and healthy. Terri, what did you eat for breakfast this morning? What are some other foods you like to eat?**
- **God made plants and animals so that we would have good food to eat. Why do you think God made food for us?** (God loves us.) Pray briefly, **Thank You, God, for loving us. Thank You for the food You give us.**

## For Younger Children

Children do not close their eyes or guess the contents of the containers. Young children will enjoy simply smelling the different containers.

## For Older Children

Write the names of the different smells on paper plates. After identifying the smells, children place the containers on the corresponding paper plate.

## Lesson 21 • Mark 6:30-44; John 6:1-14

# Bible Story Center

### Collect

Bible, Picture 33 from *Bible Story Pictures*.

## God's Word

**"God gives us what we need." (See Philippians 4:19.)**

## God's Word & Me

**I'm thankful to Jesus for His love and the good things He gives me.**

## Tell the Story

Use the pictured motions (keywords in bold) or show Picture 33. For older children, tell the version of the story on the back of Picture 33.

**What do you like to eat when you are really hungry? Listen to find out the way Jesus showed love to many hungry people.**

Jesus sat down to rest on a hillside one day. A big crowd of people—lots and lots and lots of people—came to see Him. The people wanted to hear Jesus talk about God. They listened to Jesus until supper time. Jesus knew these people were **hungry**. "Where can we buy food for all these people?" Jesus said to His friends.

"We don't have enough money to buy food for all these people!" one of Jesus' friends said.

Just then another friend said, "Here is a boy who has **five** little loaves of bread and **two** fish."

"But that's not enough food for all these people," another friend may have said.

Jesus picked up the little boy's lunch. He thanked God. He began to **break** the bread and fish into pieces. And the most surprising thing happened! Soon there were hundreds and hundreds of pieces of bread and fish! There was enough bread and fish to give to all those hungry people. Every person had plenty to eat.

When everybody had finished eating, Jesus' friends **gathered** up 12 baskets of leftover bread and fish. Jesus had made enough food out of that little boy's lunch to feed all those people—and still have lots of food left over! What a wonderful way for Jesus to show His love to people!

### God's Word & Me

**What good thing did Jesus give all the people?** (Food to eat.) **Jesus gives us good things, too. I'm thankful that Jesus loves us and gives us good things. What are some of the good things Jesus has given you?** (Food to eat. Clothes to wear. A house to live in. People who love me.)

# Worship Center

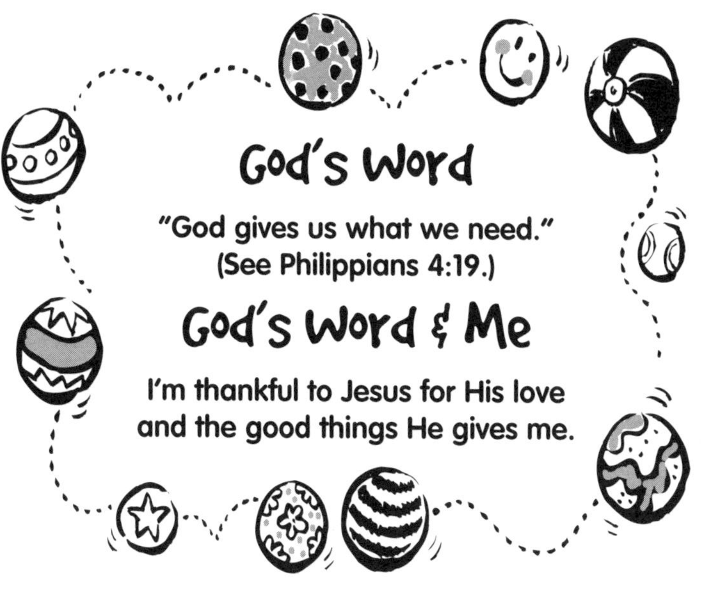
God's Word
"God gives us what we need."
(See Philippians 4:19.)
God's Word & Me
I'm thankful to Jesus for His love
and the good things He gives me.

## Collect

Bible, *Shake It Up!* songbook and cassette/CD and player, "Every Day" and "I Will Sing" word charts (pp. 27 and 30 in songbook).

## Sing to God

Play "Every Day." Invite children to sing along with you. **Let's sing a song about Jesus' love.** Lead children in singing song and doing suggested motions. **We can show our love for Jesus every day. I'm thankful to Jesus for His love and the good things He gives me.**

## Hear and Say God's Word

Holding your Bible open to Philippians 4:19, say verse aloud. **God gives us all the good things we need. God gives us these good things because He loves us. We love God, too!** Lead children in repeating the verse by echoing phrases after you: "God gives us/what we need." Point to children when it is their turn to speak. Repeat verse several times in this manner.

## Pray to God

As you say the following prayer, ask children to complete the sentence by naming their favorite foods: **We thank You, God, for loving us. We thank You for giving us __________. We love You. In Jesus' name, amen.**

## Sing to God

In closing the worship time, play "I Will Sing." Invite children to sing along with you and do suggested motions. **According to this song, when are some times we can sing? Because God always loves us, we can always show our love for Him, too!**

## Options

1. During the verse activity, vary the manner in which the first group speaks (singsong, loud, soft, whisper, low, high, etc.). Second group echoes in the same manner of speaking.
2. If you take a weekly offering during this worship time, explain to children that the money is used to help people learn about God. **Giving money is one way to thank God for His love and care for us.**

 

# Read-Aloud Story and Activity Center

## Collect

A copy of Story Picture 21 (pp. 47-48 from *Read-Aloud Story and Activity Book*) for each child and yourself, crayons or markers.

"God gives us what we need."

## Prepare

Color your copy of Story Picture 21.

## Do

**Listen to find out what a boy saw.** Read story and show completed Story Picture 21. Distribute pictures. Use conversation suggestions in Let's Talk About the Story as children complete their pages.

# Kindergarten Puzzle Center

## Collect

Copies of Puzzles 41 and 42 (p. 89 and p. 91 from *The Big Book of Kindergarten Puzzles)* for each child, pencils, crayons or markers.

## Do

Children complete the puzzles and color pages.

# Instant Activities

These activities can be used at any time during this session: when children need a change of pace, to extend the session, or during transition time at the beginning or end of the session.

## Collect

*The Big Book of Instant Activities.*

## Do

Guide children to complete "God Made My Hands" and/or "Popcorn Walk" (p. 94 and/or p. 119 from *The Big Book of Instant Activities).*

Lesson 22

# The Forgiving King

## Bible Story

Matthew 18:21-35

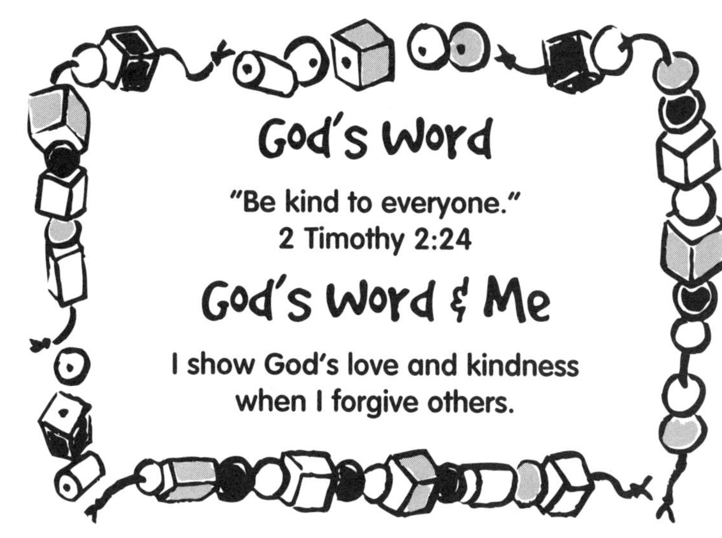
God's Word
"Be kind to everyone."
2 Timothy 2:24
God's Word & Me
I show God's love and kindness
when I forgive others.

## Teacher's Devotional

For many people, forgiveness is a sign of weakness. Revenge is considered healthy and even an accepted excuse for cruel acts. The common result of defending ourselves, however, is the creation of an expanding cycle of retaliation. According to the Bible, forgiveness is the only way to break a pattern of getting even.

The popular attitude of live and let live may seem to be a bit better than open revenge, but it's still only a poor substitute for forgiveness. The grudge remains; instead of healing, the pain of the situation is submerged. That can result in the lifelong crippling of both the spirit and the emotions.

As God's followers, however, we are able to teach forgiveness! These young ones we work with are just beginning to grasp what it means to forgive. Talk patiently with them about forgiving. Explain that to forgive others means we treat them kindly; we continue to care for them. Give children words to use in situations requiring forgiveness: "I'm sorry" and "I forgive you." And then, don't forget that your example of forgiveness is the most powerful teacher of all!

## Teacher's Planning

1. Choose which centers you will provide and the order in which children will participate in them. For tips on schedule planning, see page 7.
2. Plan who will lead each center. For staffing tips and ideas, see page 21.

# Active Game Center: Coin Hunt

## Collect

Bible, penny.

God's Word
"Be kind to everyone."
2 Timothy 2:24
God's Word & Me
I show God's love and kindness when I forgive others.

## Do

1. Children sit in a circle. Ask a volunteer to sit in the center and close his or her eyes, pretending to be the king.
2. Hand penny to a child in the circle. All children in the circle place their hands behind their backs.
3. Volunteer opens his or her eyes and guesses which child has the coin. If volunteer does not guess correctly within two or three guesses, ask child holding penny to stand up. Play resumes with child who held the penny becoming the new volunteer.

## Talk About

- **In our Bible story, a man borrowed a lot of money from a king. When the man could not pay it back, the king was kind and forgiving. Let's play a game with a coin and pretend the king is asking for our money.**
- **The king was kind. How has someone been kind to you at church today?**
- **Our Bible says, "Be kind to everyone."** Pray briefly, **Dear God, help us be kind.**
- **What should you do if a friend hits you? Instead of hitting back, you can tell that person "I don't like it when you hit me. Stop it."**

## For Younger Children

Instead of using an actual coin children might be tempted to put in their mouths, cut a circle from brown construction paper to serve as the penny.

## For Older Children

Volunteer does not close his or her eyes. In addition to penny, provide enough buttons so that every child has something to hold and pass. Play "Be Kind" or "Help Me Be Kind" from *Shake It Up!* cassette/CD as children pass buttons and penny around circle, keeping objects hidden in their fists. When you stop the music, volunteer guesses two or three times who has the penny.

# Art Center: Dough Money

## Collect

Bible, play dough, paper plates, marker, craft sticks.

## Do

1. Using approximately ¼ cup of dough, each child creates large flat coin shapes on paper plates. Write children's names on paper plates.
2. Children use craft sticks to etch designs in coins.

God's Word
"Be kind to everyone."
2 Timothy 2:24
God's Word & Me
I show God's love and kindness
when I forgive others.

## Talk About

- **In today's Bible story, a king forgave a man who owed him a lot of money. That meant the man didn't have to give the money back to the king. Let's make some large coins to remind us of our Bible story.**
- **Athena, what does it means to forgive? If Mikey was unkind to you, what would you do to forgive him? You can be kind to Mikey. You might say "I forgive you."**
- **Forgiving others is one way to show God's love. Victor, when is a time you showed God's love by forgiving someone?**
- Briefly tell about a time someone forgave you. **When we forgive others and they forgive us, we are showing God's love.**
- **Our Bible says, "Be kind to everyone." Forgiving others is a way to be kind to them.**

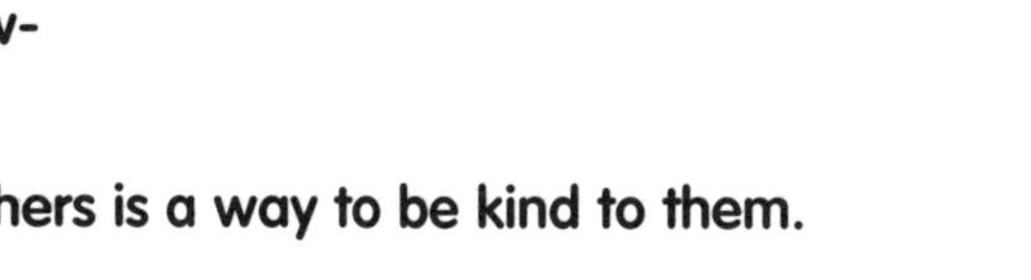

## For Younger Children

Instead of making and etching coins, children simply play with additional dough tools (rolling pins, plastic knives, etc.) as you discuss the lesson focus.

## For Older Children

Provide a variety of small objects that children can embed in dough to create designs on their coins: buttons, yarn, alphabet pasta, small stones, faux gems, etc.

Lesson 22

# Block Center: At the Races

## Collect

Bible, blocks, toy cars.

## Do

Children use blocks to create tracks on which to race toy cars.

### God's Word

**"Be kind to everyone."**
**2 Timothy 2:24**

### God's Word & Me

**I show God's love and kindness when I forgive others.**

## Talk About

- **Our Bible tells us, "Be kind to everyone." Let's look at how to be kind to others as we build racetracks for our cars.**
- **When we forgive our friends, we are being kind to them. Has anyone ever done an unkind thing to you?** Listen carefully to responses.

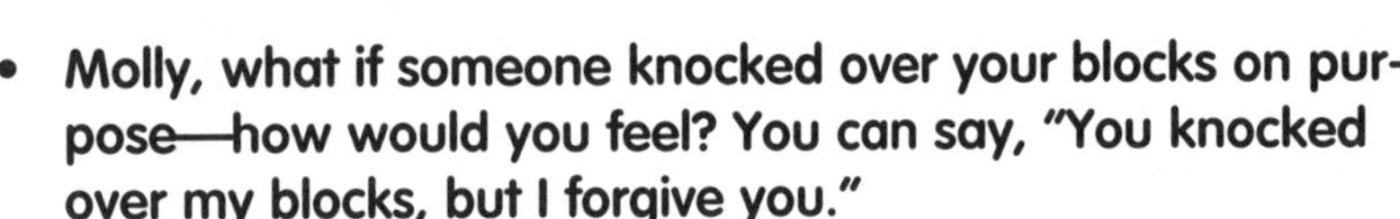

- **Molly, what if someone knocked over your blocks on purpose—how would you feel? You can say, "You knocked over my blocks, but I forgive you."**
- **To forgive means to be kind to someone who has been unkind. What could you say to show that you forgive someone?** ("I forgive you.")
- **We show God's love and kindness when we forgive others.** Pray briefly, **Dear God, help us to be kind and forgive others.**

## For Younger Children

Children use construction paper for additional features. For instance, blue construction paper becomes a lake to build a bridge across. Provide a variety of paper colors to stimulate imaginations.

## For Older Children

Children place a large piece of cardboard on a slant from a block wall to the floor. Then children race toy cars to see which goes down the ramp the fastest.

# Science Center: Cheesy Coins

## Collect

Bible, paper, marker, plastic drinking cups or circle-shaped cookie cutters, sliced cheese, bread.

## Prepare

Post a note alerting parents to the use of food in this activity. Also check registration forms for possible food allergies.

### God's Word

**"Be kind to everyone."**
**2 Timothy 2:24**

### God's Word & Me

**I show God's love and kindness when I forgive others.**

## Do

Children use drinking cups or cookie cutters to cut sliced cheese and bread into coin shapes. Children make coin-shaped sandwiches.

## Talk About

- **The man in our Bible story owed the king a LOT of money. But the king forgave the man. That means the man didn't have to pay back any of the money. Let's make some food shaped like a coin.**
- Children are probably not familiar with the concept of borrowing. **Jean, may I borrow the cookie cutter? When I'm through with it, what must I do? I must give it back to Jean.** Continue acting out situations to familiarize children with the concept.
- **Our Bible says, "Be kind to everyone." We can show God's love and kindness when we forgive others. To forgive means to be kind to someone who has been unkind to you.**
- **God is kind to us. We can be kind to others.** Pray briefly, **Dear God, help us to be kind to everyone.**

## For Younger Children

Children simply make cheese coins instead of sandwiches.

## For Older Children

In addition to cheese and bread for sandwiches, provide other circle-shaped foods for children: pickle slices, carrot slices, round crackers, cucumber slices, etc. Children select and stack their circle-shaped foods, counting each item as it is stacked.

## Lesson 22 • Matthew 18:21-35

# Bible Story Center

### Collect

Bible, Picture 35 from *Bible Story Pictures*.

God's Word
"Be kind to everyone."
2 Timothy 2:24
God's Word & Me
I show God's love and kindness
when I forgive others.

## Tell the Story

Use the pictured motions (keywords in bold) or show Picture 35. For older children, tell the version of the story on the back of Picture 35.

**Listen to what Jesus said we should do when someone has been unkind to us.**

Once there was a man who worked for a king. This man had asked the king for lots and lots of money and had promised that he would pay it all back. One day, the king told this man, "Pay back all the money you borrowed from me. And pay me right now!" But the man **didn't have** the money.

The king was angry. He called one of his helpers. The king told his helper, "Since this man cannot pay me, sell everything he has, and give that money to me!"

The man **fell** to his knees. "No! No!" the man cried. "I promise to pay you back!" The king felt sorry for this man. "I forgive you," said the king. "You do not have to pay back ANY of the money."

The man must have felt very happy that the king had been so kind. On the way home, the man saw a friend. The friend had borrowed just a LITTLE money from him. The man grabbed his friend and **shouted**, "Pay back the money you owe me! Pay it back right now." The friend got down on his knees. His friend begged, "Please wait for a little while. I promise to pay you back." But the man would NOT forgive his friend. The man had his friend put in jail.

The king heard that the man had been unkind to his friend. The king told the man to come to see him. The king said, "You are a mean person. I forgave you for ALL the money you owed me. But you would not forgive your friend for just a small amount of money." The king was very angry. He **sent** the unkind man to jail.

After the story, Jesus said, "God is like the king. God forgave you a lot. So God wants you to ALWAYS forgive other people."

### God's Word & Me

**What did the king do to be kind?** (He forgave the man who owed him money.) **We can show God's love and kindness when we forgive others. When is a time you could forgive someone?** (When people won't wait their turn. When someone takes a toy away. When someone says mean things.)

# Worship Center

God's Word
"Be kind to everyone."
2 Timothy 2:24
God's Word & Me
I show God's love and kindness
when I forgive others.

## Collect

Bible, *Shake It Up!* songbook and cassette/CD and player, "Be Kind" and "Help Me Be Kind" word charts (pp. 35 and 33 in songbook).

## Sing to God

Play "Be Kind." Invite children to sing along with you. **Let's sing a song about being kind!** Lead children in singing song and doing suggested motions. **This song tells us to be kind to everyone. I'm glad Jesus helps us be kind. Let's sing this song together again.**

## Hear and Say God's Word

Holding your Bible open to 2 Timothy 2:24, say verse aloud. **This verse tells us to be kind to everyone. We can show God's love and kindness when we forgive others.** Lead children in repeating the verse a few times. Then ask children to name people they know or types of people. (Friends, family members, neighbors, policemen, cowboys, etc.) Repeat the verse a few more times, replacing the word "everyone" with suggestions from the children.

## Pray to God

**Dear God, help us to remember to forgive people who are unkind to us. Help us to do kind things. In Jesus' name, amen.**

## Sing to God

In closing the worship time, play "Help Me Be Kind." Invite children to sing along with you and do suggested motions. **When are some times we can be kind?** Children respond with times mentioned in the song or their own ideas.

## Options

1. Add motion to the verse activity. Children line up and follow the first child in the line, walking around the classroom. Say verse aloud, replacing the word "everyone" with the name of the first child in the line. After his or her name is said, that child moves to the end of the line and the next child becomes the line leader. Repeat verse until every child has had a chance to be the line leader.
2. During prayer activity, share an age-appropriate example of a time you forgave someone who was unkind to you.

# Read-Aloud Story and Activity Center

## Collect

A copy of Story Picture 22 (pp. 49-50 from *Read-Aloud Story and Activity Book*) for each child and yourself, crayons or markers.

## Prepare

Color your copy of Story Picture 22.

## Do

**Listen to find out how these children solved a problem.** Read story and show completed Story Picture 22. Distribute pictures. Use conversation suggestions in Let's Talk About the Story as children complete their pages.

# Kindergarten Puzzle Center

## Collect

Copies of Puzzles 43 and 44 (p. 93 and p. 95 from *The Big Book of Kindergarten Puzzles)* for each child, pencils, crayons or markers.

## Do

Children complete the puzzles and color pages.

# Instant Activities

These activities can be used at any time during this session: when children need a change of pace, to extend the session, or during transition time at the beginning or end of the session.

## Collect

*The Big Book of Instant Activities.*

## Do

Guide children to complete "Rainbow Wear" and/or "Echo Game" (p. 70 and/or p. 94 from *The Big Book of Instant Activities).*

Lesson 23

# The Good Samaritan

## Bible Story

Luke 10:25-37

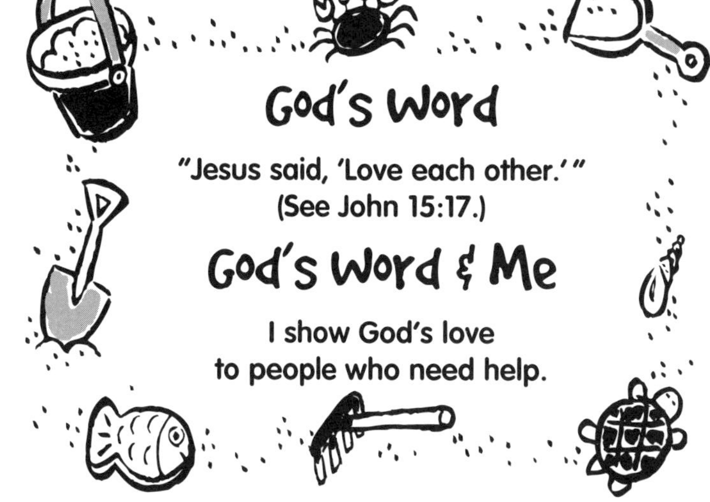

## God's Word

**"Jesus said, 'Love each other.'"**
**(See John 15:17.)**

## God's Word & Me

**I show God's love to people who need help.**

## Teacher's Devotional

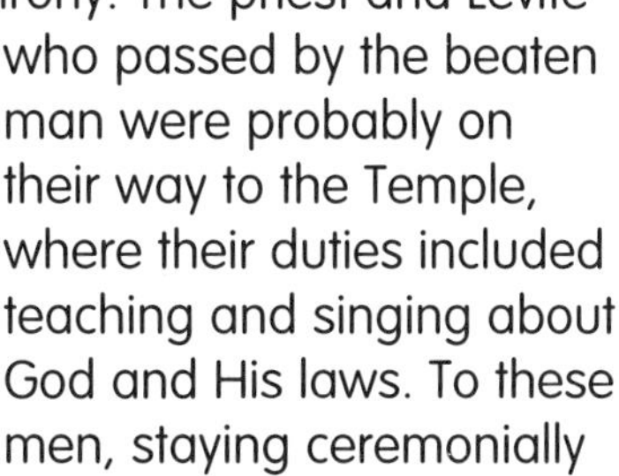

Jesus' story of love and compassion is also one of irony. The priest and Levite who passed by the beaten man were probably on their way to the Temple, where their duties included teaching and singing about God and His laws. To these men, staying ceremonially clean was more important than helping a wounded man! *After all,* they may have reasoned, *if he dies while I am touching him, I cannot serve God in the Temple!* Touching a dead body would have made them temporarily unfit for Temple duty.

Another irony is that prejudice against Samaritans ran high. Because they had intermarried with non-Jews, they were considered unclean half-breeds. The man who came along and helped from a heart of compassion was one who would be avoided or even hated by many Jews. Yet he did not take into account the wounded man's possible prejudice; he simply helped him!

Like the Samaritan, we must live out love especially to those who may not reciprocate. Never forget that when we were God's enemies (see Romans 5:10), Jesus acted in compassion that we might become His own family.

## Teacher's Planning

1. Choose which centers you will provide and the order in which children will participate in them. For tips on schedule planning, see page 7.
2. Plan who will lead each center. For staffing tips and ideas, see page 21.

Lesson 23

# Active Game Center: Ladder Walk

## Collect

Bible, masking tape.

## Prepare

Use masking tape to outline a ladder on the floor. (Note: Remove masking tape immediately after activity.)

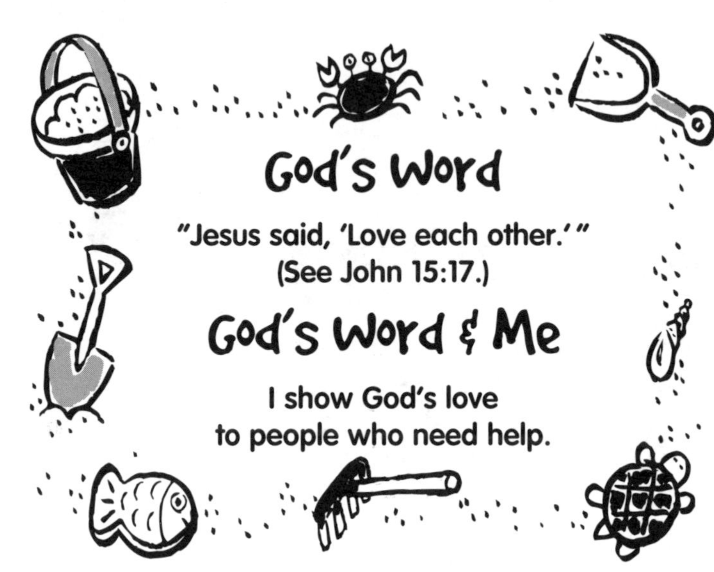
God's Word
"Jesus said, 'Love each other.'"
(See John 15:17.)
God's Word & Me
I show God's love
to people who need help.

## Do

Children take turns walking on the ladder in a variety of ways: in the spaces, on the rungs, up and down the sides, with giant steps, baby steps, jumping from space to space or rung to rung, heel to toe, etc.

## Talk About

- **Our Bible tells us, "Jesus said, 'Love each other.'" Let's play a game. We can show love by taking turns and waiting for each other.**
- **Janelle, I like the way you stood quietly while you waited for your turn. You really know about taking turns. When are some other times you have to wait? How can you show love while you are waiting?** (Don't be noisy. Don't push others. Sit quietly.)
- **What a good job Ryan is doing stepping on each ladder rung! You are big enough to step on each one carefully. I think you are big enough to know how to do kind things. How do you help your family at your house? When you go to the store?**

## For Younger Children

Taking turns may be hard for young children to do. Play the game with four to six children at a time, so waiting for turns won't take as long. If your class is very large, outline more than one ladder.

## For Older Children

As children step from rung to rung, they repeat the words of the Bible verse.

# Art Center: Mural Montage

## Collect

Bible, magazines or catalogs, scissors, 6-foot (1.8 m) sheet of butcher paper, markers, glue.

## Prepare

Cut out magazine or catalog pictures of people.

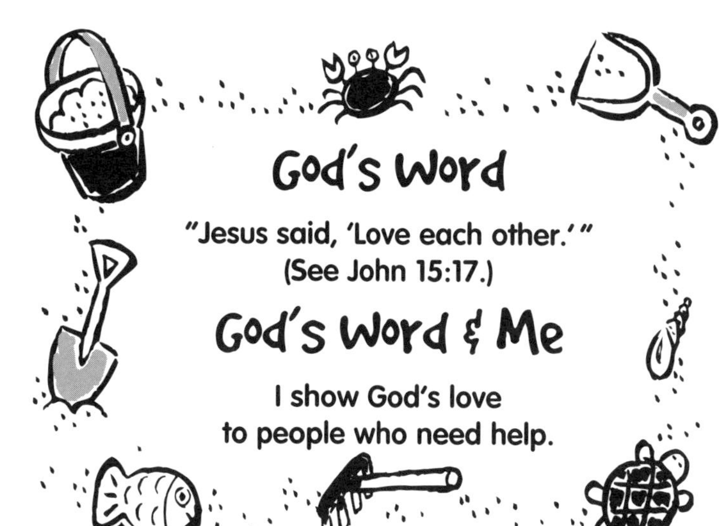
God's Word
"Jesus said, 'Love each other.'"
(See John 15:17.)
God's Word & Me
I show God's love
to people who need help.

## Do

1. Children trace each other's feet on the sheet of butcher paper. (Note: If you have a large class, provide more than one sheet of butcher paper.) Children decorate the traced feet.
2. Children select pictures of people of different ages from the magazines and glue pictures around the decorated feet.

## Talk About

- **Our Bible story today tells about a man who was hurt very badly. He waited and waited until somebody stopped to help him. Let's help each other make a picture and talk about ways to help others.**
- **Who in your family helps you? Who helps you have good food to eat? Who helps you get dressed?**
- **How do you help others? What can you do to help if someone falls down and is hurt? How can you help someone who is sad?**
- **Our Bible says, "Jesus said, 'Love each other.' " When we help others, we are showing God's love!** Pray briefly, **Dear God, help us find ways to help others.**

## For Younger Children

Trace the children's feet for them.

## For Older Children

Provide colored construction paper for children to trace feet on. Children cut out traced feet and glue them to the large paper along with the magazine pictures.

# Block Center: Block of Kindness

## Collect

Bible, blocks, toy vehicles (particularly service vehicles such as ambulances, police cars, tow trucks, fire trucks, etc.).

## God's Word

**"Jesus said, 'Love each other.'" (See John 15:17.)**

## God's Word & Me

**I show God's love to people who need help.**

## Do

Children build roads and places where people get help (service station, hospital, etc.). Children use toy vehicles on roads.

## Talk About

- **In our Bible story a man was hurt while on a trip. A kind man helped the man who was hurt. Let's build some roads and places where people help others.**
- **Andy, you were a kind friend when you gave Kristy the blocks she needed. You know how to show love.**
- **Jesse, I think Anne needs a longer block for her building. How could you help her? Jesse, you are a kind friend to give her one of yours. That's showing God's love!**
- **Our Bible tells us, "Jesus said, 'Love each other.'" Being kind and helping others are both ways to show love.**
- Pray briefly, **Dear God, thank You for loving us. Help us show love to each other.**

## For Younger Children

Building representational objects may be too advanced for your youngest children. Instead of building roads and places where people help others, children play freely with blocks. Use the conversation suggestions above to relate children's activities to lesson focus. Give smiles, hugs and pats on the shoulder to show your affection and interest. Your loving actions will demonstrate today's biblical principle to "Love each other."

## For Older Children

Instead of building roads and places where people can get help, children use blocks to build a road, boulders and an inn. Children use toy people to act out the story as you briefly retell the story events. Expect to retell the story several times during this activity.

# Science Center: Fingerprint Fun

## Collect

Bible, magnifying glass(es), white paper, washable ink pads; optional—premoistened towelettes.

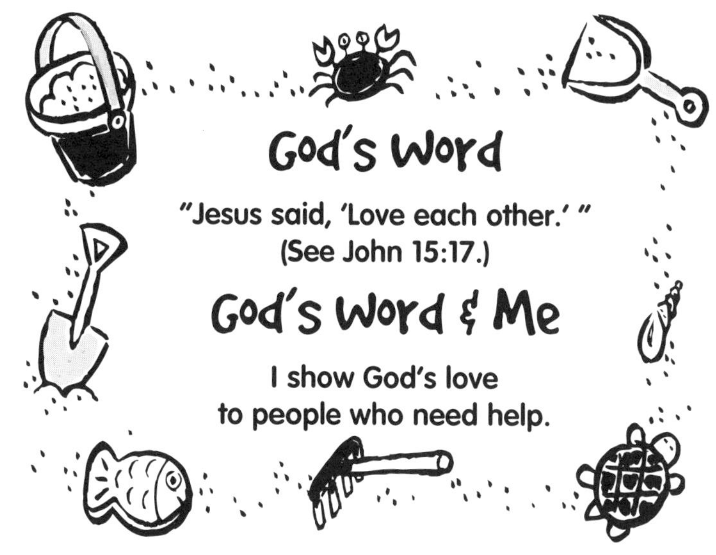
God's Word
"Jesus said, 'Love each other.' "
(See John 15:17.)
God's Word & Me
I show God's love
to people who need help.

## Do

1. Children use magnifying glass(es) to examine their fingertips. Then children make fingerprints on white paper by pressing fingers on ink pad and then on the paper. Children clean hands after making fingerprints. (Optional: If you do not have a sink nearby, distribute premoistened towelettes for children to use for clean up.)
2. Children use magnifying glass(es) to compare their fingerprints with other children's fingerprints.

## Talk About

- **In our Bible story a man helped someone in need. Often when we help, we use our hands! Let's take a closer look at our hands.**
- **How can you use your hands to help someone who has been hurt?** (Help them stand up. Put a bandage on a hurt.) **How can you use your hands to help people who are sad?** (Pat them on the back. Give them a hug.)
- **I use my hands at home to cook food to eat. What are some ways you use your hands to help at your house?**
- **Our Bible says, "Jesus said, 'Love each other.'" We show God's love when we help others.** Pray briefly, **Dear God, please help us show love to each other.**

## For Younger Children

Trace children's hands on sheets of paper. Children compare the size of their hands by placing hands on each other's tracings.

## For Older Children

Children make fingerprints in lines and curves to create letters or numbers.

 

# Bible Story Center

## Collect

Bible, Picture 36 from *Bible Story Pictures.*

## Tell the Story

Use the pictured motions (keywords in bold) or show Picture 36. For older children, tell the version of the story on the back of Picture 36.

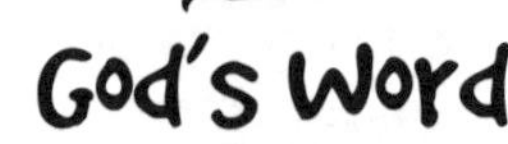


**"Jesus said, 'Love each other.' "**
**(See John 15:17.)**

### God's Word & Me

**I show God's love to people who need help.**

**I've seen many people being kind in our class today. Listen to a story Jesus told to find out which person showed love by being kind.**

A man was on a long trip. Suddenly some men jumped out from behind rocks. They beat up the man. They took away all his money and his clothes. Then they ran away. Ohhh! The man was badly **hurt**. He couldn't walk. He just lay by the side of the road.

Soon—**step**, step, step—someone was coming down the road! *Oh, maybe it's someone who will help me!* the man thought. The traveler came closer. The traveler saw the hurt man. But he didn't stop to help. The traveler stayed on the other side of the road and hurried on by! Ohhhh! The hurt man felt so sick.

Then—step, step, step—someone else was coming down the road! *Oh, surely this person will help me!* the hurt man thought. The second traveler came closer. The traveler saw the hurt man by the side of the road. But he **didn't** stop to help the hurt man. The traveler just looked at him and hurried on by! Ohhhhh! The hurt man felt worse.

Then—clippety-clop, clippety-clop—along came a traveler riding on a donkey. This man was a Samaritan. He was called a Samaritan because he came from a place called Samaria. *Maybe this traveler will help me,* the hurt man thought. When the Samaritan saw the hurt man he STOPPED! He climbed off his donkey. He bandaged the man's sore places. Then the traveler **lifted** the hurt man up on the donkey and took him to a an inn (a place like a motel). He put the hurt man in a room and cared for him all night.

Then Jesus said to the people listening to His story, "We should show love to every person who needs help."

## God's Word & Me

**Who helped the hurt man?** (The Samaritan.) **We show God's love when we help others. When is a time someone might need help at the park?** (When someone falls off the swings. When a ball rolls away.) **What is a way to help that person?** (Help that person stand up and get back on the swings. Roll the ball back to the person who was playing with it.)

# Worship Center

## Collect

Bible, *Shake It Up!* songbook and cassette/CD and player, "Help Me Be Kind" and "Be Kind" word charts (pp. 33 and 35 in songbook).

God's Word
"Jesus said, 'Love each other.' "
(See John 15:17.)
God's Word & Me
I show God's love
to people who need help.

## Sing to God

Play "Help Me Be Kind." Invite children to sing along with you. **Let's sing a song about being kind to each other.** Lead children in singing song and doing suggested motions. **God can help us be kind to others. We show God's love when we help others.**

## Hear and Say God's Word

Holding your Bible open to John 15:17, say verse aloud. **Jesus wants us to love each other. That means we should love the people in our families, the people at our church, our friends . . . everyone!** Children perform the following motions as they say the words of the verse: Cross arms over chest for "love;" point around room for "each other." Repeat several times.

## Pray to God

Volunteers say the following prayer: **Dear God, help me remember to love others. In Jesus' name, amen.**

## Sing to God

In closing the worship time, play "Be Kind." Invite children to sing along with you and do suggested motions. **According to this song, what does the Bible tells us to do?** (Be kind.)

## Options

1. With parents' permission, videotape children as they sing songs and do the motions. Show videotape at the end of the session as parents come in to pick up their children.
2. Add these additional signs while saying the verse: Alternately touch palms with middle fingers for the word "Jesus;" point to mouth for "said."

 

# Read-Aloud Story and Activity Center

## Collect

A copy of Story Picture 23 (pp. 51-52 from *Read-Aloud Story and Activity Book*) for each child and yourself, crayons or markers.

"Jesus said, 'Love each other.'"

## Prepare

Color your copy of Story Picture 23.

## Do

**Listen to find out what this lady is looking for.** Read story and show completed Story Picture 23. Distribute pictures. Use conversation suggestions in Let's Talk About the Story as children complete their pages.

# Kindergarten Puzzle Center

## Collect

Copies of Puzzles 45 and 46 (p. 97 and p. 99 from *The Big Book of Kindergarten Puzzles)* for each child, pencils, crayons or markers.

## Do

Children complete the puzzles and color pages.

# Instant Activities

These activities can be used at any time during this session: when children need a change of pace, to extend the session, or during transition time at the beginning or end of the session.

## Collect

*The Big Book of Instant Activities.*

## Do

Guide children to complete "Circle of Friends" and/or "Number Search" (p. 65 and/or p.117 from *The Big Book of Instant Activities).*

Lesson 24

# The Good Shepherd

## Bible Story

Luke 15:3-7

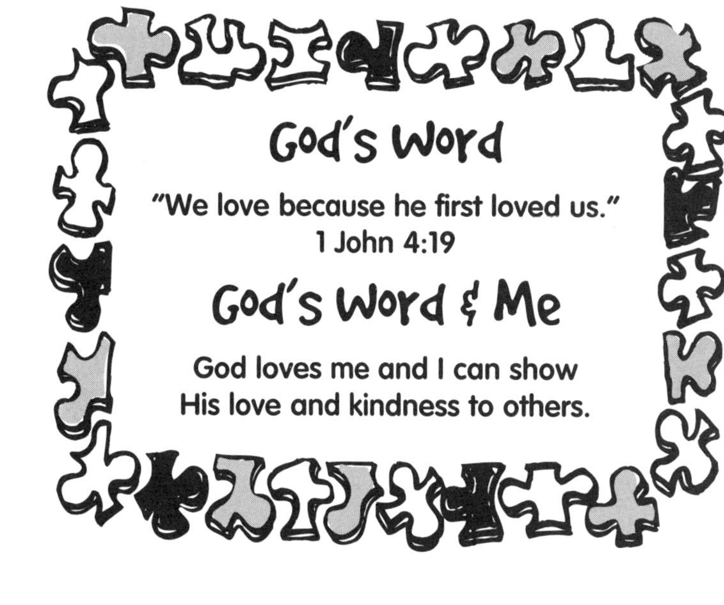
God's Word
"We love because he first loved us."
1 John 4:19
God's Word & Me
God loves me and I can show
His love and kindness to others.

## Teacher's Devotional

In Jesus' world, the relationship between sheep and shepherds was so much a part of life and so well understood that there was no more fitting illustration of God's love and care.

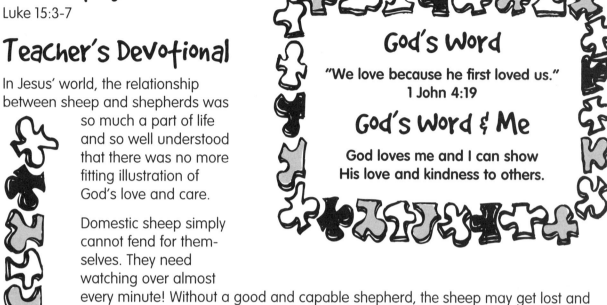

Domestic sheep simply cannot fend for themselves. They need watching over almost every minute! Without a good and capable shepherd, the sheep may get lost and eaten by predators, or they may eat too much or the wrong things and then sicken and die. We know that sheep are a great illustration of our relationship with Jesus because He said, "Apart from me you can do nothing" (John 15:5). And the better we know ourselves and our Lord, the more we know it's true!

This lesson focuses on how God's love for us can flow through us to others when we are kind. The shepherd's kindness is an example of how we can show love and be kind to others. Every child understands kindness, even if he or she can't put it into words. And your kindness is the key, for you are the living illustration of God's love and care to the little ones in your class. Shepherd them well!

## Teacher's Planning

1. Choose which centers you will provide and the order in which children will participate in them. For tips on schedule planning, see page 7.
2. Plan who will lead each center. For staffing tips and ideas, see page 21.

# Active Game Center: Balance Spoons

## Collect

Bible, cotton balls, cardboard box, plastic spoons.

God's Word
"We love because he first loved us."
1 John 4:19
God's Word & Me
God loves me and I can show
His love and kindness to others.

## Prepare

Hide cotton balls throughout room (on floor, desks, chairs, bookshelves, etc.). Open cardboard box and place in center of the activity area.

## Do

Distribute plastic spoons to children. Children find cotton balls and carry them on spoons and drop them in cardboard box. Continue until all the cotton balls are found or as time allows.

## Talk About

- **Our Bible story tells us of a shepherd who searched for one of his sheep when it was lost. The shepherd kept his sheep safe in a sheepfold at night. Let's play a game where we pretend to be shepherds, look for sheep and put them in their sheepfold.**
- **Why did the shepherd put his sheep in the sheepfold?** (To keep them safe.) **What are some of the things your mom and dad do to keep you safe?**
- **Lisa, you were careful not to bump Jimmy. You know how to show love and kindness! What are some other ways to show love to your friends?**
- **Our Bible says, "We love because he first loved us." God loves us! And we can show God's love and kindness to others!**

## For Younger Children

Instead of plastic spoons, children use paper cups to carry cotton balls.

## For Older Children

Children count aloud as cotton balls are added to the cardboard box. When the count reaches 20, begin counting again at one.

Lesson 24

# Art Center: Sheepish Faces

## Collect

Bible, white paper plates, markers, glue, cotton balls.

## Do

Children draw eyes, nose and mouths on plates and glue cotton balls to them to make sheep masks. Children hold up plates in front of their faces.

### God's Word

**"We love because he first loved us." 1 John 4:19**

### God's Word & Me

**God loves me and I can show His love and kindness to others.**

## Talk About

- **Our Bible story today tells about a kind shepherd who had LOTS and LOTS of sheep. Even though he had lots of sheep, the shepherd searched and searched to find the one that got lost. Let's make masks and pretend to be sheep.**
- **Why do sheep need a shepherd? What do you think the kind shepherd did to help his sheep?**
- **The shepherd loved his sheep. God loves us! God shows kindness to us. We can show God's love to others by being kind to them.**

- **Giving Adrienne more space was a kind thing to do, Kylee. You really know about being kind! What are some ways you can be kind when you play with others?** (Let someone else have the first turn. Share toys.)
- **Our Bible says, "We love because he first loved us." God's love shows us how to love others!** Pray briefly, **Dear God, thank You for loving us. Help us show Your love and kindness to others.**

## For Younger Children

Before class, draw eyes, nose and mouths on plates. Children glue cotton balls to sheep faces.

## For Older Children

Help children cut out eyes by beginning the eyehole. Use masking tape to attach a craft stick to the bottom of the mask for a handle.

# Block Center: Sheep in a Sheepfold

## Collect

Bible, blocks, green construction paper or towel, blue construction paper or towel, cotton balls.

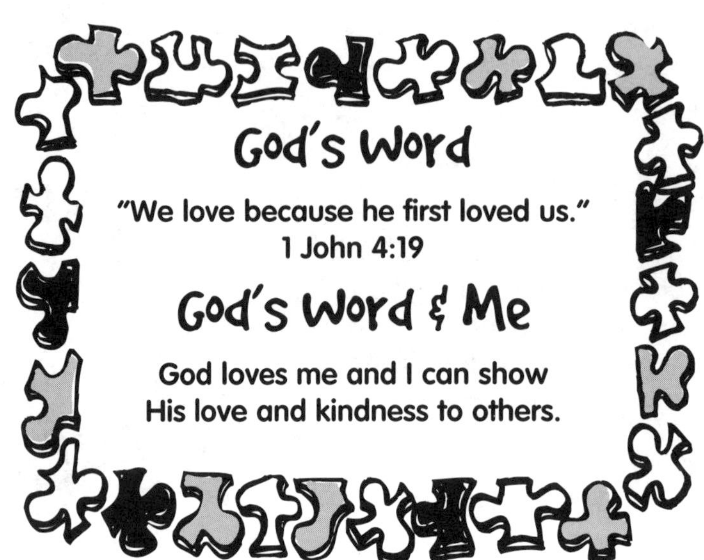
God's Word
"We love because he first loved us."
1 John 4:19
God's Word & Me
God loves me and I can show
His love and kindness to others.

## Do

1. Children use blocks to build sheepfold. Children place green construction paper or towel for a grassy field and blue construction paper or towel for water.
2. Children use cotton balls as sheep to act out caring for sheep.

## Talk About

- **Today's Bible story tells about a shepherd and the ways he cared for his sheep. Let's make a sheepfold and act out ways to care for sheep.**
- **Why do you think a shepherd often kept his sheep in a sheepfold at night? During the day, where would a shepherd need to take his sheep?** (To places with grass to eat and water to drink.)
- **Our Bible tells us, "We love because he first loved us." God loves us! And we can show God's love and kindness to others.**
- **When is it hard for you to be kind?** Pray briefly, **Dear God, help us to be kind and show love to others.**

### For Younger Children

Bring pictures of sheep from a magazine, website or encyclopedia, so children can see what sheep really look like. Bring in an object made from sheepskin (jacket, slippers, etc.) or wool (sweater, gloves, scarf, etc.) for children to touch.

### For Older Children

Hide one or more cotton balls in the classroom. Children act out story action by finding lost sheep and returning it or them to the sheepfold.

Lesson 24

# Science Center: Sorting Animals

## Collect

Bible, marker, two cardboard boxes, toy animals or magazine pictures of animals.

## Prepare

Label the boxes "Home" and "Other Places."

## Do

Show children the boxes you prepared. Children sort toy animals or pictures of animals according to where the animals live, placing animals in the appropriate boxes.

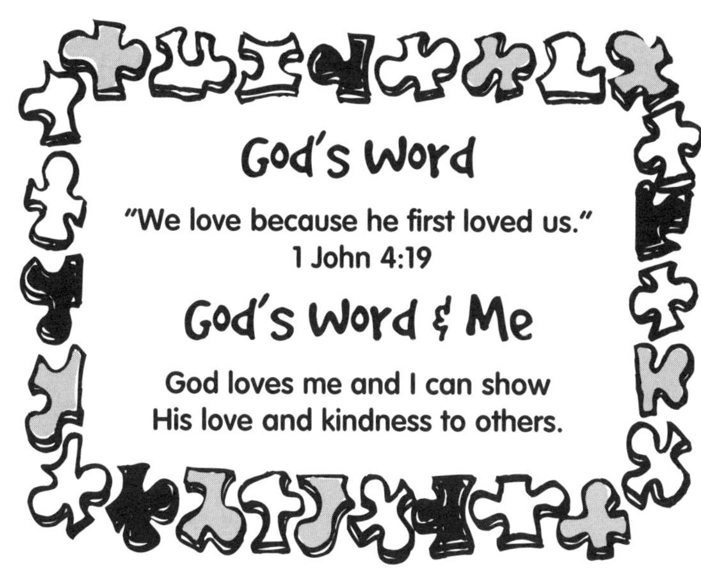
God's Word
"We love because he first loved us."
1 John 4:19
God's Word & Me
God loves me and I can show
His love and kindness to others.

## Talk About

- **Today's Bible story tells about a kind shepherd. His sheep lived outside and spent the night in a safe place called a sheepfold. Let's look at different animals and where they live.**
- **Some animals live in our homes. What are some of the animals that might live in our homes? Do we have any of those animals here?** Sort out animals kept as pets.
- **Where are some other places animals live? What animals live in a forest? In a zoo? On a farm?**
- **God wants us to show His love by being kind to others. Kelly, who are some people you can show kindness to?**
- **The shepherd in our Bible story was kind to and loved his sheep. God loves and cares for us. Our Bible says, "We love because he first loved us." We can love other people, because God loves us!**

HOME

## For Younger Children

Children play freely with boxes and toy animals or animal pictures. Use your conversation to tie children's activities to the lesson focus.

## For Older Children

Children draw pictures of other animals, such as pets they have in their homes or animals they have seen at zoos, to sort into the boxes.

 

# Bible Story Center

## Collect

Bible, Picture 37 from *Bible Story Pictures*.

## God's Word

**"We love because he first loved us."**
**1 John 4:19**

## God's Word & Me

**God loves me and I can show His love and kindness to others.**

## Tell the Story

Use the pictured motions (keywords in bold) or show Picture 37. For older children, tell the version of the story on the back of Picture 37.

**Have you ever lost something? What did you do to find it? Let's listen to a story Jesus told about a shepherd and a lost sheep.**

One day Jesus told this story. There was a shepherd who had one hundred sheep. (One hundred is many more than the number of children in our class!) This shepherd loved his sheep. He knew the name of each one of his sheep.

In the morning the kind shepherd **led** his sheep to the hillsides. The sheep ate the green grass on the hillside. And they drank cool water. The shepherd made sure the sheep had enough to eat and drink.

When nighttime came, the shepherd kept his sheep safe in a place called a sheepfold. This sheepfold was a big yard with a stone wall around it. There was no door, so the shepherd slept right across the doorway of the sheepfold. "No one can get into the sheepfold and hurt MY sheep!" he said.

One day the shepherd was counting his sheep. He **counted** 1 . . . 2 . . . 3 . . . all the way up to 98 . . . 99 but oh my! One sheep was GONE! Where was that sheep?

Right away the shepherd went out to find his lost sheep. He **looked** and looked. He called and called the sheep's name. Then the shepherd heard a BAAA! *What was that?* He wondered. Then he heard it again. BAAA! There was the lost sheep! The sheep had gotten lost and could not find its way home. The shepherd reached down and **lifted** the sheep onto his shoulders. All the way home, the kind shepherd carried the sheep. The shepherd was so happy to have found the lost sheep.

"God loves us like that," Jesus said. "He is glad when we choose to love and obey Him."

## God's Word & Me

**What did the shepherd do when he found his sheep?** (Lifted it to his shoulders and took the sheep home.) **Jesus told the story of the kind, loving shepherd to help us know that God is kind and loving, too. And God wants us to show love and kindness to each other. What is one way someone showed love to you today?**

# Worship Center

## Collect

Bible, *Shake It Up!* songbook and cassette/CD and player, "Be Kind" and "Help Me Be Kind" word charts (pp. 35 and 33 in songbook).

God's Word
"We love because he first loved us."
1 John 4:19
God's Word & Me
God loves me and I can show
His love and kindness to others.

## Sing to God

Play "Be Kind." Invite children to sing along with you. **Let's sing together!** Lead children in singing song and doing suggested motions. **Who are we supposed to be kind to?** (Everyone.)

## Hear and Say God's Word

Holding your Bible open to 1 John 4:19, say verse aloud. **This verse tells us that God loves us. God's love shows us how to love Him and how to love others.** Lead children in repeating verse as children clap their hands on each word. Vary the motion by having children stomp their feet, flap their arms, tap their heads, slap their knees, etc.

## Pray to God

Ask children to suggest ways to be kind. Pray, including several of their suggestions in the prayer.

## Sing to God

In closing the worship time, play "Help Me Be Kind." Invite children to sing along with you and do suggested motions. **We can be kind like Jesus! How can you be kind to others when you are building with blocks?**

## Options

1. During prayer activity, print children's suggestions of ways to be kind. Place list where parents can read it when they pick up their children.
2. If children give a weekly offering during this worship time, ask older children to help with the collection. Describe one or two ministries your church supports and explain to children how the money they are giving will be used to show God's love and kindness to others.

# Read-Aloud Story and Activity Center

## Collect

A copy of Story Picture 24 (pp. 53-54 from *Read-Aloud Story and Activity Book*) for each child and yourself, crayons or markers.

"We love because he first loved us."

## Prepare

Color your copy of Story Picture 24.

## Do

**Listen to find out what this boy is doing.** Read story and show completed Story Picture 24. Distribute pictures. Use conversation suggestions in Let's Talk About the Story as children complete their pages.

# Kindergarten Puzzle Center

## Collect

Copies of Puzzles 47 and 48 (p. 101 and p. 103 from *The Big Book of Kindergarten Puzzles)* for each child, pencils, crayons or markers.

## Do

Children complete the puzzles and color pages.

# Instant Activities

These activities can be used at any time during this session: when children need a change of pace, to extend the session, or during transition time at the beginning or end of the session.

## Collect

*The Big Book of Instant Activities.*

## Do

Guide children to complete "The Good Shepherd" and/or "Sticker Search" (p. 55 and/or p. 140 from *The Big Book of Instant Activities).*

Lesson 25

# The Loving Father

## Bible Story

Luke 15:11-24

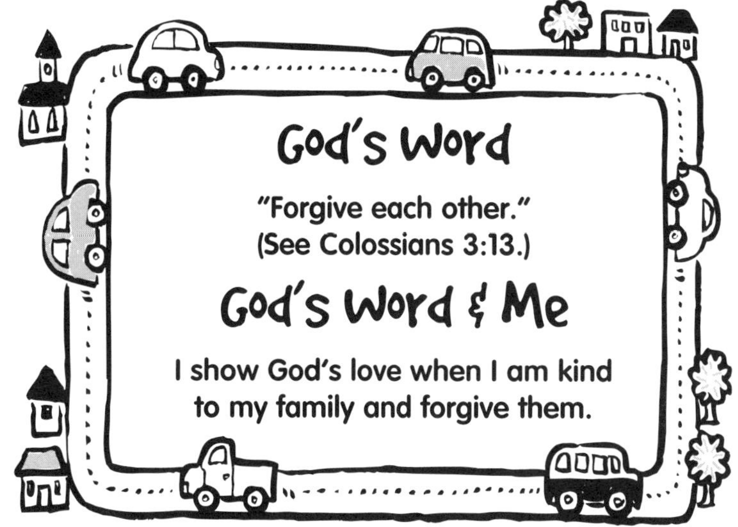

God's Word
"Forgive each other."
(See Colossians 3:13.)
God's Word & Me
I show God's love when I am kind to my family and forgive them.

## Teacher's Devotional

God graciously forgives us! He waits lovingly for us to repent. Although we may sometimes expect God to lose patience with us, His forgiveness knows no time limit. God is love and according to Psalm 103:3,4, He forgives all our sins and crowns us with love and compassion. God's forgiveness knows no end!

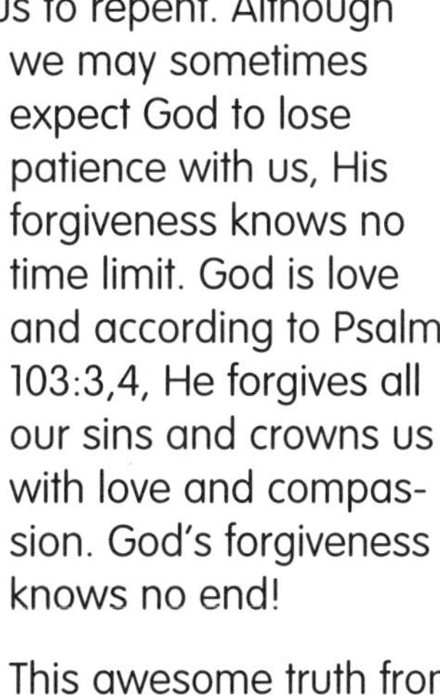

This awesome truth from God's Word can be difficult for a child to grasp due to limited experience and understanding. Understanding how to forgive and be forgiven comes partly with maturity. But concrete experiences such as being kind to others, even in difficult circumstances (something spills, a block tower gets knocked over, etc.), and then hearing the teacher say that this is a way to forgive, give a young child a foundation on which to build understanding.

Even more than that, our own expressions of forgiveness will vividly teach children. As we help young children understand what forgiveness is about, we must remember that the way we treat each child will show God's loving forgiveness to each one.

## Teacher's Planning

1. Choose which centers you will provide and the order in which children will participate in them. For tips on schedule planning, see page 7.
2. Plan who will lead each center. For staffing tips and ideas, see page 21.

 

# Active Game Center: Jumping High

## Collect

Bible; carpet squares, towels or construction paper; masking tape.

## Prepare

Place carpet squares, towels or sheets of construction paper in a line to form a continuous path. Tape to floor to prevent slipping. (Note: Remove tape immediately after activity.)

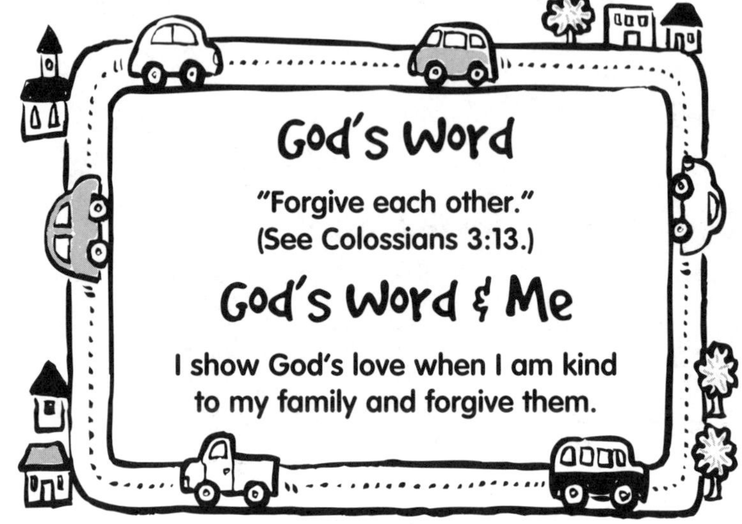
God's Word
"Forgive each other."
(See Colossians 3:13.)
God's Word & Me
I show God's love when I am kind to my family and forgive them.

## Do

Children jump from one carpet square, towel or sheet of paper to the next. Encourage children to jump using both feet. Some children may simply walk on the path while others may want to try crawling, hopping, walking backward or walking sideways on the path.

## Talk About

- **Today's Bible story is about a father who was glad his son came home. The father forgave his son for all the wrong things he had done. The father was so happy, he ran down the road to his son. Let's walk along our road!**
- **Our Bible says, "Forgive each other." Sometimes people do wrong things and ask to be forgiven. To forgive means to be kind to someone who has done wrong things or been unkind to you.**
- **Being kind is one way to show God's love to the people in our family. How can you be kind to your brothers and sisters when you go for a walk together? When you travel in the car?**

## For Younger Children

Children may hesitate to walk down the pretend road by themselves. Take each child by the hand and walk with them! Your personal involvement is the best way for children to experience kindness.

## For Older Children

Spread the carpet squares, towels or sheets of paper apart to make jumping more difficult. You can even place a small block between each carpet square, towel or paper for children to jump over.

Lesson 25

# Art Center: Heart Necklace

## Collect

Bible, poster board, measuring stick, markers, red construction paper, scissors, hole punch, string or yarn, transparent tape, plastic drinking straws.

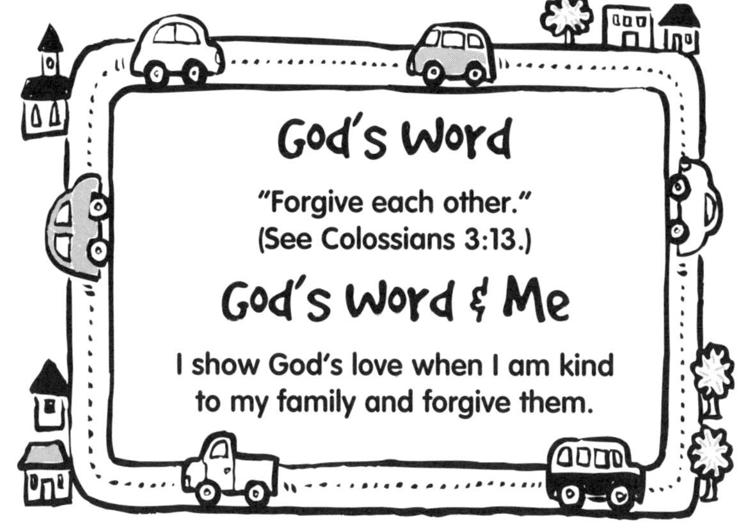
God's Word
"Forgive each other."
(See Colossians 3:13.)
God's Word & Me
I show God's love when I am kind to my family and forgive them.

## Prepare

Draw a heart approximately 3-inches (7.5-cm) wide on poster board and cut out. Use poster-board pattern to trace hearts on red construction paper. Cut out one heart for each child. Punch two holes at the top of each heart. Cut a 3-foot (.9-m) length of string or yarn for each child. Wrap a piece of transparent tape around one end of the string or yarn. Cut drinking straws into 2-inch (5-cm) pieces, about six for each child.

## Do

Children string pieces of drinking straws and heart onto string or yarn. Tie the ends together, so the necklaces fit loosely around children's necks.

## Talk About

- **Our Bible tells us, "Forgive each other." To forgive means to be kind to someone who has been unkind to you. Forgiving is one way to show love. Let's make necklaces to remind us to show God's love to our family.**
- **What are ways to show love to your family?** (Tell them you love them. Forgive them when they are unkind to us. Do kind things for them.)
- **How can you show kindness to people in your family when you are at the park? At the store? In your car?**

## For Younger Children

In addition to pieces of straws, children will enjoy making necklaces with pasta (wheels, ziti, rigatoni, etc.), beads (pony beads or larger), circle-shaped candies or circle-shaped cereal.

## For Older Children

Children trace and cut out their own heart shapes. Children also cut drinking straws into pieces of various lengths to use in making their necklaces.

# Block Center: City Blocks

## Collect

Bible, blocks, toy animals, toy people.

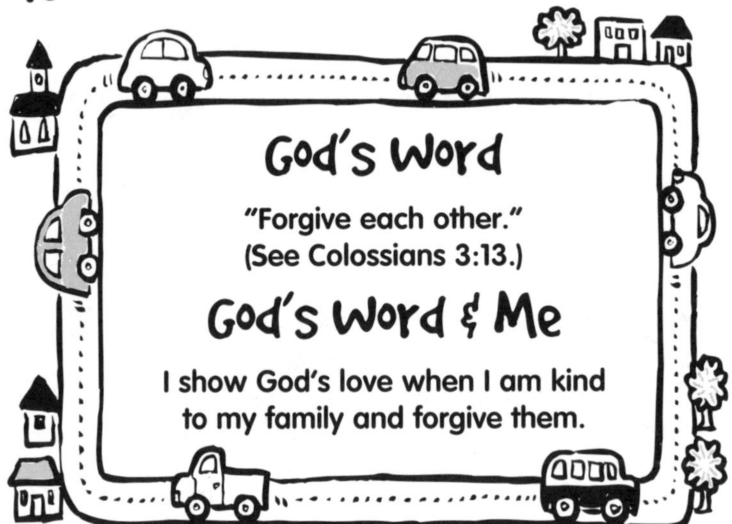
God's Word
"Forgive each other."
(See Colossians 3:13.)
God's Word & Me
I show God's love when I am kind
to my family and forgive them.

## Do

1. Children outline a long block road from one side of activity area to the other.
2. Children use toy animals and blocks to create a farm at one end of the road. Children use toy people and blocks to create a city at the other end of the road.

## Talk About

- **In our Bible story a man's son left his family and their farm. The son walked a long, long way to a faraway city. Let's build a long road!**
- **After a while, the son began to miss his father and wanted to go home again. When the son got home, his father forgave him and gave him lots of good things! What are some of the good things your parents give to you?**
- **Giving good things is one way to be kind to the people in your family. What are some other ways to be kind to the people in your family?**
- **Our Bible says, "Forgive each other." To forgive means to be kind, even when someone does wrong things or is unkind to us. We show God's love when we forgive the people in our families!**
- Pray briefly, **Dear God, help us show Your love. Help us to be kind to our families and forgive them.**

## For Younger Children

Instead of building a farm and a city, children outline a long road and walk along it.

## For Older Children

Children act out the Bible story as you describe the events. Be prepared to repeat the story several times as children come and go from the Block Center.

Lesson 25

# Science Center: Nature Families

## Collect

Bible, construction paper, scissors, nature objects (sticks, leaves, rocks, pinecones, etc.), glue, paper plates, markers.

## Prepare

Cut construction paper into a variety of geometric shapes (circles, squares, triangles, etc.).

### God's Word

**"Forgive each other."**
**(See Colossians 3:13.)**

### God's Word & Me

**I show God's love when I am kind to my family and forgive them.**

## Do

1. Each child glues nature objects and construction-paper shapes to paper plates to make a person representing someone in his or her family. Demonstrate to children how sticks, rocks and leaves can be used to form bodies. Faces can be drawn on construction-paper circles and then glued down. Feet can be made by gluing on construction-paper triangles.
2. Children may make more than one person as time permits. Print each family member's name on the paper plate.

## Talk About

- **Our Bible story today is about a father and his sons. The father was kind to his sons. He even forgave one of his sons and gave him good things. We show God's love when we are kind to our families. Let's use nature objects to make some of the people in our families.**
- **Our Bible tells us, "Forgive each other." To forgive means to stop being angry at someone who has been unkind to you. Forgiving is one way to be kind.**
- **When might it be hard to be kind to people in your family?** (When a brother or sister says mean things or does mean things.) Pray briefly, **Dear God, help us to be kind to our families and forgive them.**

## For Younger Children

Children randomly glue nature objects to paper plates to make collages to give family members.

## For Older Children

Children cut lengths of yarn and glue on for hair.

# Bible Story Center

## Collect

Bible, Picture 38 from *Bible Story Pictures.*

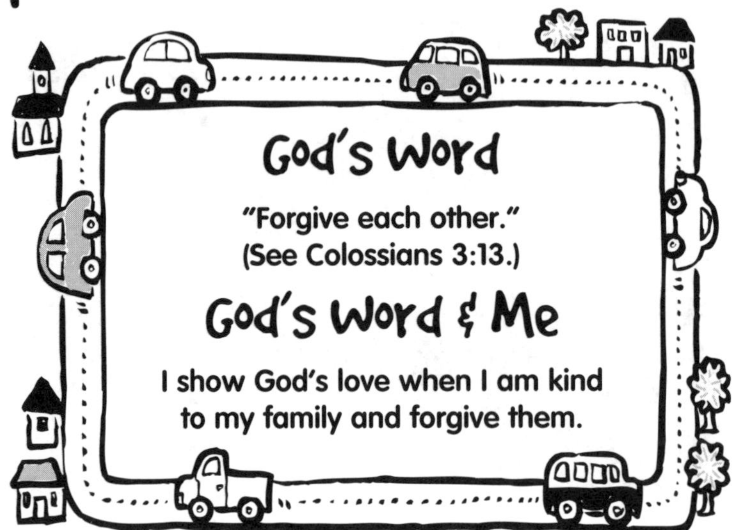
God's Word
"Forgive each other."
(See Colossians 3:13.)
God's Word & Me
I show God's love when I am kind to my family and forgive them.

## Tell the Story

Use the pictured motions (keywords in bold) or show Picture 38. For older children tell the version of the story on the back of Picture 38.

**How many people are in your family? Let's listen to a story Jesus told of a man who went far from his home and family.**

Once there was a father with two sons. They lived on a big farm. The father loved his sons. He took good care of them. One day a son said, "Father, you promised to give me **money** some day. I want it NOW!" So the father gave his son the money.

The son wanted to live far away from his family. The son packed his clothes and began walking away. The father felt sad. While the son was gone, the father waited and waited for the son to come home.

When the son got to a new place, he spent his money until it was all **gone**. His nice clothes became dirty and torn. Soon he didn't have enough food to eat.

The son went to work feeding some pigs. As he worked, the son thought, *Even the men who work for my father have food to eat.* The son decided, *I'll go back home!*

So the son began **walking** home. He walked and walked and walked. Soon he saw his father's farm. When he was almost there, he could see someone running down the road toward him! It was his FATHER running to meet him!

"Oh, Father," the son said, "I **spent** ALL the money you gave me. I am very sorry." The father loved his son and was glad he had come back home. The father gave him new clothes and other good things. How glad the son was that his father loved him and forgave him.

Jesus told this story to help us learn that God is loving and kind, just like the father in the story. We can show God's love by being kind and forgiving to each other.

## God's Word & Me

**What did the father do when his son came home?** (Showed him love and gave him good things.) **We show God's love when we are kind to the people in our families and forgive them. What is a way to show kindness to someone in your family?** (Let a brother or sister go first playing a game. Help Mom set the table for dinner.)

# Worship Center

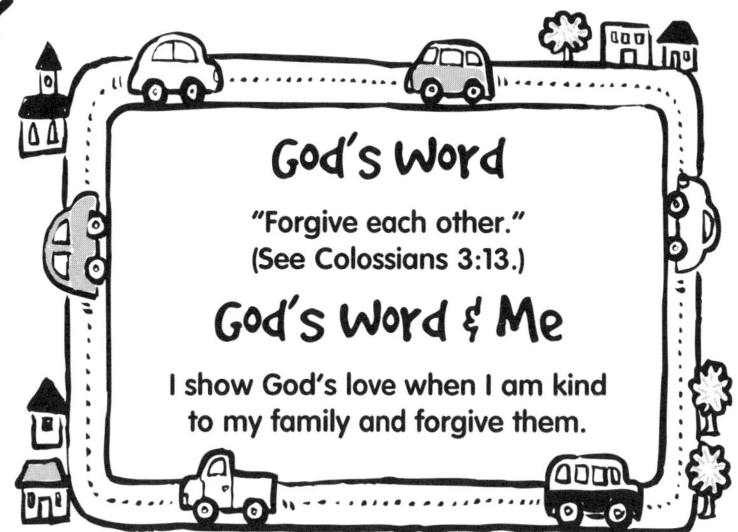
God's Word
"Forgive each other."
(See Colossians 3:13.)
God's Word & Me
I show God's love when I am kind to my family and forgive them.

## Collect

Bible, *Shake It Up!* songbook and cassette/CD and player, "Be Kind" and "Help Me Be Kind" word charts (pp. 35 and 33 in songbook).

## Sing to God

Play "Be Kind." Invite children to sing along with you. **Let's sing together!** Lead children in singing song and doing suggested motions. **When can we be kind?** Children respond with times mentioned in song or their own ideas.

## Hear and Say God's Word

Holding your Bible open to Colossians 3:13, say verse aloud. **Has anyone ever done an unkind thing to you?** Listen carefully to children's responses. **To forgive means to be kind to someone who has been unkind to you. You might say "I forgive you."** Lead children in repeating the verse while doing the following motions: "Forgive," stomp one foot on each syllable; "each," clap hands; "other," wiggle fingers in air. Repeat verse and motions several times.

## Pray to God

Lead children in repeating the following prayer, phrase by phrase: **Dear God, . . . help us to remember . . . to forgive people . . . who are unkind to us. . . . Help us to do kind things. . . . In Jesus' name, amen.**

## Sing to God

In closing the worship time, play "Help Me Be Kind." Invite children to sing along with you and do suggested motions. **Who helps us to be kind?** (God.)

## Options

1. Provide rhythm instruments for children to use while singing "Be Kind" and "Help Me Be Kind."
2. During prayer activity, ask children to name kind things they can do for others. Volunteers pray briefly, asking God for help in doing those things.

# Read-Aloud Story and Activity Center

## Collect

A copy of Story Picture 25 (pp. 55-56 from *Read-Aloud Story and Activity Book*) for each child and yourself, crayons or markers.

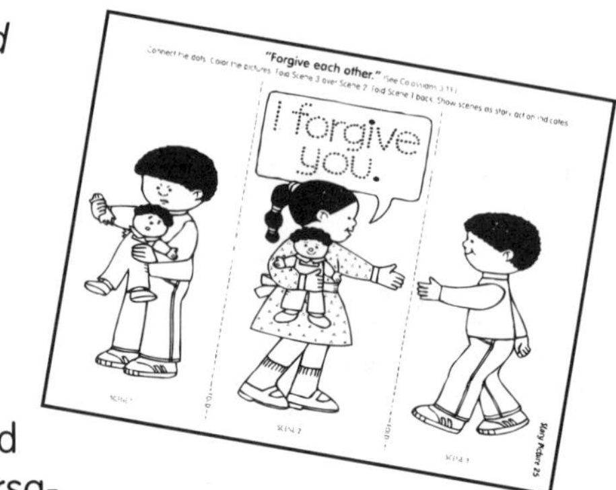


## Prepare

Color your copy of Story Picture 25.

## Do

**Listen to find out what happened in this family.** Read story and show completed Story Picture 25. Distribute pictures. Use conversation suggestions in Let's Talk About the Story as children complete their pages.

# Kindergarten Puzzle Center

## Collect

Copies of Puzzles 49 and 50 (p. 105 and p. 107 from *The Big Book of Kindergarten Puzzles)* for each child, pencils, crayons or markers.

## Do

Children complete the puzzles and color pages.

# Instant Activities

These activities can be used at any time during this session: when children need a change of pace, to extend the session, or during transition time at the beginning or end of the session.

## Collect

*The Big Book of Instant Activities.*

## Do

Guide children to complete "Mirror Me" and/or "Two Little Hands" (p. 116 and/or p. 104 from *The Big Book of Instant Activities)*.

# The Greatest of All

## Bible Story

Mark 9:33-37; Luke 9:46-48

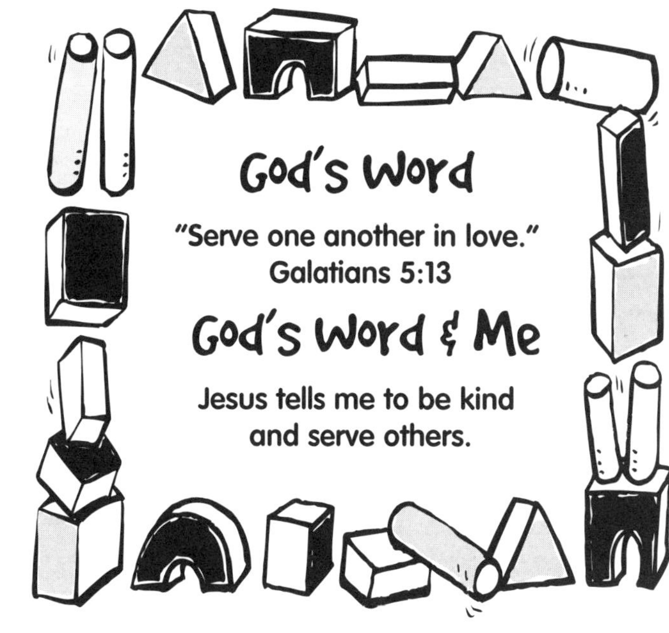
God's Word
"Serve one another in love."
Galatians 5:13
God's Word & Me
Jesus tells me to be kind
and serve others.

## Teacher's Devotional

When the question of greatness came up among the disciples, Jesus didn't even need to hear their mutterings. He knew what they were thinking: Here they were, in on the ground floor of Jesus' organization but unsure as to how to progress to a position of greatness. Perhaps their mental model was much like ours today: perform well and impress the boss. It's a familiar agenda!

Jesus' answer to His followers' struggling thoughts was to set a small boy next to Him. Here was the perfect example of the greatest man in His organization! This child had no performance to commend him; he didn't know how to impress anybody. Yet this was the very one Jesus pointed to as the most likely to succeed in His kingdom! Jesus continued, "Whoever welcomes this little child in my name welcomes me" (Luke 9:48).

Next time a little child hangs on your leg and wails, let Jesus' words transform the way you think about the situation. *Lord, help me remember I am welcoming You!* As you get down on that child's level and let the child know he or she is loved, Jesus is honored and welcomed. By your actions, you are identifying with Jesus, declaring that every little child is valuable!

## Teacher's Planning

1. Choose which centers you will provide and the order in which children will participate in them. For tips on schedule planning, see page 7.
2. Plan who will lead each center. For staffing tips and ideas, see page 21.

 

# Active Game Center: Toss It!

## Collect

Bible, magazine pictures of people (grandparents, parents, brothers, friends, babies, etc.), scissors, masking tape, beanbag.

## Prepare

Cut out pictures and place on the floor in a grid pattern. Place a loop of masking tape on the backs of pictures to hold them down.

### God's Word

**"Serve one another in love."**
**Galatians 5:13**

### God's Word & Me

**Jesus tells me to be kind and serve others.**

## Do

Children take turns tossing beanbag toward picture grid. If the beanbag lands on a picture, the child who tossed the beanbag tells one way to be kind to the person in the picture. Children continue taking turns and tossing beanbag as time allows.

## Talk About

- **In today's Bible story, Jesus' friends learned it is good to serve others. Serving others means being kind and helpful to others. Let's play a game and talk about ways we can serve others!**
- **These pictures are of different people. Whose picture do you see here?** (A grandma, a mother, a baby, a friend, etc.)

- **What are some ways you can be kind and serve your mommy?** (Obey what she says. Say kind words to her. Help her at bath time.) Repeat for all the different people shown in the pictures.
- **Our Bible says, "Serve one another in love."** Pray briefly, **Dear God, help us to serve others.**

## For Younger Children

Younger children may not be able to verbalize ways to be kind to others. Help the child identify the type of person in the picture and tell ways to be kind to that person. **Yes, Scott, that is a grandmother. We can be kind to our grandmothers. We can say "I love you, Grandma!"**

## For Older Children

To increase the challenge for older children, ask them to stand farther from the grid; or children may vary the way they toss the beanbag: over their shoulders, through their legs, etc.

# Art Center: Chalk Art

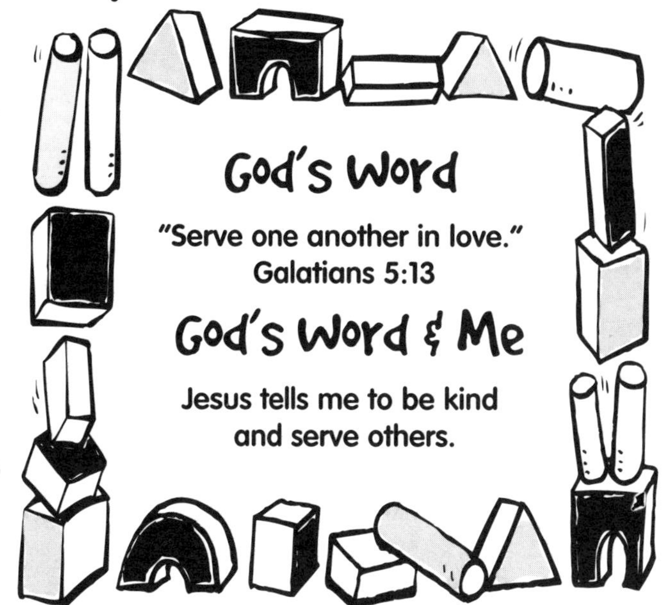
God's Word
"Serve one another in love."
Galatians 5:13
God's Word & Me
Jesus tells me to be kind and serve others.

## Collect

Bible, colored chalk, small container of water, construction paper.

## Prepare

Place chalk in water container to soak for several minutes before activity. Soaking the chalk enhances the drawings' colors.

## Do

Children roll up long sleeves and use chalk to create drawings of people. As children draw, talk about ways people can be kind and helpful.

## Talk About

- **Our Bible tells us, "Serve one another in love." Serving others means being kind and helpful to others. Let's draw people and talk about ways to serve others.**
- **Nathan, who are you drawing? What is one way you can help and be kind to your brother?**
- **Lauren, letting Reeda use the blue chalk was a kind thing to do. You are a kind friend. Jesus tells us to be kind and serve others.**
- **Joshua, thank you for putting your chalk back in the water. You know how to help and serve!**
- **Kelly, who are you drawing? What are some kind things you can do when playing with your friend Emily?** (Letting her have the first turn on the slide. Sharing toys and games.)

## For Younger Children

Young children have difficulty drawing representational objects. Ask children to simply create drawings of their choosing. As each child finishes, don't try to guess what they drew, simply say, **Tell me about your drawing.**

## For Older Children

Children dictate sentences about their drawings. Print the sentences on their papers.

Lesson 26

# Block Center: Service with a Smile

## Collect

Bible, blocks, toy people.

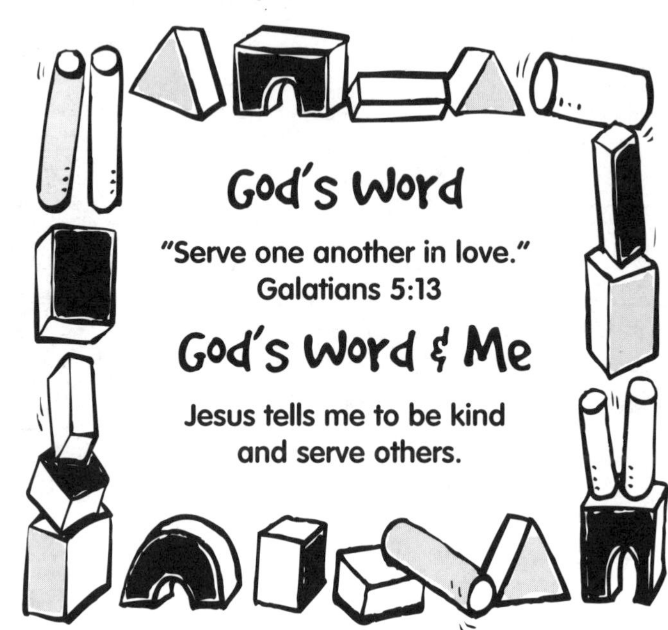
God's Word
"Serve one another in love."
Galatians 5:13
God's Word & Me
Jesus tells me to be kind
and serve others.

## Do

Children construct buildings and places of their choice. Then children use toy people to act out different situations in which people can be kind and serve others in those places.

## Talk About

- **In our Bible story today, Jesus said that God wants us to serve others. Let's build some of our favorite places and talk about ways to be kind and serve others!**
- **What kind of building are you making, Darryl? Who are some of the people who work in a restaurant? How do they help others? Being kind and helping are both ways to serve others.**
- **Who are the people in the house you are making, Donna? Let's pretend visitors are coming to the house. How will the people who live in the house get ready for visitors? Fixing food for friends is one way to serve others!**
- **Our Bible tells us, "Serve one another in love."** Pray briefly, **Dear God, help us to serve others.**

## For Younger Children

Young children will not be able to use blocks to make buildings and places. Provide baskets or buckets for children to use in block play. Children will enjoy filling their baskets or buckets with blocks and carrying them to the other side of the activity area. Use your conversation to connect children's activities to the lesson focus. **Lorie, thank you for handing Julie that block. You are kind. I see lots of kind children in our class today.**

## For Older Children

Provide pieces of cardboard so that children can construct two-story buildings.

Lesson 26

# Science Center: Measure Up!

## Collect

Bible, construction paper, markers.

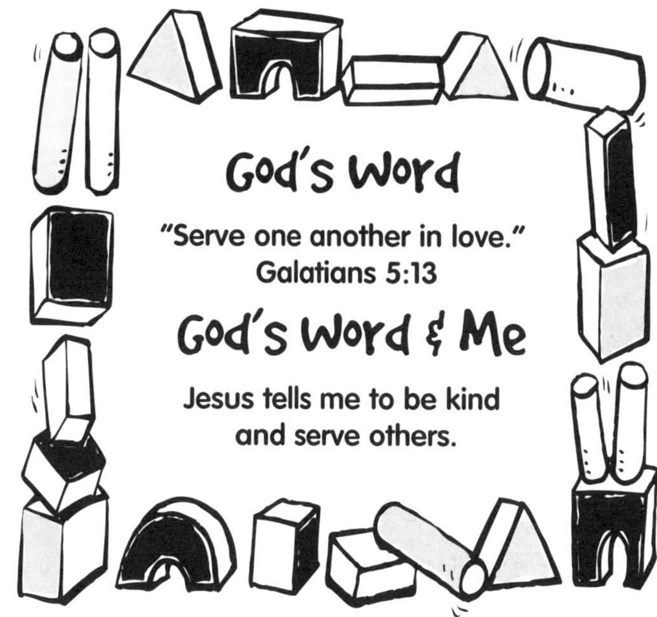
God's Word
"Serve one another in love."
Galatians 5:13
God's Word & Me
Jesus tells me to be kind
and serve others.

## Do

Trace each child's hand or foot on a sheet of construction paper. Children use hand- or footprint to find an object in the room that is as long as their hand or foot. Then children find objects that are longer or shorter.

## Talk About

- **In today's Bible story, Jesus' friends wanted to know who was the most important. But Jesus told them you don't have to be a grown-up to be important to God. Even little children can do what God wants. Let's find some things in our room and see if they are bigger or smaller than our hands or feet.**
- **Some people have big hands and some people have small hands. But all of us can use our hands to help others.**
- **Who did you help this morning at breakfast? Who did you help here at church? You showed love by serving them!**
- **Kirt, who are some of the people you love? What are some ways you can help your mommy at home?**
- **Our Bible says, "Serve one another in love." What does it mean to serve others? Serving others means helping them. It means doing good things for others.** Pray briefly, **Dear God, help us to be kind and serve others.**

## For Younger Children

Children lay objects such as crayons or blocks in a row that is as long as their arms or legs.

## For Older Children

Children use measuring sticks to find objects using exact measures. **Martin, find an object that is longer than 5 inches (12.5 cm).**

# Bible Story Center

## Collect

Bible, Picture 34 from *Bible Story Pictures.*

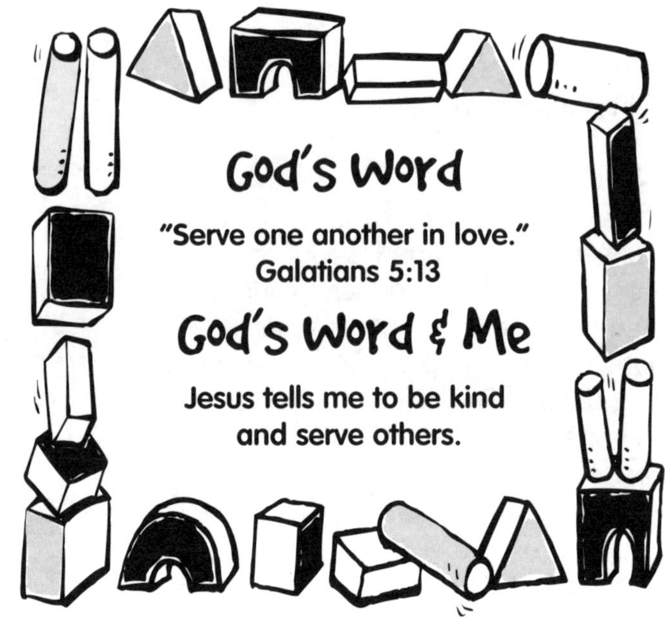
God's Word
"Serve one another in love."
Galatians 5:13
God's Word & Me
Jesus tells me to be kind
and serve others.

## Tell the Story

Use the pictured motions (keywords in bold) or show Picture 34. For older children, tell the version of the story on the back of Picture 34.

**Who are some of your friends? Let's listen to hear what some of Jesus' friends talked about one day.**

Jesus and His friends traveled from place to place. As they walked, Jesus' friends talked. One day, instead of using words that were happy and friendly, Jesus' friends said words that were unkind! One of Jesus' friends must have said he was better than someone else. Pretty soon each of them was feeling **ANGRY**! Each one wanted to be the greatest, or the best!

Jesus and His friends came into a house. Jesus said to His friends, "What were you arguing about on the road?"

Jesus' friends got very quiet. But Jesus KNEW they had been arguing about who was the greatest. And Jesus knew they had some wrong ideas.

Jesus sat down. Then He **picked up** a little child. Jesus set the child down beside the men. Jesus looked at His friends and said, "If you want God to think you are great, you must be like this little child. Don't think you are better than everyone else."

Jesus' friends were **surprised**. They thought they had to show God how good they were. Jesus was telling His friends they needed to learn that God loves a little child just as much as He loves any grown-up.

Jesus hugged the little child. He looked around at His friends. He said, "Treat children the way you would treat ME. When you are **kind** to children, it is the same as being kind to Me. God thinks you are great when you are kind and serve others."

Jesus wanted His friends to treat others with love and kindness instead of worrying about trying to be better than everyone else!

## God's Word & Me

**Jesus wanted His friends to serve others. Serving others means being kind and helpful to others. What are some ways you can serve others?** (Help Mom by obeying her. Help a brother or sister do his or her chores.)

# Worship Center

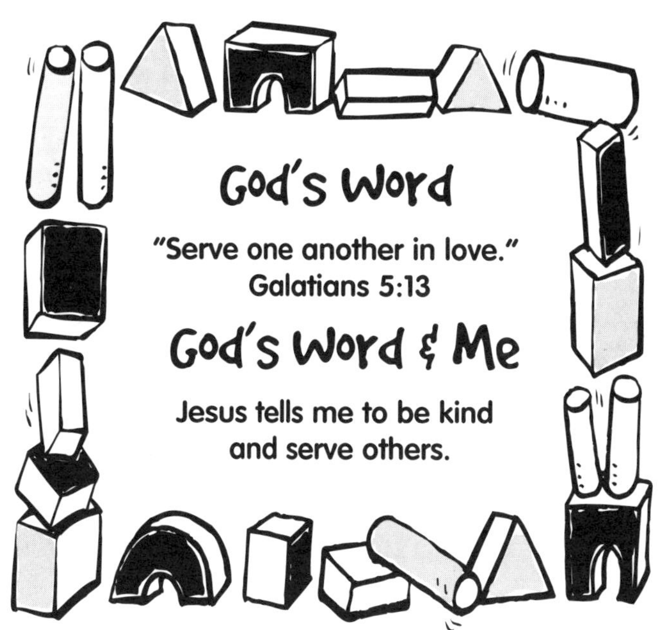
God's Word
"Serve one another in love."
Galatians 5:13
God's Word & Me
Jesus tells me to be kind
and serve others.

## Collect

Bible, *Shake It Up!* songbook and cassette/CD and player, "Help Me Be Kind" and "Be Kind" word charts (pp. 33 and 35 in songbook).

## Sing to God

Play "Help Me Be Kind." Invite children to sing along with you. **Let's sing a song about different times we can be kind.** Lead children in singing song and doing suggested motions. **Jesus tells us to be kind and serve others.**

## Hear and Say God's Word

Holding your Bible open to Galatians 5:13, say verse aloud. **When we serve others, we are showing them God's love. That's why Jesus wants us to be kind and serve others.** Lead children in repeating the verse several times. As the children are repeating the verse with you, point to one child. You and the children say that child's name instead of the words "one another." Repeat until every child has had a turn.

## Pray to God

One at a time, call on children to name a person and complete the following prayer: **Dear God, help me to love and serve __________. In Jesus' name, amen.**

## Sing to God

In closing the worship time, play "Be Kind." Invite children to sing along with you and do suggested motions. **This song tells us to be kind to others. When we are kind and help others, we are serving them like Jesus tells us to do.**

## Options

1. Lead children to experiment with singing the words of the Bible verse to the tune of "Where Is Thumbkin?" or "Twinkle, Twinkle, Little Star."

2. Invite a musician from your church to play one or more of the suggested songs for this lesson on a guitar, flute, trumpet, etc. Explain to children that by coming to play for them, the musician is serving them in love.

 

# Read-Aloud Story and Activity Center

## Collect

A copy of Story Picture 26 (pp. 57-58 from *Read-Aloud Story and Activity Book*) for each child and yourself, crayons or markers.

## Prepare

Color your copy of Story Picture 26.

## Do

**Listen to find out why this family is at the airport.** Read story and show completed Story Picture 26. Distribute pictures. Use conversation suggestions in Let's Talk About the Story as children complete their pages.

# Kindergarten Puzzle Center

## Collect

Copies of Puzzles 51 and 52 (p. 109 and p. 111 from *The Big Book of Kindergarten Puzzles)* for each child, pencils, crayons or markers.

## Do

Children complete the puzzles and color pages.

# Instant Activities

These activities can be used at any time during this session: when children need a change of pace, to extend the session, or during transition time at the beginning or end of the session.

## Collect

*The Big Book of Instant Activities.*

## Do

Guide children to complete "Which Way?" and/or "Hidden Sounds" (p. 88 and/or p. 95 from *The Big Book of Instant Activities).*

Lesson 27

# People Praise Jesus

## Bible Story

Matthew 21:1-11,15,16; Luke 19:28-38

God's Word
"Sing praises to the Lord." Psalm 9:11
God's Word & Me
I can praise Jesus and show my love for Him.

## Teacher's Devotional

The word "hosanna" plays an important part in today's lesson. Because of the way the word is often used, one might think it is interchangeable with "hallelujah," which literally means "praise the Lord." Although "Hosanna" seems to have been shouted to Jesus as a cry similar to "Long live the king!" the word in Hebrew literally means "Save!" or "Please save us!"

In Judaism today, a ceremony takes place on the last day of Sukkot (the Feast of Booths in the Bible) in which all verses that begin with "Save us" are chanted. The service is known as Hoshanot, which simply means "hosannas." The tone during this service is not one of praise but of the solemnness associated with judgment and the approaching Day of Atonement, Yom Kippur.

So as Jesus rode into Jerusalem, the "hosannas" must have sounded a bit ironic to Him. Some praised Him in hope that He would save them from Roman oppression. But even as they did, the word they used shouted out their need for salvation! And as they shouted, the sacrifice for their true and final Day of Atonement rode past them! By their very words, the people were calling to Jesus to save them and fulfill God's eternal plan!

## Teacher's Planning

1. Choose which centers you will provide and the order in which children will participate in them. For tips on schedule planning, see page 7.
2. Plan who will lead each center. For staffing tips and ideas, see page 21.

Lesson 27

# Active Game Center: Praise Parade

## Collect

Bible, *Shake It Up!* cassette/CD and player, two or three rhythm instruments; optional—palm leaves made in Art Center.

### God's Word

**"Sing praises to the Lord." Psalm 9:11**

### God's Word & Me

**I can praise Jesus and show my love for Him.**

## Do

1. Give rhythm instruments to children. Children play a game like Follow the Leader. Play "Sing Praises." Children form a line and follow the first child in the line as he or she walks around the room. Children sing and play the rhythm instruments or clap hands. (Optional: Children wave palm leaves made in Art Center.)
2. After a few moments stop music. Children freeze. The line leader moves to the end of the line. The children with rhythm instruments hand them to children who have not had a turn. Restart the music as children resume following the leader and playing instruments or clapping hands.

## Talk About

- **In today's Bible story, people stood along the road to Jerusalem. They knew Jesus was coming! Jesus rode a donkey into the city as people shouted, "Hosanna." It was a very happy parade! Let's make our own parade.**
- **Linda, what instrument are you playing? Playing your tambourine is a way to show you are glad. We're glad to show our love for Jesus!**
- **Our Bible says, "Sing praises to the Lord." "Lord" is another name for Jesus. Singing praises shows our love for Jesus. We can tell Jesus we love Him when we pray.** Pray briefly, **Dear Jesus, we love You!**

## For Younger Children

Pair younger children with older children who will hold their hands and walk beside them.

## For Older Children

Give older children additional objects with which to make music: unbreakable wind chimes, kazoos, wind-up toys, whistles, kitchen timers, music boxes, etc.

# Art Center: Paper Palms

## Collect

Bible, 9x12-inch (23x30.5-cm) green construction paper, scissors.

## Prepare

Fold sheets of construction paper in half, as indicated in the sketch. Cut out one or more paper palm leaves for each child.

God's Word
"Sing praises to the Lord." Psalm 9:11
God's Word & Me
I can praise Jesus and show my love for Him.

## Do

1. Children use scissors to cut fringe along the edges of their palm leaves.
2. Post paper palm leaves on walls of classroom, or ask children to wave leaves while singing songs in the Worship Center or the Active Game Center.

cut
cut
4½" (11.5 cm)
12" (30.5 cm)

## Talk About

- **In today's Bible story, Jesus rode a donkey into the town of Jerusalem. The people were very happy to see Jesus. They put their coats and palm leaves on the road when they saw Jesus coming. Let's make palm leaves!**
- **Jimmy, can you say "hosanna?" That is a word people used to welcome Jesus when He came to Jerusalem. Let's all say "hosanna" together.**
- **Tonya, what do you do to show you are happy to see your parents when they come home? Hugging our parents and telling them we're happy to see them shows our love for them.**
- **Even though we can't hug Jesus, we can show our love to Him. Our Bible says, "Sing praises to the Lord." "Lord" is another name for Jesus. When we sing songs about Jesus and how great He is, we show our love for Him.**

## For Younger Children

Cut palm leaves out of white paper. Younger children use markers or crayons to color leaves.

## For Older Children

Older children cut out their own palm leaves.

Lesson 27

# Block Center: Road Blocks

## Collect

Bible, blocks, old coats or lengths of fabric, green construction paper.

## Do

Children use blocks to outline a road wide enough to walk along. Then children act out walking along the road with Jesus, placing coats or fabric and sheets of green construction paper along the road. (Optional: Children use palm leaves made in the Art Center.)

God's Word
"Sing praises to the Lord." Psalm 9:11
God's Word & Me
I can praise Jesus and show my love for Him.

## Talk About

- **In our Bible story Jesus traveled to the city of Jerusalem. Jesus rode a donkey along the road as people clapped and cheered. The people laid coats and palm branches on the road in front of Jesus. Let's make a road and pretend we're watching Jesus ride by.**
- **The people were so happy to see Jesus, they shouted, "Hosanna!" "Hosanna" is a special word the people used to welcome Jesus.**
- **We can praise Jesus and show our love for Him. Singing songs about Jesus is a way to praise Him!**
- **Our Bible tells us, "Sing praises to the Lord." "Lord" is another name for Jesus. When we sing or tell how great Jesus is, we are praising Him. Singing praises to Jesus shows we love Him.**

## For Younger Children

Before class, outline road using masking tape. Children place blocks on masking-tape outline. (Note: Remove tape immediately after activity.)

## For Older Children

Children clap their hands and repeat the following poem as they walk along the block road:

**Hosanna! Hosanna! the children did sing.**
**Hosanna! Hosanna! to Jesus, our King!**

Lesson 27

# Science Center: Lovely Leaves

## Collect

Bible, a variety of leaves (real or artificial); optional—pictures of a variety of leaves or paper leaves.

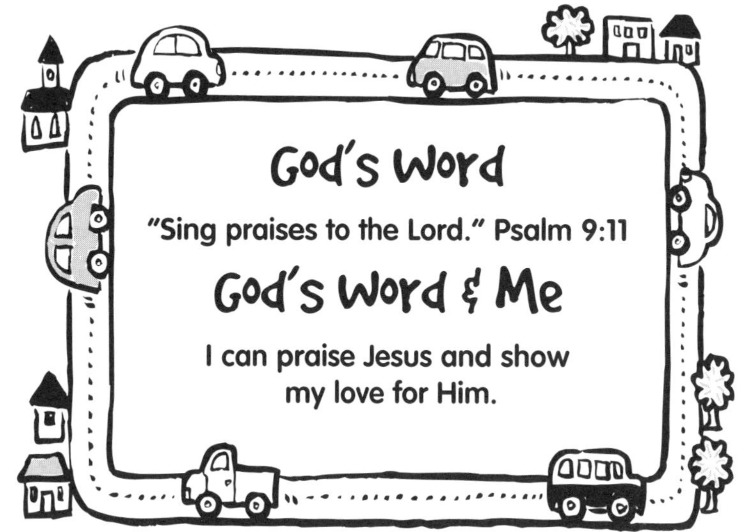
God's Word
"Sing praises to the Lord." Psalm 9:11
God's Word & Me
I can praise Jesus and show my love for Him.

## Do

1. Children each select a leaf and examine it. (Optional: Children use pictures of leaves or paper leaves in activity.)
2. Children take turns mixing their leaf with two or three leaves that were not selected. Each child examines the leaves to find their original leaf. Repeat as time allows.

## Talk About

- **In today's Bible story, Jesus rode a donkey into the city of Jerusalem. Lots and lots of people were happy that Jesus was coming. The people stood beside the road and cheered. The people threw their coats and palm branches on the road for Jesus' donkey to walk on. Palm branches are very large leaves from a palm tree. Let's look at some other kinds of leaves.**
- **Sheryl, what color is your leaf? Is it soft when you touch it? Is it crunchy? Does your leaf have a smell?**

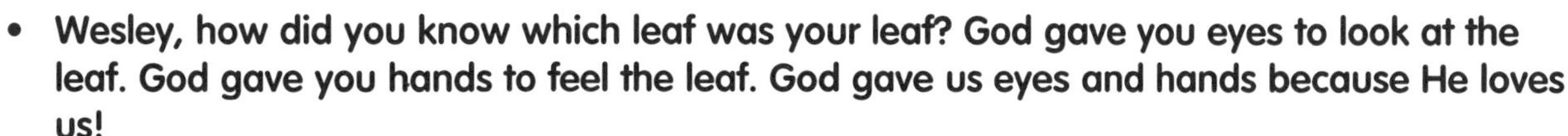

- **Wesley, how did you know which leaf was your leaf? God gave you eyes to look at the leaf. God gave you hands to feel the leaf. God gave us eyes and hands because He loves us!**
- **Our Bible says, "Sing praises to the Lord." "Lord" is another name for Jesus. We can praise Jesus by singing about our love for Him!**

## For Younger Children

Instead of mixing and finding leaves, children look at leaves with magnifying glasses and glue them to papers to make leaf displays.

## For Older Children

Children sort leaves by size, color, shape and/or texture. Children may also trace around the edges of the leaves with a crayon on a sheet of paper.

Lesson 27 • Matthew 21:1-11,15,16; Luke 19:28-38

# Bible Story Center

## Collect

Bible, Picture 40 from *Bible Story Pictures.*

God's Word
"Sing praises to the Lord." Psalm 9:11
God's Word & Me
I can praise Jesus and show my love for Him.

## Tell the Story

Use the pictured motions (keywords in bold) or show Picture 40. For older children, tell the version of the story on the back of Picture 40.

**When have you sung to someone? Listen to our Bible story to hear about a time people sang a song to Jesus.**

What a happy day it was! Jesus and His friends were going to the Temple in the big city of Jerusalem. On the way, Jesus stopped. He said to His friends, "There is a little **donkey** in the town. Untie it and bring it to Me."

Jesus' friends did just as He asked them. They found the donkey and brought it back to Jesus. Jesus climbed on the donkey's back and began riding to the big city. Clippety-clop, clippety-clop went the donkey's feet. Jesus' friends **walked** along the road with Him.

Many other people were walking along the road to Jerusalem, too. There were girls and boys, moms and dads, grandmas and grandpas. They were excited to see Jesus! Some people spread their **coats** on the road. This showed that they welcomed Jesus as if He were a king. Other people cut branches from palm trees and laid them on the road for Jesus' donkey to walk on. What a happy day it was!

Some people ran ahead to tell others, "Jesus is coming! JESUS is coming!" And even MORE people came to see Jesus. They laughed and sang. They shouted, "Hosanna! Hosanna!" (Hosanna means "please save us" and was shouted to praise someone.)

It was a wonderful day in the big city of Jerusalem! The children **praised** Jesus. The moms and dads praised Jesus. The grandparents praised Jesus. EVERYONE who loved Jesus praised Him by singing happy songs to Jesus.

## God's Word & Me

**What did the people do to welcome Jesus?** Make motions of spreading coats, cutting branches and singing to help children remember. **We can praise Jesus and show we love Him, too! What can we do to praise Jesus?** (Sing songs about Him. Pray. Tell Him we love Him.)

# Worship Center

## Collect

Bible, *Shake It Up!* songbook and cassette/CD and player, "Jesus Is Alive!" and "Sing Praises" word charts (pp. 38 and 40 in songbook).

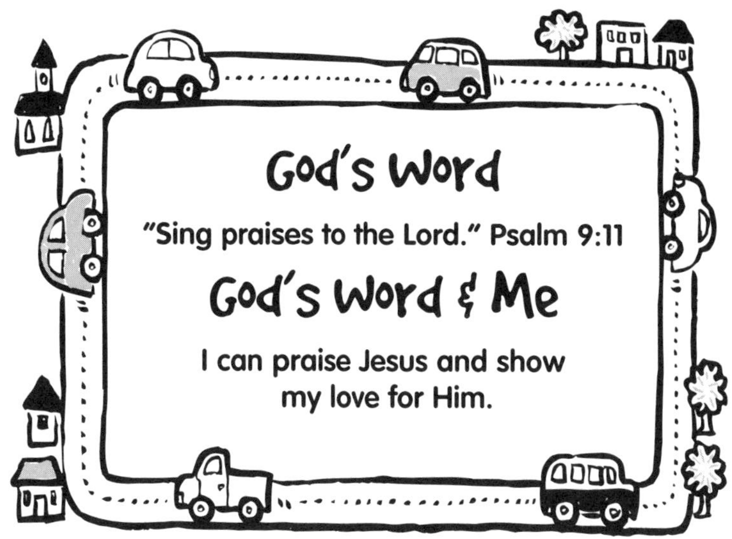
God's Word
"Sing praises to the Lord." Psalm 9:11
God's Word & Me
I can praise Jesus and show my love for Him.

## Sing to God

Play "Jesus Is Alive!" Invite children to sing along with you. **Sing a song with me about a good reason to be happy.** Lead children in singing song and doing suggested motions. **I am happy that Jesus is alive! I love Jesus. We show our love for Jesus by singing our praises to Him.**

## Hear and Say God's Word

Holding your Bible open to Psalm 9:11, say verse aloud. **"Lord" is another name for Jesus. Singing praises to Jesus shows our love for Him.** Lead children in repeating the verse and clapping their hands on each word. Repeat several times. Vary the motion by asking children to stomp their feet, pat their heads, slap their knees, etc.

## Pray to God

Volunteers say the following prayer: **Dear Jesus, we love You. In Jesus' name, amen.**

## Sing to God

In closing the worship time, play "Sing Praises." Invite children to sing along with you and do suggested motions. **When we sing praises to Jesus, we are telling others how great and good Jesus is. We are showing we love Jesus.**

## Options

1. Provide rhythm instruments for children to use while singing "Jesus Is Alive!" and "Sing Praises." You may wish to use the rhythm instruments you brought for the Active Game Center.
2. With parents' permission, videotape children as they sing songs and do the motions. Play videotape at the end of the session as parents come to pick up their children.

Lesson 27

# Read-Aloud Story and Activity Center

## Collect

A copy of Story Picture 27 (pp. 59-60 from *Read-Aloud Story and Activity Book*) for each child and yourself, crayons or markers.

## Prepare

Color your copy of Story Picture 27.

## Do

**Listen to find out why one boy is not singing.** Read story and show completed Story Picture 27. Distribute pictures. Use conversation suggestions in Let's Talk About the Story as children complete their pages.

# Kindergarten Puzzle Center

## Collect

Copies of Puzzles 53 and 54 (p. 113 and p. 115 from *The Big Book of Kindergarten Puzzles*) for each child, pencils, crayons or markers.

## Do

Children complete the puzzles and color pages.

# Instant Activities

These activities can be used at any time during this session: when children need a change of pace, to extend the session, or during transition time at the beginning or end of the session.

## Collect

*The Big Book of Instant Activities.*

## Do

Guide children to complete "Happy Parade" and/or "Body Moves" (p. 58 and/or p. 78 from *The Big Book of Instant Activities*).

Lesson 28

# Jesus Dies and Lives Again

## Bible Story

Matthew 26:1-4,47-50; 27:11-66; John 18—20:20

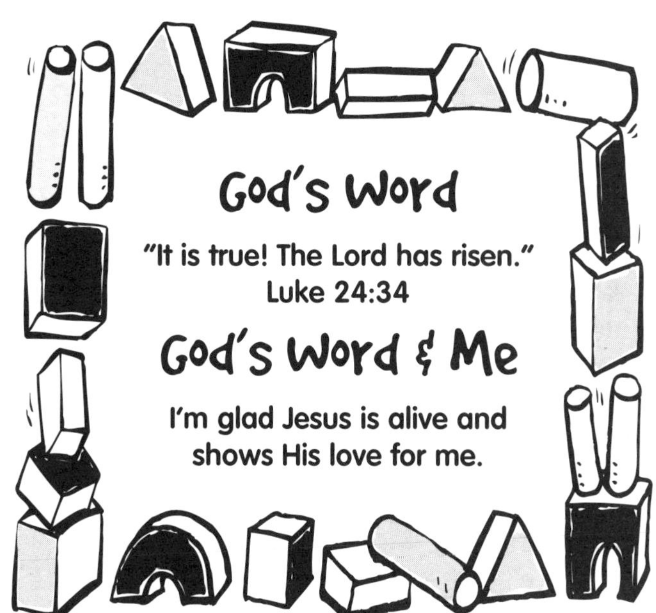
God's Word
"It is true! The Lord has risen."
Luke 24:34
God's Word & Me
I'm glad Jesus is alive and shows His love for me.

## Teacher's Devotional

On the subject of the death and resurrection of Jesus, the book of Hebrews has a beautiful idea for us to ponder: "Since the children have flesh and blood, he too shared in their humanity so that by his death he might destroy him who holds the power of death—that is, the devil—and free those who all their lives were held in slavery by their fear of death" (Hebrews 2:14,15).

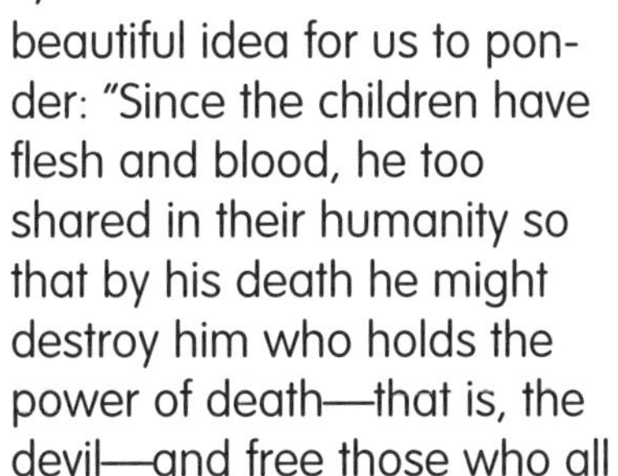

Think for a moment about how much of the world's activity is tied to the slavery that comes from the fear of death. Youth is touted as a glorious time of life by the media. Many live in fear of old age and dying; and they go to great lengths to look younger, to prolong life, even to be frozen in hope that a cure for their terminal disease might be found! Fear of death seems to hold many hostages.

But because Jesus DESTROYED him who holds the power of death, that slavery is broken for those who believe! Satan can only hold people who still refuse to believe that Jesus' victory is for them. Child of God, Jesus won this freedom for you. There is no death (see John 11:25,26). Passage out of this life will yield the final freedom that will make you fully the person God already knows you to be (see 2 Corinthians 5:1-8).

## Teacher's Planning

1. Choose which centers you will provide and the order in which children will participate in them. For tips on schedule planning, see page 7.
2. Plan who will lead each center. For staffing tips and ideas, see page 21.

Lesson 28

# Active Game Center: Plate Turnover

## Collect

Bible, paper plates, marker, beanbag.

## Prepare

Draw a happy face on several paper plates. Place these plates and several blank ones facedown on floor. (Note: If you have a large class, prepare one setup for every six to eight children.)

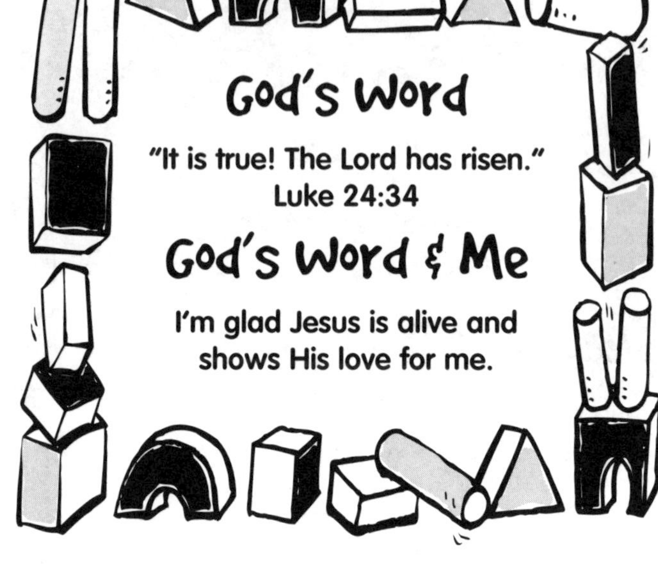
God's Word
"It is true! The Lord has risen."
Luke 24:34
God's Word & Me
I'm glad Jesus is alive and shows His love for me.

## Do

Children stand several feet from paper plates. Taking turns, each child tosses a beanbag at the paper plates. Child turns over plate beanbag lands on or near to see if there is a happy face drawn on it. Continue until all paper plates are turned over; then mix plates up, turn facedown and repeat as time and interest allow.

## Talk About

- **In today's Bible story, Jesus' friends found out that He is alive! Shanda, how do you think Jesus' friends felt to know Jesus was alive? We're happy Jesus is living, too! Let's play a game and show happy faces.**
- **Our Bible says, "It is true! The Lord has risen." "Lord" is another name for Jesus. Jesus is alive! Jesus shows His love for us. Norman, what are some of the good things Jesus helps you to have?** (Parents to care for us. Friends to play with. Food to eat.)

## For Younger Children

Prepare one happy-face plate for each child. Place plates facedown in different places around the room. Instead of waiting for a turn, children search for plates and turn them over to find a happy face.

## For Older Children

On each of five plates print one letter of the word "Jesus." Use these plates along with the ones you prepared. When all plates have been turned over, children put the letter plates in order to spell "Jesus."

Lesson 28

# Art Center: Butterfly Cards

## Collect

Bible, brightly colored tissue paper, scissors, ruler, construction paper, white paper, marker, chenille wires, transparent tape.

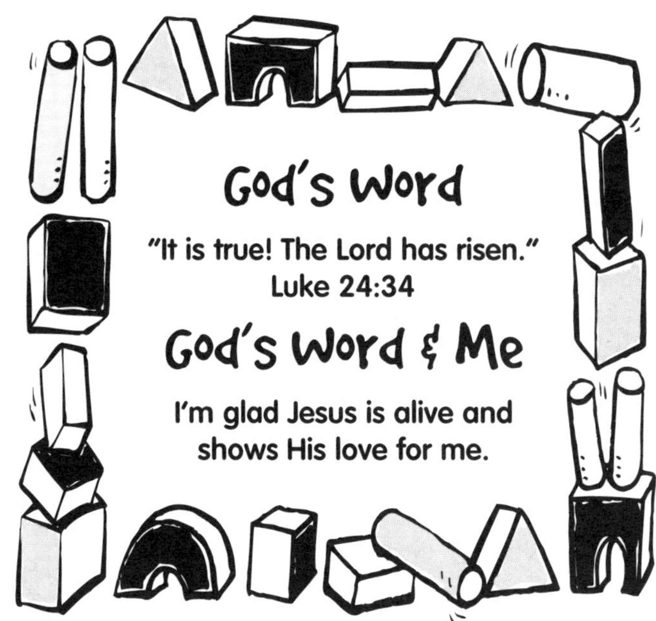
God's Word
"It is true! The Lord has risen."
Luke 24:34
God's Word & Me
I'm glad Jesus is alive and
shows His love for me.

## Prepare

Cut tissue paper into 5-inch (12.5-cm) squares, two for each child. Fold construction paper in half. On white paper, print the following sentence three or four times: "Jesus is living!" Photocopy and cut apart sentences so that there is a sentence for each child. Cut chenille wires into 6-inch (15-cm) pieces.

## Do

1. Children select a construction paper card. Distribute photocopied sentences. Children tape sentences inside their cards.
2. Assist children in bending chenille wires in half. Gather tissue in center and lay it inside wires. Twist wires. Each child makes two butterflies and tapes to card.

## Talk About

- **Our Bible says, "It is true! The Lord has risen." "Lord" is another name for Jesus. I'm glad Jesus is alive and shows His love for me. Let's make cards to tell others that Jesus is living.**
- **Rachel, what pretty colors did you use for your butterfly? We can be glad for butterflies and all the ways Jesus shows His love for us.** Pray briefly, **Thank You, Jesus, for loving us.**

## For Younger Children

Instead of making tissue-paper butterflies, children decorate cards by gluing tissue paper scraps, drawing with markers, adding stickers, etc.

## For Older Children

Instead of using tissue paper to make butterflies, children use markers to draw on a coffee filter. Then children gather coffee filters in chenille wires as described above.

Lesson 28

# Block Center: Block Garden

## Collect

Bible, brown paper, blocks, real or artificial nature objects (twigs, leaves, flowers, gravel, etc.), toy people.

## Prepare

Tear brown paper into a round rock shape.

### God's Word

**"It is true! The Lord has risen."**
**Luke 24:34**

### God's Word & Me

**I'm glad Jesus is alive and shows His love for me.**

## Do

1. Children use blocks to outline a garden and make hills. Children arrange nature objects in garden. Assist children to make a tomb by forming a cave and placing brown paper rock over the opening.
2. Children play with toy people in the garden.

## Talk About

- **Our Bible story today tells about a time when Jesus' friends were very sad. Then came the happy day when they knew Jesus was not in the tomb. Jesus is alive! Let's make a garden like the one where Jesus' friends found out Jesus was not in the tomb.**
- **This paper is like the rock that covered Jesus' tomb. His tomb was a little room made in the side of a hill. Mary, one of Jesus' friends, went to the garden to visit Jesus' tomb. When she got there, the tomb was empty. Jesus is alive!**
- **Our Bible says, "It is true! The Lord has risen." "Lord" is another name for Jesus. I'm glad Jesus is alive. I'm glad that Jesus loves us.** Pray briefly, **Thank You, Jesus, for loving us.**

## For Younger Children

Make an outline of the garden using masking tape. Children place blocks along the outline to form the garden.

## For Older Children

Children act out the Bible story as you briefly tell story events. Expect to repeat the Bible story several times during the Block Center.

Lesson 28

# Science Center: Real or Unreal

## Collect

Bible, sets of real and artificial items (a real flower and an artificial flower; hard-boiled egg and artificial egg; real food and toy food, etc.).

## God's Word

"It is true! The Lord has risen." Luke 24:34

## God's Word & Me

I'm glad Jesus is alive and shows His love for me.

## Do

Children examine items and decide which items are real and which are not real. Talk about things that are real, or true.

## Talk About

- **Our Bible story tells of a time one of Jesus' friends used her eyes to see that Jesus was not in the tomb. Jesus is alive! Mary used her ears to hear Jesus talk. She found out that it is real: Jesus is alive! Let's look at some things and decide which ones are real.**

- **Albert, which of these flowers do you think is real? What tells you that the flower is real? God gave us eyes to see. God gave us fingers to feel and noses to smell. We can use them to know if a flower is real.** Repeat for other items you brought.

- **Our Bible says, "It is true! The Lord has risen." "Lord" is another name for Jesus. It is real that Jesus is alive!**
- **We're glad Jesus is alive and shows His love for us. Jesus shows His love by listening when we pray.** Pray briefly, **Dear Jesus, thank You for loving us. We're glad that You are alive!**

## For Younger Children

Some children will need assistance to distinguish between real and unreal items. Use your conversation to explain the differences. **Todd, smell each flower. Which flower smells good? The flower that has a nice smell is the real flower.**

## For Older Children

Children group items according to whether they are real or artificial. Once items have been grouped, ask children to close their eyes. Remove one item. Ask children to identify which item was removed.

# Bible Story Center

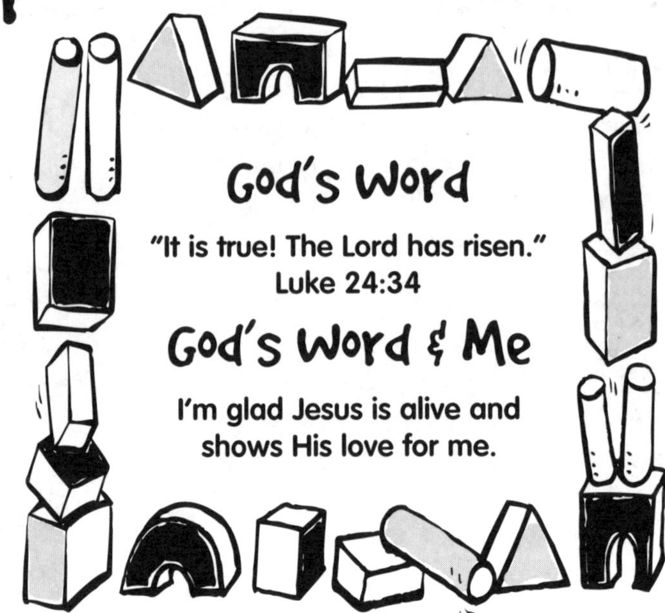
God's Word
"It is true! The Lord has risen."
Luke 24:34
God's Word & Me
I'm glad Jesus is alive and
shows His love for me.

## Collect

Bible, Picture 41 from *Bible Story Pictures*.

## Tell the Story

Use the pictured motions (keywords in bold) or show Picture 41. For older children, tell the version of the story on the back of Picture 41.

**What do people look like when they feel sad? When they feel happy? Listen to hear about a time when Jesus' friends were sad and then happy.**

One day, Jesus told His friends, "In a few days, some people are going to take Me away. I'm going to be killed." Jesus' friends were very **sad**. But Jesus knew this was part of God's good plan. Jesus knew He wouldn't STAY dead!

When the people who wanted to kill Jesus came to get Him, Jesus let them take Him. And Jesus let them kill Him on a cross. Jesus' friends were very sad to see Him dead. They took Jesus' body and put it into a **tomb**. (This tomb was a little room made in the side of a hill.) Later, a HUGE rock was rolled in front of the doorway of the tomb so that no one could go in or out.

On the third day after Jesus was killed, one of Jesus' friends named Mary **came to the tomb**. It was still a little dark, but she could see that the big rock was NOT in front of the door. Mary looked into the tomb and saw two angels. One angel asked her why she was crying. Mary said, "Because Jesus' body is gone and I don't know where He is."

She turned around and almost bumped into someone. "Mary!" the person said. Mary knew that voice—it was JESUS! Mary was so happy to know that Jesus is alive!

Jesus said to her, "Go and tell the others." And Mary did! She must have **run** very fast!

"Jesus is ALIVE! I saw Him!" she said. Jesus' other friends were so surprised, some of them did not believe her. But that night, Jesus came to the place where His friends were. Now Jesus' friends saw that Jesus is alive and knew that He loved them! The very SAD day had been turned into a very GLAD day—because Jesus is alive!

## God's Word & Me

**What did Mary do when she saw that Jesus is alive?** (Ran and told Jesus' other friends.) **Jesus' friends were glad to know Jesus is alive! We are glad Jesus is alive and shows His love for us!**

# Worship Center

## Collect

Bible, *Shake It Up!* songbook and cassette/CD and player, "Jesus Is Alive!" and "Sing Praises" word charts (pp. 38 and 40 in songbook).

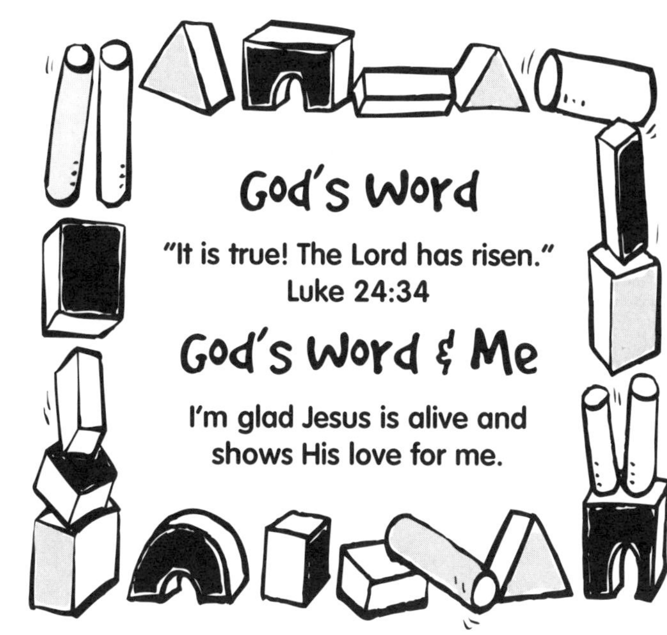
God's Word
"It is true! The Lord has risen."
Luke 24:34
God's Word & Me
I'm glad Jesus is alive and shows His love for me.

## Sing to God

Play "Jesus Is Alive!" Invite children to sing along with you. **Let's sing a song together about a very happy time.** Lead children in singing song and doing suggested motions. **Jesus is alive! At Eastertime we remember that Jesus is alive. Eastertime is a very happy time!**

## Hear and Say God's Word

Holding your Bible open to Luke 24:34, say verse aloud. **"Lord" is another name for Jesus. This verse tells us that Jesus has risen. Jesus is alive!** Lead children in repeating the verse by echoing phrases after you: "It is true!/The Lord has risen." Point to children when it is their turn to speak. Repeat verse several times in this manner.

## Pray to God

**Dear God, we love You. And we thank You that Jesus is living today. Thank You for loving us. In Jesus' name, amen.**

## Sing to God

In closing the worship time, play "Sing Praises." Invite children to sing along with you and do suggested motions. **When we sing this song, we are telling Jesus how much we love Him. We sing praises at Eastertime because we are so happy that Jesus is alive!**

## Options

1. In the verse activity, vary the manner in which you and the children speak (singsong, loud, soft, whisper, low, high, etc.).
2. Older children lead other children in doing the motions suggested in the songbook for "Jesus Is Alive!" and/or "Sing Praises."

 

Lesson 28

# Read-Aloud Story and Activity Center

## Collect

A copy of Story Picture 28 (pp. 61-62 from *Read-Aloud Story and Activity Book*) for each child and yourself, crayons or markers.

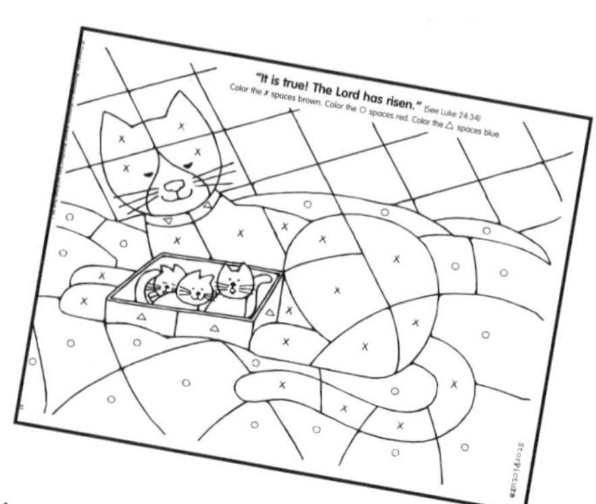
"It is true! The Lord has risen."

## Prepare

Color your copy of Story Picture 28.

## Do

**Listen to find out what Lauren was looking for.** Read story and show completed Story Picture 28. Distribute pictures. Use conversation suggestions in Let's Talk About the Story as children complete their pages.

# Kindergarten Puzzle Center

## Collect

Copies of Puzzles 55 and 56 (p. 117 and p. 119 from *The Big Book of Kindergarten Puzzles*) for each child, pencils, crayons or markers.

## Do

Children complete the puzzles and color pages.

# Instant Activities

These activities can be used at any time during this session: when children need a change of pace, to extend the session, or during transition time at the beginning or end of the session.

## Collect

*The Big Book of Instant Activities.*

## Do

Guide children to complete "Eastertime" and/or "Jumping High" (p. 58 and/or p. 83 from *The Big Book of Instant Activities*).

Lesson 29

# Thomas Sees Jesus

## Bible Story

John 20:19-31

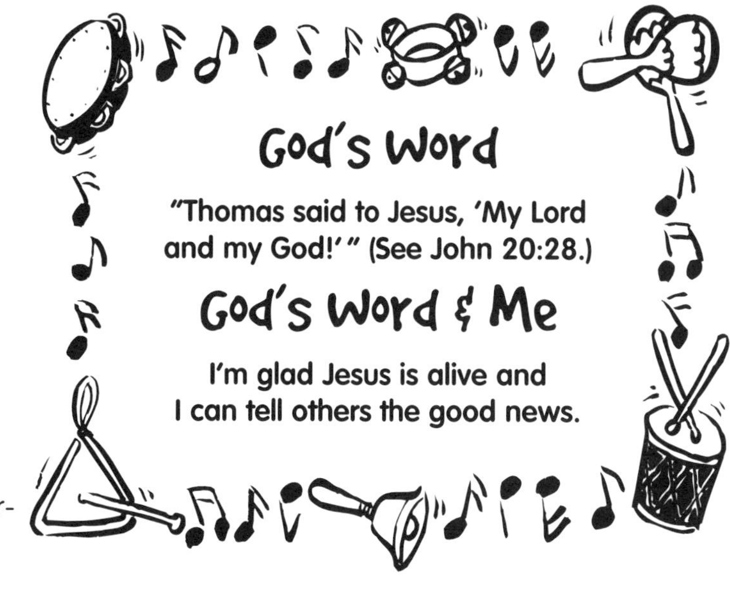

### God's Word

**"Thomas said to Jesus, 'My Lord and my God!'" (See John 20:28.)**

### God's Word & Me

**I'm glad Jesus is alive and I can tell others the good news.**

## Teacher's Devotional

Thomas had not been present when Christ came to talk with the other disciples. When the others told Thomas that Jesus was alive, Thomas refused to take their word on such a life-shaking issue. Thomas would not say that he understood what he did not understand or that he believed what he did not!

Thomas's stubborn honesty seems negative. Wouldn't it be nicer or seem more spiritual if he agreed and believed right away? But in one sense, Thomas's attitude is a positive one. All too often, Christians say they believe or understand something out of fear that others will think they aren't spiritual. Then as time goes on, their actions prove that they really didn't believe or understand at all. Thomas's humble honesty said, in effect, "This is not something I can believe. I'm not there yet. I need proof."

There are answers to all our doubts. We need only search God's Word until our own hearts are satisfied, and we shouldn't stop searching because we fear other people's opinions. Once our search is over, the end result will be, as it was for Thomas, a commitment to Jesus that is thought-out and genuine—yielding the fruit of a living, growing relationship with the same Jesus who invited Thomas to put his finger into His nail prints.

## Teacher's Planning

1. Choose which centers you will provide and the order in which children will participate in them. For tips on schedule planning, see page 7.
2. Plan who will lead each center. For staffing tips and ideas, see page 21.

# Active Game Center: Color Clues

## Collect

Bible, strips of colored construction paper.

### God's Word

**"Thomas said to Jesus, 'My Lord and my God!'" (See John 20:28.)**

### God's Word & Me

**I'm glad Jesus is alive and I can tell others the good news.**

## Do

1. Each child selects a construction-paper strip. Call out a color of paper and a motion for children to perform. **If you have a blue strip, give someone a high five.**
2. Continue calling colors and motions that show happiness (smile, clap hands, jump up and down, shake someone's hand, give a hug, etc.). Repeat until you have called each color at least once. Collect strips and let children choose again. Continue as time and interest allow.

## Talk About

- **In our Bible story, a man named Thomas was very happy to know that Jesus is alive. We're happy Jesus is alive, too! Let's play a game to show we are happy.**
- **Colleen, when do you like to give hugs? Hugs are one way to show we are happy. I'm happy that Jesus is alive. And I can tell others that good news!**
- **Our Bible says, "Thomas said to Jesus, 'My Lord and my God!'" Thomas was happy that Jesus is alive. Thomas couldn't wait to say the good news!**

## For Younger Children

Instead of using colored construction-paper strips, play a game like Follow the Leader. Lead children in walking around the room and doing motions that show happiness.

## For Older Children

Children identify and name something in the room that is the same color as their construction-paper strip.

Lesson 29

# Art Center: Fingerprint People

## Collect

Bible, white paper, washable ink pads; optional—premoistened towelettes.

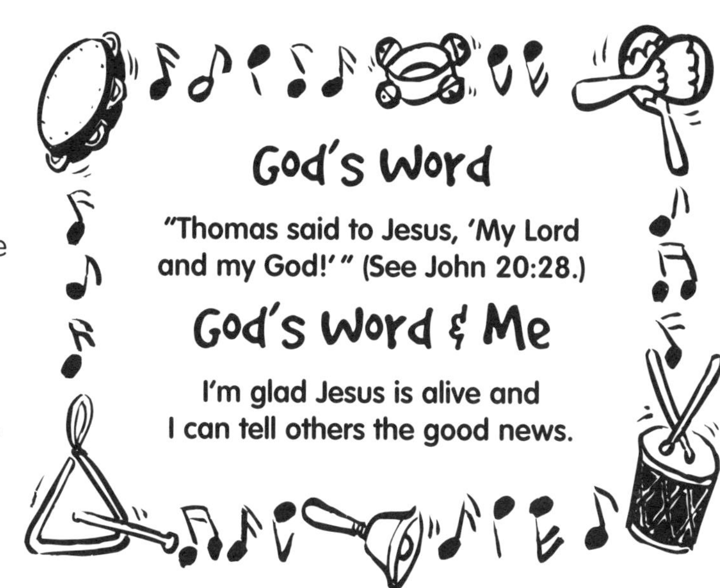
God's Word
"Thomas said to Jesus, 'My Lord and my God!'" (See John 20:28.)
God's Word & Me
I'm glad Jesus is alive and I can tell others the good news.

## Do

On white paper, children make a simple fingerprint picture of Jesus by pressing fingers on ink pad and then on the paper. Children clean hands after making fingerprints. (Optional: If you do not have a sink nearby, distribute premoistened towelettes for children to use for cleanup.)

## Talk About

- **In our Bible story today a man named Thomas was surprised when he saw that Jesus is alive. Thomas was happy to know Jesus is alive. Let's make a reminder that Jesus is alive.**
- **I'm glad Jesus is alive! That's good news we can tell everyone we know! Danny, who is someone who tells you about Jesus? Your dad tells you about Jesus because he's glad Jesus is alive. You can tell others the good news, too!**
- **Our Bible tells us, "Thomas said to Jesus, 'My Lord and my God!'" Thomas found out that Jesus was alive. Thomas was happy! He was glad Jesus was alive.**
- **Thomas was glad Jesus loved him. Jesus loves you and me, too. Let's thank Jesus for His love.** Pray briefly, **Dear Jesus, thank You for loving us.**

## For Younger Children

Instead of making figures, children make fingerprint designs of their own choosing.

## For Older Children

On a large sheet of paper, print the Bible verse. On their individual papers, children make two simple figures, Jesus and Thomas. Assist children as needed to print "My Lord and my God" in a conversation balloon next to the Thomas figure.

 

# Block Center: Block Houses

## Collect

Bible, blocks, several 12-inch (30.5-cm) squares of cardboard.

## Do

Children use blocks and cardboard to build flat-roofed, Bible-times houses.

### God's Word

**"Thomas said to Jesus, 'My Lord and my God!'" (See John 20:28.)**

### God's Word & Me

**I'm glad Jesus is alive and I can tell others the good news.**

## Talk About

- **Our Bible story today tells about a time Jesus visited some of His friends. Let's make houses like the one where Jesus visited and ate with His friends.**
- **Jesus' friends told a man named Thomas, "Jesus is alive!" But Thomas would not believe them. Then one day Jesus came into the room where Thomas and Jesus' other friends were. Thomas saw with his eyes that Jesus really was alive, and then Thomas believed.**
- **I'm glad Jesus is alive. I can tell others this good news. One way to tell others about Jesus is to tell them stories from the Bible. Nelly, who tells you stories from the Bible?**

- **Our Bible tells us, "Thomas said to Jesus, 'My Lord and my God!'" Thomas was very happy Jesus is alive! Thomas knew Jesus loved him. Jesus loves us, too!** Pray briefly, **Thank You, Jesus for being alive and loving us.**

## For Younger Children

Outline a large square with masking tape. Children place blocks on masking-tape lines to outline a room. Provide crackers or cereal for children to snack on as they sit inside the block room.

## For Older Children

Provide toy people. Children act out the story action as you use the suggestions above to briefly retell story events. Expect to repeat the Bible story several times as children come and go from the Block Center.

Lesson 29

# Science Center: Happy Faces

## Collect

Bible, flour, cornstarch, salt, warm water, food coloring, measuring cup, medium mixing bowl, large spoon, craft sticks, paper plates, markers.

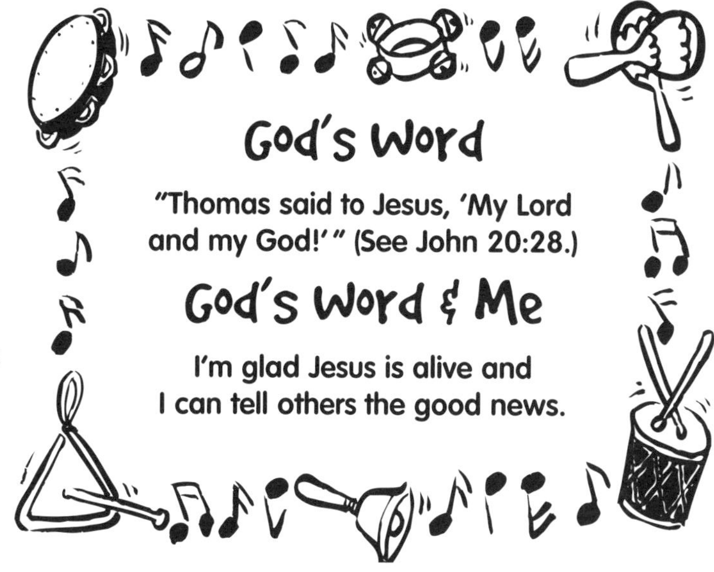
God's Word
"Thomas said to Jesus, 'My Lord and my God!'" (See John 20:28.)
God's Word & Me
I'm glad Jesus is alive and I can tell others the good news.

## Do

1. Volunteers add dough ingredients one at a time to mixing bowl: 1½ cups flour, 1 cup cornstarch, 1 cup salt, 1 cup warm water, several drops of food coloring. Children take turns stirring dough until well mixed. If dough is sticky, dust with flour. If dough is stiff, add a little water. (Note: Recipe makes about 3 cups of dough, enough for 10 to 12 children.)
2. Children use dough to create happy faces, etching details with craft sticks. When finished, children place dough faces on paper plates on which their names have been written.

## Talk About

- **In today's Bible story, Thomas didn't think Jesus was really alive until Thomas used his eyes. When Thomas saw Jesus, he knew Jesus is alive. Thomas was glad Jesus is alive! Let's use our eyes to measure ingredients and make happy faces.**
- **Our happy faces show that we are glad Jesus is alive. When people ask why we are happy, we can tell them "Jesus is alive!"**
- **Our Bible tells us, "Thomas said to Jesus, 'My Lord and my God!'" Thomas said that because he was so happy Jesus is alive. We can tell God we are happy Jesus is alive.** Pray briefly, **Thank You, God, that Jesus is alive. We love You.**

## For Younger Children

Make dough before class or purchase play dough with which children can work.

## For Older Children

Children roll additional dough into logs and form stick figures.

Lesson 29 • John 20:19-31

# Bible Story Center

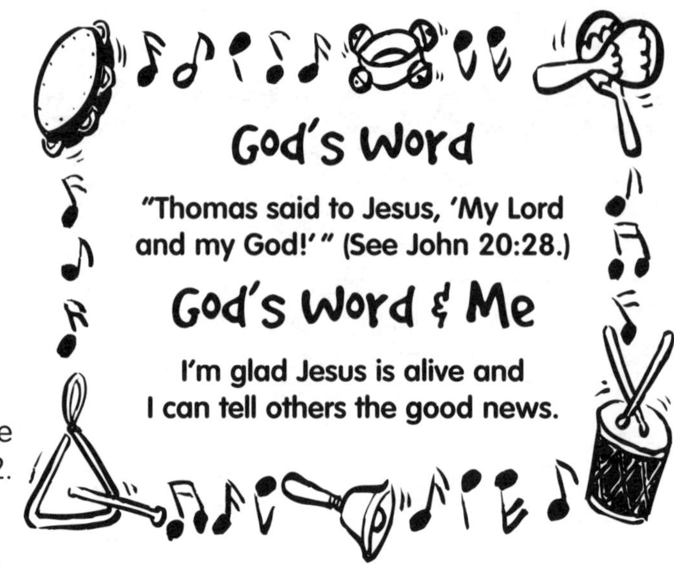
God's Word
"Thomas said to Jesus, 'My Lord and my God!'" (See John 20:28.)
God's Word & Me
I'm glad Jesus is alive and I can tell others the good news.

## Collect

Bible, Picture 42 from *Bible Story Pictures.*

## Tell the Story

Use the pictured motions (keywords in bold) or show Picture 42. For older children, tell the version of the story on the back of Picture 42.

**When have you been sad? Who helped you feel better? Listen to our Bible story to hear how Jesus helped His friend Thomas, when he was sad.**

One night some of Jesus' friends were eating together in a house. They were very sad. Their friend Jesus had been killed three days ago. They knew Jesus' body was not in the tomb. People said they had seen Jesus and that He was alive! But some of them were having a **hard time believing** that Jesus was really alive. Then Jesus came into the room. Jesus' friends were surprised and a little afraid.

Jesus must have smiled at them. "Why are you afraid?" Jesus asked. Jesus held out His **hands**, so His friends could see the hurt places on them. Jesus asked for something to eat. Then the friends knew He was really alive and they were not afraid anymore.

But Jesus' friend named Thomas was not there when Jesus came. Later, Jesus' other friends told Thomas that Jesus was alive, but Thomas **shook his head**. Thomas told the friends, "I will not believe that Jesus is alive unless I see Him and touch Him."

A week later, all the friends and Thomas were together in the same house again. Suddenly, Jesus came in the room, just as He had done before. Jesus knew that Thomas still didn't believe He was really alive. Jesus must have smiled at Thomas. "Thomas," Jesus said, "Look at My **hands**. Touch them. I want you to know that I am alive."

Thomas loved Jesus. He looked at Jesus and said, "My Lord and my God!" Now Thomas knew for sure that Jesus is alive. And he was very glad.

## God's Word & Me

**How did Thomas feel when he saw Jesus alive?** (Very glad.) **We are also glad that Jesus is alive. We can tell others the good news! Who is someone in your family who you can tell that Jesus is alive?**

# Worship Center

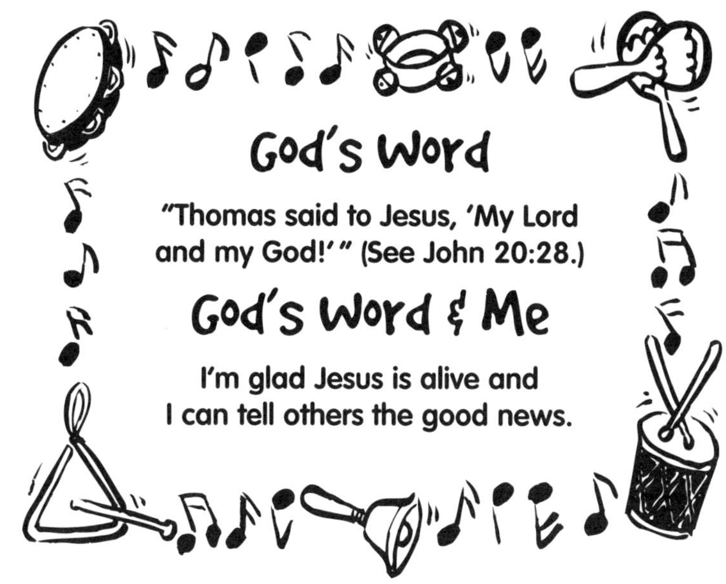
God's Word
"Thomas said to Jesus, 'My Lord and my God!'" (See John 20:28.)
God's Word & Me
I'm glad Jesus is alive and I can tell others the good news.

## Collect

Bible, *Shake It Up!* songbook and cassette/CD and player, "Jesus Is Alive!" and "Sing Praises" word charts (pp. 38 and 40 in songbook).

## Sing to God

Play "Jesus Is Alive!" Invite children to sing along with you. **I'm glad Jesus is alive! Are you glad, too? Let's sing about Jesus.** Lead children in singing song and doing suggested motions. **This song tells us that we have a reason to be happy. What's the reason?** (Jesus is alive!)

## Hear and Say God's Word

Holding your Bible open to John 20:28, say verse aloud. **Thomas said these words because he was very happy Jesus is alive. I'm glad Jesus is alive and I can tell others the good news.** Lead children in saying the verse as a group several times. Children clap their hands on each name, "Thomas," "Jesus," "Lord" and "God." Repeat several times.

## Pray to God

Children repeat the following prayer, phrase by phrase: **Dear God, . . . we believe . . . that Jesus is living today. . . . We thank You . . . for Jesus. . . . We thank You . . . for loving us. . . . We love You. . . . In Jesus' name, amen.**

## Sing to God

In closing the worship time, play "Sing Praises." Invite children to sing along with you and do suggested motions. **Singing songs is one way we can tell others about Jesus. I'm glad Jesus is alive! I can tell others this good news!**

## Options

1. If you collect a weekly offering, introduce it by saying, **Giving money to our church is one way to thank God that Jesus is alive.** Then briefly describe one or more ways the money is used to tell others about Jesus.

2. During prayer activity, share an age-appropriate example of a time someone told you about Jesus, or a time you told someone else about Jesus.

# Read-Aloud Story and Activity Center

## Collect

A copy of Story Picture 29 (pp. 63-64 from *Read-Aloud Story and Activity Book*) for each child and yourself, crayons or markers.

"Thomas said to Jesus, 'My Lord and my God!'"

## Prepare

Color your copy of Story Picture 29.

## Do

**Listen to find out what game these children are playing.**
Read story and show completed Story Picture 29. Distribute pictures. Use conversation suggestions in Let's Talk About the Story as children complete their pages.

# Kindergarten Puzzle Center

## Collect

Copies of Puzzles 57 and 58 (p. 121 and p. 123 from *The Big Book of Kindergarten Puzzles*) for each child, pencils, crayons or markers.

## Do

Children complete the puzzles and color pages.

# Instant Activities

These activities can be used at any time during this session: when children need a change of pace, to extend the session, or during transition time at the beginning or end of the session.

## Collect

*The Big Book of Instant Activities.*

## Do

Guide children to complete "Talk Show" and/or "Let Everyone Clap Hands" (p. 71 and/or p. 97 from *The Big Book of Instant Activities*).

Lesson 30

# Jesus Lives Today

## Bible Story

Matthew 28:16-20; John 21:1-14; Acts 1:3-11

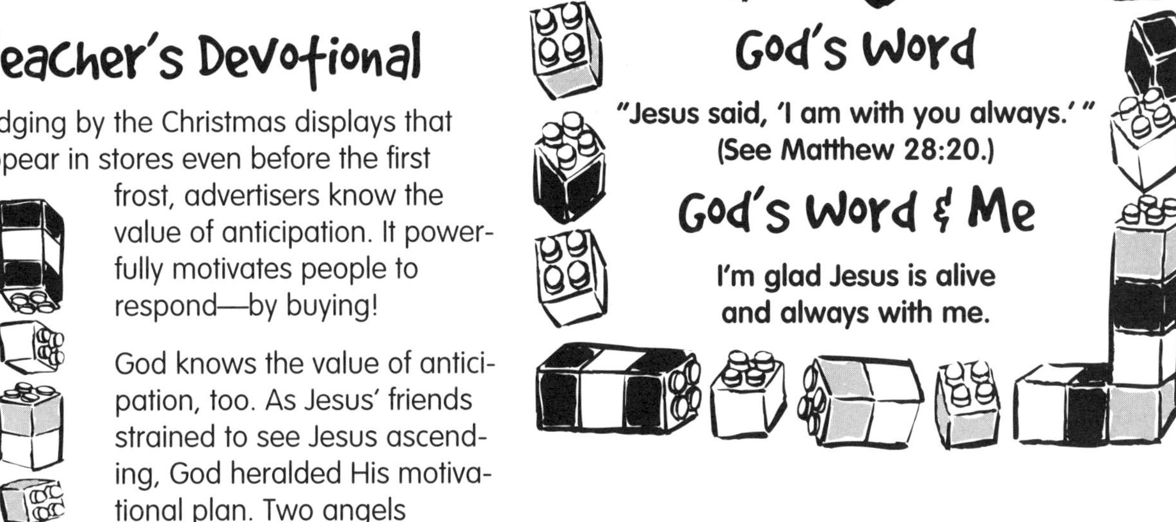
God's Word
"Jesus said, 'I am with you always.' "
(See Matthew 28:20.)
God's Word & Me
I'm glad Jesus is alive
and always with me.

## Teacher's Devotional

Judging by the Christmas displays that appear in stores even before the first frost, advertisers know the value of anticipation. It powerfully motivates people to respond—by buying!

God knows the value of anticipation, too. As Jesus' friends strained to see Jesus ascending, God heralded His motivational plan. Two angels announced, "This same Jesus . . . will come back in the same way you have seen him go into heaven" (Acts 1:11). At Pentecost, the plan was activated by the coming of the Holy Spirit. Jesus' friends were not only motivated but also empowered to spread the gospel and the news of Jesus' anticipated return. John later appealed to this anticipation, challenging God's family to "continue in him, so that when he appears we may be confident and unashamed before him at his coming" (see 1 John 2:28).

The angels caused Jesus' friends to focus on Jesus' return. Then the Holy Spirit motivated and empowered the friends to live in powerful action as they anticipated Jesus' return. They didn't just sit waiting. We also look for His return. As we do, let us be as eager as Jesus' disciples were to live in active anticipation, confident and unashamed at His coming.

## Teacher's Planning

1. Choose which centers you will provide and the order in which children will participate in them. For tips on schedule planning, see page 7.

2. Plan who will lead each center. For staffing tips and ideas, see page 21.

Lesson 30

# Active Game Center: Pack It Up!

## Collect

Bible, various household items (washcloth, slippers, comb, toothpaste, etc.), suitcase.

## Prepare

Place household items in one corner of the activity area. Open suitcase and place in a second corner.

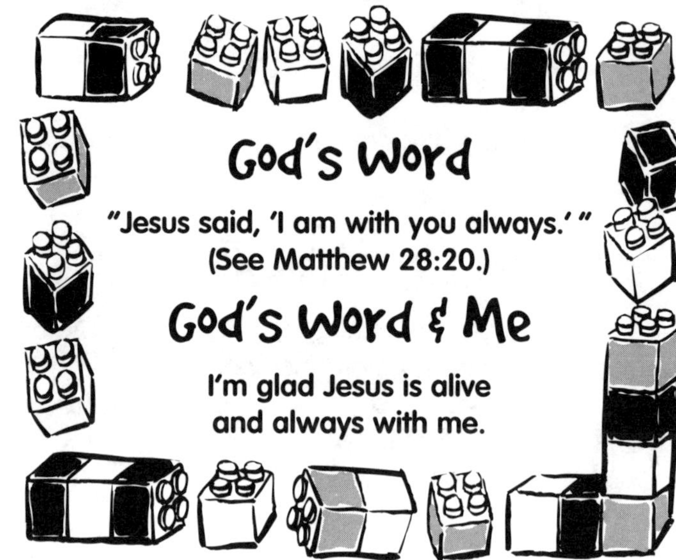
God's Word
"Jesus said, 'I am with you always.'"
(See Matthew 28:20.)
God's Word & Me
I'm glad Jesus is alive
and always with me.

## Do

1. Children line up in an empty corner of the activity area. One at a time, children walk to household items and select one. Children then place household item in suitcase and finally return to starting corner.
2. Once all the household items have been placed in suitcase, children take turns to unpack the suitcase by reversing the procedure.

## Talk About

- **Our Bible tells us, "Jesus said, 'I am with you always.'" Jesus is with us wherever we go! Let's play a game about something we do when we go to different places.**
- **Brian, what did you pack? When are some times you use a comb? Jesus is with you when you get ready for school in the morning.**
- **Dottie, where are some places you have gone? Jesus was with you there! I'm glad that Jesus is alive and always with us.** Pray briefly, **Dear Jesus, thank You for always being with us.**

## For Younger Children

Provide several suitcases, backpacks or duffel bags in addition to the household items. Instead of waiting in line for a turn, children pack and unpack all items.

## For Older Children

In addition to household items, provide classroom items such as small blocks, crayons or toy people. For each round of the game, tell a specific number of items each child is to pack.

Lesson 30

# Art Center: Shaving-Cream Art

## Collect

Bible, can of shaving cream, paper towels.

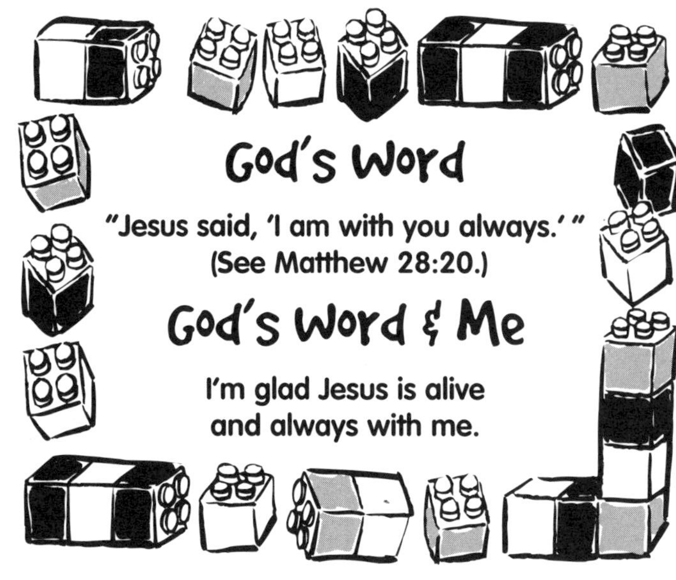
God's Word
"Jesus said, 'I am with you always.'"
(See Matthew 28:20.)
God's Word & Me
I'm glad Jesus is alive
and always with me.

## Do

Children wearing long sleeves roll up their sleeves. Squirt shaving cream on table for children to use as finger paint. Use paper towels to clean up.

## Talk About

- **In today's Bible story, Jesus rose up into the sky. Jesus rose right up into the clouds! Let's make pictures with something white and fluffy like clouds.**
- **Before Jesus went back to heaven, He told His friends that He would always care for them. Jesus cares for us, too. Cory, where are some of the places you like to go? Jesus is with you when you go to the mall. Brianne, where do you like to go with your baby-sitter? The library is a fun place. Jesus is with us at the library!**
- **Our Bible tells us, "Jesus said, 'I am with you always.'" I'm glad to know Jesus is alive and always with me! Even though we can't see Jesus, we know He is with us.**
- Pray briefly, **Thank You, Jesus, for being with us wherever we go.**

SHAVING CREAM

## For Younger Children

Instead of using shaving cream, children make cloud shapes by gluing cotton balls to sheets of blue construction paper.

## For Older Children

Print the word "Jesus" on a large sheet of paper. Children copy the letters to print the word "Jesus" in the shaving cream.

Lesson 30

# Block Center: Train of Blocks

## Collect

Bible, blocks.

## Do

Children lay blocks in the outline of a train, wide enough for the children to sit inside. When pretend train is finished, children take seats and pretend to ride the train on an imaginary journey.

### God's Word

**"Jesus said, 'I am with you always.'" (See Matthew 28:20.)**

### God's Word & Me

**I'm glad Jesus is alive and always with me.**

## Talk About

- **In today's Bible story, Jesus told His friends that it was time for Him to go back to heaven. And then something wonderful happened—Jesus went up, up, up into the clouds and back to heaven. Even though Jesus' friends couldn't see Him anymore, they knew that Jesus would always be with them. Jesus is always with us, too! Let's build a train with our blocks and pretend to go on a trip!**

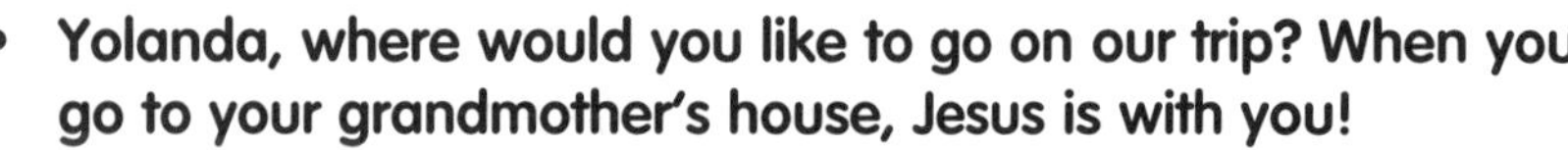

- **Yolanda, where would you like to go on our trip? When you go to your grandmother's house, Jesus is with you!**

- **Paul, did your family ever go on vacation? Where did you go? Did you know that wherever we go, Jesus is with us, always caring for us? He is! Our Bible tells us, "Jesus said, 'I am with you always.'" I'm glad Jesus loves us!**
- Pray briefly, **Thank You, Jesus, for always being with us. We love You.**

## For Younger Children

On the floor, use masking tape to outline a train. Children place blocks on masking tape for train.

## For Older Children

Children build train tracks by placing blocks in parallel lines in front of the block train. The train tracks can be straight, curved or make a large circle in the activity area.

# Science Center: Fish It Out!

## Collect

Bible, shallow baking dish, water, one or more toys or household objects (toy people, blocks, Styrofoam peanuts, pebbles, pencils, etc.) for each child, scoops (slotted or serving spoons, strainers, etc.), several towels.

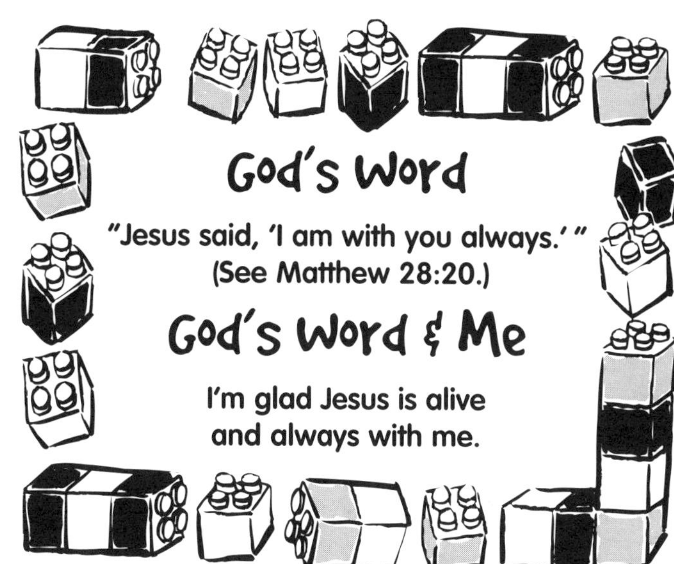
God's Word
"Jesus said, 'I am with you always.'"
(See Matthew 28:20.)
God's Word & Me
I'm glad Jesus is alive
and always with me.

## Prepare

Pour water into baking dish. Place toys and/or household objects in baking dish. (Note: If you have a large class, you may wish to prepare more than one baking dish with water and objects.) Place baking dish on a towel.

## Do

Children use scoops to fish objects out of the water. Use additional towels to clean up spills.

## Talk About

- **In today's Bible story, Jesus' friends were fishing. Jesus helped His friends catch many fish. Let's fish some things out of water!**
- **Some objects float on water and some sink. Margie, what is something that floats? Gary, what is something that sinks?**
- **Our Bible tells us, "Jesus said, 'I am with you always.'" I'm glad Jesus is alive! Jesus is always with us.**

## For Younger Children

Instead of using scoops, children use their hands to fish out objects. Make sure children wearing long sleeves roll up their sleeves before putting hands in the water.

## For Older Children

Children make sieves by using pencils to carefully poke holes in the bottoms of Styrofoam cups. Children then use sieves to fish out objects.

Lesson 30 • Matthew 28:16-20; John 21:1-14; Acts 1:3-11

# Bible Story Center

## Collect

Bible, Picture 43 from *Bible Story Pictures*.

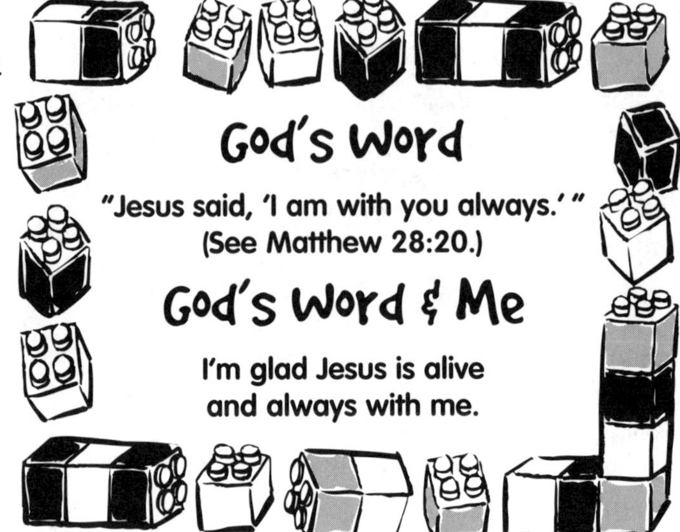

God's Word
"Jesus said, 'I am with you always.' "
(See Matthew 28:20.)
God's Word & Me
I'm glad Jesus is alive
and always with me.

## Tell the Story

Use the pictured motions (keywords in bold) or show Picture 43. For older children, tell the version of the story on the back of Picture 43.

**When have you seen a fish? Where did you see the fish? Listen to hear what happened one time when Jesus' friends were fishing.**

After Jesus died and then rose from the tomb, Jesus' friends were so happy Jesus was alive! Jesus stayed with His friends for many days. Jesus talked with them about many things. He loved His friends! Once when they were fishing, Jesus helped them catch lots of fish. Their nets were so full of fish the friends could **barely lift** them up from the water! That same day Jesus cooked some breakfast for His friends. Jesus told them that someday soon He would be going back to heaven.

Then the day came when it was time for Jesus to go back to heaven. He walked with His friends out in the country. Jesus said to His friends, "Remember that I am with you always. I will watch over you and take care of you. Someday I will come back, and we will be together in heaven." Jesus wanted them to know that even though they wouldn't see Jesus with their eyes, He was still with them. Jesus' friends **listened** quietly. "After I am gone," Jesus said, "go and tell people everywhere that I love them."

Then Jesus rose up off the ground! Jesus' friends must have been surprised! Jesus went up and up and UP, until He was in the clouds, and then His friends couldn't see Him anymore. They stood there, **looking up**.

Suddenly, there were two angels standing beside the friends. The angels said, "Why are you standing here looking into the sky? Jesus has gone to heaven! Jesus will come back again someday." Jesus' friends were very **glad**! Now they knew Jesus was going to come back, just as He had promised. And they were glad because Jesus had promised to always be with them. And He will always be with us, too!

## God's Word & Me

**What did Jesus tell His friends He would do?** (Come back. Always be with them.) **I'm glad Jesus is alive and always with me! Where do you like to go to play with your friends? Jesus is with you when you go to the park. Jesus is with us wherever we go!**

# Worship Center

## Collect

Bible, *Shake It Up!* songbook and cassette/CD and player, "Jesus Is Alive!" and "Sing Praises" word charts (pp. 38 and 40 in songbook).

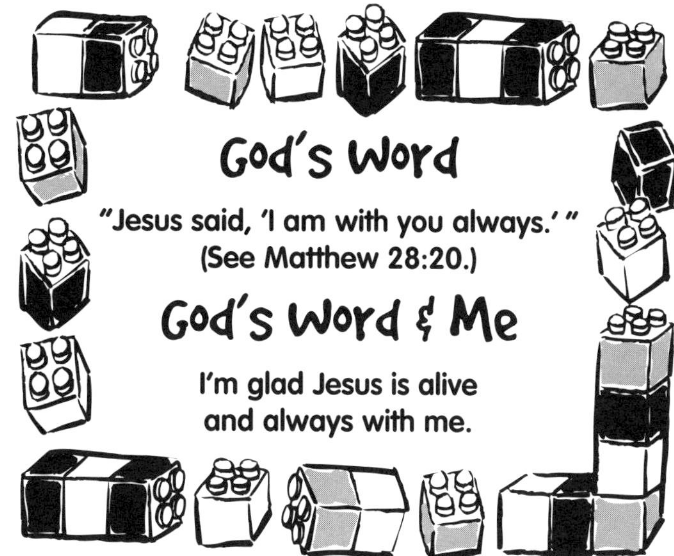
God's Word
"Jesus said, 'I am with you always.'"
(See Matthew 28:20.)
God's Word & Me
I'm glad Jesus is alive
and always with me.

## Sing to God

Play "Jesus Is Alive!" Invite children to sing along with you. **Let's sing a song about a good reason to be happy.** Lead children in singing song and doing suggested motions. **Jesus is alive! I'm glad Jesus is alive. Jesus is always with you and me.**

## Hear and Say God's Word

Holding your Bible open to Matthew 28:20, say verse aloud. **When Jesus went back to heaven, He wanted His friends to be happy. Jesus wanted His friends to know that He would always be with them.** Children perform the following motions as they say the words of the verse: Alternately touch palms with middle fingers for the word "Jesus"; point to mouth for "said"; point to self for "I"; point to person in room for "you." Repeat several times.

## Pray to God

As you say the following prayer, point to a child and pause for the child to say his or her name and complete the phrase: **Dear God, thank You for being with __________.** Repeat once for each child in your class. If you have a large class, point to more than one child each time you repeat the phrase.

## Sing to God

In closing the worship time, play "Sing Praises." Invite children to sing along with you and do suggested motions. **Singing praises to God is one way to thank God that Jesus is alive and always with us.**

## Options

1. With parents' permission, videotape children as they sing songs and do the motions. Play videotape at the end of the session as parents come to pick up their children.
2. Invite a musician from your church to play one or more of the suggested songs for this lesson on a guitar, flute, trumpet, etc.

 

Lesson 30

# Read-Aloud Story and Activity Center

## Collect

A copy of Story Picture 30 (pp. 65-66 from *Read-Aloud Story and Activity Book*) for each child and yourself, crayons or markers.

"Jesus said, 'I am with you always.'"

## Prepare

Color your copy of Story Picture 30.

## Do

**Listen to find out what this boy is doing.** Read story and show completed Story Picture 30. Distribute pictures. Use conversation suggestions in Let's Talk About the Story as children complete their pages.

# Kindergarten Puzzle Center

## Collect

Copies of Puzzles 59 and 60 (p. 125 and p. 127 from *The Big Book of Kindergarten Puzzles*) for each child, pencils, crayons or markers.

## Do

Children complete the puzzles and color pages.

# Instant Activities

These activities can be used at any time during this session: when children need a change of pace, to extend the session, or during transition time at the beginning or end of the session.

## Collect

*The Big Book of Instant Activities.*

## Do

Guide children to complete "Can You Remember?" and/or "I Stretch" (p. 110 and/or p. 42 from *The Big Book of Instant Activities*).

Lesson 31

# The Lame Man Walks

## God's Word

**"Hear the word of God and obey it."**
**Luke 11:28**

## God's Word & Me

**I can obey God by helping others.**

## Bible Story

Acts 3:1-16

## Teacher's Devotional

Imagine that you are the lame man in today's story. To stay alive, you must beg for money. Crowds of people pass you; you crane your neck, struggling to catch the eye of someone who'll give a few coins. But mostly you see legs—legs that rush, hop, skip or waddle—legs that work. And you are powerless even to crawl.

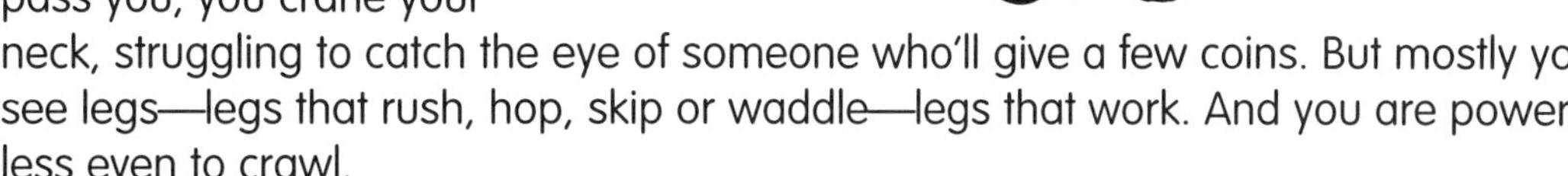

Peter and John pass by. And Peter sees you! You've made eye contact—finally! You ask for money, holding out your hand. "I have no silver or gold," Peter says. *NO MONEY?! What is this, a joke?* But instead, Peter offers what he has. By God's Holy Spirit he sees your deepest need more clearly than you do. "In the name of Jesus Christ of Nazareth, walk" (Acts 3:6).

Like the lame man, we may recognize our need for money or things or someone else's help. But like that lame man, we may not clearly see that God's power is the first thing we must have! As we take our needs for patience, for equipment, for help to Jesus, we can ask Him for His power. He knows what we need better than we do! Look as expectantly to Him as the lame man looked at Peter, "expecting to get something" (Acts 3:5). You'll see how He supplies our needs, even as He gives us power in Him to use what He gives!

## Teacher's Planning

1. Choose which centers you will provide and the order in which children will participate in them. For tips on schedule planning, see page 7.
2. Plan who will lead each center. For staffing tips and ideas, see page 21.

Lesson 31

# Active Game Center: Color Jump

## Collect

Bible, *Shake It Up!* cassette/CD and player, construction paper in four colors, scissors.

## Prepare

Cut construction paper sheets into eighths, creating one square in each color for each child. Scatter construction paper squares in activity area.

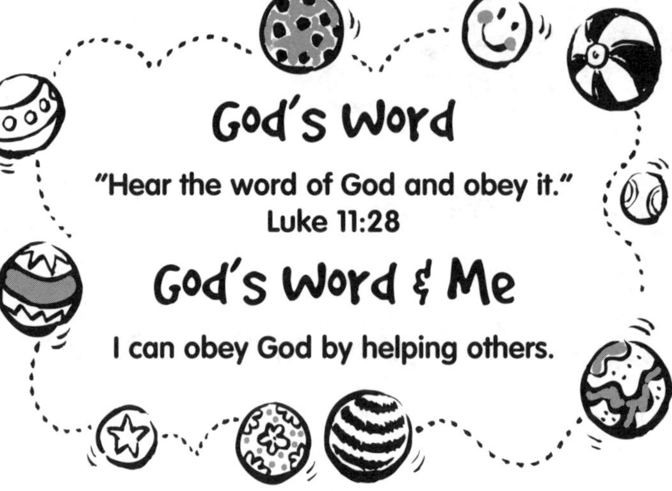
God's Word
"Hear the word of God and obey it."
Luke 11:28
God's Word & Me
I can obey God by helping others.

## Do

Play "Hear the Word" for a few moments.
Children walk around as music plays and they clap their hands on the words "hear the word." Stop the music and call out one of the colors of construction paper. Children jump to stand on a square that is the color you called and freeze until you start the music again. Repeat several times, calling out a different color each time.

## Talk About

- **Today's Bible story is about a man who couldn't use his legs. He couldn't walk, run, jump or skip! Two of Jesus' friends, Peter and John, obeyed God and helped the man. God made the man's legs work, so he could walk! Let's use our legs as we play a game.**
- **Josiah, you jumped right on that green square! You know how to listen and obey. Kathy, what is something your mom told you to do this morning? What did you do to obey?**
- **Our Bible says, "Hear the word of God and obey it." The Bible is the word of God written down. Who reads Bible stories to you? Listening to Bible stories is one way to hear the word of God!**

## For Younger Children

Instead of colors being called out and children jumping onto colored squares when the music stops, children simply freeze in place. Children begin moving again when you start the music again. Start and stop the music several times.

## For Older Children

While the music is stopped, volunteers tell ways to help others.

# Art Center: Paper-Plate Puppets

## Collect

Bible, construction paper, scissors, paper plates, glue, craft sticks, masking tape.

## Prepare

From construction paper, cut facial features as shown in sketch.

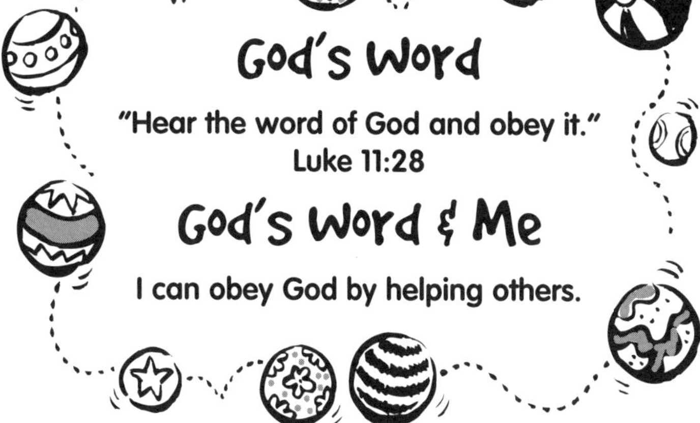
God's Word
"Hear the word of God and obey it."
Luke 11:28
God's Word & Me
I can obey God by helping others.

## Do

1. Children glue construction paper shapes onto paper plates to form faces, a happy face on one side and a sad face on the other.
2. Use masking tape to attach craft sticks to paper plates to form puppets.

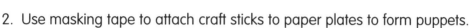

## Talk About

- **Today's Bible story is about a man who was lame. The man's legs didn't work at all. He was very sad! But two of Jesus' friends helped the man. That made the lame man very happy! Let's make puppets that have both a happy and a sad face.**
- **Our Bible says, "Hear the word of God and obey it." We obey God when we help others. Penny, you helped Rich when you moved over and gave him more room. When you helped Rich, you showed that you know how to obey.**

Front
Back

## For Younger Children

Instead of gluing on construction-paper circles, children use markers to decorate paper plates and draw happy and sad faces.

## For Older Children

Children make three paper-plate puppets, one each for Peter, John and the lame man. Children use puppets to act out story action as you briefly retell story. Expect to retell story several times as children come and go from the Art Center.

Lesson 31

# Block Center: Obey and Build

## Collect

Bible, blocks, toy cars.

## Do

Use directions below to guide children in building ramps. Children race toy cars on the ramps.

### God's Word

**"Hear the word of God and obey it."**
**Luke 11:28**

### God's Word & Me

**I can obey God by helping others.**

## Talk About

- **Our Bible says, "Hear the word of God and obey it." The Bible is the word of God. When we do what the Bible says, we're obeying God! Listen carefully to my directions. We'll build car ramps!**

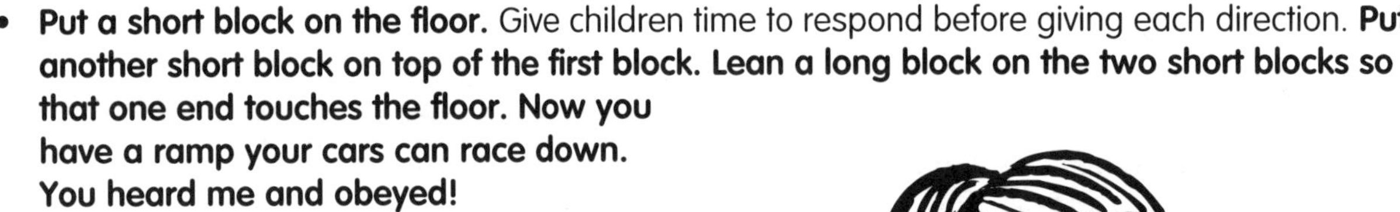

- **Put a short block on the floor.** Give children time to respond before giving each direction. **Put another short block on top of the first block. Lean a long block on the two short blocks so that one end touches the floor. Now you have a ramp your cars can race down. You heard me and obeyed!**

- **God's Word tells us to help others. We can obey God by helping others. Dwayne, Nancy needs a long block to finish building her ramp. How can you help her? Thank you for handing her a long block! You're a good helper.**
- **Noel, who fixes your breakfast in the morning? How can you help your dad fix breakfast for your family?**
- Pray briefly, **Dear God, thank You for the Bible. Help us to always obey Your Word.**

## For Younger Children

Children build towers only. Remind children to build towers no higher than their chins.

## For Older Children

Children play a stacking game to build a group tower. Children take turns placing a block on the tower. As each child places a block, he or she tells one way to help others.

# Science Center: Listen and Walk

## Collect

Bible, yarn; optional—hand bell or whistle.

## Prepare

Make a large circle out of yarn in the center of the activity area.

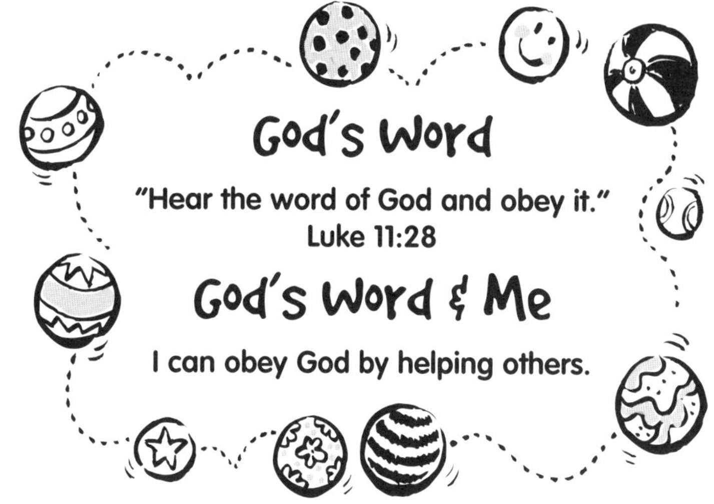
God's Word
"Hear the word of God and obey it."
Luke 11:28
God's Word & Me
I can obey God by helping others.

## Do

1. Children walk single file around the outside of the yarn circle. Clap your hands. (Optional: Ring bell or blow whistle instead of clapping your hands.) Children stop walking. At your signal children begin walking again.
2. Repeat several times, directing the children to walk in different ways around the circle (heel to toe, rubbing arms, clapping hands, straddling yarn, patting head, etc.).

## Talk About

- **Our Bible says, "Hear the word of God and obey it." The Bible is God's Word. Let's use our ears to listen and obey.**
- **Treavor, when your mom says "Help me set the table," what do you do? When you obey your mom and help her, you are obeying what God says to do, too!**
- **God has given us special rules to obey. One thing God tells us to do is help others. Brianne, what is a way you can help Howie at the Block Center today?**
- **It's not always easy to obey. Julie, when are times it might be hard to obey? We can ask God for His help.** Pray briefly, **Dear God, help us to obey, even when it's hard.**

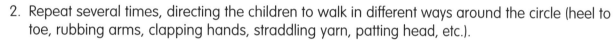

## For Younger Children

Play a game like Simon Says. Children follow you as you call out, demonstrate and tell them a specific action to do (touch noses, tap knees, jump up and down, etc.).

## For Older Children

Children repeat the words of the verse as they walk around the yarn circle.

Lesson 31 • Acts 3:1-16

# Bible Story Center

## Collect

Bible, Picture 44 from *Bible Story Pictures.*

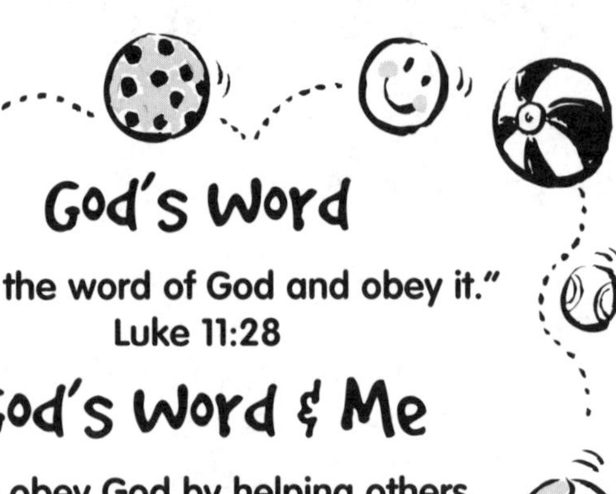
God's Word
"Hear the word of God and obey it."
Luke 11:28
God's Word & Me
I can obey God by helping others.

## Tell the Story

Use the pictured motions (keywords in bold) or show Picture 44. For older children, tell the version of the story on the back of Picture 44.

**Which do you like better—jumping or running? Listen to find out what happened to a man who couldn't jump or run.**

Near the gate outside the Temple sat a man who couldn't walk. His legs were lame. That means they didn't work. He couldn't even stand up. Every day this man's friends **carried** him up the hill to the Temple gate. The Temple was the place where many people went to pray and learn about God. Every day the lame man sat by the Temple. As people walked into the Temple, the man would ask them for money.

One day Jesus' friends, Peter and John, walked up the hill to the Temple. Peter and John heard someone call, "Please **give me** some money." They stopped. They looked down. They saw the lame man sitting on the ground.

"I have no money," Peter said, "but I do have something to give you." Peter reached out and took the man's hand. Peter said, "In the name of Jesus, stand up and walk!" and **pulled** the man to his feet.

Suddenly, the lame man's feet and legs were strong! The man began to walk! Then the man began to skip and jump and hop and RUN! He was so happy! He went into the Temple with Peter and John. The man told everyone what happened. "Thank You, God! I can walk," said the man.

The people at the Temple saw the man **walking**. They thought Peter and John had made the man walk. But Peter told them, "We did not make this man walk. Jesus made his legs strong." Peter told all those people about Jesus. And the man who now could walk learned about Jesus, too.

## God's Word & Me

**Who helped the lame man?** (Jesus. Peter. John.) **We can help others, too! When we help others, we are obeying God! How can you help your mom at dinnertime?** (Put napkins on the table. Wash my hands.) **How can you help your mom when you go to the store?** (Stay close to her. Obey what she says.)

Lesson 31

# Worship Center

## God's Word

**"Hear the word of God and obey it."**
**Luke 11:28**

## God's Word & Me

**I can obey God by helping others.**

## Collect

Bible, *Shake It Up!* songbook and cassette/CD and player, "Who Needs Help?" and "Hear the Word" word charts (pp. 42 and 44 in songbook).

## Sing to God

Play "Who Needs Help?" Invite children to sing along with you. **Let's sing a song about helping people.** Lead children in singing song and doing suggested motions. **It isn't hard to find someone to help. You can help the person standing next to you! Sometimes just saying kind words or giving a hug is the best way to help others.**

## Hear and Say God's Word

Holding your Bible open to Luke 11:28, say verse aloud. **The Bible is God's Word. We know the verses we say and stories we hear at church are true because they come from __________.** Pause to let children complete the sentence with the words "the Bible." Then lead children in repeating the verse in this manner: The boys say "Hear the word of God," and then the girls say "And obey it." Children repeat the verse in this manner several times, alternating which group says the phrases.

## Pray to God

Ask children to think of the name of someone they want to help. As you call each child's name, he or she names the person and completes the following prayer: **Dear God, thank You for Your Word, the Bible. Help us to help others. Rocky wants to help __________.** Repeat for each child.

## Sing to God

In closing the worship time, play "Hear the Word." Invite children to sing along with you and do suggested motions. **When we listen to the Bible, we listen to God's Word. When we obey the Bible, we obey God!**

## Options

1. To make the Bible verse activity more challenging for older children, ask a volunteer to repeat verse, pointing to another child and adding the child's name to the beginning of the verse. **Marcel, hear the word of God and obey it.** The named child then repeats verse, pointing to and naming another child. Continue until each child has a turn.
2. Ask children to tell ways they can help others. Print children's responses on large sheet of paper. Display paper, so parents may read it when they pick up their children.

# Read-Aloud Story and Activity Center

## Collect

A copy of Story Picture 31 (pp. 67-68 from *Read-Aloud Story and Activity Book*) for each child and yourself, crayons or markers.

## Prepare

Color your copy of Story Picture 31.

## Do

**Listen to find out what happened to this girl.** Read story and show completed Story Picture 31. Distribute pictures. Use conversation suggestions in Let's Talk About the Story as children complete their pages.

# Kindergarten Puzzle Center

## Collect

Copies of Puzzles 61 and 62 (p. 129 and p. 131 from *The Big Book of Kindergarten Puzzles*) for each child, pencils, crayons or markers.

## Do

Children complete the puzzles and color pages.

# Instant Activities

These activities can be used at any time during this session: when children need a change of pace, to extend the session, or during transition time at the beginning or end of the session.

## Collect

*The Big Book of Instant Activities.*

## Do

Guide children to complete "Jumpers in the Dell" and/or "Foot Fumble" (p. 83 and/or p. 21 from *The Big Book of Instant Activities*).

Lesson 32

# Barnabas Shares

## Bible Story

Acts 4:32-37

God's Word
"Share with God's people who are in need." Romans 12:13
God's Word & Me
I can help others by sharing with them.

## Teacher's Devotional

Jesus told His friends to seek God's kingdom—God's rule in their lives—as their first priority. He taught them that it is more blessed to give than to receive and that their Father in heaven would take care of their every need. And like the perfect teacher that He is, He demonstrated His lessons vividly, by living—and then by giving—His life for us, His family. Jesus' followers had a concrete example to follow. Then empowered by the Spirit at Pentecost, they were of one heart and one mind, giving freely and sharing everything, trusting God to meet their needs. No individual even talked as if anything belonged to him or her—everything was at the service of God's family. They practiced the love Jesus had lived: God first, others next, self last.

Barnabas was just one of many who sold his property and gave the money freely to the apostles. His real name was Joseph, but the apostles nicknamed him "Son of Encouragement"! No doubt Barnabas' attitude of God's kingdom first and his love for God's family were far more valuable than the money he gave. A group of people with hearts like his could certainly turn the world upside down!

Freely sharing and putting God's kingdom first may seem impossible these days. We're so busy, and after all, those things do belong to us. We NEED them. Yet Jesus' commands—and the principles that worked in Acts 4—are still valid! It can be done—if we want to turn the world upside down again!

## Teacher's Planning

1. Choose which centers you will provide and the order in which children will participate in them. For tips on schedule planning, see page 7.
2. Plan who will lead each center. For staffing tips and ideas, see page 21.

Lesson 32

# Active Game Center: Toss Up

## Collect

Bible, towels or baby blankets, stuffed animals.

## Do

Children form pairs. Hand each pair a towel or blanket. Each child holds on to two corners of towel or blanket. Place a stuffed animal on each towel. Children toss stuffed animal up and down by moving towel or blanket together.

### God's Word

**"Share with God's people who are in need." Romans 12:13**

### God's Word & Me

**I can help others by sharing with them.**

## Talk About

- **In our Bible story today, Jesus' friends shared with people who didn't have enough food or clothes. We can help others by sharing with them. Let's play a game by sharing with each other.**
- **Good catch, Alex and Leila! You are sharing the towel and working together. Now it is time for Craig and Lindsay to take a turn. We share with others when we take turns.**

- **It is fun to play games with this teddy bear! Erin, what stuffed animals do you have at home? We can share our toys with others by letting others play with them. What toys can you share with your sister when you play together?**
- **Our Bible says, "Share with God's people who are in need." People in need sometimes need food or warm clothes.** Briefly describe one of the charitable activities in which your church participates.

## For Younger Children

Each child takes a turn holding on to one edge of towel or blanket and dragging stuffed animals around the room.

## For Older Children

Encourage older children to count each time they toss the animal up into the air.

# Art Center: Hat Making

## Collect

Bible, yarn, scissors, measuring stick, sturdy paper plates, decorating materials (ribbons, stickers, fabric scraps, buttons, feathers, markers, etc.), glue, hole punch, mirror.

## Prepare

Cut two 18-inch (45.5-cm) lengths of yarn for each child.

### God's Word

**"Share with God's people who are in need." Romans 12:13**

### God's Word & Me

**I can help others by sharing with them.**

## Do

1. Give each child a paper plate.
   Children share decorating supplies with each other and glue decorative items to bottom of paper plates to create hats.
2. When a child is finished decorating his or her plate, punch two holes on opposite sides of the plate. Tie a string through each hole. Child puts on hat. Tie strings under child's chin. Children look in mirror to see themselves wearing their hats.

## Talk About

- **In our Bible story today, Jesus' friends shared food and clothes. We help others by sharing with them. Let's make some hats. We can help people here in our class by sharing the decorations to make hats.**
- **Gina, Michael needs some buttons. How can you help? Thank you, Gina, for sharing the buttons. We share by giving things to people who need them.**
- **Peter, please pass Megan a string. Thank you for sharing with Megan. When else can you share? What can you share with your brother or sister at home?**
- **Our Bible says, "Share with God's people who are in need." God wants us to help people in need.**

## For Younger Children

Punch holes in hats and tie strings on ahead of time. Limit the number of decorating materials by providing only markers and stickers for children to use.

## For Older Children

Children punch holes in hats themselves and tie strings into bows. Assist children as needed.

Lesson 32

# Block Center: Construction Time

## Collect

Bible, blocks, toy cars and trucks, toy people.

## God's Word

**"Share with God's people who are in need." Romans 12:13**

## God's Word & Me

**I can help others by sharing with them.**

## Do

Children use blocks to build items of their own choice and then use toy cars, trucks and people with the structures they have built.

## Talk About

- **In today's Bible story, Jesus' friends shared food and clothes with people who didn't have any of those things. Let's share our blocks to help each other build.**
- **Helena, it looks like Jesse needs one more short block. How can you help him? Yes, you can help him by giving him that short block. Thank you for sharing with Jesse! We can help people by sharing with them.**
- **Kevin and Shana are rolling a car back and forth to each other. They are sharing the car. Our Bible says, "Share with God's people who are in need."**
- **Jessica, does your sister sometimes let you play with her toys at home? She knows about sharing. Which of your toys do you share with her? We can help people by sharing with them!**
- Pray with children, **Thank You, God, for all the good things You give us. Please help us to share them with others.**

## For Younger Children

Bring three towels or large sheets of construction paper, each in a different color. Place on floor. Children carry blocks and place on different colored towels or paper. **Jenna, can you share a block from the blue towel and give it to Chris on the green towel? Thank you for sharing!**

## For Older Children

Bring several magazine pictures of different kinds of buildings (houses, office buildings, schools, etc.). Children build a road and place pictures along the road. Children use toy cars, trucks and people to act out ways people share with others.

Lesson 32

# Science Center: Bubble Fun

## Collect

Bible, measuring cups, dishwashing liquid, water, spoon, pie tins or shallow trays, bubble wands in a variety of sizes.

God's Word
"Share with God's people who are in need." Romans 12:13
God's Word & Me
I can help others by sharing with them.

## Prepare

Make arrangements for children to blow bubbles outside if possible.

## Do

1. Lead children to make bubble solution. Children measure and pour one cup of dishwashing liquid and one cup of water into pie tins or shallow trays. Children use spoon to mix solution together.
2. Children dip wands into bubble solution and experiment with blowing bubbles through a variety of wand shapes.

# Talk About

- **The Bible tells us that Jesus' friends shared food and clothes with people who did not have them. Let's share these bubble wands and make beautiful bubbles together.**
- **Kristyl, look at that big bubble you blew! What colors do you see in the bubble? Maybe you'll be ready to share the big wand with Ellie next time.**
- **Our Bible says, "Share with God's people who are in need." We are sharing our bubble wands. What can you share with your sister or brother at home? What can you share with your friends when you are playing together?**

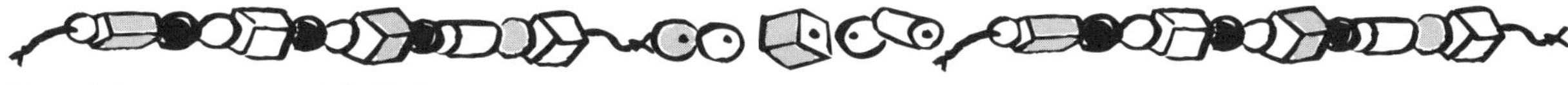

## For Younger Children

Blow bubbles for children to chase and catch. Hold wand for children so that volunteers can blow bubbles.

## For Older Children

Give each child a chenille wire. Model how to form a bubble wand. Children make wands in a variety of shapes and sizes and then share wands with one another to make different bubbles.

Lesson 32 • Acts 4:32-37

# Bible Story Center

## Collect

Bible, Picture 45 from *Bible Story Pictures*.

God's Word
"Share with God's people who are in need." Romans 12:13
God's Word & Me
I can help others by sharing with them.

## Tell the Story

Use the pictured motions (keywords in bold) or show Picture 45. For older children, tell the version of the story on the back of Picture 45.

**Who has shared a toy with you? Our story tells about a man who shared. Listen to find out what he shared.**

One of the ways Jesus' friends showed their love was by **sharing** everything they had. Nobody had to ask them to share. They wanted to share!

Some people had lots of food and clothing. But they didn't keep it all for themselves. They shared their food and clothes with Jesus' friends who had **no** food and clothing. If a family had more food than they needed, they didn't throw it away. They gave it to Jesus' friends who did not have enough food.

One of Jesus' friends helped other people so much that his friends gave him a nickname. The man's friends called him Barnabas. Barnabas meant something like "Mr. Helper." He was a cheerful, **happy** man. Barnabas was always helping people and trying to cheer them up!

Barnabas owned a field. He could have kept it for himself. Instead, Barnabas sold his field. Someone bought the land and gave Barnabas money for it. Barnabas could have spent that money on something he wanted for himself, but he didn't. Barnabas **gave** the money to the men who loved Jesus. He said, "Here, share this money with people who need it."

Barnabas had learned about Jesus and what Jesus said to do. He knew Jesus wanted him to help other people. Barnabas didn't keep his field or his money for himself. He showed he loved Jesus by sharing with other people.

## God's Word & Me

**What was the name of the man who shared?** (Barnabas.) **What did Jesus' friends share?** (Food and clothes.) **We can help others by sharing with them! Sharing means giving things to people who need them. Sharing can also mean letting others use our things. What can you share with someone who is hungry?** (Food.) **What can you share when we are playing with blocks?** (Blocks. Toy people.)

# Worship Center

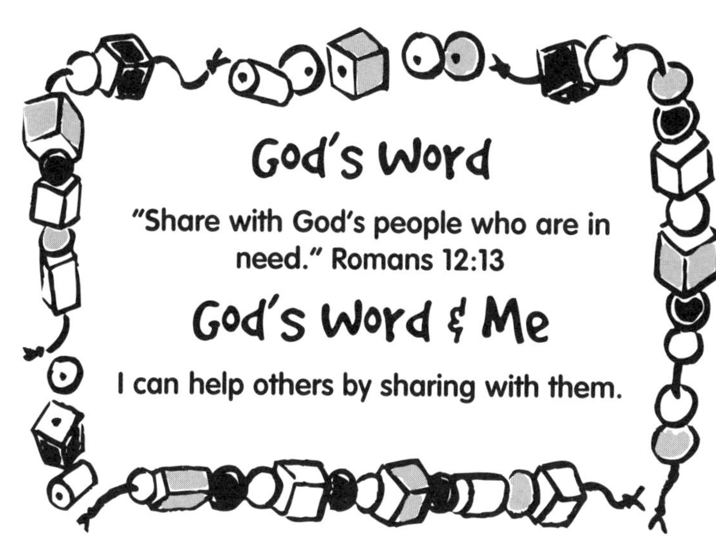
God's Word
"Share with God's people who are in need." Romans 12:13
God's Word & Me
I can help others by sharing with them.

## Collect

Bible, *Shake It Up!* songbook and cassette/CD and player, "Who Needs Help?" and "Hear the Word" word charts (pp. 42 and 44 in songbook).

## Sing to God

Play "Who Needs Help?" Invite children to sing along with you. **Let's sing a song about finding friends to help.** Lead children in singing song and doing suggested motions. **All around us are people we can help. We can help others by sharing with them!**

## Hear and Say God's Word

Holding your Bible open to Romans 12:13, say verse aloud. **I saw Jared share blocks with Grace today. Jared knows how to share! When we share with others, we help them!** Lead children in repeating the verse two or three times. Then add the word "at" and a time of day. **Share with God's people in need at lunchtime.** Children echo the phrase after you. Repeat several times, using different times of the day or days of the week.

## Pray to God

**Let's thank God that He helps us share with others.** To complete the following prayer, volunteers take turns naming people with whom they can share: **Thank You, God, that You help us share. Please help me share with __________.**

## Sing to God

In closing the worship time, play "Hear the Word." Invite children to sing along with you and do suggested motions. **God's words that we heard today are "Share with God's people who are in need." We obey God's words when we share!**

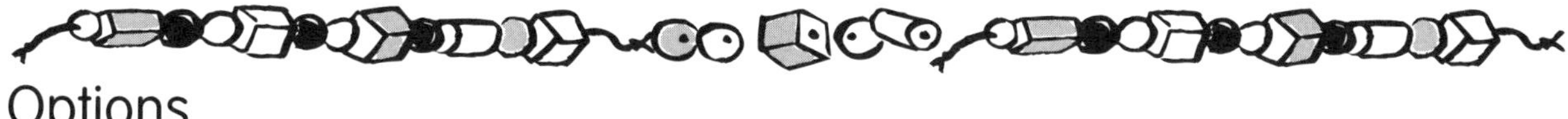

## Options

1. To make the Bible verse activity more challenging for older children, ask them to repeat verse and replace the words "God's people in need" with another child's name. The named child then repeats verse, using a different child's name. Continue until each child has a turn.
2. Ask children to tell ways they can share with others. Print children's responses on large sheet of paper. Display paper so that parents can read it when children are dismissed.

Lesson 32

# Read-Aloud Story and Activity Center

"Share with God's people in need." Romans 12:13

## Collect

A copy of Story Picture 32 (pp. 69-70 from *Read-Aloud Story and Activity Book*) for each child and yourself, crayons or markers.

## Prepare

Color your copy of Story Picture 32.

## Do

**Listen to find out what happened to this ice cream cone.** Read story and show completed Story Picture 32. Distribute pictures. Use conversation suggestions in Let's Talk About the Story as children complete their pages.

# Kindergarten Puzzle Center

## Collect

Copies of Puzzles 63 and 64 (p. 133 and p. 135 from *The Big Book of Kindergarten Puzzles*) for each child, pencils, crayons or markers.

## Do

Children complete the puzzles and color pages.

# Instant Activities

These activities can be used at any time during this session: when children need a change of pace, to extend the session, or during transition time at the beginning or end of the session.

## Collect

*The Big Book of Instant Activities.*

## Do

Guide children to complete "Shape Search" and/or "Bend Your Knees" (p. 120 and/or p. 92 from *The Big Book of Instant Activities*).

Lesson 33

# Food for Widows

## Bible Story

Acts 6:1-7

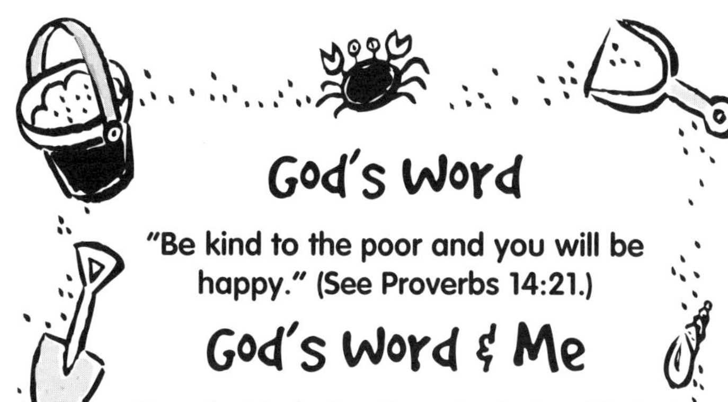

### God's Word

**"Be kind to the poor and you will be happy." (See Proverbs 14:21.)**

### God's Word & Me

**I'm glad to help others by being kind.**

## Teacher's Devotional

We want our children to grow up free of prejudice and fear, treating others fairly and seeing them as God sees them. Yet we sometimes find that it is difficult to model this kind of freedom from fear and prejudice for our children. It can be easier to label people in ways that make them seem less than God says they are.

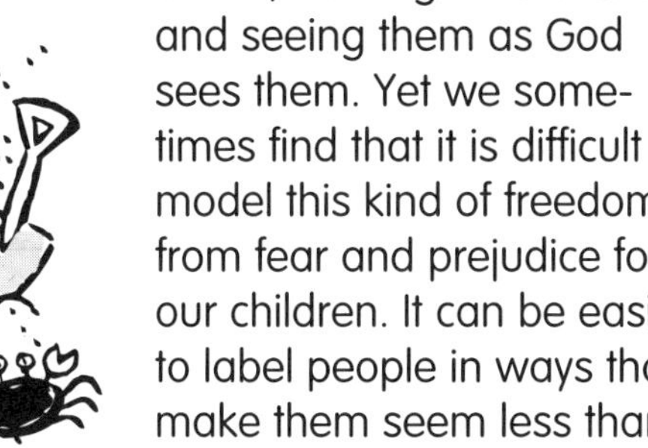

Prejudice often springs from the fear of change, fear of the unknown future. But we admit that our world is in rapid change—life will not be the same for our children as it was for us. It is sweet to know that God is in charge! He is bringing about His will, even as the waves of change roll over the society we have known. Even when these changes frighten us, we can rest, because our loving Father is turning these changes to our ultimate good—and His final glory (see Romans 8:18-39).

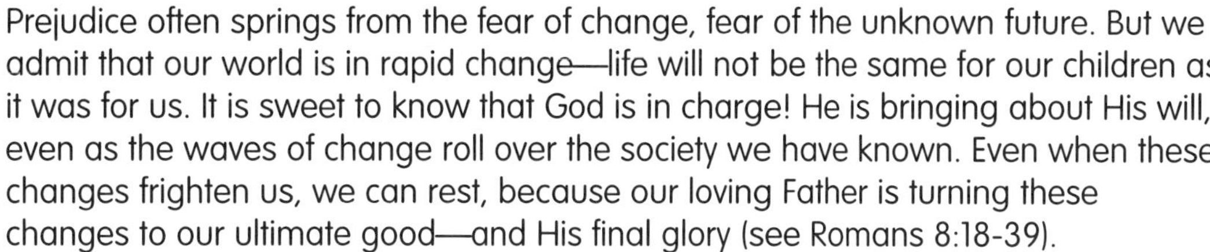

As we ask God to give us the ability to see others as He does, we can be free from prejudice and fear; for we know that in change, our perfect Father will not change. His generous love for us continues, no matter how our circumstances change. As you teach this story, help children recognize that our kind and fair actions are a result of recognizing God's overwhelming love for and kindness to us.

## Teacher's Planning

1. Choose which centers you will provide and the order in which children will participate in them. For tips on schedule planning, see page 7.
2. Plan who will lead each center. For staffing tips and ideas, see page 21.

 

Lesson 33

# Active Game Center: Ball Roll

## Collect

Bible, cardboard boxes, scissors, tennis balls.

## Prepare

Cut flaps off cardboard boxes. Place cardboard boxes on their sides against a wall with open sides facing out.

## Do

Children sit or stand about 3 feet (.9 m) from the boxes and take turns rolling the balls into the boxes. Retrieve balls and return them to the children. Invite an older child to help with retrieving balls.

### God's Word

**"Be kind to the poor and you will be happy." (See Proverbs 14:21.)**

### God's Word & Me

**I'm glad to help others by being kind.**

## Talk About

- **In our Bible story, Jesus' friends were kind to some women who had no food. They gave the women food and made sure they had enough to eat. We can help other people by being kind, too.**
- **Thank you, Jon, for straightening out the box that moved. You are being kind and helping all of us!**
- **Joy, you can be kind to Ashley by giving her a turn to roll the ball. I'm glad we can be kind and help each other with this game.**
- **What can you do to be kind and help others at your house? When you play with your friend?**
- **Our Bible says, "Be kind to the poor and you will be happy."** Pray briefly, **Dear God, help us be kind to others.**

## For Younger Children

Instead of using cardboard boxes, bring beach and/or bath towels. Children roll balls onto towels.

## For Older Children

Bring a variety of shapes and sizes of boxes and containers: smaller cardboard boxes, long mailing tubes, empty oatmeal canisters, etc. Children attempt to roll balls into target of their choice. Children may also create targets by putting long blocks across shorter blocks to create tunnels.

Lesson 33

# Art Center: Paper-Plate Faces

## Collect

Bible, red construction paper, scissors, paper plates, paper fasteners, markers.

## Prepare

Cut a curved mouth shape from red paper as shown in sketch, one for each child. Use scissors to poke a small hole in each plate where child will attach mouth.

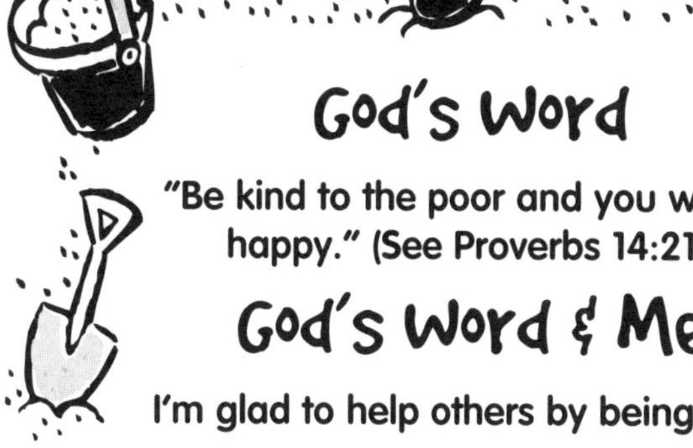

### God's Word

**"Be kind to the poor and you will be happy." (See Proverbs 14:21.)**

### God's Word & Me

**I'm glad to help others by being kind.**

## Do

Child connects mouth to paper plate with paper fastener and then draws nose and eyes on paper plate. Child rotates mouth around to show a happy or a sad face.

## Talk About

- **In our Bible story today, some women were very hungry. They were sad because they did not have enough food. Then Jesus' friends were kind and gave the hungry women food. This made the women happy! Let's make a face that can be happy or sad.**
- **Lily, show us how your paper-plate face looks when she is happy. Yes, now she is smiling. When we are kind and help other people, that makes them happy. It makes us happy, too!**
- **Our Bible says, "Be kind to the poor and you will be happy." We can be kind and help others. Claire, show with your paper plate how your mom's face looks when you help her set the table. Our moms are happy when we help!**

## For Younger Children

Make a dot-to-dot outline of a nose on children's plates. Children complete nose outline and add two dots for eyes.

## For Older Children

Provide 2-inch (5-cm) lengths of yarn for children to use for hair. Children glue yarn lengths to top edge of plate.

Lesson 33

# Block Center: Home Helpers

## Collect

Bible, blocks, toy people.

## Do

Children make the outline of a house with blocks. Children make walls to form rooms. Children use toy people to act out ways to be kind to family members.

### God's Word

**"Be kind to the poor and you will be happy." (See Proverbs 14:21.)**

### God's Word & Me

**I'm glad to help others by being kind.**

## Talk About

- **Our Bible says, "Be kind to the poor and you will be happy." When we are kind to others, we help them be happy. And we feel happy, too. Let's use our blocks to make a house. We can act out ways to be kind to the people in our families.**
- **Sophie, I see you are helping Christopher build the kitchen. You are a kind helper! That must make you and Christopher happy.**
- **Jason, how can you be kind to your sister when you are getting ready for bed? Yes, you can let your sister brush her teeth first.**
- **Hannah, how can you be kind in your home? You must be glad that you can be kind to the cat by feeding it. You are a good helper, Hannah!**
- **God is glad when we help others!** Pray briefly, **Dear God, thank You for being kind to us. Help us to help others. We love You.**

## For Younger Children

Make the outline of a house on the floor with masking tape. Children place blocks along the tape outline to form house. (Note: Remove tape immediately after activity.)

## For Older Children

Invite children to use blocks to add furniture to their house. Provide a green towel or construction paper for children to use as the yard. Children role-play helping family members in the yard as well as in the house.

Lesson 33

# Science Center: On a Roll!

## Collect

Bible, long block or sheet of wood, food items that will roll (nuts in shells, small canned food, etc.).

## Prepare

Place block or sheet of wood up against a chair or table to form a steep ramp. Make sure area around bottom of ramp is clear of furniture and children.

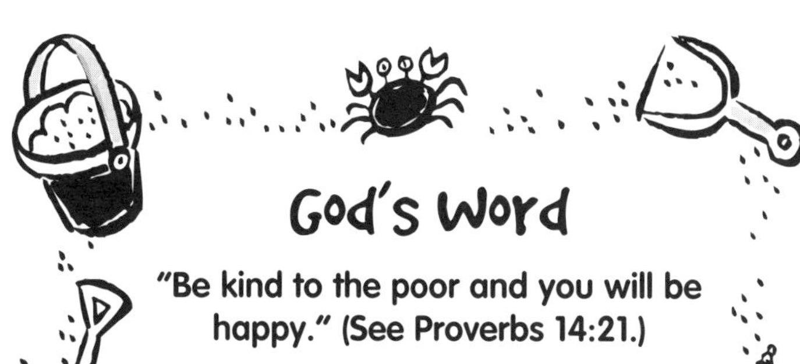

### God's Word

**"Be kind to the poor and you will be happy." (See Proverbs 14:21.)**

### God's Word & Me

**I'm glad to help others by being kind.**

## Do

Children take turns rolling food items down the ramp. Work together to find out which food item rolls the farthest and which food item rolls the shortest distance.

## Talk About

- **In our Bible story today, there were some women who didn't have enough food to eat. Jesus' friends were kind to the women and made sure they had enough food. Let's look at how some foods roll!**
- **Chris and Tyler, which rolled farther, the apple or the orange? I see you are helping each other collect the food after it stops rolling. Thank you for being kind!**

- **Jack, you can be kind and help! Will you bring the walnut here, so Lisa can take a turn?**
- **Our Bible says, "Be kind to the poor and you will be happy." It is important to be kind to ALL people! What can you do to be kind to your family? Sam, you can take turns with your sister when you play computer games.**

## For Younger Children

Make a masking-tape line. Instead of rolling food down ramp, children roll food items across the floor and over the masking-tape line. (Note: Remove masking tape immediately after activity.)

## For Older Children

Bring a tape measure or ruler for children to use to measure the distance each item rolls. Children sort food items according to how far they rolled, from the shortest to the longest distance.

Lesson 33 • Acts 6:1-7

# Bible Story Center

## Collect

Bible, Picture 46 from *Bible Story Pictures*.

**"Be kind to the poor and you will be happy." (See Proverbs 14:21.)**

### God's Word & Me

**I'm glad to help others by being kind.**

## Tell the Story

Use the pictured motions (keywords in bold) or show Picture 46. For older children, tell the version of the story on the back of Picture 46.

**What food do you like to eat? Listen to our Bible story to hear about some people who didn't have enough food to eat.**

Every day Jesus' friends told more and more people the good news that Jesus loved them. More and more people learned to love Jesus. And every day these people were **sharing** their food and clothing with people who had none. They were very happy.

However, one group of women whose husbands had died were **not happy**. These women said, "No one is sharing food with us. We are not getting enough to eat!" This was a problem!

The people who were friends of these women could have gotten angry. They could have grumbled and argued and caused lots of trouble, but they didn't. Instead, they told Jesus' friends about the problem.

When Jesus' friends heard about this, they felt sad. They wanted everyone to have enough food to eat. They wanted to be kind to everyone. So these friends of Jesus called everyone together. "We know it isn't fair that some people don't get enough food to eat." The people listened quietly.

"This is what we will do," Jesus' friends said. "Choose **seven** special helpers. These special helpers will make sure everyone gets enough food." So the people chose one, two, three, four, five, six, seven men to be special helpers. Then Jesus' friends **prayed** and asked God to help the seven men do their best work.

These special helpers did a good job. Now the women had enough food to eat, just like everyone else. Everyone worked together to be kind and show they loved Jesus.

## God's Word & Me

**What did the people do to be kind?** (Made sure the women got enough to eat. Jesus' friends chose seven special helpers to give the food to the women.) **We can be kind and help others, too. When can you be kind to your mom? Your dad? Your brothers or sisters?**

# Worship Center

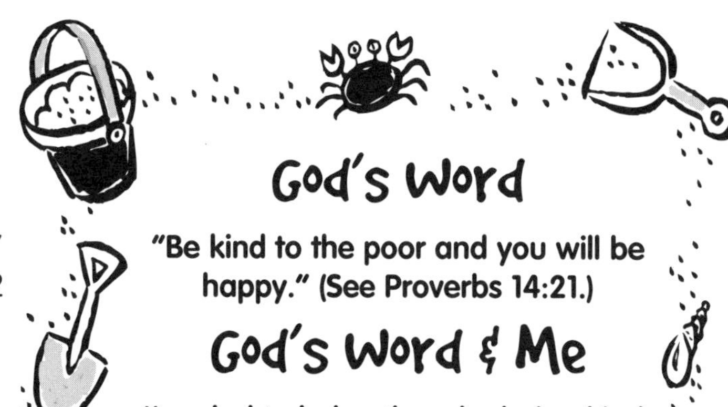

## God's Word

**"Be kind to the poor and you will be happy." (See Proverbs 14:21.)**

## God's Word & Me

**I'm glad to help others by being kind.**

### Collect

Bible, *Shake It Up!* songbook and cassette/CD and player, "Who Needs Help?" and "Hear the Word" word charts (pp. 42 and 44 in songbook).

## Sing to God

Play "Who Needs Help?" Invite children to sing along with you. **Let's sing a song about helping others.** Lead children in singing song and doing suggested motions. **Being kind to people is one way to help them. Eric, who can you be kind to when you play at the playground?**

## Hear and Say God's Word

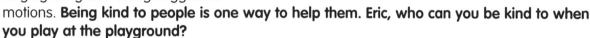

Holding your Bible open to Proverbs 14:21, say verse aloud. **We help others when we are kind. What are some of the things poor people might need?** (Food. Clothes. A place to live.) Lead children in repeating the verse after you a few times in this manner: Say the verse very quietly the first time and then a little bit louder each time you repeat the verse, until you are speaking in a normal speaking voice. Continue repeating verse, getting softer on each repetition, until speaking very quietly again.

## Pray to God

Children repeat prayer, phrase by phrase after you. **Dear God, . . . thank You that You help us . . . be kind to others. . . . Thank You that . . . when we are kind to others, . . . we will be happy, too. . . . In Jesus' name, amen.**

## Sing to God

In closing the worship time, play "Hear the Word." Invite children to sing along with you and do suggested motions. **I am glad we have ears to hear God's word. And I am glad we can obey it by being kind to others.**

### Options

1. If you take a weekly offering during this worship time, explain to children that some of the money is used to share with people who are poor. Giving money is one way to be kind to others.

2. During the verse activity, invite children to clap their hands on each word. Children clap softly when speaking softly and clap louder as they speak more loudly.

Lesson 33

# Read-Aloud Story and Activity Center

## Collect

A copy of Story Picture 33 (pp. 71-72 from *Read-Aloud Story and Activity Book*) for each child and yourself, crayons or markers.

## Prepare

Color your copy of Story Picture 33.

## Do

**Listen to find out where this family is going.** Read story and show completed Story Picture 33. Distribute pictures. Use conversation suggestions in Let's Talk About the Story as children complete their pages.

# Kindergarten Puzzle Center

## Collect

Copies of Puzzles 65 and 66 (p. 137 and p. 139 from *The Big Book of Kindergarten Puzzles*) for each child, pencils, crayons or markers.

## Do

Children complete the puzzles and color pages.

# Instant Activities

These activities can be used at any time during this session: when children need a change of pace, to extend the session, or during transition time at the beginning or end of the session.

## Collect

*The Big Book of Instant Activities.*

## Do

Guide children to complete "Can You?" and/or "What Do You See?" (p. 53 and/or p. 24 from *The Big Book of Instant Activities*).

Lesson 34

# Philip and the Ethiopian

## Bible Story

Acts 8:26-40

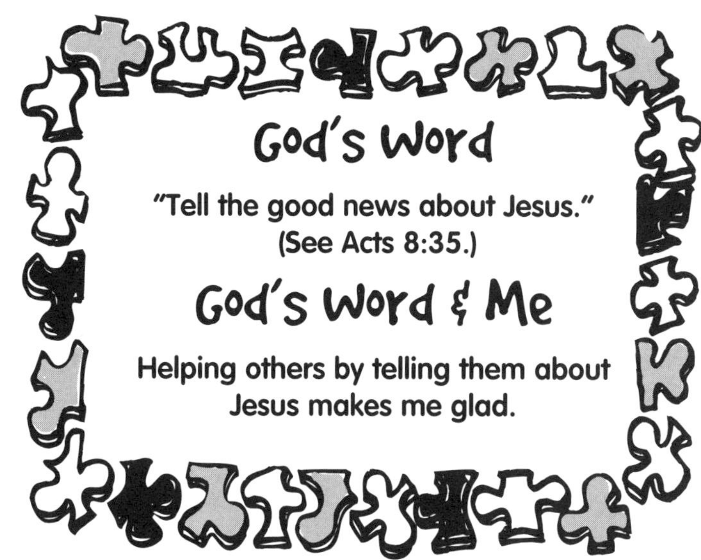
God's Word
"Tell the good news about Jesus."
(See Acts 8:35.)
God's Word & Me
Helping others by telling them about Jesus makes me glad.

## Teacher's Devotional

Imagine what Philip might have said when asked where he was headed on that road into the desert. "Oh, I don't know where I'm going. But I'm sure there's some reason for it. An angel told me to walk along here." To a stranger, Philip may have looked unusual, perhaps even silly. But to God, he looked obedient! Such obedience is the mark of a willing child of God in any age.

When God speaks to us today, we sometimes distract ourselves by wondering what others might think if we did what He told us! The opportunity to act on what God tells us may quickly pass; we could miss the opportunity God would have given us if we'd have just gotten up and obeyed.

It's common to measure our Christian growth by the expectations of other people. We must instead use Jesus as our measure! We grow to be like Jesus by obeying God as our first priority. Obeying God is very possibly going to make us look different or silly. Obeying God may even bruise our egos and in the process we may recognize our own sinfulness. That's a good thing! As we humble ourselves, we can then put Him first and move beyond worrying about what other people think.

## Teacher's Planning

1. Choose which centers you will provide and the order in which children will participate in them. For tips on schedule planning, see page 7.
2. Plan who will lead each center. For staffing tips and ideas, see page 21.

# Active Game Center: Triangle Tell

## Collect

Bible, *Shake It Up!* cassette/CD and player, masking tape.

## Prepare

Use masking tape to make several large triangles on the floor. (Note: Remove tape immediately after activity.)

### God's Word

**"Tell the good news about Jesus." (See Acts 8:35.)**

### God's Word & Me

**Helping others by telling them about Jesus makes me glad.**

## Do

1. Play "Who Needs Help?" for several moments. Children move randomly around the room while the music plays. When you stop the music, say, **Stand inside a triangle**. When all children are standing inside the triangles, talk about helping others using the conversation suggestions below.
2. Repeat game, giving a different command each time you stop the music (sit in a triangle, put one foot in a triangle, stand between the triangles, put your hands in a triangle, etc.).

## Talk About

- **Our Bible says, "Tell the good news about Jesus." We can help others by telling them the good news about Jesus!**
- **Jesus loves us. That is good news! Erin, who is a man you know? You can tell your dad Jesus loves him!**
- **Alan, who is standing next to you right now? Tell your neighbor "Jesus loves you!" This is good news!** Pray, **Thank You, Jesus, for the good news that You love us!**

## For Younger Children

When children have completed game command, say, **I will tell you some good news about Jesus. Repeat it after me: Jesus loves us.** Children repeat sentence. In other rounds, invite children to repeat other good news sentences such as "Jesus is alive" or "Jesus is God's Son."

## For Older Children

When children have completed game command, invite them to say the Bible verse aloud. **Jenny, what is some good news about Jesus? When you go home, tell your mom that Jesus is alive!**

Lesson 34

# Art Center: Paper-Bag Scrolls

## Collect

Bible, brown paper grocery bags, scissors, ruler, white paper, markers, rubber bands.

## Prepare

Cut bags into 6x10-inch (15x25.5-cm) rectangles, avoiding the print on the paper bags as much as possible. Prepare one rectangle for each child. Print "Jesus loves you!" three or four times on a sheet of white paper. Photocopy and cut apart sentences so that there is one sentence for each child.

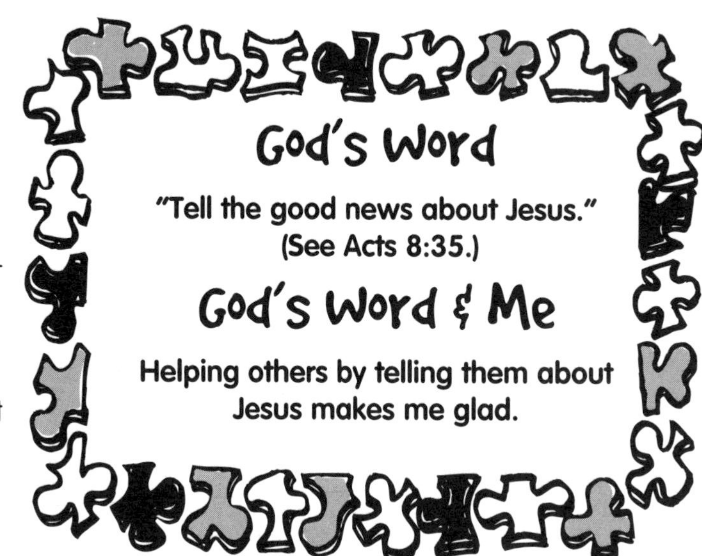
God's Word
"Tell the good news about Jesus."
(See Acts 8:35.)
God's Word & Me
Helping others by telling them about Jesus makes me glad.

## Do

Children glue sentences to paper rectangles to make a scroll. Using markers, children decorate their scrolls. Assist children in rolling up scrolls and securing them with rubber bands.

## Talk About

- **In Bible times, people read from scrolls. A scroll is like a long rolled-up sheet of paper. A man in our Bible story was reading a scroll. The scroll told about Jesus. Let's make some scrolls to tell about Jesus, too.**
- **You can help people know the good news that Jesus loves them! You can draw a heart to remind you that Jesus loves you, too.**
- **Our Bible says, "Tell the good news about Jesus." Who can you help by telling them about Jesus? What can you tell your mom about Jesus? You can show her your scroll!**

## For Younger Children

Provide stickers or rubber stamps and ink pads for children to use to decorate their scrolls.

## For Older Children

Before decorating their scrolls, children crumple the paper and then smooth it out several times to make paper look old and worn.

Lesson 34

# Block Center: Good News Trip

## Collect

Bible, blocks, paper plates.

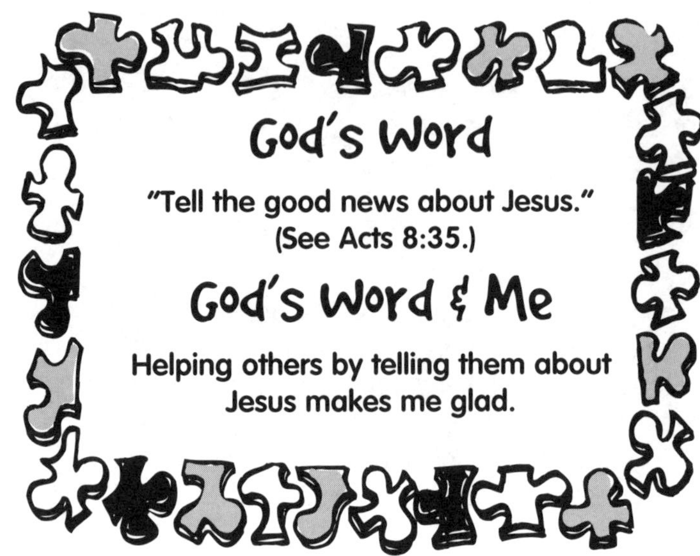

God's Word

"Tell the good news about Jesus." (See Acts 8:35.)

God's Word & Me

Helping others by telling them about Jesus makes me glad.

## Do

1. Children use blocks to outline the shape of a bus large enough for several children to sit in. Place four paper plates in corners to represent tires. Another paper plate can be used as a steering wheel by the child pretending to be the driver.
2. Children sit in the bus and pretend they are driving to church or driving home from church. (Note: If you have a large class, encourage children to build one bus for each group of four to six children.)

## Talk About

- **In our Bible story, Philip helped a man learn the good news that Jesus loved him. We learn about Jesus at church. Let's build a bus with our blocks and pretend we're driving to church.**
- **What do you see on your way to church? We can stop to pick up a friend to take to church.**

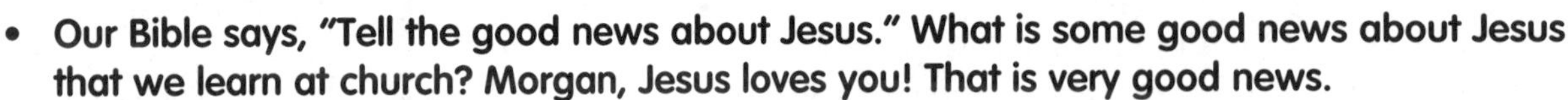

- **Our Bible says, "Tell the good news about Jesus." What is some good news about Jesus that we learn at church? Morgan, Jesus loves you! That is very good news.**
- **Let's pretend we are driving home from church. Who is in the bus with us? Let's tell each other the good news we learned about Jesus at church. Hillary, Jesus is God's Son and He came to teach us about God. That is good news!**

## For Younger Children

Make a masking-tape outline of the bus. Children place blocks along masking-tape lines. (Note: Remove masking tape immediately after activity.)

## For Older Children

Children leave openings for doors when they build the bus. After a few moments, ask children to leave through the doors, walk all the way around the bus and then enter the bus again, with a different child as the driver. Switch drivers in this manner several times.

Lesson 34

# Science Center: String Sounds

## Collect

Bible, string material (string, twine, yarn, etc.), scissors, measuring stick.

## Prepare

Cut string material into 3-foot (.9-m) lengths.

### God's Word

**"Tell the good news about Jesus." (See Acts 8:35.)**

### God's Word & Me

**Helping others by telling them about Jesus makes me glad.**

## Do

1. Demonstrate how to wrap finger with string, put wrapped finger in ear and with other hand, hold string taut. Ask a volunteer to pluck the string for you.
2. Children form pairs. In each pair, one child wraps his or her finger with string, places finger in ear and holds string as the other child plucks the string. Assist children as needed. Children switch so that everyone has a turn to hear and a turn to pluck. Children may also try making sounds while holding the string less taut.

## Talk About

- **Our Bible says, "Tell the good news about Jesus." Let's use our ears to hear some sounds we can make.**
- **What do you hear? God gave you ears, so you can hear sounds! God loves you very much! I want to tell you some good news: Jesus loves you! Who can you tell this good news to?**
- **We can help others by telling them the good news about Jesus. I'm glad God gave your brother his ears, so he can hear this good news!**

## For Younger Children

Bring stringed instruments (guitar, ukulele, Autoharp, etc.). Play instruments for children to listen to sounds. Assist children in strumming or plucking instrument strings to make sounds.

## For Older Children

Bring other items such as a large spring, a metal coat hanger and a damp paper towel. Children hang metal objects from string material. Then children pluck string or bump metal objects against wall to listen to sounds. Children listen to the sound of damp paper towel being moved along string.

Lesson 34 • Acts 8:26-40

# Bible Story Center

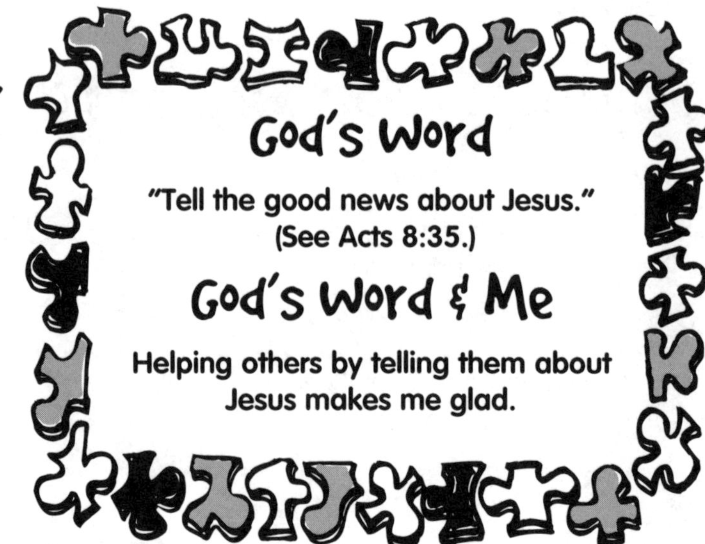
God's Word
"Tell the good news about Jesus."
(See Acts 8:35.)
God's Word & Me
Helping others by telling them about Jesus makes me glad.

## Collect

Bible, Picture 47 from *Bible Story Pictures*.

## Tell the Story

Use the pictured motions (keywords in bold) or show Picture 47. For older children, tell the version of the story on the back of Picture 47.

**Who helps you know what God's Word says?**
**Listen to this Bible story to find out about a man who needed to know what God's Word says.**

Philip was one of Jesus' friends. He told many people the good news that Jesus loved them. One day an angel came to see Philip. (Angels are God's special helpers.) This angel told Philip an important message. "There is a **road** that goes into the desert," the angel said. "God wants you to go walk on that road." Then the angel left.

Philip did exactly what the angel told him. On the road Philip saw some **horses running** toward him. Philip saw that the horses were pulling a chariot. (A chariot is a special cart to ride in.)

Riding in that chariot was a man from a country in Africa. The man was reading some words from the Bible. The words were written on a scroll. (A scroll is like a long rolled-up sheet of paper.) Philip ran up to the chariot. The man must have looked confused. "Do you understand what you are reading?" Philip asked the man.

"No, I don't. I need someone to tell me what the words mean," the man said. Then the man asked, "Will you talk with me about these words?" So Philip got into the **chariot**. Together he and the man read the Bible scroll. Philip told the man the good news about Jesus. "God sent Jesus to the earth," Philip might have said. "Jesus is God's Son! Jesus loves you."

The man was happy to hear the good news that Jesus loved him. The man believed that Jesus is God's Son. The man said, "Look! Here is some **water**. I want to be baptized." People are baptized to show that they believe in Jesus. Philip was glad he could help the man learn about Jesus. Then Philip left the man and went to tell other people that Jesus loved them, too.

## God's Word & Me

**What did Philip tell the man about Jesus?** (Jesus loves him. Jesus is God's Son.) **We can help others by telling them about Jesus! We can tell them Jesus loves them. Janna, who will you tell? You can tell your mom that Jesus loves her.**

# Worship Center

## Collect

Bible, *Shake It Up!* songbook and cassette/CD and player, "Who Needs Help?" and "Hear the Word" word charts (pp. 42 and 44 in songbook).

God's Word
"Tell the good news about Jesus."
(See Acts 8:35.)
God's Word & Me
Helping others by telling them about Jesus makes me glad.

## Sing to God

Play "Who Needs Help?" Invite children to sing along with you. **Let's sing about helping others.** Lead children in singing song and doing suggested motions. **We can help others. We can tell them Jesus loves them. I'm glad we can help others by telling them about Jesus!**

## Hear and Say God's Word

Holding your Bible open to Acts 8:35, say verse aloud. **We can tell others the good news that Jesus is God's Son. We can tell others the good news that Jesus loves us! I'm glad to help others by telling them the good news about Jesus.** Lead children in saying the Bible verse together a few times. Ask a particular group of children to say the verse together (everyone wearing pants, everyone with black hair, everyone with shoes that tie, etc.). Choose several categories and repeat the Bible verse several times.

## Pray to God

**Dear God, thank You for sending Your Son, Jesus. Thank You that He loves us and forgives us. We are glad to tell others about Jesus. Please help us tell them. In Jesus' name, amen.**

## Sing to God

In closing the worship time, play "Hear the Word." Invite children to sing along with you and do suggested motions. **God's Word says to tell others about Jesus. March in place if you can tell me something about Jesus.** Call on a child who is marching. **You're right, Keely. Jesus loves us!**

## Options

1. Briefly tell an age-appropriate example of a time someone told you about Jesus.
2. For older children, name a way to say the verse (loudly, softly, quickly, slowly, etc.) as well as the particular group of children (everyone wearing blue, everyone with brown eyes, etc.) who will say the verse in that manner.

# Read-Aloud Story and Activity Center

## Collect

A copy of Story Picture 34 (pp. 73-74 from *Read-Aloud Story and Activity Book*) for each child and yourself, crayons or markers.

## Prepare

Color your copy of Story Picture 34.

## Do

**Listen to find out what is in the letter this lady is holding.** Read story and show completed Story Picture 34. Distribute pictures. Use conversation suggestions in Let's Talk About the Story as children complete their pages.

# Kindergarten Puzzle Center

## Collect

Copies of Puzzles 67 and 68 (p. 141 and p. 143 from *The Big Book of Kindergarten Puzzles*) for each child, pencils, crayons or markers.

## Do

Children complete the puzzles and color pages.

# Instant Activities

These activities can be used at any time during this session: when children need a change of pace, to extend the session, or during transition time at the beginning or end of the session.

## Collect

*The Big Book of Instant Activities.*

## Do

Guide children to complete "Freeze" and/or "Who Is Here Today?" (p. 80 and/or p. 26 from *The Big Book of Instant Activities*).

Lesson 35

# Paul Meets Jesus

## Bible Story

Acts 9:1-20

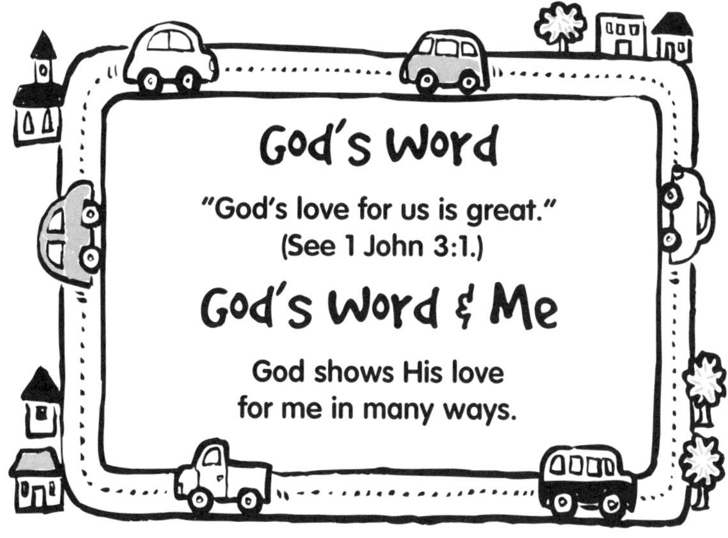
God's Word
"God's love for us is great."
(See 1 John 3:1.)
God's Word & Me
God shows His love
for me in many ways.

## Teacher's Devotional

Ananias had heard that Saul of Tarsus was coming to town with the authority to jail or kill Ananias and his closest friends. Ananias seemed to be in real danger! He may have been fervently praying for protection when the Lord told him to find Saul—and pray for him (see Acts 9:11,12).

Ananias replied, "I've heard about this man from a lot of people, Lord. He's hurt many of Your saints in Jerusalem. And now he has authority to imprison everyone here who calls on Your name" (see Acts 9:13,14). Notice that God did not strike Ananias with lightning for questioning; instead, He graciously reassured him.

This little conversation is a wonderful glimpse into Ananias's relationship with God. He seemed truly comfortable with his Lord. He didn't hesitate to tell God his worries and fears. He needed some reassurance and God didn't hesitate to give it!

God wants to have such intimacy with each of us who are His children. When we are obedient and open as Ananias was, we can feel comfortable asking Him anything. Don't let any factor in your life keep God at arm's length. He wants you to freely share with Him what is on your heart—even your deepest fears and biggest questions.

(Note: To avoid confusion for young children, the name Paul is used throughout this lesson, rather than both Saul and Paul.)

## Teacher's Planning

1. Choose which centers you will provide and the order in which children will participate in them. For tips on schedule planning, see page 7.
2. Plan who will lead each center. For staffing tips and ideas, see page 21.

# Active Game Center: Where Am I?

## Collect

Bible.

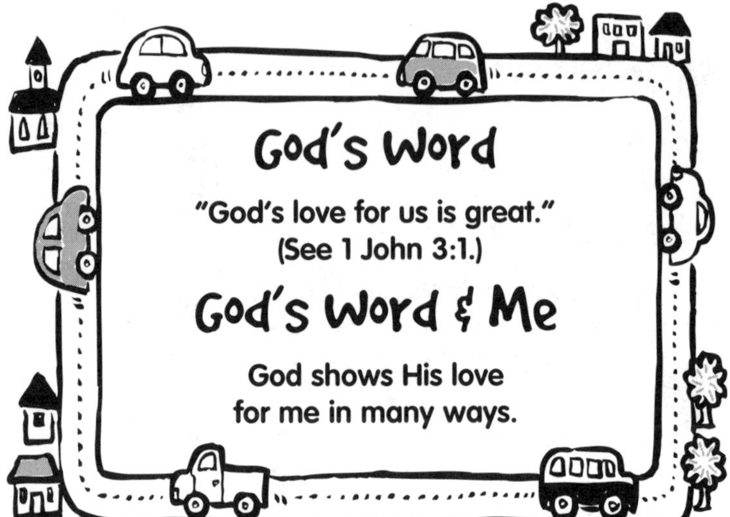
God's Word
"God's love for us is great."
(See 1 John 3:1.)
God's Word & Me
God shows His love
for me in many ways.

## Do

1. Ask two volunteers to close their eyes and keep them closed until you say to open them. Turn each volunteer around once. Take each by a hand and lead them randomly around the room for approximately 20 seconds.
2. Name four or five locations in the room, such as door, blocks area, bathroom, etc. Include location volunteers are standing near. Volunteers guess which of the locations they are closest to. Tell volunteers to open their eyes. Repeat with different volunteers as time allows.

## Talk About

- **In today's Bible story, a man named Paul was blind for three days. Paul became blind after he saw a bright light and Jesus spoke to him. Paul had good friends who helped him for the three days he was blind. Let's play a game and pretend we can't see.**
- **What are some things that would be very hard to do if you could not see?** (Catch a ball. Eat spaghetti. Climb a tree.)
- **Mario, what are some things you enjoy looking at? We can see flowers because God gave us eyes to see.**
- **Our Bible says, "God's love for us is so great." What has God given us to show how great His love is?** Pray briefly, **Thank You, God, for showing Your love for us in so many ways.**

## For Younger Children

Instead of leading child around room, provide paper and crayons. Children close their eyes and color. Then children open their eyes to see what they've drawn.

## For Older Children

If children are comfortable enough, blindfold volunteers.

Lesson 35

# Art Center: Happy Hearts

## Collect

Bible, construction paper, scissors, butcher paper, markers, masking tape, glue or tape.

## Prepare

Cut out at least one large heart from construction paper for each child. On butcher paper, print "God's love for us is great!" at the top. Tape butcher paper to table. (Optional: Draw a very large heart on butcher paper.)

God's Word
"God's love for us is great."
(See 1 John 3:1.)
God's Word & Me
God shows His love
for me in many ways.

## Do

Using markers, children decorate construction-paper hearts and glue or tape them to butcher paper. Post completed project on bulletin board, classroom wall or hallway.

## Talk About

- **Our Bible says, "God's love for us is great." God shows His love for us in many ways. Let's make a heart picture to remind us of God's love.**
- **Brandon, who helps you get ready for bed? God made your daddy to help. God loves you!**
- **One way God shows His love is by giving us moms and dads to take us places. Betty, where do you go with your mom or dad?** (Church. School. Preschool. Store. A friend's house.)
- Pray briefly, **Thank You, God, for loving us.**

God's love for us

## For Younger Children

Before class, cut out magazine pictures of people to represent moms, dads, grandparents, brothers, sisters, etc. Draw a large heart on butcher paper. Children glue pictures of people inside heart outline.

## For Older Children

Provide a variety of small items such as circle-shaped cereal, buttons, pieces of pasta, dry beans, etc. Children print their names inside their construction-paper heart and then glue on small objects to decorate their name hearts. Children glue finished name hearts to butcher paper.

Lesson 35

# Block Center: Great Things

## Collect

Bible, construction paper in a variety of colors, scissors, blocks; optional—grocery-store advertisements.

## Prepare

Cut construction paper into shapes to represent different foods grown on a farm: yellow strips for corn, orange circles for pumpkins, green oblongs for watermelons, etc. (Optional: Cut food pictures from grocery-store advertisements.)

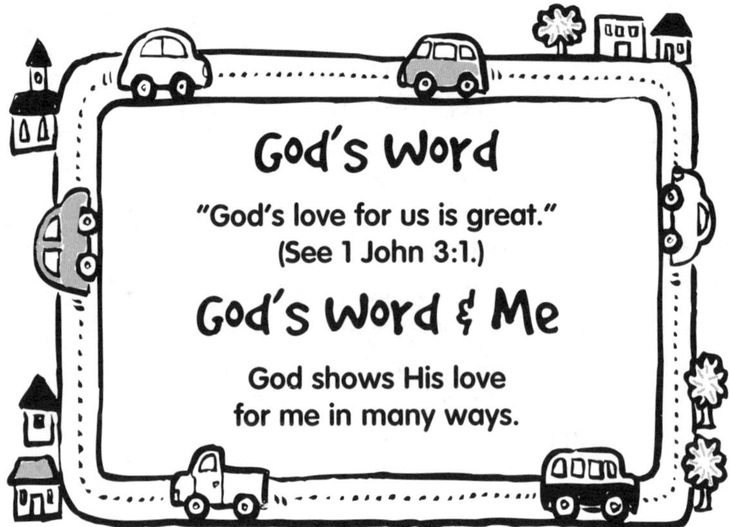
God's Word
"God's love for us is great."
(See 1 John 3:1.)
God's Word & Me
God shows His love
for me in many ways.

## Do

Children use blocks to outline fields and lay construction-paper shapes in rows as if planting rows of crops. (Optional: Use food pictures from grocery-store advertisements instead of paper shapes.)

## Talk About

- **Our Bible says, "God's love for us is great." God shows His love for us in many ways. He made the earth to grow food to care for us. Let's build a farm and talk about the great food God made for us.**
- **Nicki, what color is corn? What other foods are yellow? What foods are green?**
- Pray briefly, **Thank You, God, for all the great things You have made.**

## For Younger Children

Outline a field with masking tape. Children place blocks on masking-tape line. (Note: Remove tape immediately after activity.)

## For Older Children

Children form a letter of the alphabet with blocks. Children name things God made that begin with that letter. **Mia, you made the letter *M*. What things did God make that begin with an *M*?** (Mountains, mommies, melons, etc.) **God made all these things because He love us!**

Lesson 35

# Science Center: Sense of Touch

## Collect

Bible, large shoebox or shallow box of similar size, towel or cloth large enough to cover box, familiar small objects (spoon, cotton ball, penny, candy in wrapper, paper clip, etc.).

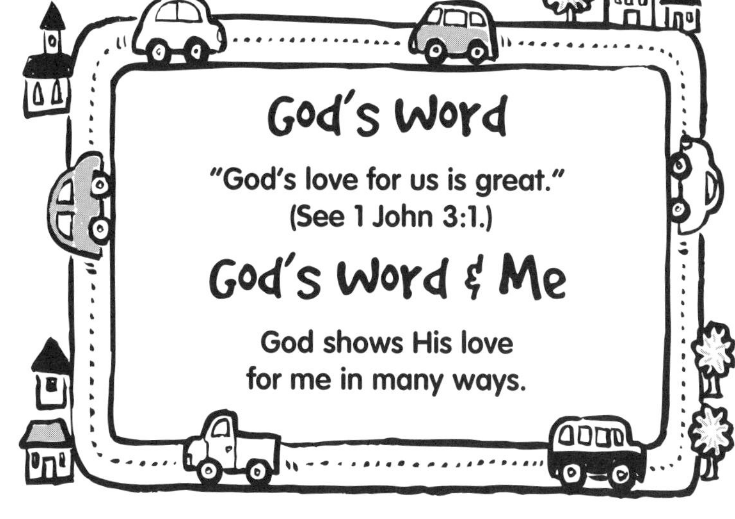
God's Word
"God's love for us is great."
(See 1 John 3:1.)
God's Word & Me
God shows His love
for me in many ways.

## Do

1. Children name the familiar objects as you place them in the box. Put the towel or cloth over the box to cover objects.
2. Children take turns sliding a hand under the towel or cloth to pick up an object from the box. The child feels the object and guesses what the object is. Child pulls the object from under the towel or cloth to see if he or she guessed correctly. Replace object in box and repeat for each child.

## Talk About

- **Our Bible story tells us about a man who became blind. Some people are blind and cannot see during their whole lives. God helps us have other ways to tell what is going on around us. Let's use our hands instead of our eyes to tell what some objects are.**
- **Even though you could not see the objects in the box, you could tell what they were by feeling them. This is called sense of touch. What is something that feels soft? Rough?**
- **I'm going to name something and you tell me how it would feel if you ran your fingers over it: kitten's fur** (soft, smooth)**, glass** (smooth, hard)**, gum** (sticky)**, driveway** (rough).
- **We can be glad that God shows His love for us by making us able to touch things and feel them. Our Bible says, "God's love for us is great."**

## For Younger Children

Use only two items at a time. Allow children to feel the objects before putting them in the box.

## For Older Children

After first time, children play a memory game. Cover box with towel. Children name as many of the items as they can.

# Bible Story Center

## Collect

Bible, Picture 48 from *Bible Story Pictures.*

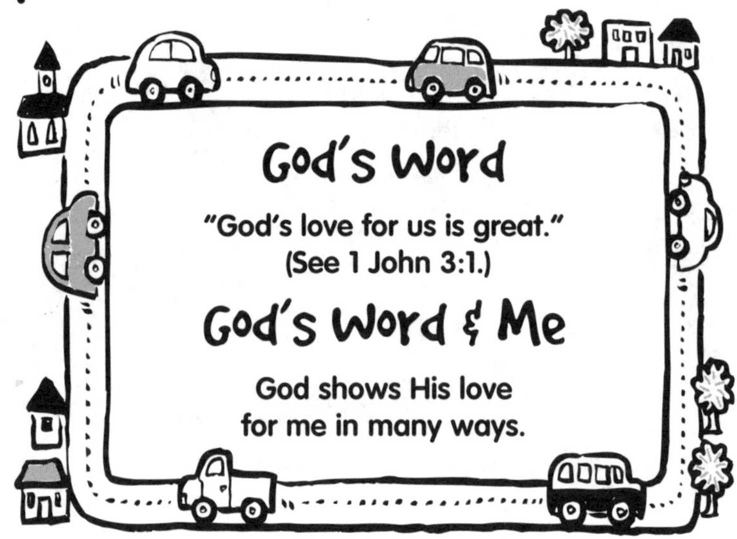
God's Word
"God's love for us is great."
(See 1 John 3:1.)
God's Word & Me
God shows His love
for me in many ways.

## Tell the Story

Use the pictured motions (keywords in bold) or show Picture 48. For older children, tell the version of the story on the back of Picture 48.

**When have you seen a bright light? Listen to hear about a man who saw a very bright light.**

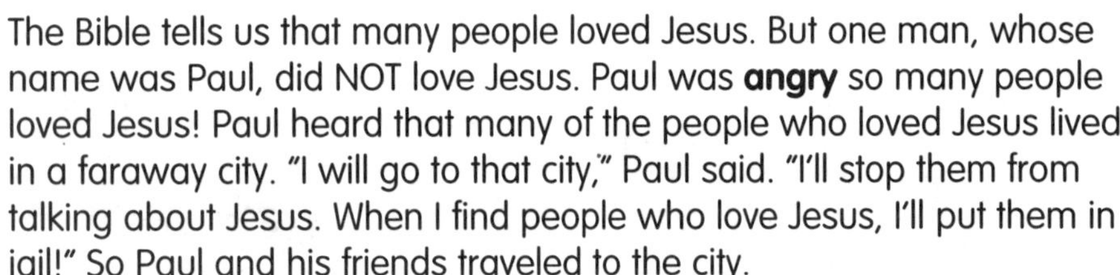

The Bible tells us that many people loved Jesus. But one man, whose name was Paul, did NOT love Jesus. Paul was **angry** so many people loved Jesus! Paul heard that many of the people who loved Jesus lived in a faraway city. "I will go to that city," Paul said. "I'll stop them from talking about Jesus. When I find people who love Jesus, I'll put them in jail!" So Paul and his friends traveled to the city.

On the road near the city, Paul and his friends saw a very **bright light**. Paul was so surprised! He fell to the ground. The light was so bright Paul could not see ANYTHING! Then Paul heard a voice! "Paul, why are you hurting Me?" the voice asked.

"Who are You, Lord?" Paul asked.

The voice said, "I am Jesus, the One you are hurting." Paul must have been surprised! Then Jesus told Paul to go to the city. With his friends' help, Paul did what Jesus said. For three days in the city, he didn't eat or drink anything. Paul still couldn't see, but he **prayed** to God. While Paul was praying, Jesus spoke to another man in the city. The man's name was Ananias. "Ananias, go to Paul and pray for him," Jesus said.

Ananias was afraid of Paul, but he trusted God. So Ananias obeyed and went to Paul. Ananias prayed for Paul and suddenly, Paul **could see** again! Now Paul loved Jesus and wanted to obey Him. Paul told others that Jesus is God's Son.

## God's Word & Me

**What happened when Paul met Jesus?** (Paul was blind for a while. Paul became Jesus' friend.) **Even though Paul used to be mean to Jesus' friends, God still loved Paul! And God loves us, too. God shows His love in many ways. God gives us many good things that show His love. What are some of the good things God has given you?** (Parents who love me. Food to eat. A home.)

Lesson 35

# Worship Center

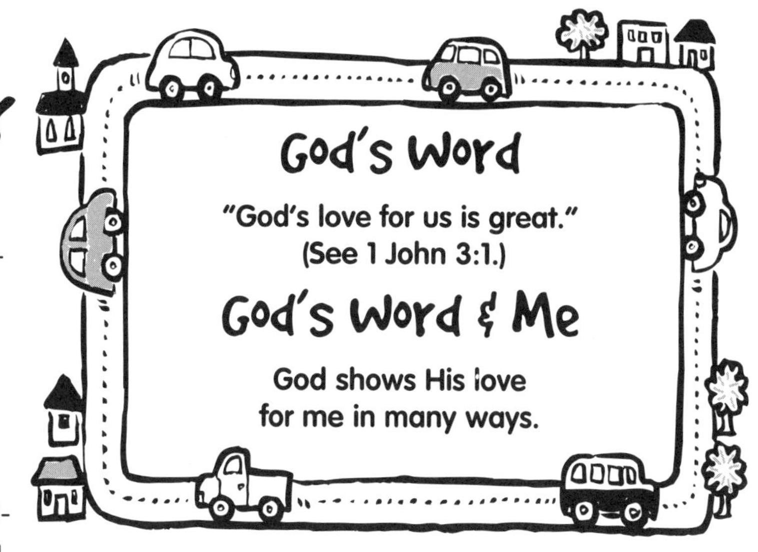

God's Word
"God's love for us is great."
(See 1 John 3:1.)
God's Word & Me
God shows His love
for me in many ways.

## Collect

Bible, *Shake It Up!* songbook and cassette/CD and player, "In a Very Big Way," and "God's Love" word charts (pp. 47 and 49 in songbook).

## Sing to God

Play "In a Very Big Way." Invite the children to sing along with you. **Let's sing a song about God's love.** Lead children in singing song and doing suggested motions. **God's love is very, very big! All around us, we can see ways God shows His love to us.**

## Hear and Say God's Word

Holding your Bible open to 1 John 3:1, say verse aloud. **When we say that God's love is great, we mean that God's love is bigger than anything! God shows His love for us in many ways.** Lead the children in saying the words of the verse softly until they come to the word "great." Children say the word "great" loudly and at the same time thrust hands upward. Repeat several times.

## Pray to God

As you say the following prayer, point to a child and pause for the child to say his or her name, thereby completing the phrase: **Dear God, thank You for Your great love for __________.** Repeat once for each child in your class. If you have a large class, point to more than one child each time you repeat the phrase.

## Sing to God

In closing the worship time, play "God's Love." Invite children to sing along with you. Lead the children in singing the song and doing suggested motions. **One way God shows His great love for us is by making our bodies to do so many things, like singing. Thank You, God!**

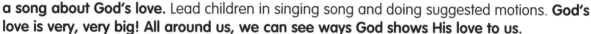

## Options

1. After singing "God's Love," talk about the five senses God gave us. Children complete each of the following sentences as you point to the corresponding body parts: **I can see with my** __________ (eyes). **I can hear with my** __________ (ears). **I can touch with my** __________ (hands). **I can smell with my** __________ (nose). **I can taste with my** __________ (mouth).
2. Invite the children to share something their body can do that is fun for them. **I like to use my legs to walk my dog. Joy, what do you like to use your legs to do?**

# Read-Aloud Story and Activity Center

## Collect

A copy of Story Picture 35 (pp. 75-76 from *Read-Aloud Story and Activity Book*) for each child and yourself, crayons or markers.

## Prepare

Color your copy of Story Picture 35.

## Do

"God's love for us is great."

**Listen to find out what these children are praying about.** Read story and show completed Story Picture 35. Distribute pictures. Use conversation suggestions in Let's Talk About the Story as children complete their pages.

# Kindergarten Puzzle Center

## Collect

Copies of Puzzles 69 and 70 (p. 145 and p. 147 from *The Big Book of Kindergarten Puzzles*) for each child, pencils, crayons or markers.

## Do

Children complete the puzzles and color pages.

# Instant Activities

These activities can be used at any time during this session: when children need a change of pace, to extend the session, or during transition time at the beginning or end of the session.

## Collect

*The Big Book of Instant Activities.*

## Do

Guide children to complete "Silent Imitation" and/or "Beanbag Fun" (p. 120 and/or p. 91 from *The Big Book of Instant Activities*).

 

Lesson 36

# Paul Escapes in a Basket

## Bible Story

Acts 9:20-28

### God's Word

**"In God I trust; I will not be afraid." Psalm 56:4**

### God's Word & Me

**When I'm afraid, God is with me and loves me.**

## Teacher's Devotional

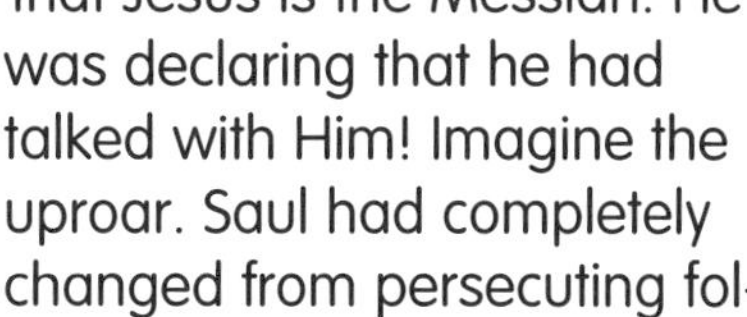

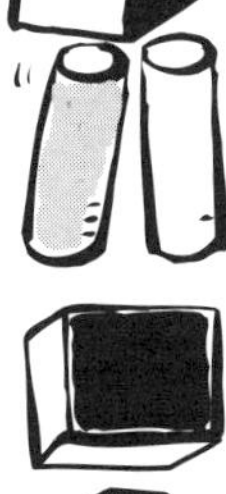

Saul was suddenly proclaiming all over Damascus that Jesus is the Messiah. He was declaring that he had talked with Him! Imagine the uproar. Saul had completely changed from persecuting followers of Jesus to being one of them. The religious leaders in Damascus were appalled. They decided that they needed to kill this troublemaker! They immediately posted spies to watch the gate. Saul was not leaving Damascus alive!

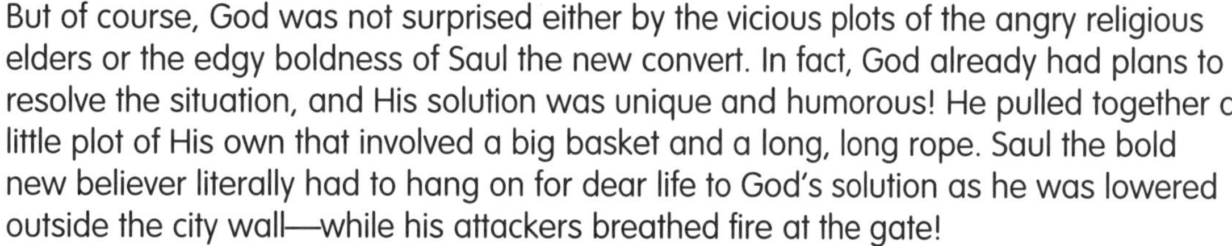

But of course, God was not surprised either by the vicious plots of the angry religious elders or the edgy boldness of Saul the new convert. In fact, God already had plans to resolve the situation, and His solution was unique and humorous! He pulled together a little plot of His own that involved a big basket and a long, long rope. Saul the bold new believer literally had to hang on for dear life to God's solution as he was lowered outside the city wall—while his attackers breathed fire at the gate!

What might be God's solution to the problems that seem to be bearing down on you today? The One who loves you best can lead you safely out of or through the most dangerous situation. This is His great adventure for you. Trust Him!

(Note: To avoid confusion for young children, the name Paul is used throughout this lesson, rather than both Saul and Paul.)

## Teacher's Planning

1. Choose which centers you will provide and the order in which children will participate in them. For tips on schedule planning, see page 7.
2. Plan who will lead each center. For staffing tips and ideas, see page 21.

Lesson 36

# Active Game Center: Over the Wall

## Collect

Bible, two blocks, yarn, construction paper, scissors, masking tape.

## Prepare

Stack two blocks. Place a yarn line on the opposite side of the activity area. Cut sheets of construction paper in half. Cut enough pieces to make a path from the yarn line to the blocks. Tape papers to floor.

God's Word
"In God I trust; I will not be afraid."
Psalm 56:4
God's Word & Me
When I'm afraid, God is with me and loves me.

## Do

1. Children line up behind yarn line. The first child follows paper path to the block wall, stepping on each paper. Then child steps or jumps over the wall. Each child does the same.
2. Play additional rounds. Children walk in a variety of ways: sideways, heel to toe, jumping, etc.

## Talk About

- **Paul escaped danger because his friends helped him get over the wall and out of the city. Let's play a game and go over a wall.**
- **God gives us our family to help us. What does Mom or Dad do to keep you safe when you are crossing the street?** (Holds my hand.) **When you are riding in the car?** (Buckles the seat belt.) **When you are sick?** (Takes me to the doctor.) **When you start to touch something very hot?** (Pulls me away from it.)
- **Our Bible says, "In God I trust; I will not be afraid." We don't have to be afraid. God is with us and loves us all the time.** Pray briefly, **Thank You, God, that we can trust in You.**

## For Younger Children

Children do not try to step from paper to paper but simply follow path to the block wall.

## For Older Children

Children trace feet on construction paper, cut out the footprints and tape them to the floor, creating the path.

Lesson 36

# Art Center: Basket Wall

## Collect

Bible, construction paper, scissors, poster board, hole punch, rope material (yarn, string or twine), measuring stick, markers, transparent tape.

God's Word
"In God I trust; I will not be afraid."
Psalm 56:4
God's Word & Me
When I'm afraid, God is with me and loves me.

## Prepare

Cut one basket shape out of construction paper for each child. Use hole punch to make holes near the top and bottom of poster board, one sheet per child. For each child, cut a 21-inch (53.5-cm) length of rope material.

## Do

1. Children draw lines on poster board to make stones in the wall. Help children thread rope material through holes, knotting in back to make a loop. Children decorate baskets with markers.
2. Pull knot in yarn to the bottom hole in the back. Help children tape basket to the top of the rope in front. This will allow basket to move all the way up and down the wall.

## Talk About

- **In our Bible story today, Paul's friends helped him by lowering him over a wall in a basket. Let's make a wall with a basket escape like Paul's.**
- **Louise, what is something you like to do? God is with you when you play in the yard! God loves you.**
- **Our Bible says, "In God I trust; I will not be afraid."** Pray briefly, **Thank You, God, that when we're afraid, we can trust in You. Thank You for being with us and loving us.**

## For Younger Children

Do not punch holes in poster board. Children decorate wall, tape construction-paper baskets to 6-inch (15-cm) lengths of rope material and tape rope to poster-board wall.

## For Older Children

Children cut a circle from construction paper, draw on a face and tape to basket for a person riding in the basket.

# Block Center: Block Wall

## Collect

Bible, blocks, rope material (yarn, string or twine), scissors, strawberry or other small baskets, toy people.

God's Word
"In God I trust; I will not be afraid."
Psalm 56:4
God's Word & Me
When I'm afraid, God is with me and loves me.

## Do

1. Children build block walls. Cut lengths of rope material longer than walls are high.
2. Tie rope material to small baskets. Children take turns placing toy people in baskets and holding onto ropes as they lower baskets over block walls. Repeat as time allows.

## Talk About

- **In today's Bible story, Paul told people about Jesus, even though Paul knew it made some leaders angry. Paul trusted God and was not afraid. God was with Paul, even when he escaped over the wall in a basket! Let's make a wall and pretend to help others escape in a basket.**
- **Janet, where is a place you go to play? God is with you when you go to the park. What do you like to play on at the park? God is with you when you go down the slide!**
- **Our Bible says, "In God I trust; I will not be afraid." When we feel afraid, we can ask God to help us. We can ask Him to help us think of the best thing to do.** Pray briefly, **Dear God, when we are afraid, please help us to remember You love us. Help us not to be afraid.**

## For Younger Children

Children simply build walls. Help children by steadying base of wall as children build higher. Children build walls no higher than their chins.

## For Older Children

Children count blocks as they add them to the walls.

Lesson 36

# Science Center: Feelings Faces

## Collect

Bible, paper plates, markers, several mirrors.

## Prepare

Prepare paper-plate faces as shown in sketch.

## Do

One at a time, hold up paper-plate faces. Ask children to describe how the person might be feeling. Children imitate the expression and look at their faces in mirrors.

God's Word
"In God I trust; I will not be afraid."
Psalm 56:4
God's Word & Me
When I'm afraid, God is with me and loves me.

## Talk About

- **Our Bible says, "In God I trust; I will not be afraid." We don't have to feel afraid, because God is with us and loves us. Let's talk about some of the feelings we have.**
- **Michael, what do you think someone making this face is feeling? Why do you think they are happy? I smile when I'm happy, too. Let's all smile and see what our faces look like. When are some times you feel happy? God is with us when we play outside.**
- **Krystal, why do you think this person is sleepy? What makes you feel sleepy? I like to go to bed at night. I know God is with me and He loves me, even when I'm asleep!**
- **It's good to feel happy and excited. But sometimes we have feelings that don't feel good. Sometimes we feel angry. Sometimes we feel sad. Sometimes we feel afraid. God is with us ALL the time. God can help us when we feel sad.** Pray briefly, **Thank You, God, for being with us and loving us. Thank You for helping us when we feel angry, sad or afraid.**

## For Younger Children

Simplify the activity by only using happy and sad faces.

## For Older Children

Children make masks by drawing faces on paper plates. Use masking tape to attach a craft stick as a handle for each mask.

Lesson 36 • Acts 9:20-28

# Bible Story Center

## Collect

Bible, Picture 49 from *Bible Story Pictures.*

God's Word
"In God I trust; I will not be afraid."
Psalm 56:4
God's Word & Me
When I'm afraid, God is with me and loves me.

## Tell the Story

Use the pictured motions (keywords in bold) or show Picture 49. For older children, tell the version of the story on the back of Picture 49.

**Who has some good news to share today? Listen to hear about a man who had good news he wanted to tell everyone!**

After Paul met Jesus, he didn't want to hurt the people in God's family anymore. He wanted to tell everyone that Jesus is God's Son. Some of the men who heard Paul talking about Jesus were **angry**! They decided, "We must stop Paul!"

The leaders sent men to watch the **gates** of the city. They knew Paul would have to come out of the city gates. They told the men to catch Paul and hurt him. But Paul found out about the leaders' plan. Paul knew he could not leave the city by walking out in the usual way. And of course, God loved Paul and had a way for Paul to escape the city.

One night, Paul's friends met him on the wall of the city. The wall was very high and wide. Paul's friends brought a very big basket and a long, long rope.

Paul climbed into the basket. His friends tied ropes tightly around the basket. And they tied a long, long rope to the basket. Paul's friends held tightly to the rope and slowly pushed the basket over the wall. The basket began to drop **down, down, down**. Soon there was a THUMP! The basket was on the ground outside the city wall.

Paul was GLAD to climb out of that basket and glad to be out of Damascus! He went to Jerusalem, but Jesus' friends there thought Paul still wanted to hurt them. They were **afraid** to be Paul's friend. One man, Barnabas, became Paul's friend. He told everyone that Paul was Jesus' friend now. And Jesus' friends in Jerusalem became Paul's friends, too.

## God's Word & Me

**How did Paul's friends help him escape?** (Put him in a basket. Tied a rope to the basket and let it drop over the city wall.) **Paul must have been afraid! But God was with Paul and loved him. When we are afraid, we can remember that God is with us and loves us! Where are some of the places you go with your mom? God is with you at the store!**

# Worship Center

God's Word
"In God I trust; I will not be afraid."
Psalm 56:4
God's Word & Me
When I'm afraid, God is with me and loves me.

## Collect

Bible, *Shake It Up!* songbook and cassette/CD and player, "In a Very Big Way," and "God's Love" word charts (pp. 47 and 49 in songbook).

## Sing to God

Play "God's Love." **Let's sing about how great God's love is for us.** Lead children in singing song and doing suggested motions. **This song tells us that God's love is great. This means God loves us all the time!**

## Hear and Say God's Word

Holding your Bible open to Psalm 56:4, say verse aloud. **We can trust God. He always does what He says He will do. God is always with us.** Lead the children in saying the verse together. Ask volunteers to raise their hands. As you repeat the verse, point to one of the volunteers. You and the children say that child's name instead of "I." **In God Joshua trusts; Joshua will not be afraid.** Repeat for each volunteer.

## Pray to God

Volunteers say the following prayer: **Dear God, I trust in You. I know You are with me. In Jesus' name, amen.**

## Sing to God

In closing the worship time, play "In a Very Big Way." Invite children to sing along with you and do suggested motions. **What are some big things you've seen? God's love is even bigger than an elephant!**

## Options

1. On large sheet of paper print "God loves me and is with me at __________." Ask children to name some of the places where they go. Print children's responses on paper. Display paper so that parents can read it when children are dismissed.
2. Older children lead other children in doing the motions suggested for "God's Love" and/or "In a Very Big Way."

# Read-Aloud Story and Activity Center

## Collect

A copy of Story Picture 36 (pp. 77-78 from *Read-Aloud Story and Activity Book*) for each child and yourself, crayons or markers.

"In God I trust; I will not be afraid." Psalm 56:4

## Prepare

Color your copy of Story Picture 36.

## Do

**Listen to find out why this girl looks unhappy.** Read story and show completed Story Picture 36. Distribute pictures. Use conversation suggestions in Let's Talk About the Story as children complete their pages.

# Kindergarten Puzzle Center

## Collect

Copies of Puzzles 71 and 72 (p. 149 and p.151 from *The Big Book of Kindergarten Puzzles*) for each child, pencils, crayons or markers.

## Do

Children complete the puzzles and color pages.

# Instant Activities

These activities can be used at any time during this session: when children need a change of pace, to extend the session, or during transition time at the beginning or end of the session.

## Collect

*The Big Book of Instant Activities.*

## Do

Guide children to complete "I Stand Up Tall" and/or "Pick a Name" (p. 42 and/or p. 69 from *The Big Book of Instant Activities*).

Lesson 37

# Peter Helps Dorcas

## Bible Story

Acts 9:32-43

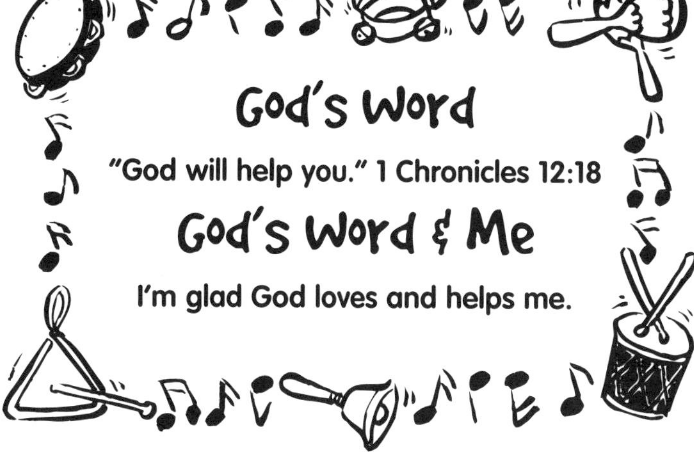
God's Word
"God will help you." 1 Chronicles 12:18
God's Word & Me
I'm glad God loves and helps me.

## Teacher's Devotional

By the time we reach adulthood, we have learned that physical death is final and inescapable. Whatever dies decomposes and eventually disappears.

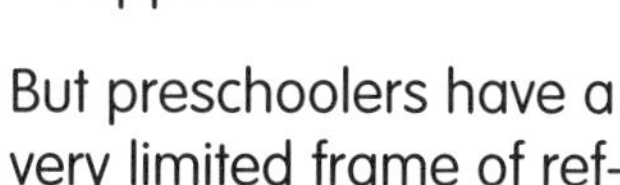

But preschoolers have a very limited frame of reference when it comes to death. Children under six have rarely encountered death; their limited frame of reference makes them more likely not to react greatly to changes death might bring into their lives. They are not usually aware of what has really happened to the one who dies. Fours and fives (perhaps influenced by cartoons) often think that death is reversible, and they often expect the person to wake up or come back.

When discussing today's story, don't use terms such as "passed away" or "went to sleep." Listen to children carefully to find out what they don't understand about death. Explain that death happens when a person's body wears out or has a problem that makes it stop working. And help them see that when God brought Dorcas back to life, it wasn't magic. It was a miracle! Help them understand that only God can give life. Your words and attitude will plant seeds that will grow in time to a proper understanding.

## Teacher's Planning

1. Choose which centers you will provide and the order in which children will participate in them. For tips on schedule planning, see page 7.
2. Plan who will lead each center. For staffing tips and ideas, see page 21.

 

# Active Game Center: Walk and Dress

## Collect

Bible, yarn, adult-sized T-shirt; optional—vest or other shirt.

## Prepare

Place a yarn line at one end of the playing area. Place T-shirt at other end. (Optional: Use vest or other shirt, instead of T-shirt.) If you have a large class, provide yarn lines and T-shirts for each group of five to six children.

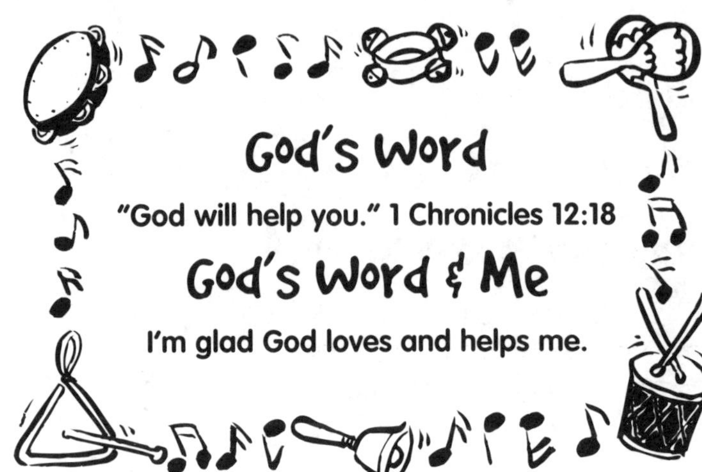
God's Word
"God will help you." 1 Chronicles 12:18
God's Word & Me
I'm glad God loves and helps me.

## Do

Children line up behind T-shirt. First child puts T-shirt on over his or her clothes, walks quickly to the yarn line and then returns to starting point. After first child takes off T-shirt, second child puts it on and repeats actions. Continue until every child has a turn.

## Talk About

- **Our Bible story today is about a woman named Dorcas. Dorcas loved God. Dorcas helped people by making clothes for them to wear. Let's play a game where we put on a T-shirt.**
- **Harry, who helps you get dressed in the morning? God helps us by giving us mommies and daddies who buy us clothes and help us get dressed. What else does your mom help you do?**
- **The Bible says, "God will help you." I'm glad God loves and helps me!** Pray briefly, **Thank You, God, for loving us and helping us. We love You!**

## For Younger Children

Instead of taking turns to put on shirt, children play dress-up with a variety of adult-sized articles of clothing.

## For Older Children

As each child reaches the yarn line, he or she says the words of the Bible verse, "God will help you."

Lesson 37

# Art Center: Sewing Cards

## Collect

Bible, lightweight poster board, markers, scissors, hole punch, yarn, transparent tape.

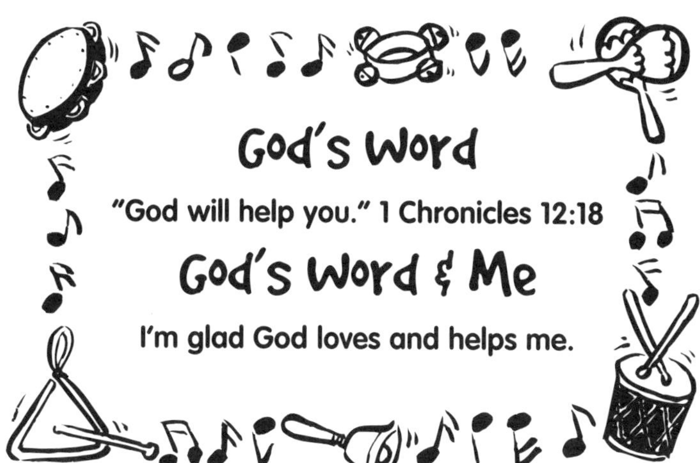
God's Word
"God will help you." 1 Chronicles 12:18
God's Word & Me
I'm glad God loves and helps me.

## Prepare

On poster board, draw robe as shown in sketch. Cut out and use as a pattern to trace one robe on poster board for each child. Cut out robes. Punch holes around edges of robes.

For each robe, cut a piece of yarn twice the circumference of the robe. Wrap tape around one end of each piece of yarn to use as a needle. Knot the untaped end of the yarn to a hole in the robe.

## Do

Children color the robe with markers. Then each child sews the yarn through the holes in the robe, sewing up and down through the holes or around the outside edges of the poster board.

## Talk About

- **In our Bible story today, Dorcas helped poor people by sewing clothes for them. Let's color and sew a robe that might have been like one Dorcas made.**
- **Pam, where do you get your clothes?** (Buy in store. Grandmother gives them.)
- **Quack like a duck if you are wearing something yellow.** Repeat with other sounds or motions and colors.
- **In our Bible we read, "God will help you."** Pray briefly, **Thank You, God, for giving me the people in my family who give me clothes and everything else I need.**

## For Younger Children

Do not punch holes or use yarn. Instead of sewing cards, children use markers to decorate robes.

## For Older Children

Children cut out robes and use hole punch to punch holes along the robes' edges.

Lesson 37

# Block Center: Building Blocks

## Collect

Bible, blocks.

## Do

Children build with blocks. To stimulate imaginative use of blocks, lay several blocks in a row. When a child asks what you are making, you might ask, **What do you think it looks like?** Often a child will immediately begin to incorporate the blocks into an idea he or she has for building.

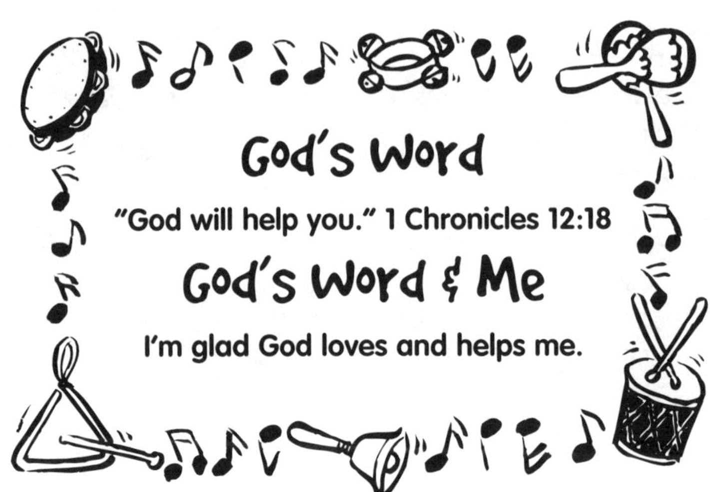
God's Word
"God will help you." 1 Chronicles 12:18
God's Word & Me
I'm glad God loves and helps me.

## Talk About

- **In our Bible story today, Dorcas is a woman who helped a lot of people. Then one day Dorcas died. Peter helped Dorcas by praying for her. God answered Peter's prayer and made Dorcas live again. Let's build with our blocks.**
- **Lance, you have strong arms to lift that long block! I'm glad God made your arms so that they can lift heavy blocks. God loves you.**
- **Eliana, what did you have for breakfast? God helps us have good food. Food helps us grow strong and healthy. God helps us because He loves us!**
- **Our Bible says, "God will help you." Let's thank God that He loves us and helps us.** Volunteers repeat the following prayer: **Thank You, God, for loving us. Thank You, God for helping us.**

## For Younger Children

Young children may have difficulty building with blocks. Place a large box in one corner of the activity area. Children carry blocks over to box and place inside. Young children will also enjoy carrying blocks from box back to the activity area.

## For Older Children

Provide clothing (shirt, skirt, pants, etc.). Lay clothing flat on floor. Children use blocks to outline or fill in the shapes of the clothing. When children are familiar with the shapes, they lay out blocks to outline other articles of clothing.

# Science Center: Fabric to Feel

## Collect

Bible, articles of clothing or fabric scraps in a variety of textures (scarf, bathing suit, undershirt, cotton dress or shirt, fleece gloves, earmuffs, wool scarf, corduroy pants, socks, burlap, terry cloth robe or washcloth, denim jeans, lace collar or tablecloth, etc.).

### God's Word

**"God will help you." 1 Chronicles 12:18**

### God's Word & Me

**I'm glad God loves and helps me.**

## Do

Children explore textures by touching the articles of clothing or fabric scraps you brought. Ask a volunteer to find an item in a texture category you request. **Aaron, find something that feels smooth.** Repeat with different volunteers and a variety of textures (silky, fluffy, bumpy, rough, etc.). Encourage volunteers to name other things that feel smooth, silky, fluffy, bumpy, rough, etc. Repeat as time allows.

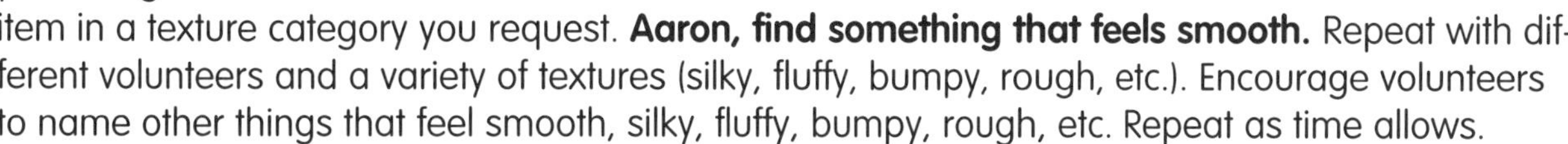

## Talk About

- **In our Bible story Dorcas died and her friends were very, very sad. They even showed Peter many clothes she had made for them. Let's look at some clothes people wear today.**
- **God helps us have clothes to wear. I'm glad God loves and helps us! We can show God's love and help others, too. How can we help people who need clothes?** (Give away clothes and shoes when we grow out of them, buy clothes to give to homeless shelters, give to clothing drives, etc.)
- **Our Bible says, "God will help you." We can help others because God always helps us!** Pray briefly, **Dear God, please help me to help others.**

## For Younger Children

Simplify activity by using only two or three articles of clothing or fabric scraps.

## For Older Children

If time allows after the regular activity, put articles of clothing or fabric scraps in a large paper bag. A volunteer feels an item, describes its texture and guesses what it is. Child removes item from bag to see if he or she guessed correctly. Repeat with other volunteers.

Lesson 37 • Acts 9:32-43

# Bible Story Center

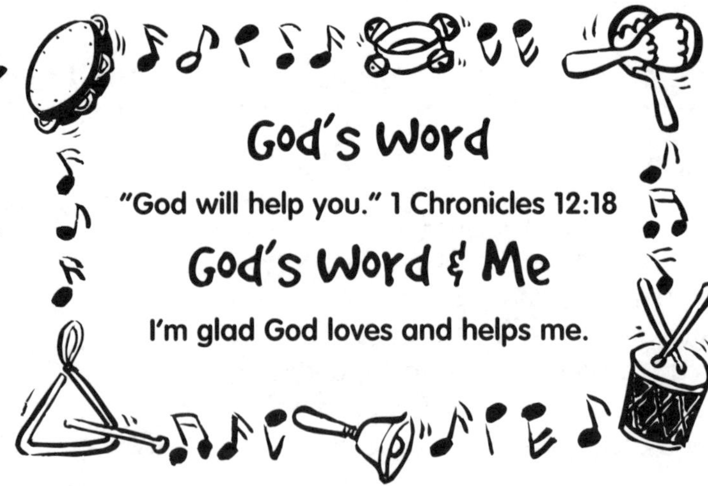

## God's Word

**"God will help you." 1 Chronicles 12:18**

## God's Word & Me

**I'm glad God loves and helps me.**

## Collect

Bible, Picture 50 from *Bible Story Pictures.*

## Tell the Story

Use the pictured motions (keywords in bold) or show Picture 50. For older children, tell the version of the story on the back of Picture 50.

**What is your favorite thing to wear? Listen to hear how a woman helped others by making clothes for them.**

Dorcas was a very kind woman. Dorcas loved Jesus. She worked hard to help people. One way she helped was by **sewing** clothes for people who needed them. Dorcas didn't just help people once in a while or whenever she felt like it. Dorcas helped people all the time. And the people Dorcas helped loved her very much.

But one day Dorcas became very sick. She got so sick that she died. Dorcas' friends were very **sad**. "Maybe Peter can help us," one of them said. Peter was one of Jesus' friends.

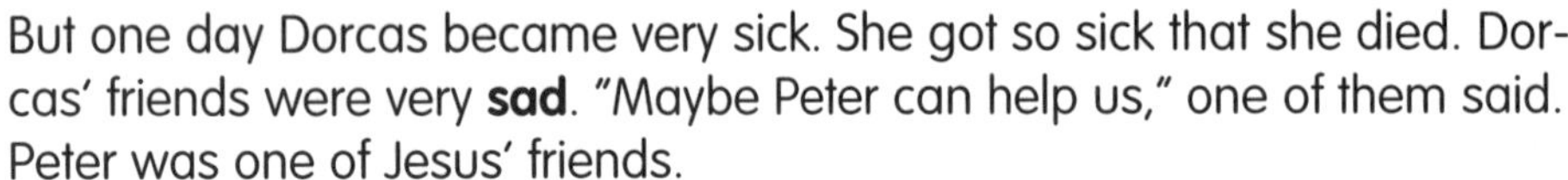

"You're right," another may have said. "Let's ask Peter to come here!"

So right away, two men went to get Peter. They hurried to where Peter was. "Peter! Come quickly!" they said. Peter hurried to Dorcas' house with them. The men told Peter what had happened.

Peter went to the room where Dorcas' body had been placed. There were many friends in the room. They were crying! They were sad because their kind friend was dead. The friends showed Peter the **clothes** Dorcas had made for them. Peter saw how much the friends loved Dorcas. Peter kindly said, "Please leave the room now."

Peter prayed to God. After he prayed, he said, "Dorcas, get up!" And Dorcas opened her eyes and got up! God answered Peter's prayer by making Dorcas alive again! Then Peter called to her friends, and they came and saw Dorcas.

Dorcas was ALIVE! She'd been dead, but now, there she was—standing and smiling at them! Dorcas' friends were so **happy** that God had made kind Dorcas live again!

## God's Word & Me

**When Dorcas died, how did Peter help her? Peter prayed and God made Dorcas live again! Dorcas' friends were glad that God loved her and made her live again. I'm glad that God loves and helps me, too. Thank You, God, for loving us and helping us!**

# Worship Center

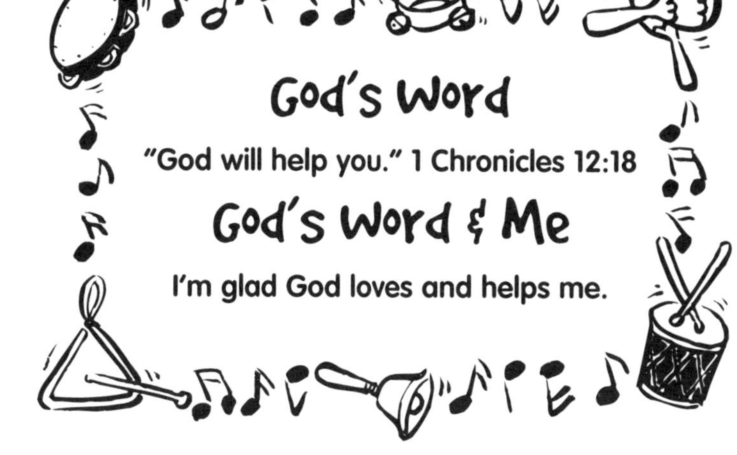
God's Word
"God will help you." 1 Chronicles 12:18
God's Word & Me
I'm glad God loves and helps me.

## Collect

Bible, *Shake It Up!* songbook and cassette/CD and player, "In a Very Big Way" and "God's Love" word charts (pp. 47 and 49 in songbook).

## Sing to God

Play "In a Very Big Way." **Let's sing about how great God's love is for us.** Lead children in singing song and doing suggested motions. **God loves us and everyone else in the world! And God always helps us and does what is best for us. That is what it means when we say God loves us in a very big way!**

## Hear and Say God's Word

Holding your Bible open to 1 Chronicles 12:18, say verse aloud. **This verse promises that God will help you. God always does what He promises. We know that God will always help us!** Point to and say the name of one of the children in your class. Children repeat the verse with you, saying that child's name instead of the word "you." The named child stands up as his or her name is said and remains standing. Repeat verse until you have used all children's names and all children are standing. (Note: If you have a large class, point to two or three children at a time.)

## Pray to God

**Thank You, God, that You are never too busy to watch over and help each one of us. Thank You for loving us in a very big way. We love You. In Jesus' name, amen.**

## Sing to God

In closing the worship time, play "God's Love." Invite the children to sing along with you, doing the suggested motions. **God's love for us is great! I'm glad God loves us and helps us. If you're glad too, clap your hands!**

## Options

1. With parents' permission, videotape children as they sing songs and do the motions. Play videotape at the end of the session as parents come to pick up their children.
2. If you take a weekly offering during this worship time, explain to children that the money is used to help people learn about God. **Giving money is one way to thank God for helping for us.**

# Read-Aloud Story and Activity Center

## Collect

A copy of Story Picture 37 (pp.79-80 from *Read-Aloud Story and Activity Book*) for each child and yourself, crayons or markers.

## Prepare

Color your copy of Story Picture 37.

## Do

**Listen to find out what this girl is doing.** Read story and show completed Story Picture 37. Distribute pictures. Use conversation suggestions in Let's Talk About the Story as children complete their pages.

# Kindergarten Puzzle Center

## Collect

Copies of Puzzles 73 and 74 (p. 153 and p. 155 from *The Big Book of Kindergarten Puzzles*) for each child, pencils, crayons or markers.

## Do

Children complete the puzzles and color pages.

# Instant Activities

These activities can be used at any time during this session: when children need a change of pace, to extend the session, or during transition time at the beginning or end of the session.

## Collect

*The Big Book of Instant Activities.*

## Do

Guide children to complete "Object Order" and/or "I Clap My Hands" (p. 117 and/or p. 39 from *The Big Book of Instant Activities*).

Lesson 38

# Peter Escapes from Prison

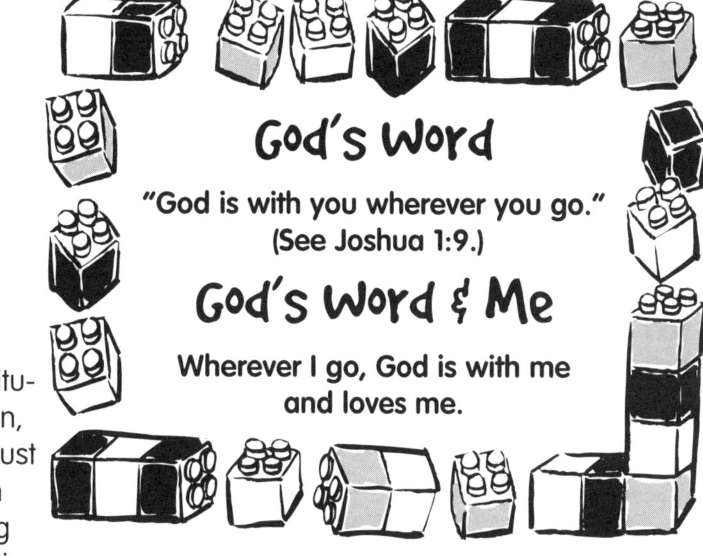
God's Word
"God is with you wherever you go."
(See Joshua 1:9.)
God's Word & Me
Wherever I go, God is with me
and loves me.

## Bible Story

Acts 12:1-18

## Teacher's Devotional

Peter was in a seemingly hopeless situation. Arrested and thrown into prison, he knew he could be killed just as James recently had been killed. Herod was attempting to eliminate Jesus' disciples in order to appease the Jewish leaders. These leaders were watching nervously as the family of Jesus' followers grew at a supernatural rate!

But the supernatural power at work building God's family was working just as effectively in Peter's prison cell! As Peter's friends prayed, an angel awakened Peter, removed all obstacles and led him out of the prison. At first, Peter didn't believe it himself—it was too fantastic to imagine! When Peter showed up at the house where his friends were praying, they did not believe it was him! They had been praying, begging God to spare Peter's life, yet when God answered their prayer in a powerful way, their lack of faith became obvious.

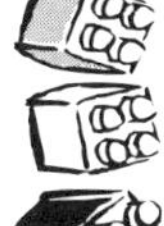

We modern Christians often show that same lack of faith. It's easy to say we believe God is with us wherever we are. It's easy to say we believe God can do anything. Yet even while we pray, we often disbelieve just as readily as Peter's friends. However, this account of Peter's deliverance clearly calls for us to pause and consider. It reminds us to ask the Lord not only to answer our prayers but to give us greater faith in His ability to answer! When we let go of our own worried agendas and invite Him to take care of our problems in whatever way He sees fit, His Spirit graces us with eyes of faith. Then we too will see who or what is at the door; we'll be ready to joyfully receive the answers to prayer God so powerfully and richly provides!

## Teacher's Planning

1. Choose which centers you will provide and the order in which children will participate in them. For tips on schedule planning, see page 7.
2. Plan who will lead each center. For staffing tips and ideas, see page 21.

Lesson 38

# Active Game Center: Knock Knock

## Collect

Bible, magazines or travel brochures, scissors, yarn.

## Prepare

Cut out pictures of different places from magazines or travel brochures. Cut at least one picture for each child. Make a yarn line at one end of the activity area.

### God's Word

**"God is with you wherever you go." (See Joshua 1:9.)**

### God's Word & Me

**Wherever I go, God is with me and loves me.**

## Do

Sit with pictures opposite yarn line. Children line up behind yarn line. Knock on a table, a wall or the floor. The first child in the line crosses the playing area to where you and the pictures are and pretends to open a door. Hand child one of the pictures. Child returns to the back of the line, and another child takes a turn. Continue until each child has a picture. Talk with children about places in the pictures.

## Talk About

- **In today's Bible story, God helped Peter get out of prison. Peter went to the house where his friends were praying and knocked on the door. When Peter's friends opened the door, they were very happy to see him. Let's play a game and pretend to open a door.**
- **Juanita, what picture do you have? Have you ever been to the beach? What did you see there? God was with you when you went to the beach. God is with you wherever you go!**
- **Our Bible says: "God is with you wherever you go." God has promised that wherever you go, He is with you and loves you.**

## For Younger Children

Hide pictures around the classroom. Children search room for pictures.

## For Older Children

For each child, knock from four to six times. The first child takes the same number of steps toward the pile of pictures. All children count each knock and each step aloud. Continue knocking and counting until the child reaches the pile of pictures. Play continues as described above.

# Art Center: Mural Map

## Collect

Bible, large sheet of butcher paper, markers, masking tape, construction paper, scissors, glue.

## Prepare

On butcher paper, draw several roads and intersections. Tape butcher paper to table. Cut construction paper into several geometric shapes (squares, rectangles, triangles, etc.).

### God's Word

**"God is with you wherever you go." (See Joshua 1:9.)**

### God's Word & Me

**Wherever I go, God is with me and loves me.**

## Do

Children glue construction-paper shapes onto butcher paper to form houses and other buildings. Using markers, children add trees, people, cars and other decorations to mural.

## Talk About

- **In today's Bible story, Peter was put in prison for telling people about Jesus. God sent an angel to help him. Peter walked right out of prison, past all the prison guards, through the town and over to the house where his friends were praying. God was with Peter all the way, and God is with us wherever we go! Let's make a picture of some of the places we go.**
- **Rusty, where does your mom take you to buy clothes? God is with you at the mall!**
- **Our Bible says, "God is with you wherever you go."** Pray briefly, **Thank You, God, for being with us and loving us wherever we are.**

## For Younger Children

Instead of working on a mural, children glue construction-paper shapes to form buildings on individual sheets of paper.

## For Older Children

Ask children to name buildings they build (Tom's house, Grocery Store, Italian Restaurant, etc.). Print the names children tell you on index cards. Children tape name cards to their buildings.

Lesson 38

# Block Center: Playground Play

## Collect

Bible, blocks, toy people; optional—small cardboard tubes and boxes.

## Do

Children stack and arrange blocks to make a playground area for toy people. (Optional: Children make playground equipment with cardboard tubes and boxes.) Children play as you talk about places God is with them.

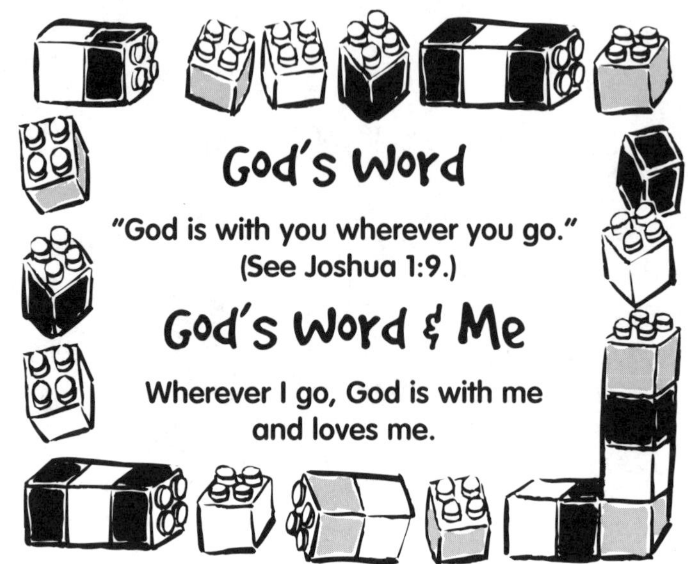
God's Word
"God is with you wherever you go."
(See Joshua 1:9.)
God's Word & Me
Wherever I go, God is with me
and loves me.

## Talk About

- **Our Bible says, "God is with you wherever you go." God is with us wherever we go because He loves us! Let's use our blocks to make a place where God is with us. Let's make a playground.**
- **Dale, what do you like to do at the playground? God is with you when you play at the playground.**
- **God is with us here in our classroom. God is with you when you go home. Kim, where are some places you like to go?**
- **Letitia, God is with you when you're at your grandpa's house. Kenny, God is with you when you go to get ice cream. God is always with us.**
- Pray, **Thank You, God, for always being with us.**

## For Younger Children

Provide several buckets or baskets. Children stack blocks in buckets or baskets and carry the blocks to other places. **Julie, where are you taking the blocks? It is fun to carry the blocks around the room. God is with you wherever you go.**

## For Older Children

Provide construction paper and markers. Children draw additional features for their playground: grassy area, pond, statue, fountain, etc.

Lesson 38

# Science Center: Who Is It?

## Collect

Bible, blank audiocassette and player.

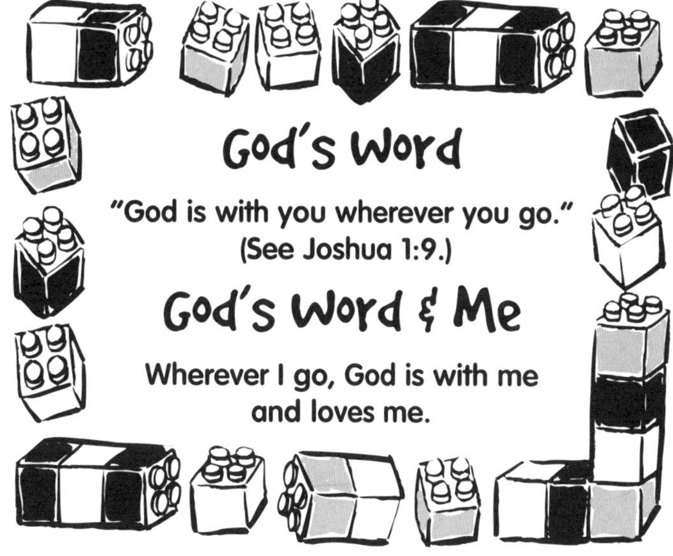
God's Word
"God is with you wherever you go."
(See Joshua 1:9.)
God's Word & Me
Wherever I go, God is with me
and loves me.

## Do

1. Holding your Bible open to Joshua 1:9, say the verse aloud. Ask children to repeat the verse together. Then tape-record individual volunteers saying the verse aloud.
2. Play back the tape. Children guess whose voice they hear saying the verse.
3. **What makes a loud noise when your dad is mowing the lawn?** (Lawn mower.) **What sound do you hear when someone telephones your mom?** Tape-record children making sounds. Play back for children to listen to.

## Talk About

- **In today's Bible story, Peter went to the house of a friend after escaping from prison. He knocked on the door. A servant girl named Rhoda went to answer the door and she recognized Peter by his voice, even before she saw him! Let's take turns and see if we can recognize a friend by his or her voice.**
- **Sometimes we can recognize things by the sounds they make. Wayne, what animal makes the sound "moo"? Let's make some other animal sounds. What animal's sound do you want to make?**
- **Our Bible says, "God is with you wherever you go." Wherever we go, God is with us and loves us.** Pray briefly, **Thank You, God, for loving us. We love You.**

## For Younger Children

Instead of asking children to identify each other, simply record children imitating various sounds as you lead them.

## For Older Children

Tape-record children reciting the alphabet. Play tape for children to identify themselves. Also play tape for parents when children are dismissed.

# Bible Story Center

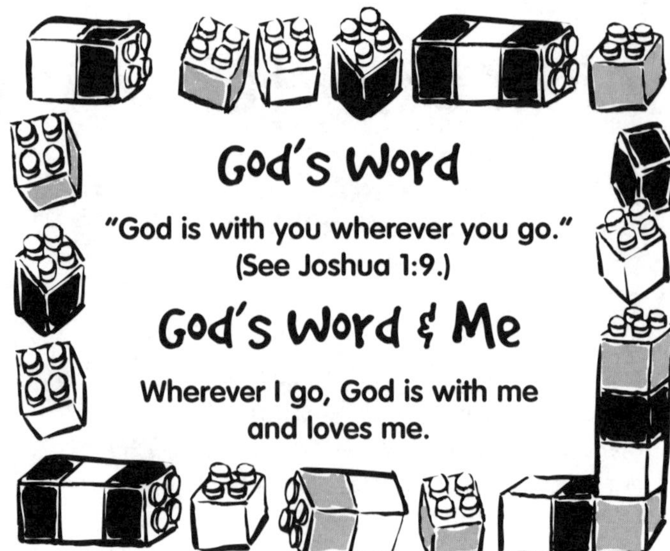
God's Word
"God is with you wherever you go."
(See Joshua 1:9.)
God's Word & Me
Wherever I go, God is with me
and loves me.

## Collect

Bible, Picture 51 from *Bible Story Pictures.*

## Tell the Story

Use the pictured motions (keywords in bold) or show Picture 51. For older children, tell the version of the story on the back of Picture 51.

**Listen to hear what happened when a man named Peter knocked on a door.**

Every day more and more people believed that Jesus is God's Son. But some leaders wanted to stop Jesus' friends from telling others about Jesus. They even put some of Jesus' friends in prison!

One day Jesus' friend Peter was put in a prison cell. Peter's friends began to **pray** to God for help. Peter had chains around him. But that couldn't stop God! One night God sent an angel to Peter.

"Quick, get up!" the angel said. Peter looked down. The chains around him fell off his **hands**! Peter got dressed and followed the angel. The guards were all asleep. The gate to the prison opened. Peter and the angel walked outside into the street.

Then the angel was gone! Peter knew that God had rescued him from the prison! Peter **walked** right to the house where his friends were praying for God's help. He knocked at the door. A servant girl named Rhoda asked, "Who is it?"

"It's me!" said Peter.

Rhoda knew that voice! She was so excited she forgot to answer the door! She ran back to tell the people who were praying. "PETER is at the door!" she shouted.

Everyone looked up at her in surprise. "You're wrong," some of them said.

"No!" she said. "It's really Peter!" All this time Peter was still **knocking** at the door! Finally his friends opened the door. Peter's friends were amazed. God had been with Peter, even in prison. And God had answered their prayer!

## God's Word & Me

**Who did God send to help Peter out of prison?** (Angel.) **Even in prison, God was with Peter and helped him. I'm glad God is with me wherever I go. God is with you and loves you wherever you go! Where do you like to go to eat food? God is with you when you go there!**

Lesson 38

# Worship Center

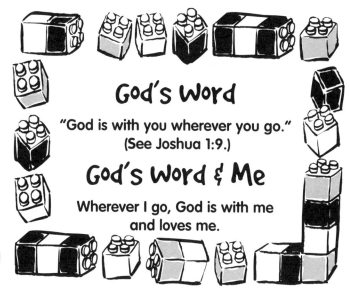

## Collect

Bible, *Shake It Up!* songbook and cassette/CD and player, "In a Very Big Way" and "God's Love" word charts (pp. 47 and 49 in songbook).

### God's Word

**"God is with you wherever you go." (See Joshua 1:9.)**

### God's Word & Me

**Wherever I go, God is with me and loves me.**

## Sing to God

Play "God's Love." Invite the children to sing along with you. **Let's sing about God's love for us.** Lead children in singing song and doing suggested motions. **God loves us so much, He promised to always be with us. I'm glad God is with me wherever I go! If you're glad God is with you wherever you go, sing this song with me again.**

## Hear and Say God's Word

Holding your Bible open to Joshua 1:9, say verse aloud. **Our Bible says that wherever we go, God is with us and loves us. Where do you go with your parents?** (Home. School. Church. Park.) **God is with us in all these places. God is with us everywhere!** Lead children in repeating the verse. Children clap their hands on each word of the verse except the word "you." Whenever children say the word "you," they each point to a different child in the class. Repeat several times.

## Pray to God

Lead the children in prayer, thanking God for being with us wherever we go. Include in the prayer the places the children mentioned in the verse activity.

## Sing to God

In closing the worship time, play "In a Very Big Way." Invite the children to sing along with you, doing the suggested motions. **We can thank God that wherever we are, He loves us and will help us. Thank you God!**

## Options

1. To make the Bible verse activity more of a challenge for older children, ask them to repeat verse and replace the first "you" with another child's name, the second "you" with "he" or "she" and "go" with "goes." The named child then repeats verse, using a different child's name. Continue until each child has a turn.
2. On the top of a large sheet of paper, print "God is with me at __________." During verse activity, as children name places they go with their parents, print children's responses on paper. Display paper so that parents can read it when children are dismissed.

# Read-Aloud Story and Activity Center

## Collect

A copy of Story Picture 38 (pp. 81-82 from *Read-Aloud Story and Activity Book*) for each child and yourself, crayons or markers.

STOP
ONE WAY
START
"God is with you wherever you go."

## Prepare

Color your copy of Story Picture 38.

## Do

**Listen to find out where this car is going.** Read story and show completed Story Picture 38. Distribute pictures. Use conversation suggestions in Let's Talk About the Story as children complete their pages.

# Kindergarten Puzzle Center

## Collect

Copies of Puzzles 75 and 76 (p. 157 and p. 159 from *The Big Book of Kindergarten Puzzles*) for each child, pencils, crayons or markers.

## Do

Children complete the puzzles and color pages.

# Instant Activities

These activities can be used at any time during this session: when children need a change of pace, to extend the session, or during transition time at the beginning or end of the session.

## Collect

*The Big Book of Instant Activities.*

## Do

Guide children to complete "Color Code" and/or "Sally, Sally" (p. 18 and/or p. 52 from *The Big Book of Instant Activities*).

Lesson 39

# Paul Helps a Lame Man

## God's Word

**"Jesus said, 'Love each other as I have loved you.'" (See John 15:12.)**

## God's Word & Me

**God loves me and I can show love to others.**

## Bible Story

Acts 14:8-20

## Teacher's Devotional

Paul and Barnabas were traveling to cities where the good news of Jesus had never been heard. There must have been a lot of cultural differences for these two Jewish men to deal with. These people were all Gentiles (people who are not Jewish), whom they had recently learned not to despise. In addition, Gentiles were worshipers of false gods. Pretty much everything they did was repulsive to Paul and Barnabas, Jewish men who had avoided Gentiles all their lives!

But God's love had been poured into these two men by His Spirit. They were compelled by that love to go into these cultures with a life-changing message. The message was that the God who made them was calling these pagan people into familial relationship with Himself through Jesus. Jesus had commanded His disciples, "Love each other as I have loved you" (John 15:12). That powerful love moved Paul and Barnabas beyond prejudice, fear and cultural conditioning.

In our lives, there is always that person, that family, that group with whom we may not feel comfortable. Those people are not like us. They have different values about some of the things we hold dear. Their political affiliations may not be the same as ours. Yet Jesus' command remains the same: "Love each other as I have loved you." Jesus' love for us led Him to make the most complete sacrifice: He sacrificed His life for us. Is there any higher call than that? Never say it's impossible to live up to that kind of love. God offers to give it to us as we drop our opinions and let Him love others through us!

## Teacher's Planning

1. Choose which centers you will provide and the order in which children will participate in them. For tips on schedule planning, see page 7.
2. Plan who will lead each center. For staffing tips and ideas, see page 21.

Lesson 39

# Active Game Center: Music Moves

## Collect

Bible, *Shake It Up!* cassette/CD and player.

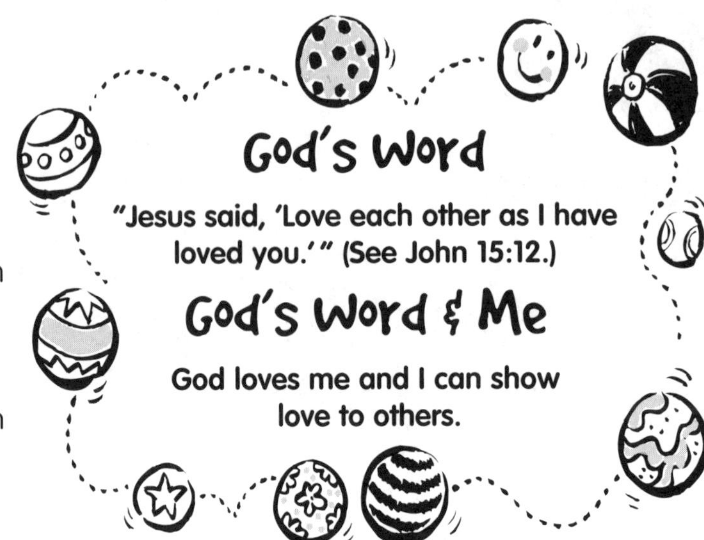

### God's Word

**"Jesus said, 'Love each other as I have loved you.'" (See John 15:12.)**

### God's Word & Me

**God loves me and I can show love to others.**

## Do

Children walk in place as you play "God's Love" for several moments. When you stop the music, children freeze in place. Children remain frozen until you start music again. Ask children to vary their movements with each round (run in place, hop on one foot, jump with both feet, tiptoe, etc.).

## Talk About

- **In today's Bible story, Paul and Barnabas showed God's love by telling people about Jesus. When the lame man heard about Jesus, he believed Jesus could make his legs well. Let's play a game using our legs.**
- **I like to use my legs to walk my dogs. Eddie, what do you like to do with your legs?** (Walk. Run. Ride a bike. Play hopscotch. Ride a scooter. Kick a ball.) **God gave us legs to walk, run, jump and skip! God loves us and wants us to show His love to others.**
- **Joleen, you moved over to give Doug more room. You showed God's love by being kind! What are some other ways you can show love today?**
- **Our Bible tells us, "Jesus said, 'Love each other as I have loved you.'" God loves us all the time! We can show God's love to others.** Pray briefly, **Thank You, God, for loving me. Please help me to love others.**

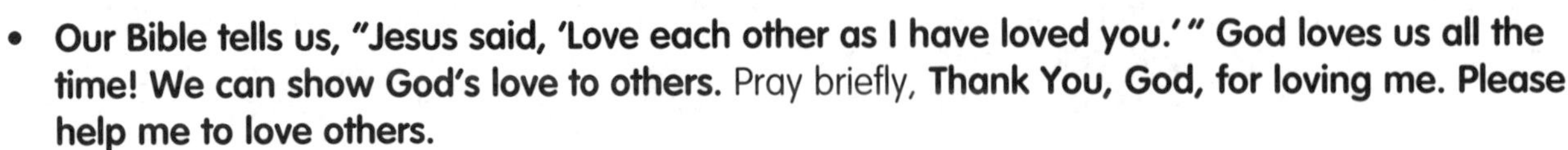

## For Younger Children

Children follow the teacher in a line for each round of the game.

## For Older Children

Ask a different volunteer to suggest the motions for each round of the game.

Lesson 39

# Art Center: Picture This

## Collect

Bible, poster board, scissors, ruler, markers, ribbon, stapler, glue; optional—instant camera.

## Prepare

Cut two 4x5-inch (10x12.5-cm) rectangles from poster board for each child. Cut a 2x3-inch (5x7.5-cm) opening from the center of half the rectangles to make frames. On the bottom of frames, print "God loves me!" Cut one 12-inch (30.5-cm) length of ribbon for each child.

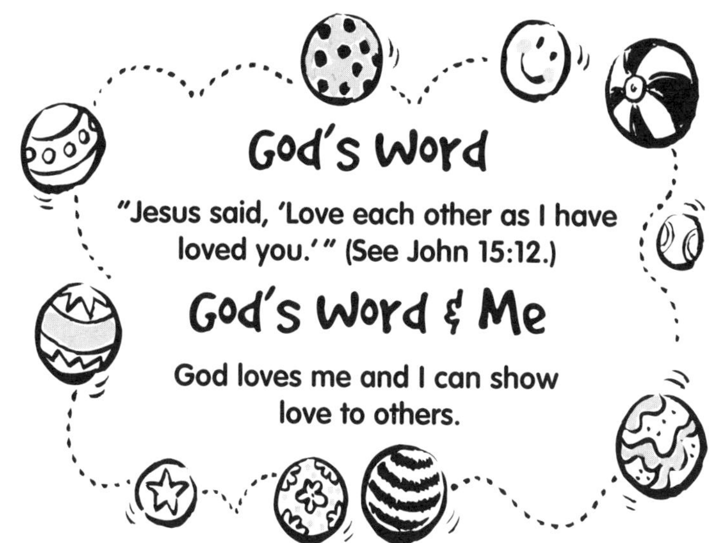
God's Word
"Jesus said, 'Love each other as I have loved you.'" (See John 15:12.)
God's Word & Me
God loves me and I can show love to others.

## Do

1. Help children staple the ends of ribbons onto the corners of uncut poster-board pieces. Children spread glue along sides and bottom of frame. With the staples and ribbon ends facing in, children place uncut poster-board piece on top of frame.
2. Using markers, children decorate frames and draw a picture of themselves in the frame opening. (Optional: Use instant camera to take a picture of each child. Children place pictures in frames.)

a. 2" (5cm) 3" (7.5cm) 5" (12.5cm) 4" (10 cm)
b. front of frame back of frame glue

## Talk About

- **In our Bible story today, God made a lame man's legs well. God helped the man because God loved him. God loves us, too! Let's make something to remind us of God's love.**
- **In our Bible we read, "Jesus said, 'Love each other as I have loved you.'" God loves us, and we can show love to others.** Pray briefly, **Dear God, please help me to show love to others.**

## For Younger Children

Before class, staple ribbon to create hanger and glue frame pieces together.

## For Older Children

Instead of printing "God loves me!" on each frame, print the sentence on a large sheet of paper. Children copy the sentence onto the bottom of their frames.

 

Lesson 39

# Block Center: Blocked Path

## Collect

Bible, yarn, blocks.

## Prepare

Use yarn to outline an obstacle course through classroom (going under tables, around bookcases, etc.).

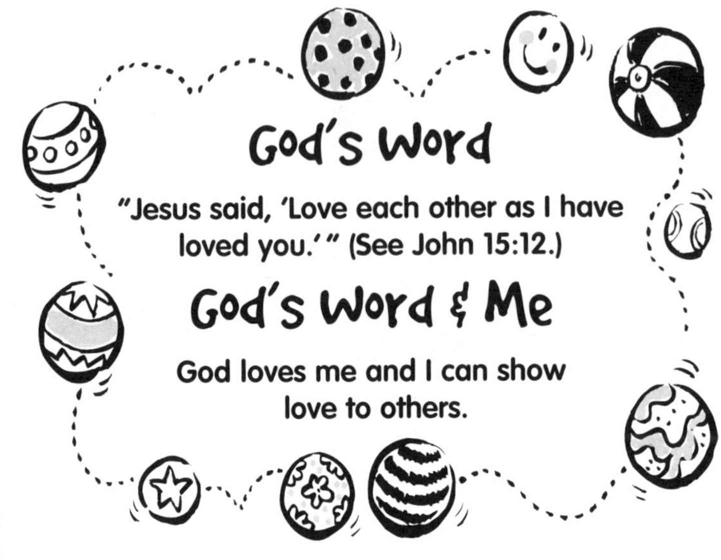
God's Word
"Jesus said, 'Love each other as I have loved you.'" (See John 15:12.)
God's Word & Me
God loves me and I can show love to others.

## Do

Children use blocks to create obstacles on or around the yarn course. Blocks may be stacked on yarn line to be jumped over, or they may be placed on yarn line to be walked on as if it were a balance beam. Children walk along the course, following each obstacle.

## Talk About

- **Our Bible story tells about a lame man. The man's legs didn't work at all. The man listened when Paul talked about Jesus. Paul helped the man by telling him about Jesus. The man believed Jesus could make his legs well. And Jesus did! Now the man could walk. Let's use our blocks to make a special course we can walk on.**
- **Thank you, Todd, for giving Andrea the first turn to walk the obstacle course. You showed God's love by being kind to her!**
- **Our Bible tells us, "Jesus said, 'Love each other as I have loved you.'" God loves us! And God wants us to show His love to others.** Pray briefly, **Dear God, help me to show love to others. I love You.**

## For Younger Children

Instead of creating obstacles, children carry blocks as they walk along the yarn course. At the end of the yarn course, children build with the blocks they've carried.

## For Older Children

Instead of preparing the yarn course before class, children create the obstacle course themselves. Children move the yarn to change the course, making and following several different courses as time and interest allow.

Lesson 39

# Science Center: Stand and Jump

## Collect

Bible, yarn, masking tape, markers.

## Prepare

Make a yarn line on floor.

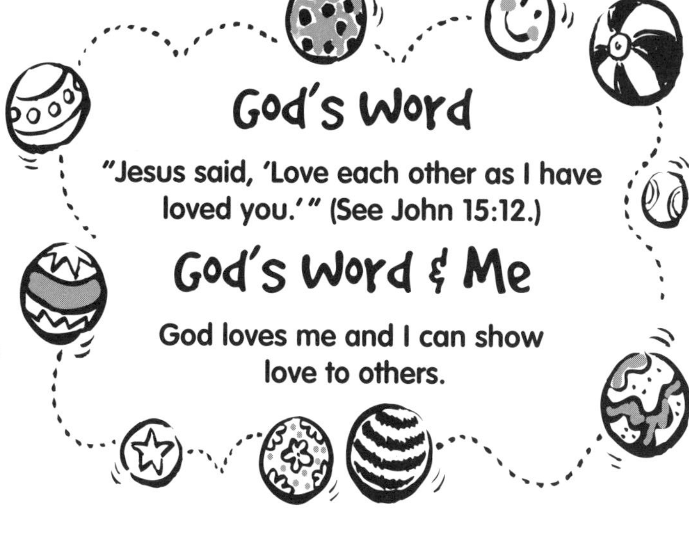

### God's Word

**"Jesus said, 'Love each other as I have loved you.'" (See John 15:12.)**

### God's Word & Me

**God loves me and I can show love to others.**

## Do

1. Children take turns standing at the yarn line and taking a big step. As the child holds the step, hand him or her a piece of masking tape. Child marks where his or her foot landed with tape. Using a marker, child writes his or her name or initials on tape (assist children as needed).
2. For the next round, each child stands at the yarn line and jumps as far as possible with both feet together. Child marks position with another masking-tape piece and writes his or her name or initials on the tape. (Note: Remove tape immediately after activity.)

## Talk About

- **In today's Bible story Paul helped a lame man by telling him about Jesus. The man's legs didn't work at all. The man believed Jesus could make his legs well. And Jesus did! Now the man could walk, leap and jump! Let's see how big a step and how big a jump you can make.**
- **Ray, what are some ways you can help your mom when you go to the store?** (Stay close to her. Wait quietly in line.) **When we help others, we show love to them!**
- **Our Bible tells us, "Jesus said, 'Love each other as I have loved you.'" God loves us and we can show love to others!**

## For Younger Children

Instead of marking their steps and jumps, lead younger children in a game of Follow the Leader, walking in a variety of ways (clapping hands, tiptoeing, etc.). Be sure to keep motions simple.

## For Older Children

Children use measuring sticks to measure the length of their steps and jumps.

Lesson 39 • Acts 14:8-20

# Bible Story Center

## Collect

Bible, Picture 52 from *Bible Story Pictures*.

## God's Word

**"Jesus said, 'Love each other as I have loved you.'" (See John 15:12.)**

## God's Word & Me

**God loves me and I can show love to others.**

## Tell the Story

Use the pictured motions (keywords in bold) or show Picture 52. For older children, tell the version of the story on the back of Picture 52.

**Can you wiggle your toes? Tap your feet? Jump up and down? Listen to hear about a man who could not use his feet at all.**

Paul and his friend Barnabas traveled together. They used their feet to **walk** from town to town. In every town, they told people about Jesus. Paul and Barnabas helped people who were sick. Many, many people believed that Jesus is God's Son because of Paul and Barnabas.

Paul and Barnabas came to a town called Lystra. They told the people there that Jesus is God's Son. They told how Jesus healed people. Paul and Barnabas told the people that God loved them. As Paul talked, he looked at **one man** in the crowd. This man had never walked in his whole life. His feet didn't work. The man looked back at Paul. Paul could see that the man believed God could make his feet well!

So Paul said to the man, "Stand up on your feet!" The man **jumped** up on his feet. He began to walk. The man may have tried to hop a little and then maybe to run a little. He must have been so happy to use his feet that maybe he twirled a little! His feet were well! God had made the man's feet work!

The people in the crowd saw the man leaping and jumping! The people got VERY excited! They thought Paul and Barnabas had made the man's feet work. But it wasn't Paul and Barnabas. They were just people like everyone else. Paul and Barnabas told the people the truth. They wanted everyone to know that God had made the man's feet work.

Paul said, "We are only here to bring the good news about **God**." Paul and Barnabas used their feet to walk to other cities to tell others about God. They wanted to show God's love to everyone!

## God's Word & Me

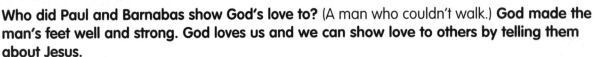

**Who did Paul and Barnabas show God's love to?** (A man who couldn't walk.) **God made the man's feet well and strong. God loves us and we can show love to others by telling them about Jesus.**

# Worship Center

## Collect

Bible, *Shake It Up!* songbook and cassette/CD and player, "In a Very Big Way" and "God's Love" word charts (pp. 47 and 49 in songbook).

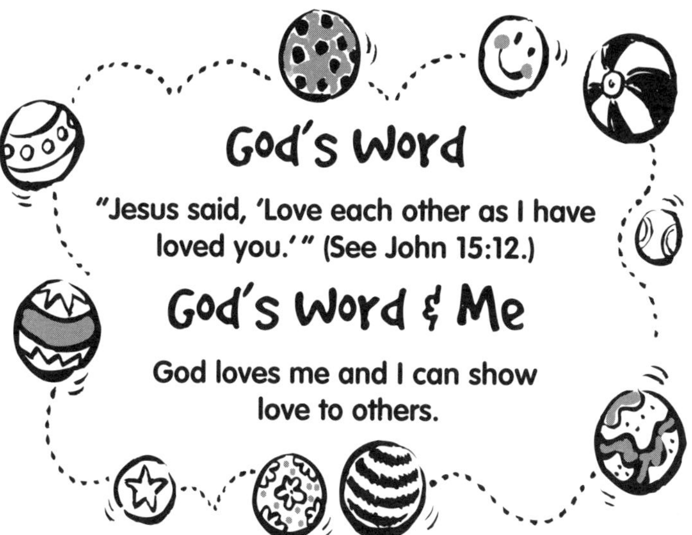
God's Word
"Jesus said, 'Love each other as I have loved you.'" (See John 15:12.)
God's Word & Me
God loves me and I can show love to others.

## Sing to God

Play "In a Very Big Way." **Let's sing about God loving us in a very big way.** Invite the children to sing along with you. Lead children in singing song and doing suggested motions. **This song tells us that God loves us and helps us when we're afraid or sad. God loves us when we're happy, too. God loves us all the time!**

## Hear and Say God's Word

Holding your Bible open to John 15:12, say verse aloud. **What does Jesus want us to do?** (Love each other.) Lead children in repeating the verse several times. As the children are repeating the verse with you, point to a child. You and the children say that child's name instead of the words "each other." Repeat until you have used every child's name.

## Pray to God

**Let's ask for God's help to show love to others.** To complete the following prayer, volunteers take turns naming people to whom they can show love: **Dear God, help me show love to** __________. After volunteers have all had a turn, close prayer: **Thank You, God, for loving us. In Jesus' name, amen.**

## Sing to God

In closing the worship time, play "God's Love." Invite the children to sing along with you and do the suggested motions. **God has given us many things to show His great love for us. What are some of the good things God has given you?**

## Options

1. During the verse activity, invite children to clap their hands on each word. Children point to the child you pointed to when they say that child's name.
2. Provide rhythm instruments for children to use while singing "In a Very Big Way" and "God's Love."

# Read-Aloud Story and Activity Center

## Collect

A copy of Story Picture 39 (pp. 83-84 from *Read-Aloud Story and Activity Book*) for each child and yourself, crayons or markers.

"Jesus said, 'Love each other as I have loved you.'"

## Prepare

Color your copy of Story Picture 39.

## Do

**Listen to find out where a girl found her shoe.** Read story and show completed Story Picture 39. Distribute pictures. Use conversation suggestions in Let's Talk About the Story as children complete their pages.

# Kindergarten Puzzle Center

## Collect

Copies of Puzzles 77 and 78 (p. 161 and p. 163 from *The Big Book of Kindergarten Puzzles*) for each child, pencils, crayons or markers.

## Do

Children complete the puzzles and color pages.

# Instant Activities

These activities can be used at any time during this session: when children need a change of pace, to extend the session, or during transition time at the beginning or end of the session.

## Collect

*The Big Book of Instant Activities.*

## Do

Guide children to complete "String Fun" and/or "Stop and Go!" (p. 122 and/or p. 85 from *The Big Book of Instant Activities*).

Lesson 40

# Jacob and Esau

## Bible Story

Genesis 25:19-28

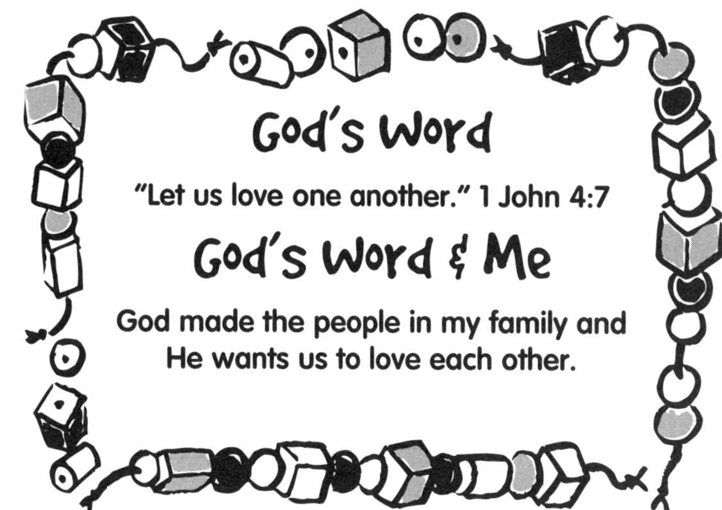
God's Word
"Let us love one another." 1 John 4:7
God's Word & Me
God made the people in my family and
He wants us to love each other.

## Teacher's Devotional

The word "brotherhood" conjures up images of familial love and harmony. Jacob and Esau were brothers—twins who grew up in the same household. But Jacob and Esau would not be considered the ideal image of brotherhood!

Even as they were born, these two struggled for dominance. Jacob literally held onto Esau's heel at birth! (That action, which looked like he was tripping his brother, earned him the name Jacob, "heel-catcher.") Once they were born, their differences were even more apparent. The ruddy, hairy Esau had little in common with his brother. Esau preferred to be outdoors hunting while Jacob preferred to stay home and cook. The differences between the brothers were only compounded by their parents' favoritism. Their father, Isaac, favored Esau while their mother, Rebekah, favored Jacob.

Young children are keenly aware of favoritism. As we teach, we express attitudes by body language, words and tone of voice. To those young observers, we constantly send messages about not only our own ways but also God's ways, for He is the source of all the sharing, the brotherhood and gentleness that we need to reflect in all we do. Pray for each little one in your class, asking God to give you sensitivity to show His love in ways that each of them can grasp.

## Teacher's Planning

1. Choose which centers you will provide and the order in which children will participate in them. For tips on schedule planning, see page 7.
2. Plan who will lead each center. For staffing tips and ideas, see page 21.

 

# Active Game Center: Chore Champs

## Collect

Bible, articles of clothing (socks, shirt, shorts, etc.), plastic dinnerware (plates, cups, bowls, etc.), small toys (toy people, blocks, etc.), large bag, laundry basket, storage box.

### God's Word

**"Let us love one another." 1 John 4:7**

### God's Word & Me

**God made the people in my family and He wants us to love each other.**

## Prepare

Place articles of clothing, plastic dinnerware and toys in large bag. Place bag, laundry basket, storage box and a table in opposite corners, forming a square playing area.

## Do

1. Children line up by bag and take turns reaching into bag and selecting an item. Child decides if the item belongs in the laundry basket (clothing), in the storage box (toy) or on the table (dinnerware) and then walks to the appropriate area and places item. Child returns to line. Continue until all the items have been placed.
2. For the next round, children choose items from the laundry basket, the storage box or the table to return to the bag.

## Talk About

- **In today's Bible story, a family had two sons. One son helped his family by getting food for them. The other son helped his family by cooking. Let's act out some ways we can help our families.**
- **Our Bible says, "Let us love one another." We show love for our families when we help them. Amanda, what are some of the jobs you do to help your family? Putting away the groceries is a way to show love! Nathan, how does your dad help you? Your dad loves you!**

## For Younger Children

Simplify game by using only the laundry basket and clothes or the table and plastic dinnerware.

## For Older Children

Place a sponge, a feather duster and a whisk broom in bag along with other items. When a child selects one of these items, he or she acts out a way to use the item to help his or her family.

# Art Center: Family Fun

## Collect

Bible, construction paper, scissors, glue, markers.

## Prepare

Cut a variety of geometric shapes (circles, squares, rectangles, triangles, etc.) of various sizes from construction paper.

God's Word
"Let us love one another." 1 John 4:7
God's Word & Me
God made the people in my family and He wants us to love each other.

## Do

Children name people in his or her family. Then children choose construction-paper shapes and glue shapes to sheets of construction paper to represent one or more family members. For example, a triangle can form the body and a circle becomes a head. Using markers, children add facial features, hair, clothing, etc.

## Talk About

- **Our Bible says, "Let us love one another." God made the people in our families and He wants us to love each other. Let's make a picture of the people in our families!**
- **Stephanie, what are the names of the people in your family? Let's count the names as you say them. One; two, three, four, and don't forget Stephanie—that makes five. You have five people in your family!**
- **Matthew, who helped you get dressed this morning? What does your big brother do to help you? Your grandma? Helping each other is one way to show love to our families.**
- Pray briefly, **Thank You, God for the people in our families. Help us to show love to them.**

## For Younger Children

Before class, cut pictures of people from magazines and catalogs. Instead of gluing shapes, children glue magazine pictures to sheets of construction paper, forming collages.

## For Older Children

Children cut shapes from construction paper.

Lesson 40

# Block Center: Kitchen Blocks

## Collect

Bible, cardboard boxes, markers, blocks.

## Prepare

On cardboard boxes, draw with markers to create various kitchen appliances. For instance, draw four circles on the top and a large square with some knobs on the front of a box to make a stove with oven. Other boxes can be left open to form cabinets or a refrigerator.

### God's Word

**"Let us love one another." 1 John 4:7**

### God's Word & Me

**God made the people in my family and He wants us to love each other.**

## Do

Children use blocks to outline a kitchen and then place cardboard-box appliances in the kitchen. Children use blocks to act out family situations, such as putting food in the refrigerator, cooking on the stove, etc.

## Talk About

- **Our Bible says, "Let us love one another." God wants us to love the people in our families. Let's build a kitchen and act out ways to show love to the people in our families.**
- **Let's pretend our family is going to eat breakfast. Luke, what food do you like to eat for breakfast? Can you get the eggs from the refrigerator? Thank you! We show love to the people in our families when we help them.**
- **We can also show love to the people in our families by being kind. Carol, what are some kind things you can do for your baby brother?** (Help Mom feed him. Be quiet when he's sleeping.)

## For Younger Children

Instead of making the outline of a kitchen, children use blocks as they play with cardboard appliances. Expect children to play individually instead of acting out family situations.

## For Older Children

Children use markers to make household appliances from cardboard boxes. Children may also cut shapes from construction paper (circles for knobs and burners, a square for an oven door or window, etc.) to glue onto boxes.

Lesson 40

# Science Center: Growing Up!

## Collect

Bible, masking tape, butcher paper, markers, measuring stick; optional—instant camera and film, transparent tape.

## Prepare

Tape butcher paper to floor or on wall with bottom edge at floor level. At top of paper, make a chart with three columns. Print "Name," "Age" and "Height," one word at the top of each column.

### God's Word

**"Let us love one another." 1 John 4:7**

### God's Word & Me

**God made the people in my family and He wants us to love each other.**

## Do

1. Children lie down with feet at the bottom of the paper on the floor, or stand next to paper on wall. Mark the height of each child. Use measuring stick to measure the height.
2. Print each child's name, age and height on chart. (Optional: Attach an instant-camera photograph of each child beside his or her name.)

## Talk About

- **In today's Bible story Isaac and Rebekah had baby boys. These babies grew up to be very different from each other. You're growing, too! Let's make a chart of your ages and heights.**
- **Our Bible says, "Let us love one another." Maria, what are some ways to tell the people in your family that you love them?** (Say "I love you." Give a hug.) **What kind things can you do for the people in your family to show you love them?** (Share toys. Help with chores.)

## For Younger Children

Bring in picture books of babies or baby dolls and a mirror. Children look at books or baby dolls and compare to their reflections from the mirror. **Dixie, you used to be a baby. What are some things people do to love and care for babies? Your family helped you eat when you were a baby, too!**

## For Older Children

Children measure their height using the measuring stick and the mark you made. Children print their own names, ages and heights on chart.

## Lesson 40 • Genesis 25:19-28

# Bible Story Center

### Collect

Bible, Picture 1 from *Bible Story Pictures.*

God's Word
"Let us love one another." 1 John 4:7
God's Word & Me
God made the people in my family and
He wants us to love each other.

## Tell the Story

Use the pictured motions (keywords in bold) or show Picture 1. For older children, tell the version of the story on the back of Picture 1.

**Do you have any brothers? Do you have any sisters? What are their names? Listen to a story about two brothers.**

Isaac was a man who loved God. Isaac married a lady named Rebekah. For a long time, they had no children. Isaac **prayed** to God. He asked God to give him children.

God answered Isaac's prayer. God told Rebekah she was soon going to have twin **babies**. Isaac and Rebekah were going to have TWO babies!

Finally it was time for the babies to be born. The twins were both boys, but they were different. The older baby was very red. He had lots of hair. His name was Esau.

The other baby was named Jacob. He had smooth skin. He didn't have a lot of hair. These boys were VERY different from each other.

As Esau and Jacob grew up, they still were very different. They looked different from each other. They acted differently from each other.

Esau became a good **hunter**. Using a bow and arrow, he was able to find food for his family to eat. Esau liked to be outdoors. Isaac was very proud of his big, strong son, Esau.

Jacob liked to stay home in the tents where his family lived. He liked to **cook** good food for his family. His mother, Rebekah, was very proud of her quiet, helpful son, Jacob.

Isaac and Rebekah were very happy that God gave them two sons to love.

### God's Word & Me

**How many sons did God give Isaac and Rebekah?** (Two.) **God made this family with two brothers, a mother and a father. God wants the people in families to love each other. Who is someone in your family?** (Mom, Dad, Grandma.) **God made the people in your family. God wants you to love each other. What can you do to show love to the people in your family?** (Help them do chores. Play games with them.)

# Worship Center

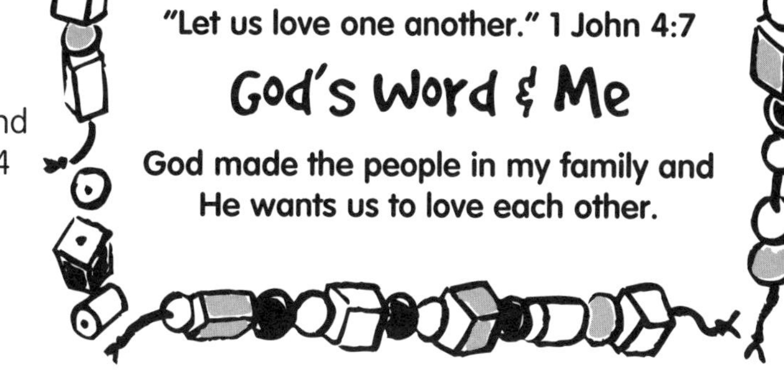
God's Word
"Let us love one another." 1 John 4:7
God's Word & Me
God made the people in my family and He wants us to love each other.

## Collect

Bible, *Shake It Up!* songbook and cassette/CD and player, "My Family" and "Let Us Love" word charts (pp.51 and 54 in songbook).

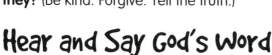

## Sing to God

Play "My Family." Invite children to sing along with you. **Let's sing a song about loving our families.** Lead children in singing song and doing suggested motions. **This song tells us several ways to show love to our family. What are they?** (Be kind. Forgive. Tell the truth.)

## Hear and Say God's Word

Holding your Bible open to 1 John 4:7, say verse aloud. **God made our families. God wants us to love the people in our families.** Lead children in repeating the verse several times. Before each repetition, ask a different volunteer to name a person in his or her family. Use that person's name instead of the words "one another." Repeat until every child has an opportunity to name someone.

## Pray to God

Invite volunteers to name people in their families, or use names mentioned in Hear and Say God's Word. Pray, using the names of the people mentioned by children. **Dear God, we love You. Please help us show love to __________. In Jesus' name, amen.**

## Sing to God

In closing the worship time, play "Let Us Love." Invite children to sing along with you and do suggested motions. **This is a song you can sing with your family. That's one way to show love for the people in your family! Let's sing the song again.**

## Options

1. If you take an offering during this time, explain to children that giving money is one way to show love to others. Briefly describe one mission project your church uses offering money to support.

2. Add motion to the verse activity. Children line up and follow the first child in the line, walking around the classroom. Say verse aloud, replacing the words "one another" with the name of the first child in the line. After his or her name is said, that child moves to the end of the line and the next child becomes the line leader. Repeat verse until every child has had an opportunity to be the line leader.

# Read-Aloud Story and Activity Center

## Collect

A copy of Story Picture 40 (pp. 85-86 from *Read-Aloud Story and Activity Book*) for each child and yourself, crayons or markers.

## Prepare

Color your copy of Story Picture 40.

## Do

**Listen to find out what this boy is doing.** Read story and show completed Story Picture 40. Distribute pictures. Use conversation suggestions in Let's Talk About the Story as children complete their pages.

# Kindergarten Puzzle Center

## Collect

Copies of Puzzles 79 and 80 (p. 165 and p. 167 from *The Big Book of Kindergarten Puzzles*) for each child, pencils, crayons or markers.

## Do

Children complete the puzzles and color pages.

# Instant Activities

These activities can be used at any time during this session: when children need a change of pace, to extend the session, or during transition time at the beginning or end of the session.

## Collect

*The Big Book of Instant Activities.*

## Do

Guide children to complete "Sometimes I'm Very Tall" and/or "Wear Pairs" (p. 103 and/or p. 73 from *The Big Book of Instant Activities*).

Lesson 41

# An Unfair Trade

## Bible Story

Genesis 25:27-34

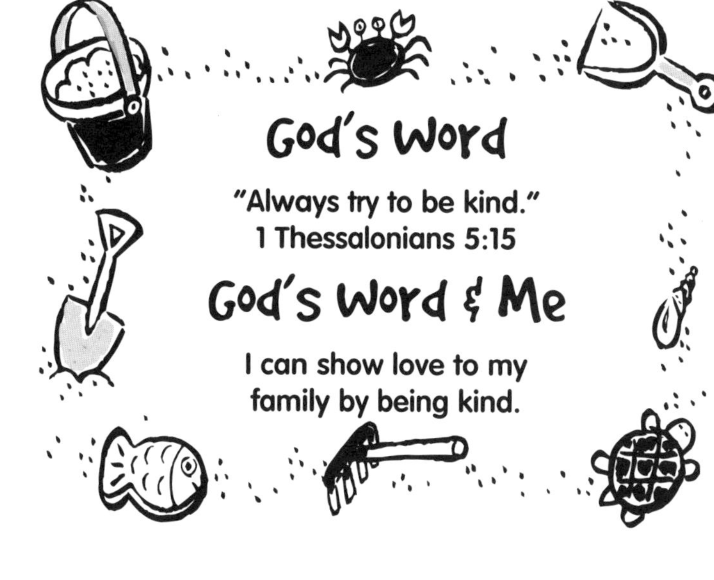
God's Word
"Always try to be kind."
1 Thessalonians 5:15
God's Word & Me
I can show love to my family by being kind.

## Teacher's Devotional

We all like to eat! There are books and magazines devoted entirely to food; cooking shows and recipe clubs entice us to try new foods. Then there is the ever-popular church potluck—if you ever thought people didn't care about eating, this is one place you'll see them really pile their plates high!

Sometimes, Bible lessons contain ideas that are somewhat abstract. The point of the story can be hard for some preschoolers to grasp. However, this lesson is about something very concrete: FOOD! Even the smallest child understands how it feels to be hungry. When most children are hungry, they are ravenously hungry, as desperately hungry as Esau was when he came in from the hunt. They need food NOW! Waiting for dinner to be ready can seem to last years to a young child. Most will also understand the feelings that come when someone is unkind.

Take advantage of the concrete nature of this lesson. Use the guided conversation to help children relate this lesson to their own experiences. Your conversation, your welcoming attitude and your model of kindness will help each one come away with greater understanding.

## Teacher's Planning

1. Choose which centers you will provide and the order in which children will participate in them. For tips on schedule planning, see page 7.
2. Plan who will lead each center. For staffing tips and ideas, see page 21.

 

# Active Game Center: Family Bowls

## Collect

Bible, magazines, scissors, several bowls, yarn, beanbag.

## Prepare

Cut out pictures to represent different family members (grandmother, dad, brother, sister, etc.). Place a picture in each bowl and place bowls on the floor. Make a yarn line on floor several feet from bowls.

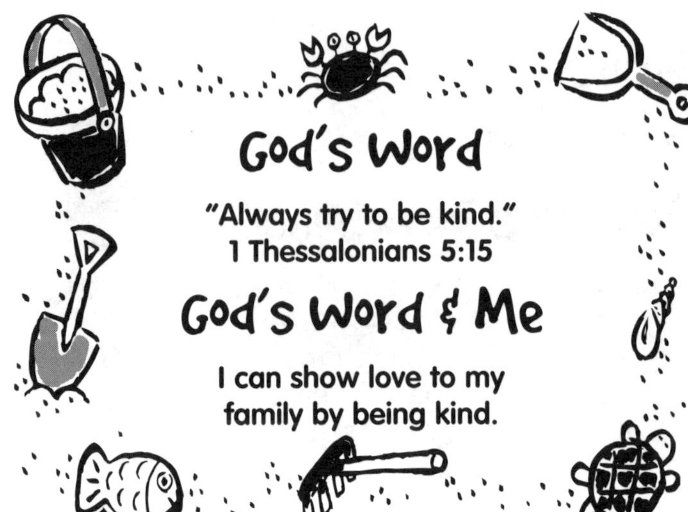
God's Word
"Always try to be kind."
1 Thessalonians 5:15
God's Word & Me
I can show love to my family by being kind.

## Do

Children take turns standing on yarn line and tossing beanbag into bowls. When a beanbag lands in a bowl, talk about ways to be kind to the person whose picture is in the bowl.

## Talk About

- **Our Bible says, "Always try to be kind." We can show love to the people in our families by being kind to them. Let's play a game and talk about ways to be kind to the people in our families.**
- **Kyle, your beanbag landed in a bowl with a picture of a girl. That girl could be someone's sister. How can you be kind to your sister when you play together?** (Take turns. Use kind words.)
- **Erica, what picture is in the bowl your beanbag landed in? That man looks like a grandfather. You can be kind to your grandpa when you visit him. What can you do to help him when he's working in the yard?**
- **Tanner, thank you for handing the beanbag to Damon. That was kind! You can be kind at home, too.**

## For Younger Children

Identify the pictures for children before playing and each time a beanbag lands in a bowl.

## For Older Children

Children stand farther from bowls when tossing beanbags or to toss beanbags over their shoulders.

Lesson 41

# Art Center: Menu Making

## Collect

Bible, magazines and/or grocery-store advertisements, scissors, construction paper, glue, markers.

## Prepare

From magazines and/or grocery-store advertisements, cut approximately five pictures of food for each child. Fold construction paper sheets in half to form menus.

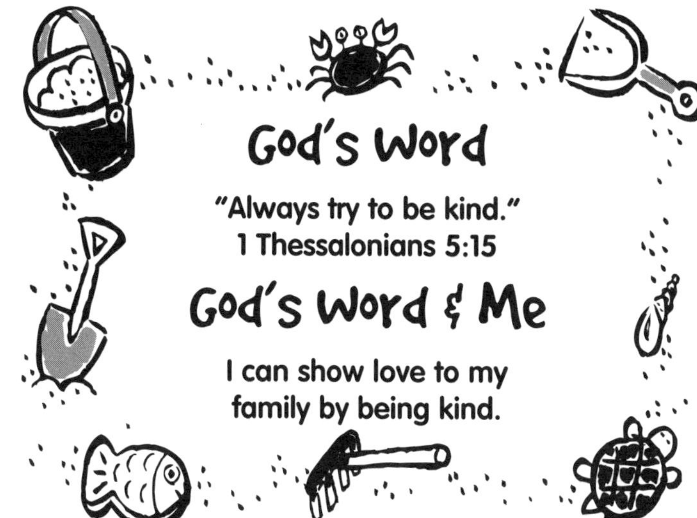
God's Word
"Always try to be kind."
1 Thessalonians 5:15
God's Word & Me
I can show love to my
family by being kind.

## Do

Children select and glue pictures of food onto construction paper to make menus. Children use markers to decorate menus.

## Talk About

- **In our Bible story today, Esau was very hungry and wanted some of Jacob's food. Jacob did not share the food. He tricked Esau and was not kind. Sharing food is one way to be kind. Let's make some menus to show the food we eat and share with our families.**
- **What can you do to be kind to your brothers and sisters when you are eating with them?** (Pass food to them. Let them choose food first.) **What food does everyone in your family like to eat? Here is a picture of grapes to put on your menu.**
- **Our Bible says, "Always try to be kind." How can you be kind when your mother makes some special food?** (Tell her thank you. Help her clean up.)
- Pray briefly, **Thank You, God, for our families. Help us to be kind to them.**

## For Younger Children

Instead of making menus, children glue food pictures to paper plates.

## For Older Children

Children print prices next to the pictures in their menus. If children ask you how to print a number, print the number on a Post-it Note and give to the child to copy.

Lesson 41

# Block Center: Block Park

## Collect

Bible, blocks.

God's Word
"Always try to be kind."
1 Thessalonians 5:15
God's Word & Me
I can show love to my
family by being kind.

## Do

Children use blocks to build items found in a park (tables, chairs, trees, slides, grills, etc.).

## Talk About

- **Our Bible says, "Always try to be kind." Who are some people we can be kind to? We can be kind to our families! Let's build some things found in a park and talk about being kind to our families.**
- **Jenna, what game do you like to play in a park? You can build a soccer field! How can you be kind to your brother when you play ball together?** (Kick the ball back to him. Go get the ball when it rolls too far away.)
- **What is a kind thing you can do when your family is having a picnic?** (Help carry out the food or plates. Let others take some food first.)
- **We show love by being kind to the people in our families. Sharing is one way to be kind. Alexis, what is something you can share with your sister?** (Dolls. Video games. Snacks.)
- Pray briefly, **Dear God, please help us show love and be kind to the people in our families.**

## For Younger Children

Use masking tape to make a large square on the floor. Children place blocks on masking tape to build a pretend sandbox. Provide sand toys for children to play with inside the block sandbox. (Note: Remove masking tape immediately after activity.)

## For Older Children

Provide toy people for children to use to act out family members being kind to one another in the park they have created.

Lesson 41

# Science Center: Bean Measuring

## Collect

Bible, a variety of beans and/or lentils (such as seven bean soup mix), shallow baking dishes, transparent tape, paper plates, measuring cups and spoons.

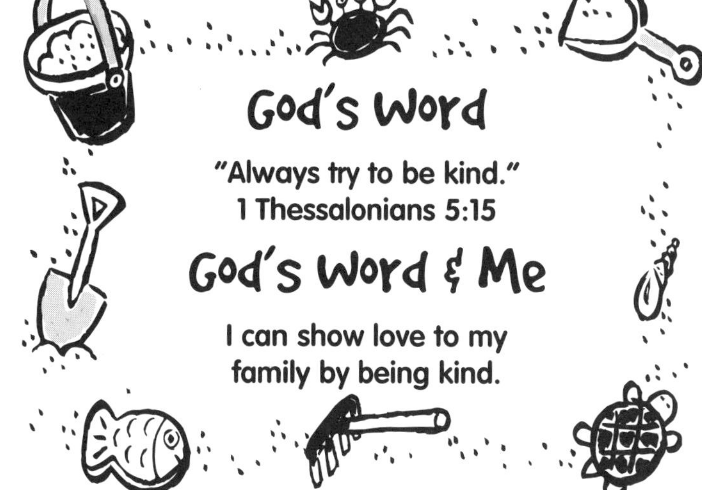
God's Word
"Always try to be kind."
1 Thessalonians 5:15
God's Word & Me
I can show love to my family by being kind.

## Prepare

Pour a mixture of the beans and/or lentils into each baking dish. Tape one of each type of bean onto a different paper plate.

## Do

1. Children examine beans by scooping and pouring them back with the measuring cups and spoons and by feeling them with their hands.
2. Children sort beans onto separate paper plates.

## Talk About

- **Today's Bible story tells about a time Jacob made some stew. Let's look at some beans like the ones Jacob might have used in his stew.**
- **Cody, what did you have for dinner last night? How can you be kind to your family when you are eating together?** (Use kind words. Help clean up the table. Thank parents for the food.)
- **When we share with our families, we are being kind and showing love to them. What is something you can share with your brother?**
- **Our Bible says, "Always try to be kind." We can show love to our families by being kind.** Pray briefly, **Thank You, God, for our families. Please help us be kind to them.**

## For Younger Children

For each child, place a spoonful of drained canned beans on a paper plate. Children use spoons to mash beans on the plate.

## For Older Children

Bring a variety of sizes of bowls. Children use measuring cups to count how many cupfuls it takes to fill each size of bowl.

Lesson 41 • Genesis 25:27-34

# Bible Story Center

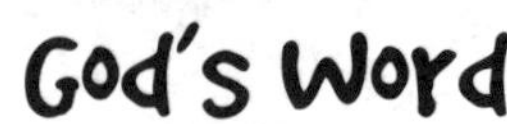

## God's Word

**"Always try to be kind."**
**1 Thessalonians 5:15**

## God's Word & Me

**I can show love to my family by being kind.**

## Collect

Bible, Picture 2 from *Bible Story Pictures.*

## Tell the Story

Use the pictured motions (keywords in bold) or show Picture 2. For older children, tell the version of the story on the back of Picture 2.

**Do you like to play inside your home? Outside your home? Which do you like most? Listen to find out what two brothers liked to do.**

Isaac and Rebekah had **two** sons, Jacob and Esau. The brothers liked to do very different things. Esau liked to be outdoors. He liked to hunt with a bow and arrow to find food. Jacob did not like hunting. He stayed home and helped his mother, Rebekah.

Esau was born before Jacob. That meant that one day Esau would be the family's leader. He would also be given most of the things his father, Isaac, owned. Jacob would only get half as much as Esau. Jacob must have thought that was not fair.

The boys grew to be men. One day, Esau went **hunting** and was gone a long time. When he got home, he was tired and very hungry! He could smell good food cooking.

Jacob was stirring a pot of stew. Esau said, "Give me some of that stew!"

Jacob did not want to share his stew. He wanted Esau to give him something for it. He said to Esau, "I'll give you stew, but first, you have to make me a promise. Promise me that I can be the family's leader."

Esau smelled the stew. He was **hungry**. All he could think about was getting food to eat. He said, "I'm going to die if I don't get some food. You can be the leader of the family. Now give me some stew!" Now Esau would not be the family leader. He would not get more of his father's gifts than Jacob.

Jacob knew the trade was **not** fair, but he did not care. And Jacob didn't care that he had been unkind to his own brother. Jacob's unkindness caused a lot of trouble for his family.

## God's Word & Me

**What did Esau get from Jacob in the trade?** (Stew.) **Jacob was unkind when he tricked Esau. But God wants us to be kind to the people in our families. How can you be kind to your brother or sister? To your mom?** (Share a toy with brother or sister. Help Mom when she asks.) **We can show love to our families by being kind to them.**

Lesson 41

# Worship Center

God's Word
"Always try to be kind."
1 Thessalonians 5:15
God's Word & Me
I can show love to my
family by being kind.

## Collect

Bible, *Shake It Up!* songbook and cassette/CD and player, "My Family" and "Let Us Love" word charts (pp. 51 and 54 in songbook).

## Sing to God

Play "My Family." Invite children to sing along with you. **Let's sing about our families.** Lead children in singing song and doing suggested motions. **We can show love to our families when we treat them with kindness. What is a kind thing you can say to your dad?** (I love you. I will help you. Thank you.)

## Hear and Say God's Word

Holding your Bible open to 1 Thessalonians 5:15, say verse aloud. **What does this verse say we should always be?** (Kind.) **What can we do to be kind when we are playing at the park?** (Share toys. Ask others to play with us.) Lead children in repeating the verse by echoing phrases after you: "Always try/to be kind." Point to children when it is their turn to speak. Repeat verse several times in this manner.

## Pray to God

Children repeat the words of this prayer after you: **Dear God, . . . please help us . . . to be kind . . . and show Your love . . . to our families. . . . In Jesus' name, amen.**

## Sing to God

In closing the worship time, play "Let Us Love." Invite children to sing along with you and do suggested motions. **What does this song tell us to do to one another? One way to love one another is to be kind.**

## Options

1. On a large sheet of paper, print the words "Always be kind to." During the prayer activity, ask children to name some of the people in their families. Print children's responses on paper and then place paper where parents can read responses when the children are dismissed.
2. Invite volunteers to pray for the family members they named.

# Read-Aloud Story and Activity Center

## Collect

A copy of Story Picture 41 (pp. 87-88 from *Read-Aloud Story and Activity Book*) for each child and yourself, crayons or markers.

## Prepare

Color your copy of Story Picture 41.

## Do

**Listen to find out what these children are looking for.** Read story and show completed Story Picture 41. Distribute pictures. Use conversation suggestions in Let's Talk About the Story as children complete their pages.

# Kindergarten Puzzle Center

## Collect

Copies of Puzzles 81 and 82 (p. 169 and p. 171 from *The Big Book of Kindergarten Puzzles*) for each child, pencils, crayons or markers.

## Do

Children complete the puzzles and color pages.

# Instant Activities

These activities can be used at any time during this session: when children need a change of pace, to extend the session, or during transition time at the beginning or end of the session.

## Collect

*The Big Book of Instant Activities.*

## Do

Guide children to complete "Where's the Pair?" and/or "How Would You Move?" (p. 125 and/or p. 82 from *The Big Book of Instant Activities*).

Lesson 42

# Jacob's Tricks

## Bible Story

Genesis 27:1-45

## God's Word

**"Speak the truth to each other." Zechariah 8:16**

## God's Word & Me

**Telling the truth is a way to show love to my family.**

## Teacher's Devotional

It seems that Jacob and Rebekah may have built up a whole lifetime of discontent which led them to collaborate on deceiving Isaac. Rebekah may have always felt that Jacob should have been the favored one, that he deserved the blessing and birthright. And she may have told Jacob this, feeding his own discontent. Discontent always exacts a high price, for it drives us to find our own solutions to our problems, instead of letting go and asking God to surprise us with His creative answers!

Jacob's discontent drove him to his first deception with the stew. After he had taken his brother's birthright, he wanted to take Esau's blessing as well. He (and his mother) saw the situation as one in which deception was the only answer. In fact, Rebekah was so convinced of this that she had a carefully thought-out plan for deceiving her husband. Getting the birthright for Jacob was far more important to her than being honest with a nearly blind loved one!

Sir Walter Scott once wrote, "Oh, what a tangled web we weave, when first we practice to deceive!" It seems basic to human nature that once we've fallen into deceit, we scramble to keep up appearances by lying again and again. We find ourselves in a far bigger mess than we ever anticipated—until we repent. Thank God, He is always ready to forgive, no matter how great our sin! He stands ready to free us from discontent and deception the moment we confess it to Him.

## Teacher's Planning

1. Choose which centers you will provide and the order in which children will participate in them. For tips on schedule planning, see page 7.
2. Plan who will lead each center. For staffing tips and ideas, see page 21.

# Active Game Center: True Moves

## Collect

Bible.

## Do

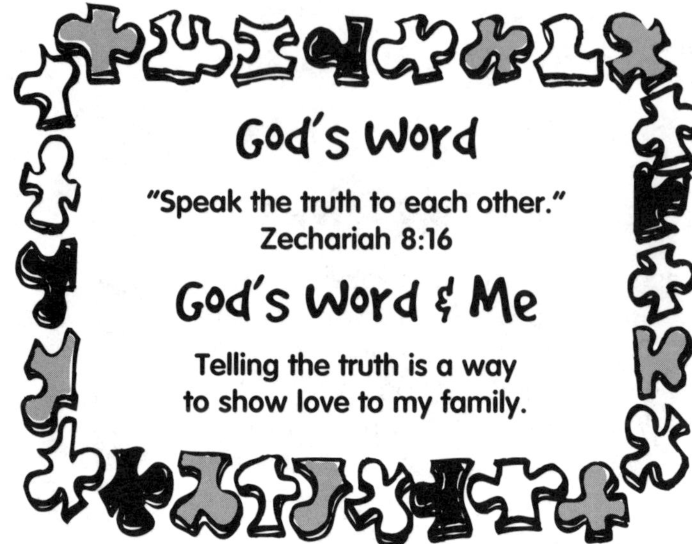
God's Word
"Speak the truth to each other."
Zechariah 8:16
God's Word & Me
Telling the truth is a way
to show love to my family.

1. Children hop like rabbits when you call out, **Rabbits hop!** When you call out, **Cows hop!** children freeze.
2. For following rounds of play, say the phrases "birds fly" (children flap arms) and "dogs fly" (children freeze); "fish swim" (children move arms as if swimming) and "birds swim" (children freeze); "kangaroos jump" (children jump up and down) and "snakes jump" (children freeze). Continue as time and interest allow, creating your own combinations of animals and motions.

## Talk About

- **Our Bible says, "Speak the truth to each other." Let's play a game and decide if some things are true or not true. If what I say is true, do the action. If what I say is not true, freeze!**
- **When I said "Rabbits hop," why did you hop? You hopped because it is true that rabbits hop. When I said "Cows hop," what did you do? You didn't hop because cows do not hop.**
- **Trent, what could happen if someone asked you if it was raining outside and you said no instead of speaking the truth? That person could get all wet!**
- **When we speak the truth to the people in our families, we show love to them.** Pray briefly, **Dear God, help us to show love to our families by speaking the truth.**

## For Younger Children

Young children may be confused by the use of conflicting statements. Instead of saying both a true and an untrue statement, say only the true statements.

## For Older Children

Children think of additional true and not-true statements to use in the game.

# Art Center: Family Talk

## Collect

Bible, index cards, markers, craft sticks, masking tape.

## God's Word

**"Speak the truth to each other." Zechariah 8:16**

## God's Word & Me

**Telling the truth is a way to show love to my family.**

## Do

On index cards, children draw the members of their families, one person per index card. Children tape cards to craft sticks to make puppets.

## Talk About

- **In today's Bible story, Jacob did not speak the truth to his father. Jacob's father was sad. Telling the truth helps the people in our families to be happy. Let's make puppets and show ways we can speak the truth to the people in our families.**
- **Brad, what could happen if you told your mom you fed the dog when you didn't feed the dog? Your poor dog would be hungry and sad! It's good to speak the truth to your mom and dad. Speaking the truth helps your mom and dad take good care of you, your dog and everyone in your home!**

- **Our Bible says, "Speak the truth to each other." Etta, who are some of the people you talk to each day?** (Parents. Brothers and sisters. Teacher. Friend.) **We show love to the people in our families by telling them the truth.**
- **Use your puppet to say something true. You can tell the name of a food you like or a game you like to play.**

## For Younger Children

Cut out pictures of people from a magazine or catalog. Children select one or two pictures of people to represent family members and glue pictures to craft sticks.

## For Older Children

Using puppets, children act out family situations, showing ways to speak the truth to each other.

Lesson 42

# Block Center: Block Tents

## Collect

Bible, blocks, blankets, pillows.

## Do

1. Children outline a large tent by laying blocks in a square on the floor.
2. Cover floor of block tent with blankets and pillows. Children pretend to live in the tent.

### God's Word

**"Speak the truth to each other." Zechariah 8:16**

### God's Word & Me

**Telling the truth is a way to show love to my family.**

## Talk About

- **In today's Bible story Jacob and Esau's family lived in tent houses. Let's use our blocks to make a tent house.**
- **We covered the inside of our tent with pillows and blankets. In Bible times, people sat on pillows and blankets instead of chairs. Will, what does your family sit on at home?**
- **If I said here in our classroom we have a diving board and tubas to sit on, would that be true or not true? Telling the truth is a way that we show love to others. Jacob said something that wasn't true and it caused a lot of trouble for his family.**
- **If your mom asks if you are wearing your seat belt in the car, you need to tell her the truth. She can help you if you need help buckling your seat belt. Why is it important to wear our seat belts?** (A seat belt helps to keep us safe.)
- **Our Bible says, "Speak the truth to each other." We tell the truth because it is a way to show love to others.**

## For Younger Children

Make a masking-tape square. Children lay blocks on the masking-tape square to form the tent. (Note: Remove tape immediately after the activity.)

## For Older Children

Provide Bible-time costumes for children to wear. You may also bring a small tent to set up.

Lesson 42

# Science Center: Touch Cards

## Collect

Bible, six to eight items with different textures (sandpaper, plastic wrap, fabric swatches, fake fur, bubble wrap, etc.), scissors, glue, index cards, large paper bag.

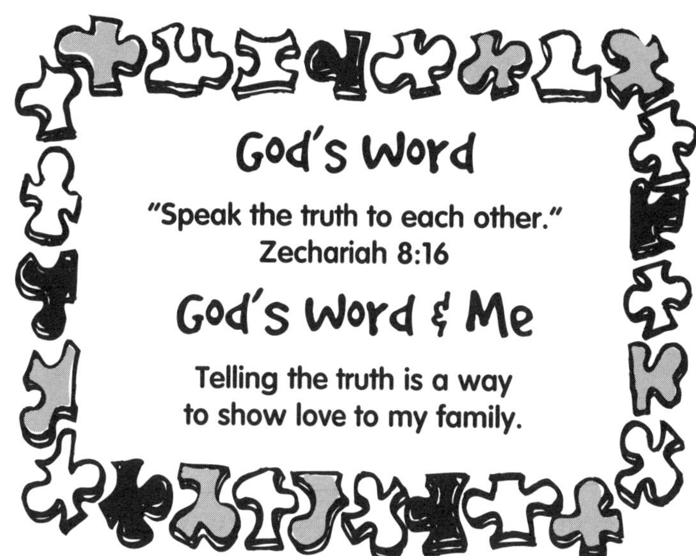

God's Word
"Speak the truth to each other."
Zechariah 8:16
God's Word & Me
Telling the truth is a way to show love to my family.

## Prepare

Cut textured items into squares small enough to glue to index cards. Make at least two texture cards for each item. Place one set of cards in paper bag. Place the other set of cards on a table.

## Do

1. Children take turns selecting a card from the paper bag. Children close their eyes and feel the cards on the table to find the card that matches the one they selected.
2. Gather the cards for the next round of play. For each round, vary the way children find the matching card (hide cards in classroom for children to find, place upside-down in a grid pattern, etc.).

## Talk About

- **Our Bible says, "Speak the truth to each other." Let's use our hands to find some things that feel the same.**
- **If I said that this sandpaper feels like the plastic wrap, would that be speaking the truth? We tell the truth to our families to show that we love them.**

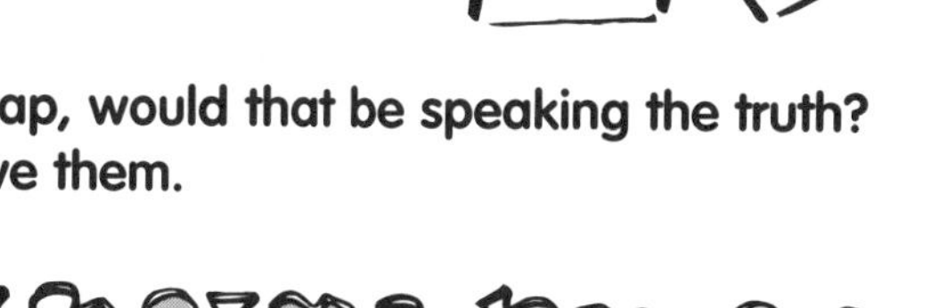

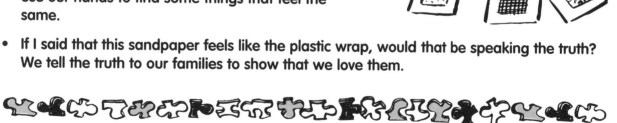

## For Younger Children

Children do not close their eyes. Children match the card they select to one on the table using both their sense of sight and their sense of touch.

## For Older Children

Increase the challenge for older children. Place only one card in the paper bag. On each child's turn, he or she feels card in bag but doesn't look at it. Then he or she finds matching card as described above.

Lesson 42 • Genesis 27:1-45

# Bible Story Center

God's Word
"Speak the truth to each other."
Zechariah 8:16
God's Word & Me
Telling the truth is a way
to show love to my family.

## Collect

Bible, Picture 3 from *Bible Story Pictures*.

## Tell the Story

Use the pictured motions (keywords in bold) or show Picture 3. For older children, tell the version of the story on the back of Picture 3.

**Do you have a brother? Do you have a sister? Listen to find out what happened when two brothers grew up.**

Jacob and Esau were all grown up now. Their father, Isaac, told Esau, "I am getting old. I want to give you my blessing before I die." Isaac wanted to promise Esau that Esau would be the new leader of the family. But first, Isaac asked Esau to go **hunting** and cook Isaac's favorite food. Esau went out hunting right away!

But Jacob and Esau's mother, Rebekah, wanted Jacob to be the new leader. She told Jacob, "We will get the blessing for YOU while Esau is gone. Do what I say, Jacob."

Isaac was so old that he **could not see** anything. Rebekah told Jacob to put on Esau's clothes. She put hairy goatskins on Jacob's hands and neck because Esau had a lot of hair. Now that Jacob smelled and felt like Esau, Isaac would think Jacob was Esau! Rebekah made Isaac's favorite meal. She told Jacob to take the food to Isaac.

Jacob took the **food** to his father. He then said something that was not true. "It's me, Esau," Jacob said. "I've made your food." Isaac asked how he found the food so quickly. "Oh, God helped me!" Jacob lied again!

Isaac smelled Esau's clothes that Jacob was wearing. He felt the goatskins on Jacob's hands. The tricks worked. Isaac said, "It sounds like Jacob's voice, but these hands feel like Esau's hands." Isaac ate, and then he said the words of blessing. Isaac thought he had blessed Esau, but he was really blessing Jacob!

When Esau found out Jacob had tricked their father, he burst out crying. Isaac was sad, too; but it was too late. Esau was so angry, he wanted to hurt Jacob! Jacob had to **go away** and stay with his uncle. He had to stay away for many, many years.

## God's Word & Me

**What happened because Jacob and Rebekah did not tell the truth?** (Isaac was tricked. Esau was angry. Jacob had to go away.) **Their lies made lots of trouble for EVERYONE in their family! Telling the truth to our families shows we love them. Telling the truth is much better than making trouble!**

# Worship Center

## Collect

Bible, *Shake It Up!* songbook and cassette/CD and player, "My Family" and "Let Us Love" word charts (pp. 51 and 54 in songbook).

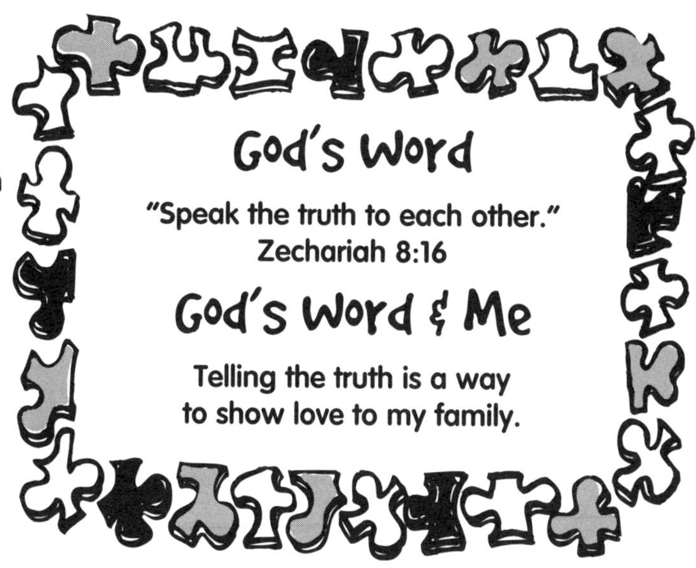
God's Word
"Speak the truth to each other."
Zechariah 8:16
God's Word & Me
Telling the truth is a way
to show love to my family.

## Sing to God

Play "My Family." Invite children to sing along with you. **Let's sing a song about loving our families.** Lead children in singing song and doing suggested motions. **This song says that telling the truth is the best way to live! Telling the truth is a way to show love to our families.**

## Hear and Say God's Word

Holding your Bible open to Zechariah 8:16, say verse aloud. **God wants us to speak the truth to each other. We can tell the truth to everyone!** Then lead children in repeating the verse several times. As the children are repeating the verse with you, point to one child. You and the children say that child's name instead of the words "each other." Repeat until every child has been named. (Note: If you have a large class, you may wish to say more than one child's name at a time.)

## Pray to God

**We can ask God to help us to speak the truth.** Invite volunteers to each say this brief prayer: **Dear God, please help me to always speak the truth.**

## Sing to God

In closing the worship time, play "Let Us Love." Invite children to sing along with you and do suggested motions. **This song tells us that God's Word says we should love one another. Telling the truth to others is one way to show love to them!**

## Options

1. Older children lead other children in doing motions suggested for "My Family" and/or "Let Us Love."
2. Add motion to the verse activity. Children stand and clap on each word of the verse. When a child's name is said, he or she remains standing and the other children sit down. Children stand and repeat activity until each child has had his or her name called.

 

Lesson 42

# Read-Aloud Story and Activity Center

## Collect

A copy of Story Picture 42 (pp. 89-90 from *Read-Aloud Story and Activity Book*) for each child and yourself, crayons or markers.

## Prepare

Color your copy of Story Picture 42.

## Do

**Listen to find out what happened to this girl.** Read story and show completed Story Picture 42. Distribute pictures. Use conversation suggestions in Let's Talk About the Story as children complete their pages.

# Kindergarten Puzzle Center

## Collect

Copies of Puzzles 83 and 84 (p. 173 and p. 175 from *The Big Book of Kindergarten Puzzles*) for each child, pencils, crayons or markers.

## Do

Children complete the puzzles and color pages.

# Instant Activities

These activities can be used at any time during this session: when children need a change of pace, to extend the session, or during transition time at the beginning or end of the session.

## Collect

*The Big Book of Instant Activities.*

## Do

Guide children to complete "Musical Circles" and/or "My Hands" (p. 99 and/or p. 44 from *The Big Book of Instant Activities*).

Lesson 43

# Esau Forgives Jacob

## Bible Story

Genesis 32:3-21; 33:1-11

God's Word
"Forgive each other."
(See Colossians 3:13.)
God's Word & Me
I can show love and forgive the people in my family.

## Teacher's Devotional

Jacob had deceived his brother and knew Esau was angry enough to kill him! After running away, Jacob lived with and worked for his uncle Laban. From his wives to his wages, Jacob, who had been the deceiver, was kept in a stranglehold of deception. Perhaps on some level, Jacob felt it was justly deserved and something to be endured.

Then one day God told Jacob to return home. Unsure of the reception he would receive from the brother he had wronged, Jacob sent messengers to Esau. They returned with distressing news: Esau was coming with 400 men! It didn't sound like a welcoming party to Jacob. He divided his household into groups and began sending herds and flocks ahead, hoping to appease his brother—or at least slow him down by the sheer number of animals coming at him!

But eventually, the moment of truth arrived. While Jacob busied himself with bowing seven times to show his submission, Esau ran to him, threw his arms around him and kissed him. No words were needed; Esau's actions spoke of his complete forgiveness. One who deserved no forgiveness at all was completely and freely forgiven by the one who had every right to condemn him.

God forgives us in the same way. When we had no way to appease God, no matter how we bowed in conciliation, Jesus' actions provided a means for forgiveness. There is no reason to try to placate God; Jesus' actions make our guilt unnecessary. He only asks us now to walk in gratitude for His grace. Since we have been forgiven, our forgiveness can flow freely to others!

## Teacher's Planning

1. Choose which centers you will provide and the order in which children will participate in them. For tips on schedule planning, see page 7.
2. Plan who will lead each center. For staffing tips and ideas, see page 21.

# Active Game Center: Who's Who?

## Collect

Bible.

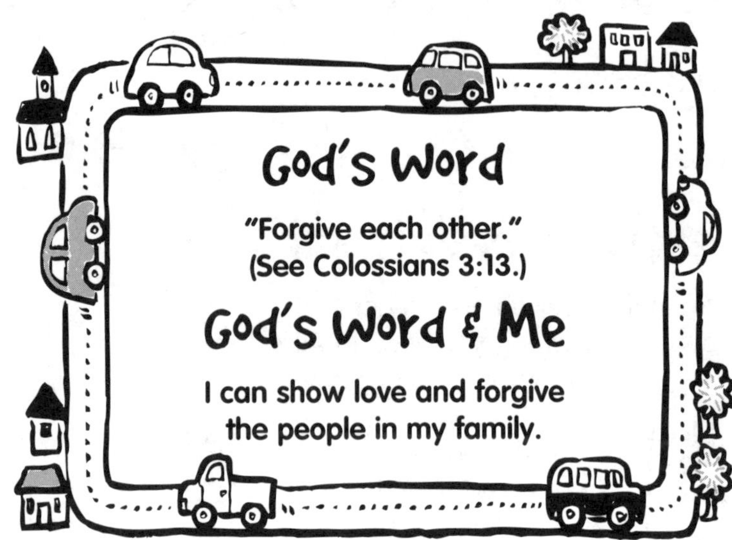
God's Word
"Forgive each other."
(See Colossians 3:13.)
God's Word & Me
I can show love and forgive
the people in my family.

## Do

1. Children sit in circle on the floor. Say, **If you are a son, stand up and clap your hands.** Children with stated characteristic respond. Children sit down again.
2. Repeat using daughter, brother, sister, mother, grandchild, cousin, nephew, niece, etc. Vary the motion for each statement (hop up and down, place hands on head, touch toes, wiggle hips, do jumping jacks, walk quickly over to a wall, etc.).

## Talk About

- **Let's play a game and talk about some of the people in our families.**
- **Our Bible says, "Forgive each other." To forgive means to be kind to someone who has been unkind to you. When someone has been unkind, we can say "I forgive you."**
- **Sometimes it's hard to forgive someone who has been unkind. We can ask God to help us forgive others.** Pray briefly, **Dear God, help us to forgive others when they are unkind.**

### For Younger Children

Young children may not know their own different roles within their families. Vary the activity by asking children to perform the motions if they have a brother, sister, cousin, etc. **If you have a brother, stand up.**

### For Older Children

Children say the words of the verse as they perform the motion. For instance, children stand and then say "Forgive each other."

Lesson 43

# Art Center: Family Album

## Collect

Bible, chenille wires or yarn, ruler, scissors, construction paper, markers, hole punch.

## Prepare

Cut one 4-inch (10-cm) length of chenille wire or yarn for each child. Cut construction paper sheets in half.

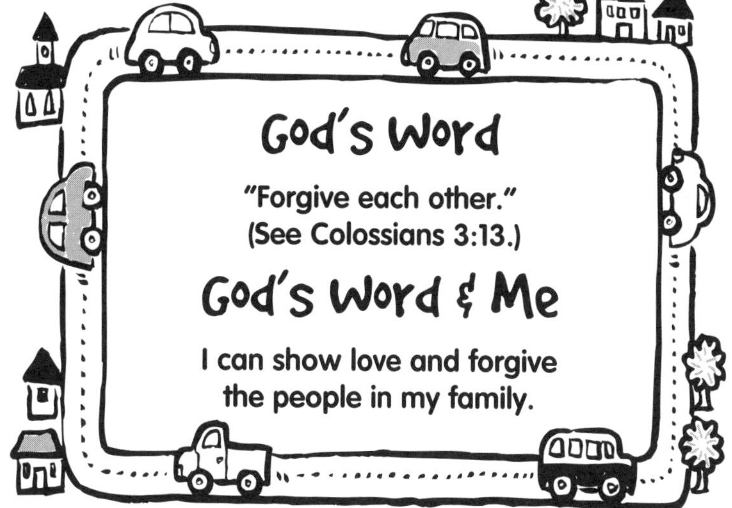
God's Word
"Forgive each other."
(See Colossians 3:13.)
God's Word & Me
I can show love and forgive the people in my family.

## Do

1. Using markers on construction-paper halves, children draw the members of their families, one person on each paper.
2. As each child finishes, gather his or her papers and place a blank paper on top. Punch a hole in the top left corner of the papers. Assist as each child threads chenille wire or yarn through the hole in his or her papers and twists or ties to secure. Child decorates top paper as a cover.

## Talk About

- **Our Bible says, "Forgive each other." When we forgive others, it means we are kind, even when others have not been kind. We show love when we forgive others. We can forgive the people in our families! Let's make a book of the people in our families.**
- **Who are the people in your family? If your brother breaks one of your toys, you might feel sad or angry. You can ask God to help you be kind to your brother, even though he made you feel sad or angry.**
- Pray briefly, **Thank You, God, for loving us. Help us to show Your love by being kind and forgiving others.**

## For Younger Children

Prepare booklets ahead of time. Children draw family members on the pages.

## For Older Children

On a large sheet of paper, print the words "My Family." Children copy the words onto their book covers. Children can also label each family member's picture with that person's name. If a child needs help spelling a word, print it on a Post-it Note and hand it to the child to copy.

Lesson 43

# Block Center: Road of Forgiveness

## Collect

Bible, blocks, toy people, toy animals or cotton balls.

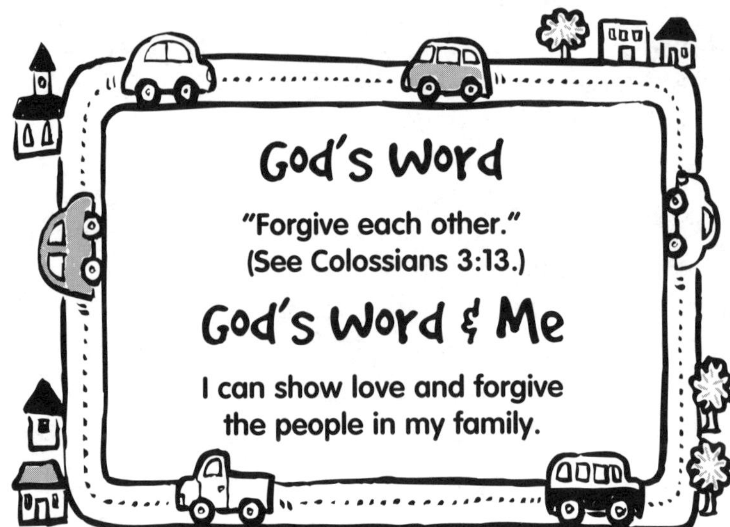
God's Word
"Forgive each other."
(See Colossians 3:13.)
God's Word & Me
I can show love and forgive the people in my family.

## Do

1. Children use blocks to outline a long and winding road.
2. Using toy people, toy animals or cotton balls, children act out traveling down the road.

## Talk About

- **In our Bible story, Esau walked down a long road. When he saw his brother, Jacob, Esau forgave him, even though Jacob had not been kind to him. Let's make a road!**
- **Our Bible says, "Forgive each other." To forgive means to be kind to someone who has done wrong things or been unkind to you.**
- **Forgiving the people in our families shows God's love. Micaela, what can you say to your brother when he says "I'm sorry"?** ("I forgive you." "I love you.")
- Pray briefly, **Thank You, God, for the people in our families. Help us to show Your love. Help us be kind and forgive them.**

## For Younger Children

Use yarn to make a road wide enough for children to walk along. Children place blocks on yarn to outline road and then walk along it.

## For Older Children

Children outline a road wide enough to walk along. Then children decide which character they want to be from the story before they walk down road. Children who decide to be Jacob, bow as they walk along the road. Children who decide to be Esau, walk down road and hug someone at the end of the road. Children may also wish to walk down road pretending to be one of the animals Jacob gave Esau: sheep, goat, camel, cow or donkey.

 

Lesson 43

# Science Center: Graphing Animals

## Collect

Bible, animal crackers, large bowl, large sheet of paper, glue, marker; optional—premoistened towelettes.

## Prepare

Place animal crackers in large bowl. Select one of each type of animal and glue crackers across the top of large sheet of paper. Using marker, draw lines down the paper between each animal cracker to make a graph.

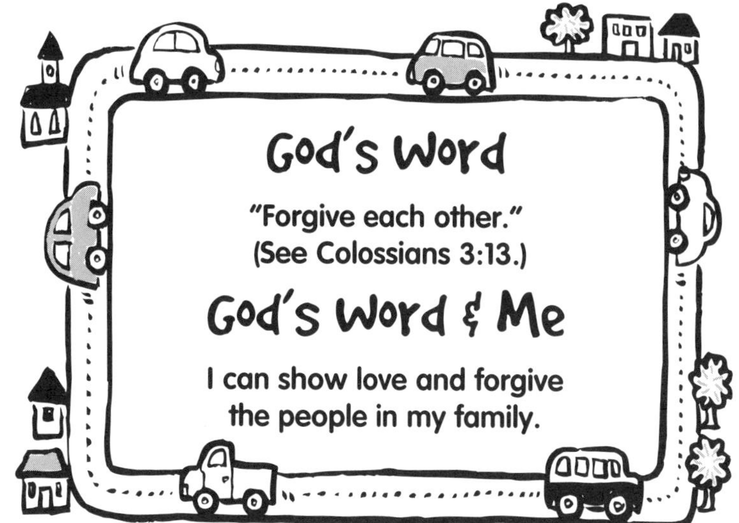
God's Word
"Forgive each other."
(See Colossians 3:13.)
God's Word & Me
I can show love and forgive the people in my family.

## Do

1. Children wash hands. (Optional: If you do not have a sink nearby, distribute premoistened towelettes with which children clean their hands.)
2. Children each select an animal cracker from the bowl and then place it in the appropriate column on the graph you prepared. When a column fills up, hand crackers from that column to children to eat, freeing up more space to place crackers.

## Talk About

- **In today's Bible story, Jacob gives his brother, Esau, lots and lots of animals. Jacob was sorry he had been unkind to Esau. Esau loved Jacob and forgave his brother! Let's look at some different kinds of animals and match them.**
- **Our Bible says, "Forgive each other." We can show love and forgive the people in our families. Forgiving means being kind to people who have been unkind to us.** Pray briefly, **Dear God, help us forgive the people in our families when they have been unkind.**

## For Younger Children

On table, lay out one of each type of cracker. Instead of asking children to sort crackers, after each child has selected a cracker, point to two crackers—one that matches and one that doesn't. Ask child to identify which of the crackers matches the one he or she selected.

## For Older Children

As children place their crackers, they count the total number of crackers in that row.

# Bible Story Center

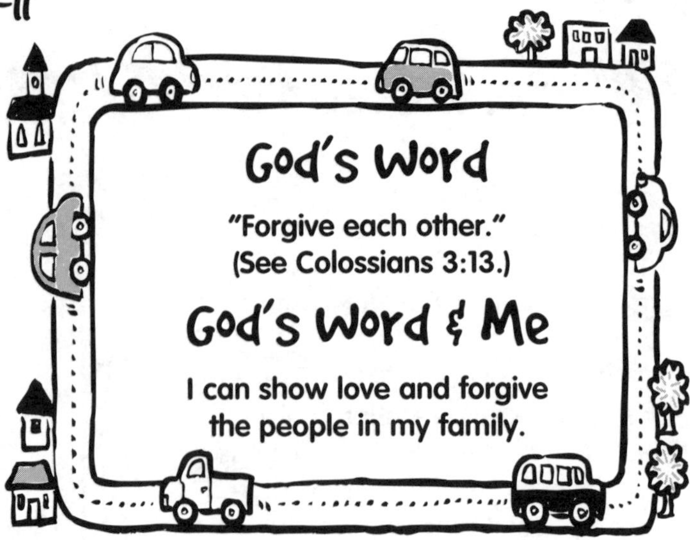
God's Word
"Forgive each other."
(See Colossians 3:13.)
God's Word & Me
I can show love and forgive the people in my family.

## Collect

Bible, Picture 4 from *Bible Story Pictures.*

## Tell the Story

Use the pictured motions (keywords in bold) or show Picture 4. For older children, tell the version of the story on the back of Picture 4.

**What is a gift you would like to get?**
**Listen to hear about gifts Jacob gave to his brother, Esau.**

Jacob and Esau grew up together as brothers. But Jacob told lies. He tricked their father Isaac. He stole important things from Esau. Jacob was afraid Esau would hurt him! So Jacob **ran** away. He went to live with his uncle for many, many years. He got married and had many children.

But one day, God told Jacob to go back home. Jacob and his family **packed** their belongings and got ready for the long journey home. Jacob sent some of his helpers to tell Esau that Jacob wanted to come home. The helpers came back and told Jacob, "We went to see Esau. He is coming to meet you. He has 400 men with him!"

Jacob was afraid. Four hundred men sounded like an army! So Jacob **prayed**. He asked God to keep him and his family safe.

Jacob decided to send Esau some gifts. He sent out a herd of goats. He sent out a flock of sheep and then a herd of camels. He also sent a herd of cattle and a herd of donkeys! Jacob thought if he sent Esau gifts, maybe Esau wouldn't be so mad.

Jacob and his family walked far behind the animals. Finally they could see Esau and his 400 men coming!

Jacob went ahead of his family. As he walked toward Esau, Jacob bowed low, over and over again, to show he was sorry for the wrong things he had done. Esau began to run toward Jacob. *Is Esau going to hurt me?* Jacob must have wondered. Esau came up to Jacob and grabbed him and **HUGGED** him! Esau had forgiven Jacob!

## God's Word & Me

**What did Esau do to show he forgave Jacob?** (Ran to meet him. Hugged him.) **To forgive means to be kind to someone, even after that person has been unkind. Forgiving the people in our families is a way to show we love them. How can you show love to your family today?** (Tell them "I love you." Forgive them when they are unkind. Do kind things for them.)

# Worship Center

## God's Word

**"Forgive each other." (See Colossians 3:13.)**

## God's Word & Me

**I can show love and forgive the people in my family.**

### Collect

Bible, *Shake It Up!* songbook and cassette/CD and player, "My Family" and "Let Us Love" word charts (pp. 51 and 54 in songbook).

## Sing to God

Play "My Family." Invite children to sing along with you. **Let's sing a song about forgiving the people in our families.** Lead children in singing song and doing suggested motions. **Forgiving means being kind to people, even though they have not been kind to you. Who are the people in your family? You show love to the people in your family when you forgive them!**

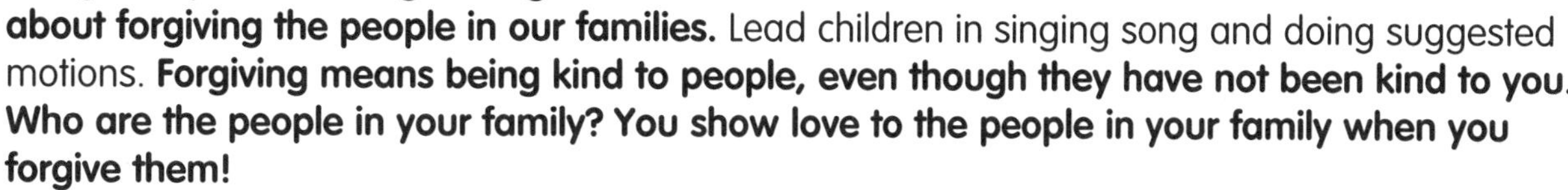

## Hear and Say God's Word

Holding your Bible open to Colossians 3:13, say verse aloud. **Has anyone ever done an unkind thing to you?** Listen carefully to children's responses. **To forgive means to be kind to someone who has been unkind to you. You might say "I forgive you."** Lead children in repeating the verse while doing the following motions: "Forgive," stomp one foot on each syllable; "each," clap hands; "other," wiggle fingers in air. Repeat verse and motions several times.

## Pray to God

Lead children in repeating the following prayer, phrase by phrase: **Dear God, . . . help us to remember . . . to forgive . . . and show love to . . . the people in our families. . . . In Jesus' name, amen.**

## Sing to God

In closing the worship time, play "Let Us Love." Invite children to sing along with you and do suggested motions. **What book tells us to love each other?** (God's Word, the Bible.)

### Options

1. Lead children in singing the words of the verse to the tune of "Are You Sleeping":

   Forgive each other. Forgive each other.
   Forgive, forgive. Forgive, forgive.
   Forgive each other. Forgive each other.
   Forgive, forgive. Forgive, forgive.

2. During prayer activity, ask children to name people in their families. Volunteers pray briefly using the names of the people in their families.

 

# Read-Aloud Story and Activity Center

## Collect

A copy of Story Picture 43 (pp. 91-92 from *Read-Aloud Story and Activity Book*) for each child and yourself, crayons or markers.

## Prepare

Color your copy of Story Picture 43.

## Do

**Listen to find out what this boy is saying.** Read story and show completed Story Picture 43. Distribute pictures. Use conversation suggestions in Let's Talk About the Story as children complete their pages.

# Kindergarten Puzzle Center

## Collect

Copies of Puzzles 85 and 86 (p. 177 and p. 179 from *The Big Book of Kindergarten Puzzles*) for each child, pencils, crayons or markers.

## Do

Children complete the puzzles and color pages.

# Instant Activities

These activities can be used at any time during this session: when children need a change of pace, to extend the session, or during transition time at the beginning or end of the session.

## Collect

*The Big Book of Instant Activities.*

## Do

Guide children to complete "The Same Game" and/or "Five Little Ducks" (p. 23 and/or p. 53 from *The Big Book of Instant Activities*).

Lesson 44

# Daniel obeys God

## Bible Story

Daniel 1

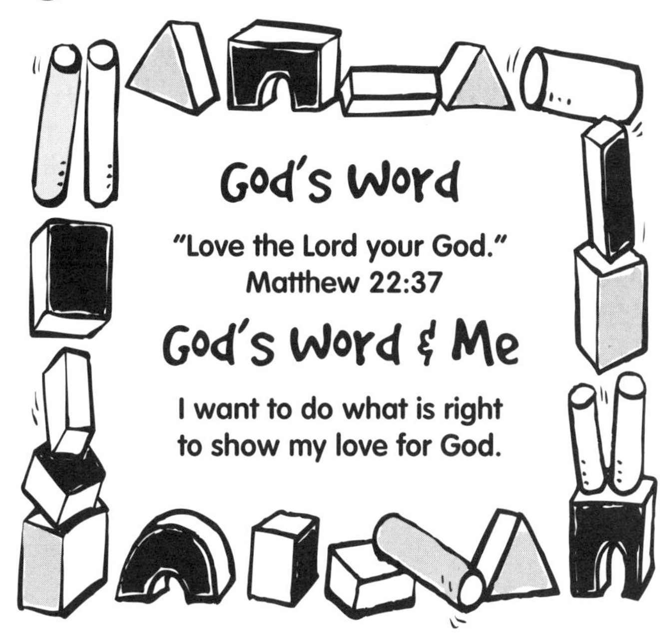
God's Word
"Love the Lord your God."
Matthew 22:37
God's Word & Me
I want to do what is right
to show my love for God.

## Teacher's Devotional

When we give in to temptation, it's fairly common to hear (or to say), "I couldn't help myself. It just happened!" We may feel that we were somehow tricked, caught off guard. When we do not choose ahead of time to avoid a temptation and plan a way of escape, we make ourselves particularly vulnerable and often find that we will give in.

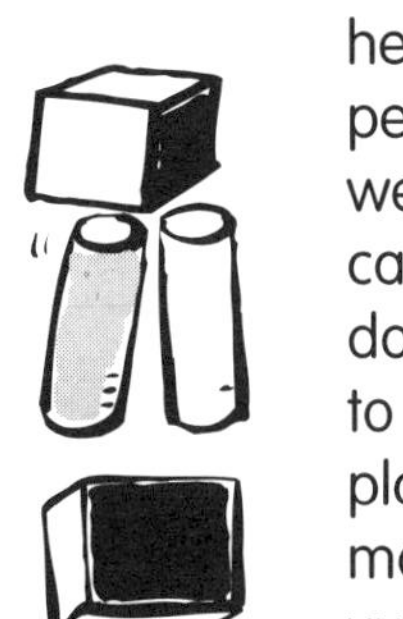

Daniel and his friends' test of eating vegetables was not about being vegetarians. It was not about being self-righteous or clinging to old cultural ways. It was an example of young men who had prepared ahead of time to face temptation. From an early age, Daniel and his friends had been taught to love and obey God. Even though the circumstances of their lives changed and they had to move from their homes in Judah, their determination to do the right thing did not change. The temptations that came with their new life in Babylon were no match for their determination to always please God and do what was right. Their love for God never faltered.

Before temptation comes, we need to determine that loving and obeying God is what we want to do. We can ask God to show us our own weaknesses and strengthen us when temptation strikes. There is no temptation we face that God will not give us grace to overcome (see 1 Corinthians 10:13). When we have determined ahead of time that we will obey God, we are prepared to face even difficult temptations!

## Teacher's Planning

1. Choose which centers you will provide and the order in which children will participate in them. For tips on schedule planning, see page 7.
2. Plan who will lead each center. For staffing tips and ideas, see page 21.

Lesson 44

# Active Game Center: Vegetable Walk

## Collect

Bible, *Shake It Up!* cassette/CD and player, magazines or grocery-store advertisements, scissors, tape, construction paper.

**God's Word**

**"Love the Lord your God." Matthew 22:37**

**God's Word & Me**

**I want to do what is right to show my love for God.**

## Prepare

Cut out pictures of vegetables from magazines or grocery-store advertisements. Tape each picture to a separate sheet of construction paper. Place vegetable pictures around activity area (on wall, on bookshelves, etc.).

## Do

1. Play "Love the Lord" for a few moments as children walk around the classroom.
2. Stop the music. Children find a vegetable picture and place a hand on it. Repeat several times. Vary the activity for each round by asking children to move in different ways as you play the music (walking heel-to-toe, hopping on one foot, jumping with both feet, hands on knees, etc.).

## Talk About

- **In today's Bible story, four friends did what was right by following God's rules. They ate only the foods God had said to eat. Vegetables were foods they could eat. Let's play a game with pictures of vegetables!**
- **Our Bible says, "Love the Lord your God." We show we love God when we do what is right. Donny, I saw you help Shawna stand up when she fell. You know how to do what is right!**

## For Younger Children

Place vegetable pictures in a circle on the floor. As you play the music, children walk around the circle. When you stop the music, each child picks up the nearest vegetable picture.

## For Older Children

When children are touching a vegetable picture, ask them to do a specific action based on the type of vegetable they are touching. For instance, **Everyone touching a carrot, say the words of the verse with me. If you are touching a green vegetable, do three jumping jacks!**

Lesson 44

# Art Center: Veggie Place Mats

## Collect

Bible, a variety of vegetables (bell peppers, celery, carrots, potatoes, etc.), knife, washable-ink pads, construction paper, art materials (markers, stickers, ribbon, glue, etc.); optional—clear Con-Tact paper.

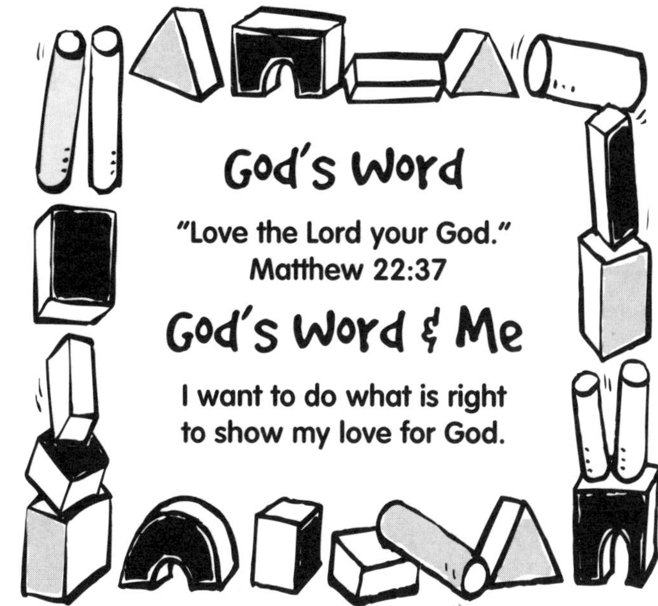
God's Word
"Love the Lord your God."
Matthew 22:37
God's Word & Me
I want to do what is right
to show my love for God.

## Prepare

Cut vegetables into chunks large enough for children to handle easily.

## Do

Children make place mats. Using cut vegetables and washable-ink pads, children make prints on sheets of construction paper. Using art materials, children add decorations. (Optional: Cover decorated construction paper with clear Con-Tact paper.)

## Talk About

- **In our Bible story, Daniel and his friends loved and obeyed God. They ate only the foods God had said to eat. Let's use some vegetables to make place mats.**
- **Daniel and his friends did what is right by obeying God. We can show our love for God by doing what is right, too.**
- **Leo, you moved over to give Candy room to work. You did what was right by being kind!**
- **Our Bible says, "Love the Lord your God."** Pray briefly, **Dear God, we love You and want to do what is right.**

## For Younger Children

Keep the activity simple by using fewer materials. Children use vegetables and washable-ink pads to make prints on place mats.

## For Older Children

On a large sheet of paper, print "Love the Lord your God." Children use markers to copy the words onto their place mats before decorating them.

# Block Center: Block Bistro

## Collect

Bible, blocks.

## Do

Children use blocks to build a restaurant and act out what people do there. Remind children of some of the people in a restaurant (cooks, servers, dishwashers, customers, etc.).

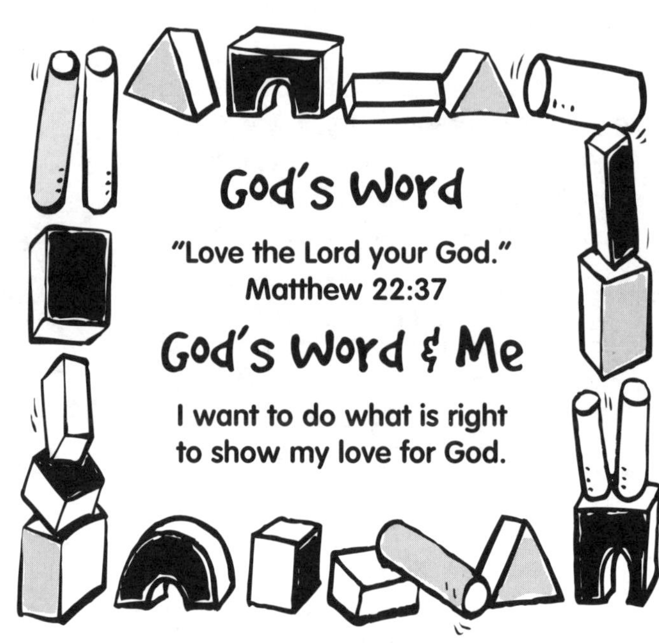
God's Word
"Love the Lord your God."
Matthew 22:37
God's Word & Me
I want to do what is right
to show my love for God.

## Talk About

- **Our Bible says, "Love the Lord your God." One way to show that we love God is to help others and share. Let's show how people in a restaurant help others and share.**
- **Hanne, what kinds of food are you cooking for our restaurant? Cooking good food to share with your family and friends is doing what is right. Who are some other people we could help by giving them food?**
- **Derek, you handed Lana the block she needed to finish building her table. Helping her was the right thing to do! When we do what is right, we show our love for God.**
- Pray briefly, **Dear God, help us to do what is right. We want to show our love for You.**

## For Younger Children

Provide serving trays. Children place blocks on trays as if blocks were food. Children carry blocks on trays to table and then place blocks on the table.

## For Older Children

Provide a variety of restaurant items (plastic dinnerware and utensils, napkins, salt and pepper shakers, chef's hat, apron, notepad and pencil, menus, toy foods, fast-food containers, etc.). Children use items to enhance their play.

# Science Center: Juice Stop

## Collect

Bible, knife, a variety of fruits and vegetables and matching juices (tomato and tomato juice, orange and orange juice, apple and apple juice, etc.), paper plates, cups, paper, marker, napkins.

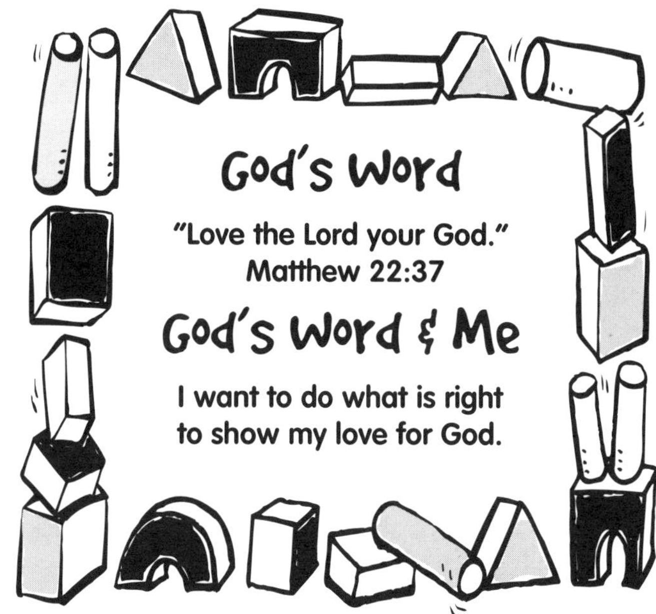
God's Word
"Love the Lord your God."
Matthew 22:37
God's Word & Me
I want to do what is right
to show my love for God.

## Prepare

Cut fruits and vegetables into wedges or chunks. Place on paper plates and place plates on table. Pour small amounts of juices into cups. Post a note alerting parents to the use of food in this activity. Also check registration forms for possible food allergies.

## Do

Children taste different juices and match the juice to the appropriate fruit or vegetable. To help them match the fruit or vegetable to the juice, children may taste the wedges and chunks you prepared.

## Talk About

- **In today's Bible story, Daniel and his friends loved God. They wanted to do what was right all the time. They obeyed God's rules about what foods to eat. They ate only vegetables. Let's taste some juices made from different vegetables and fruits.**
- **April, what did you drink with your breakfast this morning? I drank my favorite juice, grapefruit juice. Which of these juices do you like the best?**
- **Our Bible says, "Love the Lord your God." We show love for God when we do what is right.** Pray briefly, **Dear God, help us to do what is right. We want to show our love for you.**

## For Younger Children

Children may taste juices, but do not expect them to match the juice to the fruits and vegetables.

## For Older Children

Bring canned and/or frozen fruits and a blender. Children place fruits in blender and then take turns pressing the button to run the blender. Children may also add bananas, yogurt and/or ice cream.

Lesson 44 • Daniel 1

# Bible Story Center

God's Word
"Love the Lord your God."
Matthew 22:37
God's Word & Me
I want to do what is right
to show my love for God.

## Collect

Bible, Picture 22 from *Bible Story Pictures.*

## Tell the Story

Use the pictured motions (keywords in bold) or show Picture 22. For older children, tell the version of the story on the back of Picture 22.

**What is your favorite food? Would you like to eat it every day? Listen to find out what some boys chose to eat every day.**

King Nebuchadnezzar (nehb-uh-kuhd-NEHZ-uhr) went to Israel with a strong army. His army took many people from Israel back to their country, Babylon. Four boys were among the people taken from Israel. One of the boys was named Daniel. Daniel and his three friends **walked** for days and days until, finally, they came to Babylon.

When they got to Babylon, an official of the king came to choose servants for the king. The official chose the strongest, healthiest and smartest young men. Daniel and his three friends were chosen! As the king's servants, Daniel and his friends would go to a special school. They would learn to speak and **read** the king's language. They were also supposed to eat food right from the king's table—the same food the king ate!

The king's food looked and smelled very good. But God had told His people not to eat certain foods. And the king's food was not something they could eat. Daniel and his friends decided to obey God's rules.

Daniel and his friends talked to the guard who was in charge of meals. Daniel asked the guard to give them a test: For 10 days, the boys would **eat** only vegetables and drink only water. Then they would see if this was a good idea. The guard agreed!

For 10 days, Daniel and his three friends ate only vegetables and drank only water. Then the guard looked at the four boys. Daniel and his friends looked better and **stronger** than the others did! So the guard let them keep on eating the way they were supposed to. They were able to do what was right and show they loved God!

## God's Word & Me

**What did Daniel and his friends eat?** (Only vegetables.) **Daniel and his friends ate vegetables and drank water because they wanted to obey God and show they loved Him. We can obey God and show we love Him, too. What can we do to obey God when we are at our homes?** (Listen to our parents. Be kind to our brothers and sisters. Help others.)

Lesson 44

# Worship Center

## Collect

Bible, *Shake It Up!* songbook and cassette/CD and player, "Love the Lord" and "I Can Talk to God" word charts (pp. 59 and 57 in songbook).

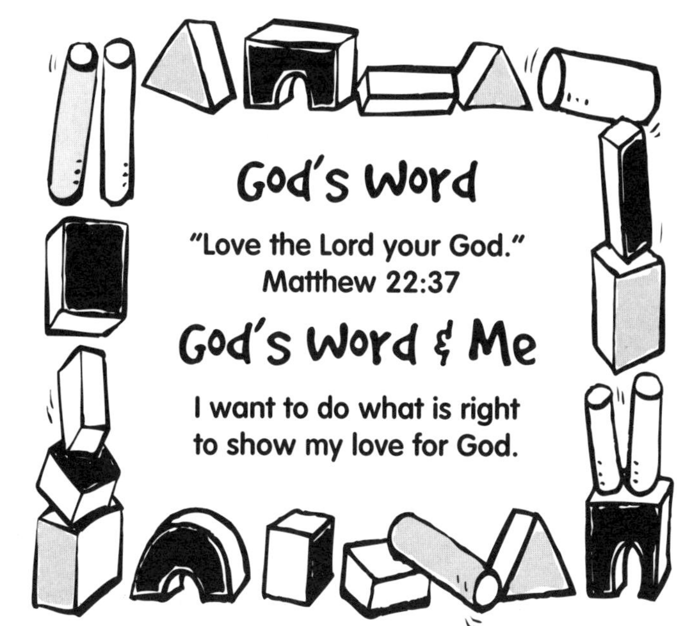
God's Word
"Love the Lord your God."
Matthew 22:37
God's Word & Me
I want to do what is right
to show my love for God.

## Sing to God

Play "Love the Lord." Invite children to sing along with you. **Let's sing a song about loving God.** Lead children in singing song and doing suggested motions. **We want to do what is right and show our love for God! One way to do what is right is to be kind. Another way to do what is right is to forgive others. What are some other ways to do what is right?** (Help others. Tell the truth. Obey parents.)

## Hear and Say God's Word

Holding your Bible open to Matthew 22:37, say verse aloud. **This verse reminds us to love God. We love God, because God loves us!** Lead children in repeating the verse. Children clap their hands on each word of the verse except the word "your." Instead of saying "your," children each point to another child in the class. Repeat several times.

## Pray to God

As you say the following prayer, volunteers say their names one at a time to complete the phrase. Repeat prayer for each volunteer. **Dear God, __________ loves You!**

## Sing to God

In closing the worship time, play "I Can Talk to God." Invite children to sing along with you and do suggested motions. **This song tells us about a lot of different times when we can talk to God. But we don't have to wait for a special time to talk to God. We can talk to God anytime! Talking to God is the right thing to do. Talking to God shows that we love Him.**

## Options

1. With parents' permission, videotape children as they sing songs and do the motions. Show videotape at the end of the session as parents come to pick up their children.
2. Invite a musician from your church to play one or more of the suggested songs for this lesson on a guitar, flute, trumpet, etc.

Lesson 44

# Read-Aloud Story and Activity Center

## Collect

A copy of Story Picture 44 (pp. 93-94 from *Read-Aloud Story and Activity Book*) for each child and yourself, crayons or markers.

"Love the Lord your God."
BIBLE STORY BOOK

## Prepare

Color your copy of Story Picture 44.

## Do

**Listen to find out what story these people are reading.** Read story and show completed Story Picture 44. Distribute pictures. Use conversation suggestions in Let's Talk About the Story as children complete their pages.

# Kindergarten Puzzle Center

## Collect

Copies of Puzzles 87 and 88 (p. 181 and p. 183 from *The Big Book of Kindergarten Puzzles*) for each child, pencils, crayons or markers.

## Do

Children complete the puzzles and color pages.

# Instant Activities

These activities can be used at any time during this session: when children need a change of pace, to extend the session, or during transition time at the beginning or end of the session.

## Collect

*The Big Book of Instant Activities*.

## Do

Guide children to complete "Where Is Kyle?" and/or "Mirror Me" (p. 24 and/or p. 116 from *The Big Book of Instant Activities*).

Lesson 45

# The Fiery Furnace

## Bible Story

Daniel 3

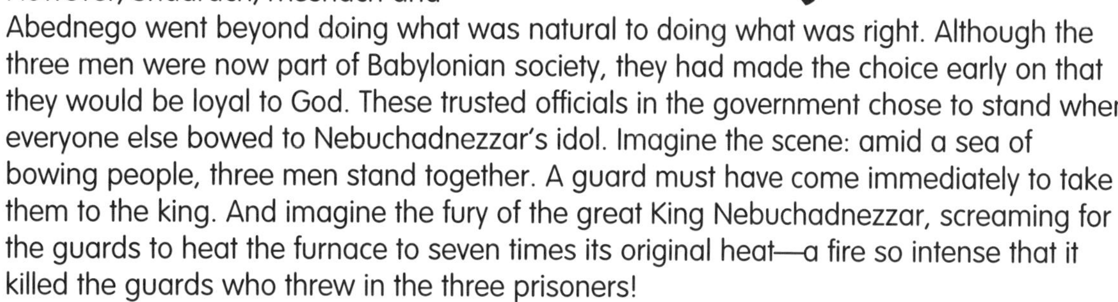
God's Word
"I trust in the Lord." Psalm 31:6
God's Word & Me
I love God and I know
He will care for me.

## Teacher's Devotional

When the pressures of life become too difficult, when debt becomes overwhelming or pain grows too great, most of us try to distance ourselves from those situations. We avoid circumstances where pain and pressure are produced. It's just natural.

However, Shadrach, Meshach and Abednego went beyond doing what was natural to doing what was right. Although the three men were now part of Babylonian society, they had made the choice early on that they would be loyal to God. These trusted officials in the government chose to stand when everyone else bowed to Nebuchadnezzar's idol. Imagine the scene: amid a sea of bowing people, three men stand together. A guard must have come immediately to take them to the king. And imagine the fury of the great King Nebuchadnezzar, screaming for the guards to heat the furnace to seven times its original heat—a fire so intense that it killed the guards who threw in the three prisoners!

These three men had a supernatural confidence. They knew that when they obeyed God, whatever else happened was God's business. They knew that their obedience presented God with the opportunity to work mighty things on their behalf, no matter how frightening the situation! When a frightening situation confronts us, there is only one thing to do: Obey the Lord. Then we can be confident He will be with us in the hottest of fires, the most difficult of times. God will work mighty things for us as well, even while we confront any trial life may present.

## Teacher's Planning

1. Choose which centers you will provide and the order in which children will participate in them. For tips on schedule planning, see page 7.

2. Plan who will lead each center. For staffing tips and ideas, see page 21.

Lesson 45

# Active Game Center: Furnace Walk

## Collect

Bible, *Shake It Up!* cassette/CD and player, yarn.

## Prepare

On floor use yarn to outline a circle large enough for several children to walk around inside.

### God's Word

**"I trust in the Lord." Psalm 31:6**

### God's Word & Me

**I love God and I know He will care for me.**

## Do

Play "Love the Lord" for several moments. Children move around inside the yarn circle as music plays. When you stop the music, call out a color. All children wearing that color jump outside the circle. Ask a volunteer outside the circle to repeat the words "God cares for me" or tell a way God cares for him or her. (Food. Friends. Family.) Repeat for several rounds, varying the color you call out and the way children move around the circle (in slow motion, like robots, like animals, backward, etc.).

## Talk About

- **Our Bible says, "I trust in the Lord." "Lord" is another name for God. Trusting God means we know He always cares for us. We know God will always love and help us. Let's play a game and talk about ways God cares for us.**
- **Peggy, who takes care of you at home?** (Grandma. Dad. Sister.) **God gives you people to take care of you!**
- **God cares for each of us! We can tell God how much we love Him.** Pray briefly, **Dear God, we love You. We trust in You.**

## For Younger Children

Instead of jumping outside the circle when the music stops, children simply freeze when the music stops.

## For Older Children

When the music stops, children say the words of the Bible verse, "I trust in the Lord."

# Art Center: Tissue-Paper Collage

## Collect

Bible, tissue paper in a variety of colors, glue, small bowls, water, paintbrushes, white construction paper or poster board.

## Prepare

Tear tissue paper into strips, approximately 2-inches (5-cm) wide. Pour some glue into small bowls, and thin glue by adding water. (Note: Crumpling and then smoothing out tissue paper before tearing it helps prevent pieces from sticking together.)

God's Word
"I trust in the Lord." Psalm 31:6
God's Word & Me
I love God and I know
He will care for me.

## Do

Children use paintbrushes to spread glue onto construction paper or poster board. Then children place tissue paper strips on glue in a design of their choice.

## Talk About

- **Our Bible says, "I trust in the Lord." "Lord" is another name for God. Trusting in God means we know that God will take care of us and help us. Let's make pictures with lots of different colors and talk about ways God cares for us.**
- **Georgio, what colors are in your picture? God cares for us by giving us eyes to see. I love God. I am so glad He cares for us.**
- **God takes care of us in many ways. Lee Anne, who takes care of you? God gave each of us people to take care of us.**
- Pray briefly, **Thank You, God, that You take care of us. We love and trust You.**

## For Younger Children

Instead of using paintbrushes and glue, children use gluesticks.

## For Older Children

Children tear the tissue papers into pieces before gluing them onto the construction paper.

Lesson 45

# Block Center: Hot Stuff

## Collect

Bible, blocks, oven mitts.

## Do

Children build an oven with the blocks. Children pretend they are baking things in the oven and wear oven mitts to remove what they are cooking.

### God's Word

**"I trust in the Lord." Psalm 31:6**

### God's Word & Me

**I love God and I know He will care for me.**

## Talk About

- **Our Bible says, "I trust in the Lord." That means that we know God loves us and will always take care of us. One way God cares for us is by giving us good food to eat. Let's build a pretend oven and pretend to cook food.**
- **Todd, what kinds of food could we cook in our oven? Mmm, that sounds good! God cares for us and gives us lots of good food to eat. I know that God will always care for us!**

- **Another way that God takes care of us is by giving us moms and dads and grandmas and grandpas who care for us. Nathan, what does your grandpa do to care for you?** (Reads a bedtime story. Cooks food for lunch. Gives hugs.)
- **I'm glad God cares for me. I love God! God cares for each of us! We can tell God how much we love Him.** Pray briefly, **Thank You, God, for caring for us. We love You!**

## For Younger Children

Bring in cardboard boxes to be pretend ovens. Children use oven mitts and move blocks in and out of the cardboard-box ovens.

## For Older Children

Children use oven mitts the entire time they are building. **It is hard to carry the blocks without using your fingers! God made us with fingers, so we can do things like carry blocks and do puzzles and draw with crayons. God cares for us very much!**

Lesson 45

# Science Center: Hot and Cold

## Collect

Bible, two large bowls, warm and cold water, water toys (measuring cups, empty plastic bottles, funnels, sieves, etc.).

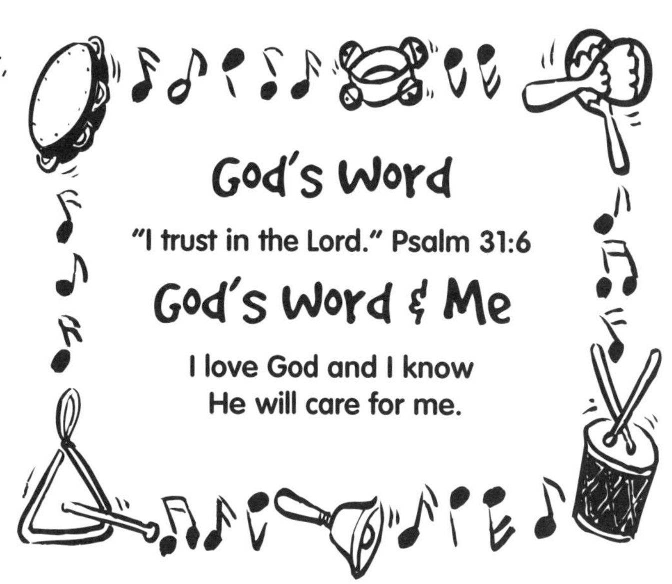

God's Word
"I trust in the Lord." Psalm 31:6
God's Word & Me
I love God and I know
He will care for me.

## Prepare

Fill one bowl with warm water and one with cold water.

## Do

Children roll up sleeves and feel the difference between warm and cold waters, touching both outside of bowls and water. Children use water toys to play with water in bowls. (Optional: Do activity outside using several bowls of water.)

## Talk About

- **Our Bible says, "I trust in the Lord." To trust God means we know that God will take care of us. One way God cares for us is by helping us feel hot and cold things. Let's feel some warm and cold waters.**
- **The water we're touching is warm. Some things are very hot. What might happen if we touched something hot?** (We could get burned.) **God made us so that we can feel hot and cold things. God cares for us by helping us stay safe.**
- **God gives us people to care for us and keep us safe, too. Who are some of the people God gave to take care of you?** (Doctors. Parents. Babysitters.)
- **How does God take care of you right now?** (Gives us parents. Gives us food and water.) **God will keep taking care of us as we get bigger, too!**

## For Younger and Older Children

A couple of days before class, fill a half-gallon milk container with water. Freeze.

Cut away container with scissors and place ice block on a shallow aluminum tray. Each child may carefully drip several colors of food coloring onto ice block to see the patterns made by the blending colors. Children may also sprinkle salt on ice block to see the texture formed as ice melts.

Older children may make ice sculptures with ice cubes. Children sprinkle ice cube with salt and then place another ice cube on top. The salt will establish a bond between the ice cubes.

# Bible Story Center

## God's Word

**"I trust in the Lord." Psalm 31:6**

## God's Word & Me

**I love God and I know He will care for me.**

## Collect

Bible, Picture 23 from *Bible Story Pictures.*

## Tell the Story

Use the pictured motions or show Picture 23. For older children, tell the version of the story on the back of Picture 23.

**What are the names of some of your friends? Listen to hear what happened to three friends.**

Daniel and his three friends worked for King Nebuchadnezzar of Babylon. One day, the king decided to make a big statue covered with shiny gold. It was a statue of himself. The statue was set up in a place where everyone could come and see it.

The king's messenger told the people, "When the music plays, **bow** down and pray to this statue. If you do not bow down, you will be thrown in a furnace and be burned up!"

But Daniel's three friends would not **pray** to a big statue. They would only pray to God! The music began to play. Everyone else bowed down low, but the three friends did not bow down. They stood tall. When King Nebuchadnezzar heard that they had not bowed to his statue, he was angry! The three friends were brought to the king. The king roared, "If you don't bow NOW, you'll be thrown into the furnace!"

The three friends said, "O king, our God is able to save us from the fire." That made the king really angry!

The soldiers tied up the friends. They threw the three men into the middle of the hot flames. Then the king **looked** in the furnace. He saw the three friends walking in the middle of the hot, hot fire. And there was someone else in there, too. It was an angel God sent to keep the three friends safe.

King Nebuchadnezzar was so surprised! Quickly, he shouted for the men to **come out** of the fire. When the three friends came out of the furnace, everyone crowded around to look at them. The friends were not burned at all. They didn't even smell like smoke! God had kept them safe, even in the fire. King Nebuchadnezzar knew God had kept the men safe, so he praised the one true God.

## God's Word & Me

**What happened when the men were thrown into the fire?** (They weren't burned.) **God took care of these men who loved Him. Who does God give to take care of us?** (Parents. Family.)

# Worship Center

## Collect

Bible, *Shake It Up!* songbook and cassette/CD and player, "Love the Lord" and "I Can Talk to God" word charts (pp. 59 and 57 in songbook).

**God's Word**

**"I trust in the Lord." Psalm 31:6**

**God's Word & Me**

**I love God and I know He will care for me.**

## Sing to God

Play "Love the Lord." Invite children to sing along with you. **Let's sing a song about loving God.** Lead children in singing song and doing suggested motions. **I'm glad we can sing about loving God. We love God. We know God will always care for us and help us!**

## Hear and Say God's Word

Holding your Bible open to Psalm 31:6, say verse aloud. **"Lord" is another name for God. When we trust in the Lord, we are sure He will always love us. What does God do to help you and care for you?** (Gives us parents to take care of us. Makes sure we have food to eat.) Lead children in saying the Bible verse together a few times. Ask all children with a certain characteristic to say the verse together (everyone wearing shoes that tie, everyone with blue eyes, everyone with a ponytail, etc.). Repeat the Bible verse several times, each time using a different characteristic.

## Pray to God

**We pray to God because we love Him. We know He takes care of us in the very best ways.** Lead children in prayer, telling God you love Him and know He will do what is best for you and the children.

## Sing to God

In closing the worship time, play "I Can Talk to God." Invite children to sing along with you. **When can we talk to God?** (Before we eat. At bedtime. Anytime.) **We can talk to God and tell Him how we feel. We know He will help us and care for us!**

## Options

1. If you take an offering during this time, explain to children that giving money is one way to show we love and trust God.

2. Volunteers pray, telling God they love Him and thanking Him that He will take care of them.

# Read-Aloud Story and Activity Center

## Collect

A copy of Story Picture 45 (pp. 95-96 from *Read-Aloud Story and Activity Book*) for each child and yourself, crayons or markers.

"I trust in the Lord." Psalm 31:6

## Prepare

Color your copy of Story Picture 45.

## Do

**Listen to find out where these people are going.** Read story and show completed Story Picture 45. Distribute pictures. Use conversation suggestions in Let's Talk About the Story as children complete their pages.

# Kindergarten Puzzle Center

## Collect

Copies of Puzzles 89 and 90 (p. 185 and p. 187 from *The Big Book of Kindergarten Puzzles*) for each child, pencils, crayons or markers.

## Do

Children complete the puzzles and color pages.

# Instant Activities

These activities can be used at any time during this session: when children need a change of pace, to extend the session, or during transition time at the beginning or end of the session.

## Collect

*The Big Book of Instant Activities.*

## Do

Guide children to complete "Listen Up!" and/or "Rainbow Wear" (p. 153 and/or p. 70 from *The Big Book of Instant Activities*).

Lesson 46

# The Writing on the Wall

## Bible Story

Daniel 5

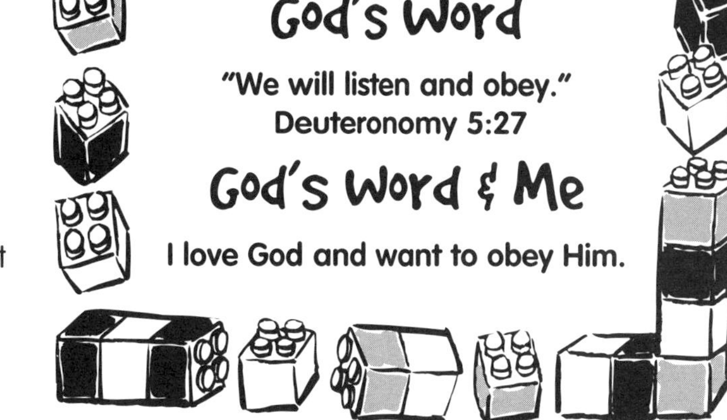

### God's Word

**"We will listen and obey."**
**Deuteronomy 5:27**

### God's Word & Me

**I love God and want to obey Him.**

## Teacher's Devotional

Many Christians work hard to bring about political and/or social change that is more in line with their beliefs. Daniel's life in Babylon, however, gives us reason to consider a very different way to bring about change: living a godly life.

Throughout his years in Babylon, Daniel never held himself aloof from the pagans around him. He simply drew his own lines of integrity and continued to live in the place where God had put him: working for a pagan king within a pagan government. He interpreted dreams, gave prophecies and was a strong, sure testimony to the power of the God of Israel. The result? Daniel's integrity had a ripple effect that was felt throughout the kingdom. Even pagan King Nebuchadnezzar praised and honored the Most High!

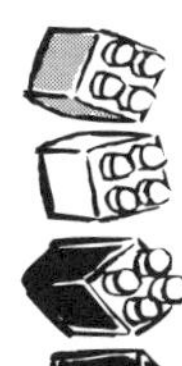

Long after Nebuchadnezzar was gone, Daniel's knowledge was summoned once again when a cryptic message burned on the wall of the royal banquet hall. Once again, in that pagan kingdom, God was mightily at work, intimately involved in every facet of the lives of those pagans! God's main tool once again was an old Hebrew man who had walked with integrity. Living a godly life among unbelievers was far more powerful than any political or social influence Daniel could have wielded.

We see the effects of pagan values even on the young children we teach. Will we despair? Complain? Or pray? How will we live? As Daniel showed, a life of integrity creates a hunger in empty hearts to know the Most High God!

## Teacher's Planning

1. Choose which centers you will provide and the order in which children will participate in them. For tips on schedule planning, see page 7.
2. Plan who will lead each center. For staffing tips and ideas, see page 21.

Lesson 46

# Active Game Center: Draw 'n' Move

## Collect

Bible, butcher paper, tape, markers.

## Prepare

Tape large sheet of butcher paper to table. Draw lines to divide the paper into several sections, one section for each child.

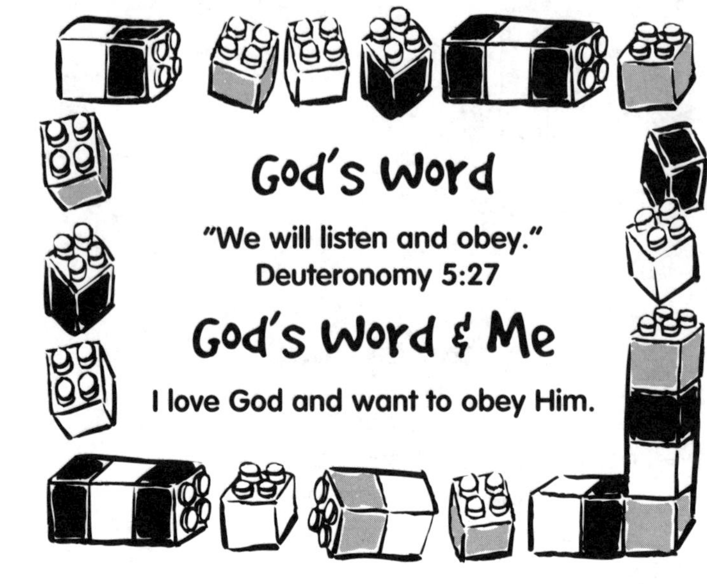
God's Word
"We will listen and obey."
Deuteronomy 5:27
God's Word & Me
I love God and want to obey Him.

## Do

1. Each child stands in front of a different section of the paper. Give children a drawing instruction. **Please draw a triangle.** Draw the object yourself in a section or on a separate piece of butcher paper. Children draw triangles in their sections on the paper.

2. Repeat several times, asking children to draw different shapes (wiggly or straight lines, dots, etc.). Instruct children to move to a new section of the paper for each new drawing instruction.

## Talk About

- **Our Bible says, "We will listen and obey." Let's play a game to practice listening and obeying.**
- **Ella, you listened to what I said and drew a triangle. You did a good job listening and obeying! In the Bible, God tells us we should obey our parents. What can you do to obey your parents when it is bedtime?** (Put toys away. Put clothes away. Brush teeth.)
- **Because we love God, we want to obey Him. In the Bible God tells us we should be kind to everyone. Tiffany, how can you obey God and be kind when you play with your sister?** (Share a toy. Use kind words.)

## For Younger Children

Young children may have difficulty distinguishing colors and drawing specific shapes. Simplify directions by telling children when to start and stop drawing, use a different marker, move to a new place at the table, etc.

## For Older Children

Add a movement command. **Hop to a new section and draw a heart.** Or add a number command. **Draw four dots.**

Lesson 46

# Art Center: Picture Surprise

## Collect

Bible, dark-colored construction paper, candle, white chalk.

## Prepare

Press firmly with candle to draw a happy face on each paper, preparing at least one paper for each child. Draw a simple flower on another paper to use as a sample.

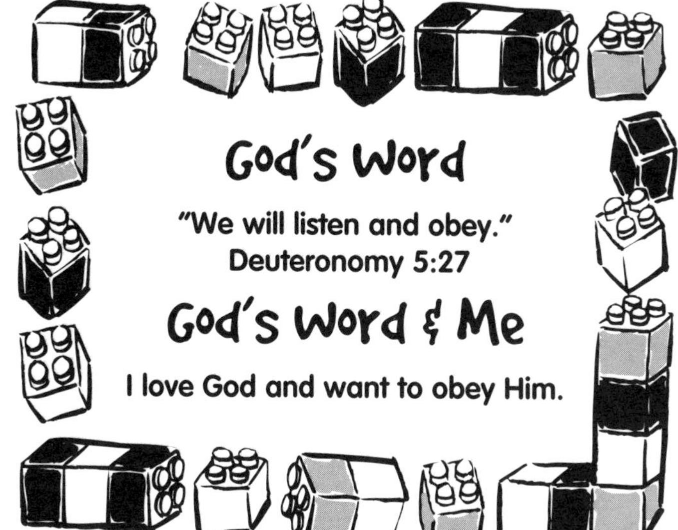
God's Word
"We will listen and obey."
Deuteronomy 5:27
God's Word & Me
I love God and want to obey Him.

## Do

1. On the flower paper, hold chalk sideways and color across the paper until flower is revealed. **What picture was hidden on this paper? Use chalk to find out if something is hidden on your paper.**
2. Children color over papers to discover the happy faces.

## Talk About

- **In our Bible story, a king saw writing appear on a wall! The writing was a special message for the king. Let's color on these papers and see what appears.**
- **What do you see on your paper? We can be happy because God loves us and we love Him! When we love God, we want to obey Him. Our Bible says, "We will listen and obey."**
- **One way to obey God is to be kind. Teri, what can you do to be kind to your friends?** (Share a snack with them. Help them pick up toys. Play games with them.)
- Pray briefly, **Dear God, We love You. Help us to obey You.**

## For Younger Children

Cut sheets of construction paper in half. Children draw happy faces on a sheet of butcher paper. Cover happy faces with a paper flap taped to butcher paper. Children lift flaps to see happy faces.

## For Older Children

Children use candles to make their own drawings. Children may color their own papers with chalk or exchange papers with others.

Lesson 46

# Block Center: Road Rules

## Collect

Bible, blocks, toy cars.

## Do

Children build roads. Children play with toy cars on roads and play a game like Red Light, Green Light. **When I say "Red light," stop your cars! When I say "Green light," you can make your cars go again.**

### God's Word

**"We will listen and obey."**
**Deuteronomy 5:27**

### God's Word & Me

**I love God and want to obey Him.**

## Talk About

- **Our Bible says, "We will listen and obey." We listen to God and obey Him because we love God. Let's build roads for our cars to drive on. We can practice obeying rules for driving cars.**
- **People who drive cars must obey rules to be safe. God loves us and wants us to be safe. Obeying God can help us be safe.**
- **One way to obey God is to obey our parents. Doris, what can you do to obey your parents when you are riding in the car?** (Wear a seat belt. Don't make a lot of noise.) **Obeying these rules can help us stay safe in a car.**
- **God loves us! And we love Him. We can obey God because we love Him.**
- Pray briefly, **Dear God, we love You. We want to obey You. Please help us.**

## For Younger Children

Bring enough toy cars so that each child can have one. Children play with cars. Talk with children about obeying stop and go signs.

## For Older Children

Children make traffic signs from construction paper (stop, yield, one way, etc.). Children place signs on the road and obey signs while playing with cars.

Lesson 46

# Science Center: Squishy Writing

## Collect

Bible, resealable plastic bags, shaving cream; optional—transparent tape.

## Prepare

Fill each bag about one-quarter full of shaving cream. Push air out. Firmly seal bag. (Optional: Secure bags to table with tape.)

God's Word
"We will listen and obey."
Deuteronomy 5:27
God's Word & Me
I love God and want to obey Him.

## Do

Demonstrate to children how to draw on bag of shaving cream with fingers and erase by smoothing bag with hand. Children use fingers to draw patterns, numbers, letters, etc.

## Talk About

- **In today's Bible story, Daniel helped a king know what a message from God said. Let's pretend to write messages.**
- **Jill, you made a straight line on your drawing bag. What message are you pretending to write?**
- **Because we love God, we want to obey Him. Our Bible says, "We will listen and obey." Erik, how can you obey God and help others in your family at home?** (Help Dad wash the car. Help baby sister by playing with her.)

## For Younger Children

Add a few drops of food coloring to each bag of shaving cream before distributing the bags to children. Children follow your directions to gently rub bags to mix in color. Comment on the way children obey and the patterns the color makes in the shaving cream.

## For Older Children

Print the words "listen" and "obey" on a large sheet of paper. Children copy one or both words, one letter at a time, on their drawing bags.

Lesson 46 • Daniel 5

# Bible Story Center

## Collect

Bible, Picture 24 from *Bible Story Pictures*.

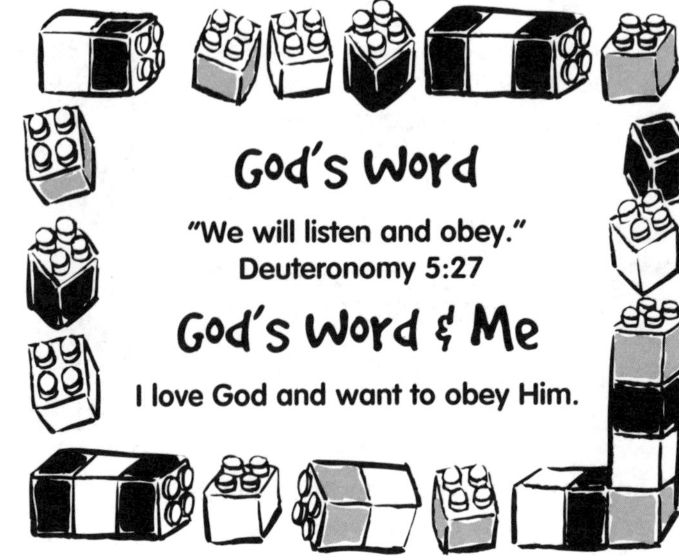
God's Word
"We will listen and obey."
Deuteronomy 5:27
God's Word & Me
I love God and want to obey Him.

## Tell the Story

Use the pictured motions (keywords in bold) or show Picture 24. For older children, tell the version of the story on the back of Picture 24.

**When have you been to a party? What kinds of things did you do at the party? Listen to hear what happened at a king's party.**

King Belshazzar (behl-SHAHZ-uhr), the king of Babylon, liked to have lots of parties. One night, King Belshazzar brought out some beautiful gold **cups**. The cups had been stolen from God's Temple in Jerusalem. The king did not care that these things belonged to God. King Belshazzar did not love or obey God. He and his friends drank from the gold cups from God's Temple.

Suddenly, something very strange happened. A big **hand** appeared out of nowhere! The finger of the hand began to write on the wall! King Belshazzar watched the hand. He grew very scared! No one could tell what the writing meant. The king called his wise helpers. None of them knew what the writing meant.

Then the queen told King Belshazzar that Daniel was very **wise**. Daniel was a man who loved God and obeyed God. The queen told Belshazzar to call for Daniel. The king asked Daniel to tell him what the writing meant. Daniel said that the words meant God had seen the ways King Belshazzar had not obeyed God.

"Now," said Daniel, "God is going to END your time as **king**. Other people will take your place."

That very same night, God's warning came true. Another king came and took over the city. And Daniel was given a new job by the new king!

## God's Word & Me

**What did Daniel tell the king?** (There was going to be a new king.) **Daniel loved and obeyed God. We love God and want to obey Him, too. One way to obey God is to do the things our parents tell us to do. How can you obey your parents at dinnertime?** (Help set the table. Share food.) **When you play with your brother or sister?** (Be kind. Share toys.)

Lesson 46

# Worship Center

## Collect

Bible, *Shake It Up!* songbook and cassette/CD and player, "Love the Lord" and "I Can Talk to God" word charts (pp. 59 and 57 in songbook).

God's Word
"We will listen and obey."
Deuteronomy 5:27
God's Word & Me
I love God and want to obey Him.

## Sing to God

Play "Love the Lord." Invite children to sing along with you. **Let's sing a song about loving God.** Lead children in singing song and doing suggested motions. **When we love God, we want to obey Him! What can you do to obey God when you are at home with your family?** (Be kind to everyone. Help parents, brothers and sisters.)

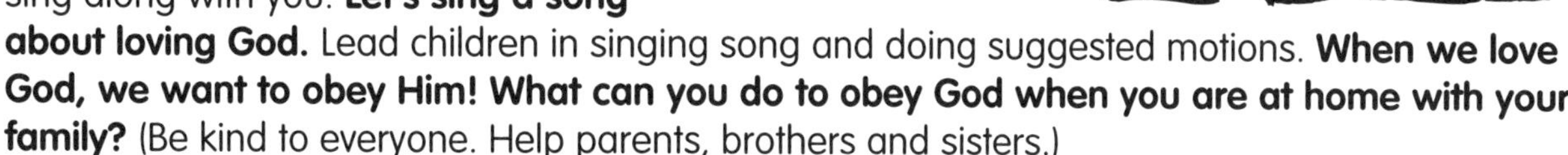

## Hear and Say God's Word

Holding your Bible open to Deuteronomy 5:27, say verse aloud. **We want to listen to God and obey Him because we love Him. Let's sing the words of this verse and tell God what we want to do!** Lead children in singing the words of the verse to the tune of "Are You Sleeping":

We will listen. We will listen.
And obey. And obey.
We will listen. We will listen.
And obey. And obey.

## Pray to God

Say the following prayer, inserting the name of a child into the prayer: **Dear God, thank You for loving __________. Help (him/her) love and obey You.** Repeat once for each child in your class. If you have a large class, name more than one child each time you repeat the prayer.

## Sing to God

In closing the worship time, play "I Can Talk to God." Invite children to sing along with you. **When we talk to God, we can tell Him we love Him and want to obey Him!**

## Options

1. Older children lead other children in doing motions suggested for "Love the Lord" and/or "I Can Talk to God."
2. Provide rhythm instruments for children to use while singing "Love the Lord" and/or "I Can Talk to God."

Lesson 46

# Read-Aloud Story and Activity Center

## Collect

A copy of Story Picture 46 (pp. 97-98 from *Read-Aloud Story and Activity Book*) for each child and yourself, crayons or markers.

## Prepare

Color your copy of Story Picture 46.

## Do

**Listen to find out why this mom is calling her children.** Read story and show completed Story Picture 46. Distribute pictures. Use conversation suggestions in Let's Talk About the Story as children complete their pages.

# Kindergarten Puzzle Center

## Collect

Copies of Puzzles 91 and 92 (p. 189 and p. 191 from *The Big Book of Kindergarten Puzzles*) for each child, pencils, crayons or markers.

## Do

Children complete the puzzles and color pages.

# Instant Activities

These activities can be used at any time during this session: when children need a change of pace, to extend the session, or during transition time at the beginning or end of the session.

## Collect

*The Big Book of Instant Activities.*

## Do

Guide children to complete "Quiet Touch" and/or "Salad Bowl Singing" (p. 119 and/or p. 102 from *The Big Book of Instant Activities*).

Lesson 47

# The Lions' Den

## Bible Story

Daniel 6

## Teacher's Devotional

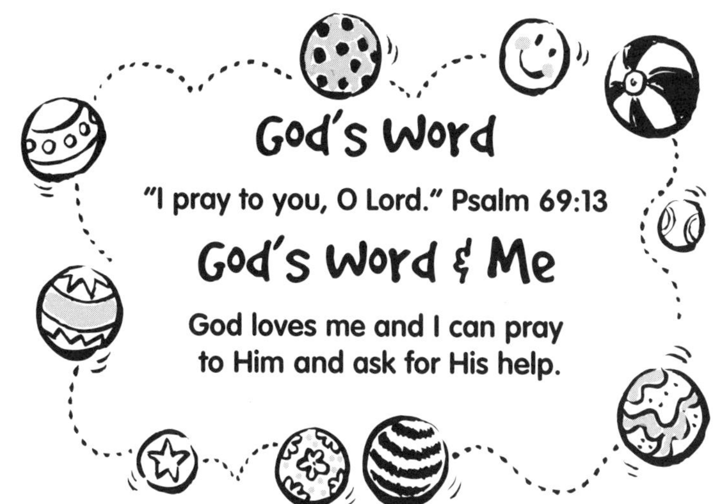
God's Word
"I pray to you, O Lord." Psalm 69:13
God's Word & Me
God loves me and I can pray to Him and ask for His help.

Today's Bible story is probably the most famous incident in Daniel's life. Most people remember the hungry lions, but Daniel's character is the crux of the story. Brought to Babylon as a young captive, Daniel was in Babylon but was not of Babylon. He didn't need the approval of the royal officials around him, for their power did not impress him. God was his helper. When he prayed, it didn't matter who saw him, because God was his focus.

This strong, unashamed man was a product of his relationship with the powerful and true God. When Daniel heard the king's ridiculous decree, he didn't lose his nerve. He did just as he had always done: opened his windows and prayed to God. Daniel recognized that when he obeyed God first, the consequences would be God's opportunity to display His power. Daniel simply depended on God to show His strength. When God shut the mouths of the lions, His power was so obvious that the king decreed that all of Babylon should pray only to the God of Daniel!

The bold and the fearless character Daniel gained from his daily relationship with God can be ours. After all, we are able to be bold when we remember that it is God's strength that will carry us. All He asks of us is faithfulness!

## Teacher's Planning

1. Choose which centers you will provide and the order in which children will participate in them. For tips on schedule planning, see page 7.
2. Plan who will lead each center. For staffing tips and ideas, see page 21.

Lesson 47

# Active Game Center: Times Three

## Collect

Bible.

## Do

Lead children as they play a game like Follow the Leader. As you and the children walk around the room, call out and lead motions for children to do three times (jumping jacks, touch toes, clap hands, hop on one foot, etc.). Count aloud with children as the motions are done.

### God's Word

**"I pray to you, O Lord." Psalm 69:13**

### God's Word & Me

**God loves me and I can pray to Him and ask for His help.**

## Talk About

- **In today's Bible story, a man named Daniel loved and obeyed God. Daniel prayed only to God. Daniel prayed to God three times every day! Let's play a game and do things three times.**
- **How many times do we eat each day? Let's name the meals we eat: breakfast, lunch and dinner. What are some other things you do more than once a day?** (Wash hands. Talk to people. Play with toys.)
- **Our Bible says, "I pray to you, O Lord." "Lord" is another name for God. We can pray to God because He loves and helps us. And we can pray to God lots of times every day!**
- Pray briefly, **Dear God, thank You for helping us every day. We love You.**

## For Younger Children

Instead of children lining up and walking around the room, children stand in a circle to perform the motions as you call them out. Each motion is performed for several moments, until you call out "Freeze!" Children remain frozen until you call out another motion.

## For Older Children

After a few rounds of play, older children volunteer to be the leaders. Join the line with the children as each volunteer leads the line in performing different motions three times.

# Art Center: Mane Event

## Collect

Bible, paper plates, scissors, hole punch, yarn, measuring stick, markers (brown, yellow and orange), stapler.

## Prepare

Cut plates in half. Following sketch a, cut one mane and ears set for each child. Punch a hole at each end of the manes. Cut two 18-inch (45.5-m) lengths of yarn for each child.

God's Word
"I pray to you, O Lord." Psalm 69:13
God's Word & Me
God loves me and I can pray to Him and ask for His help.

## Do

1. Using markers, each child colors a mane and two ears. Assist children in cutting slits in the edges of the manes and fold over every other section (see sketch b).
2. Help children place ears on mane and staple in place. Children thread a length of yarn through each hole on their manes. Assist children in tying knots. Children place manes on their heads and tie under their chins (see sketch c).

## Talk About

a.
Mane
throw away
Ear
Ear
cut
b.
c.

- **In our Bible story, Daniel prayed to God. God kept Daniel safe when he was in a cave filled with lions. Let's make lions' manes to remind us of this story.**
- **Our Bible says, "I pray to you, O Lord." "Lord" is another name for God. We can pray to God at any time! We can ask God to help us. I ask God to help me be kind.**
- Pray briefly, **Thank You, God, that we can pray to You anytime.**

## For Younger Children

Before class, thread yarn through each hole in the mane and tie into a knot. Precut sections of mane for children to fold after they color manes and ears. Staple ears to manes.

## For Older Children

Cut brown, yellow and orange construction paper into 1x4-inch (2.5x10-cm) strips. Children glue construction-paper strips to add to their manes.

Lesson 47

# Block Center: Places of Prayer

## Collect

Bible, blocks, nature items (shells, twigs, pebbles, etc.).

## God's Word

**"I pray to you, O Lord." Psalm 69:13**

## God's Word & Me

**God loves me and I can pray to Him and ask for His help.**

## Do

Children build different places with blocks and then decorate places with nature items.

## Talk About

- **Our Bible says, "I pray to you, O Lord." "Lord" is another name for God. We pray to God because He loves and helps us. Let's build some of the places where we go.**
- **Becky, what are you building? I like to go to the park, too. We can pray to God whenever we go to the park! We can pray to God wherever we go!**
- **Louis, what are you building? What are some things God can help you do at school?** (Share toys with friends. Obey the teacher. Play kindly with others. Help others.)
- **God helps us because He loves us. Praying to God is one way to show that we love Him.** Pray briefly, **Thank You, God, for helping us. We love You.**

## For Younger Children

Bring in magazine pictures of different buildings (schools, churches, homes, stores, etc.). Children build a road wide enough to walk down. Place magazine pictures along the road. Walk down the road with children, talking about the different places as you walk past them.

## For Older Children

Bring in magazine pictures of bridges, roads, city scenes, etc. Children choose one of the pictures and build the item in the picture.

Lesson 47

# Science Center: Prayer Times

## Collect

Bible, pictures of weather (clouds, rain, sunshine, snow, etc.) and/or day- and nighttime scenes, large Post-it Notes.

## Prepare

Cover each picture with Post-it Notes.

## Do

Children take turns removing Post-it Notes one at a time. As each portion of the picture is revealed, children guess what is shown in the picture. Repeat for each picture.

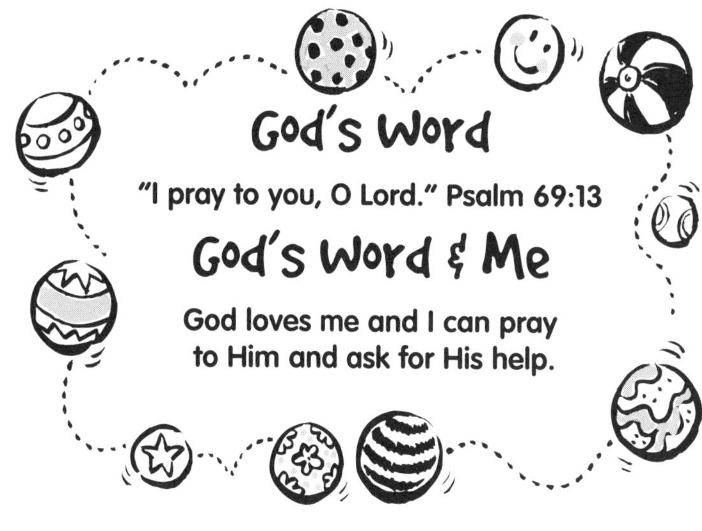
God's Word
"I pray to you, O Lord." Psalm 69:13
God's Word & Me
God loves me and I can pray to Him and ask for His help.

## Talk About

- **Our Bible says, "I pray to you, O Lord." "Lord" is another name for God. God loves us! We can pray to God every day. We can tell God how much we love Him. Let's play a game to talk about some of the times we can pray to God.**
- **Gary, what kind of weather does this picture show? We can talk to God on a rainy day.**
- **Rachel, is this a daytime or nighttime picture? We can talk to God in the morning or in the night. We can ask God to help us.**
- **Heather, what do you see in this picture? In some places, snow falls in the winter. What else might you see in a winter picture? What are the names of the other seasons? We can pray to God any time of the year!**

## For Younger Children

Simplify activity by using only daytime and nighttime pictures.

## For Older Children

Before class, glue pictures to poster board. When dry, cut pictures into four or five puzzle pieces. In addition to identifying pictures by removing Post-it Notes, children solve puzzles.

# Bible Story Center

## Collect

Bible, Picture 25 from *Bible Story Pictures.*

## God's Word

**"I pray to you, O Lord." Psalm 69:13**

## God's Word & Me

**God loves me and I can pray to Him and ask for His help.**

## Tell the Story

Use the pictured motions (keywords in bold) or show Picture 25. For older children, tell the version of the story on the back of Picture 25.

**What is something you do every day? Listen to our Bible story to find out what Daniel did every day.**

Daniel was a man who loved God. One way he showed his love was by praying to God. Daniel prayed to God one, two, **three** times every day.

Daniel had an important job. He was the king's most important helper. The king liked Daniel very much. But there were some mean men who did not like Daniel. They were angry that the king liked Daniel better than them. These mean men thought of a plan to get Daniel in trouble with the king. They went to the king and said, "King, we think you should make a rule that everyone must pray only to you. If people pray to anyone else but you, they will be thrown into a cave filled with **lions**!"

The king thought this rule was a good idea. The king sent helpers to tell all the people they must pray only to him. The angry men watched to see what Daniel would do.

The next day Daniel opened his window, just like he always did. Daniel prayed to God, just like he always did. He did not pray to the king. The mean men watched as Daniel prayed to God. Then the mean men **ran** to tell the king what they saw.

Daniel was in trouble. The king was sad. The king did not want Daniel to be hurt, but the king had to obey the rule, too. Daniel was put into a big cave where lions lived. All night the king worried about Daniel's safety. The next morning, the king ran to the lions' cave. He **called**, "Daniel! DANIEL!"

Daniel called back from inside the cave, "King, I am safe. God took care of me!" The king was so glad that Daniel was not hurt! Daniel came out of the cave. The king knew that God had helped Daniel and kept him safe from the lions. Then the king told everyone what God had done. He made a new rule that everyone should love God and pray only to Him.

## God's Word & Me

**Who did Daniel pray to?** (Only God.) **We can pray to God, too, and He will help us. What can we say when we pray to God?** (We love You. Thank You. Please help us.)

# Worship Center

## Collect

Bible, *Shake It Up!* songbook and cassette/CD and player, "I Can Talk to God" and "Love the Lord" word charts (pp. 57 and 59 in songbook).

### God's Word

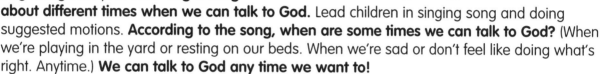

**"I pray to you, O Lord." Psalm 69:13**

### God's Word & Me

**God loves me and I can pray to Him and ask for His help.**

## Sing to God

Play "I Can Talk to God." Invite children to sing along with you. **Let's sing a song about different times when we can talk to God.** Lead children in singing song and doing suggested motions. **According to the song, when are some times we can talk to God?** (When we're playing in the yard or resting on our beds. When we're sad or don't feel like doing what's right. Anytime.) **We can talk to God any time we want to!**

## Hear and Say God's Word

Holding your Bible open to Psalm 69:13, say verse aloud. **"Lord" is another name for God. We can pray to God. God loves and helps us.** Lead children in repeating the verse two or three times. Then add the word "at" and a time of day. **I pray to you, O Lord, at bedtime.** Children echo the phrase after you. Repeat several times, using different times of the day, days of the week or seasons of the year.

## Pray to God

Children repeat the following prayer after you, one phrase at a time: **Dear God, . . . I'm so glad . . . that I can talk to You . . . anytime! . . . Thank You for loving us . . . and helping us. . . . We love You. . . . In Jesus' name, amen.**

## Sing to God

In closing the worship time, play "Love the Lord." Invite children to sing along with you and do suggested motions. **I love God. Singing songs about God is one way to show we love Him.**

## Options

1. During the verse activity, older children make up motions to do while you and other children say the verse.
2. During prayer activity, briefly tell an age-appropriate example of a time God helped you.

Lesson 47

# Read-Aloud Story and Activity Center

## Collect

A copy of Story Picture 47 (pp. 99-100 from *Read-Aloud Story and Activity Book*) for each child and yourself, crayons or markers.

"I pray to you, O Lord." Psalm 69:13

## Prepare

Color your copy of Story Picture 47.

## Do

**Listen to find out who helped this boy.** Read story and show completed Story Picture 47. Distribute pictures. Use conversation suggestions in Let's Talk About the Story as children complete their pages.

# Kindergarten Puzzle Center

## Collect

Copies of Puzzles 93 and 94 (p. 193 and p. 195 from *The Big Book of Kindergarten Puzzles*) for each child, pencils, crayons or markers.

## Do

Children complete the puzzles and color pages.

# Instant Activities

These activities can be used at any time during this session: when children need a change of pace, to extend the session, or during transition time at the beginning or end of the session.

## Collect

*The Big Book of Instant Activities.*

## Do

Guide children to complete "Measure Up!" and/or "Beach-Ball Roll" (p. 115 and/or p. 17 from *The Big Book of Instant Activities*).

Lesson 48

# Ruth Loves Naomi

## Bible Story

Ruth 1—2:23

God's Word
"Love is patient, love is kind."
1 Corinthians 13:4
God's Word & Me
I can show love for others
by being kind and patient.

## Teacher's Devotional

When faced with change, people often feel threatened and retreat to what is familiar. But even after the dramatic changes of widowhood and the loss of her home, Ruth was willing to risk change again, choosing to go with her widowed mother-in-law, Naomi, to Naomi's country. Ruth's love caused her to commit to living her life with Naomi, regardless of the consequences (see Ruth 1:16-18).

When Ruth arrived in Israel, she did not wait for Naomi's relatives to step forward with food. She was committed to doing all she could to care for her aging mother-in-law and herself. She gleaned the corners of the field diligently to take full advantage of the law God had made to help people in situations like hers. Ruth's hard work and commitment garnered Boaz's attention.

Commitment driven by love, regardless of consequence, was not only Ruth's character, but it is also Jesus' character. When teaching little ones seems too difficult a commitment and we long for the ease and familiarity of attending adult classes, we can know that God can help us be like Jesus. He can give us that deep commitment that causes us to diligently show love, even in the most difficult situations!

## Teacher's Planning

1. Choose which centers you will provide and the order in which children will participate in them. For tips on schedule planning, see page 7.
2. Plan who will lead each center. For staffing tips and ideas, see page 21.

 

Lesson 48

# Active Game Center: Food or Not?

## Collect

Bible, food items (carrot, banana, hard-boiled egg, etc.), nonfood items (rock, block, eraser, marker, etc.), large bag.

## Prepare

Place food and nonfood items in bag, reserving one item of each type. Place bag and a table on opposite sides of activity area. Place items you reserved on opposite ends of table.

God's Word
**"Love is patient, love is kind."**
**1 Corinthians 13:4**
God's Word & Me
**I can show love for others by being kind and patient.**

## Do

Children take turns reaching into bag, removing an item and identifying it as either food or not food. After identifying the item, each child walks over to the table and places the item next to the same type of item on the table. Repeat, creating one pile of items we eat and one pile of items we do not eat. Repeat game as time and interest allow.

## Talk About

- **In our Bible story, Ruth was kind and helped Naomi have good food to eat. Ruth showed love by being kind. Let's play a game to find good food to eat.**
- **Our Bible says, "Love is patient, love is kind." Kenny, you were patient when you waited quietly for your turn to play the game. Waiting for your turn is a way to show love for others.**
- Pray briefly, **Dear God, help us to show love and be patient.**

## For Younger Children

Bring additional food items. Before class, cut food items into bite-size pieces and place in different bowls. Children wash hands before selecting food items to taste. (Note: Check with parents about food allergies.)

## For Older Children

Bring additional food items. Use knife to cut food items into bite-size pieces for children to eat as a snack. Children use plastic knives to cut soft foods like bananas and hard-boiled eggs. **Andy, thank you for cutting the banana for us to eat. You know how to show kindness!** (Note: Check with parents about food allergies.)

Lesson 48

# Art Center: Surreal Cereal Collages

## Collect

Bible, dry cereal in a variety of colors and shapes (no flakes), bowls, paper, marker, glue, construction paper; optional—premoistened towelettes.

## Prepare

Place cereal in separate bowls. Post a note alerting parents to the use of food in this activity. Also check registration forms for possible food allergies.

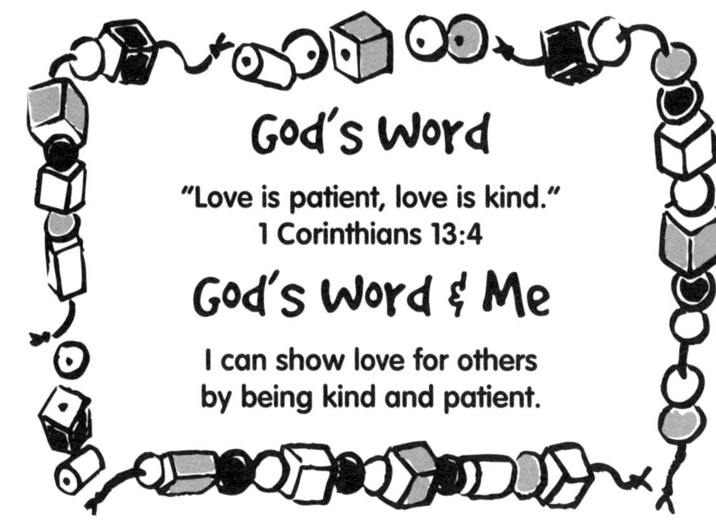
God's Word
"Love is patient, love is kind."
1 Corinthians 13:4
God's Word & Me
I can show love for others
by being kind and patient.

## Do

1. Children wash hands. (Optional: Children use premoistened towelettes to clean hands.)
2. Children glue cereal pieces onto construction paper in a design of their choosing. Children eat leftover cereal.

## Talk About

Glue

- **In today's Bible story, Ruth gathered grain to make food for herself and Naomi. Grains are little seeds used to make foods like breads and cereal. Let's use cereal to make pictures.**
- **Our Bible says, "Love is patient, love is kind." We can show love for others by being kind and patient. Being patient means waiting quietly for your turn to do something. It also means not complaining.**
- **Justine, if you want to use the glue, what do you need to do? You can ask Stefan to hand you the glue. Thank you for waiting patiently to use the glue.**

## For Younger Children

Before class, draw simple shapes on sheets of construction paper. Children choose a shape to outline and/or fill in with cereal.

## For Older Children

Children glue cereal pieces in a repeating pattern. For example, children place one square piece and then two round pieces, repeating the pattern as they make their designs.

Lesson 48

# Block Center: Heart of Blocks

## Collect

Bible, *Shake It Up!* cassette/CD and player, blocks.

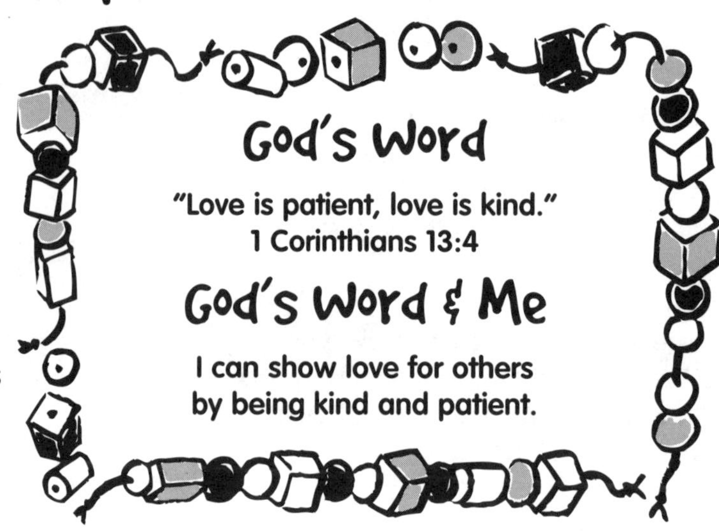
God's Word
"Love is patient, love is kind."
1 Corinthians 13:4
God's Word & Me
I can show love for others by being kind and patient.

## Do

1. Children use blocks to make a large heart on the floor of the activity area.
2. Play "Love Is" for several moments as children walk outside of heart outline. When you stop the music, children all jump to inside of heart outline. When you play music again, children jump out of the heart and begin walking around heart again.

## Talk About

- **Our Bible says, "Love is patient, love is kind." Let's make a large heart shape and talk about ways to show love for others.**
- **We can show love for others by being kind. Cindy, what are some ways to be kind to your brother when you play a game with him?** (Let him take the first turn. Say kind words.)
- **We can show love for others by being patient. Being patient means waiting quietly. Rob, you were patient when you waited for Jim to get his blocks first. That was showing love!**
- Pray briefly, **Thank You, God, that we can show love by being kind and patient.**

## For Younger Children

Children make large block shapes of their own choosing. Children jump in and out of the shapes they build.

## For Older Children

Older children move around the heart in a different way for each round: on hands and knees, in slow motion, like robots, while rubbing arms or patting head, as if swimming, etc.

Lesson 48

# Science Center: Exploring Grains

## Collect

Bible, newspaper, a variety of grains (rice, oats, corn, unpopped popcorn, wheat, barley, etc.), several bowls, paper lunch bags.

## Prepare

Cover activity area with newspaper. Place some of each grain in a different bowl and some in a different paper bag.

God's Word
"Love is patient, love is kind."
1 Corinthians 13:4
God's Word & Me
I can show love for others
by being kind and patient.

## Do

1. Children use their hands to explore the feel of the different grains in the bowls.
2. Children take turns selecting a bag and reaching in with one hand to feel the grain. Children then try to find which bowl has the same grain as is in their bags by closing their eyes and touching with their other hand. Shuffle the bags around before each child's turn.

## Talk About

- **In today's Bible story, Ruth was kind to Naomi. She gathered grain. Let's look at some grains.**
- **Grains are the seeds of plants. Grains are used to make cereals and breads.**
- **Our Bible says, "Love is patient, love is kind." Being patient means not being bossy or complaining. It means being quiet when you have to wait. Betina, you were patient when you waited for a turn to choose a bag. Tim, when is another time you might have to wait for a turn?**

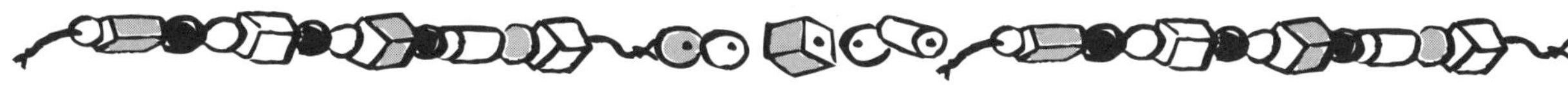

## For Younger Children

Provide only one or two types of grain. Children play with the grains using a variety of spoons (measuring spoons, teaspoons, serving spoons, slotted spoons, ladles, etc.). You may also wish to provide cups, funnels, scoops and sifters for children to use in exploring the grains.

## For Older Children

Children try to identify the grain in the bags without feeling the grains in the bowls.

## Lesson 48 • Ruth 1—2:23

# Bible Story Center

### Collect

Bible, Picture 9 from *Bible Story Pictures.*

God's Word
"Love is patient, love is kind."
1 Corinthians 13:4
God's Word & Me
I can show love for others
by being kind and patient.

## Tell the Story

Use the pictured motions (keywords in bold) or show Picture 9. For older children, tell the version of the story on the back of Picture 9.

**What do you do when you feel hungry? Listen to our Bible story to find out what a hungry woman did.**

Our Bible tells about two women who loved and obeyed God. Their names were Ruth and Naomi. Ruth and Naomi did not have any money to buy food. They were **hungry**, so Ruth went to find some food.

Ruth went to a field where workers were cutting grain. The grain was used to make bread. The workers tied the grain into bundles. Some of the grain fell on the ground. The workers left the grain on the ground to be **picked up** by people who did not have enough food to eat. Ruth asked one of the workers if she could pick up some of the grain from the ground. He said, "Yes." So Ruth picked up the grain and put it into her basket. She worked and worked.

A man named Boaz owned the field. He saw Ruth working hard. Boaz told Ruth, "From now on you may pick up all the leftover grain you can find in my field. And when you are thirsty, you may **drink** from our water jars." Boaz was kind to Ruth.

Later that day, Boaz brought some food to Ruth. She was hungry, but she didn't eat it all. She saved some food to take home to Naomi. Then Ruth went back to work. She picked up all the grain she could carry in her basket. At night, she went home.

Naomi was **surprised** that Ruth brought home so much grain. There was enough to make many loaves of bread. Ruth gave Naomi the food she had saved for her. Naomi was glad that Ruth was kind to her. She was glad that Boaz was kind, too.

### God's Word & Me

**How did Ruth help Naomi?** (Gave her food she had saved. Gathered grain for food.) **Ruth loved Naomi and that's why she was kind to her. Ruth was patient because she did not complain about the hard work she had to do. We can show love to others by being kind and patient, too. Being patient means not being bossy or complaining. How can you show patience when waiting for a turn to swing on the swings?** (Don't whine or complain. Stand and wait quietly.)

# Worship Center

God's Word
"Love is patient, love is kind."
1 Corinthians 13:4
God's Word & Me
I can show love for others
by being kind and patient.

## Collect

Bible, *Shake It Up!* songbook and cassette/CD and player, "Love Is" and "Helpin' Out" word charts (pp. 65 and 62 in songbook).

## Sing to God

Play "Love Is." Invite children to sing along with you. **Let's sing a song that tells us what love is like.** Lead children in singing song and doing suggested motions. **It isn't always easy to be patient and kind. We can pray to God and ask for His help.**

## Hear and Say God's Word

Holding your Bible open to 1 Corinthians 13:4, say verse aloud. **When we're patient, it means we wait for our turn. We show love for others when we are kind and patient.** Children sit in a large circle. Lead children in repeating the verse several times. When saying the words "Love is patient," children stand. When saying "Love is kind," children sit down.

## Pray to God

**We can ask God to help us show love and be kind to others.** Volunteers complete the following sentence prayer by adding the name of someone they know: **Dear God, help me be kind to ___________.** Close prayer by asking for God's help to show patience.

## Sing to God

In closing the worship time, play "Helpin' Out." Invite children to sing along with you and do suggested motions. **This song tells us that when we help others, we show God's love. I saw many people helping out in class today. You all showed God's love!**

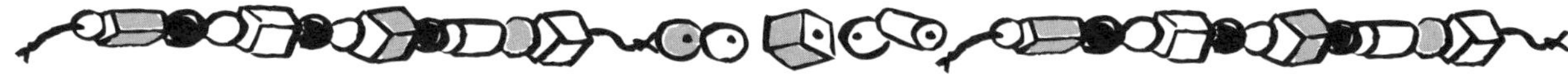

## Options

1. With parents' permission, videotape children as they sing songs and do the motions. Show videotape at the end of the session as parents come to pick up their children.
2. Children tell things they can do during the week to be kind to the people in their families. Print children's responses on a large sheet of paper. Display paper where parents will see it when they pick up their children.

 

Lesson 48

# Read-Aloud Story and Activity Center

## Collect

A copy of Story Picture 48 (pp. 101-102 from *Read-Aloud Story and Activity Book*) for each child and yourself, crayons or markers.

"Love is patient, love is kind." 1 Corinthians 13:4

## Prepare

Color your copy of Story Picture 48.

## Do

**Listen to find out what this girl is asking.** Read story and show completed Story Picture 48. Distribute pictures. Use conversation suggestions in Let's Talk About the Story as children complete their pages.

# Kindergarten Puzzle Center

## Collect

Copies of Puzzles 95 and 96 (p. 197 and p. 199 from *The Big Book of Kindergarten Puzzles*) for each child, pencils, crayons or markers.

## Do

Children complete the puzzles and color pages.

# Instant Activities

These activities can be used at any time during this session: when children need a change of pace, to extend the session, or during transition time at the beginning or end of the session.

## Collect

*The Big Book of Instant Activities.*

## Do

Guide children to complete "Put Your Hands" and/or "Color Choice" (p. 100 and/or p. 111 from *The Big Book of Instant Activities*).

Lesson 49

# Jonah and the Big Fish

## Bible Story

Jonah

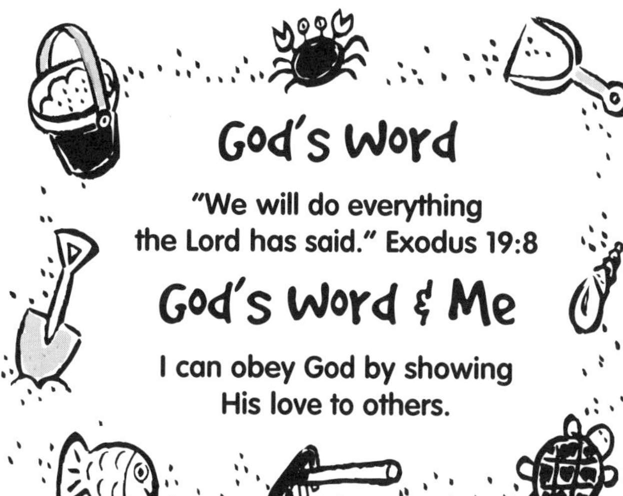
God's Word
"We will do everything the Lord has said." Exodus 19:8
God's Word & Me
I can obey God by showing His love to others.

## Teacher's Devotional

To young children, the story of Jonah may be mainly about a storm and a big fish. But to us it's much more. Truthfully, each of us probably thinks of some group of people as outsiders.

For Jonah, the outsiders were the Ninevites. Nineveh was considered the great city of the Assyrian empire and would later become its capital. At the time, Nineveh was Israel's greatest threat. The brutal and cruel acts of the Ninevites certainly showed them to be enemies of God. Wasn't Jonah right to hate God's enemies? What would possess the righteous, holy God of Israel to command Jonah to go straight into the middle of God's enemies and warn them of His coming judgment?

Love. God's love for these enemies was so serious that He didn't let Jonah run away from responsibility. Again, God was actively involved in rescuing a pagan kingdom—something righteous Israelites would never have approved!

God's powerful love for the outsiders in our lives is just as great as it is for us. The generosity of God's grace may make us a little uncomfortable. But God commands us to leave our prejudices behind and bring His love to others. Ask God to show you a way to communicate His love by action, not mere words. Then don't run. Obey!

## Teacher's Planning

1. Choose which centers you will provide and the order in which children will participate in them. For tips on schedule planning, see page 7.

2. Plan who will lead each center. For staffing tips and ideas, see page 21.

Lesson 49

# Active Game Center: Yes and No

## Collect

Bible.

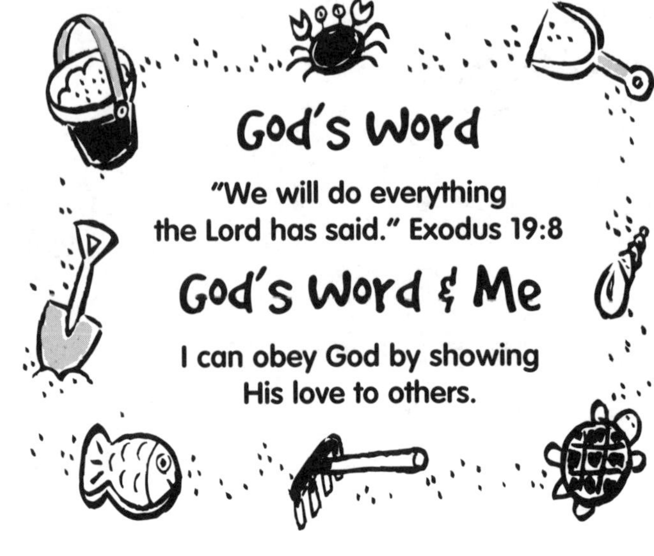
God's Word
"We will do everything the Lord has said." Exodus 19:8
God's Word & Me
I can obey God by showing His love to others.

## Do

1. Lead children in practicing ways to say "yes" and "no" with different parts of their bodies. **One way to say "yes" is to nod our heads.** Nod head with children. **We can say "no" by shaking our heads.** Shake head with children. Repeat with other body parts (elbows, shoulders, feet, etc.). For instance, children wave elbows up and down to say "yes" and wave elbows back and forth to say "no."
2. Ask children simple questions. **Do you like pizza? Answer with your elbows!** Children answer by waving their elbows up and down or back and forth. Repeat with different questions (**Do you have a brother? Do you like to play soccer? Are you wearing red?**), asking children to answer with different parts of their bodies.

## Talk About

- **Our Bible says, "We will do everything the Lord has said." "Lord" is another name for God. Obeying means we say "yes" to what God tells us to do. Let's say "yes" and "no" with different parts of our bodies.**
- **Anthony, you showed that you like pizza by moving your elbows up and down. You know how to obey!**
- **We obey God when we show love to others. Leslie, who are some of the people you love? What are some ways to show love to the people in your family?** (Obey what they tell you. Give them hugs. Say kind words to them.)

### For Younger Children

Give direct instructions instead of asking questions and have children use simple motions (stand up, sit down, touch nose) to answer. **If you like pizza, stand up!** Repeat using similar instructions.

### For Older Children

Children take turns asking questions for the other children to answer with their bodies.

# Art Center: Paper-Plate Fish

## Collect

Bible, markers, paper plates, scissors, stapler.

## Prepare

Draw lines on paper plates as shown in sketch a.

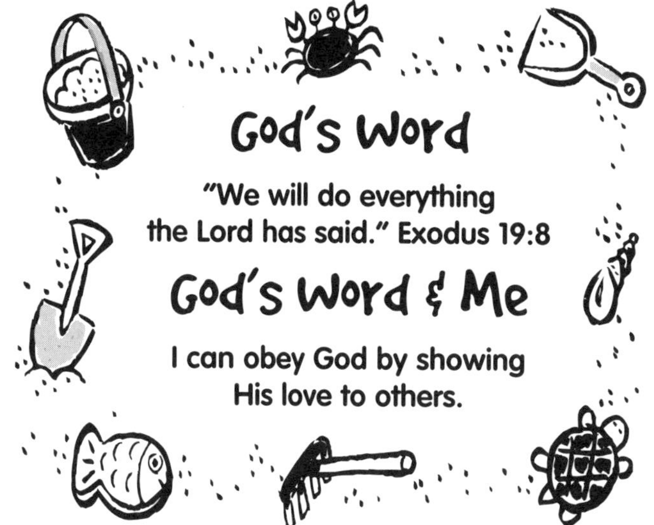
God's Word
"We will do everything the Lord has said." Exodus 19:8
God's Word & Me
I can obey God by showing His love to others.

## Do

1. Give each child a paper plate. Assist as each child cuts along lines. The opening becomes the fish's mouth. The cutoff portion is stapled opposite the opening and becomes the tail.
2. Children use markers to decorate their fish, adding facial features, scales, fins, etc. (see sketch b).

a.
cut
cut
b.

## Talk About

- **In our Bible story, God told Jonah to go to Nineveh to tell the people an important message. Jonah disobeyed God and tried to go somewhere else! But God sent a storm and a big fish to give Jonah another chance to obey. Let's make a fish to remind us of Jonah!**
- **Our Bible says, "We will do everything the Lord has said." "Lord" is another name for God. When we do what God says, we obey Him.**
- **One thing God tells us to do is to show His love to others. We obey God when we show love to others!** Pray briefly, **Dear God, please help us to show love to others.**
- **Gabriel, who is someone you can show love to? Your brother Jaime? What can you do to show love to Jaime?**

## For Younger Children

Before class, cut triangular pieces from paper plates and staple to form the fish tails.

## For Older Children

Thin glue with water in a shallow pan. Children use brushes to apply thinned glue to paper plates. Children tear off pieces of tissue paper for scales and place onto glue. Children may layer several colors of tissue paper to make fish with interesting color blends/combinations.

Lesson 49

# Block Center: Block Boats

## Collect

Bible, blocks.

## Do

Children lay blocks in the shape of a boat and then climb inside and pretend to row the boat to go on a trip.

### God's Word

**"We will do everything the Lord has said." Exodus 19:8**

### God's Word & Me

**I can obey God by showing His love to others.**

## Talk About

- **In today's Bible story, a man named Jonah did not want to obey God. Jonah tried to run away by sailing away on a boat. God sent a big storm to show Jonah that he needed to obey God. Let's use our blocks to make a boat and pretend to go on a trip.**
- **Kevin, where do you want to go in our boat? Let's pretend we're in a hurry and row very fast. Now let's pretend we're tired and row very slowly.**
- **Our Bible says, "We will do everything the Lord has said." "Lord" is another name for God. When we do what God says, we obey Him. We can obey God by showing His love to others.**
- **One way to show love is to help each other. How can we help each other build a boat? How can we help each other when it's time to clean up?**

## For Younger Children

Lay masking tape on the floor in the shape of a boat. Children place blocks on the masking-tape line to outline boat. (Note: Remove masking tape immediately after activity.)

## For Older Children

Children act out story action as you briefly retell story events (see Bible Story Center in this lesson). Provide a blanket, a pillow and some buckets or large cups. One child pretends to be Jonah and lies down to sleep. Other children pretend to be sailors, bailing water out of the boat during the storm. A large box can be the fish that swallows Jonah.

Expect to retell story several times so that different children can pretend to be Jonah.

Lesson 49

# Science Center: Sinkers and Floaters

## Collect

Bible; dishpan or baking dish with water; several towels; small objects that float or sink (toy people, rock, marker, eraser, leaf, orange, sponge, etc.), at least one item for each child.

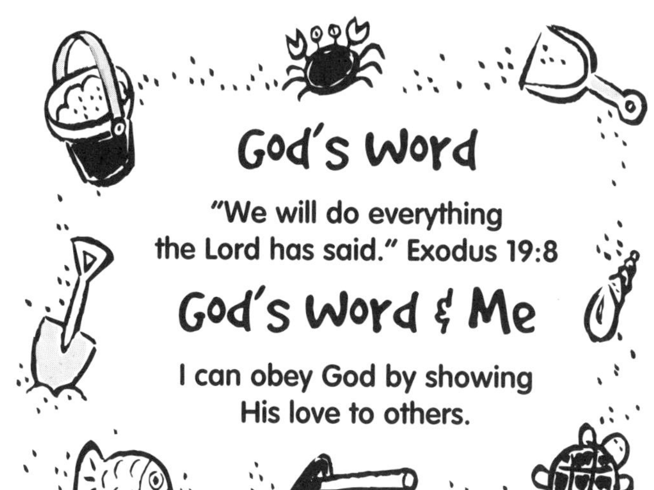
God's Word
"We will do everything the Lord has said." Exodus 19:8
God's Word & Me
I can obey God by showing His love to others.

## Prepare

Place container of water on a towel. (Note: If you have a large class, prepare one setup for every four to six children.)

## Do

1. Children take turns placing objects in water. Before each object is placed into water, ask children to predict whether the item will float or sink.
2. Children remove items from water, placing items that float in one pile and items that sink in another pile. Children dry hands and clean up spills with towels. (Optional: Do this activity outdoors.)

## Talk About

- **Our Bible says, "We will do everything the Lord has said." "Lord" is another name for God. In His Word, the Bible, God tells us to love others. When we show love to others, we obey God. Let's show God's love to others as we find things that sink and things that float.**
- **Alanna, I see you wiping up some water that spilled. Thank you for helping us. Helping others is a way to show love. What is a way you help others in your house?**
- **Max, I know you really want a turn to put something in the water. Thank you for waiting for your turn. You are patient. Being patient is a way to show love.**

## For Younger Children

Provide more than one dishpan with water so that children have several opportunities to experiment with items. If you use more than two dishpans, be sure to have additional helpers.

## For Older Children

Print "sink" on a sheet of construction paper. Print "float" on another sheet of construction paper. As children remove items from water, they place items near the appropriate sign.

 

Lesson 49 • Jonah

# Bible Story Center

## Collect

Bible, Picture 26 from *Bible Story Pictures*.

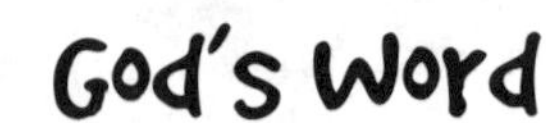


**"We will do everything the Lord has said." Exodus 19:8**

### God's Word & Me

**I can obey God by showing His love to others.**

## Tell the Story

Use the pictured motions (keywords in bold) or show Picture 26. For older children, tell the version of the story on the back of Picture 26.

**Have you ever been fishing? How big was the fish you caught? Listen to hear about a very big fish that caught a man!**

Jonah told people messages from God. One day, God told Jonah, "**Go** to Nineveh. Tell the people that they have disobeyed Me."

But Jonah did NOT like the people of Nineveh, so instead of going to Nineveh, Jonah got onto a boat that was going the other way! He did not want to obey God. He went down into the bottom of the boat and went to **sleep**.

God sent a big storm. The waves were crashing. All the sailors were very afraid! But Jonah knew that God had sent the storm because Jonah had disobeyed. Jonah told the sailors, "Throw me into the ocean. Then the storm will stop." One, two, THREE! The soldiers threw Jonah into the water. Sure enough, the waves stopped crashing.

The boat was safe. But Jonah was in the ocean! Then God sent a huge **fish**. The fish opened its mouth wide and WHOOSH! Jonah was in the belly of the big fish!

Jonah began to pray. He asked God to forgive him. He thanked God for rescuing him, even though he had disobeyed. Jonah prayed and he waited. Then God sent that big fish close to land. The fish began to cough and choke and AACK!—he coughed Jonah right up onto the beach! Then God talked to Jonah again.

God said, "**Go**! Tell those people they have disobeyed Me!" And this time Jonah obeyed! He went to Nineveh. He told everyone he saw that they had disobeyed God. The people listened. Then they obeyed God. They asked God to forgive them! And God did forgive them.

**At first, Jonah did not want to obey God. But God sent the big fish to show Jonah that he needed to obey God. What did the people in Nineveh do when Jonah told them they had disobeyed God?** (They listened and obeyed God.) **We obey God when we love other people. Who are some people you love? What can you do to show love to them?** (Give them a hug. Say kind words. Help them.)

Lesson 49

# Worship Center

## Collect

Bible, *Shake It Up!* songbook and cassette/CD and player, "Love Is" and "Helpin' Out" word charts (pp. 65 and 62 in songbook).

**God's Word**

**"We will do everything the Lord has said." Exodus 19:8**

**God's Word & Me**

**I can obey God by showing His love to others.**

## Sing to God

Play "Love Is." Invite children to sing along with you. **Let's sing a song that reminds us how to show God's love.** Lead children in singing song and doing suggested motions. **According to this song, two ways to show love are by being kind and by being patient. We obey God when we show His love to others by being kind and patient.**

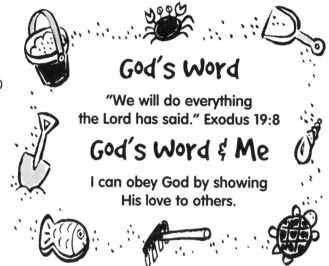

## Hear and Say God's Word

Holding your Bible open to Exodus 19:8, say verse aloud. **"Lord" is another name for God. We can learn what God says by reading His Word, the Bible. The Bible tells us ways to obey God by showing love to others.** Lead children in repeating the verse by echoing phrases after you: "We will do/everything/the Lord has said." Point to children when it is their turn to speak. Repeat verse several times in this manner.

## Pray to God

Lead children in prayer thanking God for His Word, the Bible, and that we can learn how to show love to others by reading the Bible. Close prayer by asking for His help to obey Him and show His love to others.

## Sing to God

In closing the worship time, play "Helpin' Out." Invite children to sing along with you and do suggested motions. **Helping others is way to obey God and show His love.**

## Options

1. During verse activity, lead children in saying the words in different manners (loudly, softly, in a high voice, in a low voice, whispering, quickly, slowly, etc.).
2. As part of the prayer activity, ask children to name people for whom they want to thank God and to ask for His help in showing love to them. Volunteers then choose one of the things mentioned and pray to God aloud.

 

# Read-Aloud Story and Activity Center

## Collect

A copy of Story Picture 49 (pp. 103-104 from *Read-Aloud Story and Activity Book*) for each child and yourself, crayons or markers.

## Prepare

Color your copy of Story Picture 49.

## Do

**Listen to find out how Sophie obeyed.** Read story and show completed Story Picture 49. Distribute pictures. Use conversation suggestions in Let's Talk About the Story as children complete their pages.

# Kindergarten Puzzle Center

## Collect

Copies of Puzzles 97 and 98 (p. 201 and p. 203 from *The Big Book of Kindergarten Puzzles*) for each child, pencils, crayons or markers.

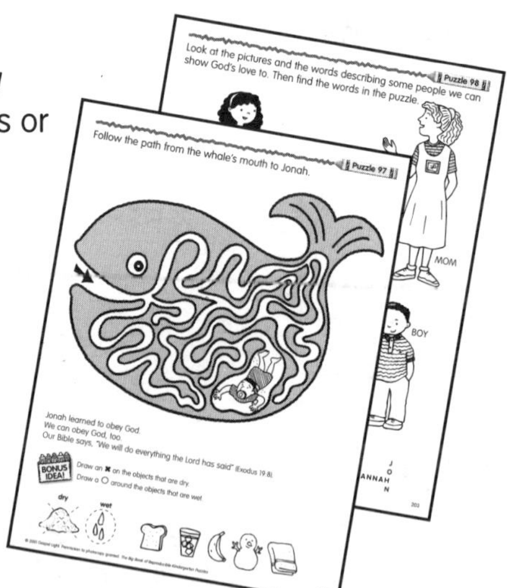


## Do

Children complete the puzzles and color pages.

# Instant Activities

These activities can be used at any time during this session: when children need a change of pace, to extend the session, or during transition time at the beginning or end of the session.

## Collect

*The Big Book of Instant Activities.*

## Do

Guide children to complete "Amazing Animal List" and/or "Popcorn Game" (p. 16 and/or p. 100 from *The Big Book of Instant Activities*).

Lesson 50

# Josiah Reads God's Words

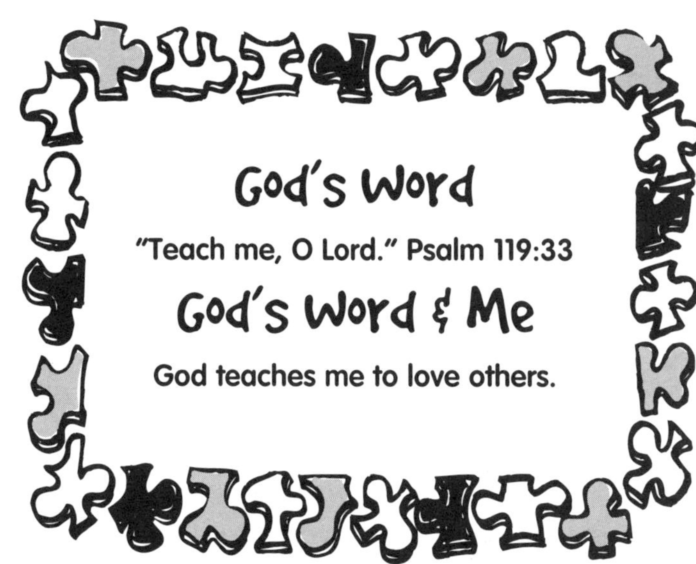
God's Word
"Teach me, O Lord." Psalm 119:33
God's Word & Me
God teaches me to love others.

## Bible Story

2 Chronicles 34—35:19

## Teacher's Devotional

Josiah was only eight years old when his father was assassinated and he was crowned king. While he was still young, Josiah turned his attention to seek the one true God (see 2 Chronicles 34). Although he did not yet know about the law of God, he had a heart full of desire to make things right. He not only removed all Baal worship in Judah but also went personally to the northern areas of Israel, even into the ruins around them, to destroy the Asherah poles and crush the idols to powder. He acted fully on everything he knew to obey God.

One way Josiah showed love for God was to repair the Temple. During the renovation, the Book of the Law was found. When Josiah heard the law God gave to Moses, he tore his clothes and humbled himself. Instead of thinking he had done enough already, Josiah called his people together to hear God's law and to promise with their king that they would obey what they had heard.

Josiah is a wonderful example of what one person can do when he or she sets out to please God by obeying everything he or she already knows to do. Help your children understand that they, too, can please God by obeying the things they already know about Him and His desires for them.

## Teacher's Planning

1. Choose which centers you will provide and the order in which children will participate in them. For tips on schedule planning, see page 7.
2. Plan who will lead each center. For staffing tips and ideas, see page 21.

 

# Active Game Center: Hearts of Color

## Collect

Bible; red, yellow and blue construction paper, scissors; tape; three boxes.

## Prepare

Cut several hearts from each color of construction paper. Tape a different colored heart to each box. Place boxes in different places in the activity area. Scatter other hearts around the classroom.

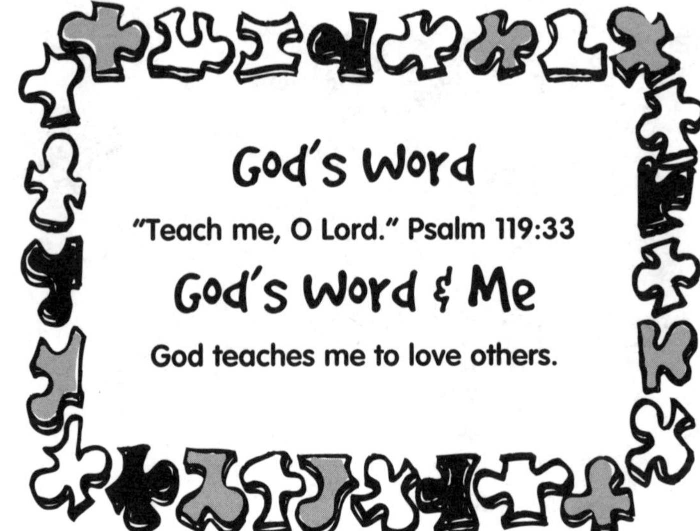

**God's Word**

**"Teach me, O Lord." Psalm 119:33**

**God's Word & Me**

**God teaches me to love others.**

## Do

1. Children search classroom to find hearts. When a heart is found, the child places it in the box with the same colored heart taped to it. Continue until all the hearts are found and placed in a box.
2. Scatter hearts and play game again, assigning a different color to each child. Vary the way children move as they search for the hearts (hopping on one foot, walking heel-to-toe, patting head, etc.).

## Talk About

- **Our Bible says, "Teach me, O Lord." "Lord" is another name for God. One of the things God teaches us is to love each other. Let's play a game with hearts to remind us to love each other.**
- **Becky, who is a person you love? What are some things you can do to show your mom that you love her?** (Obey what she says. Give her hugs. Say kind words to her. Help her.)
- Pray briefly, **Dear God, help us learn to love others.**

## For Younger Children

Children do not sort hearts but place all the hearts they find into a single box.

## For Older Children

For each heart they drop into a box, children say the words of the verse or name a person to whom they can show God's love.

Lesson 50

# Art Center: Scroll Script

## Collect

Bible, shelf paper or adding machine paper, measuring stick, scissors, markers, craft sticks, tape, rubber bands.

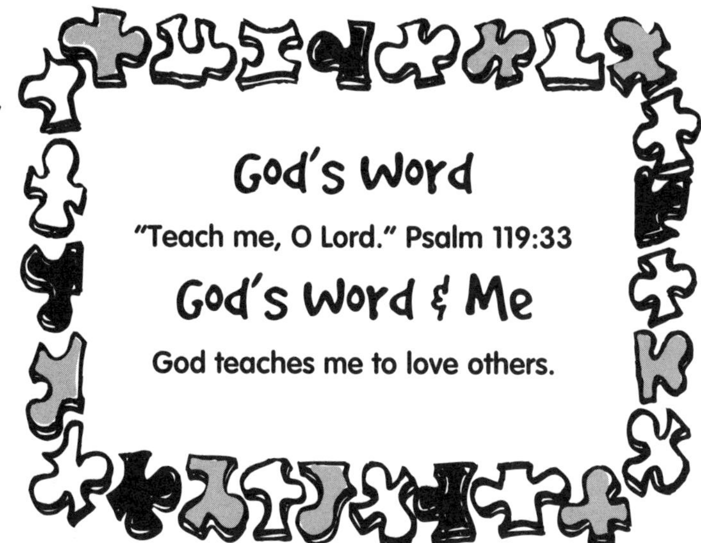
God's Word
"Teach me, O Lord." Psalm 119:33
God's Word & Me
God teaches me to love others.

## Prepare

Cut one 4x18-inch (10x45.5-cm) length of shelf paper or one 18-inch (45.5-cm) length of adding machine paper for each child.

## Do

1. Using markers, children decorate a length of paper.
2. When scrolls are decorated, give two craft sticks to each child. Children tape a craft stick to each end of their scrolls. Rolling from each end, children roll up their scrolls. Children slip rubber bands over scrolls to keep them from unrolling.

## Talk About

- **In today's Bible story, King Josiah read God's Word to all the people. In Bible times, God's Word was written on a scroll, which is like a long rolled-up sheet of paper. Let's make some scrolls of our own.**
- **King Josiah read God's Word aloud so that the people would learn from it. We learn from reading God's Word, the Bible. Sherilyn, who reads God's Word to you?**
- **Our Bible says, "Teach me, O Lord." "Lord" is another name for God. One thing God teaches us is to love others. Matthew, I saw you hand Kerry a marker. It was kind of you to help her. You know how to show love to others!**

## For Younger Children

Instead of shelf or adding machine paper, children decorate sheets of white paper. When finished, assist children in rolling up papers. Tie closed with a length of yarn or ribbon.

## For Older Children

On a large sheet of paper, print "Teach me, O Lord." Children copy the words of the verse on their scrolls.

Lesson 50

# Block Center: Tidy Up

## Collect

Bible, blocks, cleaning materials (feather dusters, dust cloths, whisk brooms, squirt bottles, paper towels, etc.).

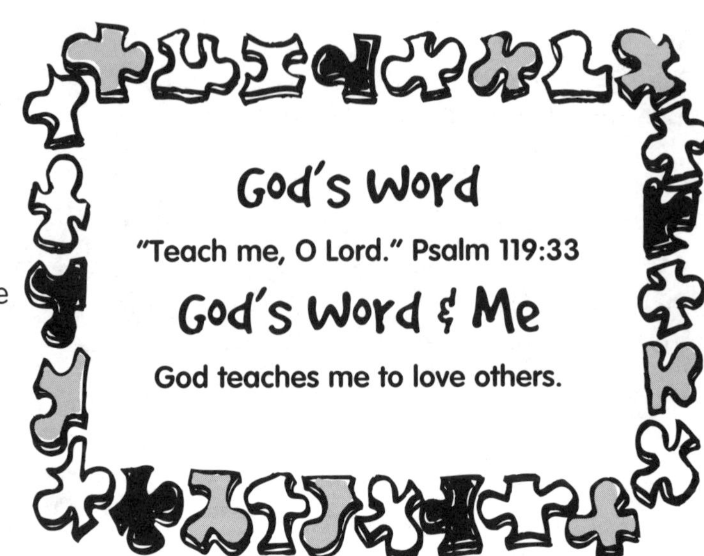

God's Word
"Teach me, O Lord." Psalm 119:33
God's Word & Me
God teaches me to love others.

## Do

1. Children use blocks to outline a square large enough to walk inside to be a pretend house.
2. Using cleaning materials, children act out cleaning up the pretend house: sweeping the floor, dusting the block walls, etc.

## Talk About

- **Our Bible says, "Teach me, O Lord." "Lord" is another name for God. God gave us His Word, the Bible, so that we can learn what God wants us to do. One thing God wants us to do is love others. We can show love to the people we live with by cleaning up our house. Let's build a pretend house and act out ways to clean up!**
- **Vicki, you are doing a good job with that feather duster. What do you dust at your home? What are some other ways you help your family at your home?** (Set the table. Feed the dogs.)
- **Neal, who taught you how to use a broom? Moms and dads teach us lots of important things. What is something else your mom taught you to do?**

### For Younger Children

Make a large square with yarn. Children build pretend house by placing blocks on yarn.

### For Older Children

Children build a pretend Temple. Print the words "Teach me, O Lord" on a sheet of white paper. Crumple paper into a ball. Crumple several more sheets of paper to create several paper balls. After children have built the Temple, scatter paper balls on its floor. Children gather paper balls as part of their cleaning of the Temple. After balls are gathered, children open papers to find the one with the Bible verse.

Lesson 50

# Science Center: Scroll Search

God's Word
"Teach me, O Lord." Psalm 119:33
God's Word & Me
God teaches me to love others.

## Collect

Bible, white paper, marker, rubber band, shallow cardboard box, sand, 1- to 2-inch (2.5- to 5-cm) paintbrushes; optional—coins, crayons, small blocks, etc.

## Prepare

Print Bible verse on a sheet of white paper, roll up tightly and secure with rubber band. (Optional: Prepare a scroll according to Art Center directions.) Fill box with a layer of sand deep enough to hide scroll you prepared. Hide scroll. (Note: If you have a large class, prepare more than one setup or take children outside to a playground sandbox and hide more than one scroll.)

## Do

Children use brushes to brush sand and find hidden scroll. Assist child who finds scroll in opening and reading scroll. Repeat as time and interest allow. (Optional: Hide coins, crayons, small blocks and other items for children to find.)

## Talk About

- **In today's Bible story, the men cleaning the Temple found a scroll. Let's search for a scroll the way scientists search for things from long ago.**
- **Scientists use brushes to find things buried in sand. Using brushes helps the scientists not to break the objects they are looking for.**
- **Our Bible says, "Teach me, O Lord." "Lord" is another name for God. God teaches us when we read His Word, the Bible. In Bible times, God's Word was written on scrolls like this one.** Pray briefly, **Dear God, help me to learn from Your Word, the Bible.**

## For Younger Children

Instead of using paintbrushes, younger children simply reach into sand and search by hand.

## For Older Children

Print "Teach me, O Lord" on paper scraps, one word on each scrap. Children hide paper scraps in the sand, use paintbrushes to find papers and then put them in correct verse order.

 

# Bible Story Center

## Collect

Bible, Picture 19 from *Bible Story Pictures*.

God's Word
"Teach me, O Lord." Psalm 119:33
God's Word & Me
God teaches me to love others.

## Tell the Story

Use the pictured motions (keywords in bold) or show Picture 19. For older children, tell the version of the story on the back of Picture 19.

**How do you help clean up here in our room? Listen to hear what some people found when they cleaned God's Temple.**

For many years, the **book** of God's Words had been lost. God's Temple was broken down and dirty. But young King Josiah loved God. One day he said, "It is time to clean the Temple. We need many helpers to make the Temple clean and beautiful."

Many people came to help. Some helpers swept and scrubbed the Temple. Swish, swish went their brooms. Some helpers fixed broken furniture. Bang, bang went their hammers. While the helpers worked hard, the Temple leader picked up something covered with dust. *What is this?* he wondered. Poof! He **blew** off the dust. "It's a scroll," he said. (A scroll is like a long rolled-up sheet of paper with writing on it.) Carefully he unrolled the scroll. He read a few words. Then he told the king's helper, "Here is a scroll with God's words written on it! King Josiah will want to see this!"

The helper **ran** to the king's house. "Look at this, King Josiah," he said. "The Temple leader found this scroll! It has God's words written on it."

King Josiah **listened** to one of his helpers read God's words. King Josiah loved God and wanted to obey God's words. He invited all of God's people to come to the Temple. Boys and girls, mothers and fathers, grandmothers and grandfathers came to hear God's words. King Josiah unrolled the Bible scroll and read God's words. The people listened.

King Josiah and the people promised to obey God's words. As long as King Josiah lived, he and the people obeyed God.

## God's Word & Me

**What did King Josiah do with God's words?** (Read them to all the people. Helped the people know how to obey God's words.) **We can obey God's words, too. God's Word teaches us to love others. Jenny, what can you do to love others in our class? When you are a good listener, you are showing love. Who can you show love to at home? How can you help your dad?**

# Worship Center

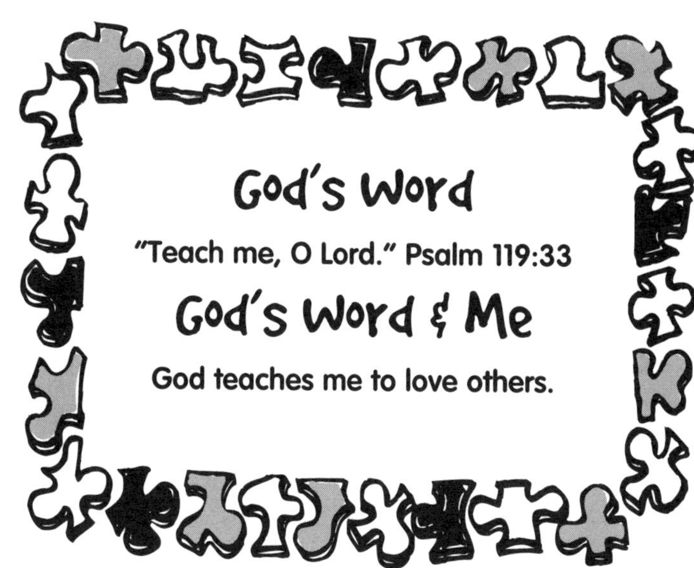
God's Word
"Teach me, O Lord." Psalm 119:33
God's Word & Me
God teaches me to love others.

## Collect

Bible, *Shake It Up!* songbook and cassette/CD and player, "Love Is" and "Helpin' Out" word charts (pp. 62 and 65 in songbook).

## Sing to God

Play "Love Is." Invite children to sing along with you. **Let's sing a song about some of the ways we can show God's love to others.** Lead children in singing song and doing suggested motions. **God's Word, the Bible, teaches us to love others. Who are some of the people you can show God's love to?**

## Hear and Say God's Word

Holding your Bible open to Psalm 119:33, say verse aloud. **"Lord" is another name for God. When we read the Bible, we are learning what God wants us to do.** Lead children in repeating the verse several times. As the children are repeating the verse with you, point to one child. Children say that child's name instead of the word "me." Repeat until every child's name has been used.

## Pray to God

**We can ask God to teach us to show love to others.** Invite volunteers to say this brief prayer individually or as a group: **Dear God, please help me learn to show love to others.**

## Sing to God

In closing the worship time, play "Helpin' Out." Invite children to sing along with you and do suggested motions. **This song tells us that the Bible tells us to show love to each other. Who is someone you are going to show love to today?**

## Options

1. If you take an offering during this time, explain to children that giving money is one way to show God's love to others. Briefly describe one mission project your church uses offering money to support.

2. Add motion to the verse activity. Children line up and follow the first child in the line, walking around the classroom. Say verse aloud, in the manner described above, pointing to the first child in the line. That child says his or her name and then moves to the end of the line. The next child becomes the line leader. Repeat verse until every child has had a chance to be the line leader.

# Read-Aloud Story and Activity Center

## Collect

A copy of Story Picture 50 (pp. 105-106 from *Read-Aloud Story and Activity Book*) for each child and yourself, crayons or markers.

## Prepare

Color your copy of Story Picture 50.

## Do

**Listen to find out who this cake is for.** Read story and show completed Story Picture 50. Distribute pictures. Use conversation suggestions in Let's Talk About the Story as children complete their pages.

# Kindergarten Puzzle Center

## Collect

Copies of Puzzles 99 and 100 (p. 205 and p. 207 from *The Big Book of Kindergarten Puzzles*) for each child, pencils, crayons or markers.

## Do

Children complete the puzzles and color pages.

# Instant Activities

These activities can be used at any time during this session: when children need a change of pace, to extend the session, or during transition time at the beginning or end of the session.

## Collect

*The Big Book of Instant Activities.*

## Do

Guide children to complete "Marching, Marching" and/or "Telephone" (p. 98 and/or p.123 from *The Big Book of Instant Activities*).

Lesson 51

# Jeremiah obeys

## Bible Story

Jeremiah 36

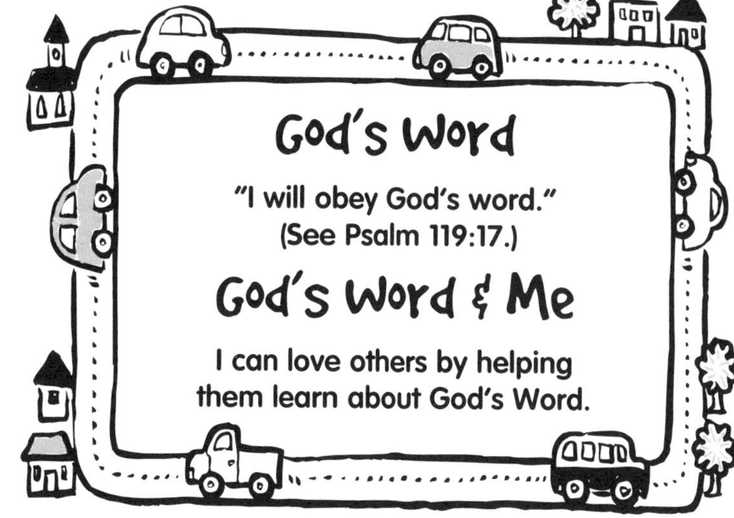
God's Word
"I will obey God's word."
(See Psalm 119:17.)
God's Word & Me
I can love others by helping them learn about God's Word.

## Teacher's Devotional

There must have been times when Jeremiah felt that being a prophet was very frustrating! God had given him strong words of warning for His people. Danger was coming!

Some people listened seriously to the reading of Jeremiah's scroll. But as King Jehoiakim listened to God's words, he cut the scroll off bit by bit with his knife, throwing the pieces into the fire. And the king's attitude didn't go unnoticed by his subjects! Even after Jehoiakim's fall from power, his subjects followed his example of rebellious disregard. They ignored the seriousness of Jeremiah's further warning and angrily threw the prophet into a cistern.

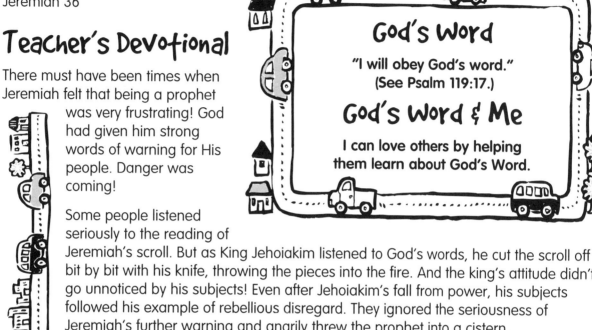

We dare not be like King Jehoiakim and disregard God's Word as it applies to any area of our lives. Just as with the king, our little "subjects" see and absorb our attitudes; they will imitate any disregard we might display. Instead, we should be like Jeremiah, diligently obeying God's commands. And when we repeat the same truths time after time as Jeremiah did, we need not feel frustrated. Instead, we can ask God to keep us faithful. Even when children seem not to hear, they absorb truth—from our attitudes first and then from our words.

## Teacher's Planning

1. Choose which centers you will provide and the order in which children will participate in them. For tips on schedule planning, see page 7.
2. Plan who will lead each center. For staffing tips and ideas, see page 21.

Lesson 51

# Active Game Center: Hidden Bible

## Collect

Bible.

## God's Word

**"I will obey God's word."**
**(See Psalm 119:17.)**

## God's Word & Me

**I can love others by helping them learn about God's Word.**

## Do

1. Select a volunteer to close his or her eyes as you hide the Bible in the classroom. Be sure Bible can be seen but is not in too obvious a place. **Let's help Kelly find the Bible. Don't make any noise when she is far from the Bible. Start clapping when she moves close to it.**
2. Volunteer begins to move around classroom. Lead children in clapping faster and louder as the volunteer moves closer and closer to the Bible. Repeat with new volunteers as time allows. (Note: If you have a large class, call on two volunteers at a time.)

## Talk About

- **In our Bible story Jeremiah said God's words out loud, so Baruch** (buh-ROOK) **could write them down. We can know God's words by reading the Bible. Let's play a game to find a Bible.**
- **Ethan, who reads to you from the Bible? I'm glad your mom reads Bible stories to you.**
- **What do we do at church to learn about God's Word, the Bible? Diego, when you listen to Bible stories and say Bible verses, you are learning God's Word!**
- **Our Bible says, "I will obey God's word." To obey God's Word means that we do the good things the Bible tells us to do.** Pray briefly, **Thank You, God, for Your Word, the Bible.**

## For Younger Children

Give verbal instructions to help children find the Bible: **The Bible is near a chair.**

## For Older Children

Instead of finding a hidden Bible, children search for an index card on which you have printed the words of the Bible verse. Each time a child finds the card, he or she reads the verse, or read the verse for the child. Other children echo the words of the verse.

# Art Center: Binding Books

## Collect

Bible, yarn, scissors, measuring stick, tape, white paper, markers, construction paper, hole punch.

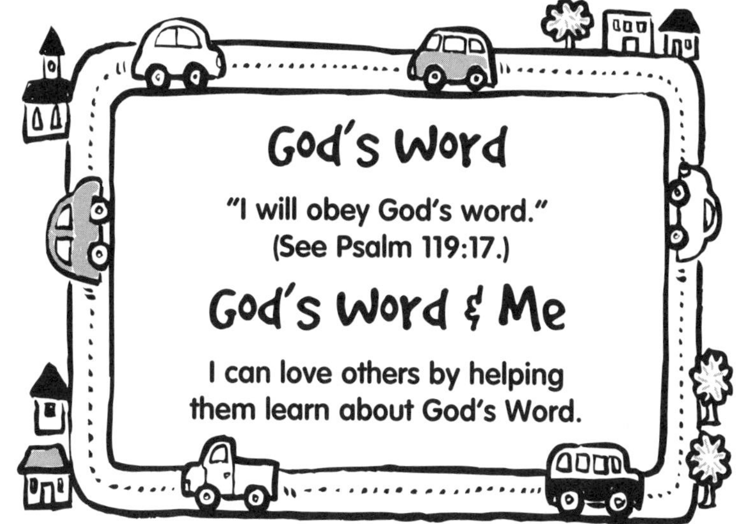
God's Word
"I will obey God's word."
(See Psalm 119:17.)
God's Word & Me
I can love others by helping them learn about God's Word.

## Prepare

Cut yarn into 18-inch (45.5-cm) lengths. Wrap tape around one end to make a needle. Three or four times on a sheet of white paper, print "obeys God's Word." Make copies and cut phrases apart so that each child has a phrase. Fold sheets of construction paper in half and punch eight holes along the folded edges.

## Do

1. Help children tie the untaped yarn end to the top hole of folded construction paper. Children sew yarn through holes to bind books. Make sure books lie flat when opened. Tie yarn around bottom hole and trim off excess yarn.
2. Children print their names inside of books. Under his or her name, each child tapes a copy of the phrase "obeys God's Word." Children use markers to decorate books.

## Talk About

- **Our Bible says, "I will obey God's word." God's Word is the Bible. Let's make books about obeying God's Word!**
- **Thank you, Pam, for handing Trey his yarn. God's Word says to help others. You obeyed God by helping Trey.**
- **Bryan, who could you show your book to? Showing others your book is a way to help them learn about God's Word.** Pray briefly, **Dear God, help us obey Your Word, the Bible. We want to help others learn about the Bible, too.**

## For Younger Children

Instead of sewing a binding, children simply decorate folded sheets of construction paper. Print children's names on insides of books.

## For Older Children

On the book covers, make dots to spell the word "obey." Children trace over dots to write the word.

 

Lesson 51

# Block Center: Building Blocks

## Collect

Bible, blocks; optional—stickers.

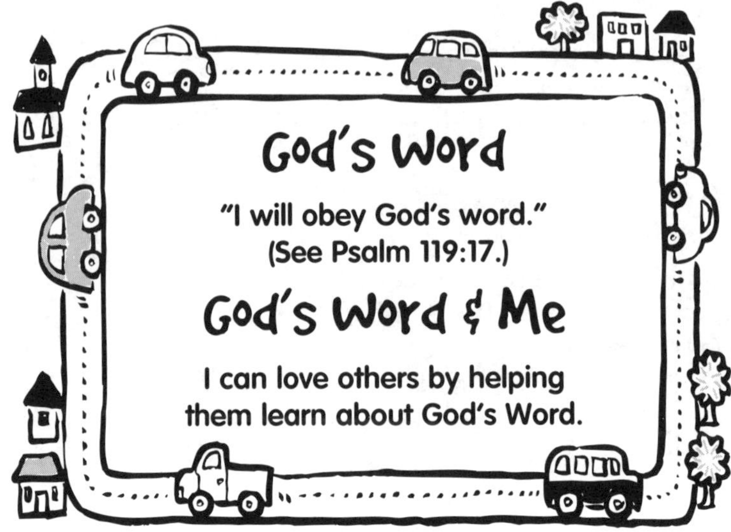
God's Word
"I will obey God's word."
(See Psalm 119:17.)
God's Word & Me
I can love others by helping them learn about God's Word.

## Do

Children build freely with blocks. Watch to observe the ways children interact with each other. When a child does something that demonstrates a biblical principle, comment on it, using the child's name. **Thank you, Sam, for handing Devon a long block. You helped her. Helping others is what our Bible tells us to do.** (Optional: Whenever you comment on the way a child is obeying God's Word, give him or her a sticker to wear. Make sure each child receives a sticker.)

## Talk About

- **In our Bible story today, people were not obeying God. They were doing many wrong things. Let's build with blocks and talk about ways to obey God's Word, the Bible. When we obey, it helps others learn God's Word, too.**
- **The Bible tells us to love each other. Claire, who is someone who showed love to you today? Your mom obeyed the Bible when she showed you love!**
- **Our Bible says, "I will obey God's word." Harry, who is someone you love? You can show love to your brother by telling him about God's Word.**
- Pray briefly, **Dear God, help us to obey Your Word. Help us tell it to others, so they can learn about Your Word, too.**

### For Younger Children

In addition to building blocks, provide a variety of cardboard boxes and other containers (grocery boxes, empty cereal boxes, potato chip cans, etc.) with which children build.

### For Older Children

Children build towers, saying the words to the verse as they add blocks to the tower. Ask children to build no higher than their chins.

# Science Center: Yarn Pictures

## Collect

Bible, yarn, measuring stick, scissors.

## Prepare

Cut one 10-inch (25.5-cm) piece of yarn and one 20-inch (51-cm) piece of yarn for each child and yourself.

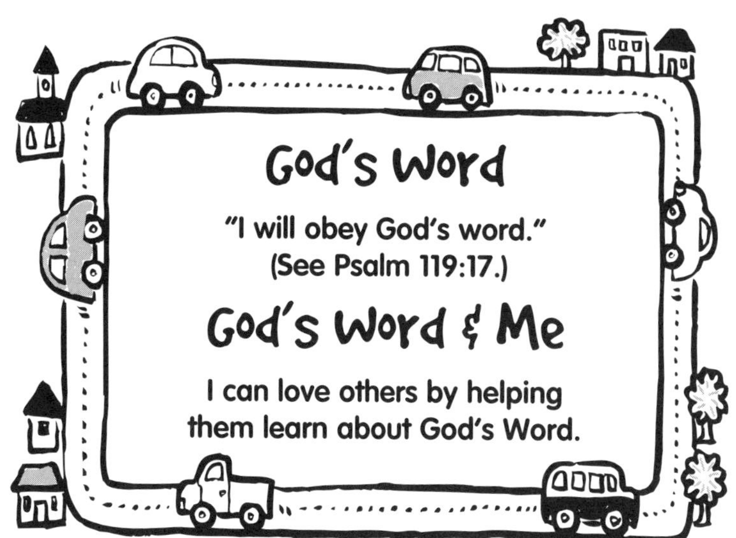
God's Word
"I will obey God's word."
(See Psalm 119:17.)
God's Word & Me
I can love others by helping them learn about God's Word.

## Do

Children sit at a table or on floor with yarn pieces. Using your own yarn pieces, make a shape (circle, triangle, square, wiggly line, numeral, letter, etc.) and ask the children to identify it. Children use their yarn pieces to duplicate the shape. Children compare the two different sizes of shapes made with the two different lengths of yarn.

## Talk About

- **Our Bible says, "I will obey God's word." To obey means to do what we are told to do. You can use your yarn to follow my directions and make different shapes!**
- **One way to learn what the Bible says is to listen to Bible stories. Justin, when are some times you listen to Bible stories?**
- **We can show love to others by helping them learn about God's Word, the Bible. Patti, who is someone you can tell God's words to? What could you tell your friend about the Bible?**
- Pray briefly, **Dear God, help us love others and help them learn about Your Word, the Bible.**

## For Younger Children

Instead of using yarn to make the shapes, children glue yarn designs to a sheet of paper.

## For Older Children

Increase the challenge by providing a third, 30-inch (76-cm) length of yarn. Children compare small, medium and large shapes.

# Bible Story Center

## Collect

Bible, Picture 21 from *Bible Story Pictures.*

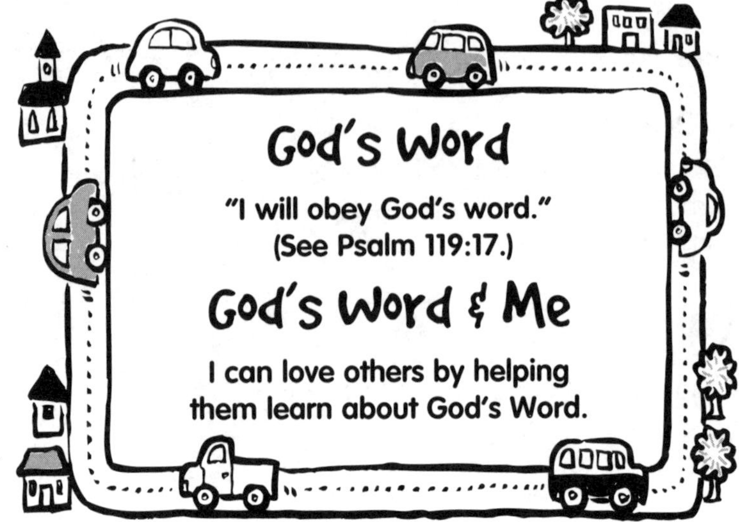
God's Word
"I will obey God's word."
(See Psalm 119:17.)
God's Word & Me
I can love others by helping them learn about God's Word.

## Tell the Story

Use the pictured motions (keywords in bold) or show Picture 21. For older children, tell the version of the story on the back of Picture 21.

**What words or letters do you know how to write? Listen to find out about some words a man wrote down.**

Jeremiah told the people to **love** and obey God. But the people were not obeying God. God still loved the people. He wanted them to stop doing what was wrong. God told Jeremiah to write down God's very important words.

Jeremiah called his helper Baruch (buh-ROOK). Jeremiah said the messages from God out loud. Baruch **wrote** the messages down on a scroll. (A scroll is like a long rolled-up sheet of paper with writing on it.)

"Take the scroll to the Temple and read it to the people," Jeremiah told Baruch. The Temple was the place where God's people came to pray and learn about God.

Baruch took the scroll to God's Temple. He read it in a loud, clear voice. Some people went to King Jehoiakim (juh-HOY-uh-kuhm) and told him about the scroll.

The king ordered one of his helpers to bring the scroll to him. One of the king's helpers read it to him. The king was **angry** about what God's words said! The king grabbed a knife. He cut the scroll apart. He burned each piece in the fire!

The king may have thought he had gotten rid of God's words. But God told Jeremiah, "**Write** the scroll again." Jeremiah and Baruch obeyed God. They wrote another scroll just like the first one. Baruch read the scroll to the people again. But the king and the people did not listen. They kept doing what was wrong, so the sad things God said would happen, did happen.

## God's Word & Me

**How did Jeremiah and Baruch help people know about God's words?** (Wrote them down. Read them to people.) **Jeremiah wanted his friends to learn from God's words. His helper, Baruch, wrote them down for the people. We can show love to our family and friends by helping them learn about God's Word. What are some ways we can help others learn about the Bible?** (Tell them what the Bible says. Invite others to church. Sing a song about Jesus.)

# Worship Center

## Collect

Bible, *Shake It Up!* songbook and cassette/CD and player, "Helpin' Out" and "Love Is" word charts (pp. 62 and 65 in songbook).

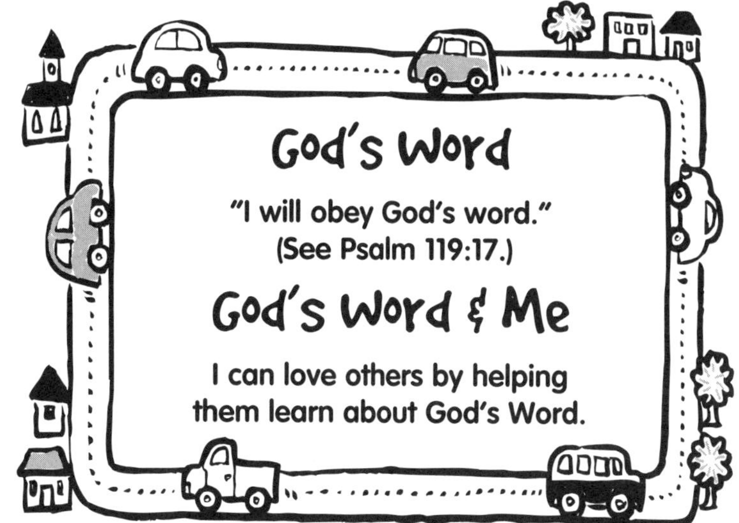
God's Word
"I will obey God's word."
(See Psalm 119:17.)
God's Word & Me
I can love others by helping them learn about God's Word.

## Sing to God

Play "Helpin' Out." Invite children to sing along with you. **The Bible says that one way to show God's love is by helping others.** Lead children in singing song and doing suggested motions. **God loves us and helps us all day long. We can love others, too! One way to love others is to help them learn about God's Word, the Bible.**

## Hear and Say God's Word

Holding your Bible open to Psalm 119:17, say verse aloud. **God loves us and will help us to obey His Word, the Bible. When we obey God's Word, it helps others learn about and obey God's Word, too.** Lead the children in repeating the verse using these motions: Point to self for "I"; point up for "God"; turn palms up and place hands together for "word" (Bible). Repeat several times.

## Pray to God

**The Bible tells us to obey God's Word. Let's pray to God and tell Him we want to obey Him.** Ask volunteers to say the words of the verse as a short prayer. Close, asking for God's help to obey His Word.

## Sing to God

In closing the worship time, play "Love Is." Invite children to sing along with you and do suggested motions. **God is patient and kind. We can show His love to others. One way to show love to others is to tell them words from the Bible.**

## Options

1. Older children lead other children in doing motions suggested for "Helpin' Out" and/or "Love Is."
2. Provide one or two rhythm instruments for children to use while singing "Helpin' Out" and "Love Is." Children hand the instruments to other children before each song is repeated.

 

# Read-Aloud Story and Activity Center

## Collect

A copy of Story Picture 51 (pp. 107-108 from *Read-Aloud Story and Activity Book*) for each child and yourself, crayons or markers.

## Prepare

Color your copy of Story Picture 51.

## Do

**Listen to find out where Daniel took a car.** Read story and show completed Story Picture 51. Distribute pictures. Use conversation suggestions in Let's Talk About the Story as children complete their pages.

# Kindergarten Puzzle Center

## Collect

Copies of Puzzles 101 and 102 (p. 209 and p. 211 from *The Big Book of Kindergarten Puzzles*) for each child, pencils, crayons or markers.

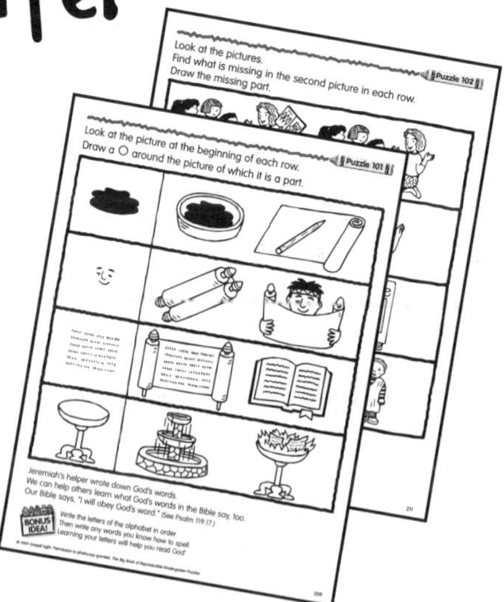


## Do

Children complete the puzzles and color pages.

# Instant Activities

These activities can be used at any time during this session: when children need a change of pace, to extend the session, or during transition time at the beginning or end of the session.

## Collect

*The Big Book of Instant Activities.*

## Do

Guide children to complete "How Does It Sound?" and/or "Growing" (p. 95 and/or p. 51 from *The Big Book of Instant Activities*).

 

Lesson 52

# Nehemiah Helps Build Walls

## Bible Story

Nehemiah 1—2; 4:1-6; 6:15,16; 12:27,43

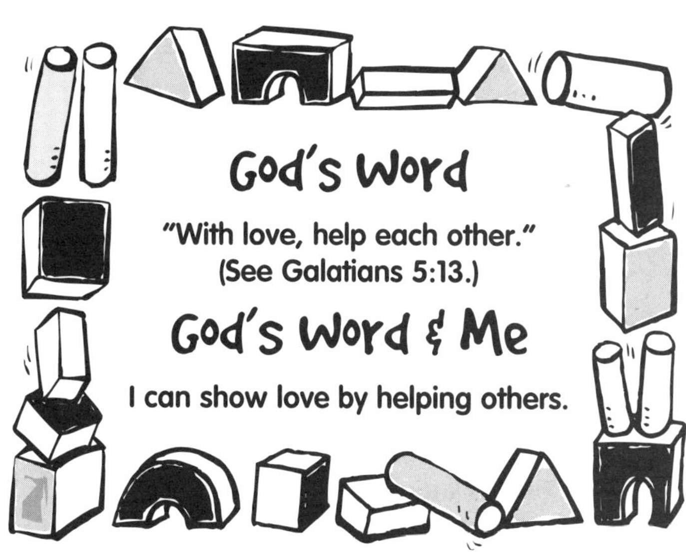
God's Word
"With love, help each other."
(See Galatians 5:13.)
God's Word & Me
I can show love by helping others.

## Teacher's Devotional

Nehemiah seemed to have all the advantages a man could have in Babylon. With an important position in the royal court, he was well taken care of. Exposed to all the culture and wealth Babylon could provide, he seemed to be set for life. He was blessed in Babylon!

When his brother visited him and told him about Jerusalem's destruction, Nehemiah could have said, "Look, things are good here. God has blessed me in Babylon. Jerusalem is a long way away. I'm sorry, but the wall isn't my problem!" However, the splendor of the royal court had not seduced Nehemiah. He could not forget the needs of his people and his family left in Jerusalem, no matter how lovely things were for him.

Sometimes it's easy to forget the larger picture. We're blessed where we are. The problems of other people in other places don't really affect us, so why bother ourselves? Maybe the problems are so big and complex, we feel there is nothing we can do to solve them, so why try? It's important to remember that although every problem doesn't affect us personally and although we won't be able to solve every problem we hear about, we are always able to pray about those problems and for the people involved. And like Nehemiah, when we begin to pray for others with an open heart, we may find that God wants to make us part of His answer!

## Teacher's Planning

1. Choose which centers you will provide and the order in which children will participate in them. For tips on schedule planning, see page 7.
2. Plan who will lead each center. For staffing tips and ideas, see page 21.

Lesson 52

# Active Game Center: Touch of Color

## Collect

Bible; construction paper in red, green, blue and yellow; ruler; scissors; masking tape.

## Prepare

Cut a 1-inch (2.5-cm) square from each color of construction paper for each child. Place a masking-tape loop on the back of each square.

God's Word
"With love, help each other."
(See Galatians 5:13.)
God's Word & Me
I can show love by helping others.

## Do

1. **Everyone take a square and place it on your arm.** Encourage children to choose different colors and direct them to place squares on different body parts (knees, elbows, feet, hands, etc.).
2. Give children different directions for touching each other according to where they put their colored squares. **Choose a partner and touch your red squares together!** Continue with other colors. Children switch partners for each round.

## Talk About

- **Our Bible says, "With love, help each other." We can show love by helping others. Let's help each other play a game.**
- **Tina, you touched your red square to Natalie's! You helped each other play the game!**
- **It is fun to help our friends. Who else can we help?** (Parents, brothers, sisters, teachers.)
- **God helps us love other people.** Pray, **Dear God, please help us to show love and help others.**

## For Younger Children

Children touch paper squares to things in the room that are the same color.

## For Older Children

Children walk across the room while continuing to touch colors.

Lesson 52

# Art Center: Building the Wall Together

## Collect

Bible, construction paper, scissors, ruler, masking tape, butcher paper, markers, glue.

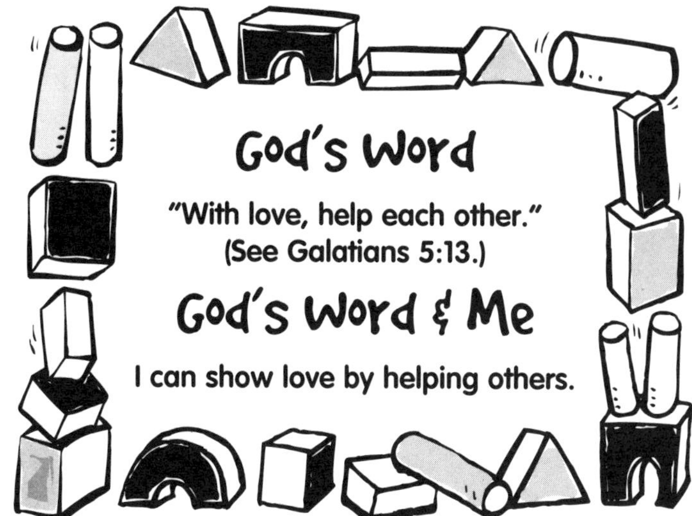
God's Word
"With love, help each other."
(See Galatians 5:13.)
God's Word & Me
I can show love by helping others.

## Prepare

Cut construction paper into differently sized rectangles with sides at least 4 inches (10 cm) long. Tape butcher paper to table.

## Do

1. Each child selects one or more construction-paper rectangles and uses markers to decorate rectangle(s).
2. Children glue rectangles to butcher paper to make a wall mural. Display mural on classroom or hallway wall.

## Talk About

- **In our Bible story today, Nehemiah and his friends rebuilt Jerusalem's broken walls. Let's help each other make a paper wall!**
- **Building the wall was hard work for Nehemiah and the people in Jerusalem. Some jobs seem hard because we don't want to do them. What is a job you or someone you know doesn't like to do?** (Make the bed. Pick up toys. Feed the dog.)
- **Jobs that are hard to do can be fun when we help each other! What is a job the people in your family help each other to do?** (Wash the car. Bake cookies.)
- **Our Bible says, "With love, help each other."** Pray briefly, **Dear God, help us obey You and show love by helping others.**

## For Younger Children

Cut rectangles that are all the same size for children to glue to butcher paper.

## For Older Children

Provide rectangles, triangles and squares for children to use in building paper walls.

Lesson 52

# Block Center: Building Together

## Collect

Bible, masking tape, marker, blocks, toy people.

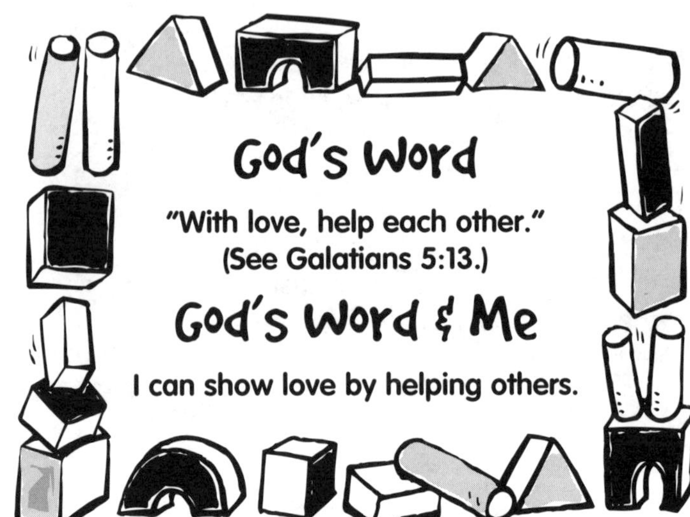
God's Word
"With love, help each other."
(See Galatians 5:13.)
God's Word & Me
I can show love by helping others.

## Prepare

With masking tape, outline an area on the floor to build a wall or walls. Use marker to divide masking tape into sections, one section for each child. (Note: Remove masking tape immediately after activity.)

## Do

1. Children choose a section of the masking-tape outline and build their section of the wall.
2. Children use toy people to carry on conversations about how the building is going, asking if someone needs help, stopping for a water break, etc.

## Talk About

- **In today's Bible story, Nehemiah and his friends rebuilt the walls of their city. Let's pretend these toy people are helping each other rebuild the city wall.**
- **The Bible says, "With love, help each other." We can show God's love by helping others.**
- **Natalie, what jobs do you have at your house? Is your job easier or harder when someone helps you?**
- **We show love to others when we help them. Dennis, how could you help your friend Aaron when you play at his house?** (Help pick up toys. Obey Aaron's mom.)

## For Younger Children

Children build constructions of their own choice. Encourage children to help each other.

## For Older Children

Provide small cardboard boxes or baskets for children to use in carrying blocks from one section of the wall to another.

# Science Center: Bread Spreads

## Collect

Bible, spreads (peanut butter, cream cheese, jelly, etc.), bowls, paper, marker, bread, paper plates, cookie cutters, plastic spoons and knives, napkins; optional—premoistened towelettes.

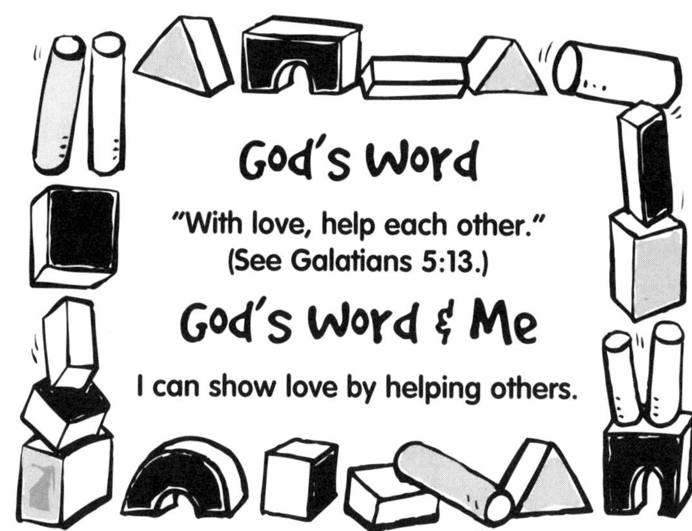
God's Word
"With love, help each other."
(See Galatians 5:13.)
God's Word & Me
I can show love by helping others.

## Prepare

Place spreads in individual bowls. Post a note alerting parents to the use of food in this activity. Also check registration forms for possible food allergies.

## Do

1. Children wash hands before beginning activity. (Optional: If you do not have a sink nearby, provide premoistened towelettes with which children clean their hands.)
2. Children help each other to make snacks. One child places a piece of bread on a paper plate. The next child cuts bread using a cookie cutter. Another spoons spread onto bread shape, and another child uses a knife to spread it. Children switch jobs occasionally. Children pass out plates of snacks and paper napkins to each other before eating.

## Talk About

- **Our Bible says, "With love, help each other." We can show love by helping others. Let's help each other and make a snack to share!**
- **Stacy, you handed Mikey a snack. Thank you for being a helper! What is one way you can help the people in your family when you eat food at home?** (Help set the table. Help clear the table afterwards.)
- Pray briefly, **Thank You, God, for friends and family we can help.**

## For Younger Children

Children make individual snacks on crackers, helping each other by sharing materials.

## For Older Children

Children make enough snacks to share with another class.

# Bible Story Center

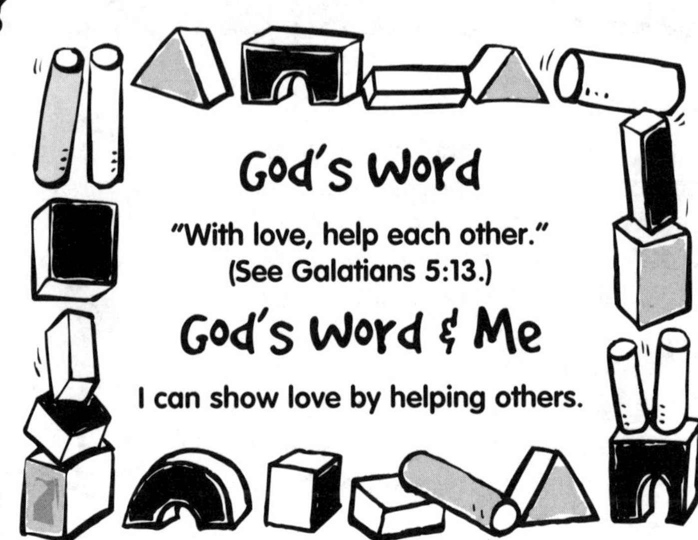

## God's Word

**"With love, help each other."**
**(See Galatians 5:13.)**

## God's Word & Me

**I can show love by helping others.**

## Collect

Bible, Picture 20 from *Bible Story Pictures.*

## Tell the Story

Use the pictured motions (keywords in bold) or show Picture 20. For older children, tell the version of the story on the back of Picture 20.

**When you feel sad, what makes you feel better? Listen to find out what made a man named Nehemiah feel sad.**

Nehemiah was a special helper to the king. He lived in a country far from his real home. One day, Nehemiah's brother came and told Nehemiah **sad** news. "The city where we used to live had strong walls. Now they are broken. The city is not safe."

Nehemiah was sad. So Nehemiah did something very important. He **prayed** to God. He knew God would hear his prayer.

When the king saw Nehemiah, he asked, "Why are you so sad, my friend?"

Nehemiah said, "I am sad because the wall around my city is broken down. I would like to go and help the people build the wall again."

The king said, "You may go and help the people build the wall. Come back when it is finished." Nehemiah was very **happy**. He thanked the king and started off to the city.

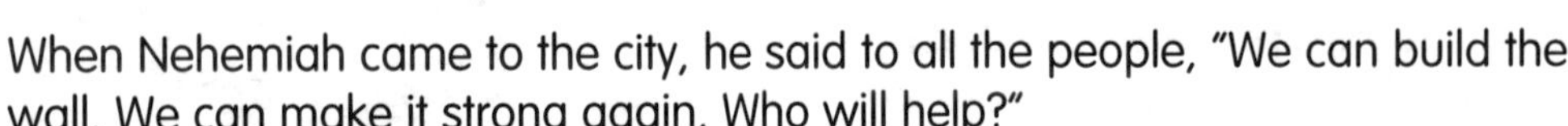

When Nehemiah came to the city, he said to all the people, "We can build the wall. We can make it strong again. Who will help?"

"My family will help," said a father. "We will cut some stones."

"My family will help," said another father. "We will cut down trees to make gates."

Bang! Bang! The **hammers** and chisels cut stone. Zzzzzz! Zzzzzz! The saws cut wood. Fathers and mothers, boys and girls all helped.

For many days, the people worked together and helped each other. Finally the wall was finished. Everyone was glad that the city was safe again. And Nehemiah was glad God had heard his prayer.

## God's Word & Me

**What did Nehemiah help people do?** (Rebuild the city wall.) **Nehemiah and the people all worked together and helped each other. We can help others and show that we love them. Who can you help at home? What can you help your mom do in the morning?**

# Worship Center

God's Word
"With love, help each other."
(See Galatians 5:13.)
God's Word & Me
I can show love by helping others.

## Collect

Bible, *Shake It Up!* songbook and cassette/CD and player, "Love Is" and "Helpin' Out" word charts (pp. 65 and 62 in songbook).

## Sing to God

Play "Love Is." Invite children to sing along with you. **Let's sing about the way God loves us and wants us to love others.** Lead children in singing song and doing suggested motions. **God wants us to help the people in our families, our friends and everyone!**

## Hear and Say God's Word

Holding your Bible open to Galatians 5:13, say verse aloud. **Helping someone with love means to help in a kind way. We show God's love when we help others.** Lead children in saying the verse. First the boys stand and say "With love" and then the girls stand and say "Help each other." Children sit down when the other group stands. Have children repeat the verse in this manner several times, alternating which group says the phrases.

## Pray to God

Children repeat the following prayer after you, one phrase at a time: **Dear God, . . . thank You for loving us. . . . Please help us show love . . . by helping others. . . . In Jesus' name, amen.**

## Sing to God

In closing the worship time, play "Helpin' Out." Invite children to sing along with you and do suggested motions. **This song tells us that the Bible tells us to help others. Helping others is a way to show God's love!**

## Options

1. To make the Bible verse activity more challenging for older children, ask them to repeat verse and replace the words "each other" with another child's name. The named child then repeats verse, using a different child's name. Continue until each child has had a turn.

2. On a large sheet of paper, print the words "People I Can Help." During the first song activity, ask children to name people other than family members whom they could help. (Friends. Teacher. Sister. Brother. Baby-sitter.) Print children's responses on paper and post where parents can read it when children are dismissed.

# Read-Aloud Story and Activity Center

## Collect

A copy of Story Picture 52 (pp. 109-110 from *Read-Aloud Story and Activity Book*) for each child and yourself, crayons or markers.

"With love, help each other."
6

## Prepare

Color your copy of Story Picture 52.

## Do

**Listen for ways this boy helped.** Read story and show completed Story Picture 52. Distribute pictures. Use conversation suggestions in Let's Talk About the Story as children complete their pages.

# Kindergarten Puzzle Center

## Collect

Copies of Puzzles 103 and 104 (p. 213 and p. 215 from *The Big Book of Kindergarten Puzzles*) for each child, pencils, crayons or markers.

## Do

Children complete the puzzles and color pages.

# Instant Activities

These activities can be used at any time during this session: when children need a change of pace, to extend the session, or during transition time at the beginning or end of the session.

## Collect

*The Big Book of Instant Activities.*

## Do

Guide children to complete "Instant Puppets" and/or "I Look at the Ceiling" (p. 113 and/or p. 96 from *The Big Book of Instant Activities*).

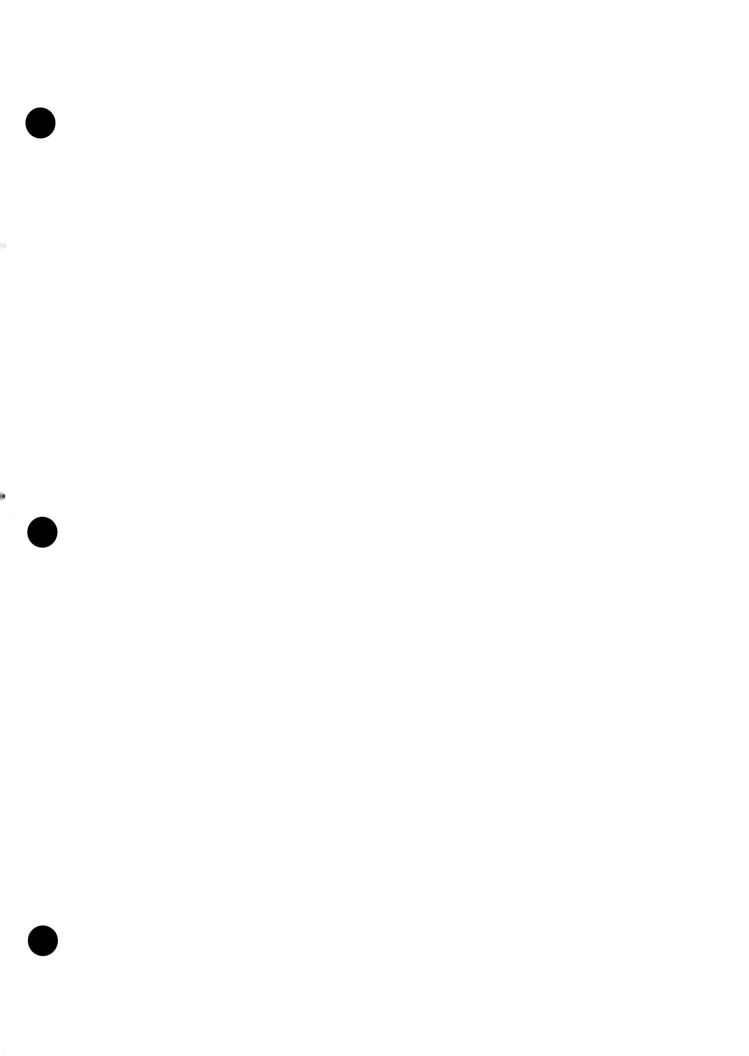